*Mississippian
Settlement
Patterns*

This is a volume in

Studies in Archeology

A complete list of titles in this series appears at the end of this volume.

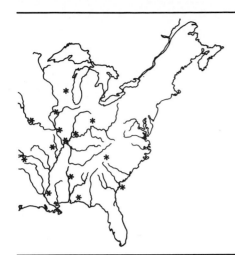

Mississippian Settlement Patterns

Edited by
BRUCE D. SMITH

Department of Anthropology
National Museum of Natural History
Smithsonian Institution
Washington, D. C.

With a Foreword by
JAMES B. GRIFFIN

ACADEMIC PRESS
New York   San Francisco   London
A Subsidiary of Harcourt Brace Jovanovich, Publishers

*Over 90% of the royalties from the sale of this book
accrue to The James B. Griffin Fund for the
support of graduate student research in archaeology
at the University of Michigan.*

ACADEMIC PRESS, INC.
111 Fifth Avenue, New York, New York 10003

United Kingdom Edition published by
ACADEMIC PRESS, INC. (LONDON) LTD.
24/28 Oval Road, London NW1 7DX

Library of Congress Cataloging in Publication Data
Main entry under title:

Mississippian settlement patterns.

    (Studies in archeology)
    Includes bibliographies.
    1.   Mississippian culture.   I.   Smith, Bruce D.
E99.M6815M57   301.32'9762   78–215
ISBN 0–12–650640–X

To the Memory of
WILLIAM H. HOLMES
CYRUS THOMAS
and the other Bureau of American Ethnology
archeologists who pioneered early research
on Mississippian settlements

Contents

3

Analysis of Late Mississippian Settlements on Ossabaw Island, Georgia / 53

CHARLES E. PEARSON

4

Fort Walton Settlement Patterns / 81

DAVID S. BROSE AND GEORGE W. PERCY

5

Mississippian Settlement Patterns in the Appalachian Summit Area: The Pisgah and Qualla Phases / 115

ROY S. DICKENS, JR.

9
Missippian Settlement Patterns in the
Central Illinois River Valley / 233
ALAN D. HARN

10
The Kincaid System: Mississippian Settlement
in the Environs of a Large Site / 269
JON MULLER

List of Contributors

Numbers in parentheses indicate the pages on which the authors' contributions begin.

ROBERT E. BELL (169), *Department of Anthropology, University of Oklahoma, Norman, Oklahoma 73069*

JEFFREY P. BRAIN (331), *Peabody Museum, Harvard University, Cambridge, Massachusetts 02138*

DAVID S. BROSE (81), *Department of Archeology, Cleveland Museum of Natural History, Cleveland, Ohio 44106*

JAMES A. BROWN (169), *Department of Anthropology, Northwestern University, Evanston, Illinois 60201*

ROY S. DICKENS, Jr. (115), *Department of Anthropology, Georgia State University, Atlanta, Georgia 30303*

PATRICIA S. ESSENPREIS (141), *Department of Anthropology, Loyola University of Chicago, Chicago, Illinois 60626*

MELVIN L. FOWLER (455), *Department of Anthropology, University of Wisconsin—Milwaukee, Milwaukee, Wisconsin*

THOMAS J. GREEN (293), *Idaho State Historical Society, Boise, Idaho 83706*

JAMES B. GRIFFIN (xv), *Museum of Anthropology, University of Michigan, Ann Arbor, Michigan 48104*

ALAN D. HARN (233), *Dickson Mounds Museum, Lewistown, Illinois 61542*

JON MULLER (269), *Department of Anthropology, Southern Illinois University at Carbondale, Carbondale, Illinois 62901*

CHERYL A. MUNSON (293), Glenn A. Black Laboratory of Archaeology, Indiana University, Bloomington, Indiana 47401

PATRICIA J. O'BRIEN (1), Department of Anthropology, Sociology, and Social Work, Kansas State University, Manhattan, Kansas 66506

DAVID F. OVERSTREET (21), Department of Anthropology and Sociology, University of Wisconsin—Waukesha, Waukesha, Wisconsin 53186

CHARLES E. PEARSON (53), Department of Anthropology, University of Georgia, Athens, Georgia 30601

CHRISTOPHER S. PEEBLES (369), Museum of Anthropology, University of Michigan, Ann Arbor, Michigan 48109

GEORGE W. PERCY (81), Division of Archives, History, and Records, Florida Department of State, Tallahassee, Florida 32303

JAMES E. PRICE (201), The Center for Archaeological Research, Southwest Missouri State University, Springfield, Missouri 65802

BRUCE D. SMITH (479), Department of Anthropology, National Museum of Natural History, Smithsonian Institution, Washington, D.C. 20560

VINCAS P. STEPONAITIS (417), Museum of Anthropology, University of Michigan, Ann Arbor, Michigan 48109

DON G. WYCKOFF (169), Department of Anthropology, University of Oklahoma, Norman, Oklahoma 73069

Foreword

JAMES B. GRIFFIN

The chapters in this volume are eloquent testimony to the progress that has been made in the last 20 years in interpreting the cultural organization of many of the prehistoric societies in the Eastern United States during the last 1000 years of their existence. In 1956, a Viking Fund publication edited by G. R. Willey presented papers on New World settlement patterns. One of these studies was on the Lower Mississippi Valley, another presented data on the Upper Mississippi Valley, and a third covered all of the Eastern United States. Only one of these studies was cited in one of the chapters in this volume. The present authors did not find it necessary or desirable to refer to the studies of 20 years ago.

The authors of the present chapters have benefited from the marked increase in archeological activity during the intervening period manifest in almost every area of archeological research. Many of the techniques of investigation were not even in existence in the mid-1950s, and much of the fieldwork had not been done. Although the title of this volume is *Mississippian Settlement Patterns* there is still some divergence among archeologists on the definition of "Mississippian" as can be seen by perusing the chapters and contrasting them with the definition given by Smith in the concluding chapter. It is to Smith's credit that he included in this volume discussions by several authors of complexes that, by his definition, are not Mississippian cultural complexes. These discussions do serve, however, to emphasize the difference between the central core of

Mississippian societies and those peripheral societies that either preceded its development or were on the margins of Smith's core area. It would probably be helpful for readers to begin their examination of this volume by reading Chapter 16 first and then read Chapters 8–13 and 15, so that they can understand the variations of patterning among societies that are commonly regarded as nascent or developed Mississippian. These chapters do not cover all of the Mississippian societies, for discussions of the Tennessee–Cumberland sites around Nashville, of complexes in the upper Tennessee Valley, or of the Mississippian development in Georgia are not included. The first three chapters present interpretations of cultural groups on the West, North, and Northeast that are not Mississippian societies, according to Smith's definition, for a variety of reasons. Chapters 4, 5, and 6 present data on late prehistoric societies that are in some ways divergent but are sometimes regarded as Mississippian, at least in their later phases.

One of the major problems in dealing with settlement patterns is to have a reasonably accurate record of the number and variety of settlement locations of a specific society at a particular moment of time. This problem has been of concern to all of the contributors, or almost all of them, for it is recognized that present knowledge of the distribution of various settlement types is incomplete because of many factors. Some of these factors are ones over which the archeologist has little or no control, such as the disappearance of sites due to natural forces or to changes in the landscape caused by our American cultural development over the past few hundred years. These changes have eliminated many sites at every level from adequate study, such as the major mound group in what is now downtown St. Louis, to the smallest farming or hunting settlements. In floodplain areas, where land leveling has been adopted, literally thousands of sites have been obliterated, many of them attributable to the Mississippian period. It can probably safely be said that no prehistoric Mississippian society settlement pattern remains in its pristine state and that all of our present data are an approximation of the former distribution of sites. In the area covered by the several authors it may also be confidently said that no single survey, whether intensive or one or another of the fashionable sampling strategies, will recover all of the locations utilized by a Mississippian society. One of the societies with which I have had an association is the Powers phase in Southeast Missouri, which is described in Chapter 8. In 1966 and 1967 we knew of Powers Fort and five nearby villages. It was also known that there were smaller locations with living debris probably attributable to the Powers phase, but their importance, number, and function were not realized. Since then, the Powers phase of the archeologist's interpretation has grown remarkably as the result of systematic survey, the uncovering of previously buried sites, the realization of the probable locational strategies of Power phase people and, to some degree, a broadening of the definition of the phase. Now there are 10 villages associated with Powers Fort and within some 6 km of it, with many hamlets, farmsteads, and limited-activity loci used for hunting, fishing, or the acquisition of lithic material, pottery clay, and other necessary industrial or ceremonial needs. This burgeoning is still only from the northern more intensively surveyed portion of what is now recognized as the Powers phase.

The authors of this volume realize the difficulty of correctly interpreting the size and distribution of a prehistoric society, let alone the interaction of its component parts, because of the difficulty in ascertaining how many sites were actually contemporary, and the varieties of settlements that were occupied during, say, any given 10- or 20-year period. Too many attempts to interpret settlement patterns, population size, and settlement systems have tended to assume contemporaneity when adequate chronological controls had not been established. It is known that radiocarbon dating, that major contribution, does not provide it, nor I fear do any of the other physico-chemical chronology assessments. Ceramic seriation or type varieties are also aids, but do not provide the fine-tuned chronology necessary for absolute contemporaneity, because of the absence of an acceptable scale recognition of the longevity attributes recognized in the manufacture of pottery. The same lack of control is present in the utilization of other prehistoric materials or behavioral patterns. Many now-utilized prehistoric "phases" are given a time span of a hundred years or more, and it is almost futile or even frivolous to present them as though they were a functioning interacting society.

The archeologists working with the Powers phase have an almost unique situation in which all of our interpretive devices indicate that all the sites were utilized during a short period of time. We cannot however say how many years it was in existence and reasonable estimates might range from 25 to 50 years for the entire phase. The villages were occupied for a shorter period of time than Powers Fort, the major ceremonial and dominant population center. Although the 10 known villages must belong to this phase, were the closely spaced paired villages occupied at the same time? Were they partially contemporary or were they sequentially occupied? There are good reasons to believe that at least some of the village pairs were like Siamese twins. It is reasonable to infer that many of the other sites in the Powers phase hierarchy were not continuously occupied during any one year but were instead utilized for short periods of time during the life span of the phase in the area. The problem of contemporaneity affects every interpretation of the size and activities of a prehistoric society and the interpretations can be suspect when this problem cannot be controlled irrespective of the other interpretive problems with which the archeologist is faced.

Even a casual reading of the several chapters should indicate that there are significant seriations in the settlement pattern. This is true even of those patterns which were left by populations normally acknowledged to be Mississippian by almost anyone's definition. Cahokia seems to be unique and of an order of magnitude and complexity significantly greater than that of any other settlement. Part of this uniqueness may be attributable to lack of chronological control, but certainly not all of it, for Cahokia at its climax during the Sterling and Moorehead phases of some 200 years duration was larger and more complex than any other presumably integrated society in the Eastern United States.

The analysis of the Kincaid settlement emphasizes the dominance of the Kincaid site itself, the presence of some "dispersed villages," the absence of specialized activity areas and an absence of the site hierarchies portrayed in some of the other discussions. For example, for many years, archeologists have uniformly recognized that the cultural complex at Kincaid had many similarities to that recovered from the Angel site some 100 miles up the Ohio in Southwest Indiana. These two settlements were almost certainly contemporary over some span of their separate life spans, yet their patterns, while having some similarities, are clearly distinct and represent different functional organizational strategies.

Up the Illinois River in Fulton County, Illinois, there are seven towns fairly regularly spaced representing a continuing occupation and reoccupation by one or more societies over some 275 years, supported by related special activity sites of different functions and size. Furthermore the towns are located on bluffs instead of in the Illinois floodplain. Be it noted that by some definitions these Fulton County societies could hardly be called Mississippian societies. Yet sites of this area and their then known cultural complex were the primary data base for early definitions of Mississippi culture. This judgment is still acceptable.

In the Lower Mississippi Valley, the cultural continuum from Coles Creek to Natchez and contemporary societies over some 1000 years changed dramatically as cultural and natural forces altered the adaptive strategies of the several societies. During the first 300 years, the Coles Creek settlements have the basic Mississippian platform mound and plaza in relatively small sites without evidence of major sites that dominated a regional area. In many features of their material culture these Coles Creek sites on both sides of the Mississippi River reflect gradual interacting shifts from the preceding non-Mississippian complexes. As a result of indigenous growth and the appearance of northern intrusions and concepts, the Plaquemine societies have markedly larger sites, mounds, and, at some locations, multiple plazas. Also in evidence are population clusters of smaller sites near major centers placed at strategic locations. This settlement pattern is closer to that expected of Mississippian societies, but does not seem to have the large permanent towns which appear for only a brief period about A.D. 1300–1400 primarily along the Mississippi River.

Subsequent to this period, there was a reorientation of settlement away from the river in many smaller population aggregates, with only a few large sites still in existence. The causes of these several shifts are still not clearly understood but recognition of them is an important step in formulating research questions.

The settlement pattern interpretation of the complex of the Kansas City area, Steed–Kisker, is primarily based on O'Brien's analysis of a survey and some site excavations on Brush Creek, a short and narrow tributary of the Missouri River northwest of Kansas City, and also on the Little Platte River Valley north of Kansas City. Her study recovered few evidences of houses, even though daub is said to have been found where there were no houses. These farmstead areas are in the valleys as they should be, with storage pit areas located on uplands or bluffs overlooking the valleys and somewhat distant from the farmstead. She also identified "trash" areas without features or extensive debris, a substantial number of burial mounds, and includes in the Steed–Kisker settlement pattern hunting and butchering sites in the Ozark area of Southwest Missouri. It is suggested that at least some of the farmsteads performed specialized tasks and were functionally akin to cottage industries. A ceramic seriation based on design with four sequent stages has been constructed for all Steed–Kisker sites, but are not tied into ^{14}C chronology. None of the Brush Creek farmstead or storage sites were occupied in Phase IV; four of the 11 sites could not be placed in the ceramic seriation; one was occupied for Phases I–III and two sites during Phases II and III. Two sites were occupied only during Phase I.

In total, this is a rather unique settlement pattern for a Mississippian complex. It is generally believed that Steed–Kisker has a close relationship to the Cahokia area, but on this interpretation of the settlement pattern it would hardly be suspected.

The interpretation of eastern Wisconsin Oneota settlement patterning suffers from lack of adequate control of most of the major factors necessary for an adequate understanding of such patterns. This the author recognizes. For example, there are no clearly identifiable sites for the hypothesis of earliest Emergent Oneota societies and very few sites with any archeological data from the Historic Oneota period. Site size for Developmental Oneota varies considerably, but at least some of this variability appears to be a reflection of temporal depth and shifting location of occupational activities and of short-term occupation of societal groups at some locations. The interpretation of Developmental Oneota settlements as relatively small and intermittently occupied is in marked contrast to that of Mississippian societies to the south. This difference, along with others, has caused many archaeologists to recognize that irrespective of a number of formal similarities of Oneota material culture to those of Mississippi complexes that it is a mistake to regard Oneota as "true Mississippian" in terms of societal organization. Oneota Developmental villages are analogous to early and marginal Fort Ancient or Monongahela sites. Oneota sites of the Classic horizon are interpreted as reflecting a marked decrease in geographical spread and a concentration of reduced overall population into a smaller number of sites. The cause of this nucleation is believed to be more effective farming but other factors may also have been involved.

The third chapter is a tight little island survey dealing with a marginal Mississippian society in an environment not normally associated with Mississippian complexes. It has the distinct advantage of relative geographical isolation and limited environmental variability. Although large population centers are not present on Ossabaw Island, there are some 47 sites whose size and location suggest different functions as well as differential length of occupation. Only one or two of the larger sites on the island appear to be actively involved with external affairs and the much larger number of sites are restricted to procurement activities on the island and the more mundane tasks of living. These island sites can be arranged in four levels of rank size, and, not surprisingly, the better soils and potentially most productive forested areas were the location for the larger sites. The locations of smaller sites are less restricted and probably reflect shorter occupations to exploit seasonal resources. This analysis has probably gone farther than almost any other in assessing the relationship of a Mississippian society to its environment.

The chapter on Fort Walton settlements of the panhandle area of Florida presents a markedly different picture of the geographical size and temporal depth of this prehistoric group. Instead of representing a late cultural intrusion from the West and Northwest, Fort Walton is seen as a relatively long-lived development from earlier Weeden Island populations which gradually changed into a Mississippian adaptation. The authors identify distinctive patterns in the several environmental zones with the more favorable ones having the larger towns and seasonal activity loci to obtain a more varied resource base. Through time with population expansion less favorable environments were occupied and exploited with considerable success. While the interpretive base for the characterization of Fort Walton is far from a complete one, the research program has already been successful in altering understanding of Fort Walton societies.

Although there has been some difference of opinion as to whether the Appalachian Summit sites of about A.D. 1100–1700 should be included in a broad definition of Mississippian, the chapter in this volume on these sites confirms such a placement. Since these sites of the Pisgah and Qualla phases have the platform mound and plaza pattern with square to rectangular houses on the major sites, and subsidiary villages and hamlets, the basic Mississippi settlement pattern is present. It is unfortunate that excavation interests have been primarily devoted to mound excavation, so that analysis and interpretation of complete town or village patterning cannot be adequately understood. The shift in area of occupation from the Pisgah to Qualla periods is a significant reflection of changes brought about by European intrusion, as is the later Qualla phase emphasis on small villages dispersed in a linear arrangement in river valleys. Such changes may well be accompanied by modifications of the social and political structure, but this cannot yet be demonstrated. I have a feeling that the authors interpretations of the Mississippian societies are an improvement over earlier constructs, but that future analysis will find that the two-phase presentation is too gross both temporally and areally.

The chapter on Fort Ancient settlements emphasizes the difficulty of categorizing a large number of components distributed over the contiguous parts of four states, in several physiographic regions and existing over at least 700 years. In the now known earliest sites their size, functions and community structure are similar to that of their immediately preceding Late Woodland settlements. While some of these seem to have existed longer than others, there is little chronological control over the possible changes and their causes that will allow archeologists to recognize such temporal depth. The major late Fort Ancient sites are primarily located along the Ohio River and in the lower reaches of its main tributary streams. Their location and size are indicative of a greater emphasis on agriculture and the importance of river transportation in the spread of concepts and specific items from Mississipian centers to the west and south. The contrast between Madisonville settlements along the Ohio and that of the Anderson and other more northern phases in Ohio is apparent. It is only the major sites that have a settlement pattern close to that of many Mississippi societies, and it is primarily in these that material objects were found that are part of the trade and exchange network of pan-Mississipian societies. For historic reasons, we are without adequate knowledge of possible subsidiary villages, hamlets, or procurement sites that should have been a part of the activities of the populations of the major centers. An understanding of Fort Ancient either as a large interacting group of regional societies or of the interplay within the regional populations has been hampered by the lack of strategies, funds, and labor that would produce such results.

Even though the chapter on the Caddoan area concentrates on settlements in the Arkansas River Valley and its major tributaries of eastern Oklahoma, both the temporal sequence and general patterning probably is applicable to the majority of the other Caddoan area settlements. With this restricted locale, the authors indicate the environmental factors that are vital to an understanding of site locations and the varied activities of the societies. Functional differences in mound construction and usage as reported in this study is one of the important characteristics representing the distinctive differences of Caddoan sites from most of the Mississippian variants to the east. These sequential changes in mound function are interpreted as indications of changes in the societal organization. Comparable studies have not yet appeared for most of the eastern Mississippian complexes. There are other analytical features of this chapter that will eventually be applied in other areas as better control and understanding of the spatial and temporal extent of distinct societal complexes is demonstrated.

The majestic Moundville site is a major Mississippian center with little or no evidence of earlier occupations. Because of its size and length of occupation it does, however, present a difficult problem of interpretation. This has been eased by decades of excavation and the preservation of the materials recovered and the records to go with them by Jones, DeJarnette, and their associates. The analysis of this data and that from related sites has produced a portrayal of Moundville societal organization that is unusual in terms of completeness and clarity. The functional differences in mound types and in the placement of dwellings and activity areas is paralleled by the differential treatment of burials reflecting status variations. The location of Moundville was carefully chosen as was the location of the several smaller communities and hamlets which were associated together in a functioning society. The interpretations of the manner in which this operated will no doubt be modified in the future as excavations at the villages, hamlets and procurement sites allow more precise examination of the role these played in the Moundville settlement and sociopolitical structure. If tribute did play a significant role in the Moundville society some concrete evidence of the goods and services should be identified, or is this too much to ask?

1

Steed–Kisker:
A Western Mississippian
Settlement System

PATRICIA J. O'BRIEN

Although individuals in the Kansas City area began collecting "Indian relics" over 100 years ago, scientific archeological research in the area began with the work of J. Mett Shippee, a long-time resident in the North Kansas City area. It was through Shippee's effort that Steed–Kisker, as a complex, was first brought to the attention of Dr. Waldo R. Wedel of the Smithsonian Institution in the late 1930s. In 1937 Wedel initiated excavations at the Steed–Kisker site (23PL13) and in 1938 examined, with Shippee, the remains of the destroyed Shepherd mound (23PL37) in the Smithville area (Wedel 1943). Shippee's earlier and later work in the area has included excavations at the Avondale mounds (Shippee 1953), the Vandiver mounds (Shippee 1958), further work at the Steed–Kisker site, and work at the McClarnon (23PL54) and Gresham (23PL48) sites. The results of this research are summarized in his monograph (Shippee 1972).

Following Wedel and Shippee, a variety of researchers have carried out excavations within the Kansas City area that have in one way or another produced information concerning Steed–Kisker archeological sites (Figure 1.1). John Mori (1967) conducted limited test excavations at the Steed–Kisker site, recovering little in the way of cultural materials from the areas he tested. Mori also tested both the Robker site (23PL63), located near the mouth of the Platte River on low ground, and the Poos site

1

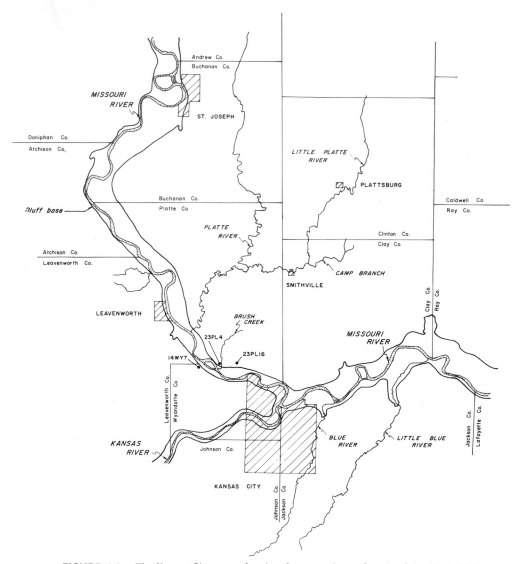

FIGURE 1.1. *The Kansas City area, showing the approximate domain of the Steed–Kisker complex, as well as some of the sites and drainages discussed in the text.*

(23PL61), located on the south bank of Bee Creek in the path of levee construction. Although Steed–Kisker materials were collected from two scattered daub areas and several dark-stained earth areas at the Poos site, subsequent testing did not reveal any subsurface structures (Mori 1967:15–18).

Research carried out in the Smithville Reservoir area during the late

1960s and 1970s has also yielded information about Steed–Kisker. Following the initial work of Thomas J. Riley (1967), F.A. Calabrese carried out research in the Smithville area in 1968 and in 1969 (see Calabrese 1969, 1974). That work was funded by the National Park Service. I carried out further work in the Smithville Reservoir area in the summers of 1975 and 1976 under the sponsorship of the U.S. Army Corps of Engineers. The location and testing of another Steed–Kisker site (23CL35) was accomplished by Evans (1974) and Butler (1974) for the Missouri Highway Department. Unfortunately no significant materials were recovered from that site.

Work on an important Steed–Kisker site outside the Kansas City area was conducted by W. Raymond Wood. His excavations at the Vista Rock Shelter (23SR20) in the Ozark Highlands of southwestern Missouri resulted in the identification of it as a specialized hunting and meat-processing camp (Wood 1968:178–179).

In the summer of 1971, Alfred E. Johnson (1974) conducted an archeological survey of Brush Creek for the Missouri State Highway Department, in relation to planned construction of a segment of Interstate 435 (I-435). Eighteen Steed–Kisker sites were found along that valley.

In addition to the location and testing of Steed–Kisker sites through various research projects that were supported either by the Smithsonian Institution or by federally funded salvage projects, a variety of Steed–Kisker sites have been found throughout Platte, Clay, Clinton, and Buchanan counties as a result of amateur surveying.

Finally, with the support of the Kansas Archeological Field School and its students, I have conducted extensive excavations on a variety of Steed–Kisker sites in the Kansas City area since 1969. In 1969, excavations were carried out at the Steed–Kisker site (23PL13), and two houses were excavated at the Young site (23PL4). In 1971, two sites on Brush Creek were tested: the White site (23PL80), and the Ley site (23PL97). The Coons site (23PL16) was also excavated in 1971, and a single structure was uncovered.

Natural Setting

Broadly speaking, the area of northwestern Missouri shown in Figure 1.1 falls within the Prairie Peninsula region. This peninsula is a wedge of grassland extending east from the Great Plains into the deciduous forest areas of Iowa, Indiana, Illinois, Michigan, Missouri, and Minnesota. This area can be further characterized as belonging to the Eastern Glaciated region of the border zone between the Prairie Penisula and the High Plains to the west. The area can be further broken down into three environmental zones: bottomland forest, upland hardwood forest, and tall grass prairie (Mori, 1967:4–7).

The bottomlands along the Missouri River and its major tributaries, of which the Platte is one, are covered with willow thickets and stands of tall cottonwood. Cutoff oxbow lakes, marshes, and swamps are also found in the river floodplains. A variety of species of bass (large and small mouth, rock, and white), as well as sunfish, black perch, pumpkin seed crappie, channel catfish, and bullheads would have been present either in the main channel or oxbow lake situations.

The bluffs bordering these river bottomlands are capped by loess deposited during the Late Pleistocene, with the Missouri River today being marked, especially along its western border, by high loess bluffs. These bluffs are more open than the bottomlands, supporting large stands of oak, ash, hickory, walnut, linden, and other deciduous trees. Woodland animal and bird populations occur with some abundance within the bottomland and bluff environmental zones.

Moving away from the drainage of the Missouri River, one comes into the prairie area proper, a rolling hilly country dissected by broad stream valleys and covered by tall grass.

The fauna that are found within this region cross cut these three environmental zones, because the open prairie, the floodplain forest, and the upland forest all interdigitate, producing a rich environment in which numerous animal forms thrive. Those animal forms that may have been important to the prehistoric inhabitants of the area include the oppossum, cottontail rabbit, a variety of squirrels, woodchuck, beaver, muskrat, coyote, red fox, racoon, mink, and skunk. Many of these, of course, are fur bearing animals and would have been hunted for pelts as well as meat. The most important animal species within the forested zones would have been the white-tail deer, whereas the most important animal in the prairie zone, particularly into the uplands, would have been the bison. Those two animals were extremely important as sources of meat. In addition, their hides and certain skeletal elements were used for the manufacture of tools.

The soils of the Kansas City area are fairly diverse. Within Brush Creek, Steed–Kisker archeological sites are located on four soil types: Wabash silt loam, Crawford stony clay loam, Wabash very fine sandy loam, and Knox silt loam (Sweet, Dunn, and Vanatta, 1912). Almost all of these soils are extremely fine grained in texture and are good agricultural soils. Most are the product of redeposition and erosion operating within the area of basically a forested bottomlands marsh. The soils of the Smithville area are marked by Sharpsburg, Grundy, Adair, and Shelby soil types, which are common to the prairie–forest transitional vegetation zone, which the Smithville area occupies (Jackson 1966).

Two aspects of the geology of Platte, Clay, and Clinton counties are significant for archeological studies. First, it is an area of former glaciation, and, as a result, the soils and the geologic members that lie above the

Pennsylvania strata are essentially gravels and glacial tills, which, in turn, are capped by thick deposits of loess (Davies 1955). Second, the underlying Pennsylvania rock is particularly significant for the prehistoric inhabitants of this region (Greene and Howe 1952). There are a number of limestone formations, which were the source of a variety of quality cherts for the prehistoric inhabitants of this area. These cherts were exposed in various areas within the larger Kansas City region. The most important cherts are Spring Hill, Argentine, Westerville, and Winterset.

Settlement Patterning

The remaining sections of this chapter will focus on three aspects of Steed–Kisker settlement patterning: (a) the character of individual sites and their function, as determined through excavation; (b) survey techniques for locating sites; and (c) the nature of the relationships that existed between the functionally different types of Steed–Kisker sites, and their relationships with broader environmental areas.

In attempting to explore the first problem—the character of sites and their function—data will be drawn from a variety of excavated sites, especially the Young site (23PL4), the White (23PL80) and Hulse (23CL109) sites, the Steed–Kisker site and cemetery area (23PL13), and the Vista Rock Shelter site (23SR20). Each of these sites reflects functional differences.

In dealing with the second and third problems—site survey and location, and the interrelationships of functionally different sites to environmental factors—archeological data will be drawn from two surveys: Brush Creek and the Little Platte River and Camp Branch (see Figure 1.1).

SITE TYPES AND FUNCTIONS

Much of the early work on the Steed–Kisker site suggested that it was a small village. Wedel (1943) refers to the Steed–Kisker habitation site as a "village site [p. 62]" and roughly approximates the area within which habitation structures may have been scattered. His description and maps suggest that the site, situated on a broad terrace, is roughly triangular in shape and covers about 380 m² (4100 ft²) within which several small concentrations of debris, or "middens" were scattered. Shippee (1972:4) refers to Steed–Kisker habitation sites as villages, and points out that they are both large and small and have been discovered along the Missouri River as well as its tributaries. Calabrese (1969:193) suggests that there are two contrastive settlement patterns in the eastern Glaciated region: individual house units located on bluffs and small clusters of houses as villages on the valley floor. He points out that there is no obvious reason for this dichotomy of settlement patterning.

O'Brien (1972b) has pointed out the difficulties of determining the character of Steed–Kisker settlement patterns because these patterns are predicated on a basic underlying assumption. That axiom is "a daub patch equals a house" and it underlies much of Plains Archeology in general. This assumption is based upon the belief that daub is derived from houses and therefore, whenever it is found, a house must be present or nearby. The fact that house structures yield daub is well known. It is equally true, though rarely mentioned, that daub could be the by-product of the simple act of baking a bird or small animal in a jacket of mud or clay, that is a product of cooking. In addition, Strong (1935:81) has pointed out that cache pits were occasionally lined with clay and then baked. Cleaning and enlarging such cache pits could easily result in daub debris. Strong (1935:80) also reported that the daub associated with caches could have been derived from fires built above them. Wilson (1917:87, Fig. 25) notes that Hidatsa storage caches were covered with a final layer of "ashes and refuse." This was done to hide the pit (Wilson 1917:94), and such refuse could easily contain daub. Daub, then, is the by-product of a number of domestic activities.

Steed–Kisker sites consist of a series of surface patches, or clusters, of daub and debris, which are typically widely scattered across the site. These clusters cover an area of about 40–100 m^2 and the area between them in the field is essentially clean. The Steed–Kisker site contains at least 11 such daub–debris clusters, whereas some smaller sites like White contained only one.

Utilizing the aforementioned axiom, the Steed–Kisker site, which contained at least 11 such daub–debris clusters, would theoretically be a village of about 11 houses. Data contradicting this axiom, especially as it relates to Steed–Kisker sites has been known since Wedel's earliest work when he (Wedel 1943:64–66) found trash filled pits but no house remains in several midden clusters.

When work was begun at the Steed–Kisker-type site (23PL13) in the summer of 1969, five such daub–debris patches were tested. Our tests revealed no structures beneath the surface patches, even though the daub extended below the plowzone; nor were any trash pits found. At that time it was assumed that somehow the house structures had been destroyed by previous agricultural activity.

Work was also begun at the Young site (23PL4) during the summer of 1969, and two daub–debris clusters were excavated, both of which revealed the structural remains of a house. In 1971 we returned to 23PL4 and excavated the seven additional Steed–Kisker daub–debris clusters that we were able to locate (Figure 1.2). This operation was slightly compounded

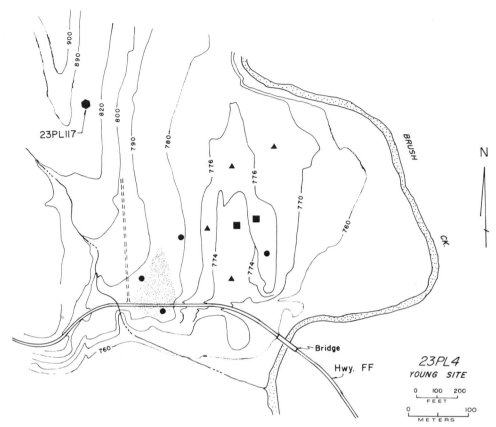

FIGURE 1.2. *Activity areas at the Young site (23PL4) and their relationships to the Burial Mound 23PL117. (●): Storage pit area; (▲): trash area; (■): house. The Kansas City Hopewell midden is indicated by stippling.*

in the southwestern segment of the site because a large Kansas City Hopewell midden is present, and two of the Steed–Kisker daub–debris clusters were found within this area. The southernmost of these had been previously excavated by Shippee. Excavation of these seven patches in 1971 yielded no clear evidence of further structures at the site. Three contained storage–trash pits, whereas four consisted primarily of daub, yielding very few artifacts or cultural debris. All seven of the daub patches extended below the plowzone, so that any structural features that might have been present could not have been destroyed plowing. In the summer of 1975, two additional Steed–Kisker storage pits were found under a daub–debris patch in the northwest corner of the Kansas City Hopewell midden. Thus, of the 10 daub–debris clusters that were excavated at the Young site, only two could be definitely identified as domestic house structures. Four definitely had storage pits within them, and can be identified as storage areas. Whether a structure was associated with them at some time in their history cannot be ascertained by the remaining evidence. Whether the remaining four daub–debris clusters are the product of specialized work areas or whether they were simply dumps for garbage has not been resolved to date. For purposes of the present analysis, these areas will be referred to as storage and trash areas, respectively.

Interpreting the available data in this manner, I suggest that approximately one of five daub–debris clusters could be expected to be clearly identified as houses at those Steed–Kisker sites with a large number of such clusters. Thus, it is apparent that Steed–Kisker sites that have been referred to as "villages" may have been little more than small two-structure habitation sites. So, when dealing with Steed–Kisker sites, we can no longer make the basic assumption that a daub–debris cluster on the ground surface represents the remains of a structure.

Indeed, some of the data from other excavations suggest that this may also be true of sites where only one daub patch is present. In 1971, for example, the White site (23PL80) on Brush Creek was excavated. This site was situated on the side of a very high, steep slope with the debris cluster of Steed–Kisker materials located on a rather flat area on the middle of the slope. Upon excavating the cluster (it was the only one in the field and was approximately 4 m²) we found that although the daub extended below the plowzone, only three storage pits were present. No structural evidence of a house was uncovered.

This surprising occurrence of isolated storage pits raised the question of whether there might exist Steed–Kisker sites that functioned only as storage areas. The full potential of this hypothesis was not recognized at the time, nor was there a way for us to test it at that specific site, since the immediately surrounding area was under cultivation. A similar site (the Richardson Hulse site, 23CL109) in the Smithville Reservoir area was, however, tested in the summer of 1976, and only a single, large Steed–Kisker storage pit was uncovered. Because the soil in this site is a clean yellow loess in which all subsurface structural features can be easily seen, and because the site was going to be destroyed by the construction of the reservoir, it was felt that this was an ideal opportunity to test the storage area hypothesis. A road grader was used, and the plowzone was completely peeled off in about 3-in. cuts over the whole area of the site. This covered a rectangular area approximately 600 m long and about 250 m wide. The materials found extending below the plowzone consisted of two additional large Steed–Kisker storage pits (Features 4, 5, and 6 of Figure 1.3), the remains of a rectangular ash area from an historic house structure (possibly the fireplace), and a very large limestone basin full of burned charcoal and remnants of pig teeth and glass. Clear evidence of a Steed–Kisker house structure was not found. This would appear to indicate that there were Steed–Kisker sites that functioned in some way as storage sites.

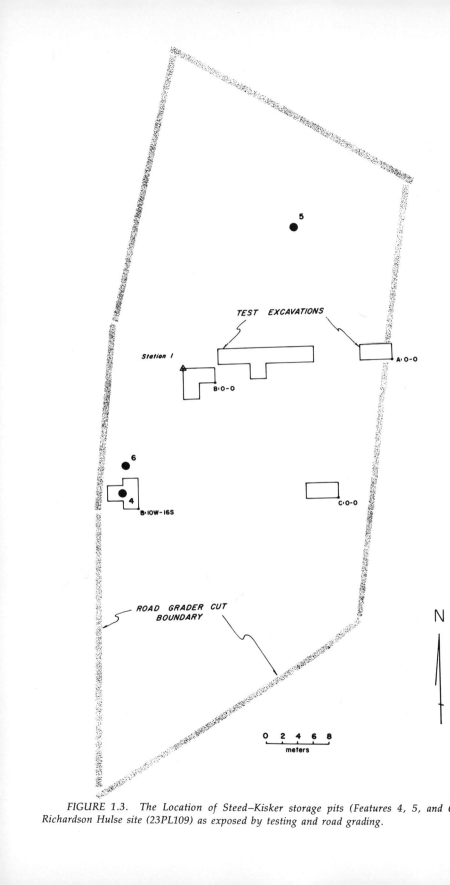

FIGURE 1.3. *The Location of Steed–Kisker storage pits (Features 4, 5, and 6) at the Richardson Hulse site (23PL109) as exposed by testing and road grading.*

Based on flotation samples from pitfill, these pits were being used to store hickory nuts and acorns, corn, amaranth, and other wild seeds. All of the known storage sites are located on extremely high, well-drained, knoll-like terraces, and were apparently used by Steed–Kisker populations for the storage of wild and domestic plant products.

If we utilize ethnographic data, we should expect that some small archeological sites will not be general living areas, but instead will be specialized work areas. For example, Wilson (1917:48–62) reports that the Hidatsa had corn stages and threshing booths in their villages and there is nothing to prevent such facilities from being used nearer the garden in earlier more peaceful times. He also reports watchers' stages with the gardens (Wilson 1917:28–30), and that beans were threshed in the fields (Wilson 1917:83–84). Finally, he mentions squash drying stages. These activities deal with the same type of agriculture that the Steed–Kisker people had, and we might expect to find their archeological equivalents as well as those of other domestic activities since Wilson states that drying stages were also used for nonagricultural activities.

Hunting and butchering camps represent a third known type of Steed–Kisker site. The Vista Rock Shelter (23SR20), located in the Ozark highlands in southwestern Missouri, is the only such site excavated to date (Wood, 1968). Species represented include woodchuck, beaver, cottontail rabbit, skunk, raccoon, canid (either wolf or dog), elk, deer, and bison. Wood concludes, based on relative bone frequencies, that the rock shelter was a hunting station. Deer and bison especially were killed in the nearby forest and dismembered where they fell. The cuts of meat were taken to the shelter for smoking and drying. The dry meat was then transported to a permanent community. This practice would certainly account for the rarity of animal bone at Steed–Kisker habitation sites in the Kansas City area. The location of the shelter itself, over 100 miles away from the Kansas City area, would suggest that Steed–Kisker populations obtained their meat resources through long ranging, and possibly annual, hunting expeditions (Wood 1968:178–179).

Burial mounds/cemetery areas constitute a fourth and final site type for the Steed–Kisker complex. Excavated by Wedel (1943), the original Steed–Kisker site (23PL13) cemetery area yielded over 80 individuals. Wedel also examined the Shepherd mound just south of the Smithville area, and Shippee has examined and excavated the Avondale mounds (1953), and the Vandiver mounds (1958). The burial population of the Calovich mound (14WY7), which was excavated by William Bass and Robert Squier, has been analyzed by Barnes (1977). Michael Finnegan and I excavated the Chester Reeves mound (23CL108) in the Smithville area. All these burial mounds yielded extended, flexed, or, more rarely, bundle burials.

In summary, Steed–Kisker populations in the Kansas City area used four functionally different types of sites: habitation areas with houses, storage pits and trash areas; storage sites with pit facilities; hunting and butchering camp sites (located in the Ozark region), and burial mound/ cemetery areas.

Brush Creek is a small tributary of the Missouri River (Figure 1.1). A survey of the Brush Creek valley was performed under the direction of Dr. Alfred E. Johnson, University of Kansas, in 1971. When he began, only three sites were known from the Brush Creek valley. That summer, 47 new sites were discovered. Johnson (1974) feels confident that at least 95% of the exposed archeological sites along Brush Creek were located. He bases this judgment on the following factors:

1. The location of the planned corridor for I-35 included both the valley floor and the surrounding hilltops on either side of the valley, and the survey teams therefore searched several topographic settings for archeological sites.
2. The majority of the valley floor, which was intensively surveyed, was under cultivation, making the detection of sites relatively easy.
3. A detailed, although less complete, survey was made of the valley hill slopes and bluff tops. This work was, however, inhibited by dense ground cover of grass, brush, and tree growth in some areas.
4. There was a complete survey made of the banks along the present course of Brush Creek in search of sites buried as the result of recent alluvial deposition.
5. Archeologists within the Kansas City area were able to supply information concerning the location of sites on Brush Creek that they gathered over a period of 40 years.

Of the 50 sites found on Brush Creek, 19 are Steed–Kisker sites (12 habitation sites or trash sites, 5 burial mounds, and 2 storage sites, Figure 1.4). For most of the archeological sites found on the Brush Creek, estimates of site size were determined by the area of surface scatter. The implications of employing surface scatter estimates to guide subsequent excavations, especially for houses, have been discussed in the previous section.

The second area that was subject to intensive site survey is the Smithville Reservoir area. This area consists of a segment of the Little Platte River and one of its tributaries, Camp Branch. The area to be inundated by the lake covers over 6475 ha. Approximately 85% of this area was surveyed during the summers of 1975 and 1976. Over 80 sites have been recorded to date north of the dam axis, 26 of which are known to be

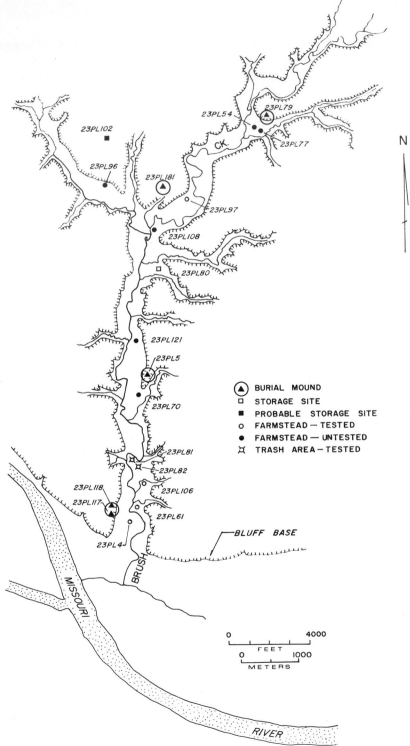

FIGURE 1.4. *The distribution of functionally distinct Steed–Kisker sites within the Brush Creek valley.*

Steed–Kisker sites. On this survey, too, estimates of site size were determined on the basis of area of surface scatter.

The survey method used varied with surface conditions. Newly plowed fields were walked by survey teams at approximately 10-m intervals. Fields with low crops were walked at 10-m intervals or less. In some cases, fields were walked at 10-row intervals. Sites in wheat stubble or newly mowed alfalfa and grass were also walked at about 10-m intervals, with generally good visibility shortly after cutting.

Ground visibility in row-crop situations ranged from good to excellent. Visibility in newly mowed grass or cut wheat was usually good. Visibility of the ground cover ranged from good to excellent for almost 75% of the land surveyed. Visibility in short grass was poor, however, and visibility in what was referred to as jungle (extremely high grass, brush, and tree cover) was minimal at best. Those areas where visibility was poor or that were categorized as jungle were checked in the following manner.

All conspicuous knolls in the fields were checked, in some cases by shovel testing, but usually by examining the knoll, scruffing the vegetation to expose the soil, checking rodent holes and other breaks in the soil pattern (e.g., small erosional gullies) for any evidence of archeological debris. Eroding gullies and upland bank areas of the tributaries of the Little Platte River were also checked.

As with the Brush Creek survey, extensive use was also made of amateur informants.

THE SETTLEMENT SYSTEM

As already indicated, there are four functionally different types of Steed–Kisker sites. Three occur in the Kansas City area, and the fourth—the hunting and butchering camp—has been found to occur in the Ozark area of southwestern Missouri. In addition to the Vista Rock Shelter, Donna C. Roper (personal communication) has found rock shelter sites where Steed–Kisker materials are present in the area within the H.S. Truman Reservoir. In the Kansas City area, habitation, storage, and burial sites have been found.

An analysis of the ceramics from all of the sites excavated in the Kansas City area has resulted in a detailed chronology based on designs and design attributes (O'Brien 1974). This has resulted in a four-phase ceramic chronology. A one-to-one alignment of that seriation with radiocarbon dates has not yet been achieved however.

Robert L. Hall (personal communication) has analyzed all available Steed–Kisker radiocarbon dates and feels that the complex dates between A.D. 1000 and 1250 A.D. This range is basically consistent with Roper's (1976) trend-surface data on Steed–Kisker dates.

Using detailed ceramic seriation it was possible to order houses, storage pits, trash areas, and burials (and therefore mounds) of the Brush Creek valley into a tight chronological framework (O'Brien 1974). One of the most interesting results obtained from the analysis was the discovery that the individual houses and pits at sites like Young (23PL4) and Steed–Kisker (23PL13) apparently overlapped in time but were not fully contemporaneous. Thus, for example, the three houses located to date on the Steed–Kisker site and the two on the Young site were apparently not occupied contemporaneously, but rather appear to have replaced each other through time. Table 1.1 shows the distribution of habitation sites on Brush Creek over the four ceramic periods.

Steed–Kisker habitation sites in the Brush Creek valley therefore probably consisted, at any point in time, of a single or small number of dwellings, probably of family units, with attendant storage and trash facilities. Such habitation sites are best characterized as being family farmsteads (O'Brien 1972b, 1973). There is also some evidence of labor specialization existing between farmsteads—implying cottage industries (O'Brien 1972a). This hypothesis is based on a χ^2 analysis of the tool types in houses at two sites, 23PL4 and 23PL16. The two houses at the Young site (23PL4) had the same array of artifacts within them, except for one artifact class (faceted hematite), suggesting the same functional and work

TABLE 1.1
The Distribution of Brush Creek Sites by Ceramic Period

	Periods			
	I	II	III	IV
Farmsteads				
23PL4	×	×	×	—
23PL61	—	—	—	—
23PL106	—	×	—	—
23PL70	—	×	—	—
23PL121	—	—	—	—
23PL108	×	—	—	—
23PL96	—	—	—	—
23PL97	×	—	—	—
23PL54	—	×	×	—
Storage sites				
23PL80	—	×	×	—
23PL102	—	—	—	—
Burial mounds				
23PL117	—	—	—	—
23PL118	—	—	—	—
23PL5	—	—	—	—
23PL181	—	—	—	—
23PL79	—	—	—	—

activities. These two house-artifact assemblages were quite different from the assemblages recovered from the Coons site (23PL16) where eight different artifact classes were present.

If sites with houses represent single or multiple family farmsteads (with or without cottage industries), a most interesting pattern emerges when the spatial distribution of Steed–Kisker sites within the Brush Creek valley is examined (Figure 1.4).

Four bluff-top burial mound sites are uniformly spaced upstream along the Brush Creek valley at intervals of 2.0, 2.8, and 1.9 km. Associated with each of these burial mound sites is a cluster of two or three farmsteads situated on the valley floor. This clear spatial clustering of several farmsteads with associated burial mound sites suggests that the mounds may represent cemeteries for a number of nuclear or extended family groupings. Two sites associated with the southernmost of the burial-mound–farmstead clusters (23PL81, 23PL82) were tested, with no clear evidence of structures being observed. They may represent trash areas for farmsteads in the cluster (23PL61, 23PL106), or be farmsteads where structures were abandoned and used as trash areas. Site 23PL80 is a known storage site, whereas 23PL102 may represent a second storage site—it is located on a well-drained knoll, and consists of a single daub–debris cluster.

A similar spatial patterning of Steed–Kisker settlements is evident in the Smithville area (Figure 1.5). A total of four bluff-top burial mounds (23CL37, 23CL208, 23CL108, 23CL155) are spaced upstream along the Little Platte valley at intervals of 5.5, 4.5, and 6.1 km. Only two of the mounds are definitely known to be Steed–Kisker. The two untested mounds (23CI55 and 23CL208) are quite likely to be Steed–Kisker, however, judging from their position close to Steed–Kisker habitation sites.

The greater spatial separation of burial mound sites in the Little Platte River valley, when compared to Brush Creek, may be a function of a slightly different environmental situation. The Smithville area sites are located in a prairie–forest transition zone, with a more tenuous potential for agricultural pursuits than Brush Creek, a direct tributary of the Missouri River. Although the Smithville area patterning of burial-mound–farmstead clusters is a little less tidy than that of the Brush Creek valley, the same basic relationship of farmsteads to mounds to storage and trash sites exists.

Conclusions

Based on the information presently available, it appears that Steed–Kisker populations inhabiting the Kansas City area lived in single or

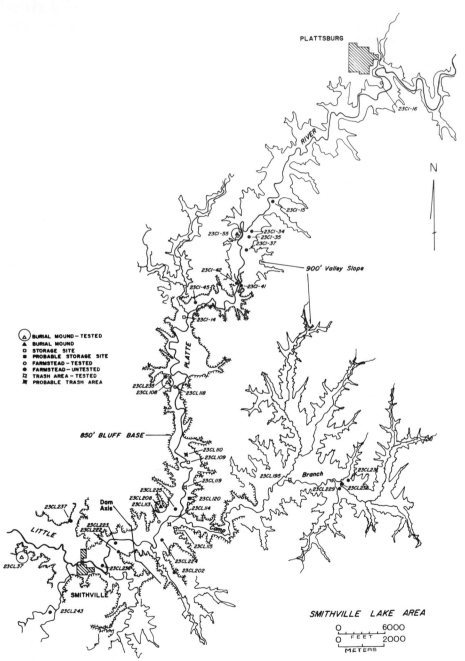

FIGURE 1.5.   The distribution of functionally distinct Steed–Kisker sites on Camp Branch
and the Little Platte River north of the Smithville Lake dam axis.

multiple-family farmsteads consisting of a habitation structure and associated trash and storage areas. A family cemetery represented by a
bluff-top burial mound was located nearby. Family groups also apparently
maintained storage sites, perhaps located near agricultural fields or
specific wild plant resources. In addition, hunting and butchering camps
located at a considerable distance from the area suggests long-distance
hunting activities, perhaps on a seasonal basis.

Research Goals

Future research concerning Steed–Kisker populations in the Kansas
City area will focus on five related problem areas.

1. To test further the hypothesis that Steed–Kisker habitation sites
are farmsteads, several more such sites should be completely excavated.
Ideally, all the sites on Brush Creek should be excavated. Careful excavation of daub–debris patches at these habitation sites should be directed
toward testing not just the hypotheses that they may represent habitation
structures or storage areas. They should also be examined with the idea
of identifying other specialized work areas which had to be a part of the
yearly round of an agricultural people. At the same time, careful stripping
of the plowzone over large areas of Steed–Kisker sites (Figure 1.3) would
reduce the possibility of missing any habitation structures not indicated
by surface materials. Ideally, all of the sites on Brush Creek should be
excavated.

2. To test the hypothesis that burial mounds represent family
cemeteries, larger and more complete skeletal populations are needed,
with analysis focusing on those metric and nonmetric traits that best show
genetic relationships. Dental anomalies observed in burials from the
Chester Reeves mound (23CL108) near Smithville, as well as the high
incidence of spina bifida in the Calovich mound (14WY7) across the
Missouri River from Brush Creek (Michael Finnegan personal communication), provide some interesting clues concerning possible family groupings. The dental anomalies in question (Carabelli's cusp and the incidence
of shovel-shaping) have been used by Hammond, Pretty, and Saul
(1975:64–65) as familial indicators on burial material from a Classic Maya
tomb at Lubaantun, Belize.

3. The tentative chronological framework that has been established on
the basis of ceramic designs and design elements should be further refined
and tested. Once this is accomplished, a detailed analysis of the ceramic
and other artifact assemblages from both burial mound and farmstead
sites might allow establishment of precise temporal relationships between
burials and farmstead structures.

4. A number of sites that have been excavated yielded neither features
nor extensive debris. For want of a better term these sites have been called

"trash" sites. It is hoped that further excavation of such sites would allow delineation of their specific function(s).

5. Surveying for Steed–Kisker sites above a farmstead level of integration is required. Since the northern, western, and southern limits of the complex are reasonably well known, examination of the Missouri River drainage east of Clay county and the Kansas City area is essential.

Acknowledgments

I have received support throughout the last 9 years of research on Steed–Kisker from the Bureau of General Research, Kansas State University. I would also like to acknowledge the invaluable assistance provided by the following amateur archeologists in the Kansas City area: R.B. Aker of Parkville, Missouri; Coy Bernard of Plattsburg, Missouri; Harold A. Harris of Smithville, Missouri; Roger Justus of Paradise, Missouri; and J. Mett Shippee of Kansas City. I would like to thank all the students and staff of the Kansas Archeological Field School (1969, 1971, 1972, 1973, 1975, and 1976), for without them this research could not have been accomplished.

Intellectually, I have received stimulation, as well as a generous use of their data from F.A. (Cal) Calabrese, J. Mett Shippee, and Waldo R. Wedel. A very special thanks is due to my colleague Alfred E. Johnson with whom I have run the Kansas Archeological Field School since 1968. I have consistently discussed the Steed–Kisker materials with him, and I have immensely profited by those discussions by being forced to greater precision of thought.

References

Barnes, E.J.
    1977   The Calovich Burials (14WY7): The Skeletal Analysis of a Plains Mississippian Population. M.A. thesis, Department of Anthropology, Wichita State University.
Butler, W.B.
    1974   Analysis of Archaeological Remains: Route I-435 from Route I-29, Clay and Platte Counties, Missouri. Report to Missouri Highway Department, Jefferson City, Missouri
Calabrese, F. A.
    1969   Doniphan Phase Origins: An Hypothesis Resulting from Archaeological Investigations in the Smithville Reservoir Area, Missouri: 1968. Manuscript submitted by the University of Missouri to the National Park Service, Midwest Region, Omaha.
    1974   Archaeological investigations in the Smithville area, Missouri: 1969. Manuscript submitted to the National Park Service, Midwest Region, Omaha.
Davies, S.N.
    1955   Pleistocene Geology of Platte County, Missouri. Ph.D. dissertation, Yale University, New Haven, Connecticut.
Evans, D.R.
    1974   Archaeological Survey and Testing of Route I-435 Platte–Clay Counties, east of Route I-29 to Route I-35. Report of Missouri Highway Department. Jefferson City.
Greene, F.C., and W.B. Howe
    1952   Geologic Section of Pennsylvanian Rocks Exposed in the Kansas City Area. *Information Circular No. 8.* Missouri Geological Survey and Water Resources. Rolla, Missouri.

Hammond, N., K. Pretty, and F. P. Saul
  1975   A classic Maya family tomb. *World Archaeology,* **7**(1):57–78.
Jackson, H.
  1966   The Soils of Kansas City North (A General Interpretation). United States Depart-
          ment of Agriculture, Soil Conservation Service. Kansas City, Missouri.
Johnson, A.E.
  1974   Settlement Pattern Variability in Brush Creek Valley, Platte County, Missouri.
          Plains Anthropologist **19**(64):107–122.
Mori, J.L.
  1967   Archaeological Salvage Work in the Kansas City, Missouri, Area: 1966. Manuscript
          submitted by the University of Missouri to the National Park Service, Midwest
          Region, Omaha.
O'Brien, P.J.
  1972a   Steed–Kisker Mississippian and Labor Specialization. Paper presented at the 37th
          Annual Meeting of the Society for American Archaeology, May 4–6, 1972. Miami,
          Florida.
  1972b   A Preliminary Review of Steed–Kisker Culture. Paper presented at the 30th Annual
          Plains Conference, November 1–4, 1972. Lincoln, Nebraska.
  1973   A New Synthesis of Steed–Kisker (Western Middle Mississippian) Culture. Paper
          presented at the 38th Annual Meeting of the Society for American Archaeology,
          May 3–5, 1973. San Francisco, California.
  1974   A Seriation of Steed–Kisker Ceramics. Paper presented at the 39th Annual Meeting
          of the Society for American Archaeology, May 2–4, 1974. Washington, D.C.
Riley, T.J.
  1967   Preliminary Salvage Work in the Smithville Reservoir Area: 1967. Manuscript
          submitted by the University of Missouri to the National Park Service, Midwest
          Region, Omaha.
Roper, D.C.
  1976   A Trend-Surface Analysis of Central Plains Radiocarbon Dates. *American Antiquity,*
          41:181–189.
Shippee, J.M.
  1953   Archaeological Salvage at Avondale Mounds. *Missouri Archaeologist* **15**(4):18–39
  1958   23PL6, Field Notes and Catalog. Manuscript on file at the Department of An-
          thropology, University of Missouri—Columbia.
  1972   Archaeological remains in the Kansas City area. *Missouri Archaeological Society
          Research Series,* No. 9. Columbia, Missouri.
Strong, W.D.
  1935   An Introduction to Nebraska Archeology. *Smithsonian Miscellaneous Collections,*
          Volume 93, No. 10. Washington, D.C.
Sweet, A.T., J.E. Dunn, and E.S. Vanatta
  1912   Soil survey of Platte County, Missouri. United States Department of Agriculture,
          Bureau of Soils. Washington, D.C.
Wedel, W.R.
  1943   Archaeological investigations in Platte and Clay Counties, Missouri. *United States
          National Museum, Bulletin* No. 183. Washington, D.C.
Wilson G.L.
  1917   Agriculture of the Hidatsa Indians, An Indian Interpretation. *Studies in the Social
          Sciences,* No. 9. University of Minnesota. Minneapolis.
Wood, W.R.
  1968   Mississippian hunting and butchering patterns: Bone from the Vista Shelter,
          23SR-20, Missouri. *American Antiquity* **33**:170–179.

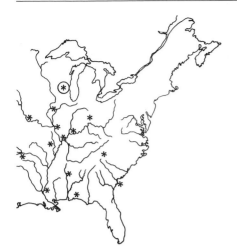

2

Oneota Settlement Patterns in Eastern Wisconsin: Some Considerations of Time and Space

DAVID F. OVERSTREET

During the last four decades, substantial effort has been directed toward various aspects of Oneota research in the Wisconsin subarea. The bulk of this research has focused on three primary research questions: (*a*) the definition of spatial units; (*b*) the explanation of the origin and development of Oneota lifeways in eastern Wisconsin; and (*c*) the demise of this prehistoric culture, which supposedly occurred ca. A.D. 1300. The term "Oneota" is interpreted in a wide variety of ways by different people, and to explain all the nuances and shades of meaning would be a lengthy task in and of itself. Used here, the term oneota most closely approximates the definition used by Faulkner:

> In the several centuries following the first millenium of the Christian Era a distinctive cultural manifestation called Upper Mississippian appeared in the Eastern United States. This socio-economic pattern was composed of several related, yet distinct cultures that made adjustments to localized environments within the prairie-deciduous forest biotic areas of the Upper Mississippi Valley through simple farming and the exploitation of the diverse and abundant natural plant and animal foods [1972:13].

Under the rubric of the midwestern taxonomic system, Will C. McKern (1945:109–285) defined two foci of the Oneota aspect in eastern Wisconsin. The first of these, the Grand River focus, was cited as concentrated in Green Lake and Marquette Counties, whereas the second, the Lake Winnebago focus, was thought to be restricted to the west side of

Mississippian Settlement Patterns

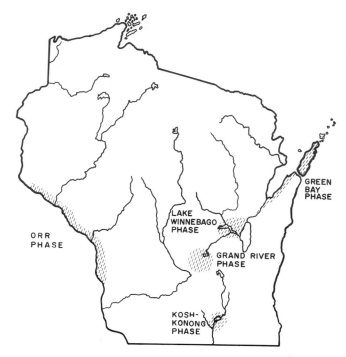

FIGURE 2.1. The distribution of the Grand River, Lake Winnebago, Green Bay, Koshkonong and Orr phases in Wisconsin.

Lake Winnebago. Based upon excavation at the Carcajou Point site, Hall (1962) later defined a third focus, the Koshkonong focus. A tentative definition has also been offered and discussed for a fourth focus, the Green Bay focus (Cleland 1966; Gibbon 1969; R. Mason 1967). McKern (1945) also defined a third focus, the Orr focus in western Wisconsin, which is not germane to this discussion. The distribution of these Oneota foci is depicted in Figure 2.1.

The use of this static terminology to define regional manifestations of Oneota prehistory in eastern Wisconsin has largely been abandoned. The impetus for this abandonment derived primarily from an Oneota conference convened at Columbia, Missouri, in 1960. Robert L. Hall proposed a more dynamic approach to interpretation of Oneota prehistory by adopting the terms "tradition" and "phase" to replace "aspect" and "focus" (Hall 1962). In addition, Hall proposed that the Oneota tradition be placed in an evolutionary framework, by segmenting it into emergent, developmental, and classic horizons. This reformulation of classification, while supported by a variety of different types of data collected by conference participants and others, was primarily based upon observed stylistic variation in ceramics (Hall 1962:106–109).

Despite the attempts of the Columbia conference participants to replace the static terminology of the midwestern taxonomic method with the more dynamic framework of Willey and Phillips (1958), the implications of the former remain. The tendency to treat these regional archeological units as isolates has persisted.

In addition to defining the spatial distribution of Oneota cultural groups on the basis of the presence or absence of material culture traits, a great deal of research has involved the formulation of alternative hypotheses concerning Oneota origins (see, for example, Baerreis and Bryson 1965, Cleland 1966, Gibbon 1969, 1972a, Griffin 1937, 1960, 1961, 1965). The most popular and persistent hypotheses concerning Oneota origins can be identified as transformationist explanations. Griffin, for example, has suggested that the emergence of Oneota lifeways might be linked in a literal genetic sense to the more southerly distributed Middle Mississippi populations (Griffin 1960, 1961). Briefly, Griffin's hypothesis proposes that Oneota culture was caused by a population movement from the Middle Mississippi occupation at the Cahokia site in southern Illinois. Upon arrival in the eastern Wisconsin subarea, these new migrants were subjected to a climatic deterioration which, in part, caused the transformation of a Middle Mississippi cultural tradition into an Upper Mississippian one (Griffin 1960, 1961).

Gibbon (1969, 1972a), on the other hand, rejects Griffin's hypothesis of Middle Mississippi ancestry for the occupants of Oneota settlements in eastern Wisconsin. His alternative hypothesis is also, however, essentially transformationist. In Gibbon's model, the resident Wisconsin Effigy Mound populations are proposed as the progenitors of Oneota culture. The causal processes of transformation are viewed as involving the development of efficient maize horticulture, accompanied by a radical alteration of material culture.

The third major research topic that has concerned individuals interested in Oneota prehistory in eastern Wisconsin is the proposition that a general debilitation and disintegration of this prehistoric group occurred around A.D. 1300. Gibbon (1972a) defines this process as *factionalization*, and argues that it ends in eastern Wisconsin with the formation of the Historic Winnebago Tribe. The causes of this proposed factionalization of eastern Wisconsin Oneota populations are both a suggested decrease in the influence of the Middle Mississippi populations to the south, and climatic change (Gibbon 1969:318–324, 1972a).

Implicit in this last research topic is the tendency to view the later and westerly distributed Oneota groups, such as those of the Orr phase, as having derived at least in part from earlier populations in eastern Wisconsin. Gibbon's factionalization hypothesis is compatible with the conclusion that movement of Oneota populations was in a westerly direction. Such relocation could correlate with the intrusion of a prairie habitat and associated species such as bison into areas east of the Mississippi River. As a result, the factionalization hypotheses also support the contention that some Oneota groups in eastern Wisconsin abandoned their characteristic mixed horticulture and hunting adaptation, relocated their settlements in a westerly direction, and adopted a prairie lifestyle as they encountered the recently expanded grassland ecosystem.

Rather than pursuing any of these three long-standing research questions, this chapter will be concerned with demonstrating that the distinctions noted between Oneota phases in eastern Wisconsin are the result of both temporal separation and changes in a basic adaptive strategy employed throughout the course of at least seven centuries of occupation (Overstreet 1976). Consequently, the models of settlement patterning presented here are based on assumptions and presuppositions quite distinct from those presented in previous Oneota research. In reconstructing the settlement patterns of eastern Wisconsin's Oneota inhabitants, I have, for example, rejected the various hypotheses which posit the emergence of Oneota culture in transformationist terms. While I have no specific alternative candidates for Oneota precursors, the present data base clearly prohibits acceptance of a Cahokia source for the emergence of Oneota populations in eastern Wisconsin. Radiocarbon chronologies which establish the contemporaneity of Upper Mississippian or Oneota populations in Wisconsin and the Middle Mississippi occupation at Cahokia represent a clear problem for those supporting the migration hypothesis. It is difficult to accept the view that the population at Cahokia, ca. A.D. 1000, could have produced a sufficient number of people to have populated the many Oneota sites known from that time period in eastern Wisconsin and have still maintained the growth in population postulated for the Cahokia site proper (Fowler 1969:1–30; Gregg 1975:126–136).

Gibbon's (1972a) transformational model is also difficult to accept. Gibbon contends that Effigy Mound populations experienced differing adjustments to a basic innovation in the economic foundations of their social units, the development of maize horticulture. This more secure subsistence base leads to the disruption of established territories and to a radical change in social patterning and external social interaction. Gibbon also proposes a rapid and radical evolution of Oneota material culture out of Effigy Mound material artifact assemblages. In support of his Effigy Mound origin hypothesis, Gibbon (1969, 1972a) points out that the distribution of early Oneota phases roughly correlates with the primary areas of Effigy Mound occupation.

There is at present, however, no evidence to demonstrate the hypothetical shift from extensive to intensive horticulture in the Effigy Mound tradition. Nor is rapid modification of Effigy Mound ceramics the only plausible interpretation for the initial development of Oneota ceramic wares. In Wisconsin, the suggested early Oneota material traits are not as new and radical as Gibbon suggests. Shell tempering, broad finger-trailing, and globular vessel form all been identified in a wide variety of contexts that predate the Oneota emergence in Wisconsin (Douglass 1946,

Wittry 1959, Hall 1962, Salzer 1969). In addition, the geographical distribution of Effigy Mound and emergent Oneota sites is certainly not clearly coincident. Finally, Hurley's (1975) lengthy and convincing monograph demonstrates the long contemporaneity of both traditions rather than the gestation and birth of one from the other.

Although adequate data are not now available to answer the question of Oneota origins, I look to the general process of regionalization that follows the demise of Southern Tier Middle Woodland traditions, such as Havana and its southern Wisconsin counterpart, the Waukesha focus (Salzer 1972), in seeking an understanding and explanation of the emergence and development of Oneota culture.

A second assumption guiding this reconstruction of Oneota settlement patterns in eastern Wisconsin relates to the omission of the Orr phase from consideration. The Orr phase is not considered, owing to my contention that it represents a clearly separate cultural unit with its own long regional history. Including it in this discussion will not add significantly to an understanding of Oneota prehistory in eastern Wisconsin. The eastern and western variants of Oneota culture resulted from lengthy *in situ* cultural development in different ecological settings. The growth and elaboration of Oneota settlements in western Wisconsin, eastern Iowa, and southeastern Minnesota parallel, but do not derive from those in eastern Wisconsin. This discussion predicts that the eastern and western variants of Oneota will be ultimately recognized as representing two distinct regional traditions, much as the Havana and Scioto traditions are considered distinct cultural phenomena; each rooted in its own past.

Finally, the theoretical concept of debilitation, factionalization, or both around A.D. 1300 has strong implications in terms of changes in Oneota settlement patterns in eastern Wisconsin. Gibbon (1969, 1972a) proposes that by A.D. 1300 large Oneota settlements had fragmented into small dispersed communities, with some relocation of population to the west. The causal factors in this hypothesized process of factionalization include climatic deterioration (the Pacific Climatic Episode; Baerreis and Bryson 1965:101–131) and the decline of Middle Mississippi influence from the south (Aztalan? Cahokia?). This process of factionalization is further viewed as involving the breakdown of higher levels of social integration, with socially and economically independent family units regrouping at a lower level of cultural complexity (Gibbon 1969:318–324, 1972a).

The presently known distribution of Lake Winnebago phase Oneota settlements (ca. A.D. 1300–1600) does indicate a greatly restricted geographic region when compared with the distribution of sites assigned to the earlier Grand River, Lake Koshkonong, and Green Bay phases (Overstreet 1976:274–275). Rather than interpreting this reduction of geographical distribution as the result of factionalization, I propose that the territorial constriction results from population and community nucleation. I further propose that, rather than being a period of cultural decline, the post-A.D. 1300 horizon witnesses the peak of Oneota cultural development in eastern Wisconsin. This proposed elaboration refers not only to material culture, but to social organizational aspects as well.

These three primary assumptions will serve as a basis for the consideration of Oneota settlement patterning to be presented in what follows. The eastern Wisconsin Oneota settlement pattern models offered here therefore rest upon the following suppositions:

1. The Oneota culture in this region is an *in situ* phenomenon resulting neither from a migration of Middle Mississippi populations nor from a rapid transformation of Effigy Mound populations.
2. Temporal differences between the Grand River, Lake Koshkonong (early component), and Green Bay phases are minimal (see Hall 1962).
3. These phases predate the Lake Winnebago phase.
4. The post-A.D. 1300 horizon is not one of factionalization and debilitation, but one of nucleation and cultural elaboration.

Environmental–Topographic Setting

Martin (1932:209–211) has defined a specific geographic province within which the great majority of Oneota settlements in eastern Wisconsin are located. Defined as the Eastern Ridges and Lowlands, this geographic province encompasses all of the state of Wisconsin between Lake Michigan on the east and the Central Plain and Western Upland to the west, as shown in Figure 2.2.

The Eastern Ridges and Lowlands province is bounded on the west by the Black River and Magnesian Cuestas, whereas the eastern boundary can be described as the contact of Lake Michigan with the backslope of the Niagara Cuesta (Martin 1932). The province comprises some 35,000 km² of unsubmerged land.

Settlements of the Koshkonong, Grand River, Green Bay, and Lake Winnebago phases are located in or immediately adjacent to the extensive and well-defined transition zone between the Carolinian and Canadian biotic zones as defined by Dice (1943). Cleland (1967:7) has noted that transition zones or *ecotones* are extremely favorable for prehistoric human occupation due to both the greater diversity and greater density of plant and animal species present within the transition zone than in adjacent, more uniform, biotic communities.

There are from 140 to 160 frost-free days in the region, the first killing frost occurring between September 30 and October 5. The mean July

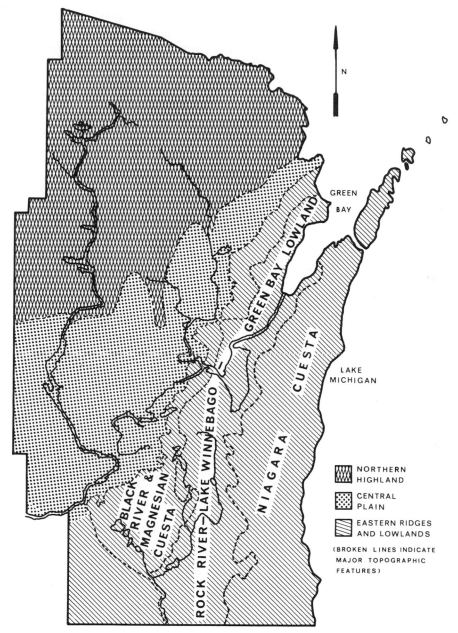

FIGURE 2.2.   The Eastern Ridges and Lowlands of Wisconsin with major topographic features shown.

temperature is 70°F, and warm season precipitation, April through September inclusive, averages 50 cm. The annual mean precipitation is 76–80 cm. For more detailed environmental studies of the area, readers are referred to Curtis (1959), Martin (1932), USDA (1941), Baerreis and Bryson (1965), Burt (1957), and Cleland (1966).

The Eastern Ridges and Lowlands province represents a relatively uniform environmental situation, with a not surprising commonality of subsistence and settlement existing throughout the Oneota continuum in eastern Wisconsin (Overstreet 1976; Peske 1966, 1971). Several similarities can be noted in the environmental setting of Oneota settlements in the Eastern Ridges and Lowlands. Immediate site environs can be described as rich riverine–lacustrine habitats, with sites often located adjacent to extensive marshlands.

Previous research has, however, focused on the environmental setting from a diametrically opposed viewpoint. Cleland (1966) has suggested that Oneota settlements in Wisconsin are located in distinctly different micro-environments, each supporting different food resources. Based on this supposition and using incomplete and varied samples of faunal remains, Cleland recognized four distinct settlement–subsistence patterns in each of four separate Oneota phases (Cleland 1966:68–90). The Lake Winnebago phase was depicted as being restricted to an area of ecological transition between grasslands and the Central Plains province. Their adaptive pattern was cited as being based primarily upon aquatic resources. Koshkonong phase populations, ostensibly located in a prairie area, were described, based on the high frequency of deer bones, as being primarily agricultural. The Grand River phase was portrayed as being restricted to an ecological transition zone between grasslands and woodlands, a situation ideal for large herbivores. Based on this environmental reconstruction, Cleland proposed that one would expect Grand River phase populations to have had an economy based on agriculture and hunting large herbivores, with bison and elk, which prefer grasslands, perhaps surpassing deer as a source of meat. Again relying on limited faunal data, Cleland further predicted a different ecological adaptation for the populations of the Green Bay phase, suggesting that in all probability the inhabitants of these Oneota settlements were oriented to exploitation of the aquatic resources of Green Bay and Lake Michigan (Cleland 1966:87).

Perhaps influenced by Cleland's portrayal of a series of differing ecological settings and subsistence patterns for the various Oneota phases, Gibbon (1969:27–28) presented a more qualitative set of distinctions regarding the location of Oneota settlements in eastern Wisconsin. Gibbon proposed that the emergence of Oneota culture took place within a series of distinct subregions rather than in a uniform environmental setting. These undefined subregions were described as having had different potentials for maize cultivation and mutually exclusive channels of communication. The major environmental differences between each region were identified as the length of the growing season, differences in vegetation, mean annual precipitation, and other (unspecified) climatic factors (Gibbon 1972a:174).

Later subsistence studies, however, have failed to support the diversity of adaptive patterns presented by Cleland as a function of dissimilarity of habitat (Overstreet 1976:197–223; Peske 1966:188–195, 1971:62–70). To the contrary, Oneota subsistence patterns are best viewed as representing a single basic exploitative strategy. Refined analysis of the ecological setting of Oneota settlements does not reveal significant differences, particularly with regard to differing potential for maize cultivation suggested by Gibbon (1969, 1972a). Yarnell (1964, 1965) has pointed out that the most important climatic factor for corn horticulture in the Upper Great Lakes is temperature, with annual precipitation being relatively unimportant when contrasted with the more significant index of warm season precipitation. Therefore, it is more reasonable to view the settlement patterns of both developmental and later Oneota populations in eastern Wisconsin as occurring in a single uniform environmental zone rather than in several distinctly different habitat situations.

Data Collection

The method of data collection used to study Oneota settlement patterns varies to a certain extent from others described in this volume. The information to be presented did not result from a specifically formulated research design in which the collection of data was carried out within a well-defined research area. Rather, the data to be considered resulted from 40 years of previous research, much of which was guided by differing research orientations. By and large, these previous research orientations were either compartmentalized, in that they were carried out at either the focus or phase level of abstraction, or they were theoretically broad to the extent that any comparative analysis of settlement and subsistence were submerged in a quest for the origins or emergence of Oneota. Because of this variability, information collected concerning patterning of settlements was often both limited and subjective.

Little information is available, for example, concerning the size of Oneota settlements. Terms such as "large," "substantial," "minor," and "small," which abound in the literature, have no solid quantitative basis. Relying on previously published information, Gibbon (1972b) cites the Grand River phase Walker–Hooper site as encompassing approximately 60 acres (26 ha), judging from the areal extent of surface materials. For the dimensions of the Bornick site, he indicates an area of 1 acre (.4 ha) defined through unspecified measures (Gibbon 1971:85). The Shrake–Gillies and Midway sites in western Wisconsin ostensibly cover approximately 40 acres (16 ha) and 35 acres (14 ha), respectively (McKern 1945). Lake Winnebago phase sites have been particularly difficult to estimate in terms of size. Peske notes that the "garbage dump" of the Lasley's Point site alone is approximately 40 acres (16 ha), and that the Furman and Eurlich sites are analogous to the former (in size?) (Peske 1966:190, 193). The Lake Winnebago phase site defined by Seurer and Faulkner (1976) as the Nile Roeder site, is considered as "the same occupation as the Overton Meadow component some ¾ of a mile to the north [p. 29]." It becomes clear from this discussion that most estimates of the extent of Oneota sites in eastern Wisconsin can at best be considered approximations.

One of the considerations that guided excavations at the Pipe site in Fond du Lac County (Overstreet 1974) was the fact that the size of Oneota settlements was largely unknown. Chemical soil tests and controlled excavations were used to determine the actual limits of intensive occupation of the site. Although a direct correspondence between high phosphate readings and intensive occupation determined by excavation was not always found to occur, the site was determined to encompass an area of 3.57 ha (Overstreet 1974:266). This would seem to provide support for McKern's (1945) hypothesis that Oneota settlements were in some cases quite large.

Although the size of the Pipe site may be comparable to at least some settlements of the Grand River, Lake Koshkonong, and Green Bay phases, it is impossible to determine the variety of site classes or the range of variation within site classes for these phases on the basis of a single excavated site.

In the absence of any systematic archeological surveys designed to demonstrate the spatial distribution of Oneota settlements in eastern Wisconsin, it should be noted, even though it is painfully apparent, that the extant data base contains significant gaps. Until more intensive regional surveys have been carried out it should be recognized that the total range of different types of settlements has not been discovered. The biases that characterize our present knowledge of Oneota settlement patterns is a result of the tendency to focus excavation efforts on large, highly visible sites that could be expected to produce large and varied artifactual data. This focus is predictable when one considers the primary goals that have guided previous research. The emphasis has been on material culture, which was, on the one hand, employed to define the "culture" of Oneota populations as compared to other prehistoric cultures throughout the state (e.g., McKern 1945; McKern and Ritzenthaler 1945, 1949), as well as being utilized to demonstrate how Middle Mississippi populations had migrated into Wisconsin and subsequently acquired Oneota characteristics (Griffin 1960, 1961; Hall 1962).

Proposed Models of Oneota Settlement Patterns

Twenty-seven sites have been considered in formulating the models of Oneota settlement patterning in eastern Wisconsin to be presented here. Although this is an admittedly small sample of sites, it represents the total data base to date. Available radiocarbon dates for these sites are presented in Table 2.1. These 27 sites encompass a time period of at least 700 years.

TABLE 2.1
Radiocarbon Chronology, Wisconsin Oneota Sites

Date B.P.	Calendric	Site	Lab and sample	Phase
1060 ± 80	A.D. 890	Carcajou Point	WIS-77	Lake Koshkonong
975 ± 105	A.D. 975	Armstrong	S-802	Blue Earth
970 ± 55	A.D. 980	Crabapple Point	WIS-609	Lake Koshkonong
960 ± 250	A.D. 990	Carcajou Point	M-786	Lake Koshkonong
960 ± 70	A.D. 990	Lasley's Point	WIS-50	Lake Winnebago
930 ± 250	A.D. 1020	Carcajou Point	M-785	Lake Koshkonong
860 ± 115	A.D. 1090	Armstrong	S-801	Blue Earth
840 ± 90	A.D. 1110	Overton Meadow	GAK-3347	Grand River, Lake Winnebago, Unidentified Woodland
840 ± 80	A.D. 1110	Overton Meadow	GAK-3348	Same as above
835 ± 115	A.D. 1115	Armstrong	S 799	Blue Earth
830 ± 105	A.D. 1120	Armstrong	S-800	Blue Earth
820 ± 60	A.D. 1130	Pipe	WIS-194	Grand River
810 ± 50	A.D. 1140	Crescent Bay Hunt Club	WIS-382	Lake Koshkonong
800 ± 50	A.D. 1150	Crescent Bay Hunt Club	WIS-384	Lake Koshkonong
795 ± 110	A.D. 1155	Armstrong	S-803	Blue Earth
780 ± 80	A.D. 1170	Lasley's Point	WIS-47	Lake Winnebago
780 ± 80	A.D. 1170	Lasley's Point	WIS-62	Lake Winnebago
780 ± 50	A.D. 1170	Crescent Bay Hunt Club	WIS-358	Lake Koshkonong
760 ± 50	A.D. 1190	Crescent Bay Hunt Club	WIS-341	Lake Koshkonong
750 ± 55	A.D. 1200	Walker-Hooper	WIS-277	Grand River
745 ± 60	A.D. 1205	Pipe	WIS-543	Grand River
740 ± 50	A.D. 1210	Walker-Hooper	WIS-290	Grand River
730 ± 65	A.D. 1220	Lasley's Point	WIS-159	Lake Winnebago
720 ± 55	A.D. 1230	Walker-Hooper	WIS-270	Grand River
710 ± 45	A.D. 1240	Walker-Hooper	WIS-268	Grand River
690 ± 60	A.D. 1260	Pipe	WIS-544	Grand River
680 ± 80	A.D. 1270	Lasley's Point	WIS-57	Lake Winnebago
660 ± 50	A.D. 1290	Bornick	WIS-288	Grand River
550 ± 70	A.D. 1400	Lasley's Point	WIS-161	Lake Winnebago
530 ± 70	A.D. 1420	Midway	WIS-61	Orr
470 ± 70	A.D. 1480	Lasley's Point	WIS-164	Lake Winnebago
470 ± 60	A.D. 1480	Lasley's Point	WIS-158	Lake Winnebago
465 ± 55	A.D. 1485	Overhead	WIS-601	Orr
440 ± 65	A.D. 1510	Overhead	WIS-573	Orr
430 ± 250	A.D. 1520	Carcajou Point	M-747	Lake Koshkonong
320 ± 60	A.D. 1630	Midway	WIS-79	Orr

This 700-year continuum of Oneota occupation of the study region has been segmented in various ways by different investigators. Hall's (1962:106–109) horizon scheme will be used here, with certain modifications. The terms *emergent, developmental, classic,* and *historic,* will be employed to refer not only to temporal horizons or stages, but also to sites that can be assigned to these temporal units.

The emergent horizon, ca. A.D. 700–1000, is viewed as the nascence of Oneota culture, reflected in subtle modifications of already existing material culture elements in resident populations of the Eastern Ridges and Lowlands. As one might expect, this emergent horizon is difficult to recognize archeologically, and thus is poorly known. However, early occupations at (*a*) the Carcajou Point site (Hall 1962), (*b*) the Lasley's Point site, as well as components of the (*c*) Sanders I site (Hurley 1975), (*d*) Watasa Lake Swamp site, and (*e*) the South Branch Chapel site (Barrett and Skinner 1932), (*f*) the Neale and McClaughry Campsites (McKern 1928), and (*g*) the Overton Meadow site (Faulkner 1974), may tentatively be assigned to this emergent horizon (Figure 2.3).

The developmental horizon, ca. A.D. 1000–1300, corresponds with the general time framework established for the Grand River and Lake Koshkonong phases. It is during this time period that resident populations acquire many of the diagnostic traits or characteristics responsible for their initial incorporation within the Oneota aspect (tradition) some 40 years ago (McKern 1939, 1945). This horizon includes, but is not limited to, the following sites or components of sites: (*a*) Carcajou Point (Hall 1962), (*b*) Crescent Bay Hunt Club, (*c*) Pipe (Overstreet 1976), (*d*) Point Sauble (Freeman 1956), (*e*) Walker–Hooper (Gibbon 1972b), (*f*) Mero (R. Mason 1966), (*g*) Porte Des Morts (C. Mason 1970), (*h*) Bornick (Gibbon 1971), (*i*) Summer Island (Brose 1968), (*j*) Little Lake, and (*k*) Winnebago Heights. The distribution of Grand River, Lake Koshkonong, and Green Bay phase ceramics is certainly wider than the geographic region indicated by these, as seen in Figure 2.4 (Hall 1962; Salzer 1969). However, in many instances the material is reported as an adjunct to other excavations and it is not clear that there was an Oneota component present. Figure 2.4 therefore represents the known distribution of Developmental Oneota settlements.

Classic horizon occupations, which should postdate A.D. 1300, are quite restricted in geographical distribution when compared with the developmental horizon. Those sites assigned to the classic horizon, depicted in Figure 2.5, include (*a*) Lasley's Point (Peske 1966), (*b*) Karow (McKern 1945), (*c*) McCauley (McKern 1945), (*d*) Overton Meadow (Faulkner 1974), (*e*) Asylum Point (Hall 1962), (*f*) Furman and Eulrich sites (Peske 1966), (*g*) Redgranite (Hall 1962), (*h*) an unnamed component on Doty's Island (Hall 1962), (*i*) the late component at Porte Des Morts (C. Mason 1970), (*j*) the late component at Carcajou Point (Hall 1962), and (*k*) the Nile

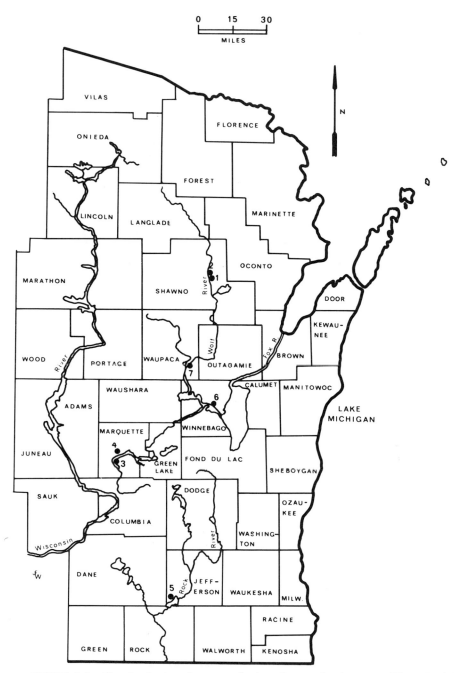

FIGURE 2.3.   *The distribution of emergent horizon Oneota sites in eastern Wisconsin: (1) South Branch Chapel; (2) Watasa Lake Swamp; (3) Neale Campsite; (4) McClaughry Campsite; (5) the early component at Carajou Point; (6) the early component at Overton Meadow; (7) Sanders I.*

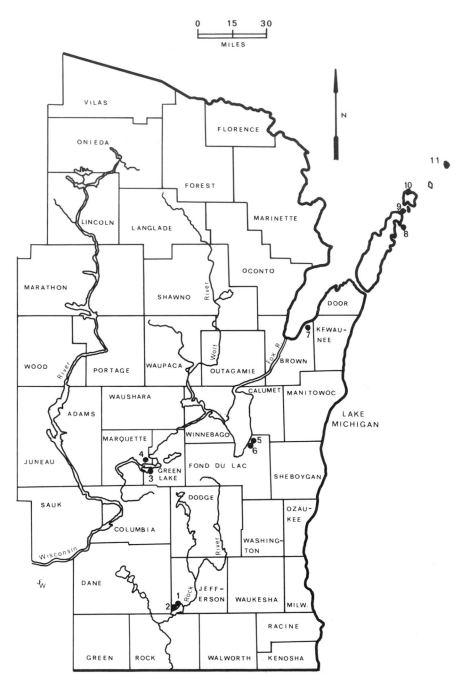

FIGURE 2.4. The distribution of developmental horizon Oneota sites in eastern Wisconsin: (1) Carcajou Point; (2) Cresent Bay Hunt Club; (3) Walker–Hooper; (4) Bornick; (5) Pipe; (6) Winnebago Heights; (7) Point Sauble; (8) Mero; (9) Porte Des Morts; (10) Little Lake; (11) Summer Island.

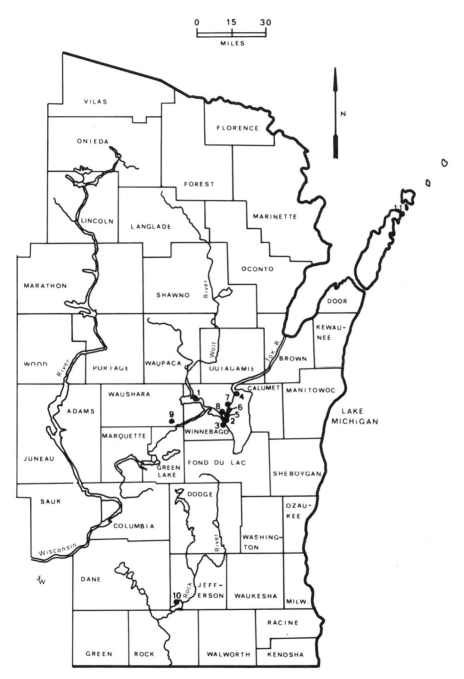

FIGURE 2.5.   The distribution of classic horizon Oneota sites in eastern Wisconsin: (1)
Lasley's Point; (2) Karow; (3) McCauley; (4) Doty's Island; (5) Asylum Point; (6) Furman; (7)
Eulrich; (8) Nile Roeder; (9) Redgranite; (10) late component at Carcajou Point; (11) late component
at Porte Des Morts.

Roeder site (Seurer and Faulkner 1976). Classic horizon artifact assemblages (i.e., decorated ceramics, end scrapers, paired sandstone abraders, catlanite disk pipes, and bison scapula hoes) comprise the basis of most traditional descriptions of Oneota material culture.

The historic horizon is, in an archeological sense, poorly known and documented. Sites that may represent settlements of this post-A.D.-1650 time period are (*a*) McCauley (McKern 1945), (*b*) Doty's Island, (*c*) Crabapple Point (Spector 1975), and (*d*) the White Crow component at Carcajou Point (Hall 1962). These four sites (shown in Figure 2.6) represent only a few of the sites that have been classified as historic Winnebago, and their identification as such is based upon ethnohistorical documentation rather than archeological investigation.

The morphology of settlement patterning varies with each defined horizon within the Oneota continuum, primarily as a result of often minor, but sometimes significant modifications of the basic adaptive strategy of the populations involved. A number of variables can certainly be identified as being potentially important in explaining Oneota settlement pattern shifts (e.g., population demography, relative stability of the resource base, technological innovation, such internal and external sociocultural factors as trade and solidarity), but the resultant effect is clear: Settlements within the Eastern Ridges and Lowlands throughout the Oneota continuum manifest differential size and geographical distribution. Adequate description of the total settlement pattern of any horizon is not possible at this time, owing to extremely limited data, particularly for the emergent and historic horizons. In this respect, the description of changing Oneota settlement patterns that follows should not be misconstrued as being solidly based upon empirical data, but rather should be recognized as a working model awaiting future confirmation or rejection.

EMERGENT HORIZON A.D. *700–1000*

The emergence of Oneota culture in eastern Wisconsin remains a poorly understood process. It should be pointed out initially that shell tempering as a paste characteristic does not coincide with the emergence of Oneota culture in Wisconsin. As Hall (1962:116) indicates, utilization of shell as a paste characteristic occurs prior to the time when resident Middle Woodland cultures had lost their identity, as evidenced by recurring rather than incidental utilization at the Cooper's Shore site and from the occurrence of Baraboo Cord Marked and Baraboo Net Marked ceramics at components of sites in Sauk County. Two additional potential early occurrences of shell-tempered ceramics may be the McClaughry and Neale Campsites in Marquette County (McKern 1928).

If the *in situ* hypothesis concerning Oneota emergence is correct, it is

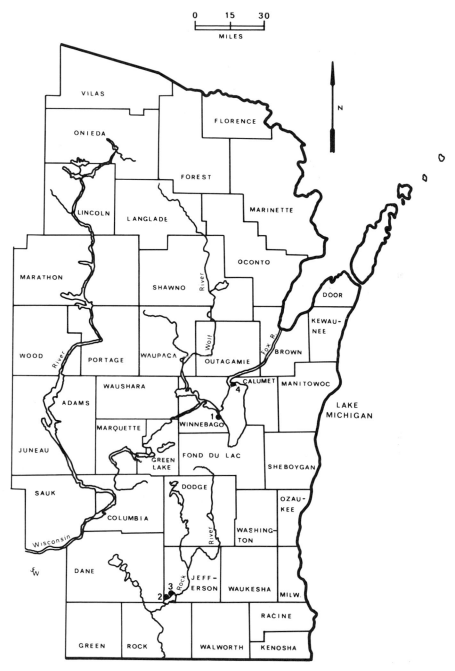

FIGURE 2.6. *The distribution of historic horizon Oneota sites in eastern Wisconsin: (1) McCauley; (2) Crabapple Point; (3) White Crow component at Carcajou Point; (4) Doty's Island.*

quite likely that settlements of this horizon will be very difficult to recognize, or even locate, archeologically. The previously discussed excavation orientation which focused on large artifactually productive village sites would, in part, explain the lack of data relating to early emergent Oneota settlements. Equally important, however, would be the nature of the settlements themselves. Hall (1962) has already indicated that the wide geographical distribution of Oneota ceramics in eastern Wisconsin does not necessarily represent the distribution of Oneota settlements. Grand River and Green Bay phase vessels have been reported from the Northern Lakes area (Salzer 1969), Summer Island (Brose 1968), and the Nicolet National Forest (Salzer, personal communication). The southernmost occurrence of these ceramic forms is the Carcajou Point site on the shores of Lake Koshkonong (Hall 1962).

The distribution of this distinctive ceramic ware can, as Hurley (1975) suggests, be explained in part as being the result of trade and interaction between populations initially acquiring the constellation of traits that ultimately result in their classification within the Oneota tradition. By logical extension, it is just as certain that somewhere within that ceramic distribution early emergent Oneota settlements must occur. Within this A.D. 700–1000 time period, prior to the appearance of maize horticulture as an habitual yet ancillary energy source of Oneota populations, and prior to the dominance of distinctive Oneota ceramic traits such as shell tempering, smooth surface treatment, and plain or finger-trailed globular vessel form, emergent Oneota cultural groups quite probably consisted of small, nonsedentary populations using a broad-spectrum hunting and gathering subsistence economy, not unlike that of preceding pre-Oneota groups.

The pattern of incipient Oneota settlements should, then, approximate or compare favorably with the settlement patterns of pre-Oneota populations. The emergent Oneota horizon in eastern Wisconsin was quite likely characterized by a broad-spectrum hunting and gathering adaptive strategy, with the corresponding settlement pattern showing seasonal occupations of varying duration and density, reflecting in turn the seasonal availability of localized versus more randomly distributed energy sources.

Almost no information reflecting the internal patterning of emergent horizon settlements has been reported. If these settlements did, in fact, represent the occupation loci of hunting and gathering populations utilizing a mobile, seasonal exploitative pattern, one would expect minimal intrasite variation. Subsistence data should indicate the season of occupation of such settlements, based upon the availability of particular resources or combinations of resources. Variability between sites of this time period, on the other hand, should be archeologically demonstrable in terms of not only the kinds and the variety of subsistence resources available on a seasonal basis, but also in terms of the size and relative number of occupants resulting from seasonal nucleation or dispersal of population. It is hoped that excavation of emergent horizon Oneota settlements will provide answers to several research questions. First, such excavations should allow for the formulation of more detailed subsistence–settlement pattern models for this important transition period. Second, the total artifact assemblage from these early occupations is critical to defining the temporal and spatial distribution of elements of material culture that serve as diagnostic traits for the subsequent developmental horizon.

DEVELOPMENTAL HORIZON A.D. 1000–1300

In contrast to the emergent horizon, a discussion of the nature and distribution of developmental horizon Oneota settlements can be based on explicit empirical data (see Hall 1962; Brose 1968; Gibbon 1969; C. Mason 1970; Overstreet 1976). The geographic distribution of developmental horizon settlements A.D. 1000–1300 (Figure 2.4), is almost as widespread as those of the preceding horizon. Settlements of this period are considered to be significantly larger than emergent horizon settlements however, and to have been occupied for significantly longer periods of time. The lengthened duration of occupation and expansion in size of Oneota settlements during the developmental horizon is best explained in terms of a modification–stabilization of the resource base resulting from the introduction of maize horticulture.

Although clear evidence indicative of the relative importance of maize cultivation in the total food procurement system is lacking, it is not likely that maize represented a focal, primary energy source for developmental horizon Oneota populations. By way of comparison with Middle Mississippi subsistence systems, Oneota maize cultivation cannot be demonstrated as having been intensive. Instead, it appears that this procurement system was only one of many energy sources in the total subsistence system. Equal expenditure of effort is indicated for the collection of wild plant foods, large and small terrestrial mammals, and aquatic resources, such as beaver, fish, and waterfowl (Yarnell 1964; Gibbon 1969; Peske 1971; Overstreet 1976).

Developmental Oneota settlements are characteristically located adjacent to major waterways such as those of the Green-Bay–Lake-Winnebago–Fox-River waterway or the Rock River drainage to the south. The settlements are normally extensive, ranging from 3.57 ha for the Pipe site to as large as 16.0 ha for the Walker–Hooper site. Determination of size at the latter site is not, however, conclusive, and represents an approximation based on the extent of surface scatter. Furthermore, Gibbon (1969) indicates multicomponency for the site, which raises the possibility that the extent of surface scatter does not represent the occupation area of a single component. Size estimates for the Carcajou Point site, also multicomponent, compare favorably with those for Walker–Hooper. An acceptable size range for these large horticultural villages would appear to be from 3.5 to 10.0 ha.

In addition to large horticultural villages, some settlements of this developmental horizon, such as the Bornick site (Gibbon 1969), the Winnebago Heights site, and the Oneota component at the Porte Des Morts site (C. Mason 1970), are quite restricted in size. Less than 1 ha in extent, these settlements may, as Gibbon (1969) suggests, represent seasonal occupations.

Gibbon (1969) notes that the Bornick site probably represents a single-family winter occupation. The range of activities carried out at these smaller settlements, as indicated by excavated data from the Bornick site as well as materials obtained through surface collections at the Winnebago Heights site, does not preclude the possibility of occupation in periods other than winter. It is possible that at least some of these small settlements represent functionally specific activity loci other than winter hunting camps. The relationships between these small occupation areas and the more characteristic large and stable villages are not clearly understood. Some regular features of the latter can nonetheless be stated.

In general terms, the larger occupation units represented stable villages often enclosed by palisades, for example, Walker–Hooper and Carcajou Point. The inhabitants of these villages practiced maize horticulture which, when coupled with several other equally important food procurement systems, provided a stable resource base, resulting in more intensive occupations and longer periods of occupation. Villages were periodically relocated, and the actual duration of habitation for any specific settlement remains to be accurately determined. While relocation could have occurred as often as every 3 or 4 years, settlements may have been occupied for as long as 10–15 years. The reasons for relocation also remain to be determined. The inhabitants may have abandoned their settlements as a result of soil depletion relating to horticultural practices, lack of firewood, or reduction of exploited animal species such as mussels, beaver, or deer. The uniformity of patterning does indicate that settlements were inhabitated for relatively short periods of time. In addition, all of the developmental Oneota sites mentioned show evidence of having been intermittently occupied. Rebuilding of the palisade at the Walker–Hooper site and extensive superimposition of features at the Pipe site support the contention that favorable occupation areas were used intermittently by Oneota populations.

A number of domestic structures have been excavated and reported for this time period. In addition to the two structures reported from the Walker–Hooper site (Gibbon 1969), a single structure has been reported at the Pipe site (Overstreet 1976), and at least three were excavated at the Carcajou Point site (Hall 1962). In addition, house structures of the Koshkonong phase were excavated at the Crescent Bay Hunt Club site by members of the University of Wisconsin–Madison staff. Some variability is indicated in this small sample of domestic dwellings, with perhaps three distinct structure forms being represented. Four of these six structures correspond to the well-known mat-covered wigwam, all having slender, arched frame poles. This type is present at the Walker–Hooper, Pipe, and Carcajou Point sites. The second type, which has so far been observed only at the Carcajou Point site, is suggested by Hall (1962) as being a gabled bark summer house of the kind used by most Wisconsin tribes during the seventeenth century. The third form, again represented by a single example from the Carcajou Point site, is a wall-trench structure with dimensions of 5.34 × 6.9 m. Because of their relatively small size, the presence of single internal hearths, and the lack of interior partitioning, all these structure forms can be interpreted as being single, nuclear-family dwellings. Until more extensive excavations are conducted on at least one site, to ascertain overall community patterning, any attempts to determine the spatial relationships and function of different dwelling types must remain highly conjectural.

Neither the excavated Pipe site (Overstreet 1976) nor the Walker–Hooper site appear to have internal functionally specific areas. Based on extensive statistical analyses to determine which artifact classes were associated with specific site areas, Gibbon (1972b:240–254) concluded that a high degree of internal site homogeneity existed, at least for those areas excavated. The Pipe site is quite similar to the Walker–Hooper site in that excavated materials and archeological features demonstrate multipurpose or multifunctional use of most of the excavated portions of the site (Overstreet 1976). This would reflect a high degree of homogeneity within and between sites of the village type.

Utilizing this admittedly limited data, some generalizations can be made with reference to Oneota settlement patterns during this developmental horizon. Villages are large and stable, intensively occupied, with encircling palisades commonly occurring. Within these villages, Oneota populations relying on widely varied resources, and depending upon maize horticulture to an unknown degree, occupied nuclear-family rather than extended- or multiple-family structures. Despite the fact that substantial effort was clearly invested in house and palisade construction, settlements were apparently abandoned after a relatively short span of from 3 to 10 years. Abandoned villages, however, were reoccupied by Oneota inhabitants after an unknown duration of abandonment. In addition to large village settlements, smaller settlements existed. These may have been seasonally occupied by some residents of the larger village units for horticultural or other functionally specific subsistence activities.

CLASSIC HORIZON A.D. 1300–1650

In contrast to the development horizon, during which settlements were distributed over an extensive geographic area (Figure 2.4), the areal distribution of Oneota sites during the classic horizon, ca. A.D. 1300–1650, is significantly reduced (Figure 2.5). Two alternative explanations for this reduction in the geographic distribution of Oneota settlements during the classic horizon are readily apparent:

1. The restriction of range indicates overall population decreases.
2. The smaller geographic area occupied by the Oneota populations of eastern Wisconsin during this period was purely a function of population concentration.

Despite the absence of extensive data collected regarding settlement patterns during this period, the second hypothesized explanation—population nucleation—because of the apparent increase in community size appears to be the more plausible.

The material culture of classic horizon Oneota populations has received some attention in the literature (e.g., Hall 1962; McKern 1945). From every indication, the material culture of this horizon, particularly in reference to ceramics, catlinite disk pipes, shell spoons and disks, bone and shell tubes and beads, and a wide range of lithic implements, reflects stylistic elaboration rather than cultural decline and decay. Indeed, this horizon should be viewed as the apex of Oneota culture in the Eastern Ridges and Lowlands of Wisconsin. The extant literature describing elements of material culture during the classic horizon, while extensive, is unfortunately devoid of conclusive settlement data. For example, the actual site boundaries of even a single Lake Winnebago Phase site have yet to be defined. Settlements are described as being substantial in size, but it is difficult to accurately document differences in the size of settlements of the Lake Winnebago phase and settlements of preceding periods. In addition to the question of settlement size, little is known of the size and form of domestic structures. With the single exception of Hall's (1962:141) description of a possible structure, which was based on his interpretation of Bullock's (1942:38–39) description of Mound 3 at the Lasley's Point site, there is no clear description of any habitation structures from classic horizon Oneota sites in eastern Wisconsin.

Despite the lack of empirical data, I would not rule out the probability of large and complex structures during this time period. This suggestion is based upon the assumption that McKern (1945) was correct in defining the Lake Winnebago phase as the precontact culture of the historic Winnebago tribal groupings. If this assumption was, in fact, correct, the dwelling structure information collected by Radin (1923) is clearly pertinent. While defining quite briefly eight distinct house forms utilized by the Winnebago "in former times," Radin describes two forms that have not been observed archeologically. These are the *ten fire gable lodge*, of which there were two types, one round and one rectangular, with some being built on platforms. In addition, Radin's (1923:56–57) informants described a long ceremonial bark lodge structure form, with interior platforms and partitions designed for such special purposes as fasting. These data are, however, both incomplete and certainly inconclusive. It is at the same time not unreasonable to hypothesize from this ethnohistorical information that Lake Winnebago phase domestic structures were large, complex, multifamily dwellings. The relative strength of this hypothesis could easily be tested through the excavation of Lake Winnebago phase occupation areas.

Recent data reported by Peske (1966, 1971) lend some support to the contention that Lake Winnebago phase settlements were larger and more intensively occupied than earlier Oneota settlements, and that they were perhaps occupied for longer periods of time. Based on excavations at the Lasley's Point, Furman, and Eulrich sites, Peske (1966) describes the location of these Lake Winnebago phase settlements as being adjacent to major waterways, with agricultural fields situated further inland. These agricultural fields may also have served as village dump or midden areas, and may have been extensive, judging from the Lasley's Point dump and garden beds, which encompass an area estimated to be approximately 16.2 hectares. In addition to yielding village debris, the dump heaps also provide indications that the importance of horticulture may have increased in the overall subsistence system. At Lasley's Point, and particularly at the Eulrich site, field preparation and clearing activities are indicated by rock piles, the by-product of removal of rocks during the preparation of horticultural fields. Peske has clearly demonstrated that these activities were carried out by Lake Winnebago populations. No such investment of time and energy relating to horticultural production is demonstrated for the earlier Grand River, Lake Koshkonong, and Green Bay phases. The remaining elements of Lake Winnebago phase subsistence do not, however, appear to represent a radical departure from the subsistence patterns of earlier Oneota populations (Cleland 1966; Peske 1966; Gibbon 1969; Overstreet 1976).

When these varying sources of information and clearly tentative data are synthesized, a working model of Lake Winnebago phase settlement patterns can be offered. This model incorporates both the qualitative and quantitative differences in settlement patterning that existed between the development horizon and the subsequent zenith of Oneota culture in eastern Wisconsin.

Classic horizon settlements, dating to ca, A.D. 1300–1650, are largely concentrated in a nuclear zone surrounding Lake Winnebago and the Lower Fox River, and are identified archeologically as the Lake Winnebago phase. This geographic constriction, does not, however, indicate population decline. Rather, it is indicative of a population concentration associated with more intensive settlement occupation. Settlements are larger than in the preceding developmental horizon, and abandonment and relocation of villages occurs less frequently. There appears to have been greater reliance on maize horticulture, based upon evidence of an increase in the expenditure of time and effort devoted to field clearing and preparation. Although maize cultivation is viewed as the keystone of subsistence during this period, there is no evidence to indicate that other elements of subsistence radically change. A wide range of wild plant and animal foods continued to play an important role in the total subsistence pattern, and the hypothesized process of economic focalization at this early a point in time, as suggested by Cleland (1966:89, 96), is rejected. Material culture, by contrast with that known for the earlier Grand River, Lake Koshkonong, and Green Bay phase populations, is both markedly flamboyant and displays stylistic standardization. Domestic structures, although not documented archeologically, are hypothesized on the basis of ethnohistorical information to be larger and internally more complex than developmental horizon dwellings, perhaps with multifamily occupancy.

HISTORIC HORIZON POST-A.D. 1650

Historic or post-A.D. 1650 settlements are largely unknown. Accepting the assumption that the historic Winnebago are genetically linked to antecedent Oneota populations does little to resolve this dilemma. Those sites shown in Figure 2.6 have traditionally been characterized as being historic Winnebago settlements, but in the absence of data that would support a direct historical connection with the Winnebago tribe, the point is moot. They could just as easily represent settlements of a number of other ethnographically described groups. Although the archeological data are extremely limited regarding the patterning of settlements during the historic horizon, substantial ethnographic and ethnohistorical literature provide pertinent data concerning the distribution and nature of historic settlements (Radin 1915, 1923, 1948; Lurie 1960). Radin's (1923) extensive investigations detail the nature of Algonkianization and the general debilitation of the Winnebago tribe. Lurie (1960:790–808) provides a lucid description of the internal processes accompanying this cultural decline. And, finally, Gibbon (1969) outlines many of these processes of debilitation and Algonkianization following of European contact and Iroquois bellicosity. The process that Gibbon defines as factionalization, although he assigns it to a ca. A.D. 1300 context rather than, more properly, post-A.D. 1650, is useful in explaining the modifications of Winnebago settlement patterns in eastern Wisconsin. His model proposes that large settlements fragmented into small, dispersed communities, with some relocation of population. Factionalization is also characterized as a process in which higher levels of sociocultural integration would have been surrendered, with functionally autonomous family units regrouping at a less complex level of organization.

On the basis of historical information, then, the patterning of historic settlements can be fairly well understood. Habitation sites were smaller, representing less complex social organizations. The population was dispersed, mobile, and, according to Lurie (1976) and others, reduced in numbers as a result of decimation by disease vectors. Radin's (1923) descriptions of single-family dwellings and strong patricentered rules of residence and descent (Radin 1915) probably also apply.

The variations between and within historic horizon settlements both in terms of artifact assemblages and internal site patterning are not demonstrated by archeologically derived data. The difficulty of recognizing characteristics that would serve to delineate differences in material culture derive largely from the rapid abandonment of aboriginal implements as European "store-boughts" became available. Despite the fact that several possible historic Winnebago sites have been excavated, the reconstruction of these communities are better served by data from the ethnographic present (e.g., Radin 1923) and by applying Gibbon's (1969) process of factionalization. The internal pattern of historic sites should reflect the internal homogeneity expected from small, dispersed, socially and economically autonomous populations.

Proposed Models of Oneota Settlement Systems

EMERGENT HORIZON A.D. 700–1000

Settlements were characteristically small, seasonal occupations in the earliest stages of development of the emergent horizon. Population size was probably not larger than that associated with a band level of sociocultural integration, perhaps no larger than several related family units. The high degree of mobility and frequent relocation of campsites would have served not only to spread the emerging characteristics of Oneota material culture over a wide geographic region, but would have also made their definition less obvious in archeological contexts where, I suspect, they are often submerged in multiple components at such sites as Watasa Lake Swamp (Barrett and Skinner 1932) and the Neale and McClaughry Campsites (McKern 1928).

DEVELOPMENTAL HORIZON A.D. 1000–1300

During the ensuing developmental horizon, ca. A.D. 1000–1300, settlements became larger and more stable areas of residence, usually encircled by palisades. The earlier hunting and gathering subsistence base was supplemented by the incorporation of maize horticulture. Activities carried out in these villages encompassed a wide range of behavior, indicating occupation throughout most, if not all, seasons of the year. In terms of material culture, there is a low degree of attribute patterning, particularly in the realm of ceramic decoration. The very low percentage of the entire ceramic assemblage that is decorated (less than 4%), consists of a wide variety of finger-trailed designs generally representing wandering or meandering horizontal lines with occasional curvilinear motif.

The strong similarities evident in material culture from components of the Lake Koshkonong, Grand River, and Green Bay phases suggests a relatively high level of interaction between the groups. The contact could perhaps be best explained in terms of intervillage trade of local commodities, with perhaps rules of exogamy maintaining tenuous ties of marriage between populations. Rules of patrilocal residence and descent, which would be probable in a cultural setting with subsistence procurement based primarily on wild plant and animal resources, would also serve to explain the lack of regionally distinct ceramic assemblages. If postmarital residence patterns were strongly male oriented, Deetz (1965, 1968:41–48) has argued that random ceramic attribute patterning, in the absence of occupational specialists, would be expected. Exchange of local commodities and marriage partners between villages would have thus served to integrate local populations in a loose confederation.

CLASSIC HORIZON A.D. 1300–1650

This loose confederation of widely scattered villages is geographically compacted, and occupation within settlements is intensified during the classic horizon, ca. A.D. 1300–1650. Large permanently occupied villages are located adjacent to major waterways with adjacent fields, perhaps also serving as village dumps. The reasons for this dramatic alteration in settlement pattern are certainly complex and multivariate. However, one of the factors promoting change is the increasing reliance on, and investment in, maize cultivation. Coupled with the intensive habitation of the core or nuclear zone surrounding the Lake-Winnebago–Fox-River waterway, the material culture of classic horizon populations takes on a new dimension of stylistic standardization. Ceramics in particular are quite standardized and embellished. A characteristically well-executed series of vertical and horizontal groupings of linear elements, often combined on the same vessel represent a common decorative motif. Vessel form as well is regularly patterned. A globular vessel form having a sharply everted rim (usually with an angle of 90° or more) is common. Unlike the plain ceramics encountered in earlier phases, vessels of the Lake Winnebago phase are invariably decorated. Finally, dwelling structures may have been both substantially larger, with internal complexity, when compared to the domestic structures of earlier phases.

Explanation of the elaboration and flamboyance of material culture and the drastic settlement pattern shift during the classic stage is difficult, especially when working with such very limited data. Some potential explanations, however, can be suggested from the existing literature. I have already noted the probability that maize cultivation was intensified during the post-A.D. 1300 period. In this light, it is plausible that rules of residence and descent became female- rather than male-oriented. Radin (1948) has cited this likelihood, indicating that evidence derived through myth, custom, and tradition all point to a period in Winnebago history where descent was reckoned through a female line. Furthermore, he discussed evidence of ranking within Winnebago society, based upon the deference shown to chiefs and their families (Radin 1948). Lurie (1976) has supported Radin's contentions and infers: "Given the Winnebago's always strong emphasis on gardening compared to neighboring Algonkians as noted even by early nineteenth century observers, matriliny is not outside the realm of possibility for the pre-contact Winnebago [p. 23]."

Assuming that there was an intensification of maize horticulture and a related shift from patricentered to matricentered rules of residence and descent, the fact that material culture (i.e., ceramics) is marked by less variation and a higher degree of standardization should come as no surprise as this process has been noted in several other instances. Deetz (1965, 1968:41–48) has provided substantial data which demonstrates this phenomenon among the Protohistoric Pawnee. He notes that with consistent matrilocal residence, ceramics exhibit a high degree of attribute association demonstrating the existence of manufacture and design procedures transmitted and reinforced by coresident groups of female potters.

Based on these data it is not unwarranted to suggest that similar processes apply to classic horizon Oneota populations and that the high degree of nonrandom spatial patterning in ceramics of the Lake Winnebago phase is a function of the emergence of matricentered rules of residence and descent related to the growing importance of maize cultivation. It is unfortunate that adequate descriptive ceramic data are not available, despite the fact that large inventories of Lake Winnebago phase pottery, excavated from several village sites, are currently housed in local repositories. In view of this, it is important to reaffirm that the intrasite ceramic homogeneity noted here is impressionistically rather than statistically derived. These changes then combine to generate new levels of social, political, and economic organization that represent the zenith of Oneota culture in eastern Wisconsin.

The historic period, post-A.D. 1650, pales by comparison. The settlement system of a previously vigorous and regionally dominant culture, through a series of both internal and external events that have been detailed by Lurie (1960, 1976) breaks down into the much less complex system described by Gibbon (1969). Rather than occupying large, permanent villages, the historic Winnebago are characterized as living in small dispersed communities of socially and economically autonomous family units.

The Directions of Future Research

The preceding discussion of changing Oneota settlement patterns is clearly, and unfortunately, largely speculative, owing to the limited and varied quality of the available data base. Still, I hope that this overview of Oneota prehistory has served to outline those research questions that necessitate further study, and will promote the collection of sufficient additional data to allow for the acceptance or rejection of the tentative settlement-pattern models presented herein. It seems clear, that the primary goals of future research should involve further analysis of the emergent and classic Oneota horizons. Small campsites such as Neale, McClaughry, and Watasa Lake Swamp should be reinvestigated to improve our level of knowledge regarding the Oneota emergence, and to test the relative strength of the *in situ* development model.

The classic horizon as exemplified by Lake Winnebago phase settlements remains poorly understood. Of highest priority is the accurate determination of the size of such settlements, perhaps through techniques such as those employed at the Pipe site (Overstreet 1974). Equally important is the excavation and reporting of at least one domestic structure from this time period. Demonstration of the time depth of this period is also important. I assume that the Lake Winnebago phase dates from ca. A.D. 1300 to ca. A.D. 1650, the early radiocarbon dates from Lasley's Point notwithstanding (Table 2.1). I feel these dates are in error, primarily because of the stratigraphic information reported by C. Mason (1970:191–227), which indicate that the Lake Winnebago occupation was superimposed upon a Grand River (or Green Bay) component. In addition, the previously cited horizon markers, catlinite disk pipes, bison scapula hoes, and the scraper-point ratio, support a later time period for Lake Winnebago phase occupations at Lasley's Point. Radiocarbon chronologies from other Lake Winnebago phase sites would certainly be welcome.

The historic horizon site distribution and the subsistence pattern of these populations is also an interesting problem, even if not of overwhelming concern to the central thesis presented here. McKern's (1945) direct historical connection, vis-à-vis Oneota and the historic Winnebago, remains, however, to be demonstrated. McKern was convinced, but many are not (e.g., C. Mason 1976:335–348). Until such time as Lake Winnebago phase cultural materials are demonstrated to be in direct association with early historic artifacts, I fear that McKern's hypothesis will not be widely accepted.

Acknowledgments

This discussion of Oneota settlement patterns is derived largely from research done for a Ph.D. dissertation at the University of Wisconsin—Milwaukee under the direction of Dr. Melvin L. Fowler and with the additional strong and helpful guidance of Dr. Edward Wellin. Support, particularly in man-hours of volunteer labor, was provided by the Wisconsin Archeological Society, and is gratefully acknowledged.

References

Baerreis, David A. and Reid A. Bryson
   1965   Climatic episodes and the dating of Mississippian cultures. *The Wisconsin Archaeologist* **47**(3):101–131.
Barrett, Samual A., and Alanson Skinner
   1932   Certain mounds and village sites of Shawano and Oconto Counties, Wisconsin. *Bulletin of The Public Museum of the City of Milwaukee* **10**(5).
Brose, David S.
   1968   The archaeology of Summer Island: Changing settlement systems in northern Lake Michigan. Ph.D. dissertation, Department of Anthropology, University of Michigan. Ann Arbor: University Microfilms.
Bullock, Harold R.
   1942   Lasley Point Mound excavations. *The Wisconsin Archaeologist* **23**(2):37–44.
Burt, William H.
   1957   *Mammals of the Great Lakes region.* Ann Arbor: University of Michigan Press.
Cleland, Charles E.
   1966   The prehistoric animal ecology and ethnozoology of the upper Great Lakes region. *Anthropological Papers, Museum of Anthropology, University of Michigan,* Number 29. Ann Arbor.
Curtis, John T.
   1959   *The vegetation of Wisconsin.* Madison: University of Wisconsin Press.
Deetz, James
   1965   The dynamics of stylistic change in Arikara ceramics. *Illinois Studies in Anthropology,* Number 4. Urbana: University of Illinois Press.

1968   The inference of residence and descent rules from archaeological data. In *New perspectives in archaeology,* edited by S.R. and L.R. Binford. Chicago: Aldine.

Dice, Lee R.
1943   *The biotic provinces of North America.* Ann Arbor, Michigan: University of Michigan Press.

Douglass, John M.
1946   Textile imprints on Wisconsin Indian pottery. *The Wisconsin Archaeologist* 27(3):71–81.

Faulkner, Alaric
1974   *Archaeological and historical survey of the Middle Fox River Passageway.* Oshkosh, Wisconsin: University of Wisconsin-Oshkosh.

Faulkner, Charles H.
1972   The Late Prehistoric occupation of northwestern Indiana—A study of the Upper Mississippi cultures of the Kankakee Valley. *Prehistory Research Series,* 5(1). Indiana Historical Society, Indianapolis.

Fowler, Melvin
1969   The Cahokia site. In Explorations into Cahokia Archeology, edited by M.L. Fowler. *Illinois Archaeological Survey Bulletin,* No. 7. Urbana: Illinois Archaeological Survey.

Freeman, Joan E.
1956   Analysis of the Point Sauble and Beaumier Farm sites. M.A. thesis, Department of Anthropology, University of Wisconsin, Madison.

Gibbon, Guy E.
1969   The Walker-Hooper and Bornick sites. Ph.D. dissertation, Department of Anthropology, University of Wisconsin, Madison.
1971   The Bornick site: a Grand River Phase Oneota site in Marquette County. *The Wisconsin Archaeologist* 52(3):85–137.
1972a   Cultural dynamics and the development of the Oneota life-way in Wisconsin. *American Antiquity* 37(2):146–185.
1972b   The Walker–Hooper site, a Grand River Phase Oneota site in Green Lake County. *The Wisconsin Archaeologist* 53(4):149–290.

Gregg, Michael
1975   A population estimate for Cahokia. In Perspectives in Cahokia archaeology, edited by J. Brown. *Illinois Archaeological Survey Bulletin,* Number 10. Urbana: Illinois Archaeological Survey.

Griffin, James B.
1937   The archaeological remains of the Chiwere Sious. *American Antiquity,* 2(3):180–181.
1960   A hypothesis for the prehistory of the Winnebago. In *Culture in history: essays in honor of Paul Radin,* edited by S. Diamond: New York: Columbia University Press. Pp. 809–865.
1961   Some correlations of climatic and cultural change in eastern North American prehistory. *Annals of the New York Academy of Sciences,* 95, Art. 1:710–717.
1965   Late Quaternary prehistory in the northeastern Woodlands. In *The Quaternary of the United States,* edited by H.E. Wright and D. Fry. New Jersey: Princeton University Press.

Hall, Robert L.
1962   *The archaeology of Carcajou Point.* Madison, Wisconsin: University of Wisconsin Press.

Hurley, William
1975   An analysis of Effigy Mound complexes in Wisconsin. *Anthropological Papers, Museum of Anthropology, The University of Michigan,* Number 59. Ann Arbor.

Lurie, Nancy O.
1960   Winnebago protohistory. In *Culture in history: essays in honor of Paul Radin,* edited by S. Diamond: New York: Columbia University Press. Pp. 790–808.

1976   An Aztalan-Winnebago hypothesis. Manuscript on file, Department of Anthropology and Sociology, University of Wisconsin–Waukesha.

McKern, Will C.
1928   The Neale and McClaughry Mound groups. *Bulletin of the Public Museum of the City of Milwaukee* **3**(3):213–416.
1939   The midwestern taxonomic method as an aid to archaeological study. *American Antiquity* **4**(4):301–313.
1945   Preliminary report on the Upper Mississippian Phase in Wisconsin. *Bulletin of the Public Museum of the City of Milwaukee,* **16**(3):109–285.

McKern, Will C., and Robert Ritzenthaler
1945   Trait list of the prehistoric cultures of Wisconsin. *The Wisconsin Archaeologist* **26**(4):66–79.
1949   Trait list of the Effigy Mound Aspect. *The Wisconsin Archaeologist,* **30**(2):39–48.

Martin, Lawrence
1932   The physical geography of Wisconsin. *Bulletin of the Wisconsin Geological and Natural History Survey,* Number 36. Madison.

Mason, Carol I.
1970   The Oneota component at the Porte Des Morts site, Door County, Wisconsin. *The Wisconsin Archaeologist* **51**(4):191–227.
1976   Historic identification and Lake Winnebago Focus Oneota. In *Cultural change and continuity, essays in honor of James Bennett Griffin,* edited by Charles Cleland: New York: Academic Press. Pp. 335–348.

Mason, Ronald J.
1966   Two stratified sites on the Door County Peninsula of Wisconsin. *Anthropological Papers, Museum of Anthropology, The University of Michigan,* Number 26. Ann Arbor.
1967   The North Bay component at the Portes Des Morts site, Door County, Wisconsin. *The Wisconsin Archaeologist,* **48**(4):267–345.

Overstreet, David F.
1974   A rapid chemical field test for archaeological site surveying: An application and evaluation. *The Wisconsin Archaeologist* **55**(4):262–270.
1976   The Grand River, Lake Koshkonong, Green Bay and Lake Winnebago Phases—eight hundred years of Oneota prehistory in eastern Wisconsin. Ph.D. dissertation, Department of Anthropology, University of Wisconsin—Milwaukee. Mikwaukee, Wisconsin.

Peske, G. Richard
1966   Oneota settlement patterns and agricultural patterns in Winnebago county. *The Wisconsin Archaeologist* **47**(4):188–195.
1971   Winnebago cultural adaptation to the Fox River Waterway. *The Wisconsin Archaeologist* **52**(2):62–70.

Radin, Paul
1915   The social organization of the Winnebago Indians, an interpretation. *Canada Geological Survey, Museum Bulletin,* Number 10. Ottawa.
1923   The Winnebago tribe. *Bureau of American Ethnology, Thirty-Seventh Annual Report, 1915–1916.* Washington, D.C.
1948   Winnebago hero cycles: A study of aboriginal literature. *Indiana University Publications in Anthropology and Linguistics, International Journal of Linguistics, Memoir,* Number 1.

Salzer, Robert J.
1969   An introduction to the archaeology of northern Wisconsin. Ph.D. dissertation, Southern Illinois University. Carbondale.
1972   The Waukesha Focus, Hopewell in southeastern Wisconsin. Manuscript on file, Department of Anthropology and Sociology, University of Wisconsin—Waukesha. Waukesha, Wisconsin.

Seurer, Daniel M., and Alaric Faulker
   1976   The Nile Roeder site: A salvage project in Winnebago County. *The Wisconsin Archaeologist* **57**(1):29–51.
Spector, Janet D.
   1975   Crabapple Point (JE 93): an historic Winnebago Indian site in Jefferson County, Wisconsin. *The Wisconsin Archaeologist,* **56**(4):270–345.
United States Department of Agriculture
   1941   *Climate and man.* Yearbook of Agriculture. Washington, D. C.: United States Government Printing Office.
Willey, Gordon R., and Phillip Phillips
   1958   Method and theory in American archaeology. Chicago: University of Chicago Press.
Wittry, Warren L.
   1959   Archaeological studies of four Wisconsin Rockshelters. *The Wisconsin Archeologist,* **40**(4):137–267.
Yarnell, Richard A.
   1964   Aboriginal relationships between culture and plant life in the upper Great Lakes region. *Anthropological Papers, Museum of Anthropology, University of Michigan,* Number 23. Ann Arbor.
   1965   Early Woodland plant remains and the question of cultivation. *The Florida Anthropologist* **18**(2).

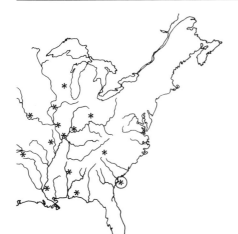

3

Analysis of
Late Mississippian
Settlements on
Ossabaw Island, Georgia

CHARLES E. PEARSON

Analysis of settlement patterns has become an increasingly important aspect of prehistoric archeology. In general, this type of analysis offers an effective and expedient means of assessing a wide variety of prehistoric cultural phenomena. The application of systemic and ecological models and methods to settlement research has enabled archeologists to examine some aspects of the interrelationships that existed between human populations and their natural and sociocultural environments. It is generally accepted that the morphology and the distribution of human settlements reflect these interrelationships to some degree and that analysis of settlement patterns should lead to meaningful statements about cultural processes and adaptation.

The configuration of settlements within a system reflects the kind of sociocultural structures and adaptive strategies used by a population. Assessment of the elements, the structure, and the relationships that occur within a settlement pattern is one of the most efficient ways to approaching the question of cultural adaptation. Settlement pattern analysis is particularly amenable to the use of surface survey data. Many relevant and quantifiable attributes of individual settlements as well as those of overall systems can be efficiently gathered through survey. This study relies largely on archeological survey data in the analysis of the settlement system of the Irene phase (A.D. 1350–1550) populations of Ossabaw Island, Georgia.

53

Inherent in the systemic approach to settlement analysis is the concept of "wholeness." This means that the settlement system under consideration must have operated as a single entity on at least some levels of cultural activity such that the major components of the system, for example, the settlements, operated "together to achieve some sort of functional stability [Odum 1971:9]." This requires that the settlement system be bounded in some legitimate manner. Establishing realistic boundaries for cultural systems is often difficult, if not impossible, when dealing with archeological data. Archeologists generally have reasonable temporal boundaries within which to view structure, but rarely in settlement system analysis have they been able to develop realistic spatial or physical boundaries. Unless cultural boundaries can be identified by distinct differences in artifactual material, it seems that distinct geographical boundaries may best serve to delimit the boundaries of prehistoric settlement systems. Ossabaw Island offers a relatively isolated and discrete geographical unit within which settlement system analysis may be carried out. It is not unreasonable to assume that the island, with its abundance of natural resources, may have supported an Irene population that was a relatively autonomous socioeconomic unit.

Four different techniques will be sequentially employed to analyze the Irene phase settlement system that existed on Ossabaw Island. Settlement-size distributional analysis will be employed initially to assess the general "state" of the settlement system. Cluster analysis will then be used to formulate a hierarchical model for the settlement system. Once this hierarchical model is formulated, frequency distributional analysis will be used to compare it with the theoretical expectations of geographical models of settlement systems. Finally, environmental analysis will be carried out to assess the relative importance of different environmental variables in determining the location of sites from different levels of the proposed settlement hierarchy.

Before undertaking this analysis, however, it is necessary to discuss the Irene phase and Ossabaw Island in more detail.

The Irene Phase

Aspects of material culture have been the focus of most previous research on the Irene phase, resulting in a rather complete knowledge of artifactual assemblages and artifact distribution. However, these data have rarely been utilized in the analysis of other aspects of the prehistoric human populations that have been termed "Irene." It should be noted that the term "phase," although used in accordance with Willey and Phillips

(1958:22), does not, in this instance, refer necessarily to a single cultural group.

The Irene phase is identified on the basis of the regional (coastal Georgia and South Carolina) distribution of a unique ceramic complex. The earliest work that recognized this distinctive ceramic complex was that of Clarence B. Moore in the 1890s (Moore 1897). Moore's excavations, centered almost entirely on burial mounds, were conducted along the Georgia and South Carolina coasts. Irene phase burial mounds and ceramics were so numerous in the area that Moore (1897) often referred to this pottery as that "of the ordinary type [p. 117]." Though it was narrowly focused, Moore's work still stands as the most extensive archeological investigations carried out on the Georgia coast.

In the late 1930s several federally sponsored WPA archeological projects were undertaken on the Georgia coast. Much of this work was carried out on Irene phase sites in the lower Savannah River area. Joseph R. Caldwell and Antonio Waring (1939:7) established a provisional ceramic chronology for the area, with Irene as the most recent ceramic complex in the sequence. Work at the Irene phase-type site (the Irene Mound, located on the Savannah River) during the years 1937–1940 provided further information concerning the Irene ceramic complex, and demonstrated stratigraphically that it was the latest prehistoric ceramic manifestation at the site (Fewkes 1938; Caldwell and McCann 1941). Dates assigned to the Irene phase range from A.D. 1350 to 1550 (Caldwell 1971:89–91).

The excavations at the Irene Mound site are the source of most of our knowledge of Irene phase material culture. Since the late 1930s, excavations have been undertaken at only a limited number of Irene phase sites (Caldwell 1943, Cook 1966, 1971, Goad 1975, Larson 1969, Pearson 1977). Several extensive archeological surveys in the area of coastal Georgia have provided valuable information on the overall spatial distribution of Irene phase sites (Caldwell 1972, DePratter 1973, 1974, 1975, Hally, Zurel, and Gresham 1975, Larson 1958a, Pearson 1977, Simpkins and McMichael 1976).

Irene phase sites are found within a narrow linear zone extending along the Georgia and South Carolina coast, which includes the Sea Islands and a narrow strip of the mainland. Their distribution corresponds generally to the area covered by a maritime live oak forest vegetation association. Only along the major rivers of the region have Irene phase sites been found at any distance inland (Figure 3.1). The pine barrens zone, which begins just inland from the coast, appears to have represented a western barrier for Irene phase populations (Larson 1969, Pearson 1977).

No Irene phase sites are reported south of the Altamaha River. It is interesting to note that the southern boundary of Irene phase ceramics corresponds to the linguistic and political boundary described as existing

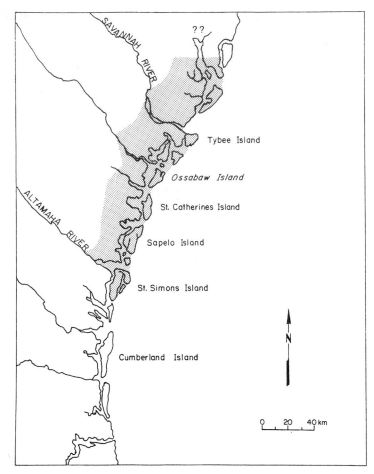

FIGURE 3.1.   *The coastal region of Georgia showing the known distribution of Irene phase sites.*

between the historic Guale and Timucua (Swanton 1922). The Irene phase appears to be the archeological equivalent of the historic Guale (see Larson 1958a). Less information is available on the northern extent of Irene phase sites. Although the Savannah River has often been considered to represent the northern boundary of the Phase, Irene or Irenelike ceramics have been found as far north as Charleston, South Carolina (Anderson 1974).

Irene phase ceramics are a variant of the much larger Southeastern ceramic manifestation that has been termed Lamar (Caldwell 1952:319, Fairbanks 1952:295, Kelly 1938, Sears 1956). Lamar or Lamarlike pottery constitutes a Late Mississippian ceramic manifestation that occurs in central and northern Georgia, much of South Carolina, and parts of Tennessee and Alabama. In broad cultural perspective, the Irene phase can be considered as the coastal manifestation of the Late Mississippian (Caldwell 1952:319, Kelly 1938:40, Larson 1958a). Mississippian cultural attributes at the Irene Mound site include square-wall trench houses, a rectangular substructural mound, shell artifacts, including engraved shell gorgets and shell dippers, and Lamarlike ceramics.

The rareness of these traits, and the lack of most of what may be considered classic Mississippian attributes, indicate that Irene phase populations were somewhat isolated from the mainstream of Mississippian cultural development. The only rectangular platform mound known for the phase, for example, is located at the Irene Mound site, and there is a general lack of the cultural elaboration that is typical of Mississippian development in the interior Southeast. Southern cult items and motifs, which are common elements in some Late Mississippian artifact assemblages, rarely occur at Irene phase sites. If, as Waring and Holder (1945) have proposed, cult items are in some way related to horticultural practices, then the rareness of cult items at Irene phase sites may reflect a lack of emphasis and reliance upon horticulture by Irene populations (Larson 1958b).

There are little published data available on Irene phase subsistence, and no attempt has yet been made to quantify subsistence data from Irene phase sites (Larson 1969, Pearson 1977). The evidence that does exist concerning Irene phase subsistence patterns indicates that heavy reliance was placed upon salt-marsh–estuary resources. Remains of shellfish, especially oyster (*Crassostrea virginica*), constitute the bulk of cultural debris at Irene phase sites. Other salt-marsh species commonly recovered include diamondback terrapin (*Malaclemys terrapin*), blue crab (*Callinectes sapidus*), and several varieties of fish and molluscs. Major mammal species found include white-tailed deer (*Odocoileus virginianus*), black bear (*Ursus americanus*), raccoon (*Procyon lotor*), gray squirrel (*Sciurus carolinensis*), opossum (*Didelphis marsupialis*), and rabbit (*Sylvilagus* sp.). Acorn and hickory nut fragments have also been recovered from Irene phase sites (Pearson 1977). Cultigens, however, are rare. Only small quantities of maize and a possible bean have been reported (Larson 1969:293–309, Pearson 1977:59). The low fertility of coastal soils combined with the unlimited abundance of marsh–estuary resources likely resulted in a minimal reliance on horticulture.

Research Universe

The study area consists of Ossabaw Island and its immediate salt marsh-estuary environs. Ossabaw Island is one of a chain of barrier islands located off the southeastern Atlantic coast that are commonly referred to as the Sea Islands (Figure 3.1). The island is geologically and ecologically young, and was formed as a result of Pleistocene and post-Pleistocene geologic forces—principally sea level fluctuation sedimentation and estuarine erosion (Johnson *et al.* 1975). An extensive salt marsh interlaced with tidal creeks and rivers separates the island from the mainland and partially bisects the island (Figure 3.2).

Topographic relief on the island is minimal, ranging from sea level to about 8 m. The western (Pleistocene) portion of the island is characterized by broad flat ridges and shallow depressions. The eastern (Holocene) section consists mainly of steep parallel dune ridges.

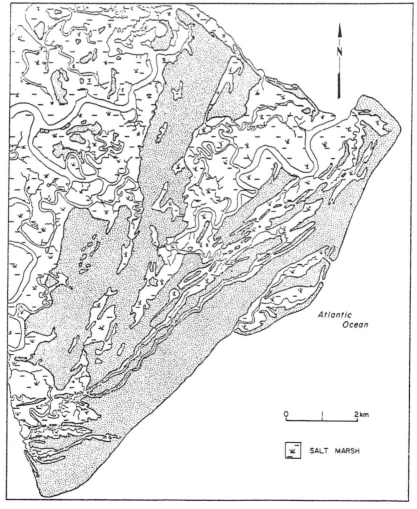

FIGURE 3.2. *Ossabaw Island.*

Soils on the island tend to be porous and subject to severe leaching. While higher areas are usually excessively drained, low areas are poorly drained, often producing ponds or swamps. Soils also tend to be acid and infertile (Johnson *et al.* 1975).

The projected climax forest for the island is a maritime live oak forest (Hillestad *et al.* 1975:76). This forest is characterized by a distinct dominance of live oak (*Quercus virginiana*) and an abundance of other oaks and nut-bearing trees. Differences in forest species composition, though slight, do exist in the mature forest covering different areas of Ossabaw Island. These differences appear to be due mainly to soil drainage characteristics. Soil data from Ossabaw Island can therefore be used to reconstruct the four major forest communities that existed on the island. Each of these communities would have offered different plant resources to Irene phase inhabitants and are considered to have been affectors of site location. These four communities are (*a*) mixed oak hardwood forest; (*b*) oak palmetto forest; (*c*) lowland mixed forest; and (*d*) high marsh.

Animal species found on the island today include the white-tailed deer, raccoon, marsh rabbit, bobcat (*Lynx rufus*), otter (*Lutra canadensis*), and mink (*Mustela vison*). Black bear are not present on the island today, although they did inhabit the Sea Islands in the recent past (Hillestad *et al.* 1975:95).

The vast salt marshes separating Ossabaw Island from the mainland support a surprising abundance of shellfish, fish, and crustacea. These include oyster, hardshell clam (*Mercenaria mercenaria*), blue crab, diamondback terrapin, shrimp (*Penaeus* sp.), and large numbers of both seasonally available and year-round fish species. The salt marshes, together with the flora and fauna of the island, would have provided abundant and easily exploited food resources for prehistoric human populations.

Data Collection

A series of archeological surveys carried out over the last several years by various individuals and institutions have provided the settlement data used in this analysis (DePratter 1974, Pearson 1977). Of the 161 prehistoric sites located on Ossabaw Island, 47 have been identified as having Irene phase components.

No systematic sampling scheme was employed in any of the surveys. In addition, heavy ground cover on the island made survey and site location difficult. During all of the surveys sites were generally recognized by the presence of surface shell scatter or shell middens. These sites were most easily found in exposed areas such as roads, or along the marsh edge.

Because of ground cover problems, plus the likelihood that many sites had been disturbed or destroyed, it can be safely assumed that other Irene phase sites either remain to be found or have ceased to exist.

Survey coverage has, however, included portions of all the various biotic and physiographic areas of the island, with sites being found in each of these areas. It is assumed that the sites found are representative of the total range of variability in site location, can provide information concerning the total range in settlement variability, and can provide information for comprehending the structure of the settlement system as a whole.

The designation of what constitutes a "site" is an important aspect of this and other studies of prehistoric settlement. The factors that lead to the determination of where one site ends and another begins are rarely stated explicitly by archeologists. Spatial separation, seemingly the most logical factor, is used in this study. A "site" is considered to be any cultural deposition at least 100 m from any other cultural debris.

Surface collections were made at all 47 Irene phase sites, and site size was determined for each by measuring the area in square meters of surface cultural debris scatter.

Since it is at present impossible to deal with time segments smaller than the 200-year span postulated for the Irene phase, the size of any site, as well as the total number of sites may possibly represent accumulation during a 200-year time span. Site distribution and variation at any one point in time is considered to reflect the sociocultural adaptation of a particular human group. Assuming generally similar patterns of behavior throughout the Irene phase, the pattern of settlement viewed over this brief period of time probably emphasizes those environmental factors that were critical to settlement throughout the time period. The 47 Irene phase sites may be considered to reflect the accumulated results of these factors and their influence on Irene phase settlement.

Analysis

SETTLEMENT SIZE DISTRIBUTION ANALYSIS

A variety of techniques and models have been developed by geographers to analyze and explain settlement systems. Analyses that deal with the size distributions of settlements have been used extensively on modern settlement systems, and appear to be particularly applicable to archeological data sets for a number of reasons. First, analysis of settlement size distributions does not require the stringent initial conditions and a priori assumptions necessary when using other geographical models such as central place theory (King 1961, Smith 1974). Size distribution analysis requires only that the settlement system in question be a single operating unit and that the elements, that is, settlements, that are used be representative of the total population comprising the system. Second, the principle variable used in size distribution analysis is that of settlement size. Settlement size is, in most instances, an easily obtainable archeological measure and is one that is common to all sites. Population rather than settlement size is the measure used by geographers in size distribution analysis of modern settlement systems. Until reliable and realistic techniques are developed for determining the population of prehistoric settlements, settlement size is seen as the most logical equivalent. In this study, site size in conjunction with location is considered to be the most adequate available measure of cultural response to environmental variation.

Settlement size is considered by most geographers and anthropologists to be a useful indicator of the number and kinds of activities carried out at a site (Haggett 1971:115–117). Within a settlement system, then, variation in site size can be considered as at least an initial indicator of possible variation in site function.

Settlement size distributions are normally viewed in terms of the relationship between the size of a settlement and its rank. In the literature these are generally referred to as *rank–size distributions* (Haggett 1971). When presented graphically, usually in logarithmic scale, rank–size distributions are considered useful in making generalized assessments of the "state" of the system (Dziewonski 1972, 1975).

Rank–size distributions have been developed and explained using actual settlement places as data. In many prehistoric settlement systems, however, smaller sites may represent occupations of brief duration. This is certainly true for the smaller Irene phase sites on Ossabaw Island. Thus, the validity of using small, possibly nonhabitation sites in size distribution analysis may be questioned.

For this study, it is argued that the inclusion of these smaller sites will provide for the graphic representation of the overall structure of the settlement system. Since other sets of prehistoric settlement data generally contain these types of nonhabitation sites, all sites must be included if we are to use size distributions as a basis for comparing the structure of prehistoric settlement systems.

For the Ossabaw Island data, it does not appear that the inclusion of these smaller sites significantly alters the explanatory power of size distributions. It was found that the shape of the size distribution curve using all sites (presented on page 63) was not appreciably different from the curve produced when the smaller and probable nonhabitation sites (the 11 smallest sites) were omitted. For these reasons all sites are included in analysis presented here.

Although a number of mathematical formulas have been developed to explain rank–size distributions, there is still considerable debate as to whether observed regularities can be explained theoretically or should be considered only as empirical regularities (Haggett 1971, Dziewonski 1972, 1975). There is a general consensus, however, that adherence to, or deviation from, a particular distribution is a reflection of identifiable socioeconomic factors (Berry 1961, Dziewonski 1972).

Two major types of distributions relating settlement rank and settlement size have been observed. A log-normal or rank–size distribution is one in which the distribution of settlements by size is truncated lognormal, whereas a primate distribution is one in which a stratum of small settlements is dominated by a single or a few very large settlements (Berry 1961). These two distributions are not mutually exclusive, but are best seen as two ends of a continuum, each of which is the result of quite different causal factors (Berry 1961, Vapnarsky 1969).

In general, log-normal distributions appear to be typical of larger countries that have a long tradition of urbanization and are politically and economically complex (Berry 1961). On the other hand, primate distributions are associated with countries that are small, have "simple" economic and political systems, have a short history of urbanization, and have generally resulted from "fewer forces" (Berry 1961:584).

Many geographers have questioned the relationship of the continuous distribution displayed by settlement size to the discrete hierarchical arrangement proposed for many settlement systems (Berry and Garrison 1958, Dziewonski 1972, 1975, Haggett 1971, Stewart 1958). Dziewonski (1972:76) suggests that rank–size distributions do possess "latent hierarchical structure" and that they "may be considered as a test in the evaluation of hierarchical models of city size." If so, then the analysis of settlement size distributions should provide information on the hierarchical characteristics proposed to exist in many Mississippian and other prehistoric settlement systems.

Despite some difficulties inherent in its application to archeological data sets, analysis of the size distributions of prehistoric settlements should allow for initial examination and assessment of the overall structure of settlement systems. In addition, rank–size distributions would appear to provide a useful way to compare prehistoric settlement systems.

In this study, rank–size analysis is used primarily to assess the overall "state" of the Irene phase settlement system on Ossabaw Island and in the formulation and examination of the probable settlement hierarchy that existed on the island.

Figure 3.3 presents the size distribution of Irene phase settlements in a form proposed by Brian Berry (1961). Berry has developed a set of settlement-size distribution curves with the conditions of primacy and log normality representing the two limiting types. He suggests evolutionary

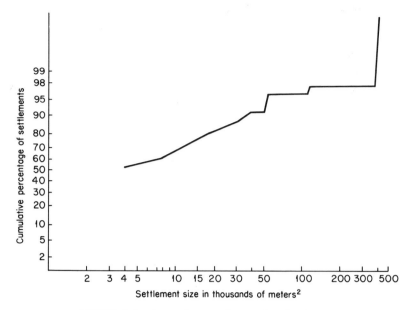

FIGURE 3.3.   *Irene phase settlement size distribution.*

implications for these curves such that the log-normal distribution is the more complex and advanced form.

Irene phase settlements (Figure 3.3) follow a primate distribution with one settlement being much larger than any of the others, and with most of the settlements falling into a log-normal distribution. This curve most closely resembles those at Berry's "intermediate" level of settlement size distributions (Berry 1961:585).

This curve can serve as a useful indicator of some broad aspects of the Irene phase settlement system on Ossabaw Island. The primate distribution suggests that most of the interaction between Ossabaw Island and the outside world was channeled through the one or two largest sites and that these two sites represented the apex of the settlement system in terms of many or most sociocultural activities (Berry 1961, Vapnarsky 1969). This distribution fits what Vapnarsky (1969:595) terms a "low closure/high interdependence" situation, in which there is a great deal of interaction among settlements within a region, with only a few settlements handling interaction outside the region. Such a situation is to be expected in a relatively small, homogeneous, somewhat isolated region like Ossabaw Island.

It would appear that although many factors affect them, settlement size distributions are useful in making low-level generalizations about settlement systems. Although more rigorous statements concerning the size distribution of Irene phase sites on Ossabaw Island are not possible with the available data, it is appropriate to note that the size distribution displayed by these sites is compatable with a priori assumptions about the type of socioeconomic system that operated on the island.

The hierarchical organization of settlement systems has been discussed extensively, primarily in terms of the relationships between the size of settlements and their functional range (see Haggett 1971). Several studies of Mississippian settlement systems have discussed site hierarchies (Brandt 1972, Fowler 1972, 1974, Peebles 1974, Price 1973, 1974, Rolingson 1976). The underlying assumption of these studies has been that functional variability, for example, range of activities, did exist among levels in the proposed hierarchies. The identification of hierarchical levels within Mississippian settlement systems has been based upon obvious features such as both the presence or absence of mounds, and the type of mounds present at a site. Although these are not considered to be usable criteria for establishing the structure of the settlement hierarchy of the Irene phase populations that occupied Ossabaw Island, site size is considered to be a practical and reasonable variable with which to identify the settlement hierarchy that may have existed. It has been suggested that site size is reflective of the range and kinds of activities being carried out at a site. Therefore, sites of equivalent size should theoretically display similar sociocultural traits and thus occupy approximately the same functional position or level in the settlement hierarchy. As mentioned earlier, Dziewonski (1972:76) argues that the settlement size continuum can be used to evaluate the hierarchical structure of settlement systems. To identify reasonably objective hierarchical levels within a continuum of site sizes some means of grouping sites into discrete size classes is necessary. Cluster analysis is used as an objective means for achieving these groupings.

CLUSTER ANALYSIS

The general computational method utilized in the cluster analysis of Irene phase settlements is Ward's method used in the computer program HCLUS, a program developed by John Wood of Northern Arizona University and modified by Donald Graybill of the University of Georgia (Graybill 1974; Wood 1974). Ward's method is a hierarchical agglomerative clustering technique in which clustering proceeds by progressive fusion beginning with the individual cases, that is, site sizes, and ending with the total population (Anderberg 1973:142–145).

Only 45 of the 47 Irene phase sites are included in the cluster analysis. The two largest sites, which are obviously much larger than any of the other sites were placed in a separate size class prior to analysis. A dendrogram of the remaining 45 sites is presented in Figure 3.4. Cluster

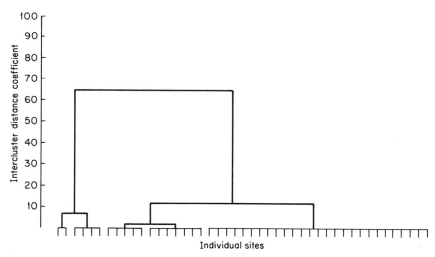

FIGURE 3.4.   Dendrogram of cluster analysis of Irene phase sites.

"merge levels," which are a measure of cluster distance, are scaled along the vertical axis of Figure 3.4.

No hard and fast rules can be used in determining the selection of a "best" cluster solution. Selection can be based partially upon a priori assumptions about the data (e.g., the expected number of hierarchical levels in a settlement system) and partially upon the amount of "information" gained or lost at any particular step in the cluster analysis (Graybill 1975).

Figure 3.5 is a graph of the percentage of change in information in relation to the number of clusters produced. This graph can best be viewed in terms of "information" as opposed to "resolution." As the number of clusters present in a solution increases the amount of information available per cluster also increases. As information (and clusters) increase there is a corresponding decrease in resolution or difference between clusters, such that the selection of a solution containing many clusters results in minimal intercluster difference. A cluster solution at a point intermediate between the extremes of maximum information and maximum resolution is desired.

Three clusters comprise a reasonable cluster solution based on the criteria of information and resolution balance. The inclusion of the two largest sites as an additional cluster produces a four-level site hierarchy. The criteria of information and resolution are simply *aids* in selecting a solution and the solution chosen must ultimately satisfy conditions of the problem at hand. This four-level hierarchy is reasonable in light of the types of hierarchies suggested for other Mississippian settlement systems (see Brandt 1972, Fowler 1972, 1974, Peebles 1974, Price 1974) as well as those suggested for settlement systems in general (Haggett 1971:114–142).

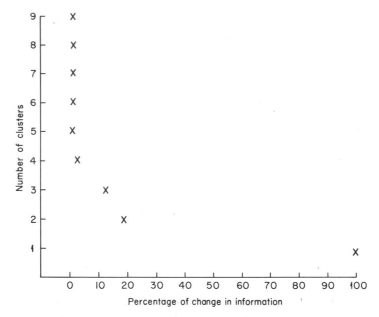

FIGURE 3.5.   Information change in cluster production.

Although the four-level hierarchy is intuitively appealing, the question remains whether this four-level hierarchy represents a realistical model of the Irene phase settlement system as it operated on Ossabaw Island. Cluster analysis, as used here, is essentially a search technique, and is not a measure of the relative strength of the hypothetical model presented. As such, it has been used to identify analytical units (site size classes or hierarchical levels) about which a variety of hypotheses can be formulated and tested. Initial examination of the proposed hierarchy will deal with it as a whole unit. Subsequent analysis will consider each level of the proposed hierarchy separately in terms of proposed functional variability.

FREQUENCY DISTRIBUTION ANALYSIS

Regularities in settlement hierarchies have been observed and discussed at length, and theoretical explanations for these distributions have been presented (Haggett 1971). The kind of settlement hierarchy expected for an accurately sampled system is of interest here. The four-level hierarchy proposed for Ossabaw Island can be compared with the sort of hierarchical configuration expected to be displayed by complete settlement systems.

Figure 3.6 is a histogram of site frequency per size class for the 47 Irene

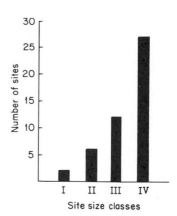

FIGURE 3.6. *Frequency distribution of Irene phase sites by size class.*

phase sites located on Ossabaw Island. The distribution shown in this figure—a large number of small sites, and a few large sites—is the typical and expected pattern. Geographers have shown that the curve that can be produced from the data in Figure 3.6, the so-called J-shaped curve, corresponds to theoretical expectations of the size distribution of settlements operating within a system (Berry and Garrison 1958, Haggett 1971).

In addition, the number of sites within each level of the proposed hierarchy conforms to the number theoretically expected. Simon (1955), utilizing stochastic processes and probability concepts, derived equations that accurately describe the frequency distributions of settlements. Berry and Garrison (1958) have modified Simon's model slightly and have shown its applicability to geographical data. Following Berry and Garrison, the modified versions of Simon's equations were applied to the Ossabaw data set to determine if the number of sites within each size class was significantly different from the number expected. The results are presented in Table 3.1. The Kolomogrov–Smirnov statistic was used to test if the observed distribution of sites in the proposed Ossabaw Island hierarchy differs from the hierarchical distribution as derived by Simon's formulas (Siegel 1956:47–52). The results indicate that there is no significant difference between the observed and the expected distributions.

This test would seem to indicate tentatively that the cluster analysis of site size has produced a reasonable settlement hierarchy—one not appreciably different from the theoretical model. Although it may be argued that this is partial validation for the technique as it is used here, there is some question as to why the hierarchical arrangement of this prehistoric settlement system is so similar to that proposed to exist in modern societies. It can only be suggested that more sets of prehistoric data be analyzed and compared with these theoretical distributions in an attempt to identify similarities and differences.

TABLE 3.1

Actual Site Size Class Composition Compared with the Expected Theoretical Distribution[a]

	Observed		Expected	
Site size class	Number	Cumulative percentage	Number	Cumulative percentage
I	2	.04	2	.05
II	6	.17	4	.16
III	12	.43	8	.38
IV	27	1.00	24	1.00

H_0: There is no difference between the observed and theoretical distributions of sites.
Statistical Test: Kolomogorov–Smirnov test goodness of fit (see Siegel 1956: 47–52).
Results: $D = .05$ There is no significant difference between the observed and theoretical
     distribution at $p = .05$ level of significance.
Expected values obtained by using the following formulas:
(1) $f(1) = nk/2$
(2) $f(i)/f(i - 1) = (i - 1)/(i + 1)$,
Where nk = total number of sites and $f(i)$ = number of sites of site size class i.

    Expected distribution of settlement sizes obtained by application of Formula (1), and
successive application of Formula (2) using $i = 2$, $i = 3$, and $i = 4$.

[a] After Berry and Garrison (1958).

ENVIRONMENTAL ANALYSIS

Ossabaw Island's Irene phase settlement system can be further analyzed by considering the relationships that existed between settlements in each of the four levels of the proposed hierarchy and sets of quantified environmental variables. It is initially assumed that the sites within each level of the hierarchy are, in the broadest sense, "functionally" similar. The variability proposed to exist between each of the hierarchical levels is therefore expected to be reflected in differential site relationships to sets of quantified environmental variables.

The environmental variables used, which are considered to be important affectors of site location, are (a) the soil type upon which a site is located; (b) the forest community within which a site is situated; (c) the distance of a site from the salt marsh; and (d) the distance of a site from tidal creeks. Within each variable set, rankings have been established based upon the assumed importance of the variable to the Irene phase population. Even though these rankings are somewhat subjective, they are considered logical and plausible in light of available data on Irene phase subsistence and adaptation.

The soil type categories used are those given in the *Soil Survey of Bryan and Chatham Counties, Georgia* (United States Department of Agriculture 1974). Soil associations were ranked primarily on the basis of drainage characteristics, the most "valued" soil type, Lakeland Fine Sand (Lp), being the best drained of the seven soil types occurring on the island. Drainage characteristics seem to be the most logical means of ranking soils since they indicate both the possibility of year-round settlement and the potential for horticultural activities. Long-term settlement would be possible only on the better drained soils since poorly drained ones are often seasonally flooded. None of the island soils is very fertile, but the better drained soils are more amenable to horticulture than the poorer ones (United States Department of Agriculture 1974).

Table 3.2 presents data on site location by size class in relation to soil type. The fact that the larger sites tend to be located on the better drained soils presumably indicates that larger sites are located to take advantage of the horticultural potential of soils as well as their potential for year-round settlement.

The smaller (Class IV) sites are distributed across all soil types. Many of these sites probably represent short-term or seasonal occupation and were therefore unaffected by possible periodic flooding. Many of these smaller sites seem to have been limited-activity extraction sites, such as shell collecting stations, and their establishment was not likely to have been related to the possible horticultural potential of the soil.

The number of sites located in each of the four forest communities present on Ossabaw Island is presented in Table 3.3. The rankings of the forest communities, 1 through 4, are based upon the exploitablity of food resources in each, mainly in terms of acorns, hickory nuts, and associated fauna (Hillestad *et al.* 1975). Larger sites tend to be associated with the highest yield forest community, the mixed oak–hardwood forest, whereas

TABLE 3.2
Site Frequency Cross-Tabulated by Size Class and Soil Type

	Soil types						
Size classes	1 Lp[a]	2 Cm[b]	3 Ol[c]	4 Lr[d]	5 El[e]	6 Kic[f]	7 Ch[g]
Class I	2						
Class II	4	1	1				
Class III	4	4	1	2	1		
Class IV	7	1	6	2	6	3	2
Total	17	6	8	4	7	3	2

[a] Lp = Lakeland Fine Sand.
[b] Cm = Chipley Fine Sand.
[c] Ol = Olustee Fine Sand.
[d] Lr = Leon Fine Sand.
[e] El = Ellabelle Loamy Sand.
[f] Kic = Kirshaw-Osier Complex.
[g] Ch = Capers soil.

TABLE 3.3
Site Frequency Cross-Tabulated by Size Class and Forest Community

Size classes	Forest communities			
	1 (Mixed oak– hardwood)	2 (Oak– palmetto)	3 (Lowland mixed)	4 (High marsh)
Class I	2	—	—	—
Class II	5	—	1	—
Class III	8	3	1	—
Class IV	11	8	6	2
Total	26	11	8	2

there is more variation with respect to the location of the smaller sites. The higher frequency of nut-bearing trees within the mixed oak–hardwood forest may have been important in supporting the long-term occupation of larger settlements. The variability evident in the distribution of smaller sites seems to indicate that the presence of mixed oak–hardwood forest was not an important factor in their location. Perhaps other factors such as accessability to a specific resource affected the choice of location for these sites.

It is difficult to interpret separately the relative importance of forest communities and soil types as factors in the location of Irene phase settlements because the two are interrelated. For example, the mixed oak–hardwood forests are associated with Lakeland Fine Sand. Perhaps soil type was more important in determining the location of many settlements because of its direct affect on the feasibility of the placement of habitation structures. The resources of the mixed oak–hardwood forest would be easily accessible from almost any part of the island. The combined value of the two resources is clearly apparent, and it must be assumed that some sites, especially the larger ones, were strategically located to take advantage of soil–vegetation associations.

Available archeological evidence indicates that extensive exploitation of salt marsh resources was undertaken by Irene phase populations (Larson 1969, Pearson 1977). It would be logical to assume that site locations were in some way influenced by these resources, depending on the types of activities occurring at sites. Although it is not possible at this time to quantify accurately the actual amounts and variation in availability of food resources in the marsh area, site distance from the marsh can be used as a plausible measure of its importance to site location.

Table 3.4 presents data on site distances from the salt marsh edge. Most of the sites (77%) are adjacent to or within 100 m of the marsh edge. Some variability does exist in distance from the marsh, mainly among the smaller sites. Even among the Class IV sites, however, 74% are located

TABLE 3.4
Site Frequency Cross-Tabulated by Size Class and Distance from Marsh

	Distance categories		
Size classes	1 (0–100 m)	2 (100–200 m)	3 (over 200 m)
Class I	2	—	—
Class II	5	—	1
Class III	9	2	1
Class IV	20	3	4
Total	36	5	6

within 100 m of the marsh edge. This pattern of site location is seen as indicative of the general importance of marsh resources to all Irene phase settlements, regardless of size.

Table 3.5 presents data on site distances from nearest tidal creek. This measure is considered to be important because creeks allow access to the marsh, thus increasing the exploitable area available to a site. Creeks are also important in providing a means of movement onto and off the island.

Table 3.5 indicates greater variability in site distances from creeks than site distances from the marsh. Only 38% of all sites are located within 100 m of tidal creeks, compared with 77% located within 100 m of the marsh edge. Variability is best seen in the difference between the largest (Class I) and the smallest (Class IV) sites. All the Class I sites are adjacent to tidal creeks and to the marsh. On the other hand, only 30% of the Class IV sites are located next to creeks whereas 74% are adjacent to the marsh. It appears that although proximity to the marsh was important for most sites, access into the marsh or off the island was not an important consideration in the location of most of the smaller sites.

In general, the data presented indicate that variability does exist among sites at different levels of the proposed hierarchy in regard to their

TABLE 3.5
Site Frequency Cross-Tabulated by Size Class and Distance from Nearest Tidal Creek

	Distance categories		
Size classes	1 (0–100 m)	2 (100–200 m)	3 (over 200 m)
Class I	2	—	—
Class II	2	2	2
Class III	6	2	4
Class IV	8	7	12
Total	18	11	18

relationship to certain environmental variables. The larger sites are associated with more "valued" environmental situations than are the smaller sites. The two largest (and presumably most important) sites on the island are associated with optimum environmental conditions. It appears that these two sites are strategically located to facilitate exploitation of not only the most valued resource zones, but also of several resource zones.

As site size decreases, there is an increasing variability in site location and a general lessening of overall "environmental quality" associated with site location. Many of the Class IV sites are located on seasonally wet or flooded soils, which may be indicative of short-term or seasonal occupation. Few are located near tidal creeks that would provide access into the marsh or away from the island. Most, however, are located adjacent to the marsh. A decrease in site size corresponds to a selection for location in areas of decreased overall environmental value. This is interpreted as indicating increasing exploitative specialization as sites become smaller, with a concomitant decrease in functional complexity and activity-range variability.

The Settlement Hierarchy

The preceding discussion has proposed a hierarchical structure for the Irene phase settlement system on Ossabaw Island. Each level of the proposed hierarchy has been shown to be differentially associated with sets of quantified environmental variables, which is seen as reflective of variability in the kind and number of sociocultural activities carried out at each level.

No extensive excavations have been undertaken at any Irene phase sites on Ossabaw Island, and only minimal archeological data are available with which to assess the proposed hierarchy. What evidence is available, however, does tend to support the proposed variability among levels of the hierarchy; it also permits generalized statements about the probable position of each site size class in the system. This basic knowledge of the structure of the settlement system permits some tentative statements about the systemic relationships that may have existed among the settlements. Site distribution by size class is presented in Figure 3.7. Site numbers are given for sites mentioned in the text.

CLASS I SITES (119,000–412,500 m^2)

This class consists of the two largest Irene phase sites on the island. Together they comprise 57% of the total area of the 47 known Irene phase

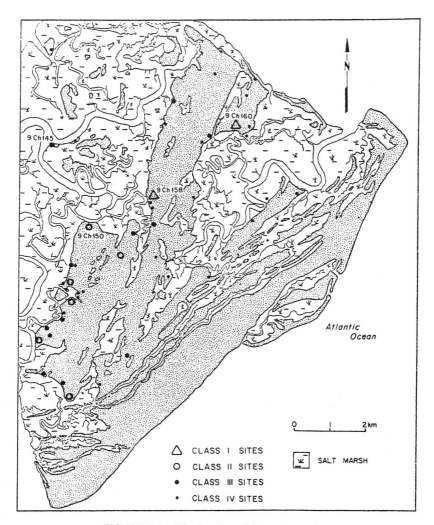

FIGURE 3.7. The location of Irene phase sites.

sites. Although site sizes are not considered exact indicators of population, they do provide relative measures of population intensity throughout the Irene phase temporal span. It can be hypothesized that the two Class I sites were important population centers.

Each of these sites has evidence of extensive pre-Irene phase occupation, and burial mounds are located at each site. The largest of these sites, 9Ch158, has five burial mounds, two of which are Irene phase mounds. The other Class I site, 9Ch160, has three burial mounds, one of which dates to the Irene phase. Clarence B. Moore (1897) totally or partially excavated all of these mounds in the 1890s. His descriptions indicate that the burial mounds at these two sites were the largest on the island. These are also the only sites on the island that contain more than one burial mound.

Both of these Class I sites are located adjacent to large tidal creeks. In fact, 9Ch158, the larger site, is located on the tidal creek that provides the most direct access to the mainland (Figure 3.7). It is likely that certain types of on- and off-island interactions were channeled through this site.

Although it cannot be clearly demonstrated at present, it is hypothesized that the Class I sites, based on their size, long period of prehistoric occupation, burial mounds, and optimum location with respect to environmental factors, were permanent year-round settlements. These sites are postulated to have been the major centers of population and many, if not all, social, political, and religious activities on the island.

CLASS II SITES (26,000–55,740 m²)

Six sites are included in the second level of the settlement hierarchy. Three of these sites have evidence of pre-Irene phase occupation. Only one Class II site has a burial mound and this mound is somewhat smaller than those found at the Class I sites (Pearson 1977). The fact that only one Class II site has a burial mound and that only three have pre-Irene phase occupation serves to differentiate these sites from those in Class I. The single Class II site with a burial mound (9Ch150), however, displays evidence of pre-Irene phase occupation. It is also located on Lakeland Fine Sand and adjacent to a tidal creek. These factors seem to indicate the possibility that this particular site was the location of sociocultural activities similar to those occurring at Class I sites, and that it should therefore perhaps be considered as a Class I site.

It is difficult to place "functional" labels on Class II sites except to say that, in general, they were less important than the Class I sites in the settlement system. The three Class II sites with no pre-Irene phase occupation may represent either population expansion during the Irene phase or seasonal dispersal of the total Irene phase population over the island. There is some evidence that the historic Guale of the Georgia coast often shifted or dispersed portions of the population seasonally to take advantage of particular resources, especially good agricultural land (see Larson 1969).

CLASS III SITES (7380–20,800 m²)

This class consists of 12 sites, most of which may best be described by the term "hamlet." These sites were permanent or semipermanent settlements which, although economically self-sufficient, were probably dependent upon and related to larger sites in certain sociopolitical spheres. These settlements likely consisted of from one to several households.

Only one of these sites (9Ch145) has any extensive pre-Irene phase occupation, and is located on a small marsh island or hammock some distance west of the island (Figure 3.7). This hammock would have provided an ideal base from which to exploit marsh–estuary resources. It may be that this site was occupied through a long period of prehistory only for this reason, and, as such, was functionally different from other Class III sites.

Five of the Class III sites have burial mounds. These mounds are much smaller than those found at any of the larger sites. Whether the mounds at these sites are small simply because they served fewer people or because they are functionally different from those at larger sites is not known, since none has been excavated.

If burial mounds are, to some extent, indicators of both permanency of settlement and socioreligious autonomy, those Class III sites with burial mounds were quite likely permanent settlements, with the mounds at each site serving only the inhabitants of that particular settlement.

Class III sites with burial mounds are postulated to have been the result of population expansion and the establishment of new settlements during the Irene phase. Class III sites without mounds are assumed to have been seasonal occupations, the result of a seasonal population dispersal over the island.

In several recent studies of Mississippian settlement patterns, sites of this general type are considered to have been small horticultural settlements (see Price 1974). The seemingly limited importance of horticulture in the overall Irene phase subsistence base suggests that in this specific situation, such small sites may not have been horticultural hamlets. They are, however, considered likely to have been economically self-sufficient.

CLASS IV SITES (1–4000 m²)

Twenty-seven sites are included in this class. Of the four levels of the settlement hierarchy, these sites demonstrate the greatest diversity of location. In general, these sites are considered to have been the location of a single, or, at most, a limited range of cultural activities. Most were probably short-term occupations, with many of the smaller ones perhaps representing only a single day's occupation. Several consist of a single shell-midden, and seem to represent short-term shellfish-gathering stations.

Variation in the location of Class IV sites does occur, and indicates that several functionally different kinds of Class IV sites may have existed.

Since most of these sites are considered to have been limited-activity, extractive sites the variability in site location probably represents variability in the type of resource being procured and possibly processed at different sites. Surface collected material indicates that many Class IV sites represent shellfish gathering stations. Excavations will be required to discern other types of activities that may have occurred.

Conclusions

Settlement size distribution analysis is one of many ways to characterize and analyze settlement systems. When used in conjunction with minimal archeological and environmental data, analysis of site size distributions has been shown to be a useful first step in the assessment of a prehistoric settlement system.

The hierarchical structure developed here, based on explicit size distinctions established by cluster analysis is tentatively supported by available archeological and environmental data. Other studies of Mississippian Period settlement hierarchies, such as those of Cahokia (Fowler 1974), Moundville (Peebles 1974), and the Powers Phase (Price 1973), although based on different criteria, also postulated three- to four-level hierarchies. A major difference exists, however, in that the Ossabaw Island hierarchy compares only to the lower levels of most other described Mississippian hierarchies. This is not surprising considering the marginal position, relative isolation, and general lack of elaboration of Irene phase development in relation to other Mississippian groups.

Ossabaw Island may have operated as a whole and discrete unit on many socioeconomic levels. At higher sociopolitical and possibly religious levels, the island appears, however, to have been part of a larger sociocultural network. This is evident in terms of observed archeological (mainly ceramic) similarities with other islands and the mainland, and in some of the early historic accounts of the area (Lanning 1935, Swanton 1922). Settlements that would be associated with the highest level or levels of the regional Irene phase settlement system would not be expected to occur on Ossabaw Island. This absence of highest-level Irene phase settlements on Ossabaw Island is indicated by the absence of platform mounds of the kind present at the Irene Mound site.

Ossabaw Island has provided a rather fortuitous situation in that it presents a distinct and obviously bounded physiographic area within which settlement data lend themselves to partial explanation. The model of settlement developed herein is a hypothetical construct, and requires further testing and refinement. The model, and the approach utilized, are considered to be initial steps toward an understanding of prehistoric settlement systems on the coast of Georgia.

Future Research

The settlement model developed here uncovers several problem areas that require further research. The most important questions to be approached involve testing the model by assessing the proposed "functional" activities occurring at sites in each level of the hierarchy and the functional variability assumed to exist among hierarchical levels. This will require the collection of artifactual material, through excavation, that can be used to test proposed site–size class function and variability. Intensive and systematic test excavations conducted at a few sites from each level of the settlement hierarchy is probably the most efficient means of acquiring the data necessary to test the model. Although a systematic and complete survey of the island is desirable, it is unlikely that additional sites uncovered by such a survey will significantly alter the structure of the proposed settlement system.

Several of the other Sea Islands have evidence of extensive Irene phase occupation. A comparison of the structure of the Irene phase settlement systems on these other islands to that on Ossabaw Island should lead to more refined statements about Irene phase settlement in general.

Geographical models and methods like those used in this study require more evaluation of their utility when applied to prehistoric data. Several of the analytical methods used here, for example, settlement size distribution analysis and cluster analysis, although apparently useful, require further testing and application with archeological data. It is hoped that archeologists will begin to use these sorts of analysis more frequently in order to test their usefulness in the assessment of prehistoric settlement systems.

References

Anderberg, Michael R.
   1973   *Cluster analysis for application.* New York: Academic Press.
Anderson, David G.
   1974   Inferences from distributional studies of prehistoric artifacts in the coastal plain of South Carolina. Paper presented at the 1974 meeting of the Southeastern Archaeological Conference, Atlanta.

Berry, Brian J.L.
  1961   City size distributions and economic development. *Economic Development and Cultural Change* **9**:573–588.
Berry, Brian J.L., and W.L. Garrison
  1958   Alternate explanations of urban rank size relationships. *Annals of the Association of American Geographers* **48**:83–91.
Brandt, K.A.
  1972   American Bottom settlements. Paper presented at the 1972 meeting of the Society for American Archaeology, Bal Harbor, Florida.
Caldwell, Joseph R.
  1943   Cultural relations of four Indian sites on the Georgia coast. M.A. thesis, Department of Anthropology, University of Chicago.
  1952   The archaeology of eastern Georgia and South Carolina. In *Archeology of eastern United States,* edited by James B. Griffin. Chicago: University of Chicago Press. Pp. 312–332.
  1971   Chronology of the Georgia coast. *Southeastern Archaeological Conference Bulletin* **13**:89–91.
  1972   Archaeological investigations on St. Catherines Island, Georgia. Department of Anthropology, University of Georgia. Mimeo.
Caldwell, Joseph R., and C. McCann
  1941   *Irene Mound Site, Chatham County, Georgia.* University of Georgia Press, Athens.
Caldwell, Joseph R., and Antonio Waring
  1939   The use of a ceramic sequence in the classification of aboriginal sites in Chatham County, Georgia. *Southeastern Archaeological Conference Newsletter* **2** (1):6–7.
Cook, Fred C.
  1966   Excavations at the Kent Mound, St. Simons Island, Georgia. Department of Anthropology, University of Georgia. Xerox.
  1971   The 1971 excavations at the Seven Mile Bend site. Department of Anthropology, University of Georgia. Xerox.
DePratter, Chester B.
  1973   An archaeological survey of Black Island, McIntosh County, Georgia. Department of Anthropology, University of Georgia. Xerox.
  1974   Archaeological survey of Ossabaw Island; a preliminary report. Department of Anthropology, University of Georgia. Mimeo.
  1975   Archaeological survey of Lewis property, Skidaway Island, Chatham County, Georgia. Skidaway Institute, Skidaway Island, Georgia. Xerox.
Dziewonski, K.
  1972   General theory of rank-size distributions in regional settlement systems: A reappraisal and reformulation of the rank-size rule. *Papers of the Regional Science Association* **29**:75–86.
  1975   The role and significance of statistical distributions in studies of settlement systems. *Papers of the Regional Science Association* **34**:145–155.
Fairbanks, Charles
  1952   Creek and pre-Creek. In *Archeology of Eastern United States,* edited by James B. Griffin. University of Chicago Press, Chicago. Pp. 285–300.
Fewkes, Vladimer
  1938   W.P.A. Excavations at Irene Mound. Savannah Chamber of Commerce, Savannah, Georgia. Mimeo.
Fowler, Melvin
  1972   The Cahokia Site: Summary and interpretations. Paper presented at the 1972 meeting of the Society for American Archaeology, Bal Harbor, Florida.

1974   Cahokia: Ancient capitol of the Midwest. Addison-Wesley Module in Anthropol-
        ogy, 48. Reading, Massachusetts: Addison-Wesley.
Goad, Sharon I.
    1975   Excavations on Skidaway Island: 9Ch112. Department of Anthropology, University
            of Georgia. Xerox.
Graybill, Donald A.
    1974   Computer programs: Program HCLUS. *Newsletter of Computer Archaeology,*
            10(1):14.
    1975   Mimbres-Mogollon adaptations in the Gila National Forest, Mimbres District, New
            Mexico. *Archaeological Report* 9. U.S.D.A. Forest Service, Albuquerque.
Haggett, Peter
    1971   *Locational analysis in human geography.* New York: St. Martins Press.
Hally, David J., R. Zurel, and T. Gresham
    1975   An archaeological survey of channel, dike and streambank protection structures,
            Big Mortar-Snuffbox Swamp watershed, Long and McIntosh Counties, Georgia.
            Department of Anthropology, University of Georgia. Mimeo.
Hillestad, H.O., J.R. Bozeman, A.S. Johnson, C.W. Berisford, and J.L. Richardson
    1975   The ecology of the Cumberland Island National Seashore, Camden County, Geor-
            gia. *Technical Report Series 75–5.* Georgia Marine Science Center, Skidaway Island,
            Georgia.
Johnson, S., H.O. Hillestad, S.F. Shanholtzer, and G. Shanholtzer
    1975   The ecology of the Georgia Coast. *National Park Service Science Monograph* 3.
            Washington, D.C.
Kelly, A.R.
    1938   A preliminary report on archaeological explorations at Macon, Georgia. *Bureau of
            American Ethnology Bulletin* **119**:1–68. Washington, D.C.
King, Leslie
    1961   A multivariate analysis of the spacing of urban settlements in the United States.
            Annals of the Association of American Geographers, **51**:222–233.
Lanning, John T.
    1935   *The Spanish Missions of Georgia.* University of North Carolina Press, Chapel Hill.
Larson, Lewis H., Jr.
    1958a   Cultural relationships between the northern St. Johns area and the Georgia coast.
            Florida Anthropologist **12**(1):11–19.
    1958b   Southern Cult manifestations on the Georgia coast. *American Antiquity* 23:426–430.
    1969   Aboriginal subsistence technology on the Southeastern coastal plain during the late
            prehistoric period. Ph.D. dissertation, Department of Anthropology, University of
            Michigan. Ann Arbor: University Microfilms.
Moore, Clarence B.
    1897   Certain aboriginal mounds of the Georgia coast. *Journal of the Academy of Natural
            Sciences* **10**(1). Philadelphia.
Odum, Eugene
    1971   *Fundamentals of Ecology.* Saunders, Philadelphia.
Pearson, Charles E.
    1977   Analysis of late prehistoric settlement on Ossabaw Island, Georgia. *Laboratory of
            Archaeology Series* 12. Department of Anthropology, University of Georgia.
Peebles, C.S.
    1974   Moundville: the organization of a prehistoric community and culture. Unpub-
            lished Ph.D. dissertation. Department of Anthropology, University of California,
            Santa Barbara.
Price, James
    1973   Settlement planning and artifact distribution on the Snodgrass Site and their

socio-political implications in the Powers Phase of Southeast Missouri. Unpublished Ph.D. dissertation. Department of Anthropology, University of Michigan.

1974   Mississippian settlement systems of the central Mississippi Valley. Paper presented at an advanced seminar on Mississippian development. Santa Fe: School of American Research.

Rolingson, Martha Ann
1976   The Bartholomew phase: A Plaquemine adaption in the Mississippi Valley. In *Cultural change and continuity,* edited by C.E. Cleland. Academic Press, New York. Pp. 99–119.

Sears, William
1956   Excavations at Kolomoki: final report. *University of Georgia Series in Anthropology* 5. Athens, Georgia.

Siegel, Sidney
1956   *Nonparametric statistics for the behavioral sciences.* McGraw-Hill, New York.

Simon, H.H.
1955   On a class of skew distribution functions. *Biometrika* **42**:425–440.

Simpkins, Daniel L., and A.E. McMichael
1976   Sapelo Island: A preliminary report. *Southeastern Archaeological Conference Bulletin* **19**:95–99.

Smith, Carol A.
1974   Economics of marketing systems: Models from economic geography. *Annual Review of Anthropology* **3**:167–201.

Stewart, C.T.
1958   The size and spacing of cities. *Geographical Review,* **48**:222–245.

Swanton, John R.
1922   Early history of the Creek Indians and their neighbors. *Bureau of American Ethnology Bulletin* 73. Washington, D.C.

United States Department of Agriculture
1974   *Soil Survey of Bryan and Chatham Counties, Georgia.* Soil Conservation Service, United States Department of Agriculture, Washington, D.C.

Vapnarsky, C.A.
1969   On rank-size distributions of cities: An ecological approach. *Economic Development and Cultural Change* **17**:584–592.

Waring, Antonio, and Preston Holder
1945   A prehistoric ceremonial complex of the Southeastern United States. *American Anthropologist* **47**(1):1–34.

Willey, Gordon, and Phillip Phillips
1958   *Method and theory in American archaeology.* Chicago: University of Chicago Press.

Wood, John J.
1974   A computer program for hierarchical cluster analysis. *Newsletter of Computer Archaeology* **9**(4):1–11.

Fort Walton
Settlement Patterns

DAVID S. BROSE

GEORGE W. PERCY

Fort Walton artifacts occur in areas with important contrasts of local environments in Florida, Georgia, and Alabama. Clear differences exist between interior and coastal sections of the Florida Panhandle, and between upland and lowland sections of the interior Panhandle and neighboring parts of Georgia and Alabama. These environmental variations present different adaptive situations, as well as different exploitative opportunities (Figure 4.1).

The Florida Panhandle and adjacent parts of southern Georgia and Alabama lie within the East Gulf Coastal Plain section of the Coastal Plain Province (Fenneman 1938:65–83). Magnolia forest climax vegetation occurs in small and scattered areas, interspersed with large areas of mixed hydric and xeric vegetation (seral stages of the climax forest, reflecting local variations in moisture and soil) (Shelford 1963:63–64).

Within the Fort Walton area, the primary physiographic divisions are the Northern Highlands, the Marianna Lowlands, and the Gulf Coastal Lowlands (Puri and Vernon 1964:7–8). The Northern Highlands and the Coastal Lowlands are separated by a relict marine scarp called the Cody Scarp.

Over the entire Coastal Lowlands zone there are two principal biotic communities. Salt marshes fringe the coastline of the eastern Panhandle, as far west as the Ochlockonee River, varying in width from less than 100 m to as much as 8 km (Kurz and Wagner 1957). They are lowlying and wet,

81

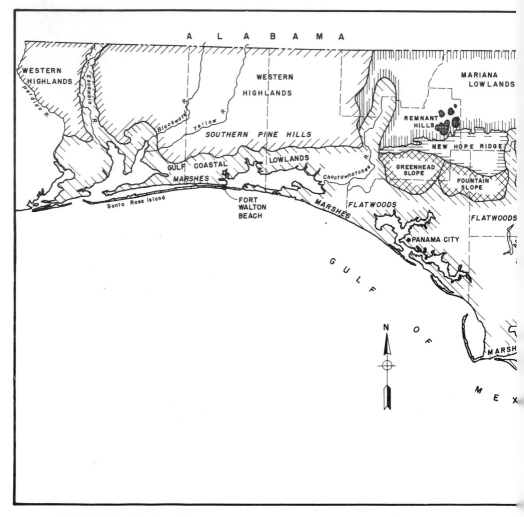

FIGURE 4.1. Physiographic zones of Northwest Florida. [Adapted from Puri and Vernon (1964).]

generally less than 1 m above mean sea level, with little relief. Salt marsh vegetation consists of grasses, rushes, and sedges. Fronting the marsh on the seaward side are sandy barrier beach ridges. These are generally under 30 m wide. Crests are about .65 m higher than the marsh, with vegetation consisting principally of live oak, *Ilex vomitoria,* and *Sabal palmetto.* Shallow mud flats extend out in front of the barrier ridges. At extreme low tides, the bay floors or flats may be exposed for 800 m or more. The barrier beaches are frequently interrupted by tidal inlets, which are connected with narrow channels that meander throughout the marsh and form tidal creeks. The marshes are subject to frequent tidal inundation.

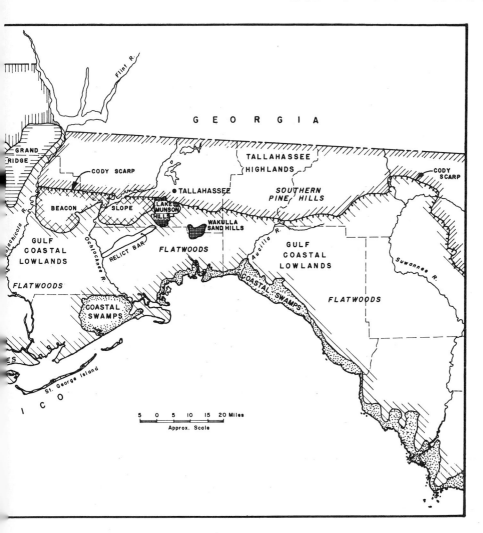

In the coastal marsh zone, the only land surfaces suitable for human settlement are the barrier beaches and occasional flatwoods islands. Inland from the marshes is the flatwoods zone, formed on the most recent Pleistocene marine terrace. Remnant flatwoods islands also occur within the marsh zone, standing .8 m or more above the surrounding marsh, with vegetation dominated by *Pinus elliottii, Sabal palmetto, Ilex vomitoria, Serenoa repens,* and *Baccharis halimifolia.*

The flatwoods extend inland, increasing gradually in elevation from a 1 m or so above sea level to as much as 60 m above sea level at the foot of the Cody escarpment, although the north-to-south slope of the zone is quite gentle. The flatwoods are poorly drained both because of their very low surface relief and because of the existence of a natural hardpan about 1 m below the surface. Vegetation consists of open pine forest dominated by longleaf pine, with slash pine and pond pine occurring locally. There is a dense understory in which saw palmetto and wire grass are major components, interspersed with a variety of low bushes, shrubs, and vines (Clewell 1971; Harper 1914:248–253, 291-313, Shelford 1963:76). Throughout the flatwoods, swamps occupy shallow depressions 1.5–3 m below the level of the surrounding pineland, and are characterized by cypress pond or bay vegetation. The sluggish streams flowing through the area are bordered by low swampy zones behind the low levees along the river banks. In general, the dense vegetation and wetness of the ground throughout much of the year make the flatwoods a relatively inhospitable place to live. In prehistoric times, settlement was confined to narrow river banks and occasional live oak xeric hammocks, slightly elevated surfaces characterized by live oak, bluejack oak, laurel oak, cabbage palmetto, and relict longleaf pine, as well as shrubs, vines, and grasses.

West of the Ochlockonee River, the coastal marsh zone is absent, and the flatwoods directly abut barrier beach ridges. West from the Ochlockonee the bay beaches seaward of the barrier ridges become wider. Between Panama City and Fort Walton, beaches are often over 100 m wide, and barrier ridges are much higher than in the eastern Panhandle.

There is a series of long and narrow offshore islands paralleling the coastline of the mainland (e.g., St. George Island and Santa Rosa Island) or islands that are small and more equilateral in area. Some combination of tidal marsh, freshwater marsh, and scrub oak and scrub pine is usually present. Larger trees are infrequent, and consist of the same species found on the crests of barrier beaches. The islands are generally less than 8 km offshore, and many small islands or islets are within 800 m of shore. Most of the Panhandle shoreline fronts on bays, sounds, or lagoons. Immediate offshore waters are very shallow. Estuarine conditions prevail in the shallow bays, and shellfish resources are plentiful and easily exploited.

The northern highlands cover the interior half of the Panhandle (Puri and Vernon 1964:10–11) and consist of a series of highland masses separated by stream valleys. The one major break is provided by the Marianna lowlands. The uplands are heavily dissected and characterized by rolling hills with sharp changes in relief and relatively few sizable areas of level land, except along the larger streams (Cooke 1939:14–21, Hendry and Yon 1958:10–11, Hubbell, Laessle, and Dickenson 1956:5–8, 15–23). In the Panhandle, higher land surfaces range between 40 and 100 m above sea level, being generally lower at the eastern end of the region. In Georgia, elevations up to 100–107 m occur.

Over the southern half of the uplands, vegetation is mostly open pine forest dominated by a longleaf-pine–scrub-oak–wire-grass association. On exceptionally sandy areas, the longleaf forest is replaced by sand pine and scrub oak. Over the northern half of the uplands is a mixed hardwood and pine forest. Shallow ponds with cypress, slash pine, and black gum occur in flatter places throughout the highlands. Such areas are less frequent in the highlands than in the flatwoods. Along streams, bottomland hardwood forests with dense growths of mesophytic broad-leaved trees are characteristic. The largest bottomlands in the Panhandle occur along the Apalachicola River, where the present floodplain through the highlands is up to 3.2 km wide.

These highlands extend up into southern Georgia as part of the Tifton upland, and they are bounded by a northward-facing escarpment that overlooks the Flint River Valley. High, steep bluffs border the Flint River Valley and are continuous with high bluffs along the east side of the Apalachicola River. Sheer drops ranging from 15.25—30.5 m are not uncommon along these bluffs. West of the Chattahoochee River, the highlands extends into southern Alabama as part of the Southern Pine Hills (Fenneman 1938:68).

The Marianna lowlands are a zone with nearly flat surfaces in the vicinity of present streams. In other parts, low, gently rolling hills are formed by the erosion of older river and marine terrace formations (Cooke 1939:18–19, Hendry and Yon 1958:11–12, W. Moore 1955:7–8). The lowlands were formed by a sequence of stream erosion and solution of underlying limestone deposits (Hendry and Yon 1958:17–20). Open forest dominated by longleaf pine is the prevailing vegetation, although numerous sinks in the northeastern part of Jackson County are fringed with narrow bands of hardwood trees. Hardwoods also occur along the banks of streams as large as the Chipola River (Harper 1914:193–208).

The lowlands are part of a larger Dougherty River Valley lowlands zone, which extends into southeast Alabama and southwest Georgia along the lower reaches of the Chattahoochee and Flint Rivers. Along the southern edge of the Marianna lowlands is a narrow remnant of the northern highlands.

Soils throughout the Panhandle are generally sandy and rather poor for agriculture, except under modern management (Florida Division of State Planning 1974). Loamy soils favorable for primitive agriculture occur in irregular patches along the larger streams, and there is also an important area of sandy loam soil in northeastern Leon County. As Harper (1914) notes

> This region was cultivated by the Indians long before the white man came, and until within the last few decades it was the leading agricultural section of the State in proportion to its size. . . . Even yet, after three-quarters of a century of cultivation by whites and negros, most of the farmers do not consider it necessary to use commercial fertilizer [pp. 278–279].

Not surprisingly, this was the most densely settled area of the Panhandle in Fort Walton and Apalachee times.

Dendritic drainage patterns are characteristic of the Panhandle, which is divided into a series of north–south drainage basins that ultimately empty into the Gulf of Mexico. The principal basins (from west to east) are the Perdido, Escambia, Blackwater, Yellow, Choctawhatchee, Apalachicola, Ochlockonee, and Aucilla (Kenner, Pride, and Conover 1967, Kenner, Hampton, and Conover 1969). Scattered throughout the Panhandle are internal drainage basins centered on karst lakes and ponds.

Climate is much the same across the Panhandle, with temperatures and precipitation slightly more moderate along the coast. The mean January temperature is 54°F, the mean July temperature is 82°F. In the summer months, temperatures regularly go above 90°F, whereas in winter, subfreezing temperatures are not uncommon (Butson 1962, Wood and Fernald 1974:58–59). The mean annual freeze-free period for the northern Panhandle is 240–270 days; for the southern half of the Panhandle it is 270–300 days. Freezing temperatures are likely to occur in the period from mid-November through early March (Wood and Fernald 1974:62–63).

Rainfall increases slightly from east to west across the Panhandle. At the eastern end, the mean annual rainfall is 132 cm, whereas from the Choctawhatchee valley, west, it exceeds 152 cm, reaching a high of 163 cm in central and southern Okaloosa and Walton counties (Wood and Fernald 1974:60). The rainy season is July–September, when there is nearly a 50% chance that some rain will fall on any given day. A second high point occurs in early spring. October and November are the driest months.

Abundant animal resources in the area include white-tail deer, puma, bobcat, black bear, the Florida wolf, and numerous smaller carnivores. Other common small mammals are the gray squirrel, fox squirrel, cottontail rabbit, marsh rabbit, and opossum (Sherman 1937, 1952). Bison (*Bison bison bison*) were documented from the mid-sixteenth to the early eighteenth century, but bison remains have not been reported from prehistoric sites. Over 300 species of birds are reported for the Panhandle (Stevenson 1960), the most important of which, from the standpoint of aboriginal use, include the wild turkey, bobwhite quail, mourning dove, ducks, and geese. The coastal marshes are important wintering grounds for migratory waterfowl (Chamberlain 1960). Oysters, clams, conchs, and many other species of shellfish, as well as fish, occur in abundance in coastal marine waters. Fish and a variety of mollusks are also plentiful in inland streams. Reptiles are common everywhere in the Panhandle.

Of the environmental zones just described, some are clearly better than others in terms of potential for human settlement. Unfortunately, archeological survey of the entire Panhandle region is not sufficiently complete to allow a claim that each of the zones is representatively sampled (Figure 4.2). In particular, the flatwoods and the northern highlands zone west of the Marianna lowlands are poorly known. However, preferred zones of settlement seem to have been the highlands (including the Marianna lowlands) and the coastal strand, which have a number of fundamental advantages over the flatwoods and marshes as places for human settlement.

The highlands zone offers a greater area of land suitable for settlement than other zones. Most of the flatwoods and coastal marshes are too wet for long-term occupation, and the few suitable places—hammocks, river banks, and remnant flatwoods islands—are small in total area. The highlands also offer better opportunity for agriculture. This is partly because there is more well-drained land in the highlands zone, and partly because patches of relatively fertile soils are more common than in the flatwoods, where soils are generally very acid and low in nutrients. Throughout the highlands, there are springheads, around which can be found small

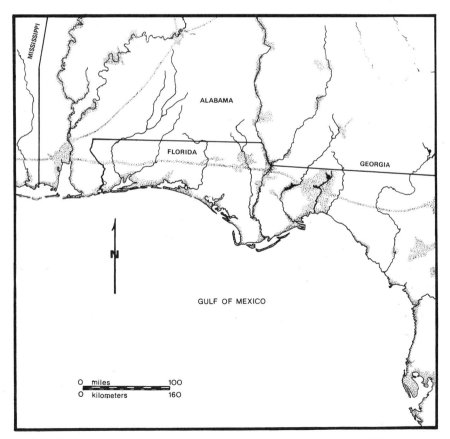

FIGURE 4.2. *Minimal archeological survey coverage within the Fort Walton area.*

patches of relatively fertile, well-watered, gently sloped ground. These places offer a significant opportunity for small-scale gardening, which is not possible in the flatwoods.

In addition, the mixed-hardwood–pine forests of the highlands offer a greater variety and abundance of edible plant resources than the pine forests of the flatwoods. For example, Harlow (1959:52) has estimated that population densities of deer could be five to six times as great in mixed-hardwood–pine communities as in the flatwoods.

The food resources available to inhabitants of the coast consist primarily of the species of marine fish and shellfish in the Gulf. These are abundantly represented in many sites situated on the barrier beaches along the coast. Other animals were exploited by coastal inhabitants, but the opportunities for hunting land animals were not as great as in the Highlands. In the same way, highland freshwater mollusks were much smaller in size on the average, and their density less than on the coast. Thus, in comparing coastal versus interior occupations, one would expect to see rather different emphases in Fort Walton subsistence and thus settlement patterns.

The character of the environment, an important factor conditioning prehistoric occupation of Northwest Florida, must be seen in relation to both the scheduling of energy source utilization by these populations and their cognitive structure of the environment. We must reconstruct selective prehistoric utilization of the microenvironmental variations to determine the native cultural changes that took place in patterns of environmental use. These must be understood in the context of changes that took place in the environment itself, including both natural changes and changes, such as burning, that were human induced (Komarek 1962–1968, Lemon 1967). The ecological conditions differ significantly between the areas where inland Lake Jackson and Apalachicola Valley Fort Walton variants occur (and both of these areas show significant ecological differences from the coastal areas where the Pensacola Fort Walton complex occurs). Sociocultural organizational responses in terms of settlement–subsistence strategies also differed between coastal and the various inland populations as a result of differences in environmental factors already described. We will further suggest that the timing and tempo of Mississippian developments show significant differences between such environmental zones.

Regional Chronology

Weeden Island (dated from A. D. 400 to 960) locally precedes Fort Walton. The Weeden Island culture has traditionally been thought of heavily oriented toward coastal resources. It is our opinion, however, that this view is not correct, but, rather, reflects sampling bias. The interior of the Northwest Florida region offers a lusher, more productive environment, and, since many interior Weeden Island sites have finally come to light in recent studies, it seems reasonable to consider the possibility that the bulk of Weeden Island populations lived inland—in the highlands— and that their use of the coastal strand area was only one aspect of the Weeden Island cultural adaptation.

Despite its temporal priority, practically no attention has been given to the developmental significance of Weeden Island culture in the sequence of culture change in Northwest Florida. Weeden Island economic and social subsystems are poorly understood and, despite all the burial mounds that have been excavated, solid demographic data are lacking. Settlement systems are a spatial reflection of interrelationships of the cultural, biophysical, and social environments, and so we should ask about the nature of the Weeden Island adaptation. How did it differ from what came before it? What basic economic and social problems did it solve for the prehistoric peoples of northwest Florida? Why was it ultimately unsuccessful? A slightly different way of putting these questions is to ask: What were the cultural processes operating in Northwest Florida that generated a system of behavior that we can label was Weeden Island culture, and what processes then caused this system to evolve into a new system state that we can label Fort Walton and that is securely dated between A. D. 1050 and 1520.

In previous papers (Percy and Brose 1974, Brose and Percy 1974), we suggested a model to describe certain basic developments in Weeden Island subsistence and settlement patterns. The model is reasonable in relation to available data and offers a processual framework for considering the significance and distinctiveness of the Weeden Island cultural system. We argued that important changes in settlement patterns occurred in Northwest Florida during the Weeden Island period, which, at least in part, were a consequence of population growth and the increasing importance of horticultural activities. A system of shifting cultivation developed, and in some Panhandle localities, land areas suitable for farming were literally filled up. This led to competition for land, and by about A. D. 1000, Weeden Island social organization and, later, economy were realigned in accordance with the Mississippian models, which were beginning to circulate in the lower southeast. Rather than thinking of Weeden Island as a sophisticated local cultural development suddenly chopped off in its prime by Mississippian invaders who established Fort Walton culture (Willey 1949:580–581; Caldwell 1958), it is more useful and more correct to think of it as the breakdown of a long-standing adaptive system under the stress of population increase. The worth of this model remains to be determined, but it provides the opportunity for generating testable hypotheses and for carrying archeological studies beyond the limited focus on material culture traits.

Historical Background

The earliest report of Mississippian material from northwest Florida appears to be Schoolcraft's illustration of Fort Walton materials from Apalachicola Bay (Schoolcraft 1849, Part 2:77ff). Sternberg (1876) excavated in a temple mound and shell midden at Fort Walton, but failed to describe the materials recovered. C. B. Moore (1902, 1903, 1907, 1918) provided the earliest detailed reports on Fort Walton materials from the Panhandle region. In addition to trenching the top of the holotype mound at Walton's camp, Moore located and excavated four extensive cemeteries, at least four distinct village middens, and four temple mounds that appear to have been, in whole or part, Fort Walton. Unfortunately, Moore's recording techniques did not match his efficiency, and other than the mounds themselves, little remains of the sites he located. It seems fair to say that much of our data base and many of our terminological difficulties are Moore's legacy. Moore's reports also indicated the rich nature of both Weeden Island and Fort Walton mounds within the area. Based upon the collections of Moore and others, W. H. Holmes (1903) produced a study of aboriginal ceramics in which he raised still unanswered questions of the relationship of this area to the Mississippi Valley and the presence of possible Caribbean and Mesoamerican influences in Northwest Florida.

Little investigation of the region was undertaken between Moore and the Federal Relief Administration program of survey and test excavations during the 1930s (Willey 1949). The first attempts at establishing a chronological and geographical framework to interpret the respective sites was initiated in 1940 by Willey and Woodbury, who visited a number of sites along a coastal strip approximately 8 km wide, conducting stratigraphic test excavations at five sites between Pensacola Bay and the Ocklochnee River and at the Lake Jackson site, north of Tallahassee (Willey and Woodbury 1942).

Willey and Woodbury retested many of Moore's sites, located several "pristine" sites, and organized their data into a geographical and temporal framework that could be integrated with contemporary regional syntheses throughout the eastern United States. Although the distinctive nature of Gulf Coast cultures was recognized, Willey and Woodbury clearly perceived the Mississippian nature of the Fort Walton materials they investigated, although it now appears that their initial reliance on the West Coast Pensacola sites may have biased their taxonomy. Willey (1949) reanalyzed extant collections from the Northwest Florida coast and assigned them to the periods defined in 1940. Willey also included summary descriptions and ceramic frequencies from work performed by others since the 1940 survey.

The latest aboriginal periods defined by Willey and Woodbury were Weeden Island and Fort Walton. Weeden Island was a manifestation of the Burial Mound period, whereas Fort Walton was representative of the Temple Mound period, which lasted in Northwest Florida to the Leon–Jefferson contact period (Boyd, Smith, and Griffin 1951, Smith 1948). Willey (1949) regarded Weeden Island as the climax of indigenous cultural development in Northwest Florida, followed by the Fort Walton period, which was considered to represent a radical shift in ceramic styles and temper and apparent settlement–subsistence patterns and socioceremonial organization, "probably as part of an actual invasion of the northward Gulf region by a people whose culture was predominantly Middle Mississippian [Willey 1949:569–570]." The significance of Weeden-Island–Fort-Wilton continuity was raised but could not be resolved (Willey 1949:537–549).

Following Willey's (1949) report, further archeological work concentrating on Fort Walton cultures has been performed in Northwest Florida, although subsistence–settlement data were not obtained in most of these research projects.

In 1948, and again in 1953, Bullen undertook survey and salvage excavation of sites that were to be destroyed by the construction of the Jim Woodruff Dam, along the lower Chattahoochee and Flint Rivers in Alabama, Georgia, and Florida and the uppermost part of the Apalachicola River in Jackson and Gadsden Counties, Florida. Bullen was able to excavate only a few of the numerous sites he located.

Bullen recorded both the first (rectangular post) structures and the first maize from a (Stage III) Fort Walton context at site JA5. His careful stratigraphic work allowed him to recognize internal chronological change within Fort Walton assemblages and to postulate four sequential stages; Stage III was radiocarbon dated to A. D. 1400 at JA5. Bullen also noted that numerous Fort Walton sites were located along the present levee systems, whereas earlier Swift Creek and Weeden Island sites were associated with earlier river channel systems (Bullen 1950, 1958).

In 1959 and 1960, William Gardner conducted test excavations at the Waddells Mill Pond site, 11.2 km northwest of Marianna. Gardner (1966) suggested that the Waddells Mill Pond site was, in fact, the Chatot Indian village of San Carlos. Further excavations by B. Calvin Jones (personal communication) have not supported this suggestion. One result of excavation at this site was a large collection of faunal remains which were analyzed and reported on by Elizabeth Wing (Wing n. d.). Gardner (1971) suggested that the site represented a refuge and ceremonial center of invading Fort Walton populations who were surrounded by hostile, autochthonous populations. Jones's recent excavations have produced significant data concerning late Fort Walton subsistence patterns, and have demonstrated that the site is fully prehistoric. Although portions of the site represent a late Swift Creek occupation, there appears to be an extensive scatter of Fort Walton occupation and a moderately large Fort Walton mound, with a number of burials extended in pits at various stages of mound construction. Few grave goods are present.

Along coastal areas of Choctawatchee Bay, serveral burial sites and midden areas pertaining to contact-period Fort Walton populations were excavated by William and Yulee Lazarus. Although published data (Adams and Lazarus 1960, Lazarus 1961, 1964, 1971, Lazarus, 1967) refer to cemetery sites, a number of Fort Walton village and midden components were also excavated, but subsistence–settlement data were not reported.

Lazarus (1971) was also convinced of a discontinuity between Weeden Island and Fort Walton occupations. It is worth noting that several of these unreported midden sites in this region display what we would interpret as an earlier varient of Fort Walton (Bullen's Stage I), unaccompanied by the classic Pensacola materials, which reflect some Moundville influence.

Fairbanks continued excavations in the Fort Walton mound during 1960 (Fairbanks 1960, 1965a) and also excavated several nonceremonial Fort Walton sites along the eastern portion of Choctawatchee Bay (Fairbanks 1964, 1971). The coastal region of Choctawatchee Bay has been one of the most intensively surveyed regions of northern Florida. The lack of numerous early Fort Walton sites might thus seem difficult to explain in terms of schemes other than dramatic Mississippian intrusions. However, as we have previously documented (Percy and Brose 1974), there is a significant shift in this region in the primary ecological correlates between Weeden Island and Fort Walton site locations, thus producing a large number of later (Fort Walton) sites along the south shore of the bay.

Continued excavations within the central portions of the Lake Jackson site, performed in 1947 (Griffin 1950), revealed midden areas and features between the mounds. Further testing at this site by Frank Fryman during 1968 and 1969 recovered evidence of wall-trench structures and associated midden accumulation suggesting several hundred years of occupation. No site limits or settlement patterning were definable (Fryman 1971).

During this period, Fort Walton components were also tested along Ochlockonee Bay by Phelps (1966, 1967, n. d.), who reported a destroyed Fort Walton temple mound at Panacea Dump. In addition, a number of small inland Fort Walton components were excavated (Anonymous 1974, Fairbanks 1971, Gardner 1971, Goggin 1971, B. Jones 1971, B. Jones and Penman 1973, Sears 1962). With the exception of Jones's excavations at the Winewood and the Borrow Pit sites near Tallahassee (Jones and Penman 1973) no intrasite settlement patterns were found, and even site limits were unknown. Most sites located were in the red sand hills of Leon and Jefferson Counties or along the Marianna limestone–lowland ecotone.

Recent survey efforts by the Florida State Archaeologist's Office have clearly revealed that in the Lake-Jackson-basin–Tallahassee-Red-Hills area, especially in northern Leon County, there is a considerably lower density of pre-Fort Walton sites than is common elsewhere in Northwest Florida. This region also displays a significantly higher density of Fort Walton sites. We suggest that late Weeden Island populations, in the process of demographic and geographic expansion, had not been committed to the intensive exploitation of the region with its lack of ecologically varied resource procurement zones. An improbable alternative explanation might view early Fort Walton in the Red-Hills–Lake-Jackson area as the contemporary of late Weeden Island in the major river valley to the west.

In 1971, Percy, working at Torreya State Park, began a survey of the upland zone along the east bank of the Apalachicola River Valley (M. Jones 1974) which located about 60 sites in the western corner of Liberty and Gadsden Counties. At the same time, B. Calvin Jones directed investigations of the proposed Interstate Route 10 right-of-way and completed a transect survey of the section from Tallahassee through the Apalachicola basin. Locating Weeden Island sites in the vicinity of Aspalaga Landing in southwestern Gadsden County (Milanich 1974, Scarry n. d.), B. Jones also reexcavated portions of the Waddells Mill Pond site (B. Jones 1974). Several late Weeden Island components and several small seasonal Fort Walton campsites and ceremonial sites were investigated in the Apalachicola basin (Brose n.d.a, Brose, Essenpreis, Scarry, and White n.d.; Brose and Wilkie n. d., Ross Morrell, personal communication).

Many of these early efforts approached Weeden-Island–Fort-Walton relationships through limited salvage excavation or were cast in the framework of earlier stratigraphic tests in mortuary and ceremonial sites along the coast. The models of settlement and cultural dynamics proposed by Willey (1949) were not seriously rethought until the last decade.

Regional Settlement Patterns: A Synthetic Model

APALACHICOLA RIVER VALLEY

In the Apalachicola River Valley, late Weeden Island villages and small Fort Walton components are common. Sets of paired, apparently partly contemporaneous Fort Walton ceremonial mound and village sites are located on opposite sides of the river 1.6 km below the Jim Woodruff Dam; again, about 48 km downstream, just below Bristol–Blountstown Bridge; a third set of paired Fort Walton mounds were reported about 48 km further south, at the confluence of the Chipola River, and about 48 km further downstream, along the coast at the mouth of the Apalachicola River (Moore 1902, 1903). Apparently one of these latter mounds had been at least partially destroyed by 1940 (Willey and Woodbury 1942; Willey 1949).

During 1974 and 1975, Brose directed limited test excavations at the Curlee site (8JA7–8JA185), the Fort Walton mound and village complex on the west bank of the Apalachicola River just below Woodruff Dam. The controlled survey and sample excavation demonstrate that significant areas of this site are still undisturbed. A major portion of the domestic activity areas appear to be intact, representing a single-component early Fort Walton or transitional Weeden-Island–Fort-Walton temple-town oc-cupation, equivalent to Bullen's Stage I Fort Walton estimated to date about A. D. 1000–1100.

The Curlee Mound is presently the remnant third of what was a multistage flat-topped mound, with at least two burned activity surfaces. The earliest of these supported a large circular-post structure, whereas the later stage supported a rebuilt rectangular wall–trench structure with at least one internal pit. Several burials with Fort Walton effigy pottery and shell ear-pendants have been recovered from this mound. The domestic zones of the site extend south for approximately 350 m and are representa-tive of two or three stratigraphically distinct horizons. Wattle-and-daub structures appear well spaced along the present levee at intervals up to 50 m in some cases. To the north of the mound, domestic zones extend along the levee for a distance of at least 100 m, to the borrow area of the U. S. Route 90 bridge embankment. All ceramics recovered thus far are early Fort Walton, with the exception of sherds representing two minimal ves-sels of Etowah Complicated stamped recovered from the upper horizon in one of the northern structures (White, n. d.).

The mound and village complex at Chattahoochee Landing, on the east bank (GD2), was noted by archeological surveys as early as 1902 (Moore 1902). Testing of this site (Bullen 1958, Brose, Essenpreis, Scarry, and White, n. d.) revealed a zone of domestic activity which ran to the south some distance from the group of six low mounds and one large, multistage platform mound, and which covered an area of approximately 30 m × 60 m. All ceramics recovered have been Fort Walton. The south-ernmost low, single-stage mound appears to have been constructed over a large sand-filled pit (still untested). Some evidence for domestic activity zones have been recovered in the Chattahoochee City picnic grounds as far as the old U. S. Route 90 embankment, approximately 200 m to the north of the mound group. Several small, single-season Fort Walton sites were investigated on levee segments in this region of the valley (Brose, *et al.*, n.d.b., Brose and Wilkie n.d., Percy 1976).

The two mound and village complexes below the Bristol–Blountstown bridge were first mentioned by Moore (1903). The Cayson site, on the west bank, was noted as a flat-topped pyramidal mound with a ramp approach, although no excavations were made (Moore 1903:467–468). The top of the Yon Mound, on the east bank, was trenched by Moore and from present indications this excavation was minimal. A small deposit of burned human bones was found. Moore (1903:473) decided the mound was domicilary, not a burial mound, and no additional excavations were made.

Sears (1962) mentions, "These two temple mound sites, apparently occupied together, constitute one of the largest Fort Walton ceremonial centers on the Chattahoochee. . . . Any future research on the Fort Walton culture might well consider major excavations here. . . [p. 30]."

Test excavations were carried out at Yon in 1962, and yielded Fort Walton and Late Weeden Island materials to a depth of at least 1.25 m. In the course of excavation, Morrell and Keel noted three distinct, stratigraphically separate zones of cultural material. At a depth of 1.83 m, a burial was encountered (Morrell and Keel 1962).

During 1972, Florida State University conducted surface collection along the bank of the Apalachicola River near the Yon Mound. This survey yielded Fort Walton material from just south of the Yon Mound itself, and north approximately 1.6 km upstream (Percy and Jones, personal communication; (Percy 1972b).

George Percy made test excavations in the plaza area at the Cayson site. Four contiguous 1.5×1.5-m units produced a total of four sherds. Percy hypothesized that the culturally sterile layer of fine gray silt constituted a prepared plaza floor. This was later confirmed by more extensive testing at Cayson in January 1973 (Brose *et al.* n.d.a.). Cultural deposits in the central portion of the site proved relatively shallow. The site was composed of a single cultural component. Excavations along the edge of the plaza revealed the presence of a well-spaced single row of large posts. Test units opened into the low mound across the plaza from the Temple mound demonstrated it to represent a Fort Walton construction that overlay the plaza level. Two adjacent wall trenches and a low, rebuilt clay wall, located about 70 m north of the central plaza area, were exposed, although structural limits were not determined. A rather deep "midden" deposit, just north of the large mound and along the river bluff edge, yielded a large quantity of pottery, but few faunal or floral remains were recovered from the rather acidic soil (Cutler 1976, Forsythe and Clapham 1975).

Further excavations by Percy in 1973 located some portion of a domestic occupation area to the northeast of the ceremonial precinct. Postholes were excavated, and Fort Walton Stage I–II artifacts mapped in place in the scattered midden deposits that grade out along a bayou to the north. Fragments of several species of nutshell were recovered, along with charred bones of turtle, deer, and several species of fish.

During the summer of 1973, excavations in the Cayson site ceremonial area revealed the first wall trench to be over 21 m long (no corners have been found) associated with burned and unburned "clay platform" areas. Testing to the south of the plaza revealed another wall trench comparable to the 21-m-long one. A line of posts 40 cm in diameter paralleled the southwest edge of the plaza and platform mound. To the south of this ceremonial precinct, salvage excavations revealed rectangular and curvilinear lines of postmolds, refuse pits, and other evidence for habitation areas. A date on one southern area wall trench (A. D. 900 ± 225) (CWRU-93) and the incidence of a much higher occurrence of Wakulla Checkstamp pottery may indicate earlier occupation for this portion of the site. Excavations into the low mound revealed a number of early Fort Walton construction stages; two with post structures and refuse-filled features—the latest of which contained maize and was dated at A. D. 1150. A penultimate burned activity surface on the large platform mound was dated A. D. 1190 (Brose *et al*. n.d.a.).

Faunal remains thus far recovered from the Cayson site have been minimal for all excavations other than those in the northern zone, but there appears to be excellent preservation of charred floral materials and pollen and spores. Maize and beans have been identified (Cutler personal communication) from dated sealed features, and preliminary palynological analyses (Forsythe and Clapham, 1975) suggest a general vegetational cover of cypress, oak, hickory, and laurel, with nearby disturbed groundcover areas yielding maize and Compositae pollen at the time of occupation.

The 1973 excavations at the Yon site (Scarry n. d.) revealed the site to be deeply stratified with well-defined separate occupations. Refuse areas immediately south of the mound possessed clear internal stratigraphy and numerous well-preserved faunal and ethnobotanical remains. Intermediate occupation levels produced a date of A. D. 1050 (CWRU-95). The associated ceramics were entirely Fort Walton, with a large amount of Wakulla Check-stamp pottery recovered. Excavations into the upstream face of the mound uncovered three distinct cultural levels. The uppermost levels produced large amounts of sand–mica tempered Fort Walton ceramics, lithic debitage, and faunal remains. Lamar Complicated stamped pottery was relatively abundant. Below these disturbed levels was a sealed, burned floor, dated to A. D. 970 (CWRU-114), and yielding Fort Walton ceramics. Pollen samples taken from this floor indicate the presence of an open area with Compositae yielding the predominant nonarboreal pollens. Below this floor was another sealed and burned living floor. The ceramics from this lower floor consisted of gross types assignable to late Weeden Island and early Fort Walton. Pollen recovered from this floor indicates that occupation occurred in a wooded environment with cypress and adler predominating.

The excavations at the Yon site suggest a shifting picture of considerable complexity, with diverse activity areas occurring in regions contiguous to the mound, whereas nearby areas were sterile.

Numerous local collections suggest considerable late Weeden Island and early Fort Walton exploitation of the Chipola River upland zone for specific economic activities that may have been seasonal in nature. Additional small sites, reported by local residents but professionally untested, occupy the wooded bluffs along the eastern valley. Examination of collections suggests a Weeden-Island–Fort-Walton temporal placement. The recent intensive Florida State University surveys of Sweetwater Creek, which drains these eastern bluffs below Torreya State Park, suggest late Weeden Island occupation for relatively permanent, small family, short-fallow swidden activities at Springheads (Jones 1974, Percy and Brose 1974). Additional information for the east bank of the Apalachicola River as far as the Ochlockonee divide is minimal. On the west bank as far as the western Chipola drainage basin, excavation on Fort Walton sites is limited to Gardner's testing in central Jackson County; the I-10 corridor salvage at Coe's Landing (Brose n.d.b.); and the salvage excavation at the Gulf Power parking lot site (Brose and Wilkie n. d.). Limited survey work (Brose *et al.* n.d.b) during 1974 and 1975 reveals the existence of several dozen small short-term seasonal extractive activity campsites along the valley rim.

In the Apalachicola River Valley, Fort Walton settlement thus appears, on both radiometric and ceramic seriation, grounds to be early (*circa* A. D. 1000). Although limited excavation data enjoin caution, it is possible to propose a model for further testing. Major sites are variable, but all lie on present levee segments and consist of a single, large, multistage pyramidal mound and plaza complex, often flanked by several smaller mounds. These ceremonial areas may be separated from the domestic areas of the site by large posts (as at the Cayson or Curlee sites) or by low (25 cm) rebuilt clay walls (as at Cayson). Associated with these ceremonial zones are extensive areas of domestic occupation which extend up to 1000 m in a linear zone along the river levee. Where internal temporal shifts can be recognized (as at Cayson, JA5, Chattahoochee Landing, and Curlee), it appears that the earlier domestic zones initially lie south of the ceremonial precinct, whereas later occupation may also occur upstream. There is some evidence for regular spacing of domestic structures in at least one of these major sites. At others, limited testing suggests no clear patterning, with rather dispersed village occupation along the levees upstream and downstream from the ceremonial centers. Structures appear to be rectangular and of wattle-and-daub construction. Although based on extremely limited data, it does appear as if both wall trench and single post structures are present, suggesting year-round occupation by at least some portion of the population. Major sites appear to be consistently located where permanent streams drain the back swamps and cut the silt–sand levee into–2-km segments. These zones normally occur within 3–5 km of hammock, upland spring, and back-swamp ecotones. Site location would thus favor varied seasonal resource procurement during the early Fort Walton period. These major temple mound villages appear as coeval pairs on opposite sides of the Apalachicola River at ecotones approximately 50 km apart; at the confluence of the Flint and Chattahoochee; at the southern edge of the highlands; at the northern edge of the coastal lowlands; and on the Gulf Coast estuary.

Macrosettlement patterns within the Apalachicola River Valley include small, special purpose, seasonal sites scattered between the major sites, along the levees and on swamp hammocks within the river valley and along the edge of the Marianna lowlands, which form the western valley rim north of the coastal flatlands. Few, if any, Fort Walton sites are located in the eastern highlands. The sites comprising the lower end of the settlement system indicate spring plant collecting, fall–winter hunting, and winter fishing activities by single or multifamily population segments, although evidence comes from only a few excavated contexts (Brose, n.d.b; Brose and Wilkie n.d. Brose *et al.* n.d.a.; Brose and White, n.d.). Numerous small Fort Walton campsites of similar demographic character are located throughout the Marianna lowlands to the west of the Apalachicola drainage, was well as throughout the upper Chipola drainage basin into Alabama (Brose and White n.d., Brose, Essenpreis, Scarry, Gardner, Bluestone, and Forsythe n.d., Gardner personal communication, n.d., Jones personal communication). Below the northern boundary of the coastal flatlands, little information is available. To the east of the Apalachicola River, a similar pattern of small group seasonal site occupation does not exist as far east as the Ochlockonee drainage (Percy 1972a, Jones 1974). Fort Walton campsites have also been recorded on flood plains below upland springs, along segmented river levees, and on isolated hammocks in the lower portions of the Flint and Chattahoochee drainage basins (Bullen 1950, 1958, Broyles 1962, Kellar, personal communication). The pattern thus suggests some continuity from the trends seen in the Late Weeden Island settlement system shift to river valley occupation in the region at about A.D. 650 (Percy and Brose 1974). Fort Walton ceremonial centers and major population concentrations occur where the river cuts a major ecotone and where both limited agriculturally productive lands and a diverse natural catchment area occurs. Topographically similar locations with differing ecological situations, as well as topographically and ecologically distinct locations, support a diversity of seasonally reoccupied special purpose campsites, utilized by some portion of the population aggregates from the major sites, but do not contain any ceremonial site (Figure 4.3).

Burial patterns, which are poorly known at present for this early Fort Walton regional manifestation, suggest a pattern of limited extended and bundle burials, sometimes with elaborate grave goods, occurring in various stages of platform mound construction, and often being associated with evidence for burned activity surfaces and structures. Flexed and extended burials with few grave goods are interred in portions of the domestic areas of these sites (as at Yon and Curlee), but associations with specific structures are uncertain. No isolated cemeteries are known for the

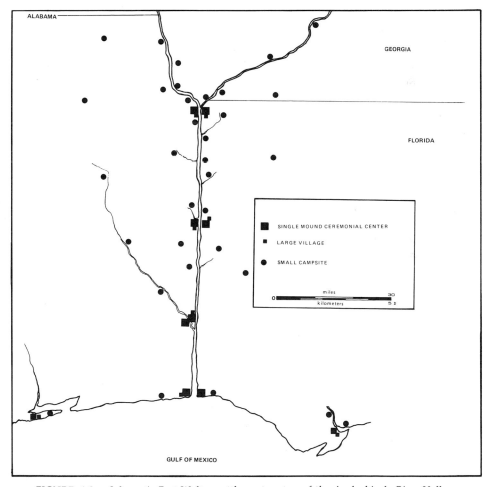

FIGURE 4.3. *Schematic Fort Walton settlement system of the Apalachicola River Valley.*

inland portions of this region, although at the Chipola cutoff mound, later Fort Walton burials were interred in the top levels of a late-Weeden-Island–early-Fort-Walton mound (Moore 1903).

TALLAHASSEE RED HILLS

Fort Walton settlement patterns in the area of the Tallahassee Red Hills display a marked difference from those in the Apalachicola River region. To some extent, this may be a factor of time. Red Hills Fort Walton seems, on the basis of available ceramic seriations, to begin somewhat later than the Apalachicola Fort Walton (Percy 1972a, M. Jones 1974). This extensive agriculturally productive region seems to display a pattern of low-intensity occupation of major ceremonial centers that contain plazas, earthen embarkments, and numerous large platform mounds. Several smaller ceremonial centers with a single platform mound also exist, with the entire ecologically homogeneous interfluvial region characterized by a dense, nearly uniform distribution of what appear to be small, single- or multifamily, year-round farmsteads such as Winewood or the Borrow Pit site (B. Jones and Penman 1973, Jones, personal communication) or even smaller, more ephemeral special purpose extractive campsites along the river and lake shores, revealed by the recent survey (Tesar 1973) in Leon and Jefferson Counties.

At the Lake Jackson site, B. C. Jones has excavated what is clearly a densely packed farmstead occupation system associated with a ceremonial center displaying a rich Southern Cult multiple burial in Mound 3. From Jefferson County, southeast of Tallahassee, a larger, 13-mound ceremonial center has been located and confirmed by state survey. The largest mound at this latter site is some 13 m high. Although systematic survey is incomplete, there is evidence to suggest that this heavy, fully packed, Fort Walton farmstead pattern extends as far east as the Aucilla River (Figure 4. 4.).

COASTAL VARIANT

What has been referred to as the coastal variant of Fort Walton represents yet a third, equally distinctive, settlement pattern. There appears to be some significant difference in at least the temporal position and the ceramic assemblages of most coastal Fort Walton sites occurring in the area between Mobile Bay and St. Andrews Bay, on the west, and those sites located between St. Andrews Bay and the Aucilla River, on the east (White n.d.). In the western coastal variant, Fort Walton ceramic assemblages generally display between 45 and 95% shell-tempering (Lazarus 1971).

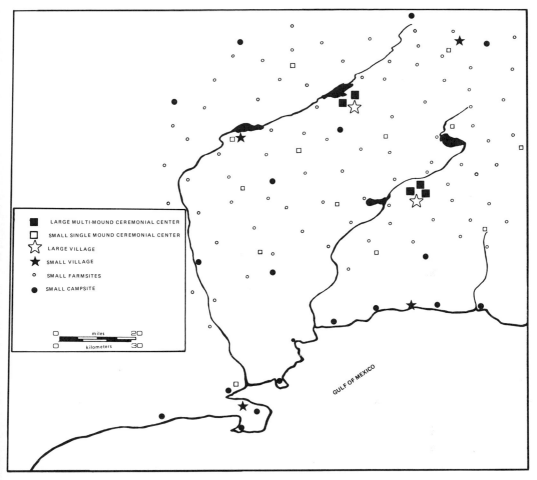

FIGURE 4.4. Schematic Fort Walton settlement pattern in the Tallahassee–Red Hills area.

Polished black ware and engraved "Moundville" motifs are also sometimes common (Fairbanks 1971; Lazarus *et al.* 1967, Lazarus 1971, Willey 1949). Furthermore, many of the sites in this area, although stratigraphically uncertain, have yielded European contact period material (Lazarus 1961, 1964, 1971, Lazarus *et al.* 1967, Moore 1902, 1918). However, we suspect that even in this "Pensacola" area, there exists a low density of dispersed early Fort Walton multifamily sites surrounding (and articulating with) small ceremonial centers. Not only do unpublished investigations tend to confirm this view, but the published reports of excavation within the Fort Walton mound itself suggest an Appalachicola River affiliation and yield little evidence for a Moundville-influence development of the major sites assigned to the Pensacola complex. Fort Walton sites from coastal areas between St. Andrews Bay and the Aucilla River generally display less than 50% shell-tempering (often none at all). Polished black wares or "Moundville" engraved motifs are rare to absent, and European contact can be inferred at few, if any, sites (Griffin 1947, Phelps 1967). Even with the absence of radiometric support, it appears judicious to consider most of the known sites of the west coastal or "Pensacola variant" of Fort Walton as quite late, with the exception of the Fort Walton mound itself.

Little recent investigation has been undertaken at the western coastal Fort Walton sites; archeology performed has been limited to stratigraphic cuts in the Fort Walton mound itself (Fairbanks 1960, 1964, 1971, Lazarus 1971); limited unsystematic surface collection in midden situations; and unsystematic test excavation in cemetery areas (Willey 1949, Fairbanks 1960, 1965a,b, 1971, Lazarus 1971), although unpublished Fort Walton villages have been located. Large portions of the west coastal area, including many barrier islands and virtually all of the coastal flatland swamps and marshes, are archeologically unknown, except for the Gulf Islands National Seashore (Tesar 1973). Utilizing existing data, it appears that the Fort Walton settlement pattern in this region is distinctive. Large ceremonial centers such as Bear Point, Fort Walton, and Pierce (which should perhaps all be considered early extensions of the Apalachicola variant) appear to consist of a large platform mound without a plaza or subsidiary mounds. Evidence of coeval domestic activity at these ceremonial sites is apparently absent, although at some sites, this may be a factor of excavation and recovery strategy. These major coastal sites are located on barrier beaches, in protected bays near a river estuary. From the Bear Point and the Fort Walton mounds, a number of flexed and extended burials (most found by Moore and thus of questionable validity), with rather meager status goods, have been recovered (Fairbanks 1964, 1971, Lazarus 1971, Moore 1903, Willey 1949). A series of late Fort Walton campsites are spaced along the western coast, from Mobile Bay to St. Andrews Bay. These small reoccupied sites yield typical "Pensacola" ceramics, unlike the large temple mounds. Such small sites do not seem to display any regular inter- or intrasite patterns. Structures are unknown. Subsistence and seasonality are also unknown, although some evidence for intensive marine resource procurement exists (Percy 1974). A number of apparently extensive Fort Walton cemeteries are located along the western coast. These are unassociated with ceremonial structures and apparently are not associated with any single occupation site of a size comparable to the inferred demographic parameters represented by the cemetery population. Apparently such cemeteries served as a ceremonial focus for a number of small occupation sites. Little evidence for major Mississippian ideotechnic material (reflecting status differentiation) is present in these cemeteries. Mississippian artifacts assigned status-indicative roles in other areas of the southeast simply do not occur in these cemeteries. At present, we have only

limited understanding of the relationships that existed between the ceremonial centers with mounds, the small sites of domestic occupation, and
the cemeteries along the the western coast. Such mounds have yielded
ceramics similar to the Early Appalachala variant of Fort Walton. The
smaller, "Pensacola" sites appear late, relative to the Apalachicola River or
Tallahassee Red Hills variants of Fort Walton, and, whereas most known
West Coast Fort Walton sites except for the major mounds themselves
display considerable evidence of at least ceramic influence from Moundville, the settlement system which can be inferred from available data
bears little resemblance to models of Moundville settlement (Peebles 1971,
1974, Chapter 13 of this volume): Rather, the "Pensacola Fort Walton"
appears to represent a continuation of Weeden Island socioeconomic coastal adaption (Percy and Brose 1974) with a late utilization of those few
ceremonial structures, derived from earlier Fort Walton influences in the
Apalachicola Valley, and with a veneer of Moundville ceramic attributes
which rapidly diminish east of Andrews Bay (Allen, 1953; Bense, 1969).

The coastal Fort Walton sites between St. Marks Bay and the Aucilla
River seem to consist entirely of small, seasonally reoccupied campsites
located along barrier beaches near flatwood ecotones. Few, if any, large
Fort Walton period ceremonial sites, mounds, or cemeteries are known to
exist in this area, although Phelps (1967) reported a mound (WA35) at the
Panacea City Dump, with three stages of construction, each with subfloor
pits and post-molds, none of which yielded Pensacola ceramics. Nor does
there appear to be any significant degree of Moundville or Pensacola
influence in these small eastern coastal sites, although some sites are
apparently quite late in time (see Griffin 1947). Internal site patterns are
unknown; but in this region, both ceramic attributes and inferred site
function suggest that some of these Fort Walton sites may represent a
seasonal coastal utilization by small population aggregates possibly derived from, or articulating with, the large populations occupying the
Tallahassee Red Hills region (Figure 4.5).

Future Research

It is clear that few areas of Northwest Florida have been adequately
surveyed. Even in those areas where reasonably adequate archeological
survey has been carried out, chronology is uncertain and practically no
Fort Walton site of any time period has been excavated to the extent that
internal settlement patterns, seasonality, or site function can be discussed
confidently. The exceptions to this generally depressing picture form sets
of noncomparable data: Cemeteries along the west coast; farmsteads in the
Tallahassee Red Hills; spring or fall collecting stations in the Apalachicola

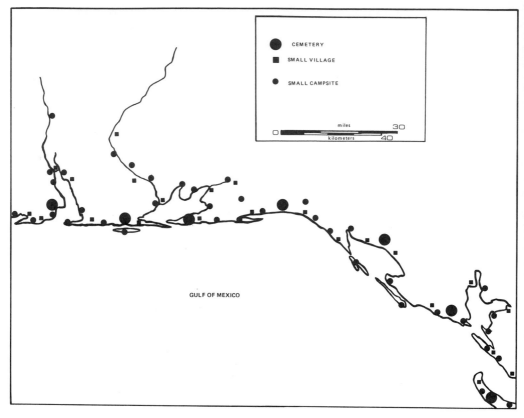

FIGURE 4.5.   Schematic Fort Walton settlement pattern along the Gulf Coast.

River Valley. Nonetheless, it is possible to create a model of Fort Walton regional settlement patterns and indicate how future research can both test derived hypotheses and provide greater accuracy for subsequent settlement studies. In addition to more extensive excavations at the known Fort Walton site, it is necessary to eliminate sampling bias by locating more sites of varied size and function within each region.

One basic problem of previous archeological work concerned with the late prehistoric period in northwestern Florida has been the attempt to characterize an unknown population from small samples of unknown or admittedly biased character (Bullen 1950, 1958, 1971, Fairbanks 1971, Sears 1954, 1958, 1962, Willey 1949). From Moore (1903) onward, only a very narrow range of possible site locations have been thoroughly investigated (Percy 1972b). To some extent, these problems can be overcome.

Following the lead of quantitative geographers, it is possible to implement archeological surveys that yield representative statistical samples of all possible site locations—samples that will minimize and control the introduction of ethnocentric or theoretical bias. In addition, portions of previously surveyed right-of-ways can be connected by transect surveys to provide continuous coverage for ecological gradients. What is required is a multilevel archeological survey to test alternative models of settlement and subsistence. In addition to testing predicted site locations in the Red Hills area, on the coast, or along the levee at secondary stream junctions in the alluvial bottom land, a statistically valid unaligned random sampling scheme, stratified by soil types, water table, topographic relief, dominant floral communities, and local drainage system patterns, should be used to locate the minimum number of points in selected, ecologically heterogeneous portions of those upland areas between major drainage systems (see Binford 1964). Such systematic investigations will be needed to test adequately alternative models of Fort Walton settlement and development.

A model developed by Brose and Percy 1974 suggests that stratified social systems in Northwest Florida are neither the result of secondary post-Colonial acculturation nor of population displacement. They represent internal rearrangements of sociocultural and technoenvironmental interrelationships, which occurred after the creation of deviation–amplification mechanisms of socially structured exchange that accompany population pressures which built up in some forms of final Weeden Island cultures and thereby created a system receptive to early Mississippian models of social reintegration. On the basis of such a model, we have predicted that the earliest manifestations of such adaptation toward a Mississippian socioceremonial pattern would occur in those regions of Northwest Florida where late Weeden Island populations practicing short-fallow swidden horticulture expanded into diverse but ecologically or socially restricted areas. These criteria appear to be met in major river valleys such as the Apalachicola River Valley. They do not exist in the Red-Hills–Lake-Jackson basin or along the coast. We have further hypothesized that the major shifts in settlement systems occur within the Weeden Island period. Following this, the gradual but consistent population increase would produce no marked increase in site frequency or density from late Weeden Island through early Fort Walton periods in such regions, but rather would result in a coalescence of population into fewer, more densely occupied year-round sites in specific ecological areas. Furthermore, the model would predict no radical shifts in ethnic styles through this period. Unpublished excavations both demonstrate this stylistic continuity from Late Weeden Island through Early Fort Walton and yield no evidence for abrupt demographic changes. In terms of models described by Ammerman and Cavalli-Sforza (1973:340–353), neither "demic" diffusion from an external source nor colonization is a relevant or applicable explanation for the occurrence of Fort Walton systems.

From this model we argue that the appearance of "Mississippian" characteristics represents something less holistic than earlier authors have implied (cf. Williams 1971) and that the socioceremonial aspects of Mississippian culture may be adopted and integrated into cultures with variant settlement–subsistence systems, all of which are undergoing structurally similar population and ecological pressure. This should necessitate considerable revision in previous concepts of the Mississippian, both in terms of its hypothesized unique origins and its subsequent "expansion." Brain (1969, 1971) has suggested much the same situation in the Yazoo region of the lower Mississippi Valley.

Several authors (e.g., Brain 1971, Brose n.d.b., Larson, 1972, Peebles 1971, Ward 1965) have demonstrated a correlation among demographic variables, site location, and the presence of culturally desirable agricultural land. In such an analysis for Pueblo I–III in the Rio Puerco Valley, Washburn (1974:325ff) has been able to demonstrate that population changes correlate cyclically with site location and agglomeration. She noted that this latter phenomenon represents a temporal lag of several generations in the readjustment of preferential site location strategies relative to demographic parameters.

Trawick Ward (1965) suggested that most major Mississippian sites were located on silt loam or sandy silt loam alluvial bottom soils for agricultural reasons. Larson (1972) argued that the development of the characteristic Mississippian agricultural subsistence pattern leads to active competition for such prime lands. Gibson's (1974) argument from the Lower Valley, which concerned the significance of ecological, as opposed to social motivation for such warfare, has accepted the underlying ecological locational analysis of major Mississippian centers.

In the most thorough analysis of Mississippian site location in the Southeast United States, Peebles's work at Moundville, Alabama expanded this hypothesis to include suitable agricultural soils as the primary locational criteria (Peebles 1974, Chapter 13 of this volume), along with an ecologically and physiographically diverse resource catchment area (Jarman, Vita-Finzi, and Higgs 1972) of 4–5 km surrounding a site within which uncultivated floral and faunal materials are available. Smith (1974) suggests that the location of most large Mississippian sites will be on natural levees of major rivers, not merely because of culturally desirable soils for agriculture but because of the large numbers of migratory waterfowl and summer fish in drying backwater areas. Smith (1974:8 5ff) also notes the desirability of locations with close proximity to ecological diversity to maximize the density of more endemic terrestrial food animals. Based on his own analyses at Moundville, and utilizing Larson's work on the Mississippian centers in Georgia, Peebles (1974, personal communication) has described a dendritic technique for the location of major Mississippian sites in the southeastern United States. If Mississippian Fort Walton cultures of Northwest Florida represent either a direct implantation or population displacements, whether from Moundville (e.g., Brain 1971, Caldwell 1958, Gardner 1966, Lazarus 1971, Peebles, 1974, Willey 1949, Williams 1971) or from Georgia (Bullen 1949, 1950, 1958, Fairbanks 1971, Goggin 1947, Griffin 1950, Milanich 1969, Sears 1954, 1958, 1962, 1973, H. Smith 1948), the ecological model of settlement location proposed by Peebles should be applicable.

If, on the other hand, the model of Weeden Island development proposed by Brose and Percy, which has been described above, is correct, then a different dendrogram can be constructed and alternative hypotheses derived for testing. On the basis of the detailed ecological parameters of the Weeden Island model, early Fort Walton in the Apalachicola River Valley will have a distinctive hierarchy for major site ecological locational preferences that will be very different than the Mississippian models just noted. The reation of a statistically controlled sampling strategy, ecologically stratified hierarchically to locate the optimal major site locations for the alternative models, and normalized to account for relative availability of the various ecological strata for either model, should produce a manageable number of potential major site locations for testing these alternative hypotheses.

It is interesting to note that Peebles has provided a further criterion for the acceptance or rejection of these alternative hypotheses. Peebles (1974) has stated clearly that for Moundville there is a consistent spatial arrangement and relative density of major-ceremonial-center–minor-ceremonial-center–hamlet settlements, so that the size and location of the Moundville site itself, as the single major ceremonial center, cannot be directly predicted from its own ecological location, but only from that of its ceremonial service area (Peebles 1974). Not all major Mississippian centers in the Southeast follow the neat nested hexagon hierarchy of Moundville. The Lower Valley (Brain 1969, 1971; Williams 1971) differs, although the Georgia area (Larson 1969, personal communication) and the Middle Mississippi Valley (Smith 1974; Ward 1965) do seem to display a somewhat similar pattern.

If the alternative model proposed herein for a Weeden Island settlement–subsistence base for Fort Walton Mississippian site locations and functions is correct, a testable hypothesis states that early Fort Walton major ceremonial sites should serve as major centers of population aggregation reoccupied for a number of years. They also should be surrounded by a number of small, short-duration hamlets or special-purpose extractive camps with no suggestion of ceremonial activity, and there should be no evidence at all for secondary ceremonial centers. There should thus be for early Fort Walton sites clear evidence for site location, relative spatial and demographic parameters, and function reflecting late Weeden Island patterns and strongly differing from the traditional models of Mississippian settlement. At the same time, the sociopolitical and ceremonial manifestations should show strong Mississippian status differentation, thus differing from evidence implying structurally egalitarian or minimally ranked lineages for Weeden Island. The research proposed here should provide some limited, but unambiguous, evidence concerning the nature and tempo of the "Mississippian phenomenon" in one portion of the Southeast. Only when several such regional studies have, in turn, illuminated the various facets of this major prehistoric culture, will we be able to discuss the arguments presently raised of unique development in the American Bottoms. Not until such studies have been made can we honestly investigate the possibility, probability, amount, tempo, timing, and presumptive importance of cultural diffusion from the "High Civilizations" of Mesoamerican areas. We will never truly know what "Mississippian" is, until we can answer what Mississippians are.

References

Adams, Grey L., and William C. Lazarus
  1960   Two skulls from a Fort Walton Period cemetary site (OK-35), Okaloosa County, Florida. *The Florida Anthropologist* **13**:92–99.
Allen, Glenn T., Jr.
  1953   A stratagraphic investigation of the Hall Site, Wakulla County, Florida. *Notes in Anthropology* **1**. Department of Anthropology, Florida State University, Tallahassee.
Ammerman, A.J., and L.L. Cavalli-Sforza
  1973   A population model for the diffusion of early farming in Europe. In *The explanation of culture change: Models in prehistory*, edited by Colin Renfrew. London: Duckworth. Pp. 343–357.
Anonymous
  1974   12-year old leads archaeologist to significant find in Tallahassee. *Archives and History News,* **5**(5):2. Division of Archives, History, and Records Management, Florida Department of State, Tallahassee.
Bense, Judith Ann
  1969   Excavations at the Bird Hammock Site (8Wa30), Wakulla County, Florida. M.S. thesis, Department of Anthropology, Florida State University, Tallahassee.
Binford, Lewis R.
  1964   A consideration of archaeological research design. *American Antiquity* **29**:425–441.
Boyd, Mark F., Hale G. Smith, and John W. Griffin
  1951   *Here they once stood: The tragic end of the Apalachee Missions.* Gainesville: University of Florida Press.
Brain, Jeffrey P.
  1969   Winterville: A case study of prehistory culture contact in the lower Mississippi Valley. Ph.D. dissertation, Department of Anthropology, Yale University, New Haven.
  1971   The lower Mississippi Valley in North American prehistory. Arkansas Archaeological Survey Report. National Park Service Contract 991 TOO 049.

Brose, David S.
  1978   Coe's Landing (8Jal37) Jackson County, Florida. A Fort Walton campsite on the
          Apalachicola River. *Report of Investigations*. Bureau of Historic Sites and Properties.
          Florida Division of Archives, History and Records, Tallahassee.
Brose, David S., Patricia Essenpreis, John Scarry, Helga Bluestone, and Anne Forsythe
  n.d.a   Contributions to the archaeology of northwestern Florida: Investigations of Early
          Fort Walton sites in the middle Apalachicola River Valley. Manuscript on file at the
          Department of Anthropology, Case Western Reserve University, Cleveland, Ohio.
Brose, David S., Patricia Essenpreis, John Scarry, and Nancy White
  n.d.b   Some Fort Walton campsites along the west bank of the Apalachicola River, Florida.
          Manuscript on file at the Department of Anthropology, Case Western Reserve
          University, Cleveland, Ohio.
Brose, David S., and Nancy White
  n.d.   Curlee Site, 8Ja7-8Jal85, A Fort Walton ceremonial center in Jackson County, Florida.
          Manuscript on file at the Department of Anthropology, Case Western Reserve
          University, Cleveland, Ohio.
Brose, David S., and Duncan Wilkie
  n.d.   Report of salvage investigations at the Gulf Power Plant Parking Lot Site (8Ja201): A
          Fort Walton camp in Jackson County, Florida. Manuscript on file at the Department
          of Anthropology, Case Western Reserve University, Cleveland, Ohio.
Brose, David S. and George W. Percy
  1974   Weeden Island ceremonialism in northwest Florida: A reappraisal. Paper presented
          at the 39th Annual Meeting of the Society for American Archaeology, Washington,
          D.C.
Broyles, Bettye J.
  1962   A Lamar Period site in southwest Georgia, 9Cla51. In Survey of archaeological sites
          in Clay and Quitman Counties, Georgia, edited by A.R. Kelly. *University of Georgia
          Laboratory of Archaeology Series* **5**:29–35.
Bullen, Ripley P.
  1949   Indian sites at Florida Caverns State Park. *Florida Anthropologist* **2**:1–9.
  1950   An archaeological survey of the Chattahoochee River Valley in Florida. *Journal of
          the Washington Academy of Sciences* **40**:101–125. Washington, D.C.
  1958   Six sites near the Chattachoochee River in the Jim Woodruff Reservoir Area,
          Florida. *Smithsonian Institution Bureau of American Ethnology Bulletin* **169**:315–357.
          Washington, D.C.
  1971   Some variations in settlement patterns in peninsular Florida. *Southeastern Ar-
          chaeological Conference Bulletin* **13**:10–19.
Butson, Keith
  1962   Climates of the states: Florida. *United States Department of Commerce Environmental
          Data Service, Climatography of the United States Reports* **60–8**. Washington, D.C.
Caldwell, Joseph R.
  1958   Trend and tradition in the prehistory of the eastern United States. *American An-
          thropological Association Memoir* **88**.
Chamberlain, E.B., Jr.
  1960   Florida waterfowl populations, habitats and management. *Florida Game and Fresh-
          water Fish Commission Technical Bulletin* **7**. Tallahassee.
Clewell, Andre F.
  1971   The vegetation of the Apalachicola National Forest: An ecological perspective.
          Report submitted to the Office of the Forest Supervisor, Tallahassee, Florida.
Cooke, C. Wythe
  1939   Scenery of Florida interpreted by a geologist. *Florida Geological Survey Bulletin* **17**.
          Tallahassee.

Fairbanks, Charles H.
  1960   Excavations at the Fort Walton Temple Mound. Report to the city of Fort Walton Beach, Florida.
  1964   The early occupations of northwestern Florida. *Southeastern Archaeological Conference Bulletin* **1**:27–30.
  1965a   Excavations at the Fort Walton Temple Mound, 1960. *The Florida Anthropologist* **18**:239–264.
  1965b   Gulf Complex subsistence economy. *Southeastern Archaeological Conference Bulletin* **3**:57–62.
  1971   The Apalachicola River area of Florida. *Newsletter of the Southeastern Archaeological Conference* **10**:38–40.
Fenneman, N.M.
  1938   *Physiography of eastern United States.* New York: McGraw Hill.
Florida Department of Administration, Division of State Planning, Bureau of Comprehensive Planning
  1974   The Florida general soils atlas with interpretations for regional planning districts I and II. Tallahassee.
Forsythe, Anne, and Wentworth Clapham
  1975   Report on preliminary pollen samples from Florida. Manuscript on file at the Department of Anthropology, Case Western Reserve University, Cleveland, Ohio.
Fryman, Frank B., Jr.
  1971   Highway salvage archaeology in Florida. *Archives and History News* **2**:1–4. Division of Archives, History and Records Management, Florida Department of State, Tallahassee.
Gardner, William M.
  1966   The Waddells Mill Pond Site. *The Florida Anthropologist* **19**(2–3):43–64.
  1971   Fort Walton in inland Florida. *Newsletter of the Southeastern Archaeological Conference* **10**:48–50.
Gibson, Jon
  1974   Aboriginal warfare in the protohistoric Southeast: An alternate perspective. *American Antiquity* **39**:130–133.
Goggin, John M.
  1947   A preliminary definition of archaeological areas and periods in Florida. *American Antiquity* **13**:114–127.
  1971   Session II part 2: Dispersal of Mississippi Culture, discussion. *Newsletter of the Southeastern Archaeological Conference* **10**:51–54.
Griffin, John W.
  1947   Comments on a site in the St. Mark's National Wildlife Refuge, Wakulla County, Florida. *American Antiquity,* **13**:182–183.
  1950   Test excavations at the Lake Jackson Site. *American Antiquity* **16**:99–112.
Harlow, Richard F.
  1959   An evaluation of white-tailed deer habitat in Florida. *Florida Game and Fresh Water Fish Commission, Technical Bulletin* **5**. Tallahassee.
Harper, R.M.
  1914   Geography and vegetation of northern Florida. *Florida State Geological Survey, Annual Report* **6**:163–437. Tallahassee.
Hendry, Charles W., Jr. and J. William Yon, Jr.
  1958   Geology of the area in and around the Jim Woodruff Reservoir. *Florida Geological Survey, Report of Investigations* **16**. Tallahassee.
Holmes, William H.
  1903   Aboriginal pottery of the eastern United States. *Twentieth Annual Report of the Bureau of American Ethnology*. Washington, D.C.

Hubbell, T.H., A.M. Laessle, and J.C. Dickinson
  1956   The Flint–Chattahoochee–Apalachicola Region and its environments. *Bulletin of the Florida State Museum, Biological Sciences* 1:1–72. Gainesville.
Jarman, M.R., Claudio Vita-Finzi, and Eric S. Higgs
  1972   Site catchment analysis in archaeology. In *Man, settlement and urbanism,* edited by P.S. Ucko, R. Tringham, and G.W. Dimbleby, London:Duckworth Pp. 61–66.
Jones, B. Calvin
  1971   Division archaeologists active throughout Florida. *Archives and History News* 4:1–2. Division of Archives, History, and Records Management, Florida Department of State, Tallahassee.
Jones, B. Calvin, and John T. Penman
  1973   Winewood: An inland Fort Walton site in Tallahassee, Florida. *Bureau of Historic Sites and Properties Bulletin* 3:65–90. Division of Archives, History, and Records Management, State of Florida, Tallahassee.
Jones, Mary Katherine
  1974   Archaeological survey and excavation in the upper Sweetwater Creek drainage of Liberty County, Florida. M.A. thesis, Department of Anthropology, Florida State University, Tallahassee.
Kenner, W.E., E.R. Hampton, and C.S. Conover
  1969   Average flow of major streams in Florida. Report prepared by the United States Geological Survey in cooperation with the Bureau of Geology, Florida Department of Natural Resources, Tallahassee.
Kenner, W.E., R.W. Pride, and C.S. Conover
  1967   Drainage basins in Florida. Report prepared by the United States Geological Survey in cooperation with the Division of Geology, Florida Board of Conservation, Tallahassee, Florida.
Komarek, Roy (Editor)
  1962–1968   *Proceedings of the Annual Tall Timbers Fire Ecology Conference,* 1–8. Tallahassee, Florida: Tall Timbers Research Station.
Kurz, Herman, and Kenneth Wagner
  1957   Tidal marshes of the Gulf and Atlantic coasts of northern Florida and Charleston, South Carolina. *Florida State University Studies* 24:105–108.
Larson, Lewis H., Jr.
  1969   Aboriginal subsistence patterns on the Southeastern Gulf Coastal Plain. Ph.D. dissertation, Department of Anthropology, University of Michigan, Ann Arbor.
  1972   Functional considerations of warfare in the Southeast during the Mississippi Period. *American Antiquity* 37:383–392.
Lazarus, William C.
  1961   Ten middens on the Navy Live Oak Reservation. *The Florida Anthropologist* 14:49–64.
  1964   The Postl's Lake II Site, Eglin Air Force Base, Florida (Ok71). *The Florida Anthropologist* 17:1–16.
  1971   The Fort Walton Culture west of the Apalachicola River. *Newsletter of the Southeastern Archaeological Conference* 10:40–48.
Lazarus, Yulee W., W.C. Lazarus, and Donald W. Sharon
  1967   The Navy Live Oak Reservation Cemetary Site (8Sa36). *The Florida Anthropologist* 20:103–117.
Lemon, Paul C.
  1967   Effect of fire on herbs of southeastern United States. In *Proceedings of the Tall Timbers Fire Ecology Conference,* edited by R. Komarek, 6:113–130. Tallahassee: Tall Timbers Research Station.

Milanich, Jerald T.
  1969   The Alachua Tradition: Extension of Wilmington-Savannah peoples into central
          Florida. *The Florida Anthropologist* **22**:17–23.
  1974   Life in a 9th centrury Indian household: A Weeden Island fall-winter site on the
          upper Apalachicola River, Florida. *Bureau of Historic Sites and Properties Bulletin*
          4:1–44. Tallahassee, Florida.
Moore, Clarence B.
  1902   Certain aboriginal remains of the northwest Florida coast, Part I. *Journal of the
          Academy of Natural Sciences of Philadelphia* **11**:420–497.
  1903   Certain aboriginal remains of the Apalachicola River. *Journal of the Academy of
          Natural Sciences of Philadelphia* **12**:439–492.
  1907   Mounds of the lower Chattahoochee and lower Flint Rivers. *Journal of the Academy
          of Natural Sciences of Philadelphia* **13**:426–456.
  1918   The northwestern Florida coast revisited. *Journal of the Academy of Natural Sciences
          of Philadelphia* **16**:513–579.
Moore, Wayne E.
  1955   Geology of Jackson County, Florida. *Florida Geological Survey Bulletin* **37**. Tallahas-
          see.
Morrell, L. Ross, and Bennie Keel
  1962   Field notes from the Yon Mound Site (8Li2). On file at the Division of Archives,
          History, and Records Management, Florida Department of State, Tallahassee.
Peebles, Christopher S.
  1971   Moundville and surrounding sites: Some structural considerations of mortuary
          practices II. In Approaches to the social dimensions of mortuary practices, edited by
          James A. Brown. *Memoirs of the Society for American Archaeology* **25**:68–91.
  1974   Moundville; the social organization of a prehistoric community and culture. Ph.D.
          dissertation, Department of Anthropology, University of California, Santa Barbara.
Percy, George W.
  1972a   A preliminary report on recent archaeological investigations in Torreya State Park,
          Liberty County, Florida. Paper presented at the 24th Annual Meeting of the Florida
          Anthropological Society, Winter Park, Florida.
  1972b   Current research: Florida. *Newsletter of the Southeastern Archaeological Conference*
          16(1):3–6.
  1974   A review of evidence for prehistoric Indian use of animals in northwest Florida.
          Bureau of Historic Sites and Properties Bulletin **4**:65–93. Florida Department of State,
          Tallahassee.
  1976   Salvage investigations at the Scholz Steam Plant Site, a Middle Weeden Island
          habitation site in Jackson County, Florida. *Bureau of Historic Sites and Properties
          Miscellaneous Project Series* **35**. Florida Department of State, Tallahassee.
Percy, George W., and David S. Brose
  1974   Weeden Island ecology, subsistence and village life in northwest Florida. Paper
          presented at the 39th Annual Meeting of the Society for American Archaeology,
          Washington, D.C.
Phelps, David S.
  1966   Early and late components of the Tucker Site. *The Florida Anthropologist* **19**:11–38.
  1967   Prehistory of north central Florida: Final report. Department of Anthropology,
          Florida State University, Tallahassee.
  n.d.   Final Report: Investigations of two prehistoric ceremonial sites. Department of
          Anthropology, Florida State University, Tallahassee.
Puri, Harbans S. and Robert O. Vernon
  1964   Summary of the geology of Florida and a guidebook to the classic exposures. *Florida
          Geological Survey, Special Publication* **5**. Tallahassee.

Scarry, John F.
    n.d.   The Sassafras Site (8Gd12), Gadsen County, Florida. A multicomponent site on the Apalachicola River. Manuscript on file at the Department of Anthropology, Case Western Reserve University, Cleveland, Ohio.

Schoolcraft, Henry R.
    1849   *Notices of some antique earthen vessels found in the low tumuli of Florida and in the caves and burial places of the Indian tribes north of those latitudes.* New York: William Van Norden, Printer.

Sears, William H.
    1954   The sociopolitical organization of Pre-Columbian cultures on the Gulf Coastal Plain, *American Anthropologist* **56**:339–346.
    1958   Burial mounds on the Gulf Coastal Plain. *American Antiquity* **23**:274–284.
    1962   An investigation of prehistoric processes on the Gulf Coastal Plain. NSF G-5019. Manuscript on file, National Science Foundation.
    1973   The sacred and the secular in prehistoric ceramics. In *Variations in Anthropology,* edited by D. Lathrap and J. Douglas. Urbana: Illinois Archaeological Survey.

Shelford, Victor E.
    1963   *The ecology of North America.* Urbana: University of Illinois Press.

Sherman, H.B.
    1937   List of recent wild land mammals of Florida. *Proceedings of the Florida Academy of Sciences* **1**:102–128.
    1952   A list and bibliography of the mammals of Florida, living and extinct. *Quarterly Journal of the Florida Academy of Sciences* **15**(2):86–126.

Smith, Bruce D.
    1974   Middle Mississippi exploitation of animal populations: A predictive model. *American Antiquity*. **39**:274–291.

Smith, Hale G.
    1948   Two historic archaeological periods in Florida. *American Antiquity* **13**:313–319.

Sternberg, G.M.
    1876   Indian burial mounds and shell heaps near Pensacola, Florida. *Proceedings of the American Association for the Advancement of Science* **24**(2):282–292.

Stevenson, Henry M.
    1960   *A key to Florida birds.* Tallahassee: Peninsular Publishing Company.

Tesar, Louis D.
    1973   Archaeological survey and testing of Gulf Islands National Seashore, Part I: Florida. Report prepared under National Park Service Contract No. CX00031438, Department of Anthropology, Florida State University, Tallahassee, Florida.

Ward, Trawick
    1965   Correlation of Mississippian sites and soil types. *Southeastern Archaeological Conference Bulletin* **3**:42–48.

Washburn, Dorothy K.
    1974   Nearest neighbor analysis of Pueblo I-III settlement patterns along the Rio Purco in eastern New Mexico. *American Antiquity* **39**:315–335.

White, Nancy
    n.d.   The Pensacola Variant of Fort Walton and the origin of Mississippian cultures in northwest Florida. Ph.D. dissertation in progress, Department of Anthropology, Case Western Reserve University, Cleveland, Ohio.

Willey, Gordon, R.
    1949   Archeology of the Florida Gulf Coast. *Smithsonian Institution Miscellaneous Collections* **113**. Washington, D.C.

Willey, Gordon R., and Richard B. Woodbury
    1942   A chronological outline for the northwest Florida coast. *American Antiquity* **7**:232–254.

114/ *David S. Brose and George W. Percy*

Williams, Stephen
    1971   Round table on definition of Mississippian Culture. *Newsletter of the Southeastern Archaeological Conference* **10**(2):1–19.
Wing, Elizabeth S.
    n.d.   Faunal remains from an Indian site in Jackson County, Florida. Manuscript on file, Florida State Museum, Gainesville.
Wood, Roland, and Edward A. Fernald
    1974   *The new Florida atlas: Patterns of the sunshine state.* Tallahassee: Trend Publications.

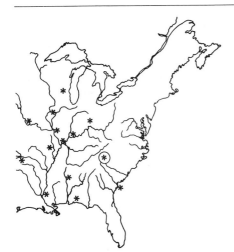

5

Mississippian Settlement Patterns in the Appalachian Summit Area: The Pisgah and Qualla Phases

ROY S. DICKENS, JR.

There are three levels of patterning in archeological settlement data. Settlement patterns include (*a*) the formal and functional characteristics of individual structures and features within a settlement; (*b*) the arrangement and functional interrelationships of structures and structural classes composing a complete settlement; and (*c*) the overall arrangements and interrelationships of settlements across the landscape, both within a single cultural–environmental system and among separate systems. Furthermore, settlement pattern data may be combined with subsistence data to reconstruct a settlement–subsistence system for a particular cultural horizon. And an analysis of settlement patterns through time can be useful in interpreting culture change and adaptive processes.

In this chapter, the three levels of settlement patterning will be examined for two successive Mississippian phases in the Appalachian Summit area of the southeastern United States. Within the limited framework of available information, it will not be possible to reconstruct the settlement–subsistence system for either phase. However, I will attempt some preliminary interpretations of changes in settlement patterns between the phases.

Mississippian Settlement Patterns

Copyright © 1978 by Academic Press, Inc.
All rights of reproduction in any form reserved.
ISBN 0–12–650640–X

Background

Settlement pattern data for the Appalachian Summit come from a number of site survey projects and from a few excavations. Most of these projects were conducted independently of one another, and for somewhat different purposes. The results of some of the work have been published, but much of the information is contained in unpublished reports to sponsoring agencies or only as maps and site survey forms. Most of the surveys utilized a walkover, surface inspection technique, and they were biased, to one degree or another, toward coverage of stream floodplains and plowed fields. Surface collections were often influenced by vegetational cover and other surface obstructions.

The survey projects referred to in this chapter are:

1. An ongoing survey of western North Carolina being carried out under the direction of Joffre L. Coe of the Research Laboratories of Anthropology at the University of North Carolina. This work, begun about 1935 and still continuing, was intensified between 1962 and 1971 during the development and execution of a project aimed at identifying the antecedents of Cherokee culture (Dickens 1976, Egloff 1967, Holden 1966, Keel 1976). The coverage was most complete in portions of the Pigeon, French Broad, and Little Tennessee drainages, as a result of long-term excavations at sites in those areas.

2. A survey of Great Smoky Mountains National Park, carried out by a team from the University of Tennessee for the National Park Service (Bass, McCullough, and Faulkner 1976). This project, the purpose of which was to identify and evaluate the significance of cultural resources on the park, was conducted as part of the agency's responsibilities under Executive Order 11593. The park contains within its boundaries a typical cross section of Appalachian Summit landforms, all of which were sampled during the course of this survey.

3. A survey of the upper Hiwassee Valley, carried out by Western Carolina University for the North Carolina Division of Archives and History (Dorwin 1975). This survey focused on stream bottomlands and currently plowed fields.

4. A survey of the upper Watauga Valley, conducted by Appalachian State University for the North Carolina Division of Archives and History (Purrington 1975). This is an ongoing survey in which all landforms, both within and bordering the valley, are being sampled.

5. A survey of the upper Saluda Valley, carried out over a several-year period by Wesley Breedlove of Marietta, South Carolina (Breedlove, personal communication). Breedlove concentrated mostly on stream floodplains, but the coverage was thorough, since areas not in cultivation on

initial visits were often revisited when they were cultivated and available for inspection.

Other sources of information on site distribution are the Hartwell Reservoir survey (Caldwell 1953), Wauchope's (1966) WPA survey of northern Georgia, the site files of the Institute of Archaeology and Anthropology at the University of South Carolina (Jackson, personal communication), and the site files of the Laboratory of Archaeology at Georgia State University.

Sites having important excavation data are the Warren Wilson site in Buncombe County, North Carolina (Dickens 1976, Keel 1976); the Garden Creek site in Haywood County, North Carolina (Dickens 1976, Keel 1976); the Coweeta Creek site in Macon County, North Carolina (B. Egloff 1967, K. Egloff 1971); the Tuckasegee site in Jackson County, North Carolina (Keel 1976); the Townson and Peachtree sites in Cherokee County, North Carolina (Keel personal communication; Setzler and Jennings 1941); the Estatoe site in Stephens County, Georgia (Kelly and de Baillou 1960); and the Chauga site in Oconee County, South Carolina (Kelly and Neitzel 1961).

Environment

The term "Appalachian Summit" was used by Kroeber (1939) to designate a cultural and natural area comprising the highest portion of the Southern Appalachian Mountains in western North Carolina and adjoining portions of Tennessee, Georgia, South Carolina, and Virginia (Figure 5.1). Physiographically, the Summit is characterized by a labyrinth of mountain ranges, most of which are oriented northeast to southwest. Bordering the Summit are the Ridge and Valley and Interior Plateau provinces on the west, and the Piedmont Plateau province on the south and east. In comparison with these surrounding provinces, the Summit has greater relief, narrower stream valleys, and a much less consistent pattern of drainage and topography (Thornbury 1965:103–108).

Alluvial soils, of demonstrated significance to Mississippian agriculturalists (Ward 1965), are limited both in distribution and gross amounts in the Summit area. Floodplains of the mountain stream valleys are narrow, often producing a linear distribution of farms in the modern-day settlement pattern. The most important exceptions to this rule are intermontane "basins" such as those found around the larger modern settlements of Asheville, Hendersonville, Canton, and Murphy (Figure 5.1).

In terms of its biota, the Summit area can be characterized as highly diverse, a by-product of the diversity of topography and hydrology.

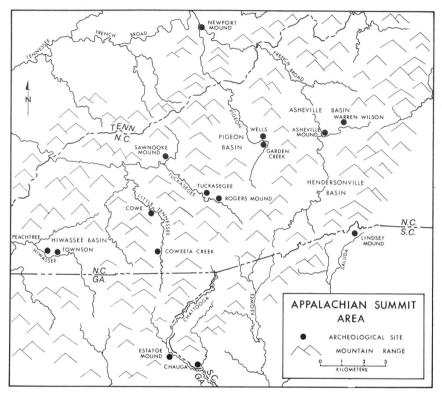

FIGURE 5.1.   *The location of important Pisgah and Qualla phase sites in the Appalachian Summit area.*

Environmental zones change frequently and abruptly—as, for example, when one moves from floodplain, to cove, to mountain slope—producing a great variety of plant and animal life within relatively short distances (Shelford 1963:17–45).

Mississippian Cultural Phases

Mississippian culture in the Summit area is represented primarily by two phases, which have been termed "Pisgah" and "Qualla" (Dickens 1976, Keel 1976). The remains of other Mississippian phases, such as Etowah, Wilbanks, Dallas, and Pee Dee, are found on sites along the margins of the area but are usually absent in the interior. It also should be noted that there are differences in the Pisgah and Qualla assemblages themselves from one part of the Summit to another. These distinctions seem to be most notable in the various Pisgah assemblages.

Six radiocarbon dates for the Pisgah phase fall between A.D. 1180 ± 150 and 1435 ± 70, with a mean of A.D. 1319. I suggest a beginning for Pisgah at about A.D. 1000–1100 and a termination at about A.D. 1400–1500. There are three radiocarbon dates for the Qualla phase of A.D. 1730 ± 100, 1745 ± 65, and 1775 ± 55. Although these three dates come from sites with European artifacts, earlier Qualla sites have been identified, and it may be that some of these sites are prehistoric. I suggest a beginning date for Qualla of A.D. 1450–1500 and a termination at removal, albeit some Qualla cultural traits persisted until the late 1800s in western North Carolina (Harrington 1922).

Elsewhere I have suggested that Pisgah and Qualla are manifestations of a cultural continuum leading from prehistoric South Appalachian Mississippian to historic Cherokee (Dickens 1976). This interpretation is based on correspondence in artifact styles, house architecture, mound construction features, and burial practices from superimposed (Qualla over Pisgah) components at several sites in the area of the Cherokee middle and out towns.

Form and Function of Individual Structures

Pisgah domestic structures have been well documented at the Warren Wilson site (Figures 5.2 and 5.3). These buildings were constructed on a square to slightly rectangular plan. The postmold patterns measured from 5.5 to 7.3 m along the outer walls, and there were always four large postmolds on the interior, marking the locations of roof supports. In all cases these roof supports were connected by rows of smaller posts, suggesting that the interior consisted of a central area (about 3 m on a side) surrounded by partitions, platforms, beds, storage racks, etc. Each house had a slightly depressed floor, a central hearth (clay platform with a depressed center), and a vestibule entrance represented by two parallel wall trenches extending outward about 1 m from one of the walls or at a corner of the building. Human burials, borrow pits, cooking pits, and storage pits were found in the house floors and immediately outside of the houses. Occasionally, a burial was located in the center of the floor, beneath the hearth; otherwise, burials commonly were positioned next to the wall, probably under the beds of the deceased (Figure 5.2). In some instances, disconnected postmold alignments were found adjacent to the outside of house walls (Figure 5.3). These posts may have served as supports for sheds or porches, or as privacy fences. Located adjacent to one house was a circular postmold pattern, about 3 m in diameter, enclosing a shallow sand- and boulder-lined pit (Figure 5.2). It is possible that

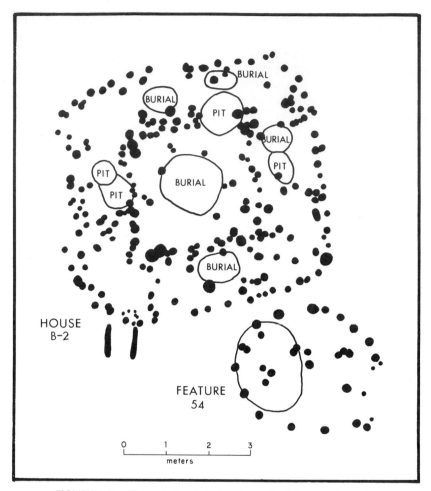

FIGURE 5.2.   *House B-2 and Feature 54 at the Warren Wilson site.*

this feature represents the remains of a conical "hot house," as described for eighteenth century Cherokee sites (Bartram 1791:296–297).

Information on "cermonial" (civic–religious) structures for the Pisgah phase comes from the Garden Creek site. The site contained three platform mounds, the largest of which, Mound 1, was entirely a Pisgah construction. In its later stages, this mound measured about 23 × 28 m at the base and about 16 × 18 m on the summit, and was about 3–4 m high (Figure 5.4, top). There was a ramp 4 m wide at the center of the east side. One of the later mound surfaces had a square structure 5 m² on a side on the western end opposite the ramp. This small building was identical in construction features to the domestic structures previously described. This same

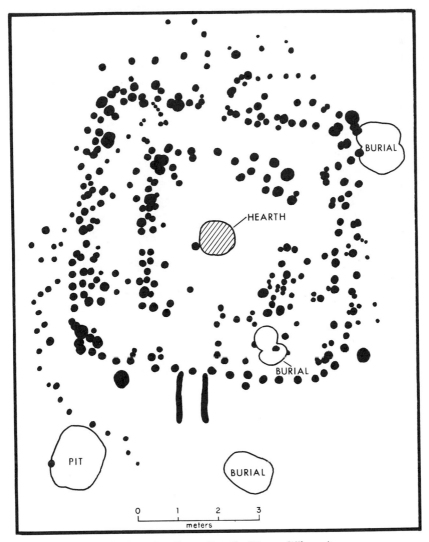

FIGURE 5.3.   House C at the Warren Wilson site.

mound surface had a palisade surrounding the summit and eight burials
on the east end between the building and the ramp.

Garden Creek Mound 1 was raised in several massive construction
stages over a complex arrangement of premound ceremonial structures,
two of which were semisubterranean earth-covered buildings. The largest
of these "earthlodges" was square and measured 8 m along a side, and the
smaller one, also square, was 6.5 on a side. Both buildings had been
constructed in shallow pits and had a layer of earth over the roofs. The

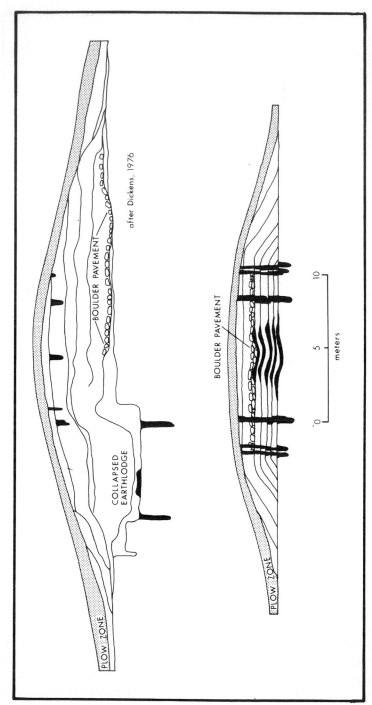

FIGURE 5.4. Profiles of Garden Creek mound 1 (top) and the Estatoe mound (bottom). [Estatoe mound, after Kelly and de Baillou (1960).]

buildings stood side-by-side on a surface that later was covered by the eastern portion of the mound. The smaller earthlodge had a vestibule entrance on the east side and a clay bench on the interior next to the entrance. The larger earthlodge had a clay bench around all four walls, and its entrance was through a passageway from the smaller building. Both buildings had central hearths.

Adjacent to the earthlodges, on a surface later to be covered by the western portion of the mound, was an arrangement of postmolds forming a 14- × 20-m rectangle, within which were nine parallel rows of slightly smaller postmolds. It is probable that these remains were part of a large arborlike structure used in conjunction with the earthlodges. Following the abandonment of the arborlike structure and probably also the earth-lodges, a pavement of boulders was laid over the western two-thirds of the area to be covered by the platform mound. In fact, the earthlodges, the arborlike structure, and the boulders, all together, demarked precisely the limits of the later mound, which suggests strongly that this complex sequence of ceremonial structures was planned. Other platform mounds of probable Pisgah affiliation include the Sawnooke, Rogers, Wells, Asheville, Lindsey, and Newport mounds (Figure 5.1).

For the Qualla phase, information on domestic structures comes from the Coweeta Creek site, the Tuckasegee site, and the Townson site. At the Coweeta Creek site, domestic structures were nearly identical to those described for the Pisgah phase (Egloff 1971:Fig. 4). They averaged about 7 m along a side, had central hearths, interior roof supports, and vestibule entrances. Burials and other pits were found in and around the houses. These houses probably date in the middle or late seventeenth century, and if so would represent the earliest Qualla structures excavated thus far.

Single Qualla structures were excavated at the Tuckasegee and Townson sites, and in both cases European artifacts were found in associa-tion. At the Tuckasegee site (Keel 1976:28–34), the building was circular in plan (6.6 m in diameter), with an outer ring of wall posts, an inner ring of roof supports, and a central clay hearth (Figure 5.5). Glass trade beads found on the floor of the structure place it in the early eighteenth century. The shape of the building demonstrates that at this time in the Qualla phase circular houses were in use along with the earlier square and rectangular houses.

At the Townson site (Keel personal communication), a structure was excavated that probably had been burned during the Rutherford expedi-tion in A.D. 1776 (Dickens 1967). This house, rectangular in plan and measuring about 3.7 × 6 m had consisted of walls of horizontal split rails, chinked with clay, and secured to upright corner posts. There was a slightly depressed packed clay floor and a central clay hearth. This struc-ture obviously contained elements of the Euro-American log cabin.

Ceremonial structures of the Qualla phase are known from excavations

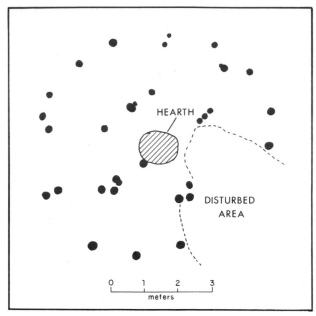

FIGURE 5.5. Circular structure at the Tuckasegee site, Jackson County, North Carolina.
[After Keel (1976).]

at the Coweeta Creek site, Garden Creek site, and Estatoe site. At Coweeta
Creek, a small platform mound was completely excavated (Egloff 1971:
42–71). The earlier phases of the mound were contemporary with the surrounding village (ca. late 1600s), whereas the later stages of the mound
probably postdate the village (ca. early 1700s). The earliest ceremonial
structure, built at ground level, was about 12 m along a side and had
interior support posts, a central clay hearth, and a vestibule entrance. A
smaller (4 × 11 m) rectanglular structure was situated immediately in front
of the entrance and probably served as an antichamber to the main building.

A succession of low platforms was raised over the location of this
initial structure. In its final stages, this mound measured about 21 m along
a side at the base and about 12 m along a side on the summit, and
probably was no more than about 2 m high. There was a ramp on the east
flank of the mound, associated with the last few building stages. Each
successive mound surface had an associated structure. One of the latest was
circular; all the earlier ones were square and had essentially the same
dimensions and orientation as the premound structure. The six extant
floors were each separated by only a few centimeters of sand and structural
debris, and the hearth of each new structure was placed directly over the
previous one. One of the structures had burned, leaving burnt daub, and

the charred remains of timbers, cane matting, and straw thatch. Although there was no boulder pavement associated with this mound, groups of boulders were found on the mound flanks.

Another early Qualla mound was excavated at the Estatoe site (Kelly and de Baillou 1960). As at Coweeta Creek, the lower stages of this mound were precontact, whereas the upper portions appear to have been constructed in the historic period. Like the Coweeta Creek mound, the Estatoe mound consisted of superimposed floors separated by thin lenses of sand and debris (Figure 5.4, bottom). The earlier structures on these surfaces were square in plan and closely resembled the Coweeta Creek mound structures (Figure 5.6), whereas a later structure, probably historic in date, was circular. One of the later stages of the mound was covered by a boulder pavement similar to the one at the base of the Pisgah mound at Garden Creek (Figure 5.7).

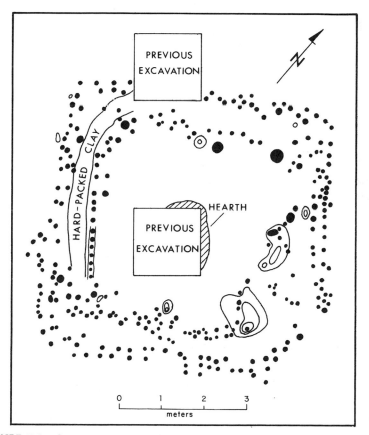

FIGURE 5.6.   Structure 3 at the Estatoe mound, Stephens County, Georgia. [After Kelly and de Baillou (1960).]

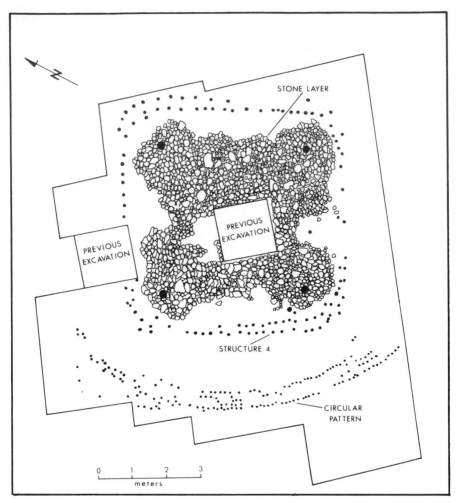

FIGURE 5.7. *Structure 4, stone layer, and circular pattern at the Estatoe mound, Stephens County, Georgia.* [After Kelly and de Baillou (1960).]

Qualla people, especially in the historic period, also made use of mounds constructed in earlier phases, but there is little evidence of Qualla alterations or enlargements of these mounds. An example of such reuse was found at the Garden Creek site, where the large Pisgah mound served as the base for a Qualla townhouse in the early eighteenth century. There was also evidence for Qualla structures on terminal stages of the Peachtree mound (Setzler and Jennings 1941) and the Chauga mound (Kelly and Neitzel 1961).

Arrangement and Functional Interrelationships of
Structures Forming a Settlement

The Warren Wilson site consists of a surface concentration of cultural debris covering about 1 ha (2.5 acres) on a low terrace adjacent to the Swannanoa River (Figure 5.8). Excavations, along with posthole testing, have confirmed that the distribution of surface remains is an accurate indication of the maximum limits of the settlement. This village initally covered no more than about 2400 m² (.5 acre), after which it was enlarged at least seven times, as indicated by palisades enclosing increasingly larger areas and by the overlap of older houses by newer ones. Houses were arranged in a roughly circular pattern, with their entrances fronting on a central "plaza" (Figure 5.9). The entire complex was surrounded by a palisade of circular, or, in at least one instance, nearly square plan. There is no evidence that this palisade had bastions. The entrance to the village, retained in approximately the same location as the village grew, was an overlap on the east side of the palisade.

At the Garden Creek site there were two surface concentrations of Pisgah cultural debris, each having a platform mound on its western margin (Figure 5.10). One of these middens covered about 2.5 ha (6 acres) and was located on a low terrace of the Pigeon River. The second midden covered about 2 ha (5 acres), and was located on a slightly higher terrace 160 m southwest of the first. A third mound, previously destroyed and having no apparent associated midden, had been situated on still higher ground about 200 m south of the other two mounds. It is not known whether this third mound was a Pisgah construction.

Excavations at the Garden Creek site were focused on the two remaining mounds, but limited work in the village area on the lower terrace did reveal three house patterns, similar to those at the Warren Wilson site, and a portion of a palisade having rectangular bastions. Although no subsurface testing was conducted in the peripheral portions of the middens at Garden Creek, the surface distributions suggest that both settlements were considerably larger than the settlement at Warren Wilson.

An important question naturally arises as to whether the two Garden Creek mound-and-midden complexes represent contemporaneous neighboring villages, or whether they are the remains of a short-distance move in the location of a single village. The latter interpretation seems most probable, since the mound associated with the midden on the higher terrace was begun earlier and apparently abandoned earlier than the mound associated with the midden on the lower terrace (Keel 1976:71–158). However, the former interpretation should not be discounted, since a settlement pattern in which two or more kin-group

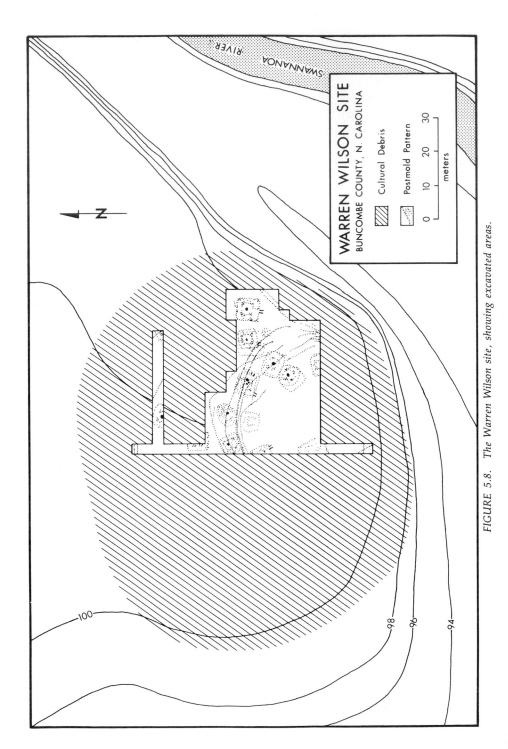

FIGURE 5.8. *The Warren Wilson site, showing excavated areas.*

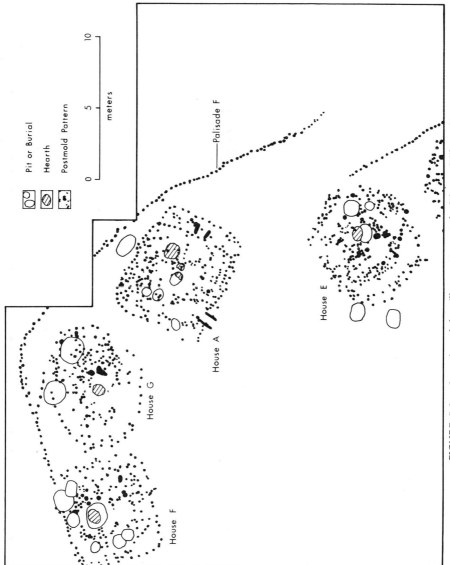

FIGURE 5.9. A portion of the village pattern at the Warren Wilson site.

129

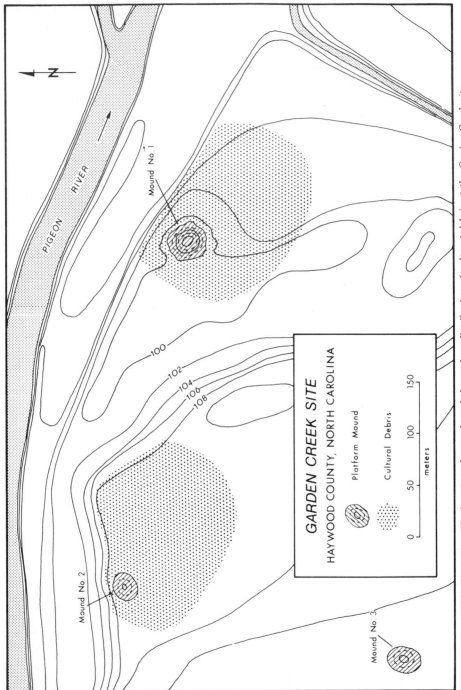

FIGURE 5.10. The location of mounds and the surface distribution of cultural debris at the Garden Creek site.

GARDEN CREEK SITE
HAYWOOD COUNTY, NORTH CAROLINA

Platform Mound

Cultural Debris

meters

0   50   100   150

Mound No. 1

Mound No. 2

Mound No. 3

PIGEON RIVER

N

100
102
104
106
108

"compounds" form a larger "village" has been documented in the ethno-graphic record for various agricultural peoples (e.g., Prussin 1969).

A compact, palisaded village, as just described for the Warren Wilson and Garden Creek sites, has been reported for other Pisgah sites in western North Carolina (Purrington personal communication), and thus seems to be the typical settlement type for river bottomlands during the Pisgah phase. That these sites were supported by approximately equal amounts of agriculture, hunting, and plant gathering, is suggested by limited analyses of subsistence remains (Dickens 1976:202–205). Outside the bottomlands, occasional Pisgah sites have been found on old terraces, benches, and uplands. These nonriverine sites usually are represented by small (less than 2000 m^2) scatters of sherds and lithic remains, or, in some instances, only lithic remains. There is almost no information on the internal organization of these sites, but it is generally assumed that they were temporary hunting or collecting camps.

Thus far, the only Qualla site to have seen large-scale excavation is the Coweeta Creek site (Egloff 1971). This site is located on a low terrace near the Little Tennessee River, and the surface remains cover about 1.2 ha (3 acres). The basic village plan closely resembles the plan for Pisgah villages, that is, a number of houses clustered around a plaza. A small platform mound, described on page 124 of this chapter, was located on the north-east side of the plaza. It is not known whether the Coweeta Creek village was palisaded, since excavations were carried to the periphery of the site in only one area, and this area was severely eroded (Keel personal communication).

At the Coweeta Creek site, the village area as well as the lower stages of the mound were virtually free of evidence of European interaction. The upper stages of the mound, however, contained abundant trade beads and other materials of European origin. This information suggests that after the village at Coweeta Creek had been abandoned, or greatly depopu-lated, the mound and its "townhouse" continued to be used. This transi-tion probably occurred in the early eighteenth century.

Surface remains at Qualla sites along the Little Tennessee, Tuck-asegee, and Hiwassee Rivers indicate that two distinct types of riverine village settlements are associated with this phase. Some sites, such as Coweeta Creek, represent nucleated villages, whereas others are com-posed of loosely grouped or even scattered structures. Sometimes, as in the case of the Townson site in the Hiwassee Valley, the houses were strung out along a river terrace at locations separated by 100 m or more (Keel personal communication). The gross size of these loosely arranged sites can be deceiving since they may have contained relatively few houses. Present evidence suggests that the nucleated type of Qualla set-tlement was earlier in time than the dispersed type.

Arrangements and Interrelationships of
Settlements across the Landscape

In a survey of the upper Watauga River drainage, Purington (personal communication) found that Pisgah phase sites were located on bottomlands, specifically on soils rated "Class 1" in terms of their modern agricultural potential. Only two Pisgah sites were located at higher elevations, and both contained only lithic remains, which suggests that they functioned as hunting camps. There were no Qualla sites, and only slight evidence for and post-Pisgah occupation, in the Watauga Valley.

A survey of Great Smoky Mountains National Park (Bass *et al.* 1976) produced nine sites on which the exclusive Mississippian component was Pisgah. Of these 9 sites, 8 were located on floodplains and 1 was on a bench adjacent to a floodplain. There were 15 sites on which the exclusive Mississippian component was Qualla, and of these sites 12 were located in floodplains and 3 were on adjacent benches. Twelve sites had both Pisgah and Qualla components, and all were located in floodplain situations. Nineteen Mississippian sites could not be identified specifically as Pisgah or Qualla since only lithic remains were present. Of these 19 sites, 3 were located in floodplains, 6 on benches, and 10 in upland situations.

In a survey of the upper Hiwassee Valley (Dorwin 1975), 49 sites were recorded on which the exclusive Mississippian component was Qualla. Of these sites, 29 were located in floodplains, 10 on secondary terraces or benches, and 10 in upland situations. Only two Pisgah sites were found, one in a floodplain and the other in an upland location.

These three surveys demonstrate that the preferred locations for village sites during both the Pisgah and Qualla phases were floodplains and adjoining terraces and benches. Some small sites, presumably hunting, gathering, or flintworking camps were found on old terraces, benches, and uplands.

When Pisgah and Qualla site locations from all available surveys are plotted on a map of the Appalachian Summit area, some important differences are evident. Pisgah sites (Figure 5.11) are found in greatest numbers in the eastern and central portions of the area, with smaller groups extending far to the north, even into the Ridge and Valley province. Qualla sites (Figure 5.12), on the other hand, are most numerous in the southern and western portions of the Summit area. Only in the central portion of the Summit—on the Pigeon, Tuckasegee, and Oconaluftee drainages—is there much overlap in occupation by the two phases. If Pisgah and Qualla do indeed represent a cultural continuum, then the site distributions indicate a major occupational shift in late prehistoric or protohistoric times.

Except for the northerly scatter of sites, the largest settlement concen-

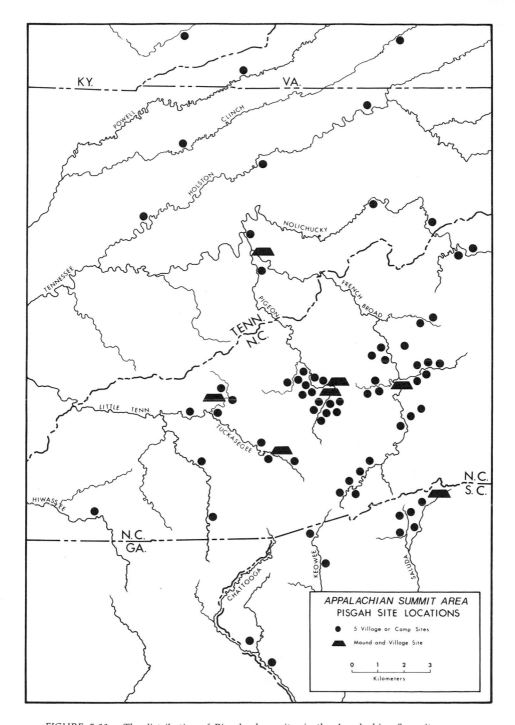

FIGURE 5.11. The distribution of Pisgah phase sites in the Appalachian Summit area.

Within the figure:

KY.
VA.

POWELL

CLINCH

HOLSTON

NOLICHUCKY

TENNESSEE

PIGEON

FRENCH BROAD

TENN.
N.C.

LITTLE TENN

TUCKASEGEE

HIWASSEE

N.C.
GA.

N.C.
S.C.

CHATTOOGA

KEOWEE

SALUDA

APPALACHIAN SUMMIT AREA
PISGAH SITE LOCATIONS

● 5 Village or Camp Sites

▰ Mound and Village Site

0   1   2   3
Kilometers

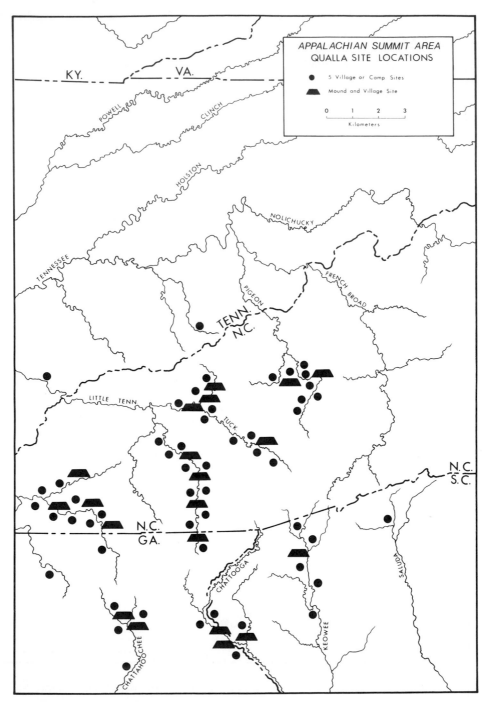

FIGURE 5.12. *The distribution of Qualla phase sites in the Appalachian Summit area.*

trations during the Pisgah phase appear to have been in the more spacious intermontane basins of western North Carolina, especially in the Asheville, Pigeon, and Hendersonville basins. Qualla sites, on the other hand, tend to follow a more linear distribution, with extensive occupations in some rather narrow stream valleys, such as the Keowee and Little Tennessee valleys. Furthermore, the Pisgah pattern, except for the more northerly sites, seems to be characterized by a clustering of village and campsites around a single larger mound-and-village center. The Qualla sites, however, do not manifest a mound-center–satellite-village pattern, but rather there are many sites with mounds, some of these sites being quite small and often in close proximity to one another.

Summary and Interpretations

At the first level of settlement data, we have found that the square to rectangular habitation structure of the Pisgah phase was maintained into the early part of the Qualla phase. A circular house type was added later in the Qualla phase, perhaps early in the eighteenth century, and finally, in the late eighteenth century, there was a shift to a structure utilizing Euro-American construction techniques. A large platform mound composed of massive construction stages for the Pisgah phase is replaced in the Qualla phase by a smaller platform composed of thinly layered, superimposed floors. Structures on the mounds are of comparable size and form in the Pisgah and Qualla phases, although a palisade around the summit of a Pisgah mound and circular structures on late stages of two Qualla mounds seem to be distinctive. Pavements of boulders have been found in both Pisgah and Qualla mounds. Ceremonial earthlodges have been documented in the archeological record only for the Pisgah phase, but there are historical descriptions of similar structures for eighteenth-century Qualla sites such as Cowe on the Little Tennessee River (Bartram 1791:297–298).

At the second level of settlement data, we have noted that Pisgah and Qualla sites are most numerous in floodplain situations. However, some small campsites of both phases are found in locations bordering floodplains and in upland settings. Pisgah bottomland sites vary in size from about 2500 m^2 to about 25,000 m^2. In western North Carolina at least, these sites represent nucleated, palisaded villages. Early Qualla sites seem to conform to a nucleated pattern similar to the Pisgah sites, but at some point in the Qualla phase there was a shift to a loosely grouped or dispersed pattern. For the Pisgah phase, mounds seem to be associated with larger village sites, whereas in the Qualla phase, mounds may be found on village sites of only moderate size.

An examination of the third level of settlement data has revealed different distributional patterns for sites of the two phases. Pisgah sites have a more widespread distribution and are found mostly in the northern and eastern portions of the Appalachian Summit area. Qualla sites are less widespread and are most numerous in the southern and western portions of the area. Much of the eastern portion of the area seems to have been abandoned or greatly depopulated following the Pisgah phase. This depopulation may have been the result of demographic shifts during the early contact period, but the possibility of late prehistoric adjustments in man–land relationships should not be ignored.

Pisgah sites tend to follow a clustered pattern in which there is a large mound site with surrounding smaller village sites, with the largest of these complexes occurring in intermontane basins. Qualla sites have a more linear arrangement with numerous, but sometimes closely neighboring sites having mounds. The change from a nucleated community pattern in the Pisgah phase to a more dispersed pattern in the Qualla phase may reflect some widespread trends in the Southeast during late Mississippian times. For example, there seems to be a similar change from the Etowah–Wilbanks phase to the Lamar phase in the Piedmont area. However, the presence of nucleated settlements in the early part of the Qualla phase in western North Carolina, and the early part of the Lamar phase in northern Georgia (Hally, Garrow, and Trotti 1975), leads me to conclude that the change was primarily related to European or European-induced disruption of the precontact cultural–environmental system. Such disruption might have been felt in the Summit area as early as the middle of the seventeenth century (Rothrock 1976:21–29).

The types of intercommunity social organization that accompanied these settlement patterns are not yet known. The Pisgah pattern appears to have involved several groupings of communities, each having allegiances to a mound center, not unlike the smaller "provincia" described in the De Soto chronicles (Varner and Varner 1951). That these groupings were chiefdoms, as interpreted by Larson (1971) for the Etowah and Wilbanks cultures and by Hatch (1975) for the Dallas culture, seems unlikely on the basis of Pisgah subsistence and burial data (Dickens 1976:210–211). The Qualla pattern, at least in the postcontact period, seems to have involved weak intercommunity organization. As with the eighteenth-century Cherokee, certain communities were larger and probably more influential than others, but it is unlikely that these "town centers" had direct political or administrative control over neighboring communities (Gearing 1962).

Recommendations for Future Research

Settlement pattern data from the Appalachian Summit area reflect the separate interests and goals of various survey projects. Some of the data come from river-basin projects, some from county-specific projects, and some from large, problem-oriented projects. It would be helpful if future survey work in the area were to use some common criteria and measurements in recording site data.

Efforts to interpret changes in settlement patterns in the area are handicapped by the lack of an accurate chronology. As stated earlier, there are only nine radiocarbon dates for the Pisgah and Qualla phases, and as yet we have no dates for early Qualla sites.

A significant bias in the settlement data has been created by a persistent emphasis on mound excavation, sometimes at the exclusion of any work in village areas accompanying those mounds or on nearby nonmound sites. To date, there have been no excavations on campsites of either phase.

Finally, there is a glaring deficiency in subsistence data from excavations in the Summit area. It will not be possible to interpret fully the settlement patterns of the Pisgah and Qualla phases without having information on the associated economic systems.

If these basic inconsistencies and deficiencies can be corrected, the Appalachian Summit area will offer an excellent opportunity to examine Mississippian settlement patterns in an environment that may well have been marginal, in the ecological sense, to the most efficient development of Mississippian economic, social, and ideological systems. The Appalachian Summit area, therefore, represents a "laboratory" for testing a variety of explanatory models of Mississippian cultural dynamics.

Acknowledgments

I am grateful to the following individuals and institutions for providing information on survey projects in the Appalachian Summit area: Wesley Breedlove, Joffre Coe, Clemens de Baillou, Stephen Gluckman, Susan Jackson, Bennie Keel, Arthur Kelly, Peter Miller, Burton Purrington, Jack Schock, Research Laboratories of Anthropology at the University of North Carolina, Laboratory of Archaeology at the University of Georgia, Department of Anthropology at Appalachian State University, Department of Anthropology at Western Carolina University, North Carolina Department of Archives and History, and the Interagency Archaeological Services of the National Park Service. Stanley Solamillo assisted in the preparation of the figures.

References

Bartram, William
    1791   *Travels of William Bartram.* 1940 edition (Mark Van Doren, editor). New York: Dover.
Bass, Quentin R., Major C.R. McCullough, and Charles H. Faulkner
    1976   Second interim report on the archaeological survey of Great Smoky Mountains

National Park. Report submitted to the Office of Interagency Archaeological Services, Southeast Region National Park Service, Atlanta, Georgia.

Caldwell, Joseph R.
1953   Appraisal of the archaeological resources of Hartwell Resorvoir, South Carolina and Georgia. Report submitted to the Southeast Archaeological Center, National Park Service, Macon, Georgia.

Dickens, Roy S., Jr.
1967   The route of Rutherford's expedition against the North Carolina Cherokees. *Southern Indian Studies* **19**:3–24.

1976   *Cherokee prehistory: The Pisgah phase in the Appalachian Summit region.* Knoxville: University of Tennessee Press.

Dorwin, John T.
1975   Upper Hiwassee River survey: 1974–75. Report submitted to the North Carolina Division of Archives and History, Raleigh, North Carolina.

Egloff, Brian J.
1967   An analysis of ceramics from historic Cherokee towns. M.A. thesis, Department of Anthropology, University of North Carolina, Chapel Hill.

Egloff, Keith T.
1971   Methods and problems of mound excavation in the Southern Appalachian Area. M.A. thesis, Department of Anthropology, University of North Carolina, Chapel Hill.

Gearing, Fred
1962   Social structures for Cherokee politics in the 18th Century. *Memoirs of the American Anthropological Association* **93**.

Hally, David J., Patrick H. Garrow, and Wyman Trotti
1975   Preliminary analysis of the King Site settlement plan. *Southeastern Archaeological Conference Bulletin* **18**:55–62.

Harrington, M. R.
1922   Cherokee and earlier remains on the upper Tennessee River. *Indian notes and monographs.* Museum of the American Indian, Heye Foundation, New York.

Hatch, James W.
1975   Social dimensions of Dallas burials. *Southeastern Archaeological Conference, Bulletin* **18**:132–138.

Holden, Patricia P.
1966   An Archaeological survey of Transylvania County, North Carolina. M.A. thesis, Department of Anthropology, University of North Carolina, Chapel Hill.

Keel, Bennie C.
1976   *Cherokee archaeology: A study of the Appalachian Summit.* Knoxville: University of Tennessee Press.

Kelly, A.R., and Clemens de Baillou
1960   Excavation of the presumptive site of Estatoe. *Southern Indian Studies* **12**:3–30.

Kelly, A.R. and R.S. Neitzel
1961   The Chauga site in Oconee County, South Carolina.University of Georgia Laboratory of Archaeology Series, Report 3. Athens, Georgia.

Kroeber, A.L.
1939   Cultural and natural areas of native North America. *University of California Publications in American Archaeology and Ethnology* **38**. Berkeley.

Larson, Lewis H., Jr.
1971   Archaeological implications of social stratification at the Etowah Site, Georgia. In *Approaches to social dimensions of mortuary practices,* edited by James A. Brown. *The Society for American Archaeology, Memoir* **25**:58–67.

Prussin, Labelle
  1969   *Architecture in Northern Ghana: A study of forms and functions.* Berkeley: University
          of California Press.
Purrington, Burton L.
  1975   A preliminary report of archaeological surveys in Watauga County, North
          Carolina, 1970–1974. Report submitted to the North Carolina Division of Archives
          and History, Raleigh, North Carolina.
Rothrock, Mary U.
  1976   Carolina traders among the Overhill Cherokees 1690–1760. *Tennessee Archaeologist*
          31:21–29.
Setzler, Frank M. and Jesse D. Jennings
  1941   Peachtree Mound and Village site, Cherokee County, North Carolina. *Bureau of
          American Ethnology, Bulletin* **131**.
Shelford, Victor E.
  1963   *The Ecology of North America.* Urbana: University of Illinois Press.
Thornbury, William D.
  1965   *Regional geomorphology of the United States.* New York: Wiley.
Varner, John G. and Jeanette J. Varner
  1951   *The Florida of the Inca.* Austin: University of Texas Press.
Ward, Trawick
  1965   Correlation of Mississippian sites and soil types. *Southeastern Archaeological Con-
          ference, Bulletin* **3**:42–48.
Wauchope, Robert
  1966   Archaeological survey of northern Georgia. *The Society for American Archaeology
          Memoir* **21**. Salt Lake City.

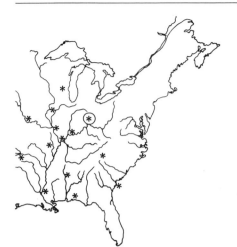

6

Fort Ancient Settlement: Differential Response at a Mississippian — Late Woodland Interface

PATRICIA S. ESSENPREIS

Sites assigned to the Fort Ancient culture are located in the Ohio River drainage area from southeastern Indiana to just east of the juncture of the Ohio and Muskingum Rivers, a linear distance of over 500 km. Sites are situated along the Ohio and extend up its tributaries as much as 300 km. When the Fort Ancient culture was described by James B. Griffin in 1943, it was thought to lie primarily within Ohio, with some extensions into southeastern Indiana, northern Kentucky, and West Virginia. However, sites assigned to this culture have since been found almost as far southeast as the Kentucky–Virginia border and throughout western West Virginia, encompassing over 50,000 km² (Figure 6.1).

Fort Ancient sites occur primarily along large water courses: the Kentucky, Licking, and Big Sandy Rivers in Kentucky; the Kanawha River in West Virginia; the Whitewater River in Indiana; and the Miami, Little Miami, Brush Creek, Scioto, Hocking, and Muskingum Rivers in Ohio. Sites of this culture are located in three physiographic provinces: the unglaciated Allegheny Plateau, the Blue Grass Region of the Interior Low Plateau, and the Till Plains of the Central Lowlands.

The Allegheny Plateau is a maturely dissected plateau with minimal amounts of flatland in both upland and lowland areas. Rivers are deeply entrenched in relatively narrow valleys with local relief of up to 400 m (McFarlan 1943:175). The Blue Grass region of the Interior Low Plateau is a rolling upland on limestone rock except near the larger rivers, which are

141

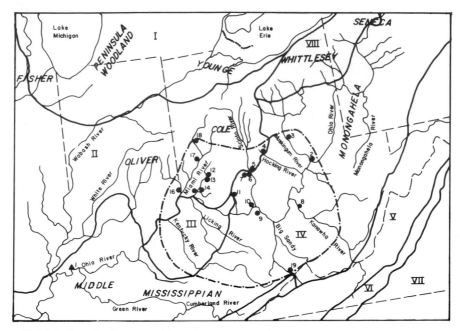

FIGURE 6.1. *The Location of Fort Ancient sites referred to in the text* (−·−·), *showing the general extent of the Fort Ancient culture within three physiographic provinces*(—). Physiographic Provinces: *II Till Plains of the Central Lowlands; III The Blue Grass Region of the Interior Low Plateau; IV Allegheny Plateau.* Sites: *1. Angel; 2. Marietta; 3. Philo; 4. Graham; 5. Gartner; 6. Blain; 7. Baum; 8. Buffalo; 9. Hardin; 10. Feurt; 11. Brush Creek; 12. Anderson Village; 13. South Fort (Fort Ancient); 14. Turpin; 15. Madisonville; 16. State Line; 17. Incinerator; 18. Erp; 19. Slone.*

deeply entrenched 30–200 m below the level of the plateau. The valley bottoms of the Kentucky, Licking, and Big Sandy Rivers are seldom more than 1.6–3.2 km wide, but the fertile uplands are suitable for agriculture (McFarlan 1943:167, Thornbury 1965:196–197). The Till Plains section of the Central Lowlands generally has very low relief, the product of at least three glaciations, although along the southern limit of glaciation just the smaller river valleys were obliterated by glaciers, leaving the larger valleys only partly filled by glacial outwash and till (Fenneman 1916) (Figure 6.1).

These three distinct physiographic provinces are also characterized by different vegetational associations. The Allegheny Plateau is an area of mixed mesophytic forests with dominance shared by a number of species—particularly beech, tuliptree, basswood, sugar maple, sweet buckeye, chestnut, red oak, white oak, and hemlock. The Blue Grass region and the areas of Illinoian glaciation in southwestern Ohio and eastern Indiana support a western mesophytic forest, an ecotone consisting of a number of unlike climax and subclimax associations. A beech–maple forest climax characterized the southern portions of the Scioto and

Miami drainages, which had been glaciated during the Wisconsin advance (Braun 1950). Within these forest types, there existed more or less distinct vegetation communities dependent on local soil type and depth, slope, exposure, drainage, and altitude, which in turn supported numerous and varied animal populations available for exploitation by aboriginal populations.

From this environmental description, it seems that few environmental constraints were placed on the subsistence activities of Fort Ancient peoples. Conditions for successful farming and hunting existed throughout the occupied range. The relatively rich ecological resource base seems to have allowed utilization of a number of different local environments, and although it may be possible to observe correlations between sites and environmental factors in local situations, no overall pattern of Fort Ancient settlement location can currently be formulated. Villages did tend to occur along major drainages but were not always located within the river valleys, suggesting that proximity to avenues of communication and transport may have been as significant a factor in settlement location as ecological considerations.

General Background of Fort Ancient

Fort Ancient does not appear simultaneously throughout the region described, but first appears in southern Ohio. The earliest dates from this culture (A.D. 950–1000) come from the Blain and Graham Village sites (Baum phase) on the central Scioto River. Fort Ancient does not appear in eastern Kentucky and West Virginia until after A.D. 1200 (Dunnell 1972:92), and continues in these regions, into the seventeenth century.

Fort Ancient is defined primarily as a particular series of ceramic attributes that often is regarded as a specific ethnic unit. It now appears, however, that there are a number of different tribal or ethnic units included within Fort Ancient. Therefore, any analysis of Fort Ancient settlement patterns should be carried out by examining individual phases, which represent more localized adaptive systems. It is not possible to formulate a single settlement–subsistence model for all of Fort Ancient that fits all of the available data. Instead, at least two settlement patterns, characterizing different Fort Ancient phases, are indicated. One pattern, found in the Madisonville phase, indicates regional structuring of sites of different functional levels whereas another, characterizing the Anderson phase, suggests that similar levels of functions were carried out at all sites. Dates from sites of these phases indicate at least partial comtemporaneity of these systems and suggest that unilineal models of Fort Ancient development are not supportable.

Thus, individual phases, rather than the Fort Ancient culture, are the foci of the following discussion of settlement patterning. There is no one Fort Ancient settlement pattern, but rather a number of systems resulting from localized responses to a number of different environmental and cultural stimuli. These stimuli include the shift to a greater dependence on agriculture and a generally more focal economy, as well as interaction with the more politically complex Mississippian cultural units to the west and south.

Initially, Fort Ancient participated in a general Mississippian system involving a shift to larger, more permanent villages, intravillage structuring with emergence of the plaza–central-post complex, and regional trade as reflected in the occurrence of nonlocal items on Fort Ancient sites. In later Fort Ancient (post-A.D. 1200), more direct Mississippian input from the west, possibly immigration, resulted in more Mississippian-like artifact traits and settlement configurations in a portion of the original area as well as expansion of this Fort Ancient pattern into eastern Kentucky and West Virginia. The settlement patterning of this later system is more organizationally complex, with sites of different sociopolitical levels represented, demonstrating a higher degree of regional organization than the system operating in the Anderson area. These two temporally and spatially distinct patterns, as represented in the Anderson and Madisonville phases, will be characterized and examined in this chapter.

Development of a Theoretical Framework

EARLY INVESTIGATIONS: DEFINING FORT ANCIENT

The archeology of the middle and upper Ohio Valley aroused the interest of prehistorians at an early date, largely because of the extensive mounds and earthworks present in this area. Early investigators of the "Mound Builder cultures" mapped these works (Squier and Davis 1848) and other investigators concentrated on proving that the historic indian tribes could have indeed built them without the aid of a now-vanished race (Thomas 1894). Along with extensive testing programs, intensive excavations were conducted by men such as Charles L. Metz and Frederick W. Putnam (at the Madisonville and Turner sites) and Warren K. Moorehead (at Fort Ancient and the Hopewell Group). This enabled the subdivision of Ohio mound builders into two distinct cultures. One culture, represented at the Turner and Hopewell sites, was demonstrably the more advanced in artistic expression and earthwork building. The other culture, named Fort Ancient by William C. Mills (1904:134–136), was represented by extensive village sites at Madisonville, Turpin, Fort Ancient, Feurt, Baum, and Gartner (Shetrone 1920).

Having attributed the more elaborate arts and constructions to the Hopewell, Mills initially considered Fort Ancient to be the earlier of the two cultures. The cultural and temporal separation of Hopewell and Fort Ancient was not established until the 1930s, when comparative studies resulted in the placement of Fort Ancient into the Upper Mississippian pattern (McKern 1933; Griffin 1937).

THE FORT ANCIENT ASPECT

Fort Ancient studies entered a classificatory stage of development during the 1930s. James B. Griffin conducted an extensive examination of notes and collections from all known Fort Ancient sites, producing a truly monumental synthesis of all data pertaining to Fort Ancient, and proposing a classificatory scheme based on the McKern taxonomic method (Griffin 1943). In *The Fort Ancient Aspect,* Griffin presented the list of traits diagnostic of Fort Ancient and further recognized four foci: Baum, Feurt, Anderson, and Madisonville. Following McKernian practice, he defined foci as the basic units for further analysis, since these were intended to represent human groups possessing nearly identical cultural habits, assuming that these habits would be reflected in the material traits by which the focus was defined (Griffin 1943:336).

The manifestation of these traits at any one site was termed a "component," with the analysis and comparison of a number of components leading to formulation of the focus level of classification. Griffin substantiated the existence of his foci primarily through ceramic analysis. He was careful not to use individual traits and attributes as indicators, preferring to rely on stabilized combinations of the elements that represented types peculiar to a limited number of sites (Griffin 1943:205).

The primary purpose of the McKernian taxonomic system was to establish a way to organize burgeoning data by grouping together components into similar classes (foci), the shared trait elements of which could then be combined to define the taxonomic unit called the "aspect." The aspect reflected a personal selection and abstraction of important features rather than a cultural reality, and acted primarily as a unit for comparison with other similarly defined units. The aspect did not, therefore, reflect the internal relationships between foci, even though it suggested a basic degree of relatedness. Thus, the Fort Ancient aspect was purely a classificatory construct and not a culture in a sociological sense. Fort Ancient was defined as a particular set of traits with no prescribed organization of elements. In an analogy with linguistics, it may be said to have possessed a vocabulary but no structure of grammar. As such, the Fort Ancient aspect was not a proper unit for analysis. Griffin implied this when he stated that one needed to understand data in their correct cultural grouping and in an approximate chronological position before defining cultural associations

(Griffin 1943:206). The valid unit of such study was stated to be the focus whose internal structure and development needed to be understood prior to formulations at the level of taxonomy. Theoretically, temporal and spatial factors were not considered in establishing a site's classification, but, in reality, the resultant site grouping or focus was implied to have covered a short temporal span and be limited to a relatively restricted geographical area (Griffin 1943:337).

Despite such implied temporal and spatial significance

> an attempt to use the classification as a means of demonstrating time horizons or cultural development would probably result in an inadequate grouping of the phenomona on the basis of likeness or dissimilarity. A clear distinction should always be made between the classification of a site as such and a temporal and spatial interpretation of the meaning of the classification [Griffin 1943:337–338].

As McKern (1939:312) admitted, one cannot establish cultural development by this classification until an independently constructed chronology is established and correlated with specific units within the cultural classification.

In summary, the framework for Fort Ancient that Griffin presented in *The Fort Ancient Aspect* utilized a system of cultural classification that was based on similar shared material traits, without specific consideration of distribution of these elements in time and space. As an analytical tool, the McKernian method offered the means for comparing "properly organized" data from sites and a means of site comparison based on the data rather than on subjective interpretations of the data. As presented, the aspect is an archeological construct the validity of which as a cultural unit has not been established. To reconstruct the way of life and historical development of "Fort Ancient peoples" it is therefore necessary first to establish the temporal and spatial distribution of elements within the individual foci by criteria not originally inherent to the establishment of these taxonomic units.

THE FORT ANCIENT TRADITION

The preceding discussion of the classificatory scheme established by Griffin was necessary because the units he defined and the criteria by which he determined placement of individual sites into the classificatory units, although modified, still provide the general framework for studies of Fort Ancient. Following Griffin's 1943 study, few other attempts were made to synthesize or study "the Fort Ancient aspect" until the mid 1960s. At that time, Olaf Prufer and Douglas McKenzie began an examination of the relationship between Late Woodland and Fort Ancient in south central

Ohio. This culminated in the publication of *Blain Village and the Fort Ancient Tradition of Ohio* by Olaf Prufer and Orrin Shane in 1970.

In this volume, Prufer and Shane discarded the McKernian terminology, replacing "focus" with "phase," and coining the phrase Fort Ancient "tradition." They replaced Griffin's four foci with four similarly defined phases, assigned two new phases (Baldwin and Brush Creek), and implied greater cultural validity for both the phase and tradition levels of classification. They then relied on the six phase- formulations to provide analytical units for reconstructing the cultural–historical development of Fort Ancient (Prufer and Shane 1970:236–264). However, although these phases can be used as organizing devices, their usefulness as analytical tools is minimal unless they are redefined so as to possess structural, functional, and organizational validity. More simply, if phases are to be used, they must be redefined to reflect the cultural system operating within definable temporal and geographical dimensions. The formal material traits identified by Griffin must be placed into cultural context, with an attempt made to reconstruct the organization and function of observed cultural practices on the local and regional level.

This is what Prufer and Shane failed to take fully into consideration when they analyzed developments within the Baum phase. Beginning primarily with ceramic criteria, they divided Griffin's Baum focus into three phases: Baum in the central Scioto Valley, Baldwin in the Hocking Valley, and Brush Creek in the Brush Creek drainage. Based on percentages of shell-tempered ceramics, and supported in some instances by radiocarbon dates, they then established site sequences for the Scioto and Hocking drainages (Prufer and Shane 1970:39–74). Again based solely on ceramic criteria, they suggested that the Feurt phase succeeded Baum in the central and eastern portion of the state, whereas the Anderson phase—the temporal equivalent of Feurt—developed out of the Brush Creek phase in the western portion of the state. The known late phase, Madisonville, occurred throughout the middle Ohio Valley, deriving its traits from new foreign influences as well as from the local Fort Ancient phases.

From a comparison of Fort Ancient and Late Woodland traits, as well as the distribution of ceramic elements, Prufer and Shane then concluded that the appearance of Fort Ancient was too abrupt (ca. A.D. 950) to allow for gradual development out of Late Woodland, even as acculturation due to diffusion of new traits and ideas. They concluded, therefore, that an invasion of Mississippian people entered the central Scioto Valley, pushing Woodland peoples into the hills, where they coexisted with the resultant Fort Ancient tradition.

One of the primary reasons Prufer and Shane saw the appearance of Fort Ancient as being abrupt was that they placed too great a reliance on use of the ceramically defined phases, which tend to obscure variability within units while maximizing it between units. This results in relatively homogeneous cultural units with well-defined boundaries. Having been established by reference to artifactual norms, these units do not operate as cultural systems in which changes in subsystems could be recognized. From this line of reasoning, it follows that it would be difficult to explain Fort Ancient as a gradual modification of the Late Woodland cultural pattern.

By defining Late Woodland groups as those that lack obvious Middle Woodland ceremonialism and also lack the Fort Ancient ceramic traits of shell tempering, strap handles, and curvilinear guilloche designs (Murphy 1975), Ohio archeologists have established a taxonomic unit which, by definition, cannot develop into Fort Ancient. Thus, classification creates a situation in which two taxonomically distinct cultures are forced into coexistance (Prufer and Shane 1970). However, the reasoning that led to this interpretation is circular, in that units established by reference to mutually exclusive formal criteria are not adequate to test hypotheses of gradual change versus replacement.

SUMMARY

Phases, as well as cultures or traditions, should be less rigid and less static constructs. Griffin's formulations were based on elements deliberately chosen to distinguish one unit from another, with concomitant emphasis on the homogeneity within the units and the differences between them. Thus, although it is valid to examine phases in relation to each other, this comparison should be preceded by an understanding of the structural elements of each phase and by an understanding of how the observed traits function within their own cultural environment.

Recognition of the range of behavioral and cultural activities subsumed within phases would allow the correlation of phases and the formulation of systemic models of Fort Ancient development. Temporal and geographical relationships suggested by ceramic evidence could then be tested by reference to the context and patterning of a number of criteria such as house form, burial patterning, and sociopolitical organization.

Fort Ancient Settlement Patterns

AN HISTORICAL PERSPECTIVE

Previous work on Fort Ancient settlement patterns has, for the most part, been of a particularistic nature. Data on architectural and structural elements were gathered beginning with investigators such as Mills, Moorehead, and Putnam. Yet the theoretical framework of these men did not encourage them to do more than describe the form and implied function of settlement elements. Their primary interest—that of establishing the "ethnic distinction" between the Hopewell and Fort Ancient cultures and determining the position of each on an evolutionary scale— led to detailed description of burial characteristics and artifact inventories, since these reflected the level of social organization and artistic expression of each group. Consequently, although prosaic elements such as house patterns were noted in excavation, descriptions of them are often of low quality.

William C. Mills presented little primary data on intrasite patterning, but made observations of significance to intrasite organization. At the Baum site, for example, he noted that, through time, house structures shifted from place to place and also that burials seemed to cluster in family groupings (Mills 1906). At the Gartner site, data as to length of occupation were provided by the observed shift in burial practices in the mound from cremation to primary extended. Also at Gartner, Mills found evidence that individual family groups could be distinguished by noting clusters of ceramic attributes (Mills 1904).

On a regional scale, Mills perceived the existence of geographically distinct cultural assemblages on Fort Ancient sites. He observed differences in burial customs and artifact types, which seemed to form regional variants of Fort Ancient. Thus, he placed the Baum and Gartner sites in one group, the Madisonville and Campbell Island sites in another, and the Feurt and Fox Farm sites in a third group (Shetrone 1926). The affinities noted by Mills were largely substantiated by Griffin (1943). In this study, Griffin went beyond earlier investigators by analyzing individual elements but he did not attempt to integrate these elements into a comprehensive settlement pattern.

The first conscious attempt to integrate settlement data from a number of sites into a settlement model was made by Prufer and Shane (1970). These investigators related excavations at the Blain mound and village site to other sites of the Baum phase, noting similarities between elements at Blain and Baum. They dealt with internal site arrangement, estimated population size, economic activities, social organization, and ceremonialism as inferred from the data from the Blain site. The internal settlement pattern of the Blain site was one of relatively closely spaced oval houses bordering a plaza that contained a burial mound. Burials placed under the mound were probably of high status, although no burials were recovered from the village area with which a comparison of mode and associations could be made. The population of the Blain Village was estimated at 100–400 individuals, assuming that the occupation of the site was of relatively short duration (Prufer and Shane 1970:246–248).

The village was a nucleated community with no evidence to suggest specialized hunting camps or hamlets in the surrounding region. Agriculture was the primary subsistence activity, with hunting focusing on deer and elk. Emphasis on utilization of the terrace–riverine zones was due to economic dependence on agriculture—and due to the presence of hostile Woodland peoples in the hilly uplands (Prufer and Shane 1970:253).

Although Prufer and Shane have considered Blain Village as a cultural system that relates to the natural environment and the presence of non-Fort Ancient populations, their analysis lacks intregration of Baum phase sites into a regional cultural system. Sites are assumed to be basically equivalent, self-sufficient entities with relatedness a function of temporal and geographical vectors. They assume a monovariant approach in the proposed settlement model as well as in the development scheme.

THE FORT ANCIENT SYSTEM

As evident from the preceding discussion, Fort Ancient settlement pattern studies have not yet reached a level of reconstructing regional settlement systems. Although comparisons among sites excavated are made, no attempt is made to fit them into an interacting and interdependent framework. Basically, the phase constructs lack the temporal and systemic components that would allow comparisons of other than formal attributes. Observed differences, if "explained" at all, are attributed to temporal variation (e.g., Prufer and Shane 1970) or are used as the basis to create new phases. Admittedly, much of the variation extant in Fort Ancient may be due to temporal differences; undoubtedly, the current phases subsume more variation than is expedient for analysis.

However, it is proposed herein that some of the observed variation in settlement patterning is due to the different functions performed by and at Fort Ancient sites, and that sites interacted in an interdependent series of relationships. As Binford has noted, there is a need to isolate and understand cultural *systems* rather than aggregates of traits in order to understand the cultural processes that are operating (Binford 1964:135–139). Furthermore, systems are complex and can be understood only in terms of this complexity as reflected in organization of behavior (Hole and Heizer 1973:443–444).

At least in regard to regional synthesis, archeologists dealing with Fort Ancient have relied on the normative approach, regarding the excavation of a single site as a typical form and thereby treating the whole as an unstructured, homogeneous entity (e.g., Hanson 1975:40). To do this however, it is necessary to seek the regular repeated relationships that existed within a region, focusing on the linkages between variables and the structural organization of cultural components. Thus, although it may be possible to describe variations as products of temporal and geographical factors, it is not possible to explain such variation functionally without attempting to understand the structural and operational significance of the variations.

A TEMPORAL FRAMEWORK

The temporal framework for Fort Ancient has its basis in the ceramic analysis completed by Griffin (1943). Although performed without regard to temporal or spatial considerations, the analysis seemed to demonstrate a basic shift from more Woodland-like characteristics of subconoidal form, grit and limestone temper, and cordmarking to the more Mississippian-like traits of shell tempering, globular vessels, smoothed-over cordmarking, and strap handles. For purposes of formulating the temporal sequence, the entire Fort Ancient culture has been treated as a single universe; temporal sequences were not first formulated for each seemingly distinct region. Thus the current temporal framework for much of Ohio Fort Ancient possesses an untested degree of validity.

The most generally used Fort Ancient temporal framework, that created by Prufer and Shane (1970), divides Fort Ancient into three periods: early (A.D. 950–1250), middle (A.D. 1250–1450), and late (A.D. 1450–1750). Early Fort Ancient consists of the Baum, Baldwin, and Brush Creek phases. In middle Fort Ancient, the Feurt phase succeeded Baum in central and eastern Ohio, whereas the Anderson phase—the temporal equivalent of Feurt—developed out of the Brush Creek phase in the western Fort Ancient area. The known late Fort Ancient phase, Madisonville, occurred throughout the middle Ohio Valley, deriving its traits from new foreign influences as well as from the local Fort Ancient phases. For each of these three periods, a uniform organizational level and a homogeneous artifactual universe is assumed.

A major problem with the framework proposed by Prufer and Shane is the assumption of a homogeneous, undifferentiated universe at one point in time. This assumption precludes consideration of Fort Ancient phases as contemporaneous rather than sequential units. Furthermore, their reliance on the ceramic criterion of shell tempering to place sites and phases in time precludes the recognition of coexisting regional groups with different ceramic assemblages.

In conclusion, it is necessary to reexamine the temporal framework proposed by Prufer and Shane, and to offer alternative models against which available data can be examined. The threefold scheme already discussed has an underlying assumption that Fort Ancient can be viewed as a sociological unit, relatively uniform in structure and trait expression at any one point in time. The nature of this framework not only places constraits on processual analysis of Fort Ancient development, but also limits interpretations at the regional or phase level. Factors other than time and geographical location need to be incorporated into an analytic framework in order to formulate hypotheses about the functioning of both the Fort Ancient system and the systems operating at the local level.

An Alternative Model of Fort Ancient Development

Examination of the distribution of phases and their attributes supports the hypothesis that all phases were at least partly contemporaneous, with many of the differences between phases resulting from differential development on the local level. Interaction among the phases can account for the presence of ceramic types of one phase at sites of another phase, rather than representing a gradual evolution of one phase into another. Studies of temporal development within phases have been hampered by collection techniques that mixed occupation levels and by a general lack of data for more than a few sites within any one phase. All Fort Ancient sites are not assumed to be functional and hierarchical equivalents, but, similar to Mississippian systems to the west and south, some Fort Ancient sites represent different organizational levels.

The culture identifiable as Fort Ancient appeared in the southern portion of Ohio by A.D. 950–1000. It was not uniform in its appearance; its defining ceramic characteristics first appeared in otherwise Woodland contexts (e.g., Voss, Sand Ridge) and were considered to constitute Fort Ancient at some point along a developmental continuum. Factors resulting in the emergence of this culture out of a Late Woodland base include an increasing reliance on maize agriculture and a corresponding increase in sedentism. This shift was largely stimulated by cultures to the west, which were also placing greater dependence on maize agriculture and were beginning to participate in a broad system termed "Mississippian." Expression of early Fort Ancient participation in this system is found in the emergence of larger and more stable villages that were often organized around a central plaza, and possibly in the appearance of a temple mound at the Baum site. The occurrence of more elaborate stylistic attributes in ceramics and more diversified bone and lithic technologies tend to separate Fort Ancient sites from the culturally ancestral Late Woodland cultures. Evidence for this Late Woodland base occurs in the continuation into early Fort Ancient of Late Woodland ceramic attributes, house forms, and burial practices.

Only sites of the Baum, Baldwin, and Brush Creek phases have so far been dated to the A.D. 950–1200 period, limiting evidence for this early period to a very restricted geographical sphere. Baum phase ceramics are "clearly derived from Late Woodland" (Griffin n.d.: 16). Vessel forms are almost entirely restricted to simple jar forms with nearly vertical rims and subconoidal to rounded bases. Shell tempering is infrequent, and vessel surfaces are predominantly cordmarked (Griffin n.d.). Traits that have been considered "Mississippian" in nature include curvilinear guilloche and line-filled triangle decorative motifs and lug and ovoid strap handles.

Baum phase houses also reflect Woodland-derived elements. Houses at Baum are circular, post structures with diameters of 3–4 m (Mills 1906:29–31). Possible Mississippian-like features include a plaza at Blain and the two-stage pyramidal mound at Baum. Two structures were found in the excavation of this mound, confirming its function. Both structures were circular, with diameters of 12 m, the upper structure having been placed immediately over the lower one (Thomas 1894:484–488).

The other phase that most closely relates to Baum and early Fort Ancient is the Anderson phase, which is centered in the Great and Little Miami Valleys to the west of Baum (Figure 6.1). The earliest dates currently known for this phase cluster at A.D. 1200 at the Incinerator site (Barber 1974:14). Additional earlier components do perhaps exist, based on typological grounds (South Fort). The Anderson Phase also demonstrates a Woodland base, as Griffin has noted:

> The pottery of this phase in basic vessel form, temper, added rim strips, and lack of variation in shape is clearly a regional variant of the late Woodland period and of contemporary ceramic practices from the Atlantic to the midwest [Griffin n.d.: 17].

Known house forms for the Anderson Phase include an almost square post-type structure at the Incinerator site on the Great Miami River (Barber 1974:11 12) and circular forms at the South Fort and Anderson Village sites in the Little Miami Valley (Moorehead 1908:86). It is possible that these variations represent development from local Woodland antecedents and further reflect the regional differentiation present in early Fort Ancient. Such variation would offer additional support to the theory of local development of these cultures out of Woodland antecedents, and would strengthen arguments that place these phases into a Woodland rather than a Mississippian system.

It is difficult to place the Feurt phase into a Fort Ancient framework at this time, owing both to a general lack of data and the number of unusual traits that occur. The Feurt site itself seems to have been occupied for a long period of time, and was subjected to greater external influences than were the Anderson or Baum phases. Griffin (n.d.) suggests that the early part of this phase was very similar to the Baum phase, yet he notes that the ceramic assemblage contains Baum and Madisonville phase ceramics as well as its own distinctive ceramic complex.

A number of late horizon markers occur in the form of Southern Cult motifs on pipes and other ornaments. A far greater number of stone pipes of all kinds occur at the Feurt site (Kuhn 1970:147). This suggests that the Feurt site, which is situated in the area where Ohio Pipestone outcrops, was perhaps a major producer and supplier of stone pipes on an extraregional scale. The specialized nature of this function may account for the occurrence of a greater variety of ceramic types, reflecting a greater degree of regularized contact with other cultural groups.

Sites of the Baum, Anderson, and Feurt phases are located along all of the major drainages north of the Ohio River and along the Ohio itself at least as far east as Portsmouth. However, no sites belonging to these phases have been found far into Kentucky or West Virginia.

The Madisonville phase appears in the southwestern portion of Ohio by about A.D. 1200–1250 (the Turpin site) and is at least partially contemporaneous with the Anderson, Feurt, and Baum phases. Through time, the Madisonville phase expanded eastward at the expense of the Feurt phase, appearing in eastern Kentucky shortly after A.D. 1200 and in West Virginia soon after that. Madisonville sites have been found far up the Big Sandy, Licking, and Kanawha Rivers in these areas, with their appearance probably being a result of invasion (Dunnell 1972). The rapidity of this movement over an area encompassing several thousand square miles supports this contention. Evidence supporting a physical intrusion of people into western Ohio is less clear, but the studies of Fort Ancient biological populations being conducted by Louise Robbins suggest there was an appearance of a Muskogid physical type in southern Ohio by this time (Robbins and Neumann 1972).

The Mississippian-like features of the Madisonville phase can be attributed to influence from the Middle Mississippi center of Angel. While a complete analysis of Angel site ceramics is not available, it does contain vessels similar to the globular jars, bowls, water bottles, and salt pans that have been found in the Fort Ancient area. Strap handles, often eared, occur on vessels that are generally plain jars (Black 1967). Thus, the Angel site could very easily have provided the influence that led both to the increasing use of strap handles, and to the increasing frequency of smoothed, plain globular jars in the Madisonville phase. It is probable that the temple mounds at the Marietta site date to this post-A.D. 1200 period, but the date of appearance of the Baum and Cedar Banks mounds has not been determined.

A complete developmental framework for Fort Ancient cannot be formulated at this time, because of the lack of an independently derived chronological framework for the Fort Ancient area. There are too few radiocarbon dates for any one area to allow more than a gross placement of components and phases, and such dates as exist have been accepted or rejected according to the investigators' preconceptions. Furthermore, the indeterminate nature of radiocarbon dating in general makes it of limited use in dealing with the narrow time span involved.

However, it is suggested that Fort Ancient development reflects the operation of at least two distinct cultural processes. The Baum, Baldwin, Brush Creek, Anderson, and Feurt phases develop as a result of incorporation of early Mississippian features into local adaptive systems. The subsequent Madisonville phase appeared as a result of population movement up the Ohio River from the west with expansion into areas of Kentucky and West Virginia that lack Fort Ancient antecedents. Its extension up the Miami and Scioto Rivers was met with resistance by earlier Fort Ancient cultures with consequent continuation of the more Woodland-like phases in these areas.

A more precise understanding of the nature of the relationship between Madisonville and the other Fort Ancient phases has yet to be obtained. Relevant to the present topic, however, are the implications regarding the existence of more than one settlement system within Fort Ancient. The possibility of the existence of more than one level of settlement organization remains to be examined. Settlement pattern models should be formulated and hypotheses tested for each of the phases rather than for the Fort Ancient culture as a whole.

Fort Ancient Subsistence

The complexity of the factors determining the nature of Fort Ancient settlement patterns preclude examination of these systems as simply a product of the interaction of environment and subsistence technology. Fort Ancient settlement patterns reflect the varying degree of importance these populations gave to different subsistence and sociopolitical functions, and also reflect a compromise among maximizing potential contacts with the environment, minimizing the amount of effort necessary to achieve such contact, and optimizing protective space and communication. Thus, Fort Ancient settlement patterns represent a resolution of economic and sociopolitical factors that vary in importance according to the local situation and temporal relationships.

Economic determinants of settlement patterning are largely dependent on subsistence strategy and degree of economic interdependence and specialization. Sociopolitical determinants are partly a function of the need to relate to groups outside the village, outside the immediate area, and outside the Fort Ancient region. These factors are interrelated, and assume greater or lesser importance depending on the level of complexity of the local system. Complexity in this situation is defined as the degree of interrelatedness of sites and the integration of settlements into a system that is of a higher organizational level than any of its constituents.

Economically, Fort Ancient settlements seem to be largely dependent on maize agriculture, with some growing of beans and squash. Maize has been recovered from the Blain, Baum, Gartner, Incinerator, Feurt, Baldwin, Madisonville, Trupin, and Campbell Island sites and generally appears to be of the 8 or 10 row variety. Several of the "refuse" or ash pits at the Baum and Gartner sites were found to contain large quantities of corn, indicating the use of some of these pits as storage facilities (Goslin 1952, Heilman personal communication, Mills 1904, Prufer and Shane 1970).

Hunting focused on deer, turkey, and elk, with secondary utilization of fish, mussels, and a number of other species of animals. In an examination of faunal remains from the Incinerator site, Barber (1974) found that mammals represented 90% of the total meat-yield estimate, and that deer constituted 61% of the total sample of skeletal elements.

An examination of the age distribution of deer at the Incinerator and Graham sites suggests that hunting techniques were nonselective, probably indicating the use of drives or surrounds; whereas at the Blain and Philo II sites, the age distributions for deer are bimodal, probably as a result of reliance on stalking in which the very young and very old were the most easily obtained (Barber 1974:19). Thus, hunting practices did not seem to be uniform for Fort Ancient, even within the same region (Graham and Blain are both Baum phase sites on the Scioto River).

Analysis of the faunal remains from the Incinerator and Buffalo sites also showed year-round hunting and butchering activities, leading Shane and Barber to postulate year-round occupation of villages by the entire population (Barber 1974, Shane and Barber 1975). However, although year-round occupation of villages is demonstrated, it also appears that hunting stations were also used. Hunting camps have been documented along the Ohio River east of Cincinnati, along the Scioto River south of the Hopeton Works, at Killen near the Wamsley site on the Ohio River at Brush Creek (Brose, personal communication), and near the Incinerator site on the Great Miami River (Heilman, personal communication). Extensive excavation of one such camp in the Fishtrap area of Kentucky (Pi-7) revealed no postmolds or pits and produced artifacts of a limited range of functional types, indicating emphasis on hunting and butchering activities (Dunnell 1972:52). The limited range of activities carried out at these sites suggest specialized short-term use as hunting camps rather than as agricultural hamlets.

Significant sociopolitical factors in settlement patterning are harder to document archeologically for Fort Ancient, and are better discussed in terms of intrasite patterning rather than in terms of regional patterns. Where examined, intrasite patterning is not uniform, but reflects differing building technologies, family structures, and undefined factors. Round houses of approximately 4 m diameter were found at the Baum and Gartner sites; oval houses were found at the Blain Village; and rectangular houses of greatly differing sizes occur at the Incinerator, Buffalo, Slone,

Hardin, and Turpin sites. At the Buffalo site, Hanson has documented three formally and functionally distinct types of houses, whereas at the Slone site, Dunnell, Hanson, and Hardesty (1971) noted specialized food preparing "porticos" attached to some of the houses (Hanson 1975:14–18, Dunnell *et al.* 1971:11). Some of this variation is probably due to persistence of local residence and building traditions, indicating differing responses to the general constraints placed by subsistence and social parameters.

The Fort Ancient System(s)

The role of subsistence has been treated as though uniform for Fort Ancient. However, it is probable that the nature, organization, and relative importance of subsistence practices as a settlement determinant differed through time and space. R. Berle Clay has proposed a developmental typology of Mississippian sites from western Kentucky based on a perceived shift in degree of importance from immediate subsistence concerns to regional coordination of activities. He used this typology, which incorporates political as well as subsistence factors, to examine Mississippian development as a system that becomes organizationally more complex through time, a situation also suggested in the early to late Fort Ancient transition in Ohio (Clay 1976).

Clay established site types of three different levels of complexity, two of which are relevant to a study of Fort Ancient settlement patterning. The simplest sites in his model tend to emphasize environmental over sociopolitical factors, and demonstrate a low level of cooperation with other sites. Such sites are basically self-sufficient, and tend to be scattered across the landscape in areas of maximum economic productivity. Villages are of minimal size for self-maintenance and represent optimum contact with exploitable resources with the least amount of effort. Such settlements demonstrate considerable change through time, reflecting greater adaptive response to changing local subsistence factors than do sites at higher levels. Short-term use of individual structures is evident at such sites, as well as a lower degree of site planning over time, as reflected by changes in the location of activity areas and structures, and rapid use–abandonment–reuse of the area (Clay 1976:139).

Such low-order settlements support few higher-order functions. Intra-site patterning reflects little status differentiation, and artifact assemblages tend to be more homogeneous, generally lacking trade items from other regions. Stylistic influences entering the regional system would appear later at these sites, possibly in modified form, or may not appear at all.

At a higher level of regional organization, sites begin to reflect greater degrees of interaction on the regional level. Such second-level sites in

Clay's classification tend to be more centrally located in areas of potential interregional communication, and demonstrate greater planning and labor investment than sites of the aforementioned type. Such regional centers sometimes lack defensive walls, but may contain mounds, plazas, and other earthworks. Less temporal change is apparent in centers, as site size remains stable and as structures are rebuilt in the same place. Greater regional cooperation is reflected in the occurrence of sites of varying size, complexity, and function (Clay 1976:140).

Differential site function is also reflected in restricted distributions of items of sociological importance as well as in the occurrence of high-status burials only at regional centers. Clay has noted that such centers contain relatively greater wealth than other sites in the system, which is reflected in an overall richness of burial accompaniments exclusive of high-status individuals (Clay 1976:149–150).

Regional centers performed a greater number and a greater variety of functions than did sites at a lower level—this made possible by support from a greater sustaining area. As the population of the supporting region increased, the center tended to take on more functions and increased in population. Thus, the highest-order settlement in a region, which performed the greatest number of functions, also tended to have the largest population and cover the largest area. The wider range of functions performed is reflected in the occurrence of burials of higher status than are found at sites of a lower level, and in greater differentiation of statuses in intrasite house patterning. Artifactual evidence for a wide sphere of interaction is found in the presence of types that were produced outside of the local system. The locations of regional center, therefore, tended to be dependent on social and political factors as well as local environmental factors, and settlements tended to be occupied for longer periods of time.

These two settlement types encompass the full range of variation in complexity and degree of village interdependence that existed in Fort Ancient. It has been suggested that not all Fort Ancient subcultures throughout the A.D. 950–1750 span had the same level of organization. Evidence, although fragmentary, suggests that significant site differentiation occurred only in the Madisonville phase (A.D. 1200–1750). The following discussion utilizes the site typology described by Clay to examine the nature of the differences between the Anderson and Madisonville phases.

THE ANDERSON PHASE SETTLEMENT SYSTEM

Anderson phase sites are located in the central portions of the Great and Little Miami River Valleys of southwestern Ohio (Figure 6.2). To the north and west are the Cole and Oliver Woodland complexes; to the south are Madisonville phase sites; and to the east are Baum phase sites. Preceding the Anderson phase in this area are Middle Woodland Hopewellian groups and an undefined Late Woodland phase, as represented at the Lichliter site. Radiocarbon dates for two Anderson phase sites, Incinerator and Erp, have produced dates of approximately A.D. 1200 and 1450, respectively, establishing the minimum temporal range for the phase.

Eleven sites have been assigned to this phase: four in the Great Miami Valley (Monteville, Steele Dam, Incinerator, and Erp), and seven along the Little Miami (Williams Village, Mangle Village, Corwin Village, Mill Grove, South Fort, Anderson Village, and Taylor Mound and Village). Five other Fort Ancient sites recorded for this region have not been assigned to a specific phase. Sites are located on bluffs as well as in valley bottoms, and lack strict association with specific soil and vegetational elements. The Erp, Monteville, South Fort, and Taylor sites are located on bluffs, whereas the remaining sites are located on the valley bottoms. The chronological placement of all sites except for Erp and Incinerator is not known at this time, although the occurrence of Madisonville ceramic types at the Anderson and Taylor sites (Griffin 1943:101, 108) suggests contemporaneity with Madisonville phase sites.

Of these 11 sites, only four have been investigated sufficiently to provide information relevant to settlement analysis. Of these, only the Incinerator site in the Great Miami Valley has been the locus of extensive excavation using modern techniques. Therefore, most data on internal settlement structuring is from one site. The Incinerator site possesses the attributes which delimit a low-level settlement. Evidence for interregional contact in the form of trade or regional high-status items is lacking. Status differentiation, although present, is of a low order, with no individuals possessing quantitatively or qualitatively superior grave offerings. Intra-site patterning lacks evidence for restricted access to site areas for burial or specialized activities limited to an elite. Organization of the village into distinct segments does suggest, however, that family structure, possibly clan-related, determined where individuals built houses, dug storage pits, and buried the dead (Heilman, personal communication).

The occupation of the Incinerator site was of relatively short duration, with little general midden accumulation and very little evidence of rebuilding of structures. The site is not large, with a diameter of approximately 130 m, and was probably occupied by as few as 100–200 individuals (Shane and Barber 1975:60). Internal functional areas were structured within a circular stockade. In the center of the site was a large post, surrounded by a plaza of approximately 25 m diameter. Encircling the plaza are burials which are in turn ringed by storage pits. Just within the stockade were square houses, each 9 m on a side (Barber 1974: 11, Heilman 1975, Griffin n.d.).

Data from other Anderson phase sites are insufficient to allow functional comparisons with the Incinerator site. However, data from the

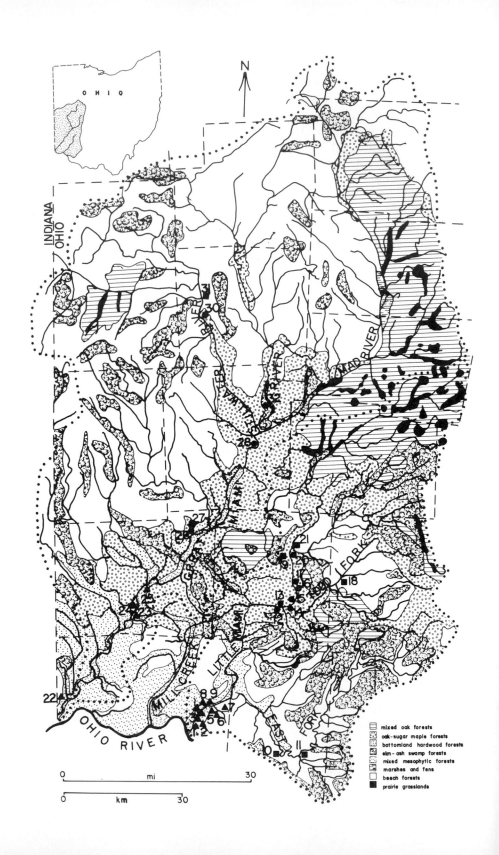

OHIO

INDIANA
OHIO

N

MAD RIVER

MIAMI RIVER

STILLWATER RIVER

GREAT MIAMI

LITTLE MIAMI

MILL CREEK

EAST FORK

SCIOTO FORK

OHIO RIVER

mixed oak forests
oak-sugar maple forests
bottomland hardwood forests
elm-ash swamp forests
mixed mesophytic forests
marshes and fens
beech forests
prairie grasslands

0   mi   30

0   km   30

Anderson Village, Taylor, and South Fort sites offer a basis for some comparisons. The Taylor site consists of a village, mound, and a gravel knoll used for burial interments. Based on surface indications, the size of the village appears comparable to the Incinerator site. Warren K. Moorehead, who excavated the Taylor site in 1891, reported finding grave goods associated with 18 of the 79 individuals buried in the mound, but found burial accompaniments with only 3 of 35 burials occurring in the village and gravel knoll. Of these grave goods, three classes of artifacts possibly indicate contracts outside the region. These include beads and pendants made of marine shell, a copper ear ornament, and a shell gorget engraved with an equal-arm cross. Contact with the Madisonville region is also indicated by the presence of a Madisonville plain jar (Griffin 1943:101–108).

Anderson Village, located about 10 km downstream of the Taylor site and about 1 km north of the Fort Ancient site, has been more extensively excavated than Taylor. Although the entire site covers a rectangular area of approximately 500 × 100 m, it actually consists of a number of discrete occupations, with evidence for fairly rapid use–abandonment–reuse of the area. A relatively low degree of site planning over time is reflected in the changes in location of activity areas and features. No structures have been excavated at either the Anderson or Taylor Village sites although Moorehead reported circular depressions of 10–12 m diameter for these sites and the South Fort of Fort Ancient (Moorehead 1908). Anderson Village did produce artifacts of extraregional origin in the form of marine shell beads, an equal-arm-cross shell gorget, and Madisonville pottery (Griffin 1943:92–101). However, the quantity and distribution of these items are not sufficient to suggest operation of Anderson as a regional center.

Therefore, the Anderson Village and Taylor sites, like the Incinerator site, can be characterized as being oriented toward maximizing the local subsistence base, rather than serving as regional sociopolitical centers. Available survey data for the Little Miami River suggests that Anderson phase sites were scattered (rather than concentrated) along the valley in an essentially random pattern.

FIGURE 6.2. Fort Ancient sites in the Great and Little Miami drainages of southwestern Ohio: 1. Ha-16; 2. Signal Hill; 3. Sand Ridge–Clough Creek; 4. Turpin; 5. Ha-201/210; 6. Ha-34; 7. Ha-138; 8. Hahn Field; 9. Madisonville; 10. Ct-109; 11. Rose; 12. Williams Village; 13. Mangle Village; 14. Corwin Village; 15. Mill Grove; 16. South Fort (Fort Ancient); 17. Anderson Village; 18. Pyle Camp; 19. Bone Stone Graves; 20. Taylor Mound and Village; 21. Burial and Pot; 22. State Line; 23. Hine Mound and Village; 24. Bu-38; 25. Campbell Island; 26. Monteville (Kemp); 27. Bu-10; 28. Incinerator; 29. My-37; 30. Erp (Pleasant Hill); 31. Maley Village; 32. Steele Dam. Key: ▲ = Madisonville phase sites; ● = Anderson phase sites; ■ = phase undetermined; . . . .: Watershed boundaries.

A MADISONVILLE PHASE SETTLEMENT SYSTEM

Madisonville phase sites are distributed over a considerably larger area than Anderson phase sites, extending from southeastern Indiana to eastern West Virginia, and from extreme southern Ohio to southern West Virginia. In fact, Madisonville extends into all of the area occupied by Fort Ancient cultures except for southern Ohio, where the Baum and Anderson phases continued, and the areas in Kentucky assigned to the Woodside phase (Dunnell 1972). Ecological parameters of site location are somewhat variable but there appears to be a strong tendency for sites to occupy valley terraces.

Dates for Madisonville phase sites range from A.D. 1275 at Turpin (Prufer and Shane 1970:237) to 1680 at Buffalo (Hanson 1975:101). Trade materials of European manufacture occur at the Madisonville, Buffalo, and Hardin sites, confirming the continuation of the Madisonville phase into the Protohistoric period (Griffin 1943:128; Hanson 1966, 1975:93).

Examination of the hypothesis that different functional orders of sites existed within the Madisonville phase utilized data from three sites: Marietta, Madisonville, and Campbell Island. The Marietta site is considered to be a primary center for the Madisonville phase, Madisonville is considered a secondary center, and Campbell Island is thought to represent the simplest site type—the agricultural village.

The Marietta site is located at the juncture of the Muskingum River with the Ohio (Figure 6.1), on a high sandy plain 15–20 m above the bottomlands of the Muskingum. It is composed of both Hopewell and Fort Ancient components of unknown extent. The Marietta Works, presumably build by Hopewell populations, consisted of two squares, one 16 ha in area and the other of 8 ha. Within the larger square were four truncated mounds, three with ramps. As described by Squier and Davis (1848:74), the largest mound was 62 × 44 m and 3 m high, and had four ramps, one to a side. The second largest mound was 50 × 40 m and 2.6 m high, and had three ramps, whereas the third mound was 40 × 16 m and 2 m high. The fourth mound was less distinct and was omitted by some observers (e.g., Sargent 1853). Evidence for a Fort Ancient origin of these mounds consists primarily of artifact collections containing shell-tempered sherds that show general Middle Mississippi influence. Mayer-Oakes (1955b) has stated,

> The Fort Ancient sherds in this collection from Marietta are perhaps the most Mississippi-like of any Fort Ancient materials; they certainly present features rare in Fort Ancient but more common in Middle Mississippi (loop handles, effigy water bottle, pottery trowel) [p. 29].

The temple mounds at the Marietta site represent a quantitatively greater degree of labor investment and planning than exists at any other

Fort Ancient site. The occurrence of more Middle Mississippi- like artifacts suggests more intensive interaction with these external cultures
than demonstrated at other sites. Owing to lack of excavation data from
the Marietta site, no other evidence can be evaluated to substantiate its
position as the primary center of the Madisonville phase. However, collections from sites in the vicinity of the Marietta site indicate stronger
relationships of this area to Middle Mississippi populations than indicated at Fort Ancient sites to the west (Mayor-Oakes 1955a:165–173).

Second-level centers, such as the Madisonville site, can be distinguished from the primary center at Marietta and from subsistence-
oriented agricultural villages. The Madisonville site is situated on the
second terrace of the Little Miami River just north of its juncture with the
Ohio River. The exact extent of the Fort Ancient component of the site is
unknown because it merges with Hopewellian earthworks and mounds
also present on this terrace. This site was intensively occupied, as evidenced from the number of refuse pits (exceeding 1200) and burials (1500)
reported to have come from this area (Griffin 1943:121). It was occupied for
an unknown length of time, with evidence for cross-cutting of pits and
burials suggesting a relatively long duration.

Besides evidence for a large population occupying the site for a relatively long temporal span, Madisonville is set apart by a series of artifactual traits not present at most Madisonville phase sites. Some of the
ceramic attributes, as noted by Griffin (1943:193), are characteristic only of
the Madisonville site. It also has an abnormally high percentage of burials
(28%) accompanied by grave goods in the form of whole pots (Hooton and
Willoughby 1920:17). Burials of special interest because they contained
different or greater quantities of grave goods were mentioned in Hooton
and Willoughby's (1920:19) report. On such burial contained several copper plates 1.5 × 2 in. which had been clasped around deer hide, a number
of shell beads made from marine shells, and a few copper beads. Another
burial contained three copper snake effigies, one on each side of the skull
and one beneath the shoulder blade. Not all data on burial goods are given
in Hooton's report, and no analysis has yet been made of the correlation of
burial goods to site area or to the sex and age of the individual burials.

Data on intrasite patterning of the Madisonville site are generally
lacking. The overall site map indicates that functions of particular areas
shifted through time. Possible house areas, consisting of eight circular
depressions 12–20 m in diameter, were located on the northeastern portion of the plateau, but Griffin feels that the distance of these circles from
the refuse and burial area casts doubt on their association with the
Madisonville phase occupation (Griffin 1943:120, Hooton and Willoughby
1920:44). The most effective way to demonstrate that Madisonville
functioned as a regional center is by comparing it to a different level site in
the same region. However, data on such sites are comparatively poor.

The Campbell Island site, located on the Great Miami River (Figure 6.2), represents a low-order site in this area. This site was apparently of rather limited extent; the excavations conducted by H. C. Shetrone in 1920 produced 21 burials and 35 storage pits in what were felt to be the most productive areas of the site. Although no data were given as to total extent or percentage of the site excavated, the materials recovered were much less dense than the remains at the Madisonville site. Two whole vessels were found as burials accompaniments, but no high-status items were recovered. Evidence of site patterning was not noted, making evaluation of the degree of site structuring impossible. However, Shetrone's general impression of the site was that Campbell Island represented an outpost of the Madisonville phase (Shetrone 1926).

There are a number of other Madisonville phase sites in southwestern Ohio (Figure 6.2), including additional sites which possess the attributes of secondary centers (State Line, Turpin). However, in most cases, published information is too limited to allow placement of sites into an areal system. A further constraint in formulating a regional model lies in the lack of adequate chronological control of sites and data.

Conclusions

The archeological construct termed "Fort Ancient" subsumes a number of different tribal or ethnic units possessing distinctive economic and sociopolitical systems that are reflected in distinctive settlement attributes and organizations. In this chapter, a comparison has been made of the Anderson and Madisonville phases, which represent two separate settlement systems. The patterns described for the Madisonville phase involves regional structuring of sites of different sociopolitical levels, whereas the Anderson phase patterns lack evidence to support functionally distinct sites. These settlement types are at least partially contemporaneous, carrying the implication that it is not possible to formulate a single settlement–subsistence model for all of Fort Ancient.

The suggestion is made that these two settlement systems may derive in part from the operation of very different developmental processes, and indicates that differences may exist in the relationships of these phases to other Mississippian groups. The Anderson, Baum, Baldwin, Brush Creek, and Feurt phases represent the adoption of maize–beans–squash agriculture by Late Woodland peoples accompanied by greater participation in the emerging Mississippian system. The Madisonville phase however, is proposed as being the result of a more direct impact from Middle Mississippi cultures to the west, and could represent a population movement into the Ohio region.

In conclusion, a number of hypotheses have been made regarding the nature of the Fort Ancient system(s)—their development and organization. It should now be possible to test these hypotheses for a particular region and to formulate more specific models of Fort Ancient settlement.

Acknowledgments

Thanks are due to the Department of Anthropology, Harvard University, and to the Peabody Museum for financial support to search for notes and collections regarding Fort Ancient, and to Martha P. Otto of the Ohio Historical Society and James Heilman of the Dayton Museum of Natural History for allowing me access to data and offering personal assistance in locating data. Special thanks are also due to Jeffrey P. Brain, David S. Brose, Michael M. Moseley, and Russell J. Barber for their critical evaluation of earlier drafts of this chapter.

References

Barber, Michael B.
  1974   Fort Ancient settlement patterns. M.A. thesis, Department of Anthropology, Kent State University, Kent, Ohio.
Binford, Lewis R.
  1964   A consideration of archaeological research design. *American Antiquity* **29**:425–441.
Black, Glen A.
  1967   *Angel Site: An archaeological, historical, and ethnological study.* Indianapolis: Indiana Historical Society.
Braun, E. Lucy
  1950   *Deciduous forests of eastern North America.* New York: Hafner.
Clay, R. Berle
  1976   Tactics, strategy, and operations: The Mississippian system responds to its environment. *Mid-Continental Journal of Archaeology* **1**:137–162.
Dunnell, Robert C.
  1972   The Prehistory of Fishtrap, Kentucky. *Yale University Publications in Anthropology* **75**.
Dunnell, Robert, Lee Hanson, and D. Hardesty
  1971   The Woodside component of the Slone Site, Pike County, Kentucky. *Southeastern Archaeological Conference, Bulletin* **14**.
Fenneman, N.M.
  1916   Geology of Cincinnati and vicinity. *Ohio Geological Survey*, 4th Series, Bulletin 19.
Goslin, Robert M.
  1952   Cultivated and wild plant food from aboriginal sites in Ohio. *Ohio Archaeologist* **2**(2):9–29.
Griffin, James B.
  1937   The chronological position and ethnological relationships of the Fort Ancient Aspect. *American Antiquity* **4**:273–277.
  1943   *The Fort Ancient Aspect.* Ann Arbor: University of Michigan Press.
  n.d.   Prehistory of the Ohio Valley, manuscript. In *Handbook of North American Indians*, edited by W. Sturtevant. Washington, D.C: Smithsonian Institution.

Hanson, Lee H.
1966   The Hardin Village site. *University of Kentucky Studies in Anthropology*, Number 4. Lexington, Kentucky: University of Kentucky Press.
1975   The Buffalo site—a late 17th century Indian village site (46 Pu 31) in Putnam County, West Virginia. *West Virginia Geological and Economic Survey, Report of Archaeological Investigations*, 5, Morgantown.
Heilman, James
1975   The Incinerator site: An Anderson Focus Fort Ancient Village in Montgomery County, Ohio. Paper presented at the Annual Meeting of the Society for American Archaeology, Dallas, Texas.
Hole, Frank and Robert F. Heizer
1973   *An introduction to prehistoric archeology*, third edition. New York: Holt, Rinehart, and Winston.
Hooton, Ernest and Charles Willoughby
1920   *Indian village site and cemetery near Madisonville, Ohio*. Peabody Museum of American Archaeology and Ethnology Paper VIII, 1.
Kuhn, D.W.
1970   The Feurt Village site, 1969. *Ohio Archaeologist* 20(1):147–149.
Mayer-Oakes, William J.
1955a   Prehistory of the upper Ohio Valley. *Annuals of Carnegie Museum, Anthropological Series* 2 Pittsburg.
1955b   Notes on selected potsherds from the Sayre collection, Marietta, Ohio. *West Virginia Archaeologist* 7:25–30.
McFarlan, A.C.
1943   *Geology of Kentucky*. Lexington: University of Kentucky Press.
McKern, W.C.
1933   Local types and the regional distribution of pottery-bearing cultures. *Transactions of the Illinois State Academy of Science* 25(4):84–87.
1939   The midwestern taxonomic method as an aid to archaeological cultural study. *American Antiquity* 4:301–313.
Mills, William C.
1904   Exploration of the Gartner Mound and Village site. *Ohio Archaeological and Historical Quarterly* 13:129–189.
1906   Explorations of the Baum Prehistoric Village site. *Ohio Archaeological and Historical Quarterly* 15:45–141.
Moorehead, Warren K.
1908   Fort Ancient, the great prehistoric earthwork of Warren county, Ohio. *Phillips Academy, Department of Anthropology, Bulletin* IV(2).
Murphy, James L.
1975   *An archaeological history of the Hocking valley*. Athens: Ohio University Press.
Prufer, Olaf and Orrin C. Shane III
1970   *Blain Village and the Fort Ancient Tradition in Ohio*. Kent, Ohio: Kent State University Press.
Robbins, Louise M. and George K. Neumann
1972   The prehistoric people of the Fort Ancient culture of the central Ohio Valley. *Anthropological Papers, Museum of Anthropology, University of Michigan* 48. Ann Arbor.
Sargent, W.
1853   Plan of an ancient fortification at Marietta, Ohio. *Memoirs of the American Academy of Arts and Sciences* n.s. 5(1):25–29.
Shane, Orrin C. III and Michael Barber
1975   Analysis of the vertebrate fauna from the Incinerator site and its implications for

Fort Ancient settlement patterning. Paper presented at the Annual Meeting of the Society for American Archaeology, Dallas, Texas.

Shetrone, Henry C.
1920   The culture problem in Ohio archaeology. *American Antiquity* **22**:144–172.
1926   The Campbell Island Village site and the Hine Mound and Village site. In *Certain Mound and Village Sites in Ohio*, 4(1), edited by William C. Mills. F. J. Heer Printing Co.: Columbus.

Squier, E.G. and E.H. Davis
1848   Ancient monuments of the Mississippi Valley. *Smithsonian Contributions to Knowledge* **1**.

Thomas, Cyrus
1894   Report on the mound explorations of the Bureau of Ethnology. Twelfth Annual Report of the Bureau of American Ethnology.

Thornbury, William D.
1965   *Regional geomorphology of the United States.* New York: Wiley.

7

Caddoan
Settlement Patterns in
the Arkansas River
Drainage

JAMES A. BROWN
ROBERT E. BELL
DON G. WYCKOFF

A research problem that has gained little attention in Mississippian settlement pattern analysis involves the degree to which such patterns are influenced by, and therefore reflect, different strategies of cultural adaptation. Much of the emphasis to date has been on the pan regional or common features of specific settlement patterns and cultural adaptations (e.g., Clay 1976, Larson 1970). From this viewpoint, the uniformity of such Mississippian cultural adaptations emerges as a dominant property in which variations are relatively unimportant (cf. Griffin 1967). But this concept of uniformity, if pursued too far, leads to neglect of ecological and settlement variability and to the disregard of important insights into the conditions affecting Mississippian settlement patterns.

It is important, therefore, to look for, and to accept, observed differences in settlement patterning as being potentially related to variation in environment and subsistence strategies. With this viewpoint, correlations between variation in settlement patterns and environmental conditions can be investigated. The adoption of this approach follows from the widely recognized notion that settlement patterns are controlled by the distribution of critical resources, density of population, exploitative technology, intergroup economic relations, and social organization (Smith 1972). Hence it becomes important to organize these components within the framework of a general model. Fortunately, analysis at the large-scale regional level has largely been focused on relevant critical resources, since

169

their distribution dominates settlement patterns (cf. Flannery 1976). Given these assumptions, the investigation of settlement patterns in different regions during the Mississippian period should be focused on those regionally specific ecological differences that determine variation in these patterns.

The purpose of this chapter is to describe settlement patterns within a Caddoan subregion according to categories recognized as important to cross-cultural description of the structure and organization of prehistoric cultural systems. A preliminary model of this subregion will be constructed from a synthesis of the available data on Caddoan settlement patterns in the Arkansas River Basin.

Four basic questions concerning settlement patterning in this subregion will be considered:

1. Does a premier center exist?
2. Is there a hierarchy of sites of a similar functional type?
3. What are the critical resources having the greatest impact on the distribution and size of sites of a similar functional type?
4. What are the factors apparently responsible for variation in settlement size and distribution?

The Arkansas Valley Caddoan

The northern portion of the Caddoan area is occupied by a distinct subregional tradition concentrated mainly along the Arkansas River and its tributaries. This tradition is known as the Arkansas Valley Caddoan to distinguish it from historically related traditions in the Red River Valley (Bell 1972:259–263, Prewitt 1974) and is distributed within the belt of dry forest and prairie groves bordering the Eastern Woodlands.

The Arkansas Valley Caddoan represents the westernmost population of advanced Mississippian cultural systems. Even though the drainage patterns favor cultural interaction to the east and west, the Arkansas Valley tradition aligns with Caddoan systems to the south to form a cultural zone west of the Mississippi lowlands. Further west lie less complex Plains agricultural groups (Bell 1973, Lintz 1974). Mississippi traditions lie downstream to the east and to the northeast beyond the Ozarks (Griffin 1967).

The Study Area

The study area is confined to eastern Oklahoma, north of the Kiamichi range of the Ouachita Mountains and roughly east of 95°40' longitude, within the limits of the physiographic provinces of the Ozark Highlands, Ouachita Mountains, and intervening Arkoma Basin. Other portions of this dry forest and prairie groves belt in northwestern Arkansas (Scholtz 1969) and southwestern Missouri (Henning 1959, McMillan 1968) were likewise occupied by this tradition. However, Caddoan manifestations in these states are beyond the scope of this chapter.

The study area is drained entirely by the Arkansas River. Originating far into the plains, it passes through the interhighland corridor formed by the Arkoma Basin, and then flows eastward to the Mississippi lowlands.

History of Investigations

The patterns of prehistoric occupation of the Arkansas Basin have slowly emerged from surface survey and site excavation over the past 30 years. At the beginning of systematic archeology in the 1930s, research focused on mounds, since they were the most conspicuous aboriginal feature on the landscape. Mounds continued to dominate excavation priorities for a few years after the discovery of the spectacular contents of the Craig mound at the Spiro site. This mound revealed an unusually well-preserved and detailed record of prehistoric material culture. Most of the Caddoan mounds in the Arkansas Basin were explored early during the period of W.P.A.-sponsored excavations, and, as a result, our knowledge of these features is limited by the unsophisticated techniques used in excavation. Fortunately, the relatively complete Harlan site remained unexcavated until later, when techniques had improved. Hence, this site forms the basis of our detailed understanding of mound construction and mound function in the Arkansas Basin (Bell 1972).

The first review of settlement patterns was Orr's (1946) study of the Spiro vicinity. Since then, several comprehensive reviews have appeared (Bell and Baerreis 1951, Prewitt 1974, Wyckoff 1970, 1974).

Settlement Pattern Controls

In a review of settlement pattern research, Parsons (1972:145) isolated four data controls critical for successful settlement pattern study: (*a*) a control over site sample, (*b*) a refined chronology, (*c*) a paleoenvironmental reconstruction, and (*d*) a functional interpretation of structures, activities, and sites. Although all of these controls remain relatively undeveloped in Caddoan-area archeology, a sufficient beginning has been made to reveal the main outlines of settlement patterning in the Arkansas Basin.

CULTURAL CHRONOLOGY

At the beginning of archeological exploration in the Arkansas Basin, it was thought that only a single sedentary culture of shallow time-depth was present prehistorically. Since the Spiro site was closely identified with this culture, it came to be called the Spiro focus (Clements 1945, Griffin 1946:85). The notion that a single culture was involved has gradually given way to the view that a sequence of distinct cultural phases existed over a span of 600 years. Further progress in our regional cultural systematics has come with the realization that the character of the material record of the major civic–ceremonial centers differs from that of the small domestic sites, especially with regard to the presence of ritual objects and items of social display (Wyckoff 1970:143).

The first step toward a cultural sequence in the Arkansas drainage was taken by Orr (1946, 1952), who defined a Spiro focus with three "periods," and a later Fort Coffee focus. The two foci became the foundation upon which subsequent classifications were based (Bell and Baerreis 1951, Wyckoff 1970). Through the apparatus of the Midwestern Taxonomic System, these two foci became the regional expression of the Gibson and Fulton aspects, which, for two decades, were the common instrument of culture–historical integration throughout the entire Caddoan area (Krieger 1946).

In the meantime, the introduction of radiocarbon dating led to the recognition of considerable time depth in the Caddoan area, and to the subsequent development of a five-period sequence of the entire area (Davis 1970). In the Arkansas River Valley subregion of the Caddoan area, research has shown that three phases can be identified with certainty, although future work will probably introduce refinements and additions. For the present, Arkansas Basin Caddoan settlement types will be examined within the framework of a threefold division into the Harlan, Spiro, and Fort Coffee phases. Summaries of the radiocarbon dates are contained in Brown (1967), Wyckoff (1970, 1974), and Bell (1972:253–258). This chronology has been confirmed through sequence ordering of selected artifact types of sites and separate components (Brown 1976:60, Cartledge 1970).

The *Harlan phase* dates between around A.D. 1000 and A.D. 1200–1250 and is largely equivalent to what used to be called the Gibson aspect. It corresponds with the Caddo I period and part of the Caddo II period (Davis 1970). Marker artifact types are Crockett Curvilinear Incised and Spiro Engraved pottery. Williams Plain domestic ware predominates, and shell-tempered Woodward Plain is a minority type (Bell 1972, Brown 1971b). Structures have four interior support posts. The Harlan site is the type component of this phase. Others are Brackett (Bareis 1955), Eufaula

(Orr 1941, 1942), the Spiro village (Brown 1967, 1971b, 1976) and Plantation sites (Briscoe 1976).

The *Spiro phase* dates between ca. A.D. 1200–1250 and A.D. 1350–1400 and includes components identified with either the Gibson or Fulton Aspect. It corresponds with Caddo III and possibly with part of Caddo II. Marker ceramic types are Woodward Applique, carinated bowls of Sanders and Poteau wares, and more specifically Sanders Engraved and Poteau Engraved types (Brown 1971b). Domestic cooking utensils are entirely shell-tempered. The greatest elaboration and diversity in ceramics occurred during this phase, the artistic complexity of which is attested to by the famous artifact trove of the Southern Cult deposited in the Great Mortuary at Spiro (Brown 1975, 1976). The specialized ritual and mortuary features of this phase are well represented at Spiro (Brown 1966, 1971a, 1975) and Norman sites (Finkelstein 1940). Residential occupations are found at Cat Smith (Wyckoff and Barr 1967), Horton (Wyckoff 1970), Sheffield (Prewitt and Wood 1969), and Littlefield I (Orr 1946). Structures have two interior support posts.

The *Fort Coffee phase* postdates ca. A.D. 1400 and includes components typically identified with the Fulton aspect. It is equivalent to Caddo IV and possibly Caddo V. Marker ceramic types are Avery Engraved, Braden Punctated, and Nash Neck Banded (Rohrbaugh 1974). This phase is represented by the Harvey (Burton 1971), Moore East (Orr 1946), Tyler (Burton, Bastian, and Prewitt 1969), Robinson–Solesbee (Bell *et al.*, 1969), and Tyler–Rose sites (Cartledge 1970).

PALEOENVIRONMENT

The environment of past centuries has not been the subject of specific study. But, when data on this aspect of prehistory become available, our understanding of the impact of Plains climate on prehistoric adaptations will become clearer. In the meantime, the climatic models of Baerreis, Bryson and others afford some insight into paleoenvironment from the baseline of historic climate and vegetation patterns.

Climate

The study area enjoys a warm, humid continental climate with relatively short mild winters and an ample growing season of at least 200 frost-free days. The mean annual precipitation ranges between 100 and 115 cm, with most rainfall occurring in May and June. Summer rainfall occurs in the form of short thunderstorms (Wahlgren 1941).

In warmth and temperateness, the study area compares well with those regions to the east that are dominated by sedentary agricultural adaptations. Both regions share a high potential for agriculture, although with respect to available moisture for plant growth the study area is a marginally humid climate. The amount of available moisture as measured by the precipitation–effectiveness index (Gray and Galloway 1959: Figure 4) ranges from 64 to 79. These isohytes currently separate the study area from both the Southern Plains on the one side and the Mississippi lowlands on the other (Thornthwaite 1948).

Vegetation

The woodlands of eastern Oklahoma reflect the transitional nature of the vegetation in the pattern of relative proportions of prairie–forest vegetation. The upland vegetation is dominated by a dry Oak–Hickory forest, which contains scattered patches of prairie. Intruding into this mosaic of forest–prairie is a floodplain vegetation distributed along the major water courses (Figure 7.1). In early historic times (ca. 1800), pockets of bottomland prairie occurred throughout the course of the Arkansas River, starting near the eastern edge of the study area. But the proportion of prairie progressively increased through time until prairie was nearly continuous and the forest was restricted to the river's edge starting at the Forks of the Arkansas (Gregg 1954, Thwaites 1905). Further evidence of environmental transition is manifest in the upstream attenuation of Southeastern floodplain vegetation. This vegetation link with the Southeast was weakly present below Webber's Falls in the study area, where oxbow lake communities and stands of pecan and persimmon existed. Canebreaks were likewise common, occurring frequently upstream as far west as the Forks of the Arkansas.

Climate Change

In the past, the boundaries of the eastern humid region were undoubtedly altered by the prevailing climatic regime. Since the summertime effective moisture is known to be governed by the strength of the westerlies, it follows that any long-term climatic cycle with stronger westerlies than at present will change the P/E index in eastern Oklahoma and consequently alter the security with which agriculture can be relied upon

---

FIGURE 7.1. *Map of the study area in eastern Oklahoma showing principal vegetation units and geographic places mentioned in the text. Upland vegetation based on Fitch (1900), bottomland after Küchler (1964). Triangles indicate civic-ceremonial centers in Table 3. Site Key: (1) Reed, (2) Lillie Creek, (3) Norman, (4) Harlan, (5) Brackett, (6) Maconnally, (7) Hughes, (8) Cat Smith, (9) Parris, (10) Harvey, (11) Eufaula, (12) Skidgel, (13) Spiro, (14) Littlefield I, (15) Cavanaugh, (16), Lf-6, (17) Lf-9. The latter two are possible centers.*

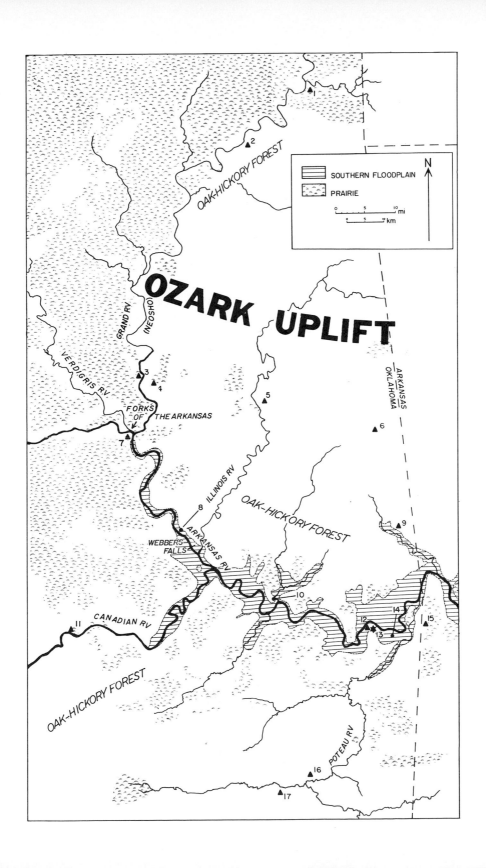

SOUTHERN FLOODPLAIN

PRAIRIE

N

0   5   10 mi

0   5   10 km

OZARK UPLIFT

OAK-HICKORY FOREST

GRAND RV. (NEOSHO)

VERDIGRIS RV.

ARKANSAS
OKLAHOMA

FORKS OF THE ARKANSAS

ILLINOIS RV.

OAK-HICKORY FOREST

WEBBERS FALLS

ARKANSAS RV.

CANADIAN RV.

OAK-HICKORY FOREST

POTEAU RV.

and probably even the food potential of the environment (Bryson, Baer-reis, and Wendland 1970). Hence, long-term climatic cycles should have exerted strong influences on the character and complexity of resident settlement patterns and sociopolitical systems through changes in subsistence security in this marginal belt of the humid East.

Research has shown that a major climatic change took place around A.D. 1200, leading to worsening rainfall patterns throughout the Plains except in the latitude of Oklahoma, where rainfall patterns benefited agriculture (Bryson *et al.* 1970). At this time, relatively drastic dislocations of cultural systems occurred in Texas (Story and Valastro 1977) and in the Central Plains (Wedel 1970). Hence, one would logically conclude that grassland–savanna-oriented cultures would be affected, but in the direction of more stable adaptations (Baerreis and Bryson 1965, Wyckoff 1970). If this were the case, then the Arkansas Valley Caddoan should have been affected through increased cultural stability and perhaps greater population in its western hinterland. Subsistence security in the Arkansas River Valley may have been enhanced as well in the A.D. 1200–1350 period. The end of the climatic cycle occurred ca. A.D. 1400.

SAMPLING CONTROLS

On the matter of sampling control, site location inventories are biased toward sites located within the floodpools of reservoirs. Outside these floodpools, site location data are spotty and basically limited to prominent sites with earthworks and to relatively rich sites within the districts to which the W.P.A. excavation crews were confined. Only three counties (Cherokee, Delaware, and LeFlore) had major W.P.A. programs. In addition, site survey data for areas outside the river basins are available along the Interstate Highway corridors. Table 7.1 shows the size of the research districts.

Although the use of sampling designs is necessary to recover many important details of settlement patterning, the valuable information that has accrued from surveys lacking explicit sampling design allows us to examine other aspects of settlement patterning.

SITE CLASSIFICATION

Basic to the investigation at hand is some control over the functional role of sites. A functional classification in this region requires that sites be distinguished in two respects. First, multipurpose and multiseasonal (base) camps and villages must be distinguished from special-purpose and seasonal camps that are part of a seasonal settlement round. Here, the span of occupation within a yearly cycle and the number of activities carried out

TABLE 7.1
Reservoirs Surveyed in Eastern Oklahoma

Reservoir	Drainage	Area (km²)
Lake O' the Cherokees	Grand (Neosho) River	188
Lake Hudson	Grand (Neosho) River	25
Fort Gibson	Grand (Neosho) River	77
Three Forks Area	Verdigris and Arkansas Rivers	54
Bayou Manard	Bayou Manard Creek	49
Webbers Falls	Arkansas River	44
Eufaula Lake	Canadian River	415
Rober S. Kerr	Arkansas River	170
Lock 14	Arkansas River	61
Tenkiller	Illinois River	51
Wister	Fourche Maline Creek	16

at a site are important. Second, sites should be distinguished according to relative complexity in settlement organization. Since both these provisions can be satisfied with the available data (even at the gross level), we propose to construct a provisional model of Caddoan settlement types.

Several crude criteria were used to make the preceding distinctions. A diverse material inventory representative of a broad spectrum of activities was used to indicate a multipurpose camp as opposed to a specialized camp (cf. Cook 1976). An occupation of more than a single season was indicated by sites evidencing permanent structures—albeit, leaving unanswered the question of actual duration of occupation within a yearly cycle. For our purpose, permanent structures had an additional utility of implying continuity of residence over several years. Determining the latter is important because the analysis of relative settlement organizational complexity assumes permanent settlement. Whereas the seasonally occupied and specialized, single-purpose sites are characterized by their low labor-investment character, the opposite is true of permanent sites, whether they are identified by permanent structures of substantial architecture or by mound-building activities. With these criteria in hand, three major site classes were recognized: extractive activity sites, permanent habitation sites, and specialized civic–ceremonial centers.

Basic Site Types

EXTRACTIVE ACTIVITY SITES

These sites lack evidence of permanent, roofed structures, and exhibit evidence of seasonal or transient use characterized by a limited set of artifacts. Typical examples are quarries, field-butchering and hunting camps, and camps utilizing the ready-made protection of rock shelters (Ray 1965, Schneider 1967). To judge from the nearby Ozark bluff shelters in Arkansas, rock shelters were used as food processing and storage stations, around which food-procurement activities were centered. Other specialized uses were made of shelters, without associated permanent constructions: For example, unusual engraved pottery was found in Owl Cave (Lawton 1964).

PERMANENT HABITATION SITES

Sites evidencing multiseasonal occupation over a number of years comprise this category. The principal evidence of permanent or sedentary seasonal use of sites are the remains of permanent roofed structures and associated features, and refuse that would be commonly associated with the principal daily activities of its residents. Hence, houses, features, and burials are found even at the smallest habitations. All examples contain the tools associated with hunting and agriculture. However, earthworks are not associated with sites of this class.

The area of scatter on moundless sites ranges up to 25 ha (Table 7.2, Figure 7.2). However, a consideration of the effects of multiple componency and other facts leads to the conclusion that the largest confirmed site of this group is 8–10 ha in size, represented with certainty only by the Spiro

TABLE 7.2
Rank Order of the 15 Largest Arkansas Basin Caddoan Sites by Size

Site number	Site name	Size in hectares	Mound "enclosure"
Lf-46	Spiro[a]	32.0	20 ha
My-6	—	19.4[b]	
Mi-45	Eufaula[a]?	20.0–16.0	?
Ck-30	—	16.0	
Wg-3	—	13.5[b]	
Sq-5	Old Courthouse	12.8	
Wg-2	Norman[a]	11.9[b]	
Ms-4	Hughes[a]	11.5[b]	1.5 ha
Lf-42	G. Bowman	9.6	
Mi-27	—	9.2	
Wg-4	—	8.1[b]	
Sq-11	Horton	8.0	
Lf-137	Kaiser-Tucker	8.0	
Ck-6	Harlan[a]	7.1[b]	7.1 ha
Ck-43	Brackett[a]	6.4[b]	2.1 ha

[a] Major civic–ceremonial centers.
[b] Size is calculated for an ellipse based on length and width measurements.

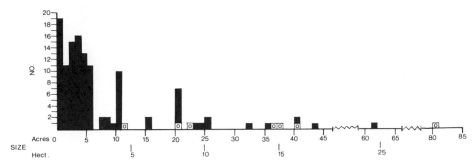

FIGURE 7.2. *Size distribution of Caddoan sites. Circled units represent civic–ceremonial centers.*

village (10 ha; see Figure 7.8). The next smaller size cluster of 14 sites are all around 4 ha in size. One, Littlefield I, was investigated sufficiently to indicate the presence of a Spiro phase component of at least 15 regularly arranged two-post structures oriented on the cardinal directions (Figure 7.4; Orr 1939, 1946). It appears to be a single-component site. Other large sites of this class are Cookson (Israel 1969, Lehmer 1952) and Horton (Wyckoff 1970). The next smaller size-cluster is around 2 ha (Figures 7.3, 7.5). Below this size cluster are a large number of hamlets and farmsteads

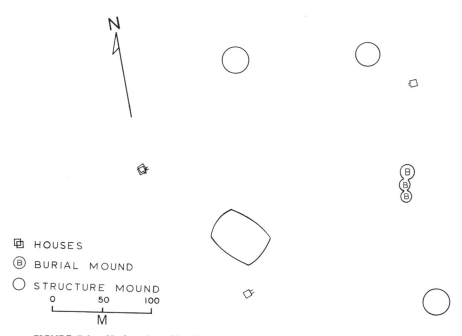

FIGURE 7.3. *Harlan sites, Cherokee county. Harlan phase civic–ceremonial center.*

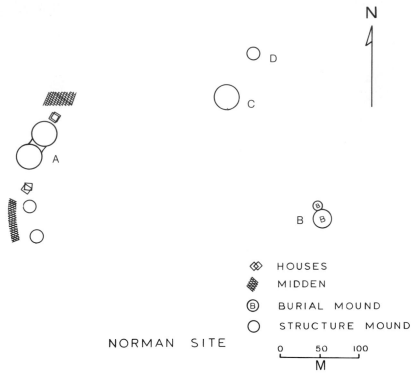

NORMAN SITE

⬦⬦ HOUSES

▨ MIDDEN

Ⓑ BURIAL MOUND

◯ STRUCTURE MOUND

0   50   100

M

FIGURE 7.4. *Norman site, Wagoner county. Spiro phase civic–ceremonial center.*

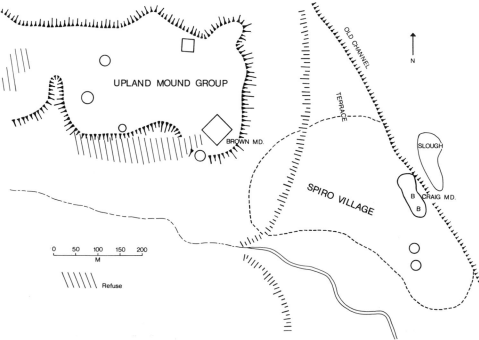

OLD CHANNEL

UPLAND MOUND GROUP

TERRACE

SLOUGH

BROWN MD.

SPIRO VILLAGE

B CRAIG MD.

B

0   50   100 150 200

M

//// Refuse

FIGURE 7.5. *Spiro site, LeFlore county. Premier civic–ceremonial center of the Harlan and Spiro phases.*

belonging to each of the cultural phases (Figure 7.2). Before discussing in detail the nature of the third site class (specialized civic–ceremonial centers) we will consider those variables influencing the location of habitation sites.

Critical Resources

AGRICULTURAL SOILS

The prime resource of mixed agriculture and hunting economies was agricultural land (Prewitt 1974, Wyckoff 1970) devoted mainly to the cultivation of corn. This food staple is amply documented from sites of all time periods (namely, Brackett, Hughes, Norman, Jones, Horton and Geren; Cutler and Blake 1973). Squash and beans were also grown, although neither is common archeologically (Cutler and Blake 1973). Additional cultivated and wild plants were probably utilized, since a long list of species is available from sites of the "Ozark Bluff Shelter" complex (Gilmore 1931). Radiocarbon dates and pottery indicate that these sites were occupied during the Mississippian period by the Arkansas Basin Caddoan (Asch and Asch 1977).

For populations with a hoe technology the most productive soils for corn cultivation would have been the floodplains of the Arkansas River and its tributaries (cf. Woodall 1969). The upland soils are either thin and acidic alfisols of low potential or tough-sodded prairie soils generally shunned under unintensive cultivation regimes (Gray and Galloway 1959, Gray and Roozitalab 1976). Where prehistoric cultivation was limited, the most productive soils in drained locations in the bottoms are the alluvials and entisols of the first and second bottoms of the major valleys. In the Arkansas River Valley, they are the Yahola–Port–Reinach association and the Lonoke–Brewer association, respectively (Gray and Galloway 1959). North of the Arkansas River they are the natural levee soils and terrace soils of the Verdegris and allied soils, as well as minor soils (Huntingdon, Razort). South of the Arkansas River the Pope series occurs on the major tributaries (Gray and Galloway 1959). The proportion of arable soils is relatively high only within counties bordering the Arkansas: ca. 10% Muskogee, ca. 8.5% LeFlore, ca. 5.5% McIntosh, and ca. 4.5% Sequoyah counties. In the Ozark highlands the proportion is much less: Less than 2% for Delaware and Cherokee Counties, and .1% for Adair County. These figures give relative differences only, since the greatest concentrations of arable soil are located in the broad floodplains of the Kerr Reservoir area and the Braden Bottom, located west and east of Spiro, respectively (see Figure 7.1).

The productivity of the bottomlands in the eastern section of the

Arkansas River was rated at the time of first white settlement at 3.0 kg of corn per hectare (Lesquereux 1860). A century later, the same soils were rated between 1.2 and 2.7 kg (Knoebel *et al.* 1931; Abernathy 1970). Generally, the terrace soils are more productive, especially in the western section, where some attain yields of 4.5 kg (Grove *et al.* 1916). These yields are moderate by comparison with productivity figures from the Mississippi lowlands (Chapters 10 and 13 of this volume, Peebles and Kus 1977).

RIPARIAN AND UPLAND RESOURCES

Riparian and bottomland vegetation associations are the major sources of small mammals, fish, and birds found in village sites; deer is cosmopolitan (Blair 1938).

Faunal remains from sites with good preservation (cf. Duffield 1969) indicate a hunting strategy probably conforming to that documented in the Mississippian Basin (Smith 1975). There is one major difference. Some sites have yielded bison bone remains, which, although generally few, are much more common in western Caddoan sites (Duffield 1969, Wyckoff 1970:141–42). This pattern of distribution points to bison hunting being undertaken well beyond the range of normal village-based procurement. Meat was transported into the easternmost settlements with a minimum of accompanying bone.

In sum, faunal remains in habitation sites attest to a riparian–bottomland foraging orientation that coincides with the dependency on arable land obtaining in the Caddoan adaptation. The hunting of bison is probably a specialized activity involving long-distance transport, since very limited amounts of bone are found in middens.

LOCATIONAL REGULARITIES

Habitation sites with permanent architecture are known largely from the river valley bottoms and along the highland overlooking arable land. Because surveys have concentrated on the river valleys, it is not surprising that our knowledge of site distribution should be heavily weighted toward this topographic zone. One exception is the immediate vicinity of the Spiro site where, as a consequence of W.P.A. activity on the bluff crests overlooking the Arkansas River, many upland farmsteads were located and excavated in addition to the bottomland sites.

As yet we do not have the means for determining the distribution and density of upland settlement in the study area. It is expected, however, that upland settlement will vary primarily in response to the corn agricultural potential of the land within a site catchment, and secondarily to the degree that a primary civic–ceremonial center such as Spiro might attract a concentration of population in its immediate vicinity.

A review of the location of habitation sites reveals that 75% are located on sandy, silty and silty clay loams in valley bottoms. More precise data are not available, since the locations of a large number of sites are under the waters of dams and are not mapped in published soil surveys. The limited available data attest to the distribution of habitation sites in and near easily tilled land. Interestingly, habitation sites located on bluff crests and other upland locations occur in the vicinity of the primary center, Spiro, and indicate the existence, here, at least, of the pull this center had in congregating population in excess of the numbers that could be maintained in residence near fields in the bottomlands.

These sites are not situated in immediate proximity to productive arable land, but on a gravel substrate that is covered with silt loams of second-rate productivity. It is doubtful that these site locations were determined by the agricultural potential of the immediately proximate soils. Adequate soils exist within a 25 km² catchment. The structures and earthworks of at least one civic–ceremonial center were built on even poorer soils. The upland ring of mounds at the Spiro site are located on poorly drained shale-derived silt loams. In this case, it is obvious that the location of this center was determined by other factors. By contrast, the Spiro village is located on one of the most productive soils in the valley (Lonoke silty clay loam).

The influence of differences in the productivity of vegetational zones on aboriginal settlement cannot be assessed at this time. Differences exist between the eastern and western sections that are potentially influential. Local differences in vegetation appear to have exercised influence. In the Grand River Valley, which flows along the edge of the Ozark Uplift and the Prairie Border, the greater density of forested vegetation to the east coincides with a greater distribution of habitation sites in the tributary valleys flowing from that direction.

SITE SIZE DISTRIBUTION

Data on the size of sites were compiled from a small sample of 124 sites, drawn chiefly from the Arkansas and Grand Valleys, and, to a lesser extent, from other portions of the study area. A histogram of these data is presented in Figure 7.2, from which it appears that habitation sites have a distribution that partially parallels that of the civic–ceremonial centers. The available data points to a regular distribution of size classes. Each class is twice the size of the smaller class. Hence, the series of site size classes conforms to a geometric series with a ratio of 1 : 2 : 4 : 8 : 16. However, such a distribution can be the product of noncultural factors such as repeated overlapping occupations of different periods, sampling bias and estimation error (Hodder & Orton 1976:73).

The calculation of site size is considerably complicated by the mixture of habitation and specialized function areas in some sites but not others. And there are several sources of error.

First, in the absence of common guidelines, different methods for determining site size have been employed over a period of 40 years. The most commonly used index of site size has been the maximal area of scatter of artifacts and related materials. But before 1942, sites were often defined solely by one or more areas of concentration within an undefined limit, since the location of rewarding excavations was the guiding principle behind site survey (Orr 1939). Although the total site area seems to have been determined in some instances (e.g., Spiro, Brackett, Norman, and Littlefield I), the older estimates are difficult to check because the sites in question are now either underwater (e.g., Norman, Eufaula, Brackett and Reed) or damaged by development and erosion.

Second, reliance has to be placed on the distribution of mounds or excavated features to estimate size in some cases. In these cases there is no available information on the relative concentration of surface material of different types that would allow some estimation of the area of distribution of prehistoric structures within a site scatter.

Third, a great percentage of the large sites are the result of overlapping distributions of smaller occupations of different ages. This can be determined from the few cases in which a site initially defined by area of surface scatter was subsequently systematically stripped over most of its area. An extreme example is the Cat Smith site, which was discovered upon excavation to be a settlement consisting of two structures, one subsurface feature, and two nearby burials that were confined to a small (15 × 30 m = .045 ha) concentration within a total area of 6 ha of thin scatter (Wyckoff and Barr 1967).

To just what extent either multiple componency or the mixture of domestic settlement with other land use types (e.g., agricultural fields) has created "large" sites has not been determined. But habitation sites greater than 4 ha are particularly suspect, since it is unlikely that they are common when the largest documented habitation site is only 10 ha. Most habitation sites are small. Half the sites in the sample are 1.5 ha or less in size, and the most numerous size group is composed of sites less than .5 ha in size.

With due consideration for these obscuring factors, the larger confirmed habitation sites are located in or near the large expanses of floodplain (e.g., Spiro village, Littlefield I, Horton).

Civic–Ceremonial Centers

INTRODUCTION

An important category of sites are the mound groups and isolated mounds, which are generally located away from permanent habitation sites. Although our information on these civic–ceremonial centers is of varying quality, sufficient information is available from early excavations to identify degrees of complexity among them, based on site layout and on the number of distinct mound types present. From these patterns a hierarchy of centers can be adduced, and a "premier center" identified.

Our interest in the hierarchy of centers is directed toward ascertaining the complexity of the cultural system, since the size of any hierarchy is one measure of that complexity (Simon 1962). The hierarchical arrangement of centers is usually conceived of as distinct levels in a ritual and regulatory network. The number of such levels is thought to be equivalent to the number of levels of information processing required to coordinate essential social events and subsistence tasks (Peebles and Kus 1977).

The number of distinct types of civic–ceremonial structures in a center provides one of the means for establishing a hierarchy of centers that are operationally indicative of organizational differences. The principle involved here is that ranks or echelons in a hierarchy are defined by a cumulative set of component elements. Expressed another way, "the higher site class has all of the distinctive features typical of the lower class in addition to a feature distinctive of it [Earle 1976:207]." The other indicator of hierarchy is the presence of organizational differences. Here, truly different echelons of a hierarchy should be distinguished by different organizational principles (Simon 1962). This means that upper levels of a hierarchy should be characterized by recombinations of the civic–ceremonial structures found in lower levels, rather than displaying a simple mechanical addition of these structures. With these general observations in mind, it is possible to establish a hierarchy of centers. First, the functionally distinct mound types require description and identification as having correspondingly distinct social and ideological functions.

MOUND TYPES

The first mound type consists of low conical mounds covering the foundations of one or sometimes a sequence of two dismantled structures. The specialized function of these structures is signified in most cases by blocked entrances and other indications of abnormal precautions to protect the entrance of a building with otherwise ordinary domestic architecture. In addition, these structures were thoroughly cleaned of trash. The type example is from the Harlan site (Bell 1972); elsewhere, low, buried structure mounds have often eroded to the point that only the unique structures themselves remain. Other examples of this mound type have been found, both as isolated structures (e.g., Choates House 1) and in groups resembling the Harlan group (Figure 7.6). Most date to the Harlan phase, with a few belonging to the Spiro phase if the number of interior roof supports is a reliable temporal marker.

Our best insight into the function of the structures buried beneath the mounds is provided by an analysis of the Harlan site (Bell 1972). Bell argued that these structures were probably mortuaries housing the dead before final interment in burial mounds (mound type 2). After the mortuary was cleared of the dead, the structure was dismantled and the site covered with a low mound (Bell 1972, Brown 1975:5).

The second mound type consists of a simple accretional burial mound. They are elongate or multilobate in plan. The Eufaula mound, Norman Mound B and the Harlan burial mound are well-defined examples of this type in the literature (Bell 1972, Finkelstein 1940, Orr 1941). They date to the Harlan phase, with the possible exception of Norman Mound A, which may date to both the Harlan and Spiro phases. Examples at the Spiro site are contained within the Craig mound as primary stages (Brown 1966). Elsewhere, this burial mound type is probably represented by round burial concentrations of the same size range (Bareis 1955; Baerreis 1954, Bell 1974). In the latter cases, the mounds may have been plowed down. Excavation shows that mounds of this type were constructed of the accumulation of burials and grave goods in distinct layers. Burials were laid on the mound surface in distinct episodes. In the case of the Craig mound primaries, these burials were laid between large sheets of cedar bark (Brown 1966). It appears that this mound type is a repository for secondary burials and burial offerings that were taken out of a mortuary facility. On the basis of the Harlan site evidence Bell (1972) has argued that these mounds grew from the deposition of burials taken from the charnel houses covered by the first mound type. The first and second mound types constitute a basic pair of earthworks that are the product of a complete mortuary program involving the storage of the dead for a period of time before final interment. The individuals so treated are probably the higher status portions of the population.

The third mound type is the pyramidal mound, a flat-topped structure with steep sides (e.g., Harlan, Lillie Creek, Norman, and Spiro sites). There is no evidence that a structure stood on the platform. Excavations at Brackett, Norman, and Skidgel mounds reveal that a large structure stood at the foot of or nearby each mound stage and at the same orientation. Since the platform was often found packed with ash, the top was perhaps devoted to long-burning fires rather than to supporting a structure. Some-times the platform of this mound was capped with a final dome of earth that lent the appearance of a conical mound after years of erosion and cultivation. The period during which this mound type was constructed was confined to the Harlan and Spiro phases; it is absent in the Fort Coffee phase.

The fourth mound type is a substructural mound having two or three lobes. The data available do not clearly show whether the platforms were pyramidal or conical. In addition, these mounds contain burials placed in pits along the mound flanks, insofar as can be determined from the avail-able records. The only two known examples are Norman Mound A and the secondary units of the Craig mound at Spiro (Brown 1966, Finkelstein 1940). Both belong to the Spiro phase, although the unit at Spiro may have been begun in the Harlan phase. The Craig mound is the more complex of the two, consisting of a sequence of distinct mound types: A multistage pyramidal mound was added to the platform mound of the fourth type (Brown 1966). This pyramidal mound was dedicated to mortuary functions that differ from other uses of pyramidal mounds (Type 3) in the interment of the dead in the top and sides of the mound. The virtually unique aspect of this latter mound is illustrated by the fact that it continues the function of the Great Mortuary on which it stood (Brown 1975).

THE HIERARCHY OF CENTERS

Each level of the site hierarchy is defined by typical combinations of mound types (Table 7.3). The lowest or first-order level consists of buried structure mounds and probably burial mounds if a complete burial pro-gram is present. The second-order level is defined by the addition of a platform mound to the set of burial program mounds defining the first-order level. The third-order level is defined by the presence of a fourth mound type that combines the features of the mortuary and platform mounds without replacing either. It is at this level that the pattern di-verges from the lower levels, thus demonstrating the existence of a dis-tinctly different level in the hierarchy of regulatory social control.

First-Echelon Centers

This basic community center served specialized social functions of a residentially dispersed group within a small area. The common facilities are a mortuary structure and associated burial dump that served a group of presumably related individuals as a common ancestral shrine. The minor centers are poorly investigated although the Sol Thompson site (Lf 16) is an excavated example. The buried structures had blocked entrances, and

TABLE 7.3

Distribution of Mound Types in Caddoan Sites

Site name (number)	Pyramidal mounds[a]	Conjoined platforms	Burial mounds	Buried structure mounds
Spiro (Lf–40,46)	H,S	H?,S	H	H (ring)
Norman (Wg-2)	H?,S	S	S?	X
Harlan (Ck-6)	H	—	H	H (ring)
Hughes (Ms-4,5)	H	—	?	? (ring)
Brackett (Ck-43)	H	—	?	H (ring)
Reed (D1-1,11)	H,S	—	?	? (ring?)
Lillie Creek (D1-41,53)	H	—	—	—
Eufaula (Mi-45)	—	—	H	—
Parris (Sk-12)	H	—	?	?
Maconally (Ad-11)	X	—	—	—
Skidgel (Lf-70)	S	—	—	?
Cavanaugh (Ark.)	S?	—	—	—

SOURCES: Brown (1966); Finkelstein (1940); Bell (1972, 1974); Bareis (1955); Orr (1941, 1942); Purrington (1970); and G. Muto, personal communication. Notes in the Oklahoma Archaeological Survey.

[a] H = Harlan phase; S = Spiro phase; X = either or both phases; ? = uncertain presence or age.

both four-post and two-post structures were buried by small mounds. A nearby small mound may be a charnel dump. The minor center is better documented outside the Arkansas River Basin (Wyckoff 1967).

Second-Echelon Centers

The presence of a platform mound in the major civic–ceremonial center in addition to the mortuary structures indicates a multicommunity service area having more centralized social and ceremonial functions than the minor centers. The type example of the major center is the Harlan site, but the primate center is Spiro of the Harlan phase (Figures 7.6 and 7.8). These sites in particular had a clear circular arrangement of low mounds of the buried structure type together with one platform mound in the case of Harlan and two at Spiro (one much smaller than the other). The other centers are smaller, and the circular arrangement is not as clear. But a strong case can be made for an essentially similar arrangement at the Brackett, Hughes, and Reed sites. At Spiro and Harlan, the center of the circle of mounds was barren of occupation, thereby suggesting that the central area had specific ceremonial functions. Ordinary domestic living quarters have not been discovered at these two centers. In fact, both are situated on high locations away from habitations. In the case of Spiro during the Harlan phase, a contemporary village lies on the terrace below.

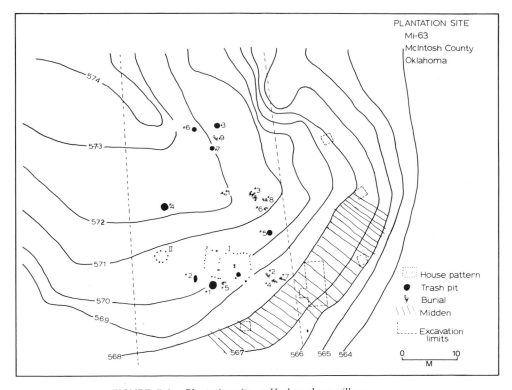

FIGURE 7.6. *Plantation site, a Harlan phase village.*

The evidence for the separation of specialized ceremonial activities and domestic occupation is not as clear in the other cases. Spiro phase centers of this level consisted of platform mounds only.

Third-Echelon Centers

At this level, distinctive architectural features of the fourth mound attest to organizational discontinuity with the lower-order centers. At the Norman and Spiro sites (of the Spiro phase) there is clear evidence that the mortuary structure complex connected with the fourth mound type is much more important than any other, and is the ancestral shrine of the regional elite (Figures 7.7 and 7.8). The ground-level charnel facilities were exceptionally large. Within this echelon, the Spiro center was clearly more complex. The ground-level mortuary was replaced by charnel facilities supported by a pyramidal mound of distinctive type. In line with the premier status of Spiro is the fact that several interment types, including the premier status litter burial, are unique to the site (Brown 1975).

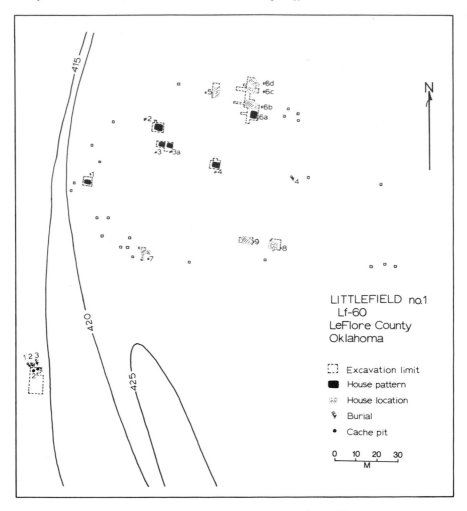

FIGURE 7.7. Littlefield I site, a Spiro phase village.

Rank Size

One method for investigating the relationship between site size and complexity within the limitations of the data set is to apply the rank-size rule. The rank-size rule specifies that the "biggest item of rank 1 is twice as big as number 2 and three times the size of number 3, and so on . . . [Fulinsbee 1977:898]." That is, the nth largest site has a size $1/n$ that of the largest site. Since the rule specifies the "ideal" size ratio among sites

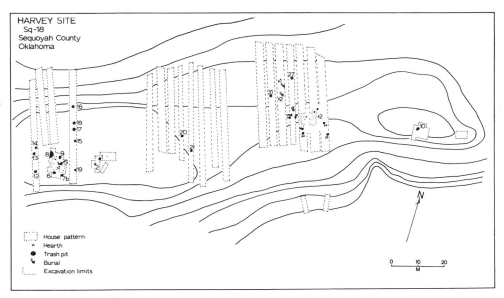

FIGURE 7.8. *Harvey site, a Fort Coffee phase village.*

belonging to a single system in which many factors affect size, a comparison of the actual rank order with the expected order on a double log graph will point to data sets in which one or both of these qualifications applies.

The lower plot of Figure 7.9 shows the rank-size order of mound group "enclosures" of Harlan phase second-level centers illustrates size relationship. The fit of the largest three centers to the rank order is very close. The complete distribution has a concave slope that is acceptable as indicative of the operation of a single underlying factor (Johnson 1977). However, because the distribution is strongly concave, there may be missing centers that would conform to the ideal third, fourth, etc. order. When the distribution remains concave after all sites are accounted for, the size distribution is said to show the effects of strongly centralized control (Johnson 1977).

Although the "mound enclosure" data appear to be conditioned by a uniform set of factors, total site size data do not. The rank-size rule can be used as a filter model to identify heterogeneous data sets. A plot of the data on overall site size is shown in the upper plot of Figure 7.9. The upper plot shows that the data from the sample of 124 sites departs greatly from the rank-size order indicated by the diagonal. The observed distribution has a convex slope, which indicates the operation of heterogeneous factors in the size data. Mixing of sites belonging to different periods and to different settlement systems would be sufficient to produce a convex size distribution (Johnson 1977).

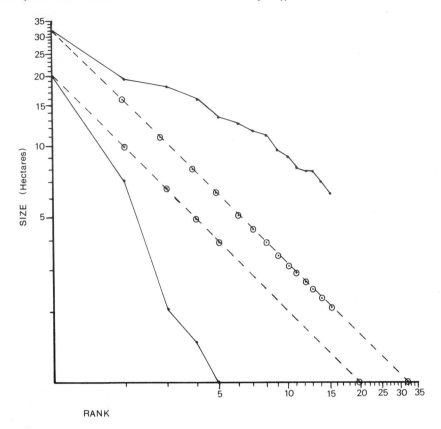

FIGURE 7.9. *Rank–size distribution of selected sites in Table 2. Upper pair of curves represent orderings by total site size (actual order is a continuous line, ideal is broken line). Lower pair of curves represent site orderings by size of mound "enclosures" of Harlan phase centers. The last dot represents the Reed site.*

Spacing of Civic–Ceremonial Centers

Central place models of site locations predict regular spacing among major sites (as well as other patterns not of concern here). The Caddoan data conform to these models when the Harlan phase pattern is separated from that of the Spiro phase (Table 7.4). In the Harlan phase, the second echelon centers are distributed over most of the region in both the Arkansas River Valley and tributary valleys of the Grand and Illinois Rivers. With the possible exception of the Harlan and Norman sites, which may be contemporary, these centers are spaced no closer than 15 km and no further than 30 km to their nearest neighbor. The Lillie Creek and Reed sites, however, are both 75 km from their second nearest neighbors. Too

TABLE 7.4
Nearest Neighbor Distances of Major Centers

Phase and sites	Nearest neighbor distance (km)
Harlan phase	
Reed—Lillie Creek	22
Lillie Creek—Harlan	75[a]
Harlan—Hughes	15
Brackett—Maconally	30
Maconally—Parris	25
Parris—Spiro	30
Spiro phase	
Norman—Spiro	90
Spiro—Skidgel	1.6
Spiro—Cavannaugh	14

[a] By river valley.

little is known about the minor first-echelon centers to evaluate their distribution with respect to major centers.

In the Spiro phase, a different pattern exists. The development of a third echelon is accompanied by an apparent decrease in the number of second-echelon centers. The two third-echelon centers, Spiro and Norman, are located at opposite ends of the study area. In the Spiro area the second-echelon centers are located within 15 km of the third-echelon center (Table 7.4). They also consist only of a platform mound and an adjoining surface public structure (e.g. Skidgel). The absence of the mortuary related Type 1 and 2 mounds may well have been due to their replacement by cemeteries, two of which are within a few kilometers (Orr 1946, Rohrbaugh 1974).

Beyond satisfying the minimal stipulations of central place models, it is not possible to stretch the data. The relatively undeveloped scale of the site hierarchy, together with the measurement and sampling problems, do not allow additional insight at the present level of our knowledge.

Settlement Patterns and Environment

In the foregoing discussion, five features of Caddoan settlement patterns in the Arkansas River subregion have been identified as conditioned to some degree by environment. First, the dispersal of households into many small settlements, with none over 10 ha in size, can be argued to be a pattern produced by a strategy designed to spread the risk of crop failure in a vulnerable growing environment, where limited soil quality sets limits to productivity. The same process is probably responsible for the separation of civic–ceremonial centers from habitation sites of the local service community. Second, the location of villages and farmsteads appears to be dependent upon available arable acreage. Third, the primary center of Spiro was centered during two continuous phases, within the largest concentration of arable floodplain and within the zone in which southeastern floodplain vegetational communities existed historically. In other words, the primary center occurred in the middle of the most productive and most stable portion of the agricultural landscape. Fourth, the larger second–level civic–ceremonial centers are distributed along the Grand River, which flows along the western edge of the Ozark Highland, whereas the smaller second-level centers are situated within the Ozark Highland and the Arkoma Basin hinterland. Fifth, a growth in system complexity accompanies a climatic cycle more favorable to corn agriculture. Increased population is implied. A collapse in complexity follows climatic reversal.

Taken together, these features attest to the extent that Caddoan settlement patterns are conditioned by those environmental variables that affect agricultural productivity at the western margins of possible intensive cultivation utilizing Mississippian technology. It remains for future research to test these relationships.

It will be useful to search for additional environmental variables. First, a west to east climb in site density in the Arkansas Valley can be expected, reflecting the greater subsistence security afforded by the higher rainfall and greater humidity in the east.

Second, habitation sites within any subarea of the region should show a bias toward catchments with a mixture of resource zones, although the bias on a regional scale is toward arable land. According to Peebles and Kus (1977:432), "Settlements should be located in areas which assure a high degree of local subsistence sufficiency. This prediction is a direct consequence of hierarchy theory: by assuring local autonomy in everyday affairs, adaptive flexibility is maintained and information costs are reduced."

Conclusions

As common and conventional as it is to consider the Caddoan cultural traditions separately from the Mississippian to the east, the one aspect in which it is more advantageous not to do so is in terms of subsistence–settlement patterns. The similar organization of communities around civic–ceremonial centers with platform mounds, combined with a basic agricultural technology based on hoe cultivation of maize, attests to the fundamental unity of the two areas (Griffin 1967). Their essential continuity can be traced to a common economic base on the one hand and to the dominating influence of Mississippian ideology on the forms of Caddoan social integration on the other.

But at a more detailed level it is obvious that differences exist, which, under closer scrutiny, can be shown to be the result of an advanced Mississippian subsistence–settlement system responding to a marginal environment for that system. In testimony for this position is the observation that the complexity of the settlement pattern supported by corn agriculture responds to significant changes in environment. This illustrates both the dependency of social complexity to the productivity of its agricultural base and to the resiliency of the Mississippian subsistence–settlement system. With these relationships as preliminary conclusions, it should be expected that further indications of subsistence–settlement adjustment to ecological variables will be found to exist in other regions of the Mississippian system.

Acknowledgments

The authors are grateful to Lois E. Sanders for compiling data on site size and site location in the southern portion of the study area.

References

Abernathy, Edward J.
  1970   *Soil survey of Sequoyah County, Oklahoma.* U.S. Dept. of Agriculture, Soil Conservation Service.
Asch, David L., and Nancy B. Asch
  1977   Chenopod as cultigen: A re-evaluation of some prehistoric collections from eastern North America. *Midcontinental Journal of Archaeology* **2**:3–45.
Baerreis, David A.
  1954   The Hufaker site, Delaware county, Oklahoma. *Bulletin of the Oklahoma Anthropological Society* **2**:35–48.
Baerreis, David A., and Reid A. Bryson
  1965   Historical climatology and the Southern Plains: A preliminary statement. *Bulletin of the Oklahoma Anthropological Society* **13**:69–75.
Bareis, Charles J.
  1955   The Brackett site, Ck-43, of Cherokee county, Oklahoma. *Bulletin of the Oklahoma Anthropological Society* **3**:1–51.
Bell, Robert E.
  1972   The Harlan site, Ck-6, a prehistoric mound center in Cherokee County, eastern Oklahoma. *Oklahoma Anthropological Society, Memoir 2.*
  1973   The Washita River Focus of the Southern Plains. In *Variation in Anthropology*, edited by Donald Lathrap and Jody Douglas. Illinois Archaeological Survey. Pp. 171–187.

1974   Mounds and fieldwork near Muskogee, Oklahoma. *Newsletter of the Oklahoma Anthropological Society.*

Bell, Robert E., and David A. Baerreis
1951   A survey of Oklahoma archaeology. *Bulletin of the Texas archaeological and paleontological society* **22**:7–100.

Bell, Robert E., and others
1969   The Robinson-Solesbee site, Hs-9, a Fulton Aspect occupation, Robert S. Kerr Reservoir, eastern Oklahoma. *Oklahoma River Basin Survey, Archaeological Site Report* 15.

Blair, W.F.
1938   Ecological relationships of the mammals of the Bird Creek region, northeastern Oklahoma. *The American Midland Naturalist* **20**:473–526.

Briscoe, J.
1976   A preliminary report on the Plantation site, Mi-63, an early Caddoan settlement in northern McIntosh County. *Newsletter of the Oklahoma Anthropological Society* **24**:9–12.

Brown, James A.
1966   *Spiro Studies, Volume 1: Description of the Mound Group.* Norman, Oklahoma: University of Oklahoma Research Institute.
1967   New radiocarbon dates from the Spiro site. *Bulletin of the Oklahoma Anthropological Society* **15**:77–80.
1971a   The dimensions of status in the burials at Spiro. In Approaches to the Social Dimensions of Mortuary Practices, edited by J. A. Brown. *Memoirs of the Society for American Archaeology* **25**:92–112.
1971b   *Spiro Studies, Volume 3: Pottery Vessels.* Norman, Oklahoma: University of Oklahoma Research Institute.
1975   Spiro art and its mortuary contexts. In *Death and the afterlife in Pre-Columbian America,* edited by E. P. Benson. Washington D.C.: Dumbarton Oaks Research Library and Collections, Washington. Pp. 1–32.
1976   *Spiro Studies, Volume 4: The Artifacts.* Norman, Oklahoma: Stovall Museum of Science and History.

Bryson, Reid A., David A. Baerreis, and Wayne M. Wendland
1970   The character of late-glacial and post-glacial climatic change. In *Pleistocene and Recent Environments of the Central Great Plains,* edited by Wakefield Dort, Jr. and J. Knox Jones, Jr., Lawrence, Kansas: University of Kansas Press. Pp. 53–74.

Burton, Robert J.
1971   The archaeological view from the Harvey site, Sq-18. *Oklahoma River Basin Survey Archaeological Site Report* **21**.

Burton, Robert J., T. Bastian, and T.J. Prewitt
1969   The Tyler site, Hs-11, Haskell County, Oklahoma. *Oklahoma River Basin Survey, Archaeological Site Report* **20**.

Cartledge, Thomas R.
1970   The Tyler-Rose site and late prehistory in east-central Oklahoma. *Oklahoma River Basin Survey, Archaeological Site Report* **19**.

Clay, R. Berle
1976   Tactics, strategy, and operations: The Mississippian system responds to its environment. *Mid-Continental Journal of Archaeology* **1**:137–161.

Clements, Forrest E.
1945   Historical sketch of the Spiro mound. *Contributions to the Museum of the American Indian, Heye Foundation* **14**:48–68.

Cook, Thomas Genn
　1976　Koster: An artifact analysis of two Archaic phases in west central Illinois. *North-western University Archeological Program, Prehistoric Records* **1**.

Cutler, Hugh C., and Leonard W. Blake
　1973　*Plants from archaeological sites east of the Rockies.* St. Louis, Missouri: Missouri Botanical Garden.

Davis, Hester A., editor
　1970　Archeological and historical resources of the Red River region. *Arkansas Archeological Survey, Research Series* **1**.

Duffield, Lathel F.
　1969　The vertebrate faunal remains from the School Land I and School Land II sites, Delaware County, Oklahoma. *Bulletin of the Oklahoma Anthropological Society* **18**:47–65.

Earle, Timothy K.
　1976　A nearest-neighbor analysis of two Formative settlement systems. In *The Early Meso-American Village,* edited by Kent V. Flannery. New York: Academic Press. Pp. 196–223.

Finkelstein, J. Joe
　1940　The Norman site excavations near Wagoner, Oklahoma. *The Oklahoma Prehistorian* **3**(3):2–15.

Flannery, Kent V., editor
　1976　*The Early Mesoamerican village.* New York: Academic Press.

Fulinsbee, R.E.
　1977　World's view—from Alph to Zipf. *Geological Society of American Bulletin* **88**:897–907.

Gilmore, Melvin R.
　1931　Vegetal remains of the Ozark Bluff-Dweller Culture. *Papers of the Michigan Academy of Science, Arts, and Letters* **14**:83–102.

Gray, F., and H.M. Galloway
　1959　Soils of Oklahoma. *Oklahoma State University Experiment Station, Miscellaneous Publications* **56**.

Gray, F., and M. H. Roozitalab
　1976　Benchmark and key soils of Oklahoma: A modern classification system. *Oklahoma State University Agricultural Experiment Station, Miscellaneous Publication* **97**.

Gregg, Josiah
　1954　*Commerce of the Prairies,* edited by Max L. Moorhead. Norman, Oklahoma: University of Oklahoma Press.

Griffin, James B.
　1946　Culture change and continuity in eastern United States archaeology. In Man in northeastern North America, edited by F. Johnson. *Papers of the Robert S. Peabody Foundation for Archaeology* **3**:37–95.
　1967　Eastern North American archaeology: A summary. *Science* **156**:175–191.

Grove, B. Jones, and others
　1916　Soil survey of Muskogee County, Oklahoma. *U.S. Dept. of Agriculture, Field Operations of the Bureau of Soils, 1913.* Pp. 1853–1891.

Henning, Dale R.
　1959　The Loftin mound (23Sn-42). *Missouri Archaeological Society Newsletter* **128**: 9–10.

Hodder, Ian, and Clive Orton
　1976　*Spatial analysis in archaeology.* New York: Cambridge University Press.

Israel, Stephen
  1969   Re-examination of the Cookson site and prehistory of Tenkiller locale in northeast-
          ern Oklahoma. M.A. thesis, Department of Anthropology, University of Okla-
          homa.
Johnson, Gregory A.
  1977   Aspects of regional analysis in archaeology. Annual Review of Anthropology 6:479–
          508.
Knoebel, E.W. and others
  1931   Soil survey of LeFlore County, Oklahoma. U.S. Dept. of Agriculture, Series 1931,
          15.
Krieger, Alex D.
  1946   Culture complexes and chronology in northern Texas. University of Texas Publication
          5670.
Larson, Lewis H.
  1970   Settlement distribution during the Mississippi Period. Southeastern Archaeological
          Conference Bulletin 13:19–25.
Lawton, Sherman P.
  1964   Test excavations in Owl Cave. Bulletin of the Oklahoma Anthropological Society
          12:87–102.
Lehmer, Donald J.
  1952   The Turkey Bluff Focus of the Fulton Aspect. American Antiquity 17:313–318.
Lesquereux, M. Leo
  1860   Botanical and paleontological report of the Geological State Survey of Arkansas.
          Second report of a geological reconnaissance of the middle and southern counties of
          Arkansas, by David D. Owen and others. Philadelphia: C. Sherman and Sons. Pp.
          295–400.
Lintz, Christopher
  1974   An Analysis of the Custer Focus and its relationship to the Plains Village Horizon
          in Oklahoma. Papers in Anthropology 15(2):1–72.
McMillan, R. Bruce
  1968   Small shelter sites in and near the Stockton Reservoir, Missouri, V: summary and
          conclusions. Missouri Archaeological Society Newsletter 226:6–11.
Orr, Kenneth G.
  1939   Field Report on the excavation of Indian villages in the vicinity of Spiro Mounds,
          LeFlore County, Oklahoma. The Oklahoma Prehistorian 2(2):8–15.
  1941   The Eufaula Mound, Oklahoma: Contributions to the Spiro Focus. The Oklahoma
          Prehistorian 4(1):2–15.
  1942   The Eufaula Mound, Oklahoma: Contribution to the Spiro Focus. M.A. Thesis,
          Department of Anthropology, University of Chicago.
  1946   The archaeological situation at Spiro, Oklahoma: A preliminary report. American
          Antiquity 11:228–256.
  1952   Survey of Caddoan area archeology. In Archeology of Eastern United States, edited
          by James B. Griffin. Chicago: University of Chicago Press. Pp. 239–255.
Parsons, Jeffry R.
  1972   Archaeological settlement patterns. Annual Review of Anthropology 1:127–150.
Peebles, Christopher S. and Susan M. Kus
  1977   Some archaeological correlates of ranked societies. American Antiquity 42:421–
          448.
Prewitt, Terry J.
  1974   Regional interaction networks and the Caddoan area. Papers in Anthropology
          15(2):73–101.

Prewitt, Terry J., and P. Wood
  1969   The Sheffield site: A Fulton Aspect component in the Short Mountain Reservoir area. *Oklahoma River Basin Survey, Archaeological Site Report* 12.
Purrington, Burton L.
  1970   *Prehistory of Delaware county, Oklahoma: cultural continuity and change on the western Ozark periphery.* Ph.D. dissertation, Department of Anthropology, University of Wisconsin—Madison.
Ray, Max A.
  1965   A report on excavations at the Pohly site, My-54, in northeastern Oklahoma. *Bulletin of the Oklahoma Anthropological Society* **13**:1–68.
Rohrbaugh, Charles L.
  1974   Fort Coffee Phase social systems as seen through the organizational structure of two mortuary systems at the Moore site, (34Lf-31). Manuscript with the author.
Schneider, Fred
  1967   Eight archaeological sites in the Webber's Falls Lock and Dam area, Oklahoma. *Oklahoma River Basin Survey, Archaeological Site Report* **7**.
Scholtz, James A.
  1969   A summary of prehistory in northwest Arkansas. *Arkansas Archeologist* **10**:50–60.
Simon, Herbert A.
  1962   *The Sciences of the artificial.* Cambridge, Massachusetts: MIT Press.
Smith, Bruce D.
  1975   Middle Mississippi exploitation of animal populations. *Anthropological papers of the Museum of Anthropology, University of Michigan* **57**.
Smith, Philip E.L.
  1972   Land-use, settlement patterns and subsistence agriculture: A demographic perspective. In *Man, Settlement and Urbanism,* edited by Peter J. Ucko, Ruth Tringham, and G.W. Dimbleby. London: Duckworth. Pp. 409–425.
Story, Dee Ann, and S. Valastro, Jr.
  1977   Radiocarbon dating and the George C. Davis site, Texas. *Journal of Field Archaeology* **4**:63–89.
Thornthwaite, C.W.
  1948   An approach toward a rational classification of climates. *Geographical Review* **38**:55–94.
Thwaites, Reuben G., editor
  1905   *Early western travels, 1748–1846. Vol. XIII, Nuttall's travels in the Arkansa Territory, 1819.* Cleveland, Ohio: Clark company.
Wahlgren, Harry F.
  1941   Climate of Oklahoma. In *Climate and Man*, Yearbook of Agriculture, 1941.
Wedel, Waldo R.
  1970   Some environmental and historical factors of the Great Bend Aspect. In *Pleistocene and Recent environments in the central Great Plains,* edited by Wakefield Dort and J. Knox Jones. Lawrence, Kansas: University of Kansas Press. Pp. 131–142.
Woodall, J. Ned
  1969   *Cultural ecology of the Caddo.* Ph.D. dissertation, Department of Anthropology, Southern Methodist University.
Wyckoff, Don G.
  1967   Woods Mound Complex: a prehistoric mound complex in McCurtain County, Oklahoma. *Bulletin of the Oklahoma Anthropological Society* **15**:1–76.
  1970   The Horton site revisited, 1967 excavations at Sq-11, Sequoyah County, Oklahoma. *Oklahoma Archaeological Survey, Studies in Oklahoma's Past* **1**.
  1974   *The Caddoan area: An archeological perspective.* New York: Garland Press.

Wyckoff, Don G., and Thomas P. Barr
  1967   The Cat Smith site: a late prehistoric village in Muskogee County, Oklahoma. *Bulletin of the Oklahoma Anthropological Society* **15**:81–106.

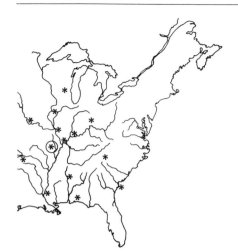

8

The Settlement Pattern of the Powers Phase

JAMES E. PRICE

The Powers phase was a short-lived Mississippian manifestation that occupied sand ridges on the extreme western edge of the Western Lowland of Southeast Missouri and Northeast Arkansas immediately adjacent to the Ozark Escarpment at ca. A.D. 1275–1320. The phase was not indigenous to the area, but represents a major population influx, probably derived from the Malden Plain of the Missouri Bootheel. The population built a major civic–ceremonial center, villages, hamlets, and limited activity sites. The occupation of the area by a Mississippian population was relatively brief, spanning little more than 50 years, and appears to have come to an abrupt halt. Settlements were abandoned and burned, and the Mississippian population deserted the area, never to return.

Powers Phase Research: Background

The archeological data discussed in this chapter resulted from 11 years of research in the Western Lowlands of Southeast Missouri by personnel

Mississippian Settlement Patterns

of the Powers Phase Project. A National Science Foundation Undergraduate Research Participant grant provided financial support in 1965 for an archeological survey by the author of a corridor along either side of the Little Black River (Price 1966). It was during this survey that several sites of the Powers phase were discovered, and test excavations carried out at the Turner site in the summer of 1966 revealed a village settlement that had been destroyed by fire.

James B. Griffin visited the excavations at the Turner site during the summer of 1966, and after visiting a number of other Powers phase sites, we discussed the unique research potential of these short-lived Mississippian sites. As a result of these discussions, further funding for the excavation of the Turner site was subsequently provided by the Museum of Anthropology, University of Michigan for both the 1966 and 1967 field seasons, and a grant proposal to the National Science Foundation was approved (NSF Grant GS 3215). Additional funding, personnel, field equipment, and field vehicles were provided by the American Archaeology Division of the University of Missouri—Columbia.

The research design of the Powers Phase Project called for the total excavation of two village settlements (the Turner and Snodgrass sites), combined with more limited excavation of numerous other sites of the phase. The complete excavation of the Turner site was accomplished over four field seasons (1966–1967; 1972–1973), and excavation of the Snodgrass site was started in 1968 and continued through 1973. A total area of approximately 3 ha (7.5 acres) was excavated at these two sites. The Neil Flurry, Wilborn, and Powers Fort sites were the location of excavation in 1969. The Gooseneck site, a pre-Powers phase locus situated on the Current River in the Ozark uplands, was excavated in 1972. The Gypsy Joint site was excavated during the summer of 1974, the Old Helgoth Farm site in 1975, and the Big Beaver site in 1976.

A number of publications have resulted from research carried out by personnel of the Powers Phase Project. The initial excavations at the Turner site are described in a brief publication (Price 1969). Two doctoral dissertations were based on analysis of Powers phase data (Price 1973, Smith 1973, 1975). Several articles dealing with the exploitation of animal populations by Powers phase hunters have also appeared in print (Hamblin 1973, Smith 1974a,b). Smith has also written a research monograph based upon excavation of the Gypsy Joint site (Smith 1978). The nature of the Powers phase settlement–subsistence strategy has been detailed in a paper presented to an advanced seminar sponsored by the School of American Research, Santa Fe, New Mexico (Price 1974). General descriptions of the Powers phase have been presented in two cultural resource assessment reports (Price, Price, Harris, House, and Cottier 1975, Price, Price, and Harris 1976).

Environmental Setting

The environmental setting of the Powers phase area has been described elsewhere (Price 1973, 1974, Price *et al.* 1975, and Smith 1973, 1975). A brief summary of these more comprehensive considerations follows.

The Powers phase area is located in the Western Lowland of the Central Mississippi Valley on either side of the Arkansas–Missouri line, adjoining the Ozark Escarpment on the west (Figure 8.1). It is an area of great environmental contrasts, a major ecotone.

The basic substrate of this area of the Western Lowland was deposited during the Early Wisconsin from glacial outwash of the Mississippi River and Missouri River drainage basins (Saucier 1974:8). The landforms are broad, flat to gently rolling stream interfluves and narrow, sinous, flat-bottomed relict braided stream channels (Saucier 1974:9). The maximum elevation of the interfluves or sand ridges is approximately 315–320 ft above sea level. Relict channels are characterized by fine-grained silty and clayey sediments slightly over 4 m thick, whereas the interfluves reveal quite sandy surface soils which grade into sand and gravel within roughly 7–8 m of the surface (Saucier 1974:9). The lowland area had a densely forested seasonally inundated floodplain, with large areas remaining swampy year round.

The adjacent Courtois Hills of the Ozark Highland (Sauer 1920:68–70) are deeply dissected with steep hills and narrow valleys. Drainage systems are dendritic, and the major streams have rock and gravel bottoms, highly contrastive to the sluggish, muddy-bottomed streams of the lowland. Soils of the area also reflect the dichotomy between the Ozark Highland and the Mississippi Alluvial Valley. In the lowland portion of the area there are two major soil associations, one on the sand ridges and one in the low areas.

The sand ridges are classified in the Beulah–Bosket–Brosely association, having relatively level to sloping, well to excessively drained soils that developed in the sandy alluvium of old natural levees of the Mississippi River. Low wet areas are composed of the Amagon–Qulin association, which consists of level, deep, and poorly drained soils with nonacid to moderately alkaline reactions.

Two loess-derived soil associations cover the eastern escarpment of the Ozark Highland. The Falaya–Waverly association lies in a band along the edge of the escarpment on the nearly level floodplain of the Little Black River, whereas the Memphis–Loring–Lax association lies just west of the Falaya–Waverly association.

The hydrology of the Little Black River is unique in Southeast Missouri in that it forms a distinct boundary between the highland and

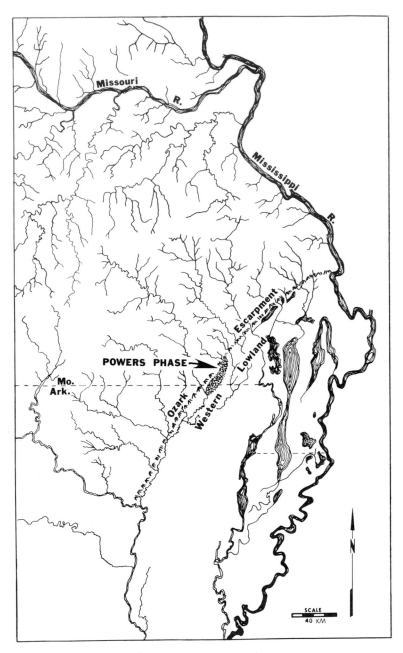

FIGURE 8.1.   The location of the Powers phase area at the extreme western edge of the Mississippi Valley.

lowland. It arises in the Ozark Highland in Carter County, Missouri, and flows first southeasterly, then southwesterly after leaving the Highland near Naylor, Missouri to flow into the Current River near Success, Arkansas (see Figure 8.1 p. 204).

The climate of the area is continental, characterized by general moderation rather than extremes of heat and cold, drought and precipitation (Moxom 1941:953). Summers are hot and winters are mild, with occasional snow flurries. The Ozarks to the west are cooler in both summer and winter than the lowland area, owing to their higher elevations.

Reconstruction of vegetation zones in the area has been carried out by Suzanne Harris (Price *et al.*, 1975:29–41). Direct evidence of the Powers phase environment has been obtained from pollen samples and charred architectural material recovered from Powers phase structures and pits. Twenty-six pollen samples from archeological context indicate a dominance of oaks and hickories (Fish 1971). Unlike the modern environment, the Powers phase functioned in an environment with almost no sweet gum and much more cypress. Higher frequencies of grass and weed pollen indicate rather widespread clearing of forest vegetation by Powers phase populations.

The exploitation of animal populations by hunters of the Powers phase has been discussed in detail by Smith (1974a,b, 1975), so it will suffice to state that a rather wide range of mammals, birds, fish, and shellfish were available in the area ca. A.D. 1300.

The topography, soil associations, and vegetation associations of the Powers phase area are summarized in Figure 8.2. The Powers phase populations lived in a world that was situated adjacent to a major ecotone. Although Powers phase sites are restricted to the sandy alluvium of the lowland sector of the area, many natural resources such as chert, galena, limonite, and hematite were extracted from the Ozarks to the west. By occupying such an area, resources from two dichotomous environments were at hand and readily exploitable.

The Location of Powers Phase Sites Relative to Elevation, Soil Types, and Proximity to Major and Minor Ecotones

As described in the preceding section, the lowland sector of the Powers phase area is composed of sand ridges that are eroded remnants of natural levees dissected by later braided streams of the Mississippi River. The areas between these ridges were covered by swamps until the area was drained in the 1920s and 1930s. Vertical relief is at a minimum, with

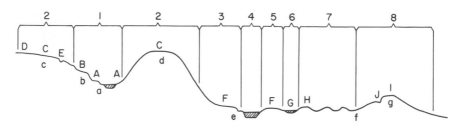

KEY

Environmental zones
1. Stream valley terraces in the Ozark Escarpment
2. Ozark Escarpment
3. Lower Ozark Escarpment slopes and terraces of the Little Black River
4. Little Black River

5. Natural levees of the Little Black River
6. Backswamps areas
7. Priarie blisters
8. Sand ridges

Vegetation
A. Sugar Maple–Bitternut Hickory
B. Sugar Maple–White Oak
C. Oak–Hickory

D. Oak–Pine
E. White Oak–Red Maple

F. Cottonwood–Willow
G. Cypress–Tupelo
H. Willow Oak–*Cherrybark Oak*–Cow Oak
I. Oak–Hickory–Sweetgum
J. Sweetgum–Nuttall Oak–Willow Oak–Pin Oak

Soils associations
a. Aston–Razort
b. Clarksville Wilderness
c. Captina–Loring–Clarksville

e. Falaya–Waverley
f. Amazon–Qulin
g. Beulah–Bosket–Broseley

FIGURE 8.2. *Vegetation and soils of the natural environmental zones of the Little Black River area.*

the sand ridges rising a maximum of 7.6 m above the level of standing water in the swamps prior to drainage. During times of abundant rainfall, the entire area was inundated except for the ridges (Hutton and Krusekopf 1916:11). Powers phase settlement was restricted to ridges above the 90-m contour interval. This phenomenon has also been noted for other Mississippian settlement systems in Southeast Missouri on Sikeston, Barnes, and Sugar Tree Ridges (Price 1974:42). This probably indicates that settlement was not adaptively feasible at lower elevations. Sites below the 91.5-m contour interval would probably have been subjected to seasonal if not permanent flooding, as indicated by the presence of swamps.

Most Powers phase sites are located between 91.5 and 95 m in elevation, but some sites are situated at elevations as high as 98 m. Powers phase populations were essentially restricted to 4.6 vertical meters in their occupation of the lowland sector of the Little Black River area. Occupation below this elevation would have been impractical, owing to the presence of water, and impossible at higher elevations, owing to the absence of land above 100 m above sea level.

Soils were an extremely important variable in the subsistence–settlement strategy of Mississippian populations, and the Powers phase was no exception. The importance of soils as a variable in Mississippian settlement has been recognized for over a decade. Ward (1965) observed that "sites which are Mississippian are located on or approximate to soils with a high degree of natural fertility and a highly friable texture. Silt loams and fine sandy loams have both of these characteristics [p. 45]."

Larson (1970) similarly observed that Mississippian settlements are located "to exploit the well-drained though moist, rich, and easily cultivated soils [p. 19]." All the major sites of the Powers phase (Powers Fort, 10 villages, and 4 hamlets) are located on a single soil association, the Beulah–Bosket–Broseley association. This locational preference for Bosket–Broseley soils has also been noted for Mississippian sites on Sikeston, Barnes, and Sugar Tree Ridges of the Eastern Lowlands (Price 1974:48). Mississippian sites throughout Southeast Missouri are restricted to one or two sandy loam soil associations, even though a wide variety of other soil types were available.

The location of Powers phase sites relative to potential energy resources is an important consideration in reconstructing the Powers phase settlement strategy. The Powers phase area lies on an alluvial plain in the Southeastern Evergreen Forest Region (Braun 1950:290). Biota of the Powers phase area were probably similar to that of the Eastern Lowlands east of Crowley's Ridge in Southeast Missouri. Some exceptions probably existed, however. For example, the Powers phase area was probably outside the Mississippi migratory waterfowl flyway. Certain species of flora such as cottonwood–willow forests were probably not as common in the Powers phase area as in the Eastern Lowlands, where stream action in the Mississippi River meander belt would have created favorable conditions for such forests.

The nature of biotic communities in the Central Valley have been discussed in detail by Smith (1973) and Lewis (1974) and need not be repeated here. Suffice it to state that generally the biotic communities were probably similar throughout much of the Central Valley, including the Powers phase area, with the exception that it is marginal to the valley and immediately adjacent to the Ozark Escarpment.

Comparable Mississippi settlement patterns throughout Southeast Missouri relative to critical site location variables probably indicates a common adaptive niche exploited by Mississippi populations in this portion of the Central Valley. I have argued elsewhere (Price 1974:72) that this common pattern reflects least-cost advantages. By positioning major sites in the most energy efficient locations, Mississippian populations would

have employed a mini–max subsistence strategy. Distributing a population throughout the natural environment in at least four orders of site size
and composition would have effectively dispersed population groups in
order to articulate with all resources of that environment, and would at the
same time have maintained them in close association for common defense,
public works, and ceremonial scheduling. A practice of situating large,
permanent settlements on the ends and margins of ridges, and placing
small, presumably seasonal farmsteads and extractive sites toward the
interior of ridges would have been an efficient exploitative strategy. Presumably, the largest mass of the population would have been closest to a
terrestrial–aquatic interface zone and would have had access to the
greatest variety of plant and animal species per unit of space in the
ecosystem.

Since major Powers phase sites occupy space adjacent to a terrestrial–
aquatic interface zone, the nature of that zone will be examined in detail.
The subtle elevation differences of ridge–swamp margins are associated
with changes from clay to sandy loam soil associations, and flood-
endangered to nonendangered zones, as well as encompassing a wide
variety of plant communities and successional stages in close association
in both the hydrosere and xerosere. A number of writers have pointed out
the nature of meander belt communities (Braun 1950, Lewis 1974, Shelford
1963). Although Lewis (1974) observed the relationship of Mississippian
sites to vegetation zones, he did not consider site size and the overall
advantage of site location in the terrestrial–aquatic interface zone.

Although the ridge margins in the Powers phase area are not exactly
like the meander belt zone, they are quite similar since they, too, represent a terrestrial–aquatic interface. Voigt and Mohlenbrock (1964:55–56)
presented a generalized succession of hydrosere in Illinois that is applicable to the Powers phase area. This interface contains a wide variety of
plant communities with a large number of species represented. These
include stages of submerged, floating leaf, reed swamp, wet meadow,
shrub, and tree vegetation. This complex array of plant species, associated
narrow- and broad-niche animal species, in combination with the highly
productive soils of the natural levee or sand ridge interior zone would
have presented an environment with a high carrying capacity per unit of
land. By locating major settlements on the terrestrial–aquatic interface
zone, Powers phase peoples would have had easy access to a wide variety
of energy resources. Not only would wild plant and animal foodstuffs have
been available in variety and quantity, but other maintenance and construction resources would have been at hand. The most obvious natural
resource would have been water. Clay for daub and ceramics, cane for
wattle, and grass for thatch would have been other important natural
resources readily available from this zone.

The Powers Phase Site Survey

The distribution of Powers phase sites is almost totally limited to the A_1 terrace defined by Fisk (1944:23). This terrace consists of a series of eight sand ridges formed by intertwined or braided stream channels at least 18,000 years old. These eight ridges extend to a height of approximately 4.6 m above the surrounding swampland (Figure 8.3). Although a

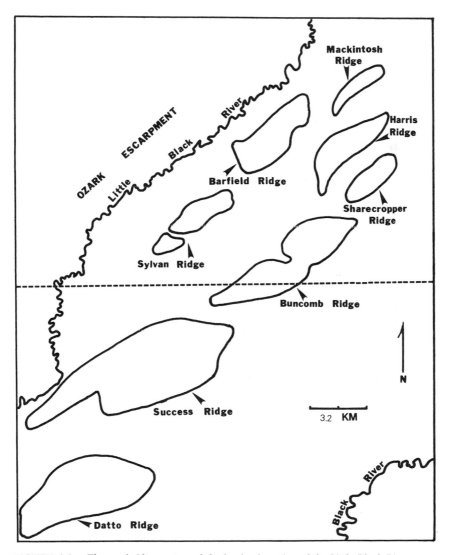

FIGURE 8.3.   *The sand ridge system of the lowland portion of the Little Black River area.*

considerable amount of effort has been directed toward the Ozark Escarpment to the west and the swamplands to the east of the A_1 terrace, no Powers phase sites have been discovered in there. Similarly, Powers phase sites have not been found either on old natural levees of the Little Black River, or on prairie blisters in the swampy areas between these ridges.

The Powers Phase Project has intensively surveyed only the northern half of the A_1 terrace located north of the Arkansas–Missouri line. The survey was restricted to this area because the whole terrace was far too large to survey adequately with the available time, personnel, and funds. Limited coverage by the Powers Phase Project and the Arkansas Archeological Survey indicates the presence of Powers phase sites throughout the southern half of the A_1 terrace. Several Powers phase villages and a large moundless site approximately the size of Powers Fort lie within this area south of the Arkansas–Missouri line. It is interesting to note that although Powers Fort is situated on the northern end of Barfield Ridge near the northern limits of the A_1 terrace, the comparably large site situated on Success Ridge lies near the southern limits of the terrace.

Thus the Powers phase settlement pattern data presented in this chapter encompasses only the northern half of the total Powers phase settlement system of the A_1 terrace in the Western Lowland.

Several years of surface reconnaissance have gone into a definition of the Powers phase settlement pattern. I conducted an initial survey in 1966, and a subsequent survey was conducted by personnel of the Powers Phase Project in 1969 and 1970. Further surface reconnaissance was conducted by James E. Price and Cynthia R. Price from 1972 to 1977 in an attempt to locate more Powers phase sites. During the spring of 1975 another survey was conducted in the area by James E. Price, Cynthia R. Price, Suzanne Harris, John House, and John Cottier. This survey focused on low areas adjacent to drainage ditches in the lowlands, as well as on several stream valleys in the Ozark Highland, in preparation of a cultural resource assessment for the United States Department of Agriculture, Soil Conservation Service.

THE RESEARCH DESIGN OF POWERS PHASE SURVEYS

The research design for the Powers Phase Project surface surveys was formulated to

1. Locate a large percentage of the Powers phase sites in various environmental zones of the Little Black River area north of the Arkansas–Missouri line.
2. Assess site size by establishing both the area of surface distribution

of material remains and the presence of midden or surface stains indicating the presence of structures.
3. Assess the location of sites relative to environmental variables of elevation, soil type, and land form.
4. Recover surface collections of cultural material for comparative purposes and for assessment of intersite variability among sites of the Powers phase.

SURVEY LIMITATIONS

It is incorrect to assume that all sites can be discovered through an intensive survey. There is a common misconception among many archeologists that a "comprehensive reconnaissance" or "complete" survey is practical and possible. In terms of the current threshold of archeological visibility in the Powers phase area, only certain kinds of sites are detectable. These are sites that yield material evidence in the form of debitage, pottery sherds, burned clay, and other evidence of human occupation from the ground surface. Examples of sites beyond the present threshold of archeological visibility are locations where such procurement activities as water drawing, basket splint extraction, or bee-tree robbing presumably took place.

Walkovers carried out in the Little Black River area have involved section by section coverage, with visual examination of the ground surface. When surface evidence of prehistoric or historic activity was noted, the approximate size of the site, local environmental setting, and nature of the material remains were recorded on standard survey forms. Sites discovered from 1975 onward have been recorded on forms designed for Southeast Missouri archeological research activities, and include more pertinent site information than previously used forms.

Surface collections in the Little Black River area have been carried out with various strategies. Collections recovered by the first surveys were "grab samples," which were limited to obvious artifacts such as projectile points, bifaces, pottery sherds, and a "representative" sample of flakes, fire-cracked rock, and other waste material. Later surface collections were sometimes gathered by rigorously controlled surface collection strategies involving "total" pickup of "all" items within randomly selected sampling quadrats. Both the Powers Fort and Snodgrass sites have been surface collected in this manner. Both sites were plowed and weathered prior to collection activities. Controlled sampling techniques were used on other sites depending upon surface conditions and expediency. One method, used in situations where sites were located in fields under row crop cultivation, was to carry out a total pickup of specimens in randomly selected crop rows across the site. Another technique involved the collection of specimens within a randomly selected circle with a 1 m radius.

Many variables have influenced the inventory of Powers phase sites in the Little Black River area. Refusal by landowners to grant access has not posed a problem since only one landowner in the area has refused permission for archeological reconnaissance. Survey in the area has been carried out for a sufficient period of time that landowners are familiar with the project and often invite survey of their property for archeological sites. Of greater importance are natural factors that affect land accessibility, such as crops, forest cover, weeds, and water. Even after a decade of survey in the area, certain locales have never been accessible for survey. Many farmers practice double cropping, and only a few hours are available each year for surface reconnaissance, since some farmers do not permit survey on planted fields. Appointments must often be made with the landowner in order to conduct a survey between summer crops of cotton or soybeans and winter wheat. Other areas have been planted as permanent pasture, which obscures the ground surface. Although a site can usually be detected in such fields, the extent and content of the sites are often difficult to ascertain. Some locales are covered by forests or farm buildings and are not easily accessible for survey, whereas other areas are covered by swamps that are full of water and vegetation throughout the year, making survey impractical.

Vegetation cover is a major factor limiting survey on the Ozark Escarpment to the west of the Little Black River. Land use in this area involves lumbering and cattle production.

Perhaps the most frustrating factor for site detection in the lowland zones of the Little Black River area involves a surface obscuring phenomenon we do not fully understand. Sites on the sandy loam ridges in the area are sometimes obvious and at other times are completely obscured. Large village sites, the Steinberg site being an example, were discovered in areas that had been repeatedly surveyed several times by at least three individuals. If surface conditions are not exactly right, no evidence of prehistoric occupation is visible. Two weeks later the surface may be littered with cultural materials. A slight shifting of surface sand by wind is probably responsible for this phenomenon. We have observed the Turner site when only about five sherds could be collected from the surface even after it had been plowed and rains had fallen on it.

There is a possibility that some sites are buried beneath duned sand. The Flurry site was first discovered in a road cut, and subsequent subsurface reconnaissance revealed that most of the western side of the site was buried under several feet of drifted sand. Many Powers phase hamlets and limited activity sites were discovered only after repeated visits to certain locales. Detection of structure stains is best immediately after a site has been plowed. Many sites have been discovered under these conditions.

Some limited activity sites have been discovered with soil coring tools in areas where the presence of Powers phase structures was suspected.

The Powers Phase Project surface reconnaissance program has been extremely intensive, but not comprehensive, owing to the limiting factors just outlined. There are no means at hand to estimate adequately the percentage of Powers phase sites that have been discovered. The survey has covered most of the study area at least once, and has covered much of the area as many as a dozen or more times. We feel that we have a significant percentage of the larger village sites inventoried, but smaller sites such as hamlets and limited-activity sites have posed many detection problems. There is no adequate means to estimate how many have gone undetected. Nonetheless, we feel that we have an adequate sample of sites of various sizes relative to landforms, soil types, and elevation to reconstruct the settlement pattern of the Powers phase.

The Range of Site Size in the Powers Phase

The settlement pattern of the Powers phase consists of sites of four orders of size. The orders are a civic–ceremonial center (Powers Fort); villages (Hunt, Taft, Malcom Turner, Flurry, Wilborn, Steinberg, Turner, Snodgrass, Smith, and McCarty–Moore); hamlets (Stick Chimney, Bliss, Harris Ridge, and Newkirk); and limited-activity sites (Gypsy Joint, Big Beaver, Old Helgoth Farm, to mention at few).

Powers Fort is approximately 4.6 ha (11.5 acres) in area. The range of village size, based on those that have been excavated or adequately mapped from surface stain evidence, is approximately .6–1.2 ha (1.5–2.85 acres). It appears from the data on hand that there are two distinct village sizes. The Turner and Steinberg sites are approximately .6 ha (1.5 acres) in size, whereas the Flurry, Wilborn, and Snodgrass sites are approximately 1.0 ha (2.5 acres) in size. Based on the distribution of surface stains and cultural material, hamlets are approximately .1 ha (.25 acres) in size. From our excavations at the Gypsy Joint, Old Helgoth Farm, and Big Beaver sites, and stain observations on numerous other sites, limited-activity sites appear to be extremely small, consisting of only one to three structures isolated on a sand ridge.

Site size appears not to be random or a continuum, but tends to cluster at certain size intervals. Powers Fort is approximately 7.0 times larger than the Turner site, 4.8 times larger than the Flurry site, and 4.0 times larger than the Snodgrass and Wilborn sites. Small villages are approximately four times larger than hamlets, large villages are approximately twice as large as small villages, and Powers Fort is approximately four times larger than large villages. Such ratios must in some way reflect the uniform size of

organized population segments on each site type, but the exact sociopolitical composition of the sites is not yet fully understood.

The Spatial Distribution of Powers Phase Sites

The primary factor influencing the distribution of Powers phase sites
is the distribution of sand ridges. Sites are restricted in location to these
sand ridges. Ridge size and elevation obviously dictated the most feasible
loci for site placement, since all surrounding areas were covered by
swamps or subject to seasonal flooding. Sufficient land was available,
however, to permit a far different site distribution than that actually
observed for the Powers phase. Second-order sites (villages) could have
been placed closer together or farther apart than they were. From locational evidence it appears that the settlement pattern is much too regular
to have been accidental (Figure 8.4). The settlement pattern is radial in
configuration on the northern half of the A_1 terrace. Powers Fort lies to the
north and west of most of the sites, with a majority of the village sites
forming an arc north, east, and south of the ceremonial center. Travel time
between sites is rather difficult to compute, but should be kept in mind as
a factor in site distribution. A very regular settlement pattern is evident,
especially along the north and east side of the settlement system. Secondary
sites occur in an arc 3.5–6.0 km (2.2–3.75 miles) distant from Powers Fort in
the northern and eastern portion of the settlement pattern. With the exception of the McCarty–Moore site, village sites are either immediately adjacent to each other or are located 2.5–3.0 km (1.55–1.90 miles) apart. Those
sites immediately adjacent to each other represent a paired-village phenomenon that is not fully understood (Figure 8.5). Known paired villages
are Taft and Hunt, Malcolm Turner and Flurry, Wilborn and Steinberg, and
Turner and Snodgrass. Intensive survey throughout various times of the
year, combined with the use of soil core tools on areas adjacent to known
single village sites such as Smith and McCarty–Moore will probably reveal
additional sites that will complete the pairs. I also feel that the Powers phase
was of such short duration that the paired village phenomenon does not
represent reoccupation of a locale by a second village after the first was
abandoned, but rather represents contemporaneous occupations.

Internal Features on Powers Phase Sites

The size range of sites, as discussed previously is obviously a direct
result of variation in the number of site elements, such as mounds,
courtyards, structures, pits, burials, and walls.

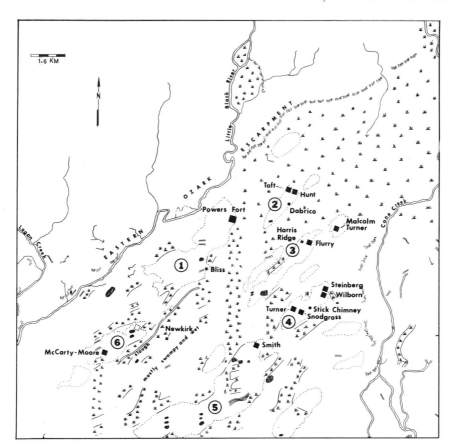

FIGURE 8.4. The distribution of Powers phase sites on the north end of the A_1 terrace. 1. Barfield Ridge; 2. Mackintosh Ridge; 3. Harris Ridge; 4. Sharecropper Ridge; 5. Buncomb Ridge; 6. Sylvan Ridge. Key: ■ = civic–ceremonial center; ■ = village; ▪ = hamlet.

Powers Fort (Figure 8.6) is the only site of the phase that has mounds and presumably a large plaza. One mound was large and flat topped, whereas three secondary mounds were hemispherical in shape. The site has large residential sectors to the northwest, west, and south of the plaza.

No data are presently available to determine whether large cemeteries exist at Powers Fort. Burials are known to be scattered throughout most of the site. Based on observed concentrations of human bone on the ground surface in certain areas, I suspect that large cemeteries are present on the site. Cemeteries exist in some Powers phase villages, but are absent from others. The major courtyard on the west side of the Turner site contained a large cemetery consisting of 106 individuals. The Snodgrass site, located only 160 m to the east, contained six adult burials distributed around the periphery of the internal compound, but no cemetery was present. Both

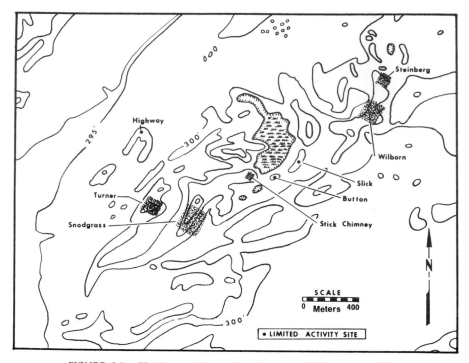

FIGURE 8.5. The Powers phase settlement pattern of Sharecropper Ridge.

sites were almost completely excavated so it is certain that some villages contain cemeteries and others do not. Cemeteries are known to exist on the Taft site and the Steinberg site. Based on the Turner–Snodgrass excavations, test excavations on the Taft site, and surface observations on other Powers phase village sites, it seems highly probable that cemeteries do not occur on the large village sites (Snodgrass, Wilborn, and Hunt), and are present on small village sites (Turner, Steinberg, and Taft). In all known cases, cemeteries appear to be in the major courtyard on the west side of these small village sites. Little information is available concerning mortuary practices at Powers phase hamlets. A burial area is known to exist on the west side of the Harris Ridge site. The size of the area is unknown, but surface evidence in the form of human bone fragments indicates that it contained several individuals. No mortuary data are available for the Newkirk, Bliss, Stick Chimney, or Dabrico sites.

Some data are available concerning mortuary practices at limited-activity sites of the Powers phase. No Powers phase burials were discovered at the Gypsy Joint site, but the Old Helgoth Farm site yielded a single-bundle burial south of two structures (see Figure 8.11, page 222), whereas the Big Beaver site had a small cemetery area consisting of at least four bundle burials located between Structures 2 and 3 on the highest part

FIGURE 8.6.   Contour map of Powers Fort.

of the sand ridge on which the site was situated (see Figure 8.12, page 223).

The number of structures present on Powers phase sites obviously varies according to site size. The exact number of structures present at Powers Fort is unknown, but from limited test excavations and surface observations, it is obvious that hundreds of structures are present. These structures apparently lie around the periphery of the site. The central area south of Mound 1 and east of Mounds 2, 3, and 4 is presumably a large plaza and is essentially devoid of cultural material. The location of specialized and public structures on this site is presently unknown. Surface evidence indicates that the largest quantity of "exotic" painted, polished, and engraved ceramics are concentrated northwest of Mound 1 and this may indicate either a public area or the location of specialized structures. Evidence of specialized structures is known to exist in Mound 1, based on data from Norris's excavations (Norris 1883).

The best data concerning the number of structures in Powers phase villages has come from the Turner–Snodgrass excavations. The Turner site (Figure 8.7) contained evidence of 48 structures and the Snodgrass site (Figure 8.8) contained evidence of 94 structures. From surface stain evidence, the Wilborn and Hunt sites contain approximately the same number of structures as the Snodgrass site. The differential number of structures present on village sites is rather conclusive evidence that there are two distinct sizes of Powers phase villages.

Apparently, there are specialized and public structures on all village sites. These large structures are usually on the west side of the sites, surrounding the major courtyard. The most important public structures, based on size, depth, and content are located to the west of the courtyard and form the last western row of structures. On both the Turner and Snodgrass sites these public structures are separated by the width of half a structure from the other structures in the western row. On the Snodgrass site this separation is to the west, on the Turner site, it is to the east. On the Snodgrass site, those structures adjacent to the courtyard on the west and east are far deeper than other structures on the site. The largest structures on village sites tend to be adjacent to or in the vicinity of the major western courtyard.

From the Turner–Snodgrass excavations, and from surface observa-

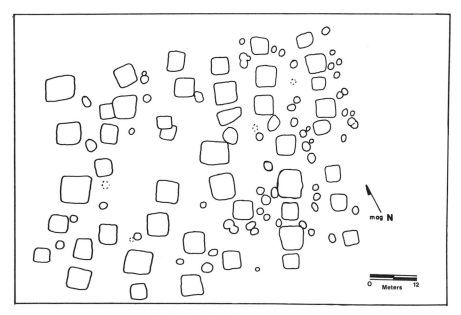

FIGURE 8.7. *The Turner site.*

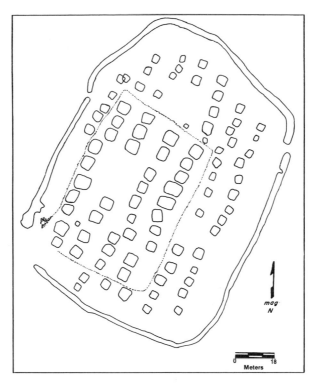

FIGURE 8.8.   The Snodgrass site.

tions on other Powers phase villages, it is evident that structures on the eastern and western sides of the village are different in terms of size, depth, and content. Structures in the western area of villages are the largest and deepest, contain the most *in situ* cultural material, and are most often burned.

The range of variation in the number of structures present on Powers phase hamlets such as Stick Chimney, Dabrico, Harris Ridge, Bliss, and Newkirk is not known because no hamlet has yet been excavated. From size and surface stain evidence these sites appear to contain from 9 to 12 structures. The best evidence for the size of hamlets comes from the Stick Chimney site, where 12 surface structure stains were observed after plowing. Structures are in rows, and the hamlets appear to be approximately square.

More complete data are available on Powers phase limited-activity sites since three such sites have been excavated to date, and surface observations have been made on dozens more. The distribution of these smaller sites on Barfield Ridge is illustrated in Figure 8.9.

The Gypsy Joint site (Figure 8.10), excavated in 1974, yielded two structures, one northeast of the other on a small sand knoll. The Old

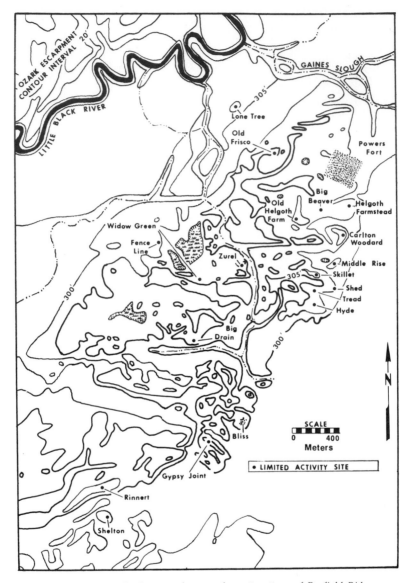

FIGURE 8.9. The Powers phase settlement pattern of Barfield Ridge.

Helgoth Farm site (Figure 8.11), excavated in 1975, yielded two structures in a similar arrangement as that observed at the Gypsy Joint site. The Big Beaver site (Figure 8.12), which lies on the small sand ridge immediately east of the Old Helgoth Farm site, contained three structures rather evenly spaced on a north–south axis.

Surface observations on other Powers phase limited-activity sites in-

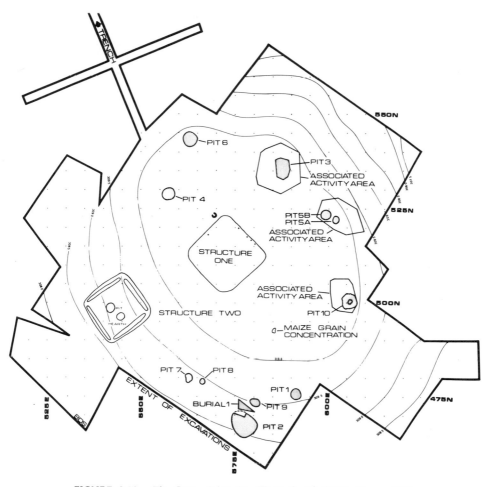

FIGURE 8.10.   *The Gypsy Joint site.* [From Smith (1978: Figure 10).]

dicate that one or two structures are usually present. From structure size and content it is evident that not all limited-activity sites are alike. The Gypsy Joint site, for example, contained huge quantities of charred hickory-nut hulls and seeds. The structures were essentially surrounded by a series of pits. In contrast, the Old Helgoth Farm site did not yield any charred vegetal materials, nor were there any pits present.

Intersite and Intrasite Variation

Since detailed analysis of cultural materials have been completed for only the Turner, Snodgrass, and Gypsy Joint sites, many of the following

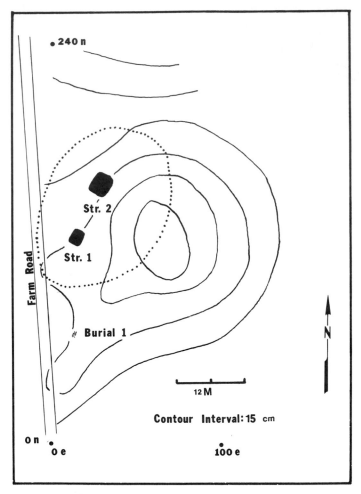

FIGURE 8.11. *The Old Helgoth Farm site.*

observations concerning other Powers phase sites are somewhat subjective. It is quite obvious from extensive surface collections and limited excavations at Powers Fort that the site contains a large volume of archeological materials, probably as much or more than all of the other villages and hamlets combined. Powers Fort contains a greater variety of vessel shapes and modes of surface treatment than any other site of the phase. Although this is probably due in some measure to the large sample of sherds available from the site, it also indicates that activities were probably performed on that site that were not performed on other sites, and that certain trade vessels reached the civic–ceremonial center that never reached lower-order sites. There are likewise larger quantities of

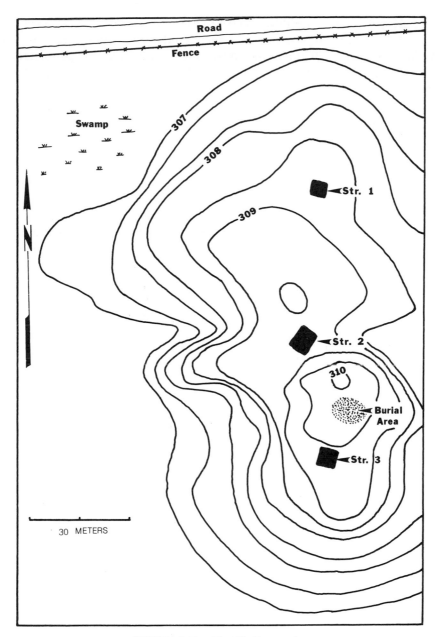

FIGURE 8.12. *The Big Beaver site.*

lithic artifacts present on Powers Fort than on other sites of the phase. The bulk of the archeological material recovered from Powers Fort is very similar to materials obtained from other sites in the phase. Examinations of surface collections and excavated materials from dozens of Powers phase sites reveals extreme homogeneity of material assemblages. The same jar, bowl, and bottle forms are present in all villages. Surface decoration was executed on a very small percentage of Powers phase ceramics, and most motifs are present at each of the village sites.

Since no hamlets have been excavated, the nature of the material assemblage associated with this site catagory is not known in detail. Surface collections indicate that the assemblage is generally similar to that of villages. The same jar, bowl, and bottle forms are present, as well as the same kinds of trade lithics such as Mill Creek Chert. Decorated ceramics are essentially lacking from hamlets, although this observation may be due to the relatively small surface samples recovered from these sites.

The material contents of Powers phase limited-activity sites varies considerably, presumably because of the different kinds of activities performed on these sites. The Gypsy Joint site yielded large quantities of lithic debris and hickory nut hulls. There was a moderate amount of ceramics present and for the most part these represented large jars. Structure 2 yielded a short-necked bottle fragment as well as a notched rim from a small jar. Other decorated ceramics from the site were a zoomorphic jar handle, a three-line-chevron-incised large jar shoulder, and an incised jar handle (Smith 1978).

The Old Helgoth Farm site yielded very little cultural material. That present was primarily ceramic body sherds, a small jar rim sherd, a projectile point, and limited lithic debris. Structure 1 at the Old Helgoth Farm site, however, yielded a round fluorite bead, the only such artifact yet recovered from a Powers phase site. No decorated ceramics were discovered at the site.

The Big Beaver site, which consisted of three rather widely spaced structures, yielded a variety of artifacts. Although Structure 1 had been almost entirely destroyed by a land leveler prior to investigation of the site, the contents, which had been dumped nearby, were thoroughly examined. The structure contained few ceramic materials, but a rather large quantity of angular chert, quartzite, and sandstone fragments were recovered. Only a small quantity of sherds and lithic debris was recovered from Structure 2 at the Big Beaver site during the land leveling procedures that destroyed the site. An adult human cranium was noted on the floor of the northeast corner of the structure. Approximately half of Structure 3 was excavated prior to its destruction. It contained a small quantity of sherds and lithic debris.

The fact that the material content of the Old Helgoth Farm site and the Big Beaver site is quite different than that of the Gypsy Joint site is probably related to their proximity to Powers Fort. It is highly likely that they functioned as some facility associated with activities performed at Powers Fort.

Powers Phase Settlement System Analysis

The Powers phase settlement pattern reflects a social, political, and economic system that was distributed over the sand ridges of the A_1 terrace in the Western Lowlands for a relatively brief period of time in the latter part of the thirteenth and first part of the fourteenth centuries A.D. The long-enduring question that has been at the root of all research conducted by the Powers phase Project has concerned the manner in which the Powers phase settlements of various sizes were integrated into a social, economic, and political system. This subject has been discussed at length by me, James B. Griffin, Bruce D. Smith, Richard T. Malouf, Suzanne E. Harris, Wilma Wetterstrom, and many other individuals involved in the project. Although the results of the project, data generated over a 10-year period, would fill several large monographs, it is appropriate to outline briefly the way I view the Powers Phase as an integrated whole.

First, I cannot escape a conclusion that the Powers phase represents a Mississippian influx into the Western Lowland of Southeast Missouri as a colonization effort that failed. Radiocarbon dates indicate that the Powers phase was short-lived. This conclusion is supported by the archeological evidence from all the sites excavated to date. Very little evidence for structure repair and replacement, the lack of midden accumulation, and the rare occurrence of overlapping pits and structures tend to support the proposition that villages, hamlets, and limited-activity sites were occupied for only a very brief time. Powers Fort, the presumed civic–ceremonial center of the phase, has qualitatively more material than other sites, and has yielded limited evidence of structure repair and replacement. But it, too, was occupied for a relatively short period of time. In comparison with the extensive Mississippian manifestations located in the Cairo Lowland of Southeast Missouri and the Lower St. Francis region, the Powers phase clearly represents a rather fleeting endeavor.

I have long maintained that Powers phase villages and lower-order sites were occupied for no more than 10 years; and probably for no more than 5 years. Without exception, all the villages that have been tested or excavated reveal the fleeting nature of the phase. They reveal that the core areas were terminated by burning. Similar evidence of burning is present at Powers Fort. Even small homesteads such as the Gypsy Joint site (Smith 1978) show evidence of burning. For the most part, portable items were removed from structures prior to or immediately after the fire that consumed them. Items left behind are large cooking and storage vessels, damaged vessels, large stone grinding slabs, solid ceramic cones, and other unwieldy or heavy objects. It appears that the Powers phase population simply picked up and left the region at ca. A.D. 1325–1350. It is highly likely that it was they who put the torch to the settlements. A total of over 10 acres of Powers phase sites has been excavated, and as yet the archeological evidence that would indicate large scale hostilities has not been observed.

Owing to the isolated and ephemeral nature of the Powers phase, certain chronological and spatial controls exist that are absent in Mississippian settlement systems elsewhere. The Powers phase represents an ideal situation—indeed, a unique opportunity—conducive to settlement system analysis. It is largely isolated from other Mississippian manifestations in the Mississippi Valley, and was of relatively short chronological duration.

In order to view the Powers phase as an integrated whole, certain variables should be examined for sites of each size category in the system These variables include the types and ranges of activities carried out on sites, the seasonality of site occupation, and the levels of social, political, and economic organization that functioned to integrate sites into a coherent system.

LIMITED-ACTIVITY SITES

Limited-activity sites, as I define them, are those sites where minimal population units articulated with the natural environment for extractive and maintenance purposes. As indicated earlier in this chapter, some limited-activity sites are beyond the threshold of archeological detection and definition. Others, such as "farmsteads" or "homesteads," are detectable. These sites represent the level of site size and composition that I can currently identify as being the minimal population and spatial unit in the Powers phase settlement system.

The best evidence for the content and range of activities carried out on such a site comes from Smith's monograph on the Gypsy Joint site (Smith 1978). After detailed analysis of the site, Smith concludes that it was probably occupied for a very brief period of time, probably less than four years; that it was probably occupied throughout the yearly cycle; that the occupying group consisted of from five to seven males and females comprising a nuclear–minimally extended family; and that a wide variety of activities ranging from the manufacture of lithic tools to the processing of both floral and faunal materials were carried out.

Other limited-activity sites located much closer to Powers Fort (the Big

Beaver and Old Helgoth Farm sites—Figure 8.9), although badly damaged by land leveling, were somewhat different from the Gypsy Joint site. The Big Beaver site, for example, had a small cemetery associated with it. Owing to their extremely close proximity to Powers Fort these small sites should not be viewed as typical limited-activity sites (if there are such typical sites). The probable role of these limited-activity sites in the social, political, and economic organization of the Powers phase will be discussed in what follows.

HAMLETS

Since no Powers phase hamlets have been excavated to date, very little can be said of the range of activities performed in them, their seasonality of occupation, and the role of their inhabitants in the social, political, and economic organization of the phase. Surface material from hamlets indicate that essentially the same activities were performed on them as on farmsteads. I doubt that they contain any of the public structures, fortifications, or courtyards that are present in the villages.

VILLAGES

As stated previously, there are apparently two village sizes in the Powers phase. The larger villages were not only occupied by more people, they also apparently had a slightly different range of activities performed in them than was taking place in the small villages. Both large and small village sites contained evidence of maintenance activities and activities related to the processing of both faunal and floral foodstuffs. Although there are courtyards, fortifications, and specialized structures on both large and small villages, they were apparently different in the way they served the population. The Turner site, for example, apparently served the community as the location of mortuary services, since it contained a cemetery with large numbers of individuals. It apparently served as the burial place for the dead generated by a larger community than the Turner site itself. The largest Powers phase structure excavated to date occurred on the Turner site (Structure 11), rather than on the larger Snodgrass site. The Turner site also contained a burned corn crib (Structure 2) which probably represents central storage of seed or surplus maize. All in all, the smaller Turner site appears to have been a more sociopolitically integrating settlement than was the larger Snodgrass site only 160 m distant. The Turner and Snodgrass sites are similar in that each has core and peripheral areas (see Figures 8.7 and 8.8). The core area of each village site occurs toward the west side of the settlement, and is bordered by the largest and deepest structures containing the most material remains present on the site. The core area on the Snodgrass site, containing 38 structures, was surrounded by a white clay wall. Some evidence also exists for the presence of a similar wall on the Turner site. Structures inside the core areas appear to have been more sturdily constructed than those outside, and often exhibit wall trench construction, which seldom occurs outside the core. Peripheral structures are smaller, shallower, more flimsily constructed, and did not burn with nearly the intensity as did those in the core area. This observed pattern holds true for the Turner, Snodgrass, Wilborn, and Flurry sites, and I suspect from surface indications on other sites, it is universal for the Powers phase.

From the evidence to date, I feel that while the villages were tied into a system that was integrated by a common civic–ceremonial center, Powers Fort, that populations on each major ridge in the Little Black River area were more or less autonomous and self-sufficient. Generally, there were paired villages on the north and south ends of the ridges, which probably maintained a core population throughout the year. The peripheral structures, those outside the core area, were probably not occupied throughout the year. Residents of these structures probably occupied small farmsteads or homesteads away from the village for a portion of the year, most likely the fall and winter, judging from the fact that the flimsy peripheral structures appear to be more suited for use in warm weather (see Smith 1978:196–200, and Chapter 16 of this volume).

Thus, I view social, political, and economic organization to have centered around paired villages on sand ridges, each village serving different functions in annual ceremonial scheduling. The divisions among and within the villages were probably along sociopolitical lines. The core versus peripheral division of the villages was probably along status or rank lines.

CIVIC–CEREMONIAL CENTER

Powers Fort, the largest site in the phase, was obviously the location of activities that were not performed on lower-order sites in the settlement system. The fortifications of this site were much more massive than those of the villages. Powers Fort is also unique in that it contains four mounds, and is the only site of the phase to contain such earthworks. Presumably, ceremonial activities were performed on that site as services for the entire phase. In addition to a ceremonial function, it housed a rather large population, based on the number of observed surface-structure stains. From such stain evidence it appears that it, too, had core and peripheral areas similar to the villages (see also the discussion of the Kincaid site by Muller, Chapter 10, and the discussion of the Angel site by Green and

Munson, Chapter 11). Archeological evidence indicates that a broad range of maintenance and floral and faunal processing activities were carried out at the Powers Fort site.

Powers Fort probably served as the major integrating force in the entire Powers phase sociopolitical system. It probably performed redistributional and ceremonial services for the entire population of the farmsteads, hamlets, and villages.

DISCUSSION

I view the Powers phase as a sociopolitical system that was integrated on two main levels—the village and the civic–ceremonial center. Villages apparently served as a central place or base of operations through which the resources of the various broad sand ridges were exploited. Villages served as the loci for local ceremonial mortuary services as well as fortified refuges from potential enemy attack. They apparently served as centers with public structures, some of which were used for storage of foodstuffs that may be indicative of redistribution. Powers Fort not only served as a dwelling place for its inhabitants, but also as a central place or base of operations for ceremonial activities involving mounds, probably for the entire phase.

Future Research Goals

Although a great deal of research has been conducted on the Powers phase, many facts concerning the settlement pattern still lie within the realm of the unknown. Perhaps the most immediate need is an intensive resurvey of the entire A_1 terrace during various seasons of the year. The survey should incorporate soil coring or limited subsurface testing to determine the presence or absence of Powers phase sites on many sand ridges. There may be hundreds of small limited activity sites that have been undetected by previous surveys. An experimental survey of .25 mi^2 of Barfield Ridge revealed nine such sites that had not previously been discovered. Several of these sites should be excavated throughout the Powers phase area to determine the range of activities performed on them.

A research program involving Sharecropper Ridge is imperative if we are ever to understand fully the sociopolitical organization of the ridge system as a whole. Since a large data base exists for the ridge from the Turner–Snodgrass excavations it would be reasonably easy to sample the Wilborn and Steinberg sites to determine if they exhibit similar internal organization as Turner and Snodgrass. The Stick Chimney site, a hamlet, should be entirely excavated in order to understand the range of activities and seasonality of occupation of such a site. Also, selected limited-activity sites on Sharecropper Ridge should be excavated to understand better their spatial and seasonal relationship to the hamlet and village sites.

It is imperative that this research be conducted in the near future, because time is running out. Agricultural land-leveling is taking place at a rapid rate. Large-scale earthmoving activities are leveling the sand ridges and filling the low swampy areas between them. Within 10–20 years over 50% of the Powers phase sites may be irretrievably lost.

References

Braun, E. Lucy
  1950   *Deciduous forests of eastern North America.* Philadelphia: Blakiston.
Fish, Suzanne K.
  1971   Archaeological pollen analysis of the Powers phase, Southeastern Missouri. Manu-
        script on file at the Museum of Anthropology, University of Michigan. Ann Arbor,
        Michigan.
Fisk, Harold N
  1944   *Geological investigation of the alluvial valley of the Lower Mississippi River*, Vicks-
        burg: Mississippi River Commission.
Hamblin, Nancy L.
  1973   The age composition of a Middle Mississippi raccoon kill. *The Missouri Ar-*
        chaeologist **35**(3–4):37–43.
Hutton, H., and H. Krusekoph
  1916   The soils of Missouri. *Soils Bulletin.* Columbia: The University of Missouri.
Larson, Lewis H.
  1970   Settlement distribution during the Mississippi period. *The Southeastern Archaeolog-*
        ical Conference, Bulletin **13**:19–25.
Lewis, R. Barry
  1974   Mississippian exploitative strategies: A southeast Missouri example. *Missouri Ar-*
        chaeological Society, Research Series **11**.
Moxom, Walter J.
  1941   Climate of Missouri. In *Climate and Man, Yearbook of Agriculture* **1941**:945–954.
        United States Department of Agriculture. Washington D.C.: United States Govern-
        ment Printing Office.
Norris, P.W.
  1883   Letter of February tenth, 1883 from P.W. Norris, ethnological assistant, to J.W.
        Powell, Director, Bureau of American Ethnology, Smithsonian Institution. On file
        at the Anthropological Archives, Smithsonian Institution, Washington D.C.
Price, James E.
  1966   *Missouri Archaeological Society, Newsletter* **98**:5–6.
  1969   Analysis of a Middle Mississippi house. *Museum of Anthropology, University of*
        Missouri, Museum Briefs **1**. Columbia, Missouri: University of Missouri.
  1973   Settlement planning and artifact distribution on the Snodgrass site, and their
        socio-political implications in the Powers phase of Southeast Missouri. Ph.D.
        dissertation, Department of Anthropology, University of Michigan. Ann Arbor,
        Michigan: University Microfilms.

1974   Mississippian settlement systems of the Central Mississippi Valley. Paper presented at an advanced seminar on Mississippian development. Sponsored by the School of American Research, Santa Fe.

Price, James E., Cynthia R. Price, Suzanne Harris, John House, and John Cottier
1975   An assessment of the cultural resources of the Little Black Watershed. Report submitted to the United States Department of Agriculture—Soil Conservation Service.

Price, James E., Cynthia R. Price, and Suzanne Harris
1976   An assessment of the cultural resources of the Fourche Creek Watershed. Report submitted to the United States Department of Agriculture—Soil Conservation Service.

Saucier, Roger T.
1974   Quaternary geology of the Lower Mississippi Valley. *Arkansas Archaeological Survey, Research Series* **6.** Fayetteville, Arkansas: Arkansas Archaeological Survey.

Sauer, Carl O.
1920   The geography of the Ozark Highland of Missouri. *The Geographic Society of Chicago, Bulletin* **7.** Chicago: University of Chicago Press.

Shelford, Victor E.
1963   *The ecology of North America.* Urbana: University of Illinois Press.

Smith, Bruce D.
1973   Middle Mississippi exploitation of animal populations. Ph.D. dissertation, Department of Anthropology, University of Michigan. Ann Arbor: University Microfilms.
1974a   Predator–prey relationships in the eastern Ozarks: A.D. 1300. *Human Ecology* **2:**31–44.
1974b   Middle Mississippi exploitation of animal populations: A predictive model. *American Antiquity* **39**(2):274–291.
1975   Middle Mississippi exploitation of animal populations. Museum of Anthropology, University of Michigan. *Anthropological Papers* **57.**
1978   *Prehistoric patterns of human behavior: A case study in the Mississippi Valley.* New York: Academic Press.

Voigt, John W., and Robert H. Mohlenbrock
1964   *Plant communities of southern Illinois.* Carbondale: Southern Illinois University Press.

Ward, Trawick
1965   Correlation of Mississippian sites and soil types. *The Southeastern Archaeological Conference, Bulletin* **3:**42–48.

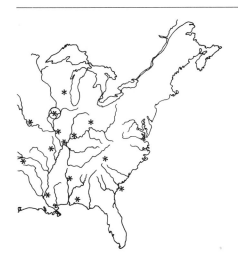

9

Mississippian Settlement Patterns in the Central Illinois River Valley

ALAN D. HARN

The Central Illinois River Valley has a long and varied history of archeological research. Few areas in North America have received such long-term and often concentrated archeological attention. Early county histories throughout the region are rife with glowing, although often accurately detailed, accounts of archeological sites (cf. *History of Fulton County, Illinois* 1879:335–339). Because they were made prior to the major period of looting and before farming activities, strip mining, and a host of other modern agencies had so drastically altered the landscape, these observations have sometimes been our only means of locating and/or interpreting the internal arrangement of features at local archeological sites.

"Professional" interest in Mississippian sites within the Central Illinois Valley was first shown by Colonel P.L. Norris, who conducted a limited archeological survey and test excavation of some of the more spectacular sites for the Smithsonian Institution. Although his work pertained specifically to archeology, and creditable maps were often included, the overall quality of the published report was little better than that produced by historians of the same period (see Thomas 1894:118–120). His handwritten notes stored in the Archives of the Bureau of

233

American Ethnology, Smithsonian Institution, have proved of somewhat greater benefit, although they are not easily accessible to most local researchers.

With the lone exception of John Francis Snyder, a local doctor with an amazing grasp of the archeological method and theory of his day, who published voluminously on his excavations through such outlets as the *Proceedings of the American Association for the Advancement of Science*, *The Archaeologist*, and the *Journal of the Illinois State Historical Society*, no creditable archeological excavation was done in the Central Illinois River Valley until the Dickson family began their explorations in Fulton County during the 1920s. Although, like much of the earlier work, a principal focus of the Dickson's efforts was to obtain artifacts, one family member, Dr. Don F. Dickson, kept notes and sketch maps of most of their excavations, and inventoried the recovered materials. Probably a majority of these records were recently donated to the Dickson Mounds Museum.

Perhaps more importantly this family, principally Don F. and Marion H. Dickson, became the prominent lay archeologists of their day. The Dickson Mound excavation became the center for lay archeologist activity, ensuring that almost no regional material was unearthed or no site discovered that did not soon come to the Dickson's attention. Although they kept only cursory records of these reportings, and published little during their lifetimes, their active involvement during the four decades following 1925 eventually ensured a completeness of archeological survey for the area that would have been otherwise impossible. Marion H. Dickson was especially instrumental in providing locations of Mississippian sites for this study, considerably reducing our survey time by both his recall of sites in obscure places and by his continuing pedestrian reconnaissance—even though he was well into his 70s at the time.

Archeology, as we define it today, came of age in Fulton County in the early 1930s. At that time, three local aboriginal burial sites had been partially excavated and were opened to public viewing on a commercial basis, drawing literally tens of thousands of visitors to this formerly secluded area.

In addition to Don Dickson's excavation at Dickson Mounds, Marion H. Dickson and his brother, Ernest, secured excavation rights to the Ogden and "haystack" mounds, the central mounds of the famous Middle Woodland Ogden–Fettie site about 1 km below Dickson Mounds. In 1928 they succeeded in driving a shored tunnel into the interior of the Ogden Mound, exposing the burials of the central tomb. The central tomb of the "haystack" mound and its associated burials was also exposed, and was protected by a frame building. These excavations were opened to the public from 1928 until 1932 by the Dicksons and from 1938 until 1941 by the Ogden family.

Some 11 km upriver from the Dickson and Ogden–Fettie area, Mr.

Robert Gooden and his son erected a small museum building over mound F°85 of the Late Woodland Maples Mills mound group and began intensive digging. Their almost total excavation of the mound in 1928 uncovered 70 human burials which were displayed, with occasional interruptions, until the mid-1950s.

Publicized by the multitude of articles in newspapers, magazines, and professional journals, the Spoon River area became a focal point of attention by prominent archeologists of that era. Foremost among these was Dr. Fay-Cooper Cole of the University of Chicago, who established the first field school in the Dickson Mounds vicinity in 1930. Over the next two field seasons, Cole and Dr. Thorne Deuel tested a series of 48 stratified mound and village sites and set forth a cultural sequence for the Spoon River area that is still used today (Cole and Deuel 1937).

After the University of Chicago era, the Central Illinois River Valley received only sporadic attention from outside institutions until 1958. In that year, Dr. Joseph R. Caldwell began test excavations on the Eveland Site, the first of several Mississippian sites he was to examine during his 11 years at the Illinois State Museum. The State Museum's association with Dickson Mounds became much closer during this period, resulting both in the latter's transfer in 1965 from the Illinois Department of Conservation to the Department of Registration and Education and in its assignment to the Illinois State Museum system. The research project discussed herein, as well as others originating at the Dickson Mounds Museum since 1965, have been coordinated with the anthropology program of the Illinois State Museum.

Other institutions and organizations recently or currently involved in local Mississippian studies include the University of Illinois—Chicago Circle; the University of Wisconsin—Madison; the University of Wisconsin—Whitewater; and the Upper Mississippi Valley Archeological Research Foundation. Archeological surveys currently being conducted by Western Illinois University are also providing data concerning the Mississippian Period in west–central Illinois.

Periodically throughout the preceding century, numerous individuals have contributed to our understanding of Mississippian site archeology in the Central Illinois River Valley. Expectedly, the single greatest group of contributors in this regard has been the excavators and collectors, many unknown, who have left behind little else than artifacts labeled "Ogden field," "near Dickson Mounds," or simply "Fulton County."

Many excavations have gone unreported, although the recovered materials and occasional notes remain. Descriptions of other excavations have been so brief that location and complete reworking of the original materials is required. This is usually the case with much of the early work, such as that undertaken at Crabtree (Snyder 1908:33–43); in the Lake Peoria area (Powell 1894:xxxix–xl); and Norris's survey and testing of

Mississippian sites in the Walsh Site area (Thomas 1894:118–120). Such brevity still typified post-1930 work done at important sites such as Fiedler (Morse, Schoenbeck, and Morse 1953) and Kingston Lake (Simpson 1952).

Many other, more detailed, reports concerning Spoon River Mississippian sites are available, but most suffer from a partial presentation of definitive data. Numbered among this group are reports dealing with excavations at Crable (Smith 1951); Dickson Camp (Cole and Deuel 1937); Dickson Mounds (Harn 1967); Fouts (Cole and Deuel 1937); Larson (Harn 1966a); Morton Mounds (Cole and Deuel 1937); and the Rose mound group (Baker, Griffin, Morgan, Neumann, and Taylor 1941:22–28). Perhaps the only published Mississippian site report coming out of the Spoon River area to include sufficient raw data is Harn's (1971a) report on the 1927–1930 excavations at Dickson Mounds.

A number of relevant dissertations have been completed, primarily dealing with the 1966–1968 excavations at Dickson Mounds, and several manuscripts pertaining to other local Spoon River sites are either nearing completion or await publication. These deal with excavations at the Berry Site (Conrad n.d.a); Dickson Mounds (Armelagos n.d., Armelagos, Moore and Swedlund n.d., Bahou n.d., Blakely 1973, n.d., Cohen n.d., Conrad 1972, Gilbert n.d., Goodman n.d., Gustav 1972, Harn n.d., Harn and Armelagos n.d., Jacobs n.d., Johnson and Gendron n.d., Lallo 1973, n.d., Lallo and Armelagos n.d.a, b, Miendl n.d., Rose 1973, n.d., VanGerven 1971, and VanGerven and Gustav n.d.); Eveland (Caldwell n.d.); and the Larson Site (Baerreis n.d., Dallman n.d., Emerson n.d., Haberman, Duncan, and Steinberg n.d., Harn and Baerreis n.d., Koeppen, Gendel, and Burch n.d., Oerichbauer n.d., Pillaert n.d., Riggle n.d., and Yerkes n.d.).

Numerous articles relating to some aspect of the Spoon River variant have appeared in various journals. These deal with explorations at Buckeye Bend (Harn and Weedman 1975); Clear Lake (Fowler 1952); Crable (McDonald 1950, Morse 1960, 1969, Neumann 1940); Dickson Mounds (Blakely 1971, Blakely and Walker 1968, Caldwell 1967b, Chapman 1962, Debusk 1967, Ditch and Rose 1972, Harn 1966b, 1972a, 1975a, b); Emmons (Emmons, Munson, and Caldwell 1960, Griffin and Morse 1961, Morse, Morse and Emmons 1961); Eveland (Caldwell 1967a, b); Frederick (Perkins 1965, Young 1960); Kingston Lake (Simpson 1952, Wray 1941); Larson (Harn 1970a, 1972b); Lawrenz Gun Club (Miller 1958); Myer–Dickson (Caldwell 1967b, Harn 1974, Shields 1969); and Orendorf (Conrad 1970, Conrad and Emerson 1974). Articles concerning surveys and general excavation of Mississippian sites have also been supplied by Buis (1940), Schoenbeck (1940) and Harn (1978).

Several unpublished or limited-edition mimeographed reports of investigations describe excavations at such Spoon River sites as Buckeye Bend (Jacobson 1959); Clear Lake (Harn 1976); Dickson Mounds (DeBusk

1966, Roberts 1938, Wells 1937); Kingston Lake (Wray n.d.b); Larson (Harn 1966a); Ogden (Wettersten n.d.); Shryock (Wray n.d.a); and Weaver (Wray and MacNeish n.d.) and include a report of archeological survey in the Rice Lake area (Stephens 1973). Mimeographed papers presenting broader syntheses of the Spoon River variant include those by Conrad (1973); Conrad and Harn (1972, 1976); and Harn (1970b). A revision of the 1972 Conrad and Harn paper has been completed (Conrad n.d.b). An early synthesis of the Mississippian occupation in the Central Illinois River Valley was contributed by Wray (1952).

A wealth of artifacts and unpublished data consisting of field notes, records, maps, and photographs of surveys and test excavations of nearly 150 Spoon River sites was also used in this study. The majority of these are now housed at the Dickson Mounds Museum.

The research to be discussed in what follows resulted not so much from a carefully implemented research program as from historical accident. Interest in the local Mississippian settlement system was probably first generated by Joseph R. Caldwell shortly after his arrival at the Illinois State Museum. By the early 1960s, several other individuals, most notably Lawrence Bowles, Lawrence A. Conrad, Patrick J. Munson, and this author had also begun informally to develop the first explanatory models of the variation in Spoon River Mississippian settlement patterns. Robert L. Hall also added stimulation during his tenure at the Illinois State Museum. No concentrated effort toward a particular end was ever made by any individual, all of us being content to pool our knowledge and add whatever data time would allow between other priorities. Although excavations at such Spoon River variant habitation sites as Larson, Myer–Dickson, Berry, Cooper, Orendorf, and V.L. Trotter were beginning to yield insights into seasonal variability and site function by the early 1970s, most of the original researchers had previously accepted employment outside the region. Only Lawrence A. Conrad and the author remained to continue actively the analysis of local Mississippian settlement patterns.

Environmental–Topographic Setting

The Central Illinois River Valley can be defined as that 210-km valley section between the present-day towns of Hennepin, Illinois, on the north and Meredosia, Illinois, on the south. This central section is separated from the upper and lower valley sections both on the basis of geographic location and because wide differences often exist in topography, hydrology, flora, and fauna (cf. Schwegman 1973). The broader central valley borders the southeastern edge of the Galesburg Plain of the Till Plains section of the Central Lowland Province. Most of the central section of the valley can be characterized as being in late youth in the erosion cycle (Wanless 1957:15).

Three major natural floristic divisions are bisected by the Central Illinois River Valley (Schwegman 1973). The Western Forest–Prairie and Grand Prairie Divisions border its western margin whereas the Illinois River Sand Area and Grand Prairie Divisions border the valley on the east. The extreme southeastern limit of the valley is bordered by a mosaic of four natural divisions, the Illinois River Sand Area, Western Forest–Prairie, Middle Mississippi Border, and Grand Prairie (Figure 9.1).

The Western Forest–Prairie Division was composed of nearly equal amounts of dense oak–hickory forest and sections of open prairie, the forest primarily situated in the heavily dissected areas along the tributaries of the Illinois River. The three principal prairies of this division, Bushnell, Carthage, and Hancock, covered much of the flat uplands with numerous fingers invading the forest region (Figure 9.2).

Extensive grasslands with numerous marshes and prairie potholes characterized the Grand Prairie Division, although limited woodlands were evident along the Mackinaw and Sangamon river valleys, the Illinios valley basin and adjacent bluff edges of the north–central section, and in the multidivisional zone bordering the southeastern valley edge.

A 60-km-long section bordering the eastern side of the Illinois River from the mouth of the Mackinaw River southward to the mouth of the Sangamon River is composed of level to rolling sand plains and dunes of the Illinois River Sand Area Division. The associated sand prairie grasslands were broken occasionally by scrubby communities of black oak, and some marshes were evident in low areas.

The Illinois River Bottomlands Division is characterized by a broad and flatly monotonous floodplain (ranging in width from about 3.25 km at Peoria to nearly 13 km at Meredosia), which is occasionally interrupted by large sand and gravel terraces. The valley edge is often bordered by terrace deposits, and alluvial fans frequently sweep outward from the bluffs. Myriad backwater lakes, marshes, and sloughs accompany the sluggish Illinois River. Forests originally covered much of this bottomland division, dominated by silver maple, American elm, and green ash. Locally large groves of pecan bordered many of the lakes and marshes.

The aquatic community is the least changed of the biotic communities and is still well represented by a variety of fish such as sunfish, bass, crappie, pike, catfish, buffalo, redhorse, drum, suckers, bowfin, and gar; numerous species of mussels; and turtles, frogs, muskrat, beaver, and large numbers of migratory waterfowl and shore birds in the early spring and fall. Once-common dwellers such as the cormorant and otter are no longer present.

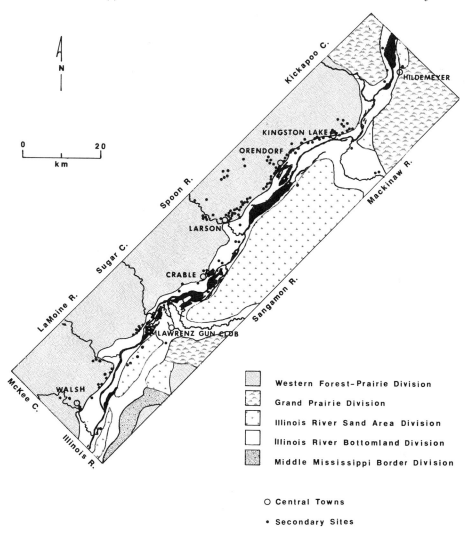

FIGURE 9.1. *The Distribution of Mississippian sites within the natural divisions of the Central Illinois River Valley.* [After Harn 1978; Natural Divisions after Schwegman 1973; Hydrology is Modern.]

The forest community originally supported large populations of deer, grey squirrel, red squirrel, raccoon, and opossum, as well as turkey, black bear, bobcat, lynx, and puma.

Prairie and bordering forest margin community members included cottontail, woodchuck, bobwhite, striped skunk, grey fox, red fox, coyote, badger, mink, weasels, numerous mouse species, passenger pigeon, ruffed grouse, prairie chicken, elk, and wolves.

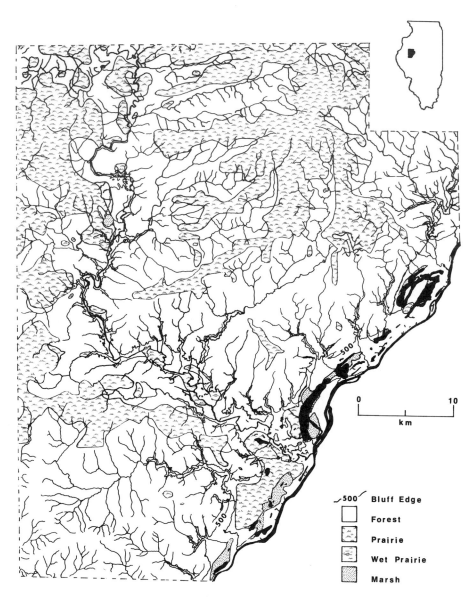

FIGURE 9.2.   *A Model of the major vegetational communities in Fulton County, Illinois, constructed from notes and plats of the original United States land surveys (Countour Interval in feet from 1949 United States Geological Survey; hydrology partially based on United States Army Corps of Engineers Maps 1902–1904).*

Additional data concerning climate, physical geography, and faunal and floristic communities of the Central Illinois River Valley can be obtained from Harn (1971a, 1978), Harn and Koelling (1974), *History of Fulton County, Illinois* (1879), and Wanless (1957).

Soil types are widely varied throughout the region, with four of the five major soil associations especially compatible to maize-horticulture requisites (Table 9.1). Fehrenbacher, Walker, and Wascher (1967) suggest that the soils holding the greatest agricultural potential would probably have been those of the Seaton–Fayette–Stronghurst and Clary–Clinton–Keomah associations. Soils of the Lawson–Beaucoup–Darwin–Haymond–Belknap association, although occasionally very productive, would probably have been exploited to a lesser degree because of problems with drainage, frequency of flooding, and weed control. Littleton–Procter–Plano–Camden–Hurst–Ginat soils are limited in distribution and are occasionally poorly drained, whereas soils of the Hagener-Ridgeville–Bloomfield–Alvin association are sandy, unfertile, droughty, and subject to considerable wind and water erosion.

Survey Methodology

Although I have personally examined by walkover nearly all Mississippian habitation sites recorded in Fulton and Mason counties and most of the larger or more significant sites elsewhere in the Central Illinois River Valley, probably an equal number of recorded sites have never been visited. Therefore, any gross assessment of Illinois Valley Mississippian settlement patterns will be heavily dependent upon data located in the site survey files of the Illinois State Museum. Unfortunately, these site forms often prove outdated and unreliable for the kinds of data required.

Since statements concerning degree of areal coverage, how site types and sizes were determined, survey biases, etc., were almost never recorded by earlier surveyors, it was felt that few positive results could be gained from an analysis of the total assemblage of Mississippian sites throughout the region. This problem is further compounded by the fact that the majority of the site forms carry only the broadest designation of cultural classification (e.g., "Mississippian"), without an attempt at further breakdown by phase. Definitive statements concerning settlement patterns throughout the region can come only after a vast majority of the sites have been far more closely analyzed with regard to cultural affiliation, sociopolitical organization, and site function.

It is for these reasons that I have confined the primary focus of this study to a limited geographical area—the core area of Mississippian occupation from the confluence of the Spoon River with the Illinois River

TABLE 9.1
Principal Associations, Distribution and Selected Characteristics of Soils in the Central Illinois River Valley Corridor[a]

Soil name	Distribution	Color of surface soil	Texture of surface soil	Permeability of subsoil	Drought resistance	Estimated average corn yield 1956–1966 (bushels per acre)
Seaton–Fayette–Stronghurst	Covers western Illinois River bluff-tops from Rice Lake southward and the eastern Illinois bluff-tops from the Sangamon River southward.	Dark gray-brown	Silt	Moderate	Good to very good	80–98
Clary–Clinton–Keomah	Covers western Illinois River bluffs from Rice Lake northward and the eastern Illinois bluff-tops from the Mackinaw River northward.	Dark gray-brown	Silt	Moderately slow	Good to very good	75–88
Lawson–Beaucoup–Darwin–Haymond–Belknap	Covers Illinois River bottomlands and extends up valleys of major tributaries.	Dark gray-brown to black	Silt and silty clay	Very slow to moderate	Fair to very good	77–107
Littleton–Procter–Plano–Camden–Hurst–Ginat	Band of soils bordering eastern bottomland of the Illinois River below the mouth of the Sangamon River.	Very dark brown to dark gray-brown	Silt	Very slow to moderate	Fair to very good	65–105
Hagener–Ridgeville–Bloomfield–Alvin	Covers eastern terraces along Illinois River between the Mackinaw and Sangamon rivers.	Dark gray-brown to very dark brown	Fine sandy loam and loamy sand	Very rapid to moderate	Fair to poor	62–83

[a] Adapted from Fehrenbacher *et al.* (1967).

northward for about 10 km. As previously mentioned, this area has received the most concentrated archeological attention over the past 50 years, producing the largest amount of data available in the region. In addition, this area is my birthplace and early training ground and that of anthropologists Patrick J. Munson of Indiana University and Lawrence A. Conrad of Western Illinois University. Our combined survey time within the core area is unknown, but hundreds of man-days are involved, since the area was located within our primary collecting universe as youngsters and within our primary research universe later. This concentrated previous reconnaissance and wealth of recovered materials have amounted to a savings of many hundreds of survey hours during the present study.

Therefore, what was begun as purely judgmental survey on our part eventually became a comprehensive survey over the next 25 years. Although heavy reliance was made upon these data, additional reconnaissance of areas lacking Mississippian sites has been undertaken during the past 6 years and reexamination by walkover of the majority of the known sites has also been carried out. Since most of the area is cultivated, with forest cover being largely limited to steep talus slopes, most of the land is readily examined. Our coverage has been complete enough to make it highly unlikely that any more than an additional few very minor Mississippian sites will be recorded in the Spoon River core area. Among these might be specialized sites such as hunting and/or gathering stations in the uplands, which have heretofore produced only chert flakes or other undiagnostic material.

Throughout the years, site size has been traditionally determined by the area of surface scatter and, in some instances, with the aid of aerial photography. In a few cases, house depressions are still evident on some well-protected sites in wooded areas, allowing us to be reasonably certain of both the physical boundaries of the sites and their estimated population. Verification of site size by complete excavation has yet to be accomplished; but at the Buckeye Bend site (Harn and Weedman 1975), the only instance in which the location of a majority of the features at a principal site has been determined, the internal structural arrangement of the site was found to correspond closely with the area of surface scatter.

Potential problems inherent to all Mississippian settlement studies are also seen in the Central Illinois River Valley. The paucity of shell-tempered pottery, due to its rapid disintegration in the highly acidic soils of the region, often gives little indication of either the type or the magnitude of the occupation below. This situation is further compounded by the fact that Spoon River Mississippian structures are usually semisubterranean, with the floors recessed as much as 1 m below the present ground surface. Normal crop cultivation procedures do not disturb the soil to that depth and in the absence of an associated artifact-bearing midden, some Mississippian sites of short-term occupation may not have yet been exposed.

These problems have been somewhat overcome at some of the major sites by the concentrated use of aerial photography.

The Regional Settlement Pattern in Broad Perspective

Mississippian occupation of the Central Illinois River Valley was apparently begun during the eleventh century A.D., according to dates from the Eveland Site of A.D. 1055 (WIS-653) and A.D. 1085 (WIS-652) (Bender *et al.* 1975:122), and probably initially represented an intrusion of small numbers of individuals from the great Mississippian center of Cahokia some 180 km (by air) to the south. How Mississippian developed in the Central Illinois Valley from that point onward is not completely understood, but it has been suggested that its composition was primarily Woodland-based with Mississippian sociopolitical overtones (Harn 1975b).

The major focus of Mississippian occupation in the Illinois valley was the 160-km section of the valley between Meredosia and Peoria, Illinois. All known temple towns are contained within this region. Causal factors for this concentration probably center on the wider abundance and variety of food resources available in the adjacent mixed forest and grassland environments of the uplands and in the mosaic of forest, grassland, lakes, rivers, marshes and sloughs that comprise the bottomland zone. It is significant that concentrated Mississippian occupation of the Central Illinois Valley virtually stops at the juncture of the Grand Prairie on the north and in the area where the valley narrows and major lakes become less numerous to the south.

Mississippian sites throughout this region are mainly restricted to the Illinois riverfront zone—terraces in the bottomlands, the bluff edge, and bluff edges overlooking secondary stream valleys within 1.5 km of the Illinois River bluff edge. Only occasional sites, which probably represent loci of specialized hunting or gathering activities, are positioned along secondary valleys farther inland (Figure 9.1).

In general, site locations of this period appear primarily within the heavily forested zone along the western bluffs and terraces of the Illinois River. With the lone exception of the Clear Lake Site, which has been proposed as being seasonally exploited for farming purposes (Harn 1976:8), Mississippian sites do not occur along the eastern side of the Illinois River throughout the main Illinois River Sand Area Division, and occur only in the secondary sand areas in association with upland and floodplain forests. Prairies were similarly avoided as habitation sites. In an earlier analysis of the relationship of Mississippian sites to natural environment, I proposed that site locations were nonrandomly distributed; that they were influenced in descending order of importance by access to favorable biotic zones, water sources, landforms, and soil types; that a predictable set of physiographic zones was selected over all others; and that the variables of site type, size, physical location, and permanence of occupation appear to be closely correlated with these zones (Harn 1978:The Settlement Pattern). These proposals will be dealt with further.

Briefly stated, the Mississippian settlement pattern in evidence in the Central Illinois River Valley consists of a series of seven towns that occur at fairly regular intervals along the valley. These are, from north to south, Hildemeyer, Kingston Lake, Orendorf, Larson, Crable, Lawrenz Gun Club, and Walsh (Figure 9.1). Distances between towns range between 18 and 36 km, with an average of about 23.5 km. All seven towns are positioned near the outlets of river or major stream drainages, or are in close proximity to large lakes. Work at three towns, Crable, Larson, and Orendorf, has yielded insights into site structuring that may be applicable to other town sites (*History of Fulton County, Illinois* 1879, Conrad and Emerson 1974, Harn 1966a, Stephens 1976). The internal patterning of the town sites generally consists of a single pyramidal mound fronting onto an open plaza. (The two southernmost towns have multiple platform mounds, however.) A concentrated 4–8-ha village area is usually associated with the mound and plaza areas. A fortification wall usually encloses the mound, plaza, and several hectares of the core area of the village, but related occupation often extends the town limits over a considerable adjacent area up and down the bluff or terrace edge. Extensive. midden deposits are common at towns, although they are rarely seen on secondary habitation sites. Borrow pits and large cemeteries are often positioned outside the fortification wall on the edge of town. Such town sites appear to have served as centers for related hamlets, farmsteads, and hunting-and-gathering camps positioned at intervals for up to 15 km up and down the valley.

Evidence has previously been presented suggesting that little contemporaneity existed between the majority of the town sites, and that they represented a continuum of occupation as populations shifted from one area to another within the valley from the late twelfth to the early to middle fifteenth centuries A.D. (Harn 1978: The Community Concept). Four of five radiocarbon dates from Orendorf, the first of the town sites to be erected, range between A.D. 1105 and 1180 (Bender, Bryson, and Baerreis 1975:123). The fifth date (A.D. 1085) is considered too early. The Larson town, which is chronologically later than Orendorf, is also well dated (WIS-655, 659, 688, and 689) (Bender *et al.* 1975:123–124). Unfortunately, although the dates are very consistent internally, their average of A.D. 1156 is at least a century too early to be consistent with the remainder of the Spoon River series. Dates of A.D. 1385 and 1435 (WIS-648 and WIS-644) for the Crable site, the latest of the Spoon River towns, are about as expected (Bender *et al.* 1975:125). The range of radiocarbon dates from Larson (75 years), Orendorf (75 years), and the clustering of dates from Crable at around A.D. 1400 suggest that major occupations of Mississippian towns in the Central Illinois River valley were relatively short term.

Although the Orendorf site and the Crable site have no temporal counterparts among the other towns, ceramics from the remaining towns suggest varying degrees of contemporaneity. An earlier discussion of occupational variability among Mississippian towns in the Illinois Valley clearly demonstrates the ceramic individuality of each of these centers (Harn 1978:Table 3).

No town had a major early Mississippian occupation. Although classic early Mississippian ceramics such as Powell Plain and Ramey Incised appear in both the Kingston Lake site and Lawrenz Gun Club site assemblages, their actual frequency is quite low, accounting for about 1% of the jar types at Kingston Lake and less than .5% at Lawrenz Gun Club.

The major occupation of Orendorf postdated the classic early Mississippian or Eveland phase period (Conrad n.d.b), in light of the replacement of Ramey Incised by its apparent successor, Trotter Trailed. Black polishing of vessel surfaces had also dropped away considerably, constituting only 2% of the total assemblage; but red filming had greatly increased, being present on nearly 79% of our sample of 694 sherds from Orendorf. Cordmarking had yet to gain popularity, and was present in only 2% of the sample.

The major period of temple-town construction followed the abandonment of the Orendorf site and extended for at least the next century. Five towns—Hildemeyer, Kingston Lake, Larson, Lawrenz Gun Club, and Walsh—were probably erected during this span. The ceramic assemblages of these towns are very cohesive in many respects in terms of percentage distribution of modes of surface treatment, jar type, and vessel and rim form (Harn 1978:Table 3), placing all within the Larson phase of the Spoon River variant. It is only by closer examination of specific stylistic elements that postulations for the possible succession of occupation can be generated.

Three sites positioned in the northern half of the survey area, Hildemeyer, Kingston Lake, and Larson, share many similarities, the most important of which is the relative frequency of jars of the Dickson ceramic series—Dickson Plain, Dickson Cordmarked, and Dickson Trailed. They also show a higher frequency of jar forms and plain globular jar types than the southernmost towns.

Walsh and Lawrenz Gun Club, the southernmost towns, lack the trailed design elements on jar shoulders that are prevalent in the northern region and show a much greater employment of cordmarking as a surface treatment. Pie-crust and scalloped rims were recorded only at these southern towns, and, although they may or may not be an important element of segregation, cordmarked bowls were also restricted to that region.

The trailed design elements of the northern towns, which evolved out of Ramey Incised (Harn 1971a:20–21, 1975b:423), suggest that occupation of the Hildemeyer, Kingston Lake, and Larson towns probably began sometime before occupation of the towns of Lawrenz Gun Club and Walsh. How much before and how much occupational overlap may have existed between the two regions can only be speculated at present.

The scalloped and pie-crust rims on some jars from the Lawrenz and Walsh sites suggest that their occupations extended late enough to have been influenced by the Spoon River–Oneota expressions at Crable. This is also supported by design elements on some associated plate rims, which include nested arcs with either radiating triangular rays or bordering punctates which are also seen in the degenerated Wells Incised motifs at Crable. These particular late plate motifs are also recorded at Hildemeyer along with the earlier trailed motifs on jar shoulders.

On the basis of these data, it is suggested that the major Mississippian occupation in the Central Illinois River Valley began in the Orendorf area and blossomed locally before emphasis was shifted to the south–central section of the valley. Kingston Lake and Larson appear to be roughly contemporaneous, with Kingston Lake perhaps being a generation or two older. It is conceivable that their occupations little overlapped those of Lawrenz Gun Club and Walsh. In fact, the erection of these latter towns may have been accomplished by groups abandoning Kingston Lake and Larson. The Hildemeyer site is another matter, because it seems to contain elements of both the earlier and later occupations. Since it is a very small town, Hildemeyer may represent a splinter group from the Kingston Lake site that had moved upriver to Lake Peoria either at the time of or shortly before the exodus of the major town populations into the south–central valley.

Crable, like Orendorf, functioned without a sister city. In fact, the intensity of occupation at Crable seems to suggest consolidation of a majority of the Mississippian population at Anderson Lake by A.D. 1400. The settlement pattern associated with the occupation of Crable may prove to be somewhat different than that associated with the other temple towns, for no definable network of secondary sites surrounds the main center. Although there are a few nearby sites producing pottery that is late in the Spoon River sequence, only two very small sites with diagnostic Oneota-influenced, Crable-like ceramics appear in that region; one 8 km upriver in the Illinois bottomlands, the other some 32 km downriver. However, although Crable is often thought of as being a site with intense Oneota association, Smith's (1951:Table 1) and Harn's (1978:Table 3) ceramic distribution tables suggest that the classic Crable Trailed design elements occur in only minor percentages. Most of the Crable assemblage is comparable to that of Lawrenz Gun Club and Walsh, except that a higher percentage of all pottery is plain-surfaced; shallow bowls are more frequent; there is greater stylistic variability among Wells Incised motifs on plates; and Crable Deep Rimmed Plates appear only at Crable. Therefore, it is entirely possible that nearby sites such as Emmons and Fiedler were contemporaneous with the main occupation of Crable, even though no "classic" Crable Trailed elements have been associated with them.

In the preceding pages it has been demonstrated that there is an abundance of potential data relating to Mississippian settlement patterns in the Central Illinois River Valley. An attempt has also been made to enumerate some of the pitfalls involved in attempting to synthesize the settlement pattern on a broad scale; for until we can satisfactorily identify all sites that were temporally and spatially associated and determine the function of each, one to the other, we cannot advance much beyond speculation.

It is for these reasons that the primary focus of this study has been limited to the clustering of related Larson Phase sites in the vicinity of the juncture of the Illinois and Spoon River valleys (Figure 9.3), a clustering now referred to as the Larson community (Harn 1978). As indicated previously, we feel that each town and clustering of habitation sites represents a distinct sociopolitical entity which falls under the following concept of the term community.

> In essence, the clusters of related Mississippian sites in the Central Illinois River Valley comprised what appear to have been somewhat self-contained communities. The term *community* is used to define the sum total of related sites within a particularly defined geographic area or procurement territory which can be attributed to activities relating to a specific phase of human occupation which does not appreciably change throughout its life within that region. The term *settlement* is used in reference to individual areas of habitation which include towns, hamlets, and specialized camps. In this concept of the term *community*, we will propose that the settlement pattern stems from a single communal base; that it represents an integrated extractive system with religious/political roots; and that there is seasonal variability of occupation, with a majority of the total population occupying the main town during colder seasons and dispersing into the surrounding biotic zones during the warmer months. In this respect the term *conjoined community* might more appropriately describe the united population and *dispersed community* the scattered population. However, at present we view the single term *community* as encompassing all types of occupation within the defined territory [Harn 1978].

Internal Site Patterning and
the Larson Community

Our discussion of the Larson community is limited to those sites producing only diagnostic Larson phase ceramics. Other sites having less distinctive Mississippian artifacts were not considered, even though some (such as those producing occasional unnotched triangular projectile points, but not ceramics) may have been specialized camps of the Larson phase. Ten sites of this category are presently recorded. Five are situated on terraces and natural sand levees in the Illinois bottomlands; three are located on terraces in the Spoon River bottomland; and two are located on Big Creek, a tributary of Spoon River. Excavation of one of the Big Creek sites, Scovill, has been nearly total, but has failed to produce evidence of any form of Mississippian habitation (Munson, Parmalee, and Yarnell 1971). We suspect that most of the other outlying Larson phase sites will also have a paucity of subsurface features.

Rather than representing actual habitation areas or temporary camps, scattered surface finds of projectile points may sometimes be indicative of favored hunting areas, especially when occurring in conjunction with the natural feeding and watering areas of animal species. However, in the case of white tail deer, the most economically important food resource, the most productive hunting areas would not necessarily have been those directly associated with feeding or watering, unless those activities involved spatially and seasonally limited resources (e.g., persimmon groves during the late fall or isolated water holes during droughts). If movement patterns of modern deer in any way reflect those of their ancestors, the most productive hunting areas would have been near deer runs along natural corridors linking bedding areas with feeding zones. The points of those narrow ridges which served to funnel deer traffic into lower elevations would have provided optimum ambush sites; but little is known about these locations because most are still heavily forested or are in pasture.

The 39 sites comprising the Larson community are limited to an area of approximately 40 km². This area is essentially bordered on the north by the Sister Creeks, on the west by Big Creek, on the south by Spoon River, and on the east by the Illinois River (Figure 9.3). The settlement pattern is dominated by the central town, Larson, which is situated on the bluff spur at the juncture of the Illinois and Spoon River valleys. A series of five hamlets are positioned at regular intervals along the Illinois River bluff tops moving upstream from Larson, with one hamlet on Big Creek at the headwaters of the Sisters Creeks and another on Spoon River below the mouth of Big Creek. Numerous ancillary sites surround the hamlets. Al-

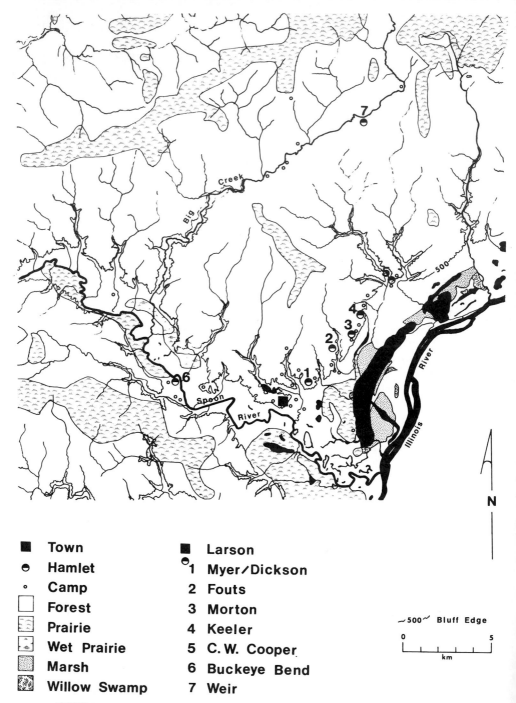

	Town		Larson
	Hamlet	1	Myer/Dickson
	Camp	2	Fouts
	Forest	3	Morton
	Prairie	4	Keeler
	Wet Prairie	5	C. W. Cooper
	Marsh	6	Buckeye Bend
	Willow Swamp	7	Weir

~500~ Bluff Edge

0   5
km

FIGURE 9.3. *The distribution of Larson phase sites within the Larson community. (Vegetational communities and hydrology constructed from notes and plats of the original United States land surveys, with hydrology partially based on United States Army Corps of Engineers Maps 1902–1904; contour interval in feet from 1949 United States Geological Survey).*

though many of the larger camps are limited to the same bluff-top zone as the hamlets, other progressively smaller sites appear on the terraces and slopewash near the bluff base, on natural sandy levees along bottomland lakes, and in upland locations overlooking small stream valleys (Figure 9.3).

The settlement pattern of the Larson community is atypical for the Illinois valley, in that the town is positioned at one end of the occupation area rather than being more centrally located. It is probable that its placement at such a strategic location as the merger of the valleys of the Spoon and Illinois rivers was deemed more important than an idealized central location, even though that location may have restricted the overall size of the community because of natural water-related barriers to the east and south.

THE CENTRAL TOWN

The Larson site is the largest settlement in the community, with concentrated village debris spread over about 8 ha of its core area. If the scattered occupation extending away from the main site to the west is included, approximately 40 ha would be involved. However, concentrated aerial reconnaissance of that area shows a scattering of less than 30 structures, probably representing a potential population increase of only another 100 persons or so, considering the probable lack of contemporaneity among all of the structures (Harn 1978:Figure 5a–b). The 1970 excavations at Larson suggested a ratio of between 32 and 40 houses per hectare in the primary habitation area, representing about 234 contemporaneous structures at peak population and 120 contemporaneous structures during the final occupation, when the living area was more restricted. From this, an average population of 885 individuals has been projected for the town (Harn 1978:The Larson Community—Summary).

Larson is characterized by a single truncated pyramidal mound flanking a plaza slightly more than 2 ha in extent. The mound is square approximately 60 m on a side and was originally as much as 5 m high. Prior to its alteration to facilitate cultivation (this was done by my grandfather in the 1890s), the eastern ramp must have conspicuously extended into the plaza, for Chapman describes the mound as a "pyramid with a road up the east side" in 1879 (*History of Fulton County, Illinois* 1879:337).

A fortification wall enclosed at least 6 ha of the south portion of the site including the mound and plaza. The west, south, and east walls of the palisade have been verified by aerial photography and by excavation, but the north wall crosses a heavy midden deposit and has not yet been located. No bastions were evident along the excavated portion of the palisade. Larson is the only site in the community that has been found to have been fortified. Large cemeteries are positioned on the bluff edge outside the east wall, and substantial borrow pits are located both on the east and north edges of the village (Harn 1966a:Map 1).

The 1970 excavations at Larson revealed that large portions, if not all, of the site had burned on more than one occasion, presenting a unique opportunity to study complete artifact inventories and interpret related domestic activities among various structural units within a .18-ha section of the village. Although the final analysis of the faunal and floral materials has been completed by the University of Wisconsin—Madison and the Missouri Botanical Gardens, only preliminary analysis of the artifact assemblage has been completed by Dickson Mounds Museum. On the basis of this preliminary analysis, however, I have presented data suggesting that the major occupation of Larson was in part seasonal, with emphasis on the months between fall and early spring (Harn 1970b, 1974, 1978:The Town).

Included among seasonal indicators were the presence of internal hearths in domestic structures at Larson and either their absence or infrequency coupled with the presence of external hearths at hamlets; differences in artifact inventories; a higher incidence of food storage at the town linked with a correspondingly higher incidence of fall-ripening nuts, seeds, and corn; a high frequency of adult animal and migratory bird bones, deer skulls with shed antlers, and dog remains at the town; and a manner of placing burials in storage–refuse pits (inhumations of winter dead in readily available graves?) that is not duplicated elsewhere within the community. Although not all of the above data have been quantified and comparisons drawn between Larson and Myer–Dickson, the only well-excavated hamlet, preliminary observations suggest a definite trend toward seasonal occupation of sites within the community.

Occupational scatter at the town is very heavy, due in part to a large midden accumulation, with quantitites of pottery, bone, chert, and fire-cracked rock. All types of artifact categories are present, creating conspicuous differences between the artifact inventories of Larson and its subsidiary sites. Categories well represented at Larson but rare or absent at other sites include fabricating and processing tools, woodworking tools, ornaments, caches of equipment, and ceremonial equipment dominated by sandstone block pipes of the frog-effigy form, plus pottery cones, thick pottery palettes, galena, and loose human bones. Quantities of mussel shells also are conspicuous at Larson, but rather than representing food resources, it is just as probable that they were more economically important as sources of lime or tempering material for pottery manufacture.

SECONDARY SITES OF IMPORTANCE: THE HAMLETS

Seven sites in the Larson community are distinct from the others because of their greater size and concentration of occupational debris.

These are Myer–Dickson, Fouts, Morton, Keeler, C.W. Cooper, Buckeye Bend, and Weir. Although size and debris concentration served as the initial segregating criteria for inclusion into the hamlet category, other identifying elements have become evident and will be briefly discussed. Work at Buckeye Bend and Myer–Dickson has added support to the proposition that all other sites currently viewed as hamlets were intermediate in importance to the town and the smaller camps; but the assignment of sites to this category is still largely intuitive because our knowledge of internal structuring is primarily limited to the two excavated hamlets. It is probable that two hamlet-designates, Morton and Weir, will conform to the patterning to be described whereas two others, Keeler and C.W. Cooper, are not as confidently identified, if for no reason other than the fact that they have received the least archeological attention. The actual function of the seventh possible hamlet, Fouts, is unclear.

Five of the seven hamlets (Myer–Dickson, Fouts, Morton, Keeler, and C. W. Cooper) are positioned along the Illinois River bluff-top moving upstream from the town at approximate 1.5-km intervals. Their locations do not appear to be dependent upon close proximity to large, permanent bodies of water or even to minor stream drainages for that matter. Rather, they appear to have been positioned at junctures of a number of natural resource zones.

Locations of the two other hamlets, Buckeye Bend and Weir, would have imposed restrictions upon the availability of a variety of natural resources. Weir is located on the bluff edge of Big Creek at the headwaters of the Sisters Creeks some 12 km to the west of the Illinois River. Available resources would have been almost entirely limited to those found in an oak–hickory forest situation, although a small stream environment does bisect the area and prairie and bordering forest margin zones also occurred within 6 km to the northest. Excavation of Scovill, a terminal Middle Woodland or early Late Woodland site on Big Creek about 16 km downstream from Weir, produced faunal remains composed primarily of deer, turkey, and fish along with quantities of nuts, and generally suggested a narrower variety of available resources than would have been found in the Illinois River corridor (Munson *et al.* 1971:Tables 1–8).

Buckeye Bend is situated on a low terrace overlooking Spoon River some 6 km to the west of Larson. Its local environment probably more nearly approached that of the Illinois corridor but on a more restricted scale. The terrace on which Buckeye Bend is located is low and very wet (it is actually listed as floodplain, although it has flooded only once in memory) and probably supported a forest transitional between that of the talus slope and floodplain. The heavy oak–hickory forest bluff-top site situation that characterized the locations of the town and all other hamlets was not utilized by the occupants of Buckeye Bend, even though it existed about 1 km to the west. Site selection appears to have been influenced by direct access to the river.

Although adequate data concerning internal structuring are available for only two hamlets in the Larson community (Buckeye Bend and Myer–Dickson), the physical composition of these sites appears to be similar in many respects to that of the town except that there are no for-tification walls or temple mounds. Houses are arranged in rows around open plazas, with a large and obviously important building(s) positioned on the plaza edge (cf., Harn and Weedman 1975). Hamlets are smaller than the central town, generally ranging in size between 1.5 and 6 ha, and suggest populations that may have ranged between 88 and 440, averaging about 219 individuals (Harn 1978:Table 4).

Occupational scatter at these sites is considerably less than at the town, with no real accumulation of midden. Less variety in the artifact inventories is also suggested; but broken pottery, chert, fire-cracked rock, projectilepoints, end scrapers, simple flake knives and scrapers, and grooved sandstone abraders are commonly recovered along with occa-sional drills, manos, celts, faunal remains, and, rarely, hoes.

One hamlet, Myer–Dickson, has a large associated cemetery that con-tains several hundred individuals (Dickson Mounds). Another, Morton, has a smaller cemetery of perhaps less than 200 total burials (Cole and Deuel 1937:57–111). Most of the other hamlets have cemeteries consisting of only one or two small mounds which surely have burial populations of far less than 100. No burial areas have been identified with Fouts or with Weir, the most distant hamlet. One explanation for the paucity of burials is that duration of occupation of a majority of the hamlets was shorter-term than the 75 years we have projected for the town, with the occupation of hamlets in closest proximity to the town being either larger (which does not necessarily seem to be the case) or of longer duration. Another possi-bility is that a higher ratio of deaths occurred during the winter months. These possible explanations assume that there was no differential treat-ment regarding the disposition of the dead among the town and the various hamlets and that individuals were interred at the place of their death. This glaringly unknown aspect of Spoon River social organization bears heavily on all settlement pattern and demographic studies currently being undertaken in the area. Yet we have not even begun to formulate possible solutions to the problem.

SUBSIDIARY SITES: CAMPS AND DAY-ACTIVITY AREAS

Information regarding subsidiary sites is meager indeed. Only one Larson Phase camp, Berry, has been excavated to any extent (by the Illinois State Museum, in 1967), and it is doubtful that its complete habita-tion area has been exposed. Knowledge of sites of this class is almost entirely limited to surface observation, limited aerial photography, and considerable walkover.

Thirty-one sites in the Larson community are included within the broad category traditionally identified as "camps." These appear to be distributed around the hamlets, but remain in fairly close proximity. The degree of concentration of camps varies within the three principal areas of occupation in the Larson community—the Illinois River Valley, Spoon River Valley, and Big Creek Valley. Along the Illinois River, 18 of the 20 camps are within 1.5 km of either a hamlet or the town. In fact, the concentration of these ancillary sites along the Illinois River bluff-top zone is such that no gaps exist between the supposed occupation "territories" of each hamlet. It is presently impossible to identify which camp is attributable to which hamlet. Only in the isolated instances of Weir and Buckeye Bend does a clearer picture of the relationship of size, number, and spatial distribution of the camps to the hamlet become evident. Camps associated with Weir range in distance from 2.90 to 6.12 km from the hamlet, averaging about 4.52 km. The Buckeye Bend grouping is much tighter, with distances ranging between .33 and 5.96 km and averaging 1.94 km. Unfortunately, the physiographic environments of both Buckeye Bend and Weir are unlike that of the hamlets along the Illinois River, disallowing, for the present, many extrapolated comparisons.

It is assumed that the subsidiary camps were attributable to a variety of activities which centered around food procurement—farming, hunting, fishing, and gathering. No camps that were representative of other types of exploitive activities (e.g., sites positioned at unique resources such as quarries or mineral deposits) were recorded within the community.

Site size is as diverse as is their probable function. Some have such small concentrations of occupational debris that a single structure is indicated, or perhaps no permanent structure at all. It has been previously suggested—from their small size, specific placement in a variety of ecological zones, and frequent proximity to permanent settlements—that many of the smaller camps may have functioned as temporary day-activity stations (Harn 1978:The Camps).

Of the three camps that are sufficiently intact that well-defined house depressions remain (Eskridge, Newlun, and M.S.D. No. 1), no more than seven structures are evident. In these cases, the depressions are clustered on a bluff point, ridge top, and on a bench of a talus slope. Maximum size for camps appears to be less than 1 ha, but it is not known if this represents an appreciably larger population than is suggested by the occupations of Eskridge, Newlun, or M.S.D. No. 1 or if it is simply a more dispersed pattern of structures or surface scatter. One current problem is the functional interpretation of the Fouts Site (Cole and Deuel 1937:111–120), which is presently viewed as a hamlet although it is small and has no apparent internal structuring or associated cemetery. If it is eventually included in the category of "camp," the maximum camp size would increase somewhat since Fouts has 15 house depressions over an area of about 1.5 ha. Portions of the site are not in cultivation and the limits of occupational scatter cannot be determined; but it is suspected that debris would be spread over at least 2 ha.

Camps associated with the Illinois River drainage system show greater locational diversity within the environment, but only because the environments of the Spoon River and Big Creek are less diverse. Only 1 of the 20 Larson Phase camps associated with the Illinois River settlement pattern (Norris Farms No. 1) is located on a natural levee along a bottomland lake, although occasional triangular projectile points have been recorded elsewhere in that zone. All sites in this zone would have been subjected to occasional flooding. Six camps are positioned on terraces or on slopewash in the Illinois River bottomland; 10 occur in the bluff-edge zone; and three are positioned on the bluffs bordering Sepo Creek within between 1.0 and 2.6 km of the Illinois River bluff edge. All upland, slopewash, and bottomland terrace camps were probably located in heavy forest situations, barring clearing by the inhabitants, whereas camps on levees bordering bottomland lakes were probably located in more open forest situations dominated by pecan groves. However, the only lakes-associated camp with a definite Larson phase occupation was located in an area that historically was covered with prairie.

Triangular projectile points and Larson phase ceramics are only occasionally recovered at bottomland camps. Although we would assume that these sites were oriented toward hunting, fishing, and gathering activities, extensive surface reconnaissance has given little indication of function, since each site is multicomponent and the Mississippian occupation is of relative insignificance. Testing of one bottomland camp, Ogden, produced one Mississippian storage–refuse pit, but its contents were not analyzed because they did not pertain to the Middle Woodland occupation being studied (Wettersten n.d.). Bluff-top camps appear to have been more heavily occupied. Larger assemblages of artifacts, including occasional manos, end scrapers, and, rarely, horticultural tools are evident on these sites, but the occupational scatter is still very light. Upland camps are characterized by occasional triangular projectile points although ceramics are infrequently recovered and one polished hoe of Mill Creek chert has been found at the Boo site. Little occupational scatter is associated.

The Larson phase occupation of the Big Creek area consisted of a hamlet, Weir, and six subsidiary sites. All sites are positioned in the same environment as the hamlet, the bluff-edge zone, in a probable heavy oak–hickory forest situation. Five camps occur along the bluff-top of Big Creek, whereas the sixth is situated at the head of a branch of Evelen Branch, a tributary of Big Creek, some 3 km to the west. Occupational scatter on all of these sites, including Weir, is very light and is probably indicative of short-term occupation. It is expected that additional small camps eventually may be recorded on Big Creek because its survey has not been exhaustive.

The Larson phase occupation of the Spoon River Valley also consisted of a hamlet, Buckeye Bend, and five subsidiary sites; but the settlement pattern is directly opposite of that evidenced on Big Creek. Buckeye Bend and four of its associated camps are located on bottomland terraces, in what was probably a transitional forest situation. Only one camp was located on the adjacent Spoon River bluff-top. Although there is the usual sparseness of artifacts on these sites, some differences seem to exist. One site, Frazier, may have functioned primarily as a gardening area for the nearby hamlet of Buckeye Bend, since a number of hoes and hoe fragments have been collected there. In support of this hypothesis, concentrated aerial reconnaissance of the site has failed to reveal any indication of subsurface features, even though central tombs of the numerous Middle Woodland mounds at the site could be clearly defined as could the subsurface features at Buckeye Bend (Harn and Weedman 1975). Another Spoon River area camp, Lockard (west), actually has burial mounds in association—the only such association in the Larson community. However, there is the possibility that the only Larson phase burial recovered to date was intrusive into an earlier (Middle Woodland?) burial mound since only a small hole in one mound has been dug by a local collector. Like the Larson Phase occupation of Big Creek, that of Spoon River appears to have been short-lived.

Discussion

Many factors influenced the settlement pattern evidenced within the Larson community. While no particular emphasis was placed on nucleation by the early Mississippian groups in the Central Illinois River Valley, whether from lack of adequate population or perhaps in the absence of stress, by the beginning of the thirteenth century A.D., related Mississippian sites were beginning to cluster into smaller areas. It is at this time that the first fortifications appear, probably resulting from social stresses developed from competition for the same resources or new concepts of land control or ownership brought on by the introduction of maize horticulture or both. Whatever the causal factors, post-A.D. 1200 Spoon River variant populations expressed a definite need for nucleation that, with their increasing numbers, directly opposed their need for dispersal into the various ecological zones. Any attempt at an ideal settlement arrangement, whether for economic, political, or defensive reasons, would have been somewhat restricted by the available natural resources.

Evidence to suggest that there was seasonal variability of occupation among related sites within the Larson community has previously been presented (Harn 1970b, 1974, 1978:The Town). In general, I have proposed that the major occupation of the central town took place during the colder months and, although there may have been a number of permanent residents in the town, a substantial population dispersed into the surrounding countryside during warmer weather. Occupation of these outlying areas was nuclear-based at permanent centers (hamlets), which were located in close proximity to or at junctures of a variety of major natural resource zones. Exploitation of these various zones was further facilitated by smaller semipermanent camps and day-activity stations placed within specific microenvironments.

Several hypotheses for the construction and occupation of the hamlets and subsidiary sites have been presented (Harn 1978:The Larson Community). These proposals have centered around exploitive and political factors. (For example, were the hamlets positioned at precise locations to allow maximum exploitation of a number of natural resource zones or were their locations assigned by political process or determined by the distance necessary to provide adequate resources without encroaching upon the territory of the nearest neighbor?) I have also touched on the subject of contemporaneity, considering four alternative models:

1. All hamlets were contemporaneous.
2. Hamlets represent successive occupations as the population became larger and expanded outward from the town.
3. Hamlets represent successive occupations as a single group exploited new areas.
4. Hamlets represent both contemporaneous and successive occupations as more than one population segment exploited new areas.

If the projected average population estimates for the town and the hamlets are reasonably accurate (Harn 1978:Table 4), then the combined population of all hamlets would have been about 1.7 times that of the town. Assuming that the town had a number of permanent residents, and considering the fact that occupation of some hamlets was probably very short-term, it is proposed that no more than three of the larger hamlets could ever have been occupied simultaneously if they remained at peak population. In light of this, it appears that the fourth of the above hypotheses is the most plausible. The settlement pattern of the Larson community probably represents both contemporaneous and successive occupations as separate community factions exploited new areas, but the length and sequence of occupation of these areas cannot be even speculated at present. A successful solution of this problem will hinge on our ability to determine both intersite contemporaneity and the range of population variation within the central town; for a previous study has suggested that the population of Larson may have fluctuated significantly through time (Harn 1978).

The reasons for the abandonment of hamlets were probably varied but may have centered on both the depletion of natural food resources and on soil fatigue by unrestricted crop-growing. Perhaps, as in the cases of Weir and Buckeye Bend, the combination of a marginally favorable environment and isolation from the principal Illinois Valley community center sometimes ensured short-term occupation.

The former reasons may also have been instrumental in the eventual abandonment of the entire community, possibly compounded by other unknown factors of stress or political change. However, a potentially greater deterrent to residential stability, especially with regard to sites as large as Larson, would have been the lack of sufficient firewood and green wood of suitable size for building and palisade construction. The amount of firewood and gathering time consumed by normal cooking and heating operations is staggering and can only be appreciated by personal involvement in a winter camping situation. Access to building materials becomes very important when one considers that the entire town was apparently leveled by fire on a number of occasions.

In general, we view the mundane lifeways of the Spoon River variant as closely paralleling lifeways of contemporaneous cultures of the western Prairie and eastern Plains regions. This is not viewed as a political confederation of cultures so much as it is seen as a generalized adaptation to a similar environment. Innovations and expressions of contact throughout the region are almost exclusively secular in nature and reflective of daily living (Harn 1975b:430). Throughout the northern Mississippian frontier, basic daily subsistence may have been continued in much the same form as it had been for the previous several hundred years and as it would be continued until Europeanization took place. The addition of maize horticulture added another dimension to the subsistence pattern; but its introduction certainly had less impact upon the Spoon River settlement system than did the continued exploitation of wild food resources—if for no other reason than the fact that maize was transportable and would have flourished in almost any local soil.

Although the suggested Mississippian orientation toward natural energy sources rather than horticultural produce may seem contrary to popular archeological tradition, I believe that the "Mississippian-horticulturalist" subsistence concept is partly the product of primary research focus on Mississippian urban centers. The relationship and implied ramifications of horticultural tools and equipment for harvesting natural products in the Cahokia–Mississippian hinterlands have been previously discussed, and it has been concluded that wide differences existed between the subsistence patterns of the Cahokia area and those of the Mississippian frontier (Caldwell 1967a, Hall 1967, Harn 1971a, 1975b).

A superficial overview of the settlement pattern evidenced within the Larson community inevitably invites comparisons to developmental plateaus of emergent state-level societies in areas such as Mesoamerica or the American Southeast. I believe any comparisons are premature. Although Late Aztec settlement patterns in the Central Mexican highlands were also characterized by principal centers, secondary centers, and rural villages, it is suggested that the settlement patterns and associated social organization was governed by a multilevel political heirarchy with an extensive market system as a principal medium of integration at local and regional levels (cf. Parsons 1971:45–83). The beginnings of similar developments were also evident among some historic tribes of the American Southeast such as the Natchez, Cherokee, and other groups with that region (cf. Swanton 1911) and may also have been functioning during late prehistory in the core area around Cahokia (cf. Conrad n.d.b, Fowler 1974, Harn 1971b, Porter 1969). Whether the state-centered, symbiotic–extractive exchange system proposed for the Cahokia region can be stretched into the northern Mississippian frontier remains to be seen.

It is unquestioned that the particular expressions of ranked society and the distinct secular innovations accompanying the Cahokia–Mississippian movement initially created contrasts between Late Woodland and early Mississippian groups inhabiting the Spoon River area; but I have previously suggested that all durative aspects of the Cahokia presence, including sociopolitical organization, were soon modified by the host population (Harn 1975b:414–434). In attempting to interpret local social organization, the significance of the Larson central town as a principal religious political center is clear; but the secondary centers and camps should not be viewed in the same political context as their approximate counterparts in state-level societies, or even urban Mississippian societies for that matter.

While it is probable that political organization played some part in the local settlement system and that surpluses of natural products and commodities manufactured from natural products may have been regularly transported out of the Central Illinois Valley, I cannot see Cahokia as being a direct governing or major extractive factor locally. Primary articulation with the natural environment appeared to govern the size, function, and location of sites within the Larson community, and the resulting settlement pattern reflects an expediently interrelated extractive system as opposed to a complexly interrelated sociopolitical organization.

Some Research Goals for the Future

It is probable, unfortunately, that many of our present research goals ultimately will have to be compromised by limitations of funding and research time. I cannot foresee easy or immediate answers to any of the research problems outlined herein, but the accomplishment of the first of the goals to be discussed should be of critical importance to all research that is to follow.

To facilitate future Mississippian settlement pattern studies in the Illinois Valley, data-recording methods could be improved by the common use of a records-keeping system in which the same types of information would be recorded by all investigators. This would ensure more compatible recording of such natural variables as elevation, landform, water source, soils, vegetation, adaptive use, and other environmental relationships. To further control recovery biases, the system should also outline standards for recording such judgmental variables as ground cover and areal coverage of survey or excavation units, site size, density of occupational scatter, classification and quantification of the types of cultural materials recovered, and a host of other variables relative to the presence or absence of cultural features.

Although ceramics have been satisfactorily used in gross determination of occupational chronology throughout the Central Illinois River Valley, other, more sensitive, indicators must be found if we are to develop the precision required for analysis of social organization at the community level. One immediate goal involves the recovery of dendrochronology samples from as many Mississippian sites as possible and the development of at least a floating master chart for tree-ring growth in the area.

Our primary research goal includes complete excavation and analysis of a hamlet and its associated subsidiaries to determine the precise nature of the relationships existing among an assumed group of internally functioning units which are spatially demarcated within the settlement system. Analysis of the associated burial population must also be undertaken. The isolated Buckeye Bend site and its subsidiaries would appear to be ideally suited to this research orientation for a number of reasons. Locations of most of the structures and features are already known at Buckeye Bend (Harn and Weedman 1975), and the lack of structural superimposition suggests short-term occupation of the area, perhaps less than 5 years. The fact that Buckeye Bend and at least two other camps were apparently destroyed by fire also presents the potential for gaining considerable evidence about life patterns within the structures, as has been gained in similar situations at the Larson and Myer–Dickson sites (Harn 1970b, 1974, 1978). A major deterrent to the goal of total excavation of the complete Spoon River faction would be the 5.24 ha size of Buckeye Bend, but controlled sampling procedures would help offset this situation.

Considering the length of time already expended in one Mississippian community in the Central Illinois River Valley and the few positive statements that have been forthcoming, it is obvious that immediate research goals should not include a "comprehensive" study of the total Mississippian population. Although sufficient data are available to suggest that spatial organization and internal structuring can be studied on a regional level, research focus must be severely reduced. Only through qualification and quantification of the various factors involving the simplest life patterns at the smallest sites can we expect to unravel the complex organization expressed in the settlement patterns of the Spoon River variant communities. We must take an infinitely longer look through the other end of the telescope.

References

Armelagos, George J.
  n.d.   Skeletal biology and the Dickson Mounds population. In *Dickson Mounds: Cultural change and demographic variation in the life of a Late Woodland–Middle Mississippian cemetery*, edited by Alan D. Harn and George J. Armelagos (in preparation).
Armelagos, George J., James Moore, and Alan Swedlund
  n.d.   The analysis of mortality in skeletal populations. In *Dickson Mounds: Cultural change and demographic variation in the life of a Late Woodland–Middle Mississippian cemetery*, edited by Alan D. Harn and George J. Armelagos (in preparation).
Baerreis, David A.
  n.d.   Untitled chapter concerning the analysis of gastropods from the Larson site. In *The Larson site (11F 1109): A Spoon River variant town in the Central Illinois River Valley*, edited by Alan D. Harn and David A. Baerreis (in preparation).
Bahou, Wadie
  n.d.   The role of trace elements in infectious disease. In *Dickson Mounds: Cultural change and demographic variation in the life of a Late Woodland–Middle Mississippian cemetery*, edited by Alan D. Harn and George J. Armelagos (in preparation).
Baker, Frank C., James B. Griffin, Richard G. Morgan, Georg K. Neumann, and Jay L.B. Taylor.
  1941   Contributions to the archaeology of the Illinois river valley. *Transactions of the American Philosophical Society* 32:22–28. Philadelphia.
Bender, Margaret M., Reid A. Bryson, and David A. Baerreis
  1975   University of Wisconsin radiocarbon dates XII. *Radiocarbon* 17(1).
Blakely, Robert L.
  1971   Comparison of the mortality profiles of Archaic, Middle Woodland, and Middle Mississippian skeletal populations. *American Journal of Physical Anthropology* 34:43–54.
  1973   Biological variation among and between two prehistoric populations at Dickson Mounds. Ph.D. dissertation, Department of Anthropology, Indiana University, Bloomington.
  n.d.   Biological distance between Late Woodland and Middle Mississippian inhabitants of the central Illinois river valley. Manuscript on file at the Dickson Mounds State Museum, Lewistown, Illinois.
Blakely, Robert L., and Phillip L. Walker
  1968   Mortality profile of the Middle Mississippian population of Dickson Mounds, Fulton County, Illinois. *Proceedings of the Indiana Academy of Science for 1967* 77:102–108.
Buis, A.R.
  1940   The prehistoric villages and camp sites of the Peoria Lake area. *Transactions of the Illinois State Academy of Science* 33(2):42–44.

Caldwell, Joseph R.
  1967a The house that "X" built. *The Living Museum* **28**(12):92–93. Illinois State Museum, Springfield.
  1967b New discoveries at Dickson Mounds. *The Living Museum* **29**(6):139–142. Illinois State Museum, Springfield.
  n.d.   Untitled report of excavations at the Eveland site (F^{v}900) in preparation. Manuscript on file at the Dickson Mounds State Museum, Lewistown, Illinois.
Chapman, Florence H.
  1962   Incidence of arthritis in a prehistoric Middle Mississippian Indian population. *Proceedings of the Indiana Academy of Science* **72:**59–62.
Cohen, Janice
  n.d.   The dental morphology of Dickson Mound and Cahokia Mound 72 populations. In *Dickson Mounds: Cultural change and demographic variation in the life of a Late Woodland–Middle Mississippian cemetery*, edited by Alan D. Harn and George J. Armelagos (in preparation).
Cole, Fay-Cooper, and Thorne Deuel
  1937   *Rediscovering Illinois.* Chicago: University of Chicago Press.
Conrad, Lawrence A.
  1970   Test in Fulton County. *Quarterly Newsletter, Illinois Association for Advancement of Archaeology* **2**(1):4.
  1972   1966 excavation at the Dickson Mound: A Sepo-Spoon River burial mound in the central Illinois valley. M.A. thesis, Department of Anthropology, University of Wisconsin—Madison. Madison.
  1973   The nature of the relationships between Cahokia and the central Illinois river valley. Paper presented at the fifty-second annual meeting of the Central States Anthropological Society in St. Louis, Missouri, March 29–31. (Mimeographed).
  n.d.a. The Berry Site: A multicomponent site in the central Illinois river valley. Manuscript in preparation.
  n.d.b. The Spoon River culture in the central Illinois river valley. Manuscript in possession of the author.
Conrad, Lawrence A., and Thomas E. Emerson
  1974   1973 excavations at the Orendorf site (11F 1284). *Quarterly Newsletter, Illinois Association for Advancement of Archaeology* **6**(1):1–2.
Conrad, Lawrence A., and Alan D. Harn
  1972   The Spoon River culture in the central Illinois river valley. Manuscript on file at Dickson Mounds State Museum, Lewistown, Illinois.
  1976   Evidence for contact between the Spoon River area and the plains: Some observations. Paper presented at the 21st Annual Midwest Archaeological Conference in Minneapolis, Minnesota, October 20–22, 1976. (Mimeographed).
Dallman, John
  n.d.   Untitled chapter concerning the analysis of turtles, snakes and amphibia from the Larson site. In *The Larson site (11F 1109): A Spoon River variant town in the central Illinois river valley*, edited by Alan D. Harn and David A. Baerreis (in preparation).
DeBusk, Charles R.
  1966   A pre-mound occupational level in the Dickson Cemetery Mound (F°34)—summer of 1966. Manuscript on file at the Dickson Mounds State Museum, Lewistown, Illinois.
  1967   Sleuths with spades. *The Living Museum* **29**(3):116–119. Illinois State Museum, Springfield.
Ditch, Larry E., and Jerome C. Rose
  1972   A multivariate dental sexing technique. *American Journal of Physical Anthropology* **37**(1):61–64.

Emerson, Thomas E.
  n.d.   Untitled chapter concerned with the analysis of cranial elements of deer from the
          Larson site. In *The Larson site (11F 1109): A Spoon River variant town in the central
          Illinois river valley*, edited by Alan D. Harn and David A. Baerreis (in preparation).
Emmons, Merrill, Patrick J. Munson, and Joseph R. Caldwell
  1960   A prehistoric house from Fulton County, Illinois. *The Living Museum* 22(5):516–517.
          Illinois State Museum, Springfield.
Fehrenbacher, J.B., G.O. Walker, and H.L. Wascher
  1967   Soils of Illinois. *Bulletin* 725, University of Illinois College of Agricultural Experi-
          ment Station in cooperation with the Soil Conservation Service, U.S. Department
          of Agriculture.
Fowler, Melvin L.
  1952   The Clear Lake site: Hopewellian occupation. In *Hopewellian communities in Illinois*,
          edited by Thorne Deuel. *Illinois State Museum Scientific Papers* 5.
  1974   Cahokia: Ancient capital of the midwest. *An Addison–Wesley Module in An-
          thropology* 48:1–38.
Gilbert, Robert
  n.d.   Trace elements, diet and pathology in Dickson Mounds. In *Dickson Mounds: Cul-
          tural change and demographic variation in the life of a Late Woodland–Middle Missis-
          sippian cemetery*, edited by Alan D. Harn and George J. Armelagos (in prepara-
          tion).
Goodman, Alan
  n.d.   Dental hypoplasia. In *Dickson Mounds: Cultural change and demographic varia-
          tion in the life of a Late Woodland–Middle Mississippian cemetery*, edited by Alan
          D. Harn and George J. Armelagos (in preparation).
Griffin, James B., and Dan F. Morse
  1961   The short-nosed god from the Emmons site, Illinois. *American Antiquity* 26:560–
          563. Salt Lake City.
Gustav, Bonnie
  1972   Sexual dimorphism in the adult bony pelvis of a prehistoric human population
          from Illinois. Ph.D. dissertation, Department of Anthropology, University of Mas-
          sachusetts, Amherst.
Haberman, Tom, Dana Duncan, and Linda Steinberg
  n.d.   Untitled chapter concerning the analysis of seeds and other plant material from the
          Larson site. In *The Larson site (11F 1109): A Spoon River variant town in the central
          Illinois river valley*, edited by Alan D. Harn and David A. Baerreis (in preparation).
Hall, Robert L.
  1967   The Mississippian heartland and its Plains relationship. *Plains Anthropologist*
          12(36). Lincoln.
Harn, Alan D.
  1966a   A surface survey and salvage of the Larson site in Fulton County, Illinois. Manu-
          script on file at the Dickson Mounds State Museum, Lewistown, Illinois.
  1966b   *Skeletons and artifacts from the Dickson Cemetery Mound: Sketchbook.* Illinois State
          Museum Society. Springfield.
  1967   Dickson Mounds: An evaluation of the amateur in Illinois archaeology. *Earth
          Science* 20(4):152–157.
  1970a   Dickson Mounds Museum excavations in the central Illinois valley. *Quarterly
          Newsletter, Illinois Association for Advancement of Archaeology* 2(4):35.
  1970b   Notes on the Mississippian occupation of the central Illinois river valley. Paper
          presented at the 69th annual meeting of the American Anthropological Association
          in San Diego, California, November 19–22; revised February, 1971. (Mimeo-
          graphed).

1971a   The prehistory of Dickson Mounds: A preliminary report. *Dickson Mounds Museum Anthropological Studies* **1**. Illinois State Museum, Springfield.

1971b   An archaeological survey of the American Bottoms in Madison and St. Clair counties, Illinois. In Archaeological surveys of the American Bottoms and adjacent bluffs, Illinois. *Illinois State Museum Reports of Investigations* **21**. Springfield.

1972a   A long-nosed god mask from Dickson Mounds. *The Living Museum* **34**(4):112–117. Illinois State Museum, Springfield.

1972b   A Mississippian house, A.D. 1972. *The Living Museum* **34**(5):124–126. Illinois State Museum, Springfield.

1974   New excavations at the Myer–Dickson site. *Quarterly Newsletter, Illinois Association for Advancement of Archaeology* **6**(4):27–32.

1975a   Another long-nosed god mask from Fulton County, Illinois. *The Wisconsin Archaeologist* **56**(1):2–8.

1975b   Cahokia and the Mississippian emergence in the Spoon River area of Illinois. *Transactions of the Illinois State Academy of Science* **68**(4):414–434.

1976   An archaeological survey of the Statewide Hatchery site, Sand Ridge State Forest, Mason County, Illinois. An archaeological assessment and impact statement prepared for Kramer, Chin & Mayo, Inc., Seattle, Washington. Copy on file at the Dickson Mounds State Museum, Lewistown, Illinois.

1978   Variation in Mississippian settlement pattern: The Larson community in the Central Illinois River Valley. In Mississippian site archaeology in Illinois: II. *Illinois Archaeological Survey Bulletin* **11**, Urbana.

n.d.   The archaeology of Dickson Mounds. In *Dickson Mounds: Cultural change and demographic variation in the life of a Late Woodland–Middle Mississippian cemetery*, edited by Alan D. Harn and George J. Armelagos (in preparation).

Harn, Alan D., and George J. Armelagos (Editors)
n.d.   *Dickson Mounds: Cultural change and demographic variation in the life of a Late Woodland-Middle Mississippian cemetery*. Manuscript on file at the Dickson Mounds State Museum, Lewistown, Illinois.

Harn, Alan D., and David A. Baerreis (Editors)
n.d.   The Larson site (11F 1109): A Spoon River variant town in the central Illinois river valley (in preparation).

Harn, Alan D., and Alfred C. Koelling
1974   The indigenous drug plants of Fulton County, Illinois. *Transactions of the Illinois State Academy of Science* **67**(3):259–284.

Harn, Alan D., and William Weedman
1975   Archaeology, aircraft, and answers. *The Living Museum* **27**(6):348–352. Illinois State Museum, Springfield.

History of Fulton County, Illinois
1879   Peoria: Charles C. Chapman and Co.

Jacobs, Kenneth
n.d.   The uses of skeletal analysis in archaeological populations. In *Dickson Mounds: Cultural change and demographic variation in the life of a Late Woodland–Middle Mississippian cemetery*, edited by Alan D. Harn and George J. Armelagos (in preparation).

Jacobson, Jerome F.
1959   Buckeye Bend site survey report. Manuscript on file at Dickson Mounds State Museum, Lewistown, Illinois.

Johnson, Dennis, and Gregory Gendron
n.d.   Sexual dimorphism of the bones of the foot. In *Dickson Mounds: Cultural change and demographic variation in the life of a Late Woodland–Middle Mississippian cemetery*, edited by Alan D. Harn and George J. Armelagos (in preparation).

Koeppen, Robert C., Peter A. Gendel, and Patricia Burch
  n.d.   Untitled chapter concerning the analysis of wood charcoal from the Larson site. In
          *The Larson site (11F 1109): A Spoon River variant town in the central Illinois river
          valley*, edited by Alan D. Harn and David A. Baerreis (in preparation).
Lallo, John
  1973   The skeletal biology of three prehistoric American Indian societies from Dickson
          Mounds. Ph.D. dissertation, Department of Anthropology, University of Massa-
          chusetts, Amherst.
  n.d.   Skeletal pathology as a measure of stress in the Dickson Mounds population. In
          *Dickson Mounds: Cultural change and demographic variation in the life of a Late
          Woodland–Middle Mississippian cemetery*, edited by Alan D. Harn and George J.
          Armelagos (in preparation).
Lallo, John, and George J. Armelagos
  n.d.a. Analysis of mortality pattern in the Dickson Mounds population. In *Dickson
          Mounds: Cultural change and demographic variation in the life of a Late Woodland–
          Middle Mississippian cemetery*, edited by Alan D. Harn and George J. Armelagos (in
          preparation).
  n.d.b. Dental paleopathology. In *Dickson Mounds: Cultural change and demographic varia-
          tion in the life of a Late Woodland–Middle Mississippian cemetery*, edited by Alan D.
          Harn and George J. Armelagos (in preparation).
McDonald, S.E.
  1950   The Crable site, Fulton County, Illinois. *Journal of the Illinois State Archaeological
          Society* **7**(4):16–18.
Miendl, Richard
  n.d.   Multivariate analysis of the Dickson Mound crania. In *Dickson Mounds: Cultural
          change and demographic variation in the life of a Late Woodland–Middle Mississippian
          cemetery*, edited by Alan D. Harn and George J. Armelagos (in preparation).
Miller, David
  1958   The Mound Lake site spade cache. *Central States Archaeological Journal* **4**(3):96–97.
Morse, Dan F.
  1960   The southern cult: The Crable site. *Central States Archaeological Journal* **7**(4):124–
          135.
  1969   The Crable site. In Ancient disease in the Midwest, *Illinois State Museum Reports of
          Investigations* **15**, Appendix 2:63–68.
Morse, Dan F., Phyllis Morse, and Merrill Emmons
  1961   The southern cult: The Emmons site. *Central States Archaeological Journal* **8**(4):124–
          140.
Morse, Dan, George Schoenbeck, and Dan F. Morse
  1953   Fiedler site. *Journal of the Illinois State Archaeological Society* **3**(2).
Munson, Patrick J., Paul W. Parmalee, and Richard A. Yarnell
  1971   Subsistence ecology of Scovill, A terminal Middle Woodland village. *American
          Antiquity* **36**(4):410–431.
Neumann, Georg K.
  1940   Evidence for the antiquity of scalping for central Illinois. *American Antiquity*
          5(4):287–289.
Oerichbauer, Edgar S.
  n.d.   Untitled chapter concerning the analysis of large mammal fauna from the Larson
          site. In *The Larson site (11F 1109): A Spoon River variant town in the central Illinois
          river valley*, edited by Alan D. Harn and David A. Baerreis (in preparation).
Parsons, Jeffrey R.
  1971   Prehistoric settlement patterns in the Texcoco Region, Mexico. *Memoirs of the
          Museum of Anthropology* **3**. Ann Arbor:University of Michigan Press.

Perkins, Raymond W.
  1965   The Frederick site. *Illinois Archaeological Survey Bulletin* **5**. Urbana.
Pillaert, Elizabeth
  n.d.   Untitled chapter concerning the analysis of small mammal and avian fauna from
          the Larson site. In *The Larson site (11F 1109): A Spoon River variant town in the
          central Illinois river valley,* edited by Alan D. Harn and David A. Baerreis (in
          preparation).
Porter, James W.
  1969   The Mitchell site and prehistoric exchange systems at Cahokia: A.D. 1000±300. In
          Explorations into Cahokia archaeology, edited by Melvin L. Fowler. *Illinois Ar-
          chaeological Survey Bulletin* 7:137–164. Urbana.
Powell, J.W.
  1894   *Twelfth annual report of the Bureau of American Ethnology. Washington, D.C.*
Riggle, R. Stanley
  n.d.   Untitled chapter concerning the analysis of freshwater bivalves from the Larson
          site. In *The Larson site (11F 1109): A Spoon River variant town in the central Illinois
          river valley,* edited by Alan D. Harn and David A. Baerreis (in preparation).
Roberts, Alvin B.
  1938   The history of the Dickson Mound builders. M.A. thesis, State University of Iowa,
          Ames.
Rose, Jerome C.
  1973   Analysis of dental microdefects of prehistoric populations from Illinois. Ph.D.
          dissertation, Department of Anthropology, University of Massachusetts, Amherst.
  n.d.   Microdefects of the Dickson Mounds population. In *Dickson Mounds: Cultural
          change and demographic variation in the life of a Late Woodland–Middle Mississippian
          cemetery,* edited by Alan D. Harn and George J. Armelagos (in preparation).
Schoenbeck, Ethel
  1940   Prehistoric aboriginal pottery of the Peoria region. *Transactions of the Illinois State
          Academy of Science* **33**(2):44–45.
Schwegman, John E.
  1973   *Comprehensive plan for the Illinois Nature Preserves system part two: The natural
          divisions of Illinois.* Illinois Nature Preserves Commission in cooperation with the
          Illinois Department of Conservation.
Shields, Wayne F.
  1969   Recent archaeology at Dickson Mounds. *The Living Museum* **31**(5):132–135. Illinois
          State Museum, Springfield.
Simpson, A.M.
  1952   The Kingston village site. *Journal of the Illinois Archaeological Society* **2**(1):63–79.
Smith, Hale G.
  1951   The Crable site, Fulton County, Illinois. *Anthropological Papers, Museum of An-
          thropology, University of Michigan* **7**. Ann Arbor.
Snyder, John Francis
  1908   The Brown County ossuary. *Journal of the Illinois State Historical Society* **1**(2–3):33–
          43.
Stephens, Jeanette E.
  1973   An archaeological survey of the Banner Reservoir area, Fulton County, Illinois.
          Manuscript on file at the Dickson Mounds State Museum, Lewistown, Illinois.
  1976   Mississippian settlement relocation at the Orendorf site. Paper presented at the
          21st annual meeting of the Midwest Archaeological Conference in Minneapolis,
          Minnesota, October 20–22. (Mimeographed).
Swanton, John R.
  1911   Indian tribes of the lower Mississippi valley and adjacent coast of the Gulf of
          Mexico. *Bureau of American Ethnology Bulletin* **46**. Washington, D.C.

Thomas, Cyrus
  1894   Report on mound explorations of the Bureau of Ethnology. *Bureau of American Ethnology,* 12th Annual Report. Pp. 118–120.
VanGerven, Dennis
  1971   The contribution of size and shape variation to patterns of sexual dimorphism of the human femur. Ph.D. dissertation, Department of Anthropology, University of Massachusetts, Amherst.
VanGerven, Dennis, and Bonnie Gustav
  n.d.   Shape and size of the pelvis and femur. In *Dickson Mounds: Cultural change and demographic variation in the life of a Late Woodland–Middle Mississippian cemetery,* edited by Alan D. Harn and George J. Armelagos (in preparation).
Wanless, Harold R.
  1957   Geology and mineral resources of the Beardstown, Glasford, Havana, and Vermont quadrangles, Illinois. *Illinois State Geological Survey Bulletin* **82.** Urbana.
Wells, Lewis Bruce
  1937   Comparative study of the long-bones of Indians buried in Dickson and other mounds of Fulton County, Illinois. M.A. thesis, State University of Iowa, Ames.
Wettersten, Vernon H.
  n.d.   Ceramic analysis of a Hopewell village. Manuscript on file at Northwestern University.
Wray, Donald E.
  1941   Middle Mississippian grit tempered ware. *Transactions of the Illinois State Academy of Science* **34**(2):66–67.
  1952   Archaeology of the Illinois valley: 1950. In *Archaeology of the eastern United States,* edited by James B. Griffin. Chicago: University of Chicago Press.
  n.d.a. The Kingston Lake sequence. Manuscript on file at the Illinois State Museum, Springfield.
  n.d.b. The Shryock site–Fulton County, Illinois. Manuscript on file at the Illinois State Museum, Springfield.
Wray, Donald E., and Richard S. MacNeish
  n.d.   The Weaver site: Twenty centuries of Illinois prehistory. Manuscript on file at the Illinois State Museum, Springfield.
Yerkes, Richard
  n.d.   Untitled chapter concerning the analysis of fish remains from the Larson site. In *The Larson site (11F 1109): A Spoon River variant town in the central Illinois River valley,* edited by Alan D. Harn and David A. Baerreis (in preparation).
Young, Philip D.
  1960   The Frederick site–S^c-11. *Illinois Archaeological Survey Bulletin* **2**:71–79.

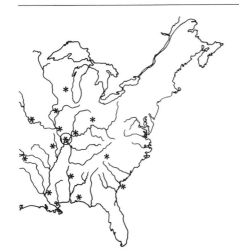

10

The Kincaid System: Mississippian Settlement in the Environs of a Large Site

JON MULLER

The Kincaid locality has been an area of archeological interest for some time. The local records (Page 1900) first mention the site at the latter part of the last century, but the first description by an archeologist was by Clarence Moore in 1916. Moore, however, was denied permission to dig at the site and his steamship, the *Gopher,* sailed on to visit and revisit other places. At the beginning of the 1930s, Fay-Cooper Cole and his associates at the University of Chicago were looking for an area to balance the information they were obtaining from work in northern Illinois. Through the agency of Fain King of Wycliffe and others, the Chicago investigators became interested in the Kincaid site as a place to establish a chronological sequence (Cole *et al.* 1951). This project continued over a number of years, and involved a cast of hundreds. Even though many of the students involved in the project were primarily interested in areas of anthropology other than archeology, the list of participants includes many of the top names of archeology. The long list of social anthropologists who had field experience at the Kincaid site is equally impressive, but it is difficult to determine how important this archeological experience was to their career choice.

In any event, it would not be an exaggeration to say that this initial

269

research at the Kincaid site played a vital role in the development of archeology in the eastern United States. The files and records of this work are now in the possession of Southern Illinois University, and examination of these has shown that the planning, organization, and execution of the research was excellent, even by modern standards.

The involvement of Southern Illinois University with this area dates from the founding of the Department of Anthropology, although survey work in the locality by various staff members of the Museum and department was not extensive until a visit to the Kincaid site by myself and others in early 1967. At that time, we discovered that a portion of the site had been damaged by clearing for agriculture. With support from the Office of Research and Projects of the University, we initiated small-scale salvage operations in the affected area (University of Chicago site number Mx^{f}36) (Weigand and Muller, in press). During the course of this work, it became apparent that delineation of the boundaries of the site left something to be desired. Phil C. Weigand and I began surface site-location surveying at the Kincaid site in an effort to define more accurately the limits of the site. A series of subsequent flights over the area revealed further details of site structure, and University Museum personnel started to explore the possibilities of protecting the site as a state park. As a result of the initial efforts of Phil Weigand and the subsequent enormous amount of work done by Frank Rackerby, a portion of the site was finally purchased by the State of Illinois as the first archeological preserve in the state. During this time, I noted the increasing clearing of the land in the Black Bottom area, which surrounds the Kincaid site. For this reason, a systematic site-location survey of the locality was initiated. This survey has continued up to the present time. To date, over 60 million m^2 of area have been surveyed within the Black Bottom locality and well over 500 site locations of all time periods have been recorded for the immediate environs of the Kincaid site. Additional surveys have been carried out at selected locations in the adjacent upland areas in both Illinois and Kentucky.

The major source on the University of Chicago work in the Black Bottom during the 1930s is *Kincaid, a Prehistoric Illinois Metropolis* by Fay-Cooper Cole and others (1951). Preliminary reports on Southern Illinois University's work are in press by the Illinois Archaeological Survey. Berle Clay also has discussed the archeology of the area (Clay 1976).

Environment

The Kincaid archeological locality is roughly the area of the confluence of the Cumberland, Tennessee, and Ohio Rivers. The Kincaid site is located in the approximate center of an extensive bottomland, which is a large point bar of the Ohio River. Evidence suggests that the Ohio River channel has been essentially stable here for thousands of years (Alexander and Prior 1971:371). The Black Bottom, as the area is known, is about 5 km wide and some 16 km long at the widest point. The Black Bottom itself consists of ridges and swales with standing water in lower places. Almost all past and present human settlement in the locality is restricted to the higher ridges, which are today above normal winter and spring flooding. Sedimentation in the Black Bottom is variable, but average sedimentation on the ridges is approximately .027 cm per year, whereas sedimentation in the swales is on the order of .19 cm per year (Alexander and Prior 1971:370). Both geological and archeological evidence from the Black Bottom suggest that rates of sedimentation may be slightly greater during the historic period, but that regular sedimentation on the order of .01 cm per year on the ridges has been characteristic of the area for the last 3000 years. This steady, but slow, sedimentation process has meant that soil exhaustion due to agriculture has not been, and is not today a serious problem. It appears likely that in Mississippian times, as today, occasional floods reached very high levels in the Black Bottom (Cole *et al.* 1951:15, 43). Modern floods in 1913 and 1937, for example, put some 5 to 6 m of water over most of the high ground in the Black Bottom, leaving only the mounds at the Kincaid site above the water.

Climatic evidence for the last 400 years in the form of tree-ring analysis (Bell in Cole *et al.* 1951, Estes 1969) suggests that there has not been any major change in rainfall patterns. Botanical evidence supports the tentative conclusion that the climate in the Black Bottoms area during Mississippian times was very similar to the historically documented climate. Over the last 100 years, the driest months have been September and October, with about 7 cm of precipitation each, and the wettest month has been May, with 11 cm of rain. Rainfall is relatively constant throughout the year, however; and the monthly average is 9.4 cm (with a standard deviation of 1.2 cm).

In general, the soils of the Black Bottom are very fertile. The most fertile soils are nearer to the river. These have modern yields of maize as high as 7740 kg per hectare (125 bushels per acre), although average yields for the area today are closer to 5000 kg per hectare (about 80 bushels per acre). These soils are resistant to drought.

The plant life of the Black Bottom is fairly typical Southern Lowland vegetation. The deep swamps of the area have cypress and water tupelo trees with swamp rose and many other species occurring in the shrubby understory layer. In shallower water, the water tupelo is replaced by pumpkin ash and the shrubby layer is composed of virginia willow. Higher areas within the Black Bottoms support a lowland forest vegetation association, with a gradation from cottonwood to various oaks, hickories, and sweet gum. The terraces above the Black Bottom are predominantly characterized by post oak flats, although poorly drained areas on the terraces may show vegetation more characteristic of the adjacent bottom-land. Very large areas of the Black Bottom, however, were covered by cane brakes at the time of the initial land survey. The spatial distribution of these extensive stands of cane corresponds very closely to the most fertile soils of the bottom as well as to the distribution of Mississippian settlements. In terms of vegetation as well as in climate, then, the Black Bottom and the Kincaid area are very closely related to the Coastal Plain (Mohlenbrock and Voight 1959, Voight and Mohlenbrock 1964). At the same time, the Kincaid area is very close to the boundaries of the Coastal Plain with the Central Lowlands, the Ozark Plateau, and the Interior Low Plateaus. Like so many other areas of Mississippian settlement, there is an incredibly diverse range of environments within a few hundred kilometers of the Kincaid site. In the course of our work, a detailed reconstruction of the environment at the time of the original land survey was done by Brian Butler (1972, 1977).

Research Orientation

From the start of our survey of the Kincaid locality, our work has had two basic goals. The first was to utilize the potential of the area for assessing the usefulness of a series of more or less traditional assumptions concerning Mississippian organization. The second was conservation of the archeological resources. The Black Bottom area today is almost entirely open and in cultivation. Much of this development took place after 1960 and agricultural development and impact on the archeological resources of the area are both increasing.

The particular hypotheses concerning Mississippian organization being tested in the Black Bottom are diverse, and range from general statements about the size and complexity of the Kincaid site made by the University of Chicago investigators to suggestions that Kincaid may have been a "militaristic state" (Sears 1968). Sears's definition of *state*, however, is not consistent with more recent usages (e.g., Service 1975). If states are taken to differ from chiefdoms in the lack of institutionalized force (Service 1975:14–15), then there is very little indication in the ethnographic record from the Southeast for the existence of states. Whether or not the distinction is important to archeologists, most of the archeological evidence relating to Mississippian societies in general and to Kincaid in particular seems consistent with the lower chiefdom levels as opposed to the higher state level of organization. Evidence of long-term planning at the Kincaid site does seem more in line with the kinds of organization suggested by the concept of "chiefdom," but this view cannot be tested if only large sites are considered. Most views of Mississippian society do postulate ranked societies, dense population at certain regional centers, and ranking in the size and function of smaller sites. Yet examination of the literature relating to the size and distribution of Mississippian sites shows relatively little information to be available concerning such things as actual site size and distribution, particularly of sites that cannot be described as "centers." Concentration on large and dramatic sites is understandable, but does not yield representative data on the total character of Mississippian settlement systems. For this reason, surveys and selection of sites for excavation in the Black Bottom were carried out in such a way as to ensure representativeness in terms of the total settlement system.

Survey Methodology

The initial survey of the Black Bottom began with a transect from the terrace down into the bottomland in the northern portion of the floodplain. This area was chosen because a number of different habitats were represented and because the area had mostly been in forest or otherwise unavailable for walkover at the time of the University of Chicago's work. We had noted that the sites located by the University of Chicago were predominantly in a zone about 2 km back from the Ohio River. However, we doubted the representativeness of this survey because we also noted that this same zone was the major area of the Black Bottom under cultivation at that time. It was expected that similar sites would be found elsewhere in the Black Bottom, with perhaps some local variation in site function dependent upon locally available resources. Although a number of sites were located in this first transect, they were almost all Archaic. Only one possible nonceramic Mississippian site was located.

The results of this initial survey suggested that there were some significant differences in settlement patterning during different periods of occupation. With this in mind, the survey was expanded out of the transect zone. At this time, neither adequate soil nor vegetation data were available for the construction of sampling strata. Since the Black Bottom as a whole was a well-defined and relatively small zone, a complete survey was carried out of those areas in cultivation. Since almost the entire area was being cultivated, this amounted to a virtually complete survey of the Black Bottom. Every environmental zone present in the area is well represented in areas under cultivation. Since that time, more than 49 km² of the Black Bottom has been surveyed—approximately 80% of the total area. In addition, more than 10 km² have been intensively surveyed in areas across the river, in the uplands, and on terraces near the Black Bottom.

Survey was carried out by parties of from 10 to 15 individuals who walked across fields at intervals of approximately 5 m. All finds of lithic and other materials were located on topographic maps and aerial photographs. Since the majority of the area surveyed is alluvial floodplain, the presence of any lithic material is a fair indication of human agency. Needless to say, human agency does not necessarily imply Indian occupation, since the area has been exploited by European farmers for 150 years. All historic and modern locations were also recorded, in any case. For areas with more than one item, an attempt was made to define the limits of surface scatter and these limits were recorded on maps and aerial photographs. In general, any discrete area of scatter was recorded separately. The limit of resolution was approximately 10 m, however; and concentration of surface materials closer than that were sometimes recorded as subareas depending on field judgment of the degree of continuity among concentrations. In all cases, however, apparent concentrations and areas of scatter were collected separately. An effort was made to take representative collections, but the collection procedure was systematic rather than random.

The accuracy of site size estimation in the Black Bottom is primarily affected by alluviation. The major problem with regard to Mississippian sites is that site extent may be greater with lower areas of the site buried under slope wash from the tops of ridges. Extensive test excavation at Mississippian sites has shown, however, that the actual size of sites is usually very close to the area of observed surface scatter. Some more deeply buried sites do, however, appear to be very small, based on surface survey. Nonetheless, it seems unlikely in light of known alluviation rates, elevation, and other variables that there are substantial errors in our site size estimates based on area of surface scatter. The one area where our surface survey can yield no results at all is in the zone within 500–1000 m of the river bank. In some areas of this zone, alluviation has added more than 2 m of deposits in the last century; but inspection of both the eroded bank (which is up to 10 m high) and eroded channels have not yielded a single trace of prehistoric occupation or use. In addition, the nature of the soils and the character of flooding in this zone make it unlikely that this part of the Black Bottom had substantial Mississippian settlement. The survey coverage of the Black Bottom and surrounding areas is such that all environmental zones have been adequately represented.

Settlement Pattern

Of the more than 500 sites that have been recorded in our survey, over 100 are Mississippian. The total span of Mississippian occupation in the Black Bottom may range from A.D. 900 to 1500 or later. The bulk of evidence strongly suggests that a peak in the Mississippian use of the area occurred in the thirteenth century. The mean of all radiocarbon dates (tree-ring corrected) on Mississippian components in the locality is A.D. 1180. If two rather early (tenth century) dates are excluded, the mean date is A.D. 1212. Of 17 radiocarbon dates from Mississippian contexts in the Kincaid locality, the range of those that are obviously not erroneous (e.g., GX-2715 which gave a date of 1460–1480 B.C., corrected, for a pit with beans, corn, and shell-tempered pottery) is from A.D. 920 to 1330. Moreover, 10 of the 15 reasonable dates fall in the period from A.D. 1190 to 1290. Although information on earlier Mississippian occupation of the area is limited, similarities in location of sites and other data suggest the possibility of a gradual shift from Lewis Late Woodland to the Kincaid Mississippian phase. Ceramic materials and the style of a shell gorget found in the Mx^{v}1A area at Kincaid support the view that Kincaid was occupied approximately the same time as other Mississippian settlements in the area. It should be noted that these dates do not agree with the University of Chicago tree-ring dates nor with Clay's belief that Kincaid area settlement is largely between A.D. 1300 and 1650 (Clay 1976:14). Although I had earlier been impressed by the reasonableness of the position taken by Munson (1966) that the dendrochronological sequence of Kincaid was basically correct (e.g., Weigand and Muller, in press), more recent work in the area now makes it seem very unlikely that Kincaid and other settlements in the Black Bottom were at a dense level of population as late as the sixteenth or seventeenth century. Although the evidence is still not conclusive in regard to Kincaid itself, there are increasing indications that it is contemporary with its immediate hinterlands settlement. If this is so, then Clay's (1976) model for Mississippian settlement in the region must be considerably revised (cf. Butler's discussion of this problem, 1977). Robert Riordan (1975), in his dissertation on Kincaid ceramics, also argues that Kincaid is later than other Mississippian sites in the Black Bottom.

The distribution of sites by size within the Black Bottom is essentially trimodal. There are, as might be expected, a number of very small sites of less than .01 ha in size. Undoubtedly, many of these are somewhat larger sites that were poorly represented by surface materials at the time of survey. Nonetheless, it seems likely that at least some of these locations represent temporary or special-purpose Mississippian use stations. Unfortunately, such sites have a way of "melting" away under archeological investigation, but further work on such sites is a high priority of the project. By far the most important site size grouping is made up of those sites that are approximately .3 ha in area. The greatest part of the energies of the project has been devoted to researching this kind of site. Sites of this size level have often been either ignored by archeologists if they are spatially isolated, or have been grouped together with other such sites if they are close to one another. Yet it is this size of site that makes up the minimal unit of Mississippian permanent settlement. A site covering .3 ha has usually one, but sometimes as many as three structures occupied at any one time. The indications are that these structures were occupied at least through the entire growing season of some 9 months, and were probably occupied throughout the year except for times of flooding (for a discussion, see Blakeman 1974). Toward the top end of the size scale in the Black Bottom are a few larger sites of approximately .9–1.0 ha in area. These sites appear to be made up of a group of small "farmsteads" that are contiguous and contain from 10 to 15 structures. In general, the larger sites appear to be located near the center of an area of smaller, .3-ha sites. Riordan (1975) and Butler (1977) have argued that these sites are "nodal" in terms of social organization, although a great deal remains to be done before their hypotheses can be fully tested.

At the very top of the site size ranking is the Kincaid site, which has an area of approximately 70 ha enclosed within its palisade. It should be emphasized however, that the total area of occupation at Kincaid covered only some 6 ha, or about 8% of the total area enclosed within the palisade, not including the mounds. In effect, Kincaid is similar in its internal organization to other ridge areas in the Black Bottom in consisting of a series of farmstead-like settlements occurring either singly or grouped into hamlets. The difference, of course, lies in the existence of a palisade and in public works manifested in mound construction. One class of site, in terms of function and size, that is lacking from the Black Bottom proper is what has been described as a secondary center, which is essentially a large hamlet or village with two platform mounds. It can be argued, as Butler (1977) has done, that the presence of a large mound center has a suppressive effect on mound construction in its immediate environs. Manpower requirements of the large center certainly might well have this effect, and it is possible that intermediate levels of political and social organization were either concentrated at the main center or that such levels or organization were superfluous in the neighborhood of a major center.

Mississippian sites in the Black Bottom proper are almost entirely restricted to the area that Butler (1972) has termed the "cane bottoms," which are basically the same as the area of the Armiesburg silty clay loam soil type. Approximately 80% of the Mississippian sites in the Black Bottom are located in the cane bottoms and on Armiesburg or Huntington soil (Figure 10.1). Of the 112 Mississippian sites used in Butler's analysis, 92 were in this environmental zone. Of the remaining 20 Mississippian sites, all but four were within 300 m of the cane bottoms, and it is likely that this simply reflects conservatism in defining the environmental zones. Three of the four sites that are definitely not in the cane bottoms have no shell-tempered pottery and could very well represent either Late Woodland sites or specialized Mississippian locations (Butler 1977:177).

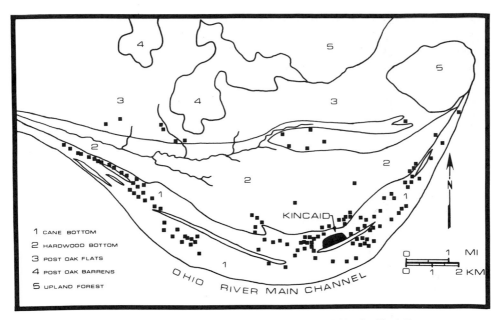

1 CANE BOTTOM
2 HARDWOOD BOTTOM
3 POST OAK FLATS
4 POST OAK BARRENS
5 UPLAND FOREST

OHIO RIVER MAIN CHANNEL

KINCAID

FIGURE 10.1.   The distribution of Mississippian sites within the Black Bottom.

It is not clear exactly what features of the environment were being selected by the Mississippian farmers, but it is clear from the distribution of Mississippian sites that they were highly selective. As indicated earlier, these soil types are very fertile for maize agriculture. The concentration of Huntington soils close to the river edge in a somewhat high-risk flood situation make this soil less important in terms of Mississippian settlement than Armiesburg soils.

Another major characteristic of the location of Mississippian settlements in the Black Bottom is elevation. Mississippian habitation sites are located more than 4 m above normal river pool. This elevation (99–100 m above sea level) is the normal crest of winter and spring flooding today. However, fertile soils and relatively high elevations are not enough. There must also be enough land above normal flooding to support the minimal occupation unit. For this reason, there normally must be more than 2–3 ha of land available that meets the criteria before a Mississippian habitation site can be expected. A site located in the minimal settlement location of 2 ha would be expected to belong to the one-structure class ("farmstead") and might be expected to have a population of approximately five persons in a structure having 9–36 m² of floor area. This general relationship does, in fact, hold. Population estimates based on actual observed site area and population estimates based on the amount of support area (with Mississippian settlement meeting the three criteria given above) have a correlation coefficient of .918 with an R^2 of .843! It should be noted that the estimates of potential support areas used here do not include zones adjacent to the river, which appear to be subject to flooding (for a discussion of these estimates, see Muller, in press). Only auguring or other forms of deep testing will resolve the question of Mississippian use of these heavily sedimented areas. However, as already indicated, survey along the bank and in eroded areas has not revealed any trace of Mississippian occupation.

Thus, there are four major variables that can be used in a model of Mississippian settlement in the alluvial valley proper:

1. Soil fertility and vegetation cover.
2. Elevation high enough to avoid annual innudation.
3. Sufficient area meeting Criteria 1 and 2 to allow support of the minimal settlement unit.
4. Location away from the main channel of the Ohio River (which may be locational selection for proximity to swales, rather than distance to the river).

It is, however, much more difficult to predict the location of settlements outside the alluvial bottom. For one thing, survey coverage of this zone is less adequate than in the bottomland proper. With elevations more than 9 m above the river level, flooding is rarely a problem on the terraces. Yet, in general, soils on the level, and often poorly drained terraces are not as fertile as those of the Black Bottom. Under modern agricultural conditions, however, these terrace soils can produce yields that are in some cases still very high. Nonetheless, under basic levels of management, these soils are much less fertile than the bottomland soils. Although the differences in productivity at basic level of management are not enormous, it is not without significance that more fertile soils in the Black Bottom were passed up for settlement by Mississippian groups in favor of relatively less fertile soils on the terrace. It may well be that the deciding factor is that the terrace sites are almost completely free from flooding hazard to crops. The bottomland areas are extremely productive, but they are also hazardous. It is quite possible that Mississippian groups occupying the Kincaid locality used a divided risk strategy such as that used by the farmers in the area today, who like to have land under cultivation both in the Black Bottom and on higher ground. In this way, late flooding in the valley will not completely destroy their crop for the year, whereas extremely dry weather, which may reduce yields in upland areas, will have relatively less effect on crop yields from bottom soils (Russell Angelly, personal communication).

Settlement patterning away from the river bottom and terrace areas is poorly known. Although surveys have covered a few sections of transect into the upland area, no Mississippian sites have been detected to date. Present data on diet and settlement in the Black Bottom suggest that it is quite possible that there is no permanent settlement by Mississippian populations in the areas away from the alluvial valleys and the tributaries. Among the test implications for this hypothesis would be the existence of only temporary Mississippian sites, such as hunting camps, in upland areas, or a total lack of any evidence of Mississippian use of the area. At present there is no indication of how Kincaid populations exploited the upland areas between the Ohio and the Cache Valley. In the Cache Valley itself and its hinterlands to the north, however, there are some rock shelters with petroglyphs of diamond-shaped eyes and bi-lobed arrows, which indicate Mississippian occupation. However, the nature of this presence is not known. It seems reasonable that such sites might be hunting stations similar to those investigated by Wood in Missouri (Wood 1968:172). It should be noted that there are considerable problems in determining the relationship between Cache Valley Mississippian populations and groups occupying the Black Bottom and Lower Ohio River Valley. Moreover, the dietary evidence from the Black Bottom does not show much evidence for a strong hunting pattern. Admittedly, bone preservation is very poor in the area as a whole, but the species that are represented at Kincaid, Angel, and at IAS Mx109 (a small Mississippian terrace site) suggest that the animals taken by Mississippians in this area are predominantly those that compete with human beings for maize and other resources in close proximity to human residences (for a discussion, see Davy 1976; also Martin, Zim, and Nelson 1951). Certainly, the data on plant foods in the diet of the Mississippian populations suggest that all essential nutrients are present with relatively low need for animal food (Blakeman 1974:102). Of course, animal foods may well have been very important for reasons divorced from any absolute need for such foods in the diet. Thus, it is possible that Mississippian populations may have made very little use of upland resources. The dietary requirements of the population were not such as to force intensive hunting in the upland, but could have been satisfied by exploitation of the game that was drawn to agricultural fields. This is not to say that there were no seasonal forays into the upland for hunting or other purposes, but future survey in these areas will most likely show little use of the environmental zones after the beginning of Mississippian times.

In fact, Late Woodland settlement patterning in the area, as it is presently known, shows considerable similarity to the distribution of Mississippian sites. The major difference lies in the increasing restriction of settlement through time to the bottomland and terrace zones occupied by Mississipian peoples, as already outlined. It is not clear whether this increasing restriction of sites to the bottomland is a developmental sequence of local "Mississippian." It is clear, however, that throughout the history of settlement of the locality there is an overall trend toward the eventual Mississippian pattern. Each succeeding phase shows greater restriction on the range of environments that are "settled" (Lafferty 1976). Although the Late Woodland settlement pattern is strikingly similar to the Mississippian, there is no evidence that maize agriculture plays an important subsistance role in Late Woodland times in this area (Davy 1976, Gilreath 1976), or further north (Kuttruff 1974). Aside from maize, the dietary pattern of Late Woodland populations is not very different from that of Mississippian populations in the actual species represented, but the percentages are very different. Nonetheless, the Late Woodland settlement pattern seems to be different from the Mississippian system primarily in terms of having a slightly greater choice of environments for site location, and in having fewer people to settle. The change from Late Woodland to Mississippian in the Black Bottom is not marked by an dramatic change regardless of whether the change represents the "Mississippianization" of indigenous peoples or whether there is actual immigration. The only two Late Woodland dates from the Black Bottom environs at this time are A.D. 650–670 (DIC-396, tree ring corrected) and A.D. 970 (DIC-394, tree ring corrected). There are three relatively good Mississippian dates that overlap with the latter date for "Lewis": A.D. 920 (DIC-136, IAS Mx66); A.D. 930 (DIC-357, IAS Mx109); and A.D. 980–1000 (DIC-395, IAS Mx109) (all tree-ring corrected). In any case, there does not appear to be any clear chronological or cultural hiatus between Late Woodland and Mississippian in the Kincaid locality.

Internal Site Patterning

One of the more interesting results of the work in Kincaid locality has been the definition of a kind of "building block" of Mississippian settlement in this area. As already indicated, the small Mississippian sites (about .3 ha) appear to have consisted of from 1 to 3 structures at any given time. It is likely that in many cases these structures were arranged in an L or U pattern and occurred together with ramadas and perhaps corn cribs. This same internal site pattern appears to hold throughout the size range of Mississippian sites. Each "hamlet" of 8–15 structures appears to have been made up of a number of "farmsteads" in close association with one another. Aerial photographs that show details of structure location at Kincaid itself show the same pattern. If "hamlets" are small groups of associated "farmsteads," then the Kincaid site can be described as consisting of "hamlets" clustered around mounds and partly surrounded by a palisade.

Internal organization of the sites is not easily described in terms of activity areas, since each structure appears to be the center of a wide range of domestic activities. There are some exceptions to this pattern, in that the total area of a "hamlet" is somewhat less than the multiple of the number of "farmsteads" of which it is composed. There are some indications of task-specific activity areas within sites, but factor analysis of the spatial distribution of surface materials does not clearly sort these out (v. Butler 1977). The clear exceptions to this general lack of patterning within sites are directly related to probable social variables. Whereas some sites have distinct burial areas associated with them, only Kincaid also has the distinctive substructure mounds characteristic of Mississippian centers. The nearest Mississippian mound site is the Rowlandtown Mound site on the west edge of Paducah, Kentucky, located across the Ohio River, approximately 15 km west of Kincaid. The next closest small, one- or two-mound Mississippian sites are at least 30–40 km from Kincaid. In any event, for the survey area, it is not possible at present to determine the internal structure of any of these "intermediate" or "secondary" centers, although it may be predicted that their internal structuring, so far as residence is concerned, will be similar to the pattern just described.

Although the presence of burial areas at .9–1.0-ha sites like IAS Mx66 in the Black Bottom is part of the evidence for considering these sites to have played a somewhat "nodal" role in the settlement system, the presence of these burial areas seems to have made little difference in terms of internal site patterning. The substructure mounds at Kincaid, however, clearly have considerable impact on the internal patterning of the site. The mounds themselves are located in the center of an area of high agricultural potential which is, for various reasons, less prone to flooding than many surrounding areas. The mounds are set around the sides of a level area or plaza. In addition to this main plaza, there are other such areas that yield little surface debris and that have little indication of occupation. In view of the tremendous impact of mounds on overall site planning, however, it is still true that the village areas of Kincaid are basically similar in pattern to the smaller .9–1.0 ha settlements such as IAS Mx66.

Thus, the two western occupation zones at Kincaid (UC Mx^{v}1A, 1B, 1A–41; and the distinct UC Mx^{v}1C) contain about 30 structures in all, with about 15 structures in each area. However, some of these structures are much larger than those found at other sites, having apparent maximum dimensions of as much as 15 m; but this is judged from aerial photographs and may simply reflect surface "spread" as a result of cultivation. The University of Chicago excavations in these areas found no structures approaching these dimensions. In general, the maximum structure dimensions are less than 6 m on a side, usually in the neighborhood of 3 m on a side, both at Kincaid and at the outlying sites.

Cemetery areas consist of what are called "stone-box" graves of the sort found elsewhere. In many cases, the graves are clustered together in a small, more or less conical mound feature. It seems likely that this resemblance to pre-Mississippian burial mounds is often fortuitous and results from accretion of stone box graves in a small area. At Kincaid, UC Pp°2, however, there is evidence of actual mound stages (Cole *et al.*, 1951:108–109); and similar features may be present at other sites.

The major mound constructions at Kincaid are substructure mounds, with a total volume of 95,000 m^3 of earth in the major mounds. Assuming that only one mound was being constructed at any one time, the greatest volume of any one stage (presumably representing one year's construction) can be estimated to have been between 6000 and 8000 m^3 of earth. At a conservative estimate of construction capabilities (v. Muller, in press), this level of construction in a year could have been attained with 27 person-days of labor per household, given a total population of 1300–1500. This level of community labor is lower than that observed for Big Man societies in New Guinea (Erasmus 1965:280–281). Whatever the population of Kincaid, the mounds themselves clearly cannot be used to argue for extremely dense population in the Black Bottom area.

Another distinctive feature of the Kincaid site is the presence of a palisade on the north side of the site. A section of this palisade was trenched by the University of Chicago workers (Cole *et al.* 1951:54ff.). A search for clear traces of palisade on the sourth side of the site, however, was inconclusive (Cole *et al.* 1951:57). Examination of the 1936 aerial photographs taken of the site by the Tennessee Valley Authority have shown very clear indications of a major portion of the palisade line on the north. These photographs show bastions spaced at intervals of approximately 30–30 m. This spacing is consistent with an interpretation of the palisade as a defensive structure with an estimate of optimum arrow range at circa 40 m (Lafferty 1973:133ff.). A spacing of 30 m would allow highly effective flanking fire from bastion to bastion, and thus it would be unnecessary to man the palisade curtain wall. The total length of the palisade seems to have been from 1100 to 1400 m, depending upon the interpretation of the site limits and aerial photographs. This may well represent no more than 5600 person-hours of labor (Lafferty 1973:96ff.); and clearly does not appear to have required anything like the investment of labor required by construction of the mounds. Even so, the manning of the bastions on the north side of the site would appear to have severely strained the estimated manpower of the Kincaid site (Muller in press). It may be that the site formed a refuge for outlying populations in times of difficulties, that population was much greater than estimated, or that the main function of the palisade was not actually defensive. Which of these, or other, possibilities is actually correct is uncertain.

Another special feature that has been detected in the Black Bottom so far only at the Kincaid site is the presence of circular wall-trench structures in the UC Mx^{f}36 area. Unfortunately, these structures were badly disturbed by bulldozing along the edge of Avery Lake (Weigand and Muller in press) so that information on their possible function is sparse. Somewhat similar, more or less round structures were found in the area by the University of Chicago excavators, but the actual correspondence to the round structures along the swale edge is not great. The presence of considerable amounts of broken sandstone in the vicinity of the UC Mx^{r}36 structures might indicate some sort of sweat lodge use of the sort postulated at Angel Mounds for similar structures (Black 1967:300, 306, 352). Other Mississippian sites in the Bottom do have areas of broken sandstone scatter; and, if these are not of more recent origin (cf Butler 1977:100), they might be associated with similar features. Excavations to date have not confirmed this, however.

At present, it appears that all Mississippian sites in the Black Bottom, including Kincaid, had a similar pattern of domestic life. Although features like the palisade and mounds at Kincaid and the stone box graves at some smaller sites are important indications of specialized site functions, these features seem to have relatively little impact on the internal organization of settlements; even though the overall layout of such sites is strongly altered by the presence of features such as plazas and mounds. Finally, these conclusions on the internal organization of Mississippian sites in the Black Bottom must be viewed as being tentative, since investigation of this aspect of Mississippian occupation of the area has been peripheral to the primary goals of Phase One of the research project, which was concerned with locating sites and determining their primary productive functions. The second phase of the project has as a primary goal the analysis of the distribution of goods in the Black Bottom and this will require larger-scale excavations that will reveal more about the nature of internal patterning of sites.

Settlement System Analysis

As already indicated, there are basically three or four types of settlements in the Black Bottom area surrounding the Kincaid site. First, there are a number of very small sites (about .01 ha) that may represent special-purpose locations. For example, one aceramic site that may date to the Mississippian time period is located in the center of a large swamp. The only artifacts from the site that can be assigned to the Mississippian time period are six small, triangular projectile points. These points could also date to the Late Woodland period, although they are of a size and shape that are more common in later times. If this is a Mississippian site, then it is possible that it represents an exploitative site for swamp resources such as waterfowl, fish, and plants. The vast majority of such small sites that are tentatively identified as Mississippian have the same distribution as larger Mississippian locations. Thus, there is really no good evidence to support an idea of widespread specialized extractive sites for resource areas other than the cane bottoms. Most of the small sites quite likely represent either ephemeral Mississippian sites such as "field houses," or are perhaps traces of sites that are buried more deeply or plowed more shallowly. If the latter is taken to be the case, the amount of occupied area known in the locality would be increased by some 13%, but the conclusions expressed later in this chapter in regard to population level would not be materially affected. There is no evidence to suggest that terrace occupations are either special-function sites or that they are the seasonal settlements of people seeking to escape the flooding of the bottomland, although it may well have been advantageous to have members of ones own corporate group (of whatever kind) in residence on this higher ground during the flood season. Indeed, all the evidence we have to date supports the hypothesis that terrace sites played the same basic economic role in the Kincaid system that was played by similar-sized sites in the Bottom, at least in terms of horticulture and exploitation of wild plant foods (Blakeman 1974:123ff). Butler (1977) has discussed a number of possible hypotheses to explain Mississippian settlement of the terrace, but available data are not sufficient to resolve these questions at this time.

As already indicated, the major class of Mississippian site in terms of numbers is made up of sites that are in the general range of .2–.3 ha in surface extent. These are the "building blocks" of the system, and all larger sites are built up from clusters of such units. When such a site stands alone, it can justifiably be called a farmstead in the Black Bottom. Our evidence from botanical, faunal, locational, and artifactual data all strongly support the hypothesis that the basic function of this kind of unit was the production of horticultural goods and the harvesting of other kinds of resources in the Bottom (Blakeman 1974, Butler 1977, Muller, Lafferty, Rudolph, and Blakeman 1975). There is considerable evidence that this kind of unit was self-sufficient if productivity was high enough (Blakeman 1974). The quality of the diet, as represented in the archeological record, is high, given sufficient quantities. The planting and harvesting of maize, bean, perhaps some *Chenopodium* species, and other crops would, of itself, have provided a reasonable diet. When combined with the many wild species of plants (such as hickory and pecan) that were exploited, and with the harvesting of animals such as squirrels concentrating around agricultural fields, the diet was probably more than adequate in nutritional terms. Indeed, this apparent abundance raises some evolutionary problems. Why would people in such a rich and productive environment *need* the kind of centralized authority that seems to be represented at the Kincaid site? There is probably no single, simple answer to this question; but one obvious possibility is that population pressure had begun to approach carrying capacity, and centralized redistribution was essential to long-term survival. Another possibility is that there were external pressures from other groups that forced greater interdependence for these people. I shall return to these problems later.

The next largest class of sites is made up of the groups of 8–15 structures that are normally described as hamlets. As already indicated, such a site is essentially a group of farmsteads brought together. Here, as at the smaller level, there is evidence of all basic activities for economic production. Farming and harvesting of wild foods appears to be pursued at the household level in the same way as in the farmsteads. It is possible that some of the evenness of this pattern is due to redistribution of foodstuffs, but it should be noted that the tools required for primary production occur with essentially the same pattern at hamlets as at farmsteads. There is little evidence to support the idea that some residential groups (families?) in these hamlets were exempt from farming and other basic productive tasks. There are, however, some indications that some households may have somewhat greater access to exotic materials and fine ceramics (Riordan 1975:137–138). Some hamlets with special features such as grave areas may play what Riordan (1975) has termed "nodal" roles in the social system, but not all larger sites did play such roles. The picture that seems to be supported best by present data is that, if there were some individuals in these nodal sites who did perform social functions as redistributors, these roles were not so highly ranked nor involved so much time as to relieve their households of basic productive tasks. "Leadership" on the hamlet level appears to have been added to the other functions of the household, rather than replacing them. In the second phase of the project, more time is being devoted to examination of variables that might yield information on patterns of economic distribution. As always, our task is to recover the information we need at the cost of minimal damage to the sites.

In any given part of the Black Bottom cane bottom area there are a number of Mississippian sites of both farmstead and hamlet size. In general, these appear to cluster into larger units or "dispersed villages" (e.g., Butler 1977). It is very difficult to judge the reality of these clusters of sites in cultural terms, simply because the topography of the ridge and swale area to some extent forces clustering of occupation and isolates other settlements from one another across swales and wet areas. However, it is these whole areas of sites that have normally been recorded as single sites in archeological survey in the past. By such site definition criteria there are nine reasonably distinct groups of sites or "sites" from Mississippian times in the Black Bottom rather than the 100 plus discussed here. While it may prove to be true that these site clusters did function as some kinds of units in social terms, this remains to be demonstrated, and should not simply be assumed. Radiocarbon dates suggest that these nine "dispersed villages" were contemporaneous, ca. A.D. 1240. However, when the concern is with questions of social interaction, the scale of contemporaneity that is possible from radiocarbon dates is much too coarse. For this reason, considerable effort will have to be expended on dendrochronology and on other means that may help to date individual structures relative to one another. For example, we hope to be able to obtain archeomagnetic samples from different hearths to test for contemporaneity on a finer level. The tree-ring picture is rather more difficult. There is what appears to be an excellent sequence for the Kincaid area. Unfortunately, the dates that were given for materials at Kincaid are 200–300 years later than any radiocarbon dates for the Black Bottom, although there are some comparable radiocarbon dates further up the Cumberland and Tennessee Rivers. Given sufficient funding for a restudy of the material, tree-ring dating is perhaps the most promising avenue to tight chronological control in the locality.

Even though it is very difficult to determine the exact contemporaneity of the sites, the radiocarbon information suggests that most Mississippian occupation did fall in a relatively narrow period. If we may, for the moment, assume some considerable overlap of occupation in the thirteenth century, the picture that emerges is that a typical Mississippian settlement consisted of an area with a few scattered farmsteads surrounding somewhat larger groups of houses at more or less central locations. Ridges that meet the occupation criteria discussed earlier range from 10 to nearly 200 ha in area. On the average, there is about 27 ha of such ridge for each hectare of site area actually observed in survey, but the actual figure is somewhat lower since this estimate makes no allowance for unsurveyed areas on the east side of the Bottom. On the more intensely surveyed west side of the Bottom there are about 16 ha of "support area" for each hectare occupied.

Botanical data from these sites show that the sites were occupied for at least the 9 months of the growing season. Unfortunately, data indicating winter occupation are limited, and poor bone preservation in the Black Bottom makes it difficult to approach this problem. Thus it is possible that the bottomland sites were largely abandoned during the winter, but it is also reasonably clear that the terrace sites that are known were also occupied during the rest of the year and cannot simply be treated as winter camps away from the flooded bottom. As has already been indicated, the location of bottomland sites above the normal modern winter and spring flooding has been established. This suggests that these sites could have been, and probably were, occupied during periods of high water. Certainly, there were occasions of greater flooding that may well have caused movement to higher ground. The modern cycle of flooding is such that the whole Bottom is flooded about every 5 or 6 years, with even larger floods occurring roughly every 20 years. Farmers of European culture tolerated this state of affairs for about 130 years. After the great flood of 1936–1937, however, most moved up onto the terrace and upland permanently. For what it is worth, these modern farmers also erected a number of mounds in the Black Bottom to supplement those of Indian origin as platforms for buildings and particularly for corncribs. These European mounds are scattered across the locality, not showing the concentration characteristic of the Mississippian period.

The small and moderate-sized sites on the terrace do not show any strong indications of specialization beyond that characteristic of the bottomland sites of similar size classes. The exceptions to this statement at present concern slightly greater proportions of lithic resources that are of local origin (terrace gravels) on the terrace, and an indication at IAS Ms109 (which may date from the early Mississippian period) that there may be an underrepresentation of the choicer cuts of meat of the deer. There is a corresponding overrepresentation of the same deer body parts at the Kincaid site, but on a quite different time level (Davy 1976, Muller *et al.* 1975). Because of the disparity in time, it would be premature to interpret either of these patterns too glibly, but it does agree with other evidence that there are some differences in the access to certain types of material between smaller sites and Kincaid. All in all, the differences among the various smaller site classes are not striking and are in line with a general conclusion of homogeneity outside of Kincaid itself.

Finally, there is Kincaid. This site is enormous when the total area within the palisade is calculated. Even when allowance is made for the lack of actual habitation, the total area is still very large, although not much larger than some of the "dispersed villages." When the mounds with some 95,000 m³ of earth are taken into account, it can be seen that Kincaid is, after all, something more than a simple farming settlement. Yet, ironically, it is that too. The size of the area above flooding and the amount of actual settlement at the site are at the same ratio as at the other sites in the locality; and other evidence suggests that most, if not all, of the nonmound inhabitants were as involved in subsistence activities as their counterparts outside the palisade.

Of course, the people who may have lived on the mounds were probably also involved with subsistence, but the traditional view that their role was primarily with distribution and administration is reasonable, if not firmly established archeologically. The scale and continuity of construction imply centralized direction and control. The mounds do suggest greater continuity than would seem usual in societies where authority was achieved anew in each generation. Hereditary authority without force is the essence of the chiefdom, and it is possible that Kincaid, like many examples in the ethnographic literature from the Southeast, may well have been a chiefdom. The problem is whether a concept like *chiefdom* is really useful for archeologists. If it provides a focus for archeological activity in seeking to test ideas about the nature of status and rank, social continuity, political organization and the like, then its discussion is fully justified. If, on the other hand, we devote our energies to a typologizing of political structures and are merely concerned with pigeon-holing archeological systems, then the long-term progress from our potsherd-shuffling days can be seen to be very slight. Ultimately, it is less important to know whether Kincaid was a "tribal," "big man," "chief," or even "state-level" organization than it is to understand the dynamics of adaptation to the conditions of the Lower Ohio Valley.

With the extremely detailed information that we have on the settlement system of the Kincaid locality, it is possible to make some estimates of the maximum population of the area. The first estimate is based on the actual areas of Mississippian occupation recorded in our survey, and as interpreted as a result of our extensive testing program. Although there may be some question as to the representativeness of the present sample so far as testing is concerned, the limited variability from site to site seems to justify the assumption that present data are not badly biased. The controlled surface collection and excavation data suggest that there is a maximum of from five to eight structures for each hectare of occupation. There are some variations from site to site according to size, but this estimate is fair for an indication of maximum population. The total area known to have been occupied at Kincaid and in its environs is no less than 36 ha, implying some 250 structures. If all of these were contemporary and if all were habitations, the population of the locality, at five persons per structure, might have been 1250 people. By the same process, Kincaid alone would have slightly less than 400 people. Although the population of the total Kincaid society might have been much larger, this estimate is clearly lower than the estimates usually given for large Mississippian sites. Nonetheless, I feel that the estimate is reasonable for several reasons. First, this is not so very different from the scale of Amerindian society described in many of the historic records from the sixteenth century. The second reason has to do with other ways of coming to an estimate of population for the area.

A number of sources for rather diverse areas suggest that aboriginal horticulture in the eastern United States was able to support one person for 1 year on the produce of .4 ha (Sauer 1971:295, Will and Hyde 1917). If the total area of the zone of Mississippian settlement just defined is taken, there are 621 ha of such land in the Black Bottom. This 621 ha, under continual cultivation, could support some 1500 people. Taken area by area, estimates of population from "support area" and actual occupied area agree, with a correlation coefficient of .9, as indicated earlier.

In addition, if horticulture labor investment for the Black Bottom was roughly equivalent to digging stick horticulture in Mexico (Lewis 1951), then these 621 ha of land would have required about 590 workers over a 5-month season. If one worker is estimated for each household of five, this would imply a total population of 2960 people. At a figure of two worker equivalents per household of five, the population required to cultivate this land would have been 1480 people, strikingly close to the estimates of population just derived.

Thus, several different ways of looking at population and labor requirements in the Black Bottom locality all agree on the approximate maximum of population. The population of the Black Bottom was, in fact, probably lower than these estimates. It is unlikely that the twin assumptions of all sites being contemporary and all structures being occupied are actually true. It should be emphasized, however, that the estimates of numbers and areas of sites for this area are based on actual observation and testing, and are not merely guesses. It is possible that some of the smallest sites are somewhat larger, but even assuming that all such small sites are actually .3 ha in area results in a population estimate of only 1423 people. I do not think that we have missed very many sites, and our information on the lack of Mississippian sites in certain areas is supported by the presence of earlier-period sites in those locations.

Research Goals for the Future

Many of the needs for future work in the Kincaid locality have already been indicated. Among the highest priorities is additional survey of areas outside the immediate environs of the Kincaid site. The survey data for areas further away from the large site are simply not comparable to our own survey, even where there is some information. Additional surveys are necessary to determine the actual limits of the Kincaid system. Although ceramic similarities cannot be expected to be very helpful in this regard, the distribution of sites may assist in establishing such boundaries.

A second important task is to recover additional information on very small sites, to test whether any of these do show characteristics of specialized economic or social functions. A third important task, one that is just beginning, is to determine the nature of relationships among sites in a site "cluster." In order to discuss the nature of economic and social relationships, it will be necessary to control dating of structures and settlements on a much finer level than has been characteristic of past work on Mississippian sites. Our project will continue to address these kinds of problems in the future. Additional testing and resurvey can assist in refinement of the estimates made here. Whether or not we can prove that Kincaid was a "chiefdom" or that the economy was "redistributive," it is clear that archeological work in this locality can test hypotheses about population density, "capital" investment, and social interaction. I am sure that these research topics may turn out to be as important as deciding whether the people living on the mounds had achieved or ascribed status.

Acknowledgments

Most of this work has been supported by the Department of Anthropology and the College of Liberal Arts of Southern Illinois University—Carbondale. In addition, support for a special project on evidence for prehistoric seismic activity was supported by the United States Geological Survey. I particularly wish to thank Dr. Frank McKoewn of the USGS for his assistance. The research has predominantly been carried out within the Field School in Archaeology program. Although this has undoubtedly meant that work has progressed more slowly than might otherwise have been the case, the benefits to the program as a whole have been substantial, especially in allowing long-term planning. I want to thank all of the students who have worked with me on this project over the years. Many of them are individually cited in this paper, but even those who are not have made many important contributions. Last, but by no means least, I wish to thank all of the landowners and farmers in the Black Bottom locality who have shown patience and kindness in allowing hordes of students to tromp over and dig around in their fields. Although there are too many to name all of our local benefactors individually, I do want to single out Mr. and Mrs. Russell Angelly of Unionville, Illinois for our special thanks.

References

Alexander, C.S. and J.C. Prior
  1971   Holocene sedimentation rates in overbank deposits in the Black Bottom of the lower Ohio River, southern Illinois. *American Journal of Science* **270**:361–372.
Black, Glenn A.
  1967   *Angel site: An archaeological, historical, and ethnological study.* Indianapolis: Indian Historical Society.
Blakeman, Crawford
  1974   The late prehistoric paleoethnobotany of the Black Bottom, Pope and Massac Counties, Illinois. Ph.D. dissertation, Department of Anthropology, Southern Illinois University—Carbondale.
Butler, Brian
  1972   Early vegetation of the Kincaid area. Manuscript on file with the Southeast Archaeology Laboratory, Department of Anthropology, · Southern Illinois University—Carbondale.
  1977   Mississippian settlement in the Black Bottom, Pope and Massac Counties, Illinois. Ph.D. dissertation, Department of Anthropology, Southern Illinois University—Carbondale.
Clay, R. Berle
  1976   Tactics, strategy, and operations: The Mississippian system responds to its environment. *Midcontinental Journal of Archaeology* **1**(2):137–162.
Cole, Fay-Cooper *et al.*
  1951   *Kincaid: A prehistoric Illinois metropolis.* Chicago: University of Chicago Press.
Davy, Douglas
  1976   Mammalian remains at IAS-Mx-109. Manuscript on file in Southeast Laboratory, Department of Anthropology, Southern Illinois University—Carbondale.
Erasmus, Charles J.
  1965   Monument building: Some field experiments. *Southwestern Journal of Anthropology* **21**(4):277–301.

Estes, Eugene T.
1969   The dendrochronology of three tree species in the central Mississippi valley. Ph.D. dissertation, Department of Botany, Southern Illinois University—Carbondale.
Gilreath, Amy
1976   Floral analysis at IAS-Mx-109. Manuscript on file in Southeast Laboratory, Department of Anthropology, Southern Illinois University—Carbondale.
Kuttruff, Carl
1974   Late Woodland settlement and subsistence in the lower Kaskaskia River valley. Ph.D. dissertation, Department of Anthropology, Southern Illinois University—Carbondale.
Lafferty, Robert H., III
1973   An analysis of prehistoric Southeastern fortifications. M.A. thesis, Department of Anthropology, Southern Illinois University—Carbondale.
1976   Mississippian settlement systems in the Black Bottom. Manuscript on file in Southeastern Laboratory, Department of Anthropology, Southern Illinois University—Carbondale.
Lewis, Oscar
1951   *Life in a Mexican village: Tepoztlan revisited.* Urbana: University of Illinois Press.
Martin, A., H.S. Zim, and A.L. Nelson
1951   *American wildlife and plants: A guide to wildlife food habits.* New York: McGraw-Hill. (Reprint, 1961, Dover Books.)
Mohlenbrock, R.H. and J.W. Voigt
1959   *A flora of southern Illinois.* Carbondale: Southern Illinois University Press.
Muller, J., R. Lafferty, J. Rudolph, and C. Blakeman
1975   Kincaid environs archaeology. *Southeastern Archaeological Conference, Bulletin* **18**:148–157.
Muller, Jon
in press Mississippian population and organization: Kincaid locality research, 1970–1975. *Illinois Archaeological Society, Bulletin.*
Muller, Jon and Frank Rackerby
in press The Kincaid Site and its environs. *Illinois Archaeological Survey. Bulletin.*
Munson, Patrick
1966   Midwestern dendrochronology and archaeological dating. *Transactions of the Illinois Archaeological Society, Bulletin.*
Page, Oliver J.
1900   *History of Massac County, with life sketches and portraits.* Metropolis, Illinois.
Riordan, Robert
1975   Ceramics and chronology: Mississippian settlement in the Black Bottom, southern Illinois. Ph.D. dissertation, Department of Anthropology, Southern Illinois University—Carbondale.
Sauer, Carl O.
1971   *16th century North America.* Berkeley: University of California Press.
Sears, William
1968   The state and settlement patterns in the New World. In *Settlement archaeology,* edited by K.C. Chang. Palo Alto: National Press Books. Pp. 134–153.
Service, Elman R.
1975   *Origins of the state and civilization: The process of cultural evolution.* New York: Norton.
Voigt, J.W., and R.H. Mohlenbrock
1964   *Plant communities of southern Illinois.* Carbondale: Southern Illinois University Press.

Weigand, Phil, and Jon Muller
  in press   Preliminary report on investigations at the Kincaid site. *Illinois Archaeological Survey, Bulletin.*
Will, George F., and George E. Hyde
  1917   *Corn among the Indians of the Upper Missouri.* Reprint edition (n.d.). Lincoln: University of Nebraska Press.
Wood, W. Raymond
  1968   Mississippian hunting and butchering patterns: Bone from the Vista Shelter, 23SR-20, Missouri. *American Antiquity* **33**:170–179.

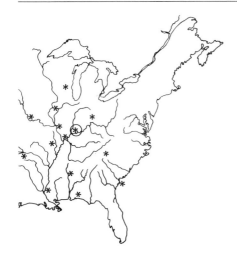

11

Mississippian Settlement Patterns in Southwestern Indiana

THOMAS J. GREEN
CHERYL A. MUNSON

The importance of a detailed knowledge of settlement patterns as a basis for social and economic interpretation of prehistory is widely accepted. Willey's (1953) Viru Valley study and Winters's (1967) Wabash Valley study have demonstrated the value of settlement pattern data for facilitating inferences about the character of prehistoric society and culture that are not readily observable in the archeological record. With the introduction of the goals and methods of geography into archeology (Clarke 1968), settlement patterns have become more than a methodological tool for reconstructing other aspects of prehistoric society, they have become a focus of study which can lead to generalizations concerning cultural development and change (Clay 1976, Larson 1970).

Archeological research spanning 80 years can be brought together to describe the areal settlement patterns of two Mississippian phases in the Ohio River Valley of southwestern Indiana and the adjacent portions of Kentucky: the Angel phase and the Caborn–Welborn phase. The Angel phase (Honerkamp 1975) is the earliest Mississippian occupation in the area and it is also the most extensive in areal distribution. The phase is dominated by the Angel site. Located on the Ohio River near the mouth of the Green River, this site is a large (40 ha) palisaded village with a plaza

293

and substructure mounds (Black 1967). Numerous small villages, hamlets, and farmsteads of the Angel phase are known to occur in the river valley near the Angel site.

The Caborn–Welborn phase represents a late Mississippian occupation centered near the mouth of the Wabash River in the Ohio Valley. This phase was defined by Munson and Green (1973). Unlike the Angel phase, the Caborn–Welborn phase does not have a single large village or town dominating the settlement pattern; instead it is characterized by a number of smaller settlements dispersed along the floodplains and terraces.

The settlement patterns of these two Mississippian phases will be briefly contrasted with the less well-known, terminal Late Woodland Yankeetown phase (Blasingham 1953, Dorwin and Kellar 1968). Settlements of this phase are smaller than those of both the Angel and Caborn–Welborn phases.

The following discussion is based on research by the authors using primarily the already-existing site data and collections from southwestern Indiana. Our goal will be both to propose possible models of Mississippian settlement patterning and to outline how these models might be tested. We will focus on "areal settlement patterns" as opposed to either "community patterns" (Trigger 1968) or "settlement systems" (Winters 1969:110–111). Winters uses "settlement pattern" to refer to the geographic and physiographic distribution of sites within a single culture, whereas "settlement system" refers to the interrelationships among the sites in the pattern. We will be concerned with the location and geographic distribution of the various settlement types characteristic of the Angel and Caborn–Welborn phases and thus primarily with "settlement patterns," but references will also be made to interrelationships among sites within each phase and to the variables that influence the location of settlement types.

Background and History

Our latest research in southwestern Indiana is part of a long history of archeological exploration in the area. The first excavations were conducted in 1826 by the French naturalist and artist Charles Alexander Lesueur. Lesueur, while employed as a land surveyor for the New Harmony settlement, found numerous aboriginal mounds in the area. Curious of their contents, and, with the help of other interested persons in New Harmony, he opened many of them, kept notes of his excavations, and made sketches of the artifacts he found. From his descriptions we can identify Woodland and Mississippian components at sites he explored (Black 1961, Hamy 1904, Hemphill 1976, Thwaites 1906:172–177). References to archeological sites in southwestern Indiana occurred sporadically in various publications for the next 70 years (Kellar 1973:14–15). The Indiana Geological Survey published reports in the 1870s and 1880s describing the geology of each county and also including descriptions and discussions of the major archeological sites found in the course of each geological survey. These documents are valuable for their descriptions of sites that have now been destroyed.

In 1898, Clifford Anderson, working for Warren K. Moorehead of the Phillips Academy, excavated a large Mississippian village in Posey County, Indiana. From the "Mouth of the Wabash" site, or the Murphy site as it is now called, Anderson recovered 157 burials, numerous pottery vessels, and other artifacts (Adams 1949:25–57, Moorehead 1906:62–86). These collections are now stored at the Glenn A. Black Laboratory of Archeology at Indiana University.

No further archeological work was initiated in southwestern Indiana until 1938, when the Indiana Historical Society purchased Angel Mounds, the large Mississippian town located near Evansville, Indiana. Under the direction of Glenn A. Black the archeological program of the Indiana Historical Society was based at the Angel site until 1965. Throughout this 30-year period most of the archeological effort in Indiana was concentrated at the Angel site. Extensive excavations were conducted using WPA employees from 1939 to 1942, and from 1947 to 1962 the Angel site was also the location of a summer field school in archeological training sponsored jointly by Indiana University and the Indiana Historical Society. Owing to these efforts, the site is one of the most extensively excavated large Mississippian settlements in the eastern United States.

Concurrent with the excavations at the Angel site, the Indiana Historical Bureau sponsored archeological surveys of various counties in Indiana. Because of the activity at the Angel site, one of the explicit goals of these surveys in southwestern Indiana was to locate other Mississippian settlements in the area. As a result, a number of counties, including Posey (Adams 1949), Gibson (Dragoo 1955), Warrick (Curry 1954), Spencer (Kellar 1956) and Perry (Kellar 1958) were surveyed in the Indiana "pocket" during the 1940s and 1950s. More recently, several surveys have been conducted in the area in response to federal projects (T. Green 1972a, Hoffman 1966).

Beginning in 1960, Glenn Black devoted his full energies to the preparation of the final report for the 20 years of research at the Angel site. Unfortunately, at his death in 1964 much of the analysis remained uncompleted. The collections, site records, and equipment accumulated by him were transferred from Angel Mounds to the Glenn A. Black Laboratory of Archeology at Indiana University (Kellar 1973:20).

During the 1960s Indiana University conducted field schools at the Mann site, a large settlement with Woodland and Mississippian components, near Mount Vernon in Posey County, Indiana. Surveys in Posey County were also conducted by Indiana State University and the Wabash Valley Archaeological Society. The Wabash Valley Archaeological Society also excavated a Mississippian site in southern Posey County (Henn 1971).

By 1970, it was quite obvious that a considerable body of data had been gathered over a 75-year period on the archeology of southwestern Indiana. In 1971 and 1972 the Glenn A. Black Laboratory of Archaeology funded the authors to review systematically the information housed in the laboratory pertaining to the Ohio River Valley. Basically the project was to organize and assess the archeological collections and site survey information for curatorial, cultural resource management, and research purposes.

One research goal formulated in the project was to place the Angel site in a regional perspective by determining its relationship with other Mississippian sites in southwestern Indiana. It was quite clear that additional information was necessary prior to the formulation of even preliminary statements concerning the settlement pattern of the Angel phase. In 1973 the Glenn A. Black Laboratory funded the excavation of the Ellerbusch site (T. Green 1977), a small Mississippian hamlet northwest of Angel. This research was initiated to provide detailed information on one of a number of small Angel phase habitations in the vicinity of the Angel site. The goals of the excavations were to determine the season of occupation of the Ellerbusch site, its community structure, and the range of economic activities carried out by the occupying group.

Additionally, the need for systematically collected survey data was clear. The focus of previous archeological survey in southwestern Indiana was the floodplain areas and terraces of the Wabash and Ohio Rivers. The areas away from the river, the uplands, had generally been neglected. For this reason in 1974 a 4-week survey was conducted in the uplands of Vanderburgh and Warrick Counties. This survey provided valuable information on the intensity of Mississippian utilization of the upland portions of southwestern Indiana.

Despite excavation at the Ellerbusch site, and the 1974 survey, the description and analysis of Mississippian settlement patterns presented here is based primarily on the compilation of existing data that was collected over a 40-year period by the Indiana Historical Society. Information concerning the site location and descriptions utilized in the present study was obtained from the county survey records of the Glenn A. Black Laboratory of Archaeology at Indiana University and the Laboratory of Anthropology at Indiana State University. The site information for Kentucky was obtained from Michael Hoffman's (1966) survey of the Ohio floodplain in Union, Henderson, and Daviess Counties, Kentucky. Additional information was obtained from Honerkamp (1975) and from Funkhouser and Webb's *Archaeological Survey of Kentucky*. Finally, avocational archeologists and collectors provided additional site data. From all these sources, a total of 97 sites were defined and used to construct the settlement patterns of the two phases.

Despite many years of archeological reconnaissance in southwestern Indiana, it is doubtful that all Mississippian sites have been found in the area, or will ever be found. As already indicated, the Indiana Historical Society and Indiana University have had an interest in this area for over 40 years, and numerous surveys have been initiated by both organizations. It seems unlikely that very many of the larger Mississippian sites have been overlooked, but large areas remain unsurveyed in the adjacent portions of Kentucky. Numerous sites have also been destroyed by human and other natural factors. Modern urban developments in Indiana and kentucky are situated on ideal locations for Mississippian villages, while coal and oil exploitation have increased site destruction.

Additional factors limiting site inventories are the riverine processes of alluviation and erosion. Sites are known to be alternately covered by flood-deposited silts and scoured. Even though the Ohio River is considered to be relatively stable (Alexander and Nunnally 1972), sites are often destroyed by riverbank cutting. The Yankeetown site (Dorwin and Kellar 1968) and the Crib Mound site (Kellar 1956) are obvious examples. The Wabash River is notorious for its frequent meandering and the destruction of sites in its floodplain is probably greater than in the Ohio River Valley. Bone Bank (Adams 1949) is a well-known site that has all but been destroyed by the Wabash River. It is difficult to estimate how many prehistoric settlements have been destroyed by these causes. These limitations on the data base must be taken into account in any analysis of settlement patterns that relates site characteristics to the reconstructed natural environment.

NATURAL ENVIRONMENT

The section of the Ohio Valley under study is called the Wabash Lowland physiographic zone in Indiana (Malott 1922, Wayne 1956) and the western Coal Field region in Kentucky (McFarlan 1943). Thornbury (1965) has arbitrarily used the Ohio River to divide two of his major geomorphological zones. That portion of the study area lying north of the Ohio River is included in his Central Lowlands province, and that area lying south of the Ohio River is included in his Interior Low Plateau province. Although the Ohio River has been a convenient boundary for physiographic studies, the Kentucky and Indiana portions of the valley are quite similar in climate, soils, vegetation, and geomorphology.

The general topography of southwestern Indiana and the adjacent portions of Kentucky is characterized by broad alluvial valleys that merge almost imperceptively into rolling uplands. The Ohio River Valley itself is composed of a wide floodplain and two terraces. The upland portions of the area have a sandstone bedrock that is capped with extensive loess deposits. The uplands are low hills with gentle slopes and moderate relief.

Climate in this area can be considered mild. The mean minimum temperature in January is 26–28°F, whereas the mean maximum temperature is 42–46°F. In July, the mean minimum temperature is 66–68°F, whereas the mean maximum is 90°F. The region is generally humid, with the relative humidity usually above 50%. Precipitation is uniform throughout the year with a rainfall average of 106–112 cm and an average snowfall of only 38 cm (Schall 1966). The area enjoys long growing seasons (200–210 days) and mild winters.

According to Indiana land survey records, the area was covered with oak–hickory forest in the early 1800s (T. Green 1972b, Potzger, Potzger, and McCormick 1956). Compared with the central and northern portions of Indiana, the vegetation in southwestern Indiana has a distinctive southern composition. Many southern plant species are at their most northern distribution in this area. Deam (1953) lists pecan, lowland hackberry or sugarberry, bald cypress, and overcup oak as trees occurring in the area that are typical of the lower Mississippi Valley flora. There are also numerous smaller plant species as well as several small mammals that are at their most northern distribution in this area.

Based on the geomorphology of this portion of the Ohio Valley, five broad environmental zones can be defined. Included are the floodplain bottoms, the low terrace, the high terrace, the lacustrine plains and the uplands. Within these broad categories, are a number of microenvironmental zones that are defined on the basis of vegetation, soils, and minor variations in landform.

The floodplain is that portion of the river valley that normally floods annually or semiannually. Floodplain soils belong to the Huntington–Lindside association, and are generally fertile, well drained, alluvial silt deposits. The floodplain climax forest was characterized by a variety of species of trees. Hickory was the most common, followed by ash, elm, oak, and box elder. A common understory plant in the floodplain was southern cane.

There are two terraces in this section of the Ohio Valley. Alexander (1974) has named the high terrace the Brownfield terrace and the lower terrace he calls the "upper floodplain." The high terrace is a result of the aggradation of the river valley during Tazewell times (18,000–21,000 B.P.). This Ohio Valley terrace correlates with the Shelbyville terrace (Fidlar 1942) in the Wabash Valley. The lower terrace is less than 13,000 years old, and prior to this time it was the Ohio River floodplain associated with the Cary advance (Ray 1965:46). This terrace is approximately 3 m above the current floodplain and 4 m below the high terrace, but rarely do sharp escarpments separate the three features. The lower terrace in the Ohio Valley correlates with the Maumee terrace in the Wabash Valley (Ray 1965).

The terrace soils belong to the Weinbach–Sciotoville association. These lack the fertility of the floodplain soils and are quite variable in permeability. Forest composition of the two terraces is similar. Different varieties of oak are the dominant tree species in the low terrace forest, with hickory, gum, and ash also common. The high terrace forest is composed of gum, hickory, ash, and oak. The land surveyors also describe large "brushy areas" occurring on the terraces. The vegetation of these brushy areas was not described in detail, but seem to indicate early successional stages of forest development. Additionally, two small tracts of prairie, both less than 400 ha in size, were located on the low terrace in Posey County. These are the only references to prairie in the entire study area.

The lacustrine plains in southern Indiana are relatively flat areas dissected by creeks. Both Fidlar (1942) and Ray (1965) argue that the lacustrine zones were caused by the rapid aggrading of the Wabash and Ohio floodplains with glacial debris, which caused the smaller tributaries to be ponded. Ponding formed extensive lake beds, which correspond with the Shelbyville terrace in the Wabash Valley and the Brownfield terrace in the Ohio Valley, dating between 18,000–21,000 B.P. With the erosion of these terraces the lakes were drained, and their beds are now situated about 4 m above the low terrace in the Ohio and Wabash Valleys. Lacustrine plains soils are composed of heavy clays and silts and typically are poorly drained. According to the land survey records the lake plain forests were of varied composition, with elm, oak, gum, hickory, and ash dominating.

The uplands in southwestern Indiana and neighboring Kentucky are low undulating features with few sharp escarpments. Bluffs are rare but do occur on the Ohio River near Newburgh and West Franklin, Indiana. Upland soils are composed of thick loess deposits attributed to strong winds blowing silts across the Ohio and Wabash valley-trains during the Tazewell advance (Fidlar 1942, Ray 1965). Soils vary in their fertility, depending primarily on the effects of slope, but upland soils are equally as productive on level surfaces as the floodplain soils (Shively and McElrath 1973, Williamson and Shively 1973). Prior to massive land-clearing, over 50% of the trees in the uplands were oaks, with hickory accounting for another 15%. Within the uplands are extensive areas described by the land surveyors as "brushy" or "barren." Despite this designation, the surveyors had little trouble finding witness trees in these areas and the tree composition was similar to the oak–hickory forests that surrounded them.

The Angel and Caborn–Welborn Phases

MATERIAL CULTURE

Mississippian settlements can be clearly separated from the preceding but not yet well-defined terminal Late Woodland or Yankeetown phase settlements. The Yankeetown phase is characterized by grog-tempered rather than shell-tempered pottery, similar to the'Baytown series (Phillips 1970:47–57), and certain rarely occurring but diagnostic pottery decorations. The Yankeetown phase also lacks mounds and large sites. However, the presence of salt pans, pottery disks and trowels, discoidals, triangular points, and large flint hoes has led some researchers to consider the Yankeetown sites in the study area as "emergent Mississippian" (Dorwin and Kellar 1968, Honerkamp 1975:312, 331, Kellar 1973:53–54).

Angel phase and Caborn–Welborn phase settlements of the Mississippian period are distinguished primarily by stylistic differences in the decorative features of their ceramics. Both phases have the characteristic Mississippian vessel shapes of bowls, jars, plates, pans, and bottles. Typical Angel phase pottery is shell-tempered and undecorated, with most vessels having smooth, plain surfaces (Figure 11.1). The predominant decorative techniques used on Angel phase pottery are modeled animal and human effigies attached to bowls and the red filming and negative painting of plates and occasionally bottles. Although the Angel site is well known for its filmed and negative-painted pottery, only .8% of the sorted collection has these characteristics (Kellar 1967:473). Negative painting and red filming are also quite rare as decorative modes at other Angel phase settlements.

Other forms of pottery decoration at the Angel site and at other Angel phase sites are exceedingly rare. Of the half-million sherds from the sorted Angel site collection, 138 have fine-line incising or broad trailing. The incising occurs on plates in the form of chevron designs, and the broad trailing is limited to arches on jar forms. Additionally, the collection includes 107 punctated sherds comparable to Parkin Punctate (Kellar 1967:468–470). The overall similarity of the ceramics from Angel and those from Kincaid, 130 km west of Angel, has been pointed out by several researchers (Cole *et al.* 1951:161–162, Kellar 1967:484–485).

In contrast, the decorated shell-tempered pottery of the Caborn–Walborn phase is characterized by slightly outflaring jars that have a band of incised and punctated triangular motifs. This decoration forms a band of repeated triangles that may be filled with oblique parallel lines, chevrons, punctations, or combinations of oblique parallel lines and punctations (Figure 11.2). The decoration is limited to the shoulder area and is frequently zoned by an incised line on both sides of the decoration. In

FIGURE 11.1. Angel phase pottery. [From Kellar (1967:Figure 544).]

decoration and form, the Caborn–Welborn incised and punctated jars are most similar to Barton Incised, variety Arcola (Phillips 1970:45). However, a number of sherds have been found with ticked lines bordering the incised decorations and their similarity to late Oneota motifs has been noted (Munson and Green 1973) and confirmed (Dale Henning personnal communication). Also characteristic are beaded- or notched-appliqué bowls similar to the Dallas bowls illustrated by Lewis and Kneberg (1946:Plates B, C, G), and to bowls from the lower Mississippi Valley illustrated by Phillips, Ford, and Griffin (1951:Figure 100h, o, w).

With the exception of the decorated jars and beaded bowls, the bulk of the Caborn–Welborn ceramic complex differs little from that of the Angel phase; salt pans, plain jars and bowls, plates, bottles, and rare pieces of red-filmed and negative-painted ware have been found. However, the large sites with excavated, looted, or flood-scoured cemeteries can easily be distinguished from Angel phase sites because of the occurrence of such unusual ceramic effigy vessels as seated humans (Adams 1949:28–29),

FIGURE 11.2. *Caborn–Welborn phase pottery: reconstructed designs.*

human heads (Hathcock 1976:Figures 570, 582), and cat-serpents and op-posums, as well as such rare forms as double pots and stirrup spout bottles (Adams 1949:Plate Xa). The rare occurrence of vessels or sherds of a number of Lower Mississippi Valley types further distinguishes Caborn–Welborn sites: Barton Incised, variety Kent; Campbell Appliqué, Incised, and Punctated; Carson Red on Buff; Mathews Incised, varieties Beckwith, Mathews and Manly; Nodena Red and White; and Wallace Incised (Phillips 1970).

Nonceramic artifacts such as hoes and gouges of Mill Creek and Dover cherts and triangular points and knives characterize both Angel phase and Caborn–Welborn phase sites. The latter can be distinguished, however, by the occurrence of large numbers of snubnose end scrapers, small leaf-shaped Nodena points, humpbacked knives, and small tapered and bipointed drills. It is also not uncommon to find catlinite, limestone, and sandstone disk pipes, some unfinished and some with "thunderbird" or "weeping eye" images, on Caborn–Welborn settlements. Other Southeastern Ceremonial Complex or Southern Cult motifs are also occasionally found on slate gorgets and cannel coal disks. Shell-mask gorgets and a number of minature monolithic axes and maces also occur. Interestingly, although the three symbolic categories of the cult (war, falcon, and death: Brown 1976) occur on the major Caborn–Welborn sites, the same sites produced such characteristic Oneota artifacts as copper snakes and ear coils as well as disk pipes.

AREAL DISTRIBUTION

It is difficult to place specific limits on the actual territory occupied by the two phases. Angel phase settlements are found in an approximately 100-km-long segment of the Ohio River Valley, with a distribution centered near the mouth of the Green River (Figure 11.3). The western border

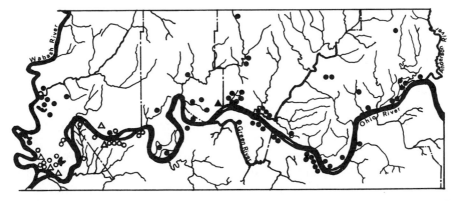

FIGURE 11.3.   *The Distribution of Angel phase and Caborn–Welborn phase sites in southwestern Indiana and north–central Kentucky.*

extends to just beyond the mouth of the Wabash River, although the westernmost sites cannot yet be distinguished from sites related to Kincaid and to Mississippian sites in the lower Tennessee River and Cumberland River area. The eastern limit of the phase is, for most purposes, the Anderson River (Honerkamp 1975:260). East of this tributary stream, which marks the eastern limit of the Wabash Lowlands in Indiana, Angel phase materials have been found in a few rock shelters in Perry County, Indiana (Kellar 1958). In the Wabash Valley the phase extends 35 km to the north, near New Harmony, Indiana (Kellar 1958). North of this town, there are only a few small and scattered Mississippian sites in Indiana until one reaches Vincennes, where there is another center of Mississippian activity (Winters 1967). There are a few sites in the Green River Valley in Kentucky (Hoffman 1966), but it is presently unclear where the limits of the Angel phase are in this area.

The spatial distribution of the Angel phase can be contrasted only generally with the preceding, less well-known Yankeetown phase, whose eastern limit in the Ohio Valley also is the Anderson River (Kellar 1956:51) The coincidence of the distributions of the Angel and Yankeetown phases in this area is not surprising; upriver, the Ohio Valley floodplain and terraces are markedly restricted and the valley margin is marked by steep bluffs. Except for occasional rock-shelter occupations and isolated finds of triangular points, Mississippian manifestations are not encountered until one reaches the Falls of the Ohio region (Honerkamp 1975:246–251), where emergent or at least early Mississippian sites have been described (Guernsey 1939, 1941, Honerkamp 1975:142–170, Janzen 1971). Up the Wabash River Valley, Yankeetown and the related or synonymous Duffy complex extends at least 110 km (Gillihan and Beeson 1960:68, Winters 1967:60–70). To the west, the distribution of Yankeetown pottery seems to extend further than Angel ceramics, occurring in the Shawneetown area (Blasingham 1953:44–74), at Saline Springs (Winters 1967:70), in the lower Cumberland River Valley (Schwartz 1962), and possibly as far as the Missouri Bootheel (Williams 1968:117–159, Figure 32). Finally, Yankeetown's southern distribution, about 90 km up the Green River (Martha Rolingson personal communication), may also be more extensive than the Angel Phase.

The Caborn–Welborn phase has a much more limited distribution than the Angel phase. In Indiana, the phase occurs only in southern Posey County; in Kentucky, its distribution is in western Henderson County and northern Union County. The western limits of the Caborn–Welborn phase are imperfectly known, although sites are reported to occur as far west as the mouth of the Saline River. Collections from southeastern Illinois at the Saline Springs site indicate a Caborn–Welborn component at this salt-processing location.

CHRONOLOGY

Ten radiocarbon dates exist for the Mississippian settlements in this portion of the Ohio Valley (Figure 11.4). Six of these dates are from the Angel site, two are from the Ellerbusch site (Green 1977), and two are from the Leonard site (Henn 1971), the only Caborn–Welborn settlement yet to yield radiocarbon dates.

Three of the Angel site dates are from Mound F (Black 1967:272). Dates of 20 B.C. ± 130 (M-9c), A.D. 620 ± 120 (M-2c), and A.D. 1430 ± 100 (M-4c) have been obtained. The first two dates are unreasonable for the Mississippian occupation at Angel and have been rejected by Black. The A.D. 1430 ± 100 assay dates Feature 12, part of a religious structure, on the surface of the primary building stage of Mound F. After Black had written the Angel report, an earlier building stage was discovered under the primary mound, and Mound F is now known to have three building stages, of

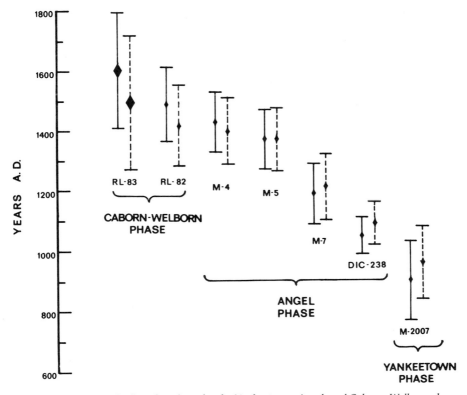

FIGURE 11.4.   *Radiocarbon dates for the Yankeetown, Angel, and Caborn–Welborn phases (solid lines indicate uncorrected date ranges, dashed lines indicate date ranges corrected for atmospheric fluctuation).*

which the primary mound is the middle construction stage. Kellar (1967:484) argues that this data falls late within the development of the site.

Black did not discuss three radiocarbon dates from the village area in the text of the Angel report. Samples were collected in 1941 and submitted to the Michigan Laboratory in the early 1950s. With the exception of one date obtained from shell, we know of no reason why these dates would not be acceptable. A date of A.D. 1190 ± 100 (M-7) was obtained from a piece of charcoal found in a house wall trench in Block 9-L-3 of subdivision W11A. Charcoal found in a wall trench in Block 0-R-1 of subdivision W10B was dated A.D. 1370 ± 100 (M-5). The third date was obtained from a mussel shell found in Block 9-R-5 of subdivision W11A and dated A.D. 100 ± 120 (M-10).

The two dates from the Ellerbusch site were thought to date the Mississippian component of the site when submitted. One date, A.D. 260 ± 60 (DIC-237), is unreasonable for this component, whereas the other date of A.D. 1050 ± 60 (DIC-238) is plausible, but seems about 100 years early.

The chronological relationship of the terminal Late Woodland Yankeetown phase and the Angel phase is relevant to dating the beginning of the latter. A single date from the Yankeetown component at the site of the same name is A.D. 900 ± 130 (M-2007) (Dorwin and Kellar 1968:61). This date ties in well with the rare occurrence of Yankeetown pottery in the Cahokia area, where it has been found in Fairmount phase contexts, which, one the basis of numerous radiocarbon dates, has been assigned the time range of A.D. 900–1050 (Fowler and Hall 1975:3–4). The standard error of the single date from the Yankeetown site overlaps that from Ellerbusch by 20 years, and indicates that the chronological relationships between the Yankeetown and Angel phases are by no means clear.

The Leonard site of Caborn–Welborn phase, located near the mouth of the Wabash River, has two dated samples: A.D. 1490 ± 125 (RL-82) and A.D. 1605 ± 190 (RL-83). Again, the standard deviations overlap some of the Angel phase dates, although these two can be safely considered later than one of the Angel site samples and the sample from Ellerbusch.

Correcting radiocarbon dates to approximate calendrical dates is of considerable importance when dealing with the late prehistoric period. The chronological spans of the two phases is somewhat modified by correcting the mean dates for atmospheric fluctuation of carbon-14 (Ralph, Michael, and Han 1974). The uncorrected Angel phase mean date span of A.D. 1050–1490 is shortened by 110 years to a corrected span of A.D. 1090–1420, owing to fluctuation in the correction curve, which makes the earlier dates later and the later dates earlier. The Caborn–Welborn phase mean date span of 105 years, A.D. 1490–1605, is not greatly changed by this correction, but the mean values are considerably different. Adding an additional ±10 years to the standard statistical error (Ralph, Michael, and

Hank 1974:4) the Leonard site date of A.D. 1490 ± 190 date is corrected to a range of A.D. 1470–1520 ± 200. The high standard statistical error and the calibration range necessitate cautious use of the latter sample. As can be noted in Figure 11.4, corrected radiocarbon dates for the two phases indicate that Caborn–Welborn, with a corrected mean date span of A.D. 1420–1520, is only slightly later than the Angel phase.

The cultural sequence indicated by the radiocarbon dates is supported by the material culture of the two phases. "Intrusive" sherds in the Angel site collection of Ramey Incised and Cobbs Island Complicated Stamp suggest twelfth and thirteenth century dates (Kellar 1967:484). On the other hand, modes of incised and punctated decoration that occur on Caborn–Welborn pottery are considered late in the overall Mississippian tradition, and particularly in the Tennessee–Cumberland cultures (Clay 1963). At Hiwassee Island these techniques only occur in the Dallas component (Lewis and Kneberg 1946:Table 19). The rare-occurring, possibly nonlocally made incised or punctated pottery designs found on Caborn–Welborn sites that clearly fit within the Lower Mississippi Valley typology have been dated to the late and terminal Mississippi periods (Phillips 1970). The Caborn–Welborn beaded- or notched-appliqué bowls also occur late in the Mississippian tradition. At Hiwassee Island they occur only in the Dallas component (Lewis and Kneberg 1946:100). Other bowls of this nature are common in late contexts in the Nashville, Tennessee region (Ferguson 1972).

Additional important evidence for the lateness of the Caborn–Welborn phase is the occurrence of historic European trade goods. With the exception of an intrusive historic (ca. A.D. 1800) burial in Mound F at the Angel site (Black 1967:251–256), no earlier historic trade materials have been found in aboriginal contexts at Angel phase sites. Surface collections and burial contexts from no less than seven Caborn Welborn sites, on the other hand, contain brass artifacts, sometimes in considerable numbers: tinklers, bracelets, rings, labrets(?), tweezers, and kettle fragments. Additionally, large blue spherical glass beads and Dutch and French gunflints are known from some of the same as well as other sites. Bison astraguli, a bison tooth pendant, and bison scapula hoes have also been excavated from a few Caborn–Welborn sites, which is a relevant fact since it has been argued that bison did not appear east of the Mississippi River in any large numbers prior to A.D. 1600 (Black 1967:579, Griffin and Wray 1945, Parmalee 1961). These data point to a period of A.D. 1650–1700 for the end of the Caborn–Welborn phase.

Considering the radiocarbon dates, the modes of pottery decoration, and the presence or absence of historic artifacts and bison, the Angel phase is clearly later than the Yankeetown phase and earlier than the Caborn–Welborn phase. With so few radiocarbon dates, and lacking dated European trade goods, we will estimate that the duration of the

Angel phase is ca. A.D. 1050–1450, and that the duration of the Caborn–Welborn phase is ca. A.D. 1400–1700. We should note, however, that for a number of reasons, Black (1967:549) extended the Angel site occupation to ca. A.D. 1600 and that Honerkamp (1975:331) considered climatic deterioration as a cause of site abandonment and proposed an end date of ca. A.D. 1550 for the Angel phase.

DISCUSSION OF PROBLEMS

There are three major gaps in our knowledge that hinder the description and analysis of the Angel phase and Caborn–Welborn phase settlement patterns. One is the lack of chronological control. At the moment, there are no data that would permit a division of either phase into more discrete units. Thus, in terms of settlement analysis, the sites within each 300-year phase have to be treated as contemporary. This is a necessary, albeit unreasonable, assumption.

The second problem concerns the attributes and characteristics of the Caborn–Welborn settlements. Since the Caborn–Welborn phase occurs somewhat later in time than the Angel phase, and since the areas occupied by the two phases overlap in part, it is possible that many of the Mississippian sites in southern Posey County, Indiana and the adjacent portions of Kentucky have both Angel components and Caborn–Welborn components. For example, at three of the large Mississippian villages, Murphy, Welborn, and Mann (Lilly 1937:30) and reportedly at Alzie and Bone Bank, distinctive Caborn–Welborn pottery, disk pipes, and large quantities of end scrapers have been found in concurrence with one or more mounds. Each of these sites also has (or had) large amounts of plain pottery that are indistinguishable from Angel phase ceramics. The problem is then, that there is at the moment no way to associate either the mounds or the plain pottery with definitely the Caborn–Welborn artifactual complex that occurs at these sites. One can certainly envision a superposition of Caborn–Welborn materials on to an Angel phase site, but with only surface collections to deal with, it is impossible to determine the true relationships. For the time being, and for purposes of analysis, we will assume that the attributes characteristic of sites containing the distinctive Caborn–Welborn material culture are characteristic of this later Mississippian phase, and are not the results of Angel phase peoples.

Third, owing to insufficient data, our goal of settlement pattern description cannot yet be achieved for what is now considered the pre-Angel occupation of the study area, the Yankeetown phase. The little available data suggest that the largest Yankeetown sites are less than 1 ha, lack mounds and middens, and are greatly outnumbered by smaller sites. Settlement pattern data for the terminal-Late-Woodland–emergent-Mississippian period has been shown to be of special importance for developing general models of subsequent settlement at Cahokia (Gregg 1975), and we would expect they would be equally important in southwestern Indiana. Unfortunately the Yankeetown data are not yet adequate for inclusion in the following analysis.

Settlement Patterns

SETTLEMENT CATEGORIES

The various categories of Angel phase and Caborn–Welborn phase settlements to be presented were empirically determined on the basis of the presence or absence of mounds, site size, the intensity of occupation, the nature of the inferred activities that took place at each site, and whether there was evidence for cooking utensils and house structures (T. Green 1977).

A fourfold classification of site size was used. Small sites are less than .25 ha, medium sites are between .25 and 1 ha, large sites are between 1 and 4 ha, and very large sites are over 5 ha in size.

Intensity of occupation refers to the density of artifacts and debitage found on the surface. This attribute was not quantified, and sites were divided into two categories based on either a low or high intensity of surface debris. The presence of a midden that was definitely attributable to the Mississippian occupation at a site was taken as an indicator of a high-intensity occupation.

The identification of the activities that took place at each site was based on the artifactual materials recovered from the surface and surface features. Projectile points were taken as evidence for hunting activities. Shell and flint hoes, hoe flakes from flint hoes (Witthoft 1967), and actual cultivated plant specimens were assumed to be evidence of horticultural activities. Gathering activities were generally indicated by the presence of manos and metates, but these tools lack diagnostic traits that would allow them to be assigned to a specific component at a site. The presence of houses was determined from wall daub or other observable surface features that could be interpreted as indicating houses.

It is acknowledged at the onset that these criteria are very simplistic indicators of the range and duration of activities that took place at any one site. This is especially true when compared with the more sophisticated methods of activity analysis such as Winters's (1969) systemic index. However, in order to utilize activity indicators, based on the differential frequency of tool types at different sites, temporal control is necessary. Of the 97 Angel phase and Caborn–Welborn phase sites utilized in this study, fully 96% have Archaic and/or Woodland components, and given current knowledge it is difficult to assign many tool categories collected from the surface to a specific occupation at a site.

A sixfold settlement typology reflecting the Mississippian occupation in southwestern Indiana has been generated by the attributes just discussed:

1. Towns (Angel Site)
   A. Very large size, over 5 ha.
   B. Substructure mounds present.
   C. Intensive occupation (midden present).
   D. Horticultural, hunting, and gathering activities.
   E. Houses present.
   F. Estimated population: 3000 people.
2. Large Villages
   A. Large size, 1–4 ha.
   B. Mounds present or reported.
   C. Intensive occupation (midden present).
   D. Horticultural, hunting, and gathering activities.
   E. Houses present.
   F. Estimated population: 200–500 people.
3. Small Villages
   A. Medium size, .25–1 ha.
   B. Mounds absent.
   C. Intensive occupation (midden present).
   D. Horticultural, hunting, and gathering activities.
   E. Houses present.
   F. Estimated population: 25–75 people.
4. Hamlets
   A. Medium size, .25–1 ha.
   B. Mounds absent.
   C. Low density of surface debris.
   D. Horticultural, hunting, and gathering activities.
   E. Houses present.
   F. Estimated population: 10–25 people.
5. Farmsteads
   A. Small size, less than .25 ha.
   B. Mounds absent.
   C. Low density of surface debris.
   D. Horticultural, hunting, and gathering activities.
   E. Houses present.
   F. Estimated population: 5–10 people.
6. Camps
   A. Small size, less than .25 ha.
   B. Mounds absent.
   C. Low density of surface debris.
   D. Hunting and gathering activities.
   E. Houses absent.
   F. Population variable, probably seasonal.

POPULATION

A population estimate has been listed for each settlement category, indicating the estimated number of people occupying a particular type of settlement. Although the accuracy of these figures can certainly be questioned, they do allow for a comparison between the Angel phase and Caborn–Welborn phase in terms of the proportions of the total population living in the various settlement categories, and hence, can be used to help describe the relative degree of nucleation and dispersion of the populations.

Population estimates are based on what little empirical evidence is available. Population figures were estimated for a town (the Angel site), a small village (12 Po 56), and a hamlet (the Ellerbusch site) and then extrapolated to other settlement categories.

The Angel site (Black 1967) is the dominant settlement of the Angel phase. This town covers approximately 40 ha and is enclosed by a bastioned stockade (Figure 11.5). Near the center of the site is a large, multilevel, flat-topped mound designated Mound A. Just west of this mound is a large plaza area bordered by individual houses. Near the western edge of the town and across the plaza from Mound A is Mound F, another rectangular truncated mound. Other mounds occur north and east of

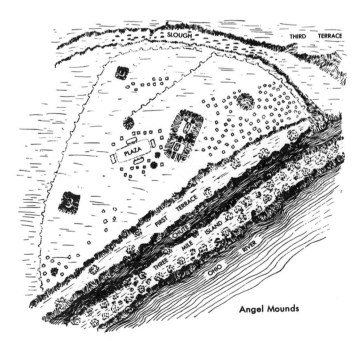

FIGURE 11.5.   The Angel phase town: a diagramatic representation. [From Black (1967: Figure 546).]

Mound A. To the east of Mound A is a heavily occupied area composed of numerous remains of individual houses (Figure 11.6).

Black (1967:547) estimated the population of the Angel site at approximately 1000 people. He considered this a minimum estimate predicated on the presumed spatial requirements of an individual household of five people. Based on historic documents, the possibility exists that each household would have had a small garden plot, a summer and winter house, corn cribs, and other structures within the settlement. Black estimated that 223 m² per household may have been needed. He stated that there was evidence of dense habitation on only about one-eighth of the site, and by dividing the estimated required household space into this area he estimated that only 200 households existed at the Angel site at any one time. Using a standard figure of five people per household, Black concluded that 1000 people inhabited the site.

Black's figure is a minimum estimate, but it still seems unreasonably low. Excluding the plaza area, the portion of the site covered by mounds, and a very low wet area that was possibly a barrow pit, there is approximately 330,855 m² (about 33 ha) available for habitation within the stockade perimeter. Using Black's figure of 223 m² per household, there is room for 1483 households within the stockade. If an average household

FIGURE 11.6. *The Angel site: an excavated area showing house wall postholes.* [From Black (1967:Figure 121).]

had five members, then the site could have been populated by 7400 people.

It is doubtful that this many people would have occupied the site at any one time. Nevertheless, house patterns have been found in all areas of the site where excavations have been conducted, with the exceptions of the mounds and plaza areas. While some areas of the site have been more heavily occupied than others, Black (1967:57) states that surface debris covers the whole site area.

One reason Black felt his population estimate of 1000 people was a minimum estimate was that this population would only include approximately 200 men. In view of the overall size of the stockade at the Angel site, and including that portion of the site adjacent to the river, 200 men would find it hard to defend such a large town. The known stockade was close to 1.9 km long and had 51 bastions. The portion of the site adjacent to the river was 1.3 km long and may have been stockaded (Black 1967:541). Black felt that the additional manpower needed to protect such a large perimeter would have to come from the small villages in the vicinity of the Angel site. Based on what we know today about smaller sites near Angel, it is doubtful that an additional 1000 people or 200 men could be found within a 15–25-km radius of the site. Based on this fact and on the overall size of the Angel site, it does not seem unreasonable that 3000 people (90 people per hectare of habitation area) could have occupied Angel at its zenith, and this figure will be used in the discussions that follow.

The Ellerbusch site (T. Green 1977) is a hamlet approximately .3 ha in size, has a low density of surface debris, and has evidence of horticultural, hunting and gathering activities. The remains of four houses were found during excavation, but no more than three of these houses were occupied concurrently (Figure 11.7). Following Black it is estimated that five people lived in each house, and hence the site at any one time period had a population of from 10 to 15 people. Other hamlets range in size from about .3 to about 1 ha in size, with the larger sites perhaps having a population of 10–25 people.

Evidence from one other smaller settlement (12 Po 56) permits some estimate concerning the population range of small villages. Covering approximately .5 ha, 12 Po 56 has a very intensive single component Mississippian occupation, and has yielded evidence of horticultural, hunting and gathering activities. When surface conditions are right the remains of at least eight houses can be observed (Figure 11.8). Again, by estimating five people per house, approximately 40 people lived at the site, assuming that all houses were occupied contemporaneously. Small villages range from about .3 to 1 ha in size and, by employing the population-size–site-size ratio derived for 12 Po 56, it is estimated that anywhere from 25 to 75 people occupied small village settlements.

With little empirical evidence, it is difficult to estimate the population

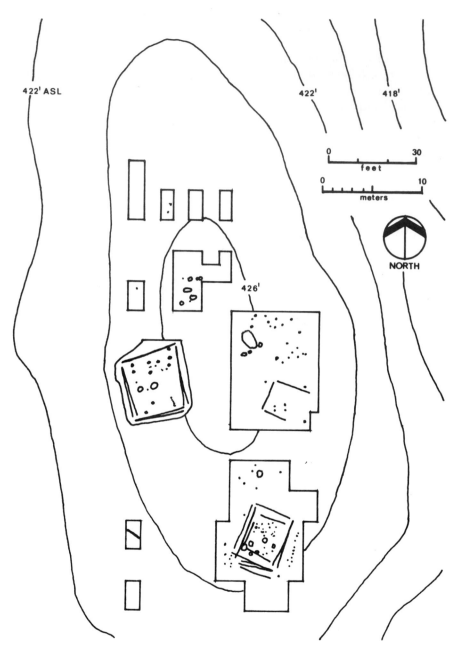

422' ASL

422'   418'

0   30
feet

0   10
meters

NORTH

426'

FIGURE 11.7.   *The Ellerbusch site: an Angel phase hamlet.* [From Green (1977:Figure 5).]

FIGURE 11.8.   *Infrared aerial photograph showing houses(?) At 12 Po 56: an Angel phase
small village.* [Photograph Courtesy of Robert E. Pace.]

sizes of large villages and farmsteads, but a rough estimate can be extrapolated from the estimates for other settlement categories. Large villages
with dense middens are most similar to Angel site for which we have
projected approximately 90 people per hectare. With most large villages
covering about 4 ha, we estimate an average population size of approximately 350 people for this category. Farmsteads are most similar to hamlets
which have an estimated population size-site size ratio of about 25 people
per hectare. Farmsteads which are less than .25 ha in size, then, would
have about 5–10 people per site.

SETTLEMENT LOCATIONS AND NATURAL ENVIRONMENT

The locations of the Angel phase and Caborn–Welborn phase sites
with respect to the major geomorphic zones are shown in Table 11.1 and
Figures 11.9 and 11.10. As can be seen, the majority of sites from both
phases are located on the floodplain and terraces of Ohio Valley. What few
sites do occur in the lacustrine plains and uplands are small hamlets,

TABLE 11.1
The Distribution of Angel Phase and Caborn–Welborn Phase Settlements in Different Geomorphological Zones

Geomorpholog- ical zones	Town	Large village	Small village	Hamlet	Farm- stead	Camp	Total
			The Angel phase				
Floodplain			56% (5)	50% (3)	38% (6)	39% (14)	41% (28)
Low Terrace	100% (1)		44% (4)	17% (1)	31% (5)	22% (8)	28% (19)
High Terrace					6% (1)	6% (2)	4% (3)
Lacustrine Plain						6% (2)	3% (2)
Upland				33% (2)	25% (4)	28% (10)	24% (16)
Total	(1)		(9)	(6)	(16)	(36)	(68)
		The Caborn–Welborn phase					
Floodplain	40% (2)	57% (4)	60% (3)	43% (3)		20% (1)	45% (13)
Low Terrace	40% (2)	43% (3)	40% (2)	57% (4)		60% (3)	48% (14)
High Terrace	20% (1)					20% (1)	7% (2)
Lascustrine Plain							
Upland							
Total	(5)	(7)	(5)	(7)		(5)	(29)

farmsteads, and hunting and gathering camps; no sites of any size have been found in these zones.

The choice of river valleys as the location of settlement is characteristic of Mississippian populations. Within river valleys correlations have been observed between Mississippian sites and the more fertile soils (Bennett 1944, Larson 1972, Ward 1965; and most convincingly by Butler (1976). Usually, these fertile soils also support a plant understory of cane, which can easily be cleared for horticulture (Lewis 1974; Phillips *et al.* 1951). These same soils are also usually above the annual or semiannual floods, making them even more attractive for settlement.

In southwestern Indiana these three factors of elevation, fertility, and cultivability of soils also appear to be significant environmental variables affecting the choice of Mississippian farming settlements within the river valley. Most of the sites are located on natural levees, old point bars, eroded terrace remnants, and other higher portions of the floodplain. Large cane brakes were recorded in these areas historically by the land surveyors (T. Green 1972b), and the characteristic soils are the Huntington–Lindside associations, which are well drained, friable, and fertile.

Explanations for the correlation of Mississippian sites with alluvial soils have emphasized the economy of farming these fertile and friable soils as opposed to other soil types (Butler 1976, Lewis 1974). The argument is that these soils are more productive with less labor input than other soils in the area, and that it is desirable to settle on or near these soils to minimize the travel distance to and from the fields. Similar least-cost

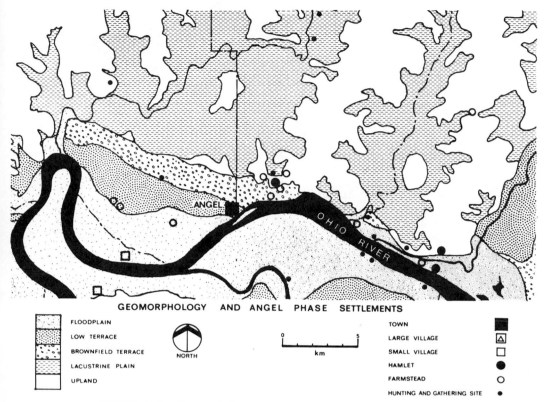

GEOMORPHOLOGY AND ANGEL PHASE SETTLEMENTS

FLOODPLAIN			TOWN	■
LOW TERRACE	NORTH		LARGE VILLAGE	▣
BROWNFIELD TERRACE		0 km 5	SMALL VILLAGE	□
LACUSTRINE PLAIN			HAMLET	●
UPLAND			FARMSTEAD	○
			HUNTING AND GATHERING SITE	•

FIGURE 11.9. *Geomorphology and Angel phase settlement distribution.*

location analyses are widely used in archeological explanation (Eddy 1974, Ellison and Harriss 1972, E. Green 1973, Hill 1971).

We concur generally with this reasoning for the explanation of Mississippian site locations, but it is important to emphasize that Mississippian sites do occur in the uplands. Six small sites have been found in the uplands with surface evidence of horticultural activities, and excavations at the Ellerbusch site have confirmed that horticulture was an important activity at these sites. Not surprisingly, such upland sites are located on the most fertile soils available, the Alford silt loams. On a level surface, these soils are as productive as floodplain soils (Shively and McElrath 1973), and being loess, they are quite friable and can be easily cultivated with hoes. Upland horticulture is clearly possible for Mississippian farmers in southwestern Indiana; there are no environmental constraints on farming these soils and, in fact, since some of the upland soils are as productive as the floodplain soils, it is surprising that more horticultural sites have not been found in the uplands. One explanation for their paucity is that there are other important resources in the floodplain.

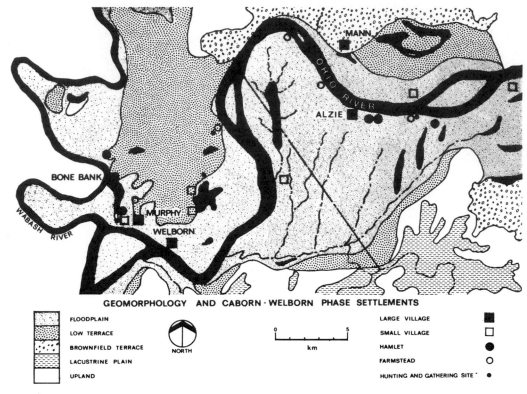

FLOODPLAIN

LOW TERRACE

BROWNFIELD TERRACE

LACUSTRINE PLAIN

UPLAND

NORTH

0 _____ 5

km

GEOMORPHOLOGY AND CABORN - WELBORN PHASE SETTLEMENTS

LARGE VILLAGE

SMALL VILLAGE

HAMLET

FARMSTEAD

HUNTING AND GATHERING SITE '

FIGURE 11.10. Geomorphology and Caborn–Welborn phase settlement distribution.

Chisholm (1968:102) states that arable land, water, building materials, fuel, and grazing land are universal economic needs of an agricultural society. If animal food products are substituted for grazing land these five goods are equally applicable to the prehistoric societies in the Eastern Woodlands. Based on a qualitative least-cost analysis of obtaining these goods in different environmental zones in southwestern Indiana (T. Green 1977), it appears that large quantities of all of these resources can be obtained more cheaply in the floodplain than in other ecological zones. If economy of obtaining these resources from the floodplain is coupled with ease of transportation and communication provided by the Ohio River, it is not hard to understand why the floodplain was chosen for settlement.

SETTLEMENT LOCATIONS AND SOCIAL ENVIRONMENT

Both the Angel phase and the Caborn–Welborn phase populations chose to settle on or near the floodplain of the Ohio River, but the manner in which they settled the river valley was very different. Table 11.2 shows the distribution of the estimated population within the different settle-

TABLE 11.2
Estimated Populations of the Angel Phase and Caborn–Welborn Phase[a]

Settlement category	Angel phase		Caborn–Welborn phase	
	Number of sites	Estimated population	Number of sites	Estimated population
Towns (300 people)	1	3000 (85%)	—	—
Large villages (350 people)	—	—	5	1750 (80%)
Small villages (50 people)	9	400 (11%)	7	350 (16%)
Hamlets (10 people)	6	60 (2%)	5	50 (2%)
Farmsteads (5 people)	16	80 (2%)	7	35 (2%)
Camps	36	—	5	—
Total	68	3540	29	2185

[a] Population estimates were determined by using average population estimates discussed in the text and by assuming that all known horticultural sites were occupied both contemporaneously and continuously throughout the year, while camp sites were occupied seasonally.

ment categories of the two phases. The Angel phase population had a relatively nucleated settlement pattern with the majority of people occupying a central town, the Angel site. In contrast the Caborn–Welborn population had a more dispersed settlement pattern, with the population distributed in a number of large village settlements.

The Angel phase as it is presently known, is composed of one large town, nine small villages, six hamlets, 16 farmsteads, and 36 hunting and/or gathering camps (we feel that additional research will reveal that many of the sites located in the river valley and presently identified as hunting and gathering camps are in fact farmsteads). Angel phase sites have a very distinctive distribution. Only two small villages, three hamlets, 10 farmsteads and 19 hunting and gathering camps are located within a 25-km radius of the Angel site. With the exception of the two small villages all the farming sites within this 25-km circle lack a midden that would indicate a permanent or substantial occupation.

To the west of this 25-km circle there are four small villages, four farmsteads, and three camps that can be assigned to the Angel phase. With one exception, all of these sites are located on the Wabash River about 50 km west of the Angel site. To the east of the 25 km circle there are three small villages, five farmsteads and 18 hunting and gathering camps. Although we have used a 25-km circle solely for descriptive purposes, Clay (1976:149) has noted that clusters of Mississippian settlements have a patterned organizational field with major settlements spaced at distances of 32–40 km.

The Caborn–Welborn settlement pattern is in comparison, quite different from the Angel phase pattern. Instead of one central town dominating the settlement pattern, as in the Angel phase, there are five large villages located within 15 km of each other. These are Murphy, Welborn, Bone Bank, and the Mississippian components at Mann, and Alzie. In addition there are seven small villages, five hamlets, seven farmsteads, and five hunting and gathering camps, none of which is located more than 12 km (or a half-day's walk) from one of the large villages. With the exception of their size and the observed or reported presence or substructure mounds, there is little to distinguish the large villages from the small villages. There is no surface evidence of stockades or plazas and the "finer" artifactual classes—such as disk pipes, worked flourite, and decorated pottery—are found on all categories of Caborn–Welborn settlements except camps.

One additional point needs to be clarified. In the vicinity of Alzie, which is located on a natural levee in Kentucky, numerous Caborn–Welborn sites have been identified. Based on Hoffman's (1966) description this whole area might be better characterized as a continuous series of farmsteads and small villages, rather than one large village with numerous smaller sites adjacent to it.

The different patterns of population distribution between the settlements of the two phases have been contrasted as nucleated and dispersed. However, it is important to note there is an overall similarity in the distribution of the majority of the estimated populations. In the study area, both the Angel phase and the Caborn–Welborn phase had approximately 80% of their estimated populations concentrated into a town or large villages, each of which contained observed or reported substructure mounds; the remainder of both populations was similarly distributed in a number of small villages, hamlets, and farmsteads. The major difference in the settlement patterns is that 80% of the population was nucleated into 1 central town in the Angel phase, whereas the same percentage was dispersed into five large villages in the Caborn–Welborn phase.

There are many factors that might have caused the relative nucleation of the Angel phase settlement pattern and the subsequent dispersion of the Caborn–Welborn phase settlement pattern (cf. Everson and FitzGerald 1969, Rowlands 1972, Trigger 1968). Green (1977) has brought together the ethnohistoric data relating to settlement patterns in the Eastern Woodlands. There is ample evidence in this data to support the claim that large nucleated, fortified towns, such as the Angel site, were responses to warfare. A corollary to this thesis is that in relatively peaceful times the peoples of the Eastern Woodlands preferred to live in dispersed small-village settlement patterns that excluded large population centers.

The best example of this pattern is the Huron. Trigger's (1969:17) analysis of the Huron settlement pattern indicates that those tribes living nearest to the Iroquois, and hence the most threatened, had the fewest but the largest villages, and they were palisaded. In contrast, the Attignawantan Huron who lived the farthest from the Iroquois had small but more numerous villages, only one being stockaded. When the Attignawantan were directly threatened by the Iroquois, they debated whether to build one large fortified town for protection, but this plan was abandoned when the threat diminished.

Other examples occur in the Southeast. Adair (1930:442–443) states that the Chickasaw lived in compact villages during times of strife but preferred a dispersed pattern. Adair (1930:302) also states that the Choctaw had only compact villages on their frontiers adjacent to the Creek and Chickasaw, and that in the interior of Choctaw country they lived in "scattered plantations." Among the Cherokee, Fogelson and Kutsche (1961:113) claim that palisaded villages were rare, and occurred only with towns that were near the edge of their territory; the towns in the interior of Cherokee territory were groups of dispersed individual house sites organized around a central rotunda. Based on DeSoto's descriptions, Swanton (1928:438) states that the Creek had fortified towns only on their borders, and in the interior a dispersed pattern was characteristic. Finally, the Natchez lived in dispersed house sites, loosely organized into five villages, but when attacked by the French, their immediate response was to build two fortified villages (Neitzel 1965).

The advantages of a nucleated settlement for defense are widely recognized. Rowlands' (1972) study of the influence of warfare on settlement patterns shows that this response to warfare is common throughout the world. Rowlands stresses, though, that warfare does not always cause nucleated settlements, nor do prehistoric nucleated settlements always indicate warfare. There are other reasons, particularly economic, for the concentration of peoples at fewer settlements. However, with the exception of Cahokia, which is still problematical, it appears that warfare was the primary cause for nucleated settlements in the Eastern Woodlands.

The advantage of a dispersed settlement pattern of small villages were primarily economic, in that basic resources could be obtained more cheaply (Trigger 1969:17, 1976:30). For example, if the Angel site contained 3000 people, between 400 and 1200 ha of land under cultivation would have been needed each year to feed the population (Green 1977). Assuming they followed the usual Southeastern pattern of farming permanent fields in the floodplain, their fields would have been situated immediately southwest of the Angel site in the broad floodplain located there. To get to these fields some people would have had to walk over 3–4 km. If, on the other hand, these people were located in small villages, they would have been closer to their fields, thus saving considerable travel time. Similar arguments can be made for each of Chisholm's critical resources. A population of 3000 people would have eventually exhausted the surrounding sources of fuel, building materials, and game within a reasonable walking distance of the Angel site more quickly than if this same population were dispersed over the landscape. The advantage of a dispersed settlement pattern, then, is in terms of a reduction in the labor cost of subsistence production, because fewer man-hours are needed to travel to and from the desired resources. Conversely, a large population concentration increases the costs of producing these same goods.

It is safe to conclude that the Angel phase population was involved in warfare. The palisade surrounding the Angel site, with its additions and repairs, is evidence of conflict. Defense was the only function of stockades historically in the Eastern Woodlands and presumably this was their function prehistorically. It is necessary to emphasize that although a large stockaded settlement is good evidence of warfare it does not necessarily indicate that a large population lived at the site. It is possible, and may even be likely, that the majority of the Angel population could have lived in the surrounding country and fled to the Angel site only in times of strife. Such a strategy would have provided protection while still allowing the economic advantages of a dispersed settlement pattern. But, based on our interpretation of the survey data currently available for the Angel phase and on our population estimate for the Angel site, this does not appear to have been the case with the Angel phase pattern.

As already stated, Angel phase settlements within 25 km of the Angel site all lack middens that would suggest permanency. These sites appear to be seasonal farming settlements presumably established by Angel site population segments to minimize the distance to and from the agricultural fields. There are no substantial populations living near the Angel site. It would seem, in view of the surprise-attack nature of Eastern Woodland warfare (Gibson 1974, Trigger 1969:68), that the populations occupying Angel phase settlements located over 25 km from the Angel site would not have had sufficient time to flee to the stockade and hence would either have had their own stockades or would have occupied these sites only in peaceful times.

The Caborn–Welborn phase settlement pattern is most similar to the dispersed village pattern of the historic Eastern Woodlands Indians. The settlement pattern is composed of a relatively uniform linear distribution along the Ohio River of small and large villages, hamlets, farmsteads, and camps. It is tempting to attribute the dispersed settlement pattern of the Caborn–Welborn phase to a lack of warfare. This is a logical conclusion, and there is no evidence to negate it; but neither is there any independent archeological evidence to support it.

Preliminary Models of Mississippian Settlement Patterns in Southwestern Indiana

Our current knowledge of the settlement patterns of the Angel phase and the Caborn–Welborn phase are deficient in a number of respects. We

need more accurate chronological control, more accurate population estimates, more accurate information on site function and seasonality, and
very importantly, we need more accurate information on the exact nature
of the Caborn–Welborn settlements. For these reasons we can only present
our conclusions concerning the settlement patterns of these two phases
in the form of alternative models that need to be tested with further
archeological research.

There are two alternative settlement pattern models for the Angel
phase that would appear to explain the variable density of habitational
debris at the Angel site and the distribution of the smaller settlements in
the area. One would be a nucleated settlement pattern with the majority of
the Angel phase population living at the Angel site because of the threat of
warfare. During the spring and summer, subsidiary farming settlements
would be established near Angel to minimize the time needed to travel to
and from the fields and to protect the crops from birds and other wildlife.
These farming settlements would be located close enough to the Angel site
so that the people could seek refuge at the site in time of need. An
alternative model of the Angel phase settlement pattern would have a
greater percentage of the population distributed over a wide area in small
farmsteads, hamlets, and villages leaving only about 1500 people as residents at the Angel site. Presumably this pattern would occur during
relatively peaceful times.

It is probable that through time both of these models characterized the
pattern of settlement used by the Angel phase population. During periods
of hostility, people would have moved into the Angel site for protection.
When the threat diminished, the people would have dispersed into
smaller settlements in order to minimize the costs of basic subsistence
goods. This simple dynamic has been identified in historic aboriginal
societies, and there is no reason why it would not have occurred in
prehistoric societies.

If the population of the Angel site varied through time in response to
warfare, this would explain the variability in the intensity of habitational
debris at the site. Black (1967) stated that one-eighth of the Angel site was
intensively occupied. This portion of the site would represent the permanent population at the site, and following Black this would be around 1000
to 1500 people. The lighter habitational debris and house patterns found
in other portions of the site would represent population segments moving
to the Angel site temporarily for protection.

These two models used sequentially would also help explain the
distribution of the other Angel phase settlements. Those sites located far
from the Angel site would have been settlements occupied during peaceful
periods, whereas the sites located near the Angel site would represent
seasonal habitations of the permanent residents of Angel.

A single model for the Caborn–Welborn settlement pattern would be a series of small villages, occasional large villages and nearby farmsteads that were occupied on a year-round basis. It is possible, though, that one or more of the large villages were stockaded and that the majority of the population chose to live in close proximity to these settlements. An ethnographic parallel to this pattern might be the Creek. Swanton (1928:170) states that Creek towns consisted of a succession of villages or neighborhoods scattered in the woods along rivers and streams but that stockaded towns did occur along the margins of Creek territory.

As a final consideration, we would expect that the social and political organization of a population dispersed into what appear to be autonomous large villages and subsidiary settlements may be very different from that of a population that looks to one center or town. Unfortunately, there is not sufficient evidence to allow us to incorporate these factors into the preliminary models.

Summary and Prospects

Two Mississippian cultures of southwestern Indiana, the Angel phase population (A.D. 1050–1450) and the Caborn–Welborn phase population (A.D. 1400–1700), have been described and shown to reflect similar responses to the available choices for location of major settlements. It has also been proposed that the choices of floodplain and terrace locations represented the optimum solution for satisfying subsistence, domestic maintenance, transportation, and communication needs. Given the same resource base and the same extractive technology, we have argued that the dispersed Caborn–Welborn phase settlement pattern is a more economic distribution of population than is the nucleated Angel phase pattern. On the basis of empirical evidence and ethnographic analogy, it is proposed that the Angel phase settlement pattern is a response to another need— defense. It is not to be inferred, however, that the Caborn–Welborn population was not concerned with defense. The dispersion of this population within a restricted area does not preclude a response to defense and as such appears to be the optimum solution to considerations of both economy and defense. Finally, we can speculate that the two distinct settlement patterns also reflect different structures of social and political organization.

The models we have presented of the Mississippian settlement patterns in southwestern Indiana are initial formulations and remain untested. In order to establish the relative strength any of these models, explicit regional research designs such as those outlined by Binford (1964) and Struever (1968) will have to be implemented in this area. The problem is clearly regional in scope and excavations at any one site will not provide all the data necessary.

Special problems that will be important to address include (*a*) the question of the ethnicity of the late prehistoric–protohistoric Caborn–Welborn phase (Munson and Green 1973); (*b*) the strength and nature of the relationship that existed between the five large village sites of the Caborn–Welborn phase; (*c*) the continuity or discontinuity that existed between the Caborn–Welborn and Angel phase occupations; and (*d*) the relationship of the Angel phase to the Yankeetown phase and the nature of the initial Mississippian emergence in the study area. Certainly, the interpretation that the Angel phase is an intrusive culture in the area (Honerkamp 1975:314, Kellar 1973:59) is based on both the absence of good chronological data for the Angel site and smaller Angel phase settlements and the discrete nature of the Yankeetown and Angel phase ceramic assemblages. We are of the opinion that the complex and very rapid "Mississippianization" and nucleation of Late Woodland populations is not necessarily a process restricted to Cahokia (Fowler and Hall 1975, Gregg 1975), but is certainly a process understood through analysis of well controlled data sets. Clearly, the preliminary models we have proposed will be subject to refinement or alteration when there is better control of data relating to chronology, subsistence, mound association, defense, social stratification, and intrasite as well as extraregional relationships.

Acknowledgments

We would like to acknowledge the assistence of many people who contributed to this study. James H. Kellar (Director, Glenn A. Black Laboratory of Archaeology) and Patrick J. Munson (Department of Anthropology, Indiana University), offered support, comments, and criticism. Many individuals contributed site data: Robert E. Pace (Indiana State University), Gilbert Apfelstadt, Joseph Ford (Owensboro Museum), Robert Henn, George and Frances Martin, Gary Morrison, Denzil Stephens, and especially Charles Lacer and Edmund Lewis. We offer these people our sincere appreciation, but of course assume responsibility for errors in judgment and interpretation.

References

Adair, James
    1930   *Adair's history of the american Indian*, edited by Samuel C. Williams. Johnson City, Tennessee: The Watauga Press.
Adams, William R.
    1949   Archaeological notes on Posey County, Indiana. Indianapolis: Indiana Historical Burea.

Alexander, Charles S.
   1974   Some observations on the Late Pleistocene and Holocene of the lower Ohio Valley. *Occasional Papers of the Department of Geography, University of Illinois* **7.**
Alexander, Charles S. and Nelson R. Nunnally
   1972   Channel stability on the lower Ohio River. *Annals of American Geographers* **62**:411–417.
Bennett, John W.
   1944   The interaction of culture and environment in the smaller societies. *American Anthropologist* **46**:461–478.
Binford, Lewis R.
   1964   A consideration of archaeological research design. *American Antiquity* **29**:425–441.
Black, Glenn A.
   1961   "... that what is past may not be forever lost..." *Indiana History Bulletin* **38**:51–60.
   1967   *Angel Site: An archaeological, historical, and ethnological Study*. Indianapolis: Indiana Historical Society.
Blasingham, Emily J.
   1953   Temporal and spatial distribution of the Yankeetown cultural manifestation. M.A. thesis, Department of Anthropology, Indiana University. Bloomington.
Brown, James A.
   1976   The Southern Cult reconsidered. *Midcontinental Journal of Archaeology* **1**:115–135.
Butler, Brian M.
   1976   Mississippian settlement in the Black Bottom: Environment, community, and site distribution. Paper presented at the 41st Annual Meeting of the Society for American Archaeology. St. Louis, Missouri.
Chisholm, Michael
   1968   *Rural settlement and land use*. London: Hutchinson and Co.
Clarke, David L.
   1968   *Analytical archaeology*. London: Methuen and Co.
Clay, R. Berle
   1963   Ceramic complexes of the Tennessee–Cumberland regions in western Kentucky. M.A. thesis, Department of Anthropology, University of Kentucky.
   1976   Tactics, strategy, and operations: The Mississippian system responds to its environment. *Midcontinental Journal of Archaeology* **1**:137–162.
Cole, Fay-Copper *et al.*
   1951   *Kincaid, a prehistoric Illinois metropolis*. Chicago: University of Chicago Press.
Curry, Hilda
   1954   *Archaeological notes on Warrick County, Indiana*. Indianapolis: Indiana Historical Bureau.
Deam, Charles
   1953   *Trees of Indiana* (3rd edition). *State of Indiana, Department of Conservation, Division of Forestry*.
Dorwin, John T. and James H. Kellar
   1968   The 1967 excavation at the Yankeetown site. National Park Service. Manuscript on file at the Glenn A. Black Laboratory of Archaeology, Indiana University.
Dragoo, Don W.
   1955   *An archaeological survey of Gibson County, Indiana*. Indianapolis: Indiana Historical Bureau.
Eddy, Frank W.
   1974   Resource management and locational strategies of certain prehistoric sites in central Texas. *Plains Anthropologist* **19**:99–106.
Ellison, A. and J. Harriss
   1972   Settlement and land use in the prehistory and early history of southern England: A

study based on locational models. In *Models in Archaeology,* edited by David Clark. London: Methuen and Co.

Everson, J.A. and B.P. FitzGerald
1969   *Settlement patterns.* London: Longmans.

Ferguson, Robert B. (Editor)
1972   The Middle Cumberland Culture. *Vanderbilt Publications in Anthropology* **3**. Nashville, Tennessee.

Fidlar, Marion M.
1942   Physiography of the lower Wabash valley. Ph.D. dissertation, Department of Geology, Indiana University. Bloomington.

Fogelson, R.D. and P. Kutsche
1961   Cherokee economic cooperatives: The Gadugi. In Symposium on Cherokee and Iroquois Culture, edited by William N. Fenton. *U.S. Bureau of American Ethnology, Bulletin* **180**.

Fowler, Melvin L. and Robert L. Hall
1975   Archaeological phases at Cahokia. In Perspectives in Cahokia Archaeology. *Illinois Archaeological Survey, Bulletin* **10**. Urbana. Pp. 1–14.

Funkhouser, W.D. and W.S. Webb
1932   Archaeological survey of Kentucky. *University of Kentucky Reports in Archaeology and Anthropology* **2**. Lexington.

Gibson, Jon L.
1974   Aboriginal warfare in the protohistoric southeast: An alternative perspective. *American Antiquity* **39**:130–133.

Gillihan, James E. and William J. Beeson
1960   The Bamble Site. In Indian mounds and villages in Illinois. *Illinois Archaeological Survey, Bulletin* **2**. Urbana. Pp. 31–70.

Green, Ernestene L.
1973   Location analysis of prehistoric Maya sites in northern British Honduras. *American Antiquity* **38**:279–293.

Green, Thomas J.
1972a   An archaeological survey of the Wabash river valley in Posey and Posey and Gibson Counties Indiana. Manuscript on file at the Glenn A. Black Laboratory of Archaeology, Indiana University.
1972b   The vegetation of southwestern Indiana in 1800: An archaeological perspective. Manuscript, Glenn A. Black Laboratory of Archaeology, Indiana University.
1977   Economic relationships underlying Mississippian settlement patterns in southwestern Indiana. Ph.D. dissertation, Department of Anthropology, Indiana University. Bloomington.

Gregg, Michael L.
1975   A population estimate for Cahokia. In Perspectives in Cahokia Archaeology. *Illinois Archaeological Survey, Bulletin* 10. Urbana. Pp. 126–136.

Griffin, John W. and Donald E. Wray
1945   Bison in Illinois archaeology. *Transactions of the Illinois Academy of Sciences* **38**:21–26.

Guernsey, E.Y.
1939   Relationships among various Clark County sites. *Proceedings of the Indiana Academy of Science* **48**:27–32.
1941   The culture sequence of the Ohio Falls sites. *Proceedings of the Indiana Academy of Science* **51**:60–67.

Hamy, E.T.
1904   Les Voyages du naturaliste Ch. Alex Leseur dans l'Amerique du Nord, ... *Journal de la Societé des Americanistes* **5**:65–77.

Hathcock, Roy
  1976   *Ancient Indian pottery of the Mississippi River valley.* Camden, Arkansas: Hurley
          Press.
Hemphill, Marie-Louise
  1976   The Bone Bank skull and the fossil shells of Walnut Hills. Manuscript, Paris.
Henn, Robert
  1971   A preliminary report on the Leonard site. *Proceedings of the Indiana Academy of
          Sciences* **80**:67–73.
Hill, J.N.
  1971   Research propositions for consideration, Southwestern Anthropological Research
          Group. In *The distribution of prehistoric population aggregates,* edited by G.J. Gum-
          merman. Prescott, Arizona: Prescott College Press. Pp. 55–62.
Hoffman, Michael A.
  1966   An archaeological survey of the Newburgh and Uniontown Lock and Dam areas.
          National Park Service, Southeast Region Office.
Honerkamp, Majory W.
  1975   The Angel phase: An analysis of a Middle Mississippian occupation in southwest-
          ern Indiana. Ph.D. dissertation, Department of Anthropology, Indiana University.
          Bloomington.
Janzen, Donald E.
  1971   Report of 1971 excavations at the Prather site: A Mississippian site in Clark County,
          Indiana. Manuscript on file at Centre College of Kentucky.
Kellar, James H.
  1956   *An archaeological survey of Spencer County, Indiana.* Indianapolis: Indiana Histori-
          cal Burea.
  1958   *An archaeological survey of Perry County, Indiana.* Indianapolis: Indiana Historical
          Bureau.
  1967   Material Culture. In *Angel Site: An archaeological, historical and ethnological study,*
          by Glenn A. Black. Indianapolis: Indiana Historical Society.
  1973   *An introduction to the prehistory of Indiana.* Indianapolis: Indiana Historical Society.
Larson, Lewis H., Jr.
  1970   Settlement distribution during the Mississippian Period. *Southeastern Archaeologi-
          cal Conference, Bulletin* 3:19–25.
  1972   Functional considerations of warfare in the southeast during the Mississippi
          Period. *American Antiquity* **37**:38–392.
Lewis, R. Barry
  1974   Mississippian exploitative strategies: A southeast Missouri example. *Missouri Ar-
          chaeological Society, Research Series* **11**.
Lewis, T.M.N. and Madeline Kneberg
  1946   *Hiwassee Island.* Knoxville: University of Tennessee Press.
Lilly, Eli
  1937   *Prehistoric antiquities of Indiana.* Indianapolis. Indiana Historical Bureau.
Malott, C.A.
  1922   The physiography of Indiana. In *Handbook of Indiana Geology.* Indiana Depart-
          ment of Conservation, Publication No. 21 (2): 59–256. Indianapolis.
McFarlan, Arthur C.
  1943   *The geology of Kentucky.* Lexington: The University of Kentucky Press.
Moorehead, Warren K.
  1906   Explorations at the mouth of the Wabash. *Phillips Academy, Bulletin* 3:62–86.
Munson, Cheryl A., and Thomas J. Green
  1973   The Caborn–Welborn complex of southwestern Indiana and Oneota relationships
          with the lower Ohio Valley. Paper presented to the Central States Anthropological

Society, St. Louis. Manuscript on file at the Glenn A. Black Laboratory of Archaeology, Indiana University.

Neitzel, Robert S.
1965   Archaeology of the Fatherland site: The Grand Village of the Natchez. *Anthropology Papers of the American Museum of Natural History* **51**(1).

Parmalee, Paul W.
1961   Faunal materials from the Zimmerman Site (Ls13), LaSalle County, Illinois. In The Zimmerman Site, by James A. Brown. *Illinois State Museum, Report of Investigations* **9**. Springfield.

Phillips, Philip
1970   Archaeological survey in the lower Yazoo River basin, Mississippi, 1944–1955. *Papers of the Peabody Museum of Archaeology and Ethnology* **60**.

Phillips, Philip, James A. Ford, and James B. Griffin
1951   Archaeological survey in the lower Mississippi valley, 1940–1947. *Papers of the Peabody Museum of Archaeology and Ethnology* **25**.

Potzger, J.E., M.E. Potzger, and Jack McCormick
1956   The forest primeval of Indiana as recorded in the original U.S. land surveys and an evaluation of previous interpretations of Indiana vegetation. *Butler University Botanical Studies* **13**:95–111.

Ralph, E.K., H.N. Michael, and M.C. Han
1974   Radiocarbon dates and reality. *Archaeology of Eastern North America* **2**:1–20.

Ray, Louis
1965   Geomorphology and Quaternary geology of the Owensboro quadrangle, Indiana and Kentucky. *U.S. Geological Survey, Professional Paper* **488**. Washington, D.C.

Rowlands, M.J.
1972   Defense: A factor in the organization of settlements. In *Man, settlement, and urbanism,* edited by Peter J. Ucko, Ruth Tringham, and G.W. Dimbleby. Cambridge: Schenkman Publishing Company.

Schall, Lawrence A.
1966   Climate. In *Natural features of Indiana*, edited by Alton Lindsey. Indianapolis: Indianapolis Academy of Science. Pp. 156–170.

Schwartz, Douglas
1962   The Driskill site: A Late Woodland occupation in the lower Cumberland River valley. *Transactions of the Kentucky Academy of Science* **23**:1–13.

Shively, Jerald L., and George McElrath, Jr.
1973   *Soil survey information and interpretations, Warrick County, Indiana.* U.S.D.A. Soil Conservation Service. Washington, D.C.

Struever, Stuart
1968   Problems, methods and organization: A disparity in the growth of archaeology. In *Anthropological archaeology in the americas,* edited by Betty Meggars. Washington D.C.: Anthropological Society of Washington.

Swanton, John R.
1928   Social organization and social usages of the Indians of the Creek confederacy. *U.S. Bureau of American Ethnology, 42nd Annual Report.* Washington, D.C.

Thornbury, W.D.
1965   *Regional geomorphology of the United States.* Bloomington: Indiana University Press.

Thwaites, Reuben G.
1906   *Early western travels, 1748–1846.* Vol. 22. Cleveland: The Arthur H. Clark Co.

Trigger, Bruce
1968   The determinants of settlement patterns. In *Settlement archaeology,* edited by K.C. Chang. Palo Alto: National Press.

1969   *The Huron: Farmers of the north.* New York: Holt.

1976   Inequality and communications in early civilizations. *Anthropologica* **18**:27–52.

Ward, Trawick

1965   Correlation of Mississippian sites and soil types. *Southeastern Archaeological Conference, Bulletin* **3**:42–48.

Wayne, William J.

1956   Thickness of drift and bedrock physiography of Indiana north of the Wisconsin glacial boundary. *Indiana Geological Survey, Report of Progress* **7**. Bloomington.

Willey, Gordon R.

1953   Prehistoric settlement patterns in the Viru Valley, Peru, *U.S. Bureau of American Ethnology, Bulletin* **155**. Washington, D.C.

Williams, Ray

1968   *Southeast Missouri, land leveling salvage archaeology: 1967.* National Park Service.

Williamson, H.F. and Jerald I. Shively

1973   Soil survey conservation service and Purdue University agricultural experiment station. Washington, D.C.

Winters, Howard D.

1967   An archaeological survey of the Wabash Valley in Illinois. *Illinois State Museum, Reports of Investigations* **10**. Springfield.

1969   The Riverton Culture. *Illinois State Museum, Reports of Investigations* No. 13 and *Illinois Archaeological Survey, Monograph 1.* Springfield.

Witthoft, John

1967   Glazed polish on flint tools. *American Antiquity* **32**:383–388.

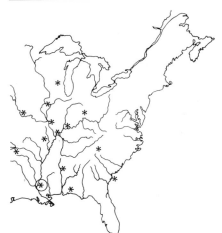

12

Late Prehistoric Settlement Patterning in the Yazoo Basin and Natchez Bluffs Regions of the Lower Mississippi Valley

JEFFREY P. BRAIN

It will be noticed that the key word "Mississippian" is missing in the title of this chapter. The reason for this omission lies in the confusion of definitions attached to the term in the studies of eastern United States prehistory and, more importantly for these considerations, the historical perspective of Lower Mississippi Valley archeology. The genesis and exegesis of the term is the subject of a forthcoming publication (Williams in press) and need not be detailed here. However, it will be recalled that what began as nomenclature for a ceramic assemblage (Holmes 1885, 1886, 1903), was broadened to include a greater range of archeological data (e.g., McKern 1939), and subsequently became a basic unit in culture–historical integration of traditional prehistoric expositions (e.g., Willey and Phillips 1958). More recently, "Mississippian" has been used as a vehicle for processual studies, where it has come to identify the greatest sociopolitical and economic elaborations that occurred during the later prehistory of the eastern United States (e.g., Brown 1971, Griffin 1967, Mosenfelder 1975). There is no quarrel with any of these usages, but the confusion points up an obvious need for clear definition in each case of application.

The late prehistory of the Lower Mississippi Valley is characterized by cultural developments as elaborate as most any to be found in the eastern

331

United States. In fact, the earliest indications of such elaboration in the East might be identified in the indigenous development of the Coles Creek culture, which was well underway by A.D. 700 in the southern part of the valley (Phillips 1970, Williams and Brain in press). The fact of this precedence and subsequent continuity expressed by the Coles-Creek–Plaquemine cultural tradition throughout the last millennium of prehistory, even in the face of mounting external pressures during the final five centuries, make it important to recognize the continuum as a distinctive phenomenon in its own right. The most important external pressures that came to influence this tradition—and that were instrumental in transforming the Coles Creek culture into the Plaquemine culture—came downriver from the northern part of the valley, an area equivalent to the old Middle Mississippi province in the terminology of Holmes (1903). These influences were not in the form of a single isolated event, but rather consisted of a series of multifaceted phenomena (Brain in press). Although separate episodes of northern influence may have been sponsored by different sociocultural groups for very different reasons, all are archeologically recognized as similar artifactual complexes, site plans, settlement patterns, and inferred behaviors, which, in the context of the regions of study, are not seen as indigenous, but did have contemporary counterparts farther upriver. It is this traditionalist set of criteria for the definition of Mississippian which is used here, because such criteria *can* be recognized archeologically. It is conceptually important to be able to distinguish the interplay of two highly developed but very different cultural traditions, and their overall environmental adaptations, in the analysis of late prehistoric settlement patterning in the Yazoo and Natchez regions of the Lower Mississippi Valley.

Background

The focus of this study will be that part of the Lower Mississippi Valley lying between 31°15' and 34°00' north latitude in the state of Mississippi. In physiographic terms, these coordinates describe that portion of the east bank of the Mississippi River defined on the south by the Homochitto River and on the north by the confluence of the Arkansas River, and containing the Natchez Bluffs and Lower Yazoo regions (Figure 12.1).

THE ENVIRONMENT

A particular value of this study lies in the opportunity to contrast these two contiguous regions that were subjected to similar cultural influences

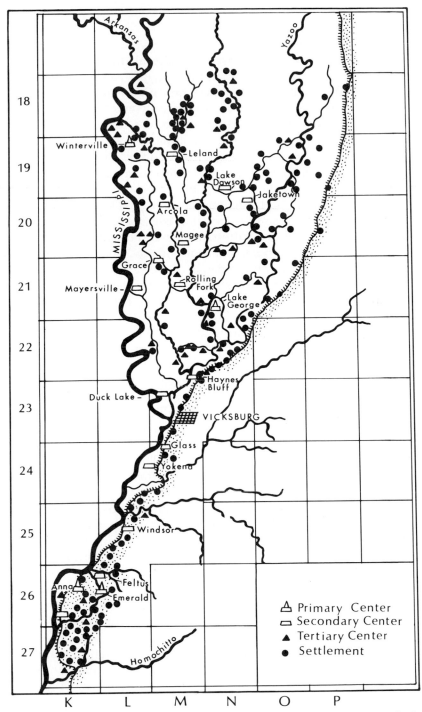

FIGURE 12.1. *The settlement pattern of the Mississippi period occupation in the Lower Yazoo and Natchez Bluffs regions.*

333

and yet often manifest distinctively different responses, as well as important similarities, in details of observed cultural development. The two regions exhibit some very diverse environmental features, but it is to be emphasized that the cultural differences may not be attributed entirely to contrasts in the natural setting. Still, geologically and topographically, the Yazoo and Natchez regions could hardly be less similar.

The alluvial bottomlands of the Yazoo Basin are, of course, the creation of the Mississippi River. Deposited during the recent period of aggradation, approximately the last 10,000 years, myriad soils drawn from a continental drainage some 1,000,000 mi^2 in extent have been interbedded into an immensely heterogeneous pedology. However, the significance of this complicated soil composition is considerably overshadowed by the nature of alluvial deposition, which sorts water-carried particles into two major categories: clays and sandy loams. The sandy loams were deposited as natural levees on the banks of the active channel of the river and lower reaches of tributary streams. They were the highest, best drained, most easily worked soils in the valley. The most favored landforms of all were the older natural levees on recently abandoned channels, for they had the highest elevations and so the best drainage. For agriculturists who also wished to keep their feet dry these were the choice settlement locations. In fact, this choice was very circumscribed since such locations constituted a very small percentage of the total alluvial surface, with the greater part consisting of young levees still in the process of formation, backslopes, and swamps—all subject to seasonal overflow or permanent inundation. Interlacing all, of course, were the riverine and lacustrine features that dominate the land. The topographic diversity is not expressed in dramatic topographic relief. The valley floor is a flatland in which less than 1 m difference in elevation may be as important ecologically as 30 m in a hilly upland region.

The loess bluffs of the Natchez region are composed of an extremely homogeneous silty loam of aeolian origin. The Natchez Bluffs are among the largest loess deposits in the world. Literally rising in a sheer face, sometimes over 100 m high, the bluffs dramatically define the eastern margin of the valley, and often the bank of the river itself. In fact, since the river hugs the east side of the valley in this region, there are only small pieces of alluvial bottomland on the east side of the river in the meander loops swinging away from the bluffs. These were continually reworked by the river. The obvious locations for permanent settlements were the bluff tops, particularly along the interior drainages, although the talus slopes and small stretches of alluvial bottoms could also be profitably exploited. However, for agricultural purposes, loess is one of the most productive soil groups in the world, when adequately watered and drained, so that there was considerable latitude for settlement patterning in this region. Or, perhaps, better to say longitude, for the Natchez Bluffs, as an environmental and topographic feature, stretch for a considerable distance north–south, but quickly thin out to the east and within 8–32 km of the valley are replaced by the more limited potential sandy soils and piney woods so characteristic of the Gulf coastal plain. Archeological investigations have revealed that aboriginal occupation generally fades sharply 5–8 km from the bluff edge. Clearly, the attenuated bluffs were not choice locations, except where they were penetrated by a major tributary stream.

Beyond the dissimilarities of geology and topography, the Yazoo Basin and Natchez Bluffs regions share certain environmental advantages: 127–152 cm of annual rainfall and moderate temperatures create an almost subtropical climate, which originally supported a lush natural biota, as well as nearly ideal conditions for the agriculturists of late prehistory. Because of the great variability between and within the two regions there was a wide array of flora and fauna that could be exploited. From the swamps of the lowlands, in which cypress and tupelo gum, alligators and other reptiles predominated, to the oaks, honey locusts, cottonwoods, canebrakes, and associated mammals and birds of the levees, to the mixed-hardwood forests and faunal communities of the hilly uplands, to the riverine products of the great and small streams cross-cutting all, most conceivable requirements for human sustenance were available. To what degree these resources were exploited is not presently known in detail, but the possibilities were great. It is probable that different populations at different times concentrated on different resources, their orientation toward different energy sources being reflected in settlement distributions. By the late prehistoric period, however, the most productive aspects of the natural environment must have been recognized and selectively incorporated into the broadly based subsistence–settlement patterns the success of which is being documented for other parts of the valley (e.g., Lewis 1974, Price, in press, Smith 1975). This said, such concerns will largely be ignored in the following pages, for reasons to be given in the summary of this chapter.

THE ARCHEOLOGY

The Yazoo and Natchez regions have been the object of considerable archeological investigation. The period of modern archeology began with James A. Ford (1936), and has continued at an intensive level to the present (Phillips, Ford, and Griffin 1951, Ford, Phillips, and Haag 1955, Greengo 1964, Neitzel 1965, Brain 1969, 1970a, 1971b, 1975, 1977, 1978, in press, n. d., Phillips 1970, I. W. Brown 1973, 1975, 1978, Brain, Brown, and Steponaitis n. d., Brain, Toth, and Rodriquez-Buckingham 1974, Steponaitis 1974, Brown and Brain 1977, Williams and Brain in press). This work was carried out largely under the auspices of the Lower Mississippi

Survey, an informal collaboration of scholars who share a research interest in the archeology of the Mississippi Valley (Williams and Brain 1970). Support has been provided by the National Endowment for the Humanities, National Science Foundation, National Geographic Society, and private contributions.

The archeological data accumulated for over 50 years (Ford began work in 1927) was gathered in a variety of ways. Field procedures were determined by the varied objectives of the investigators, limited by the actual condition of the land. Because the regions have been surveyed and resurveyed a number of times, the overall survey coverage has been relatively complete except where archeological surfaces have been destroyed or are inaccessible owing to modern conditions of terrain, vegetation, and development. Although intensive archeological survey was perhaps not an integral aspect of the original research strategy in any given case, the cumulative results of these projects represents as close to a total site sample as may ever be achieved. An obvious drawback of such a data base is that because it is derived from a number of sources it is of unequal quality, which often makes comparison difficult. Compounding this problem are the forces of man and nature, which have literally changed the face of the land during the last century and a half.

In the alluvial valley, modern man, with his emphasis upon a single-crop agricultural economy, has drastically changed the natural environment rather than adapted to it. By the construction of great artificial levees to contain the Mississippi, the draining and leveling of the land, the clearing of the floodplain forests, and the implementation of modern agricultural methods, the original physical appearance and the biotic community of the valley have been completely altered. Similarly, the archeology has been affected. Although land clearing has revealed many sites, mechanized methods of agriculture have also disturbed or destroyed at least as many. Thus, determination of original site size and structure is often impossible.

The Natchez Bluffs were stripped of their natural vegetation cover and intensively farmed during the nineteenth century. The beautifully rugged hills melted away, for once erosion commences, loess is subject to terrible dissection and deflation. This has occurred to some degree in all parts of the bluffs, with the worst damage evident in the more desirable locales— those most favored by prehistoric populations as well as by modern farmers. The erosion has had a devastating impact on archeological sites. All too often, although we may be able to identify the locus of past occupations, the sites themselves have been irretrievably altered. Furthermore, in recognition of past mistakes (but seeming more like a cabal against the archeologist), much of the Natchez Bluffs region is once again covered by forests, a conservation effort that hampers archeological survey to an almost impossible degree.

In both regions, the larger the site, the better the archeological features have withstood the ravages of man and nature. Fortunately, most of the mound sites were recorded before modern machinery made it too easy to tear down a mound, so that even where such destruction has occurred we still have some usable data regarding site size and structure. Thus, in both regions, there is probably a nearly complete record of the major sites, whereas the representation of sites in the smaller categories decreases proportionally as the chance of archeological recovery diminishes. The problem is especially serious in the Natchez region, for reasons already noted. Although there may be problems with the sample, there is nevertheless a large corpus of archeological data available for interpretive studies of the late prehistoric occupation of the Lower Yazoo and Natchez Bluffs regions.

THE PREHISTORY

As a result of previous research, we now have relatively good control over the culture history ("cultural" continuity and change) of this part of the Lower Mississippi Valley. The broadest cultural trends may be traced, and a fair discrimination of the prehistoric record has resulted in a coarse framework of regional chronologies (Table 12.1).

Highly evolved patterns of cultural development in the Lower Valley can be traced to the first millennium A.D. The most important of these is the Coles Creek culture, which began to take form about the middle of the millennium. This culture was similar to Mississippian in a number of respects, most notably in the construction and use of pyramidal mounds, a trait it seems to have pioneered. A particular characteristic of the development of Coles Creek which is important to the following discussion is that it was quite provincial in its manifestation. Coles Creek populations seem to have independently developed a closely ordered and highly successful cultural adaptation, which was restricted to the rich bottomlands of the southern part of the valley. The Lower Yazoo and Natchez regions, together with the Tensas Basin on the west side of the river, were the core area of Coles Creek development. The strength of this early cultural adaptation to these regions formed an important foundation for subsequent events.

By A.D. 1100, Coles Creek had expanded as far north as the latitude of the Arkansas River (Figure 12.2). At that time, it was a strong, well-organized, remarkably homogeneous culture (in archeological terms). The homogeneous material culture probably reflects the close interaction of well-developed but independent sociopolitical units. This was the cultural background with which the growing Mississippian phenomena would interact.

TABLE 12.1
Late Prehistoric Chronologies for the Lower Yazoo and Natchez Bluffs Regions of the Lower Mississippi Valley

Period	Calendar	Natchez Bluffs	Lower Yazoo	Culture	¹⁴C[a]
MISSISSIPPI	A.D. 1700 / 1600	Natchez	Russell	MISSISSIPPIAN	1585 ± 100(F)
					1540 + 100(F)
	1500	Emerald	Wasp Lake		1420 + 125(G)
					1410 ± 110(W)
	1400	Foster	Lake George		1330 ± 125(W)
					1310 ± 110(W)
	1300	Anna	Winterville	PLAQUEMINE	
	1200	Cahokia Horizon			1230 ± 110(W)
					1220 ± 90(W)
BAYTOWN	1100	Gordon	Crippen Point	COLES CREEK	1090 ± 115(G)
	1000				1040 ± 80(W)

[a]F = Fatherland, G = Lake George, W = Winterville.

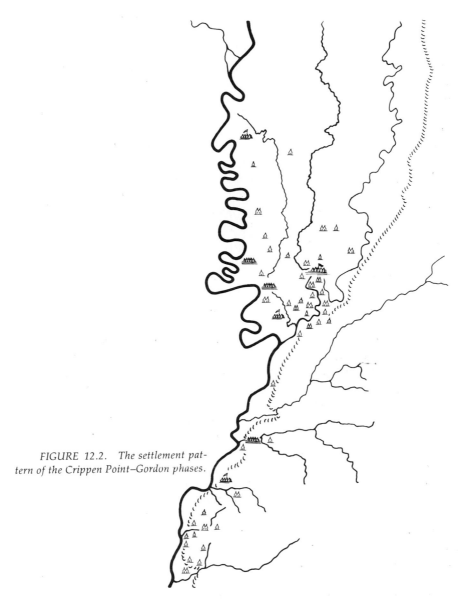

*FIGURE 12.2.   The settlement pat-
tern of the Crippen Point–Gordon phases.*

Through time, the indigenous Coles Creek cultural tradition was increasingly affected by the influence of Mississippian developments farther north in the Lower Valley. Because the Yazoo region was closer to this external stimulus it might be expected that the cultural impact would be greater—and so it proves. The Yazoo and Natchez regions thus also allow for a comparative analysis of the influence of Mississippian cultural systems on this area of the Lower Valley.

Systems of Late Prehistoric Settlement Patterning

More than 200 sites can be identified in the Yazoo and Natchez regions which date to the half millennium ca. A.D. 1200–1700, labeled by Phillips (1970) as the Mississippi period. Sites are identified as belonging within this period on the basis of recovery of diagnostic artifactual materials, usually ceramic types and modes. In the Yazoo Basin, diagnostic ceramics are strongly "Mississippian" in character, especially in terms of an increasing use of shell tempering. In the Natchez Bluffs region, the influence is not as strong, but is present so that solid correlations can be made with the indigenous Plaquemine ceramic types and modes. Sites dating to this temporal period range from small loci—apparently minimal residential or other functional units, yielding a mere handful of artifactual data from the surface—to the great multimound groups presumed to be primary "ceremonial" centers.

In Table 12.2 Mississippi period sites are ranked according to the number and size of mound features present. The sites listed in Table 12.2 were not occupied continually throughout the 500-year-long Mississippi period, and will be discussed within a more detailed temporal context later in this chapter. For the moment, however, it is worthwhile to assume that such a detailed chronological chart of the Mississippi period as shown in Table 12.1 does not exist. How would the "Mississippian" (A.D. 1200–1700) occupation of these two regions be interpreted? A distributional map, purporting to represent the settlement pattern of the Mississippi period in the Lower Yazoo and Natchez Bluffs regions, would appear as in Figure 12.1. The picture is one of high population density and an obvious hierarchy of stratified sites, inviting the archeologist to apply sophisticated models of analysis that would lead to interpretations of social, political, and economic significance.

For example, it might be seen in the apparent settlement pattern of the Yazoo Basin shown in Figure 12.1 that there are two large primary centers spaced some 80 km apart. In between, situated with considerable spatial regularity, are a number of secondary centers. Tertiary centers are relatively evenly spaced over the entire landscape, considering the broken nature of the terrain. Altogether, an apparent hierarchical distribution can be seen which would seem to lend itself to the locational and nearest-neighbor analyses of central-place theory (e.g., Christaller 1966). But there is a significant disconformity when the smallest settlement units are considered. Although these are distributed throughout the Yazoo Basin, many are located some distance away from the primary and secondary centers, some of which have very few "satellite" sites. If these smaller sites were the basic production–extraction units within the system, then factors other than efficiency of transportation and redistribution of goods within the system would seem to be operating.

TABLE 12.2
Mississippi Period (A.D. 1200–1700) Settlements in the Lower Yazoo and Natchez Bluffs Regions.[a]

PRIMARY

Centers: Multimound sites with at least one dominant mound more than 15 m in height

Winterville (19-L-1)	Anna (26-K-1)
Lake George (21-N-1)	Emerald (26-L-1)

Total: 4

SECONDARY

Centers: Multimound sites with one mound about 10 m in height

Leland (19-M-1)	Haynes Bluff (22-M-5)
Lake Dawson (19-N-6)	Duck Lake (23-M-6)
Arcola (20-M-1)	Yokena (24-M-1)
Magee (20-M-2)	Glass (24-M-2)
Jaketown (20-O-1)	Windsor (25-L-15)
Mayersville (21-L-1)	Linwood (26-K-5)
Rolling Fork (21-M-1)	Feltus (25-K-42)
Grace (21-M-7)	

Total: 15

TERTIARY

Centers: Mound sites with one or more mounds ca. 5 m in height

Neblett Landing (18-L-1)	Silver City (20-O-5)
Perkins (18-L-2)	Mount Helena (21-M-2)
Shadyside Landing (18-L-3)	Lowery (21-M-4)
Huntington Camp (18-L-6)	Cary (21-M-5)
Lipe (18-M-4)	Shellwood (21-O-9)
Choctaw (18-M-6)	Jeff Davis (22-M-2)
Marlow (18-N-1)	Aden (22-M-3)
Boyer (18-N-7)	Manny (22-M-6)
Metcalfe (19-L-4)	Hardee (22-M-8)
Refuge (19-L-6)	Leist (22-N-1)
Ash Bayou (19-L-7)	Enola Landing (22-N-5)
Kinlock (19-N-1)	Dornbusch (22-N-6)
Failing (19-N-5)	Landrum (22-N-10)
McLean (19-O-1)	Gammel (22-N-21)
Shell Bluff (19-O-2)	Bayou Pierre (25-L-26)
Law (20-L-1)	Fatherland (26-K-2)
Griffin (20-L-3)	Foster (26-K-3)
Swan Lake (20-M-5)	Quitman (26-K-6)
Midnight (20-N-1)	Mazique (27-K-1)
Summerfield (20-N-2)	Shieldsboro (27-K-15)
Fort (20-O-3)	

Total: 41

Settlements: Mound(s) may be present, but are less than 3 m in height. (Many of these sites are multicomponent and have minor occupations assigned to this period on the basis of a handful of Mississippi Plain potsherds.)

Total: 148

[a] Site categories were determined on the basis of the number and the size of mound features.

The Natchez Bluffs region presents a very interesting contrast in overall site distribution (Figure 12.1). The two primary centers, Anna and Emerald, are situated within 16 km of each other—an unusual concentration of power—whereas secondary centers are strung along the entire bluff edge at fairly regular intervals. The small number of tertiary centers, however, are concentrated in the south, as are the fourth-order sites, which group most closely around the primary centers. This is certainly a much different pattern, requiring a locational model different from that which might have been developed for the Yazoo Basin.

But it is all an illusion. Or, at least, it is a badly distorted view of prehistory which ignores an important aspect of archeological studies— the measure of change through time—by the reduction of a complex series of patterns to a single synchronic surreality. Let us now see what happens when, as is now possible, this mélange is discriminated into its component phases.

The regional chronologies of the Yazoo and Natchez regions are parallel in structure (Table 12.1). That is, each is composed of a series of phases similarly ordered in time, a convenience that makes it possible to structure the following presentation in equally comparable segments. Thus, commencing with a brief background description of the settlement pattern of the latest Coles Creek phases in the two regions, the developments that occurred during the succeeding phases of the Mississippi period will be examined similarly region to region.

Figures 12.2, 12.4, 12.5, 12.7, and 12.8 show the sites that were occupied during the different phases of the Mississippi period. The phases are brief enough segments of time so that the sites assigned to each phase may be considered contemporaneous. Those sites that have not yielded specific phase artifact diagnostics have been omitted, which limits the sample, but, it is hoped, keeps each individual pattern as accurate as possible. All the sites excluded from consideration belong to the smaller categories (Table 12.2). Those small sites that can be identified according to phase of occupation are plotted on the regional maps (Figures 12.2, 12.4, 12.5, 12.7, 12.8), and those with an especially strong assemblage of artifact diagnostics are indicated by a double symbol. Tertiary sites are small mound sites with appropriate artifact diagnostics, but the evidence indicates that most "tertiary" sites were actually earlier mound centers that were reoccupied during the Mississippi period with no appreciable construction or other modification. Primary and secondary sites are not ranked by size, per se, but rather according to their relative importance, as determined by apparent emphasis on site construction and usage during each phase of occupation: in other words, as foci of human activity.

A major weakness of the following settlement pattern formulations is that although it is possible to discriminate sites according to relative size and number of platform mounds, and to presume that there is some atten-

dant functional significance along one or more scales, it is not now possible to determine particular site functions in any satisfactory detail. Thus,
the value of this study is in terms of establishing a series of synchronous
site occupations and their geographic interrelationships. Some hypotheses will be offered concerning the settlement patterns to be described,
but it should be kept in mind that these hypotheses are recognized as
being only a partial, and perhaps inaccurate, description of past events.
The basic theme to be elaborated upon here is simply an appreciation of
the dynamic changes in settlement patterning which can be seen to have
occurred through time in the Lower Yazoo and Natchez Bluffs regions.

CRIPPEN POINT—GORDON

The patterning of late Coles Creek settlements in the Yazoo and
Natchez regions appear remarkably similar, considering the great
physiographic differences (Figure 12.2). There is clearly a marked preference for settlement near the main channel of the Mississippi River along
the lower courses of tributary streams, especially where they coincided
with the bluff margins. The arable bottomlands along these streams would
have been especially suitable for a developing agricultural capability, such
as that hypothesized, but not yet documented, for Coles Creek; and the
bluff ecotone would have allowed equal access to the varied resources of
both the uplands and the alluvial valley.

Insofar as can be determined, the sites of the Crippen Point and
Gordon phases are modest in dimensions, and when mound features are
present they are small in size and number. The late Coles Creek settlement
pattern seems to have been one of population dispersal in hamlets and
small villages scattered over the prime bottomland. Some of the larger
villages had mounds, typically two to four in number, approximately
equal in size, with none higher than 7 m (Williams 1956:58). These
mounds are usually concentrated on the south side of the plaza. The
largest known site—in all probability, an illusion, due to the fact that only
there has sufficient archeology been done—appears to have been Lake
George at the center of the population concentration along the lower Yazoo
River. A number of smaller mound sites were also distributed along the
Mississippi River in both regions. The settlement pattern is apparently
one of small local centers serving local populations while interacting directly at the regional level on a relatively equal footing. In other words,
there is no evidence that any site, including Lake George, was preeminent
over the rest, or that there was a highly structured regional sociopolitical
organization that would have enforced such a hierarchy. The absence of
such a hierarchy is especially evident if the simple pattern of disposal of
the dead is sufficient indication (the mortuary practices of some Islamic

sects, however, should give pause for reconsideration): Even at the larger mound sites, burials of all ages and sexes were equally consigned to the earth with a minimum of differential treatment (e.g., Ford 1951, Williams and Brain in press).

Overall, the distribution of sites within the Yazoo Basin and Natchez Bluffs regions demonstrates a general population orientation toward the main channel of the Mississippi River, which should be expected since the Tensas Basin on the west side of the main channel was an equal partner in the Coles Creek culture. This segment of the Mississippi River, then, was a central artery for Coles Creek interaction and development. It was also to become an avenue for new introductions.

Toward the end of the twelfth century, a striking intrusion appears in the archeological record of the Yazoo Basin. At a number of sites, artifacts diagnostic of Cahokia have been found (Brain 1969, Phillips 1970, Williams and Brain in press). Although these sites are more widely dispersed than the Crippen Point occupation of the Basin, most of the contact seems to have been with sites located at strategic demographic or natural points. The nature and the possible motivations for this contact are explored elsewhere (Brain in press) and need not be a matter of concern here beyond the fact of its occurrence, the external source, and the dramatic impact it apparently had upon the settlement patterning of the Yazoo Basin and Natchez Bluffs regions. This external contact set the stage for, and almost certainly prompted, the great developments that were to come.

WINTERVILLE—ANNA

The direct Cahokia contact that intruded into the late Coles Creek occupations seems to have been of brief duration. Strongly and widely manifest, but of no great duration, at least in the Lower Mississippi Valley, it thus provides a secure reference point, a bright horizon for other events to be measured against. This is especially important when the developments that next transpired in the Lower Yazoo Basin and Natchez Bluffs regions are considered.

The most striking development in the Lower Valley during the thirteenth and fourteenth centuries is a grand florescence. In the area of focus this was the zenith of prehistoric aboriginal achievement, if the construction of major mound centers is an adequate criterion. The most fascinating aspect of this florescence is that although it seems to have been stimulated by outside influences, it was largely an indigenous affair. That is, although the Mississippian cultural tradition generally, and Cahokia specifically, were perhaps responsible for some inspiration and continuing input, the phenomenon found in the Yazoo and Natchez regions was not transplanted Mississippian of whatever genre. Rather, as archeologically manifested, it was a distinctive blend of northern and southern elements, quite literally a hybridization that led to unusual achievements. This is the Plaquemine culture. Quite simply, the concept of Plaquemine, as used here, is best expressed as "Mississippianized" Coles Creek—that is, neither one nor the other, but the vigorous product of both [this is quite different from the concept offered by Quimby (1942, 1951), Cotter (1951), Ford (1951), and Phillips (1970)].

Nowhere is the process and the product better expressed than in artifactual materials, especially ceramics. Pottery types of both northern and southern origin are present, and there are many instances of unusual combinations of modes from both traditions. But whereas this ceramic evidence documents the process, and helps to define the product, it is of little interpretive value in and of itself.

The most observable archeological evidence of this Plaquemine florescence is earthwork construction. Pyramidal mounds arranged around a plaza were noted to be characteristic of the Coles Creek culture, but there is a striking quantitative and qualitative change that occured in the Yazoo and Natchez regions. There are more mound sites than ever before, they are considerably larger, and they have more mounds, sometimes arranged around multiple plazas. Furthermore, the mounds themselves are larger: The principal mounds at Winterville, Lake George, and Anna are nearly 20 m high and cover up to 1.6 ha, which is four times the size of the average Coles Creek mound. Altogether, there is an emphasis that has been labeled, with some lack of felicitation, "megalomoundia."

In the Yazoo Basin, the primary sites, Winterville and Lake George, boast more than two dozen mounds each (Figure 12.3), and although there may have previously been modest Coles Creek mounds present on the site, they represent but a small portion of the great bulk of earthen construction (Brain 1969, Williams and Brain in press). Thick mantles were added to Coles Creek mounds and many new mounds were constructed. At both Winterville and Lake George, new plazas were established to the east of the large focal mound, and all of the mounds situated around these eastern plazas were built during this phase. The emphasis upon one mound above all others and its placement on the west side of the principal plaza are distinctly non-Coles-Creek traits, but were characteristic of contemporary Mississippian sites (Reed 1969). The Windsor and Anna sites in the Natchez region also display this basic site plan.

Although the Yazoo Basin sites tend to be of greater magnitude and complexity than their Natchez counterparts, the disparity was often compensated for by taking advantage of the spectacular topography of the Bluffs region. In the Natchez region, the river followed the eastern margin of the valley, and often touched the very base of the bluffs. Where those bluffs arose almost straight up from the river in imposing splendor, sites were placed in a commanding position at the summit. As striking exam-

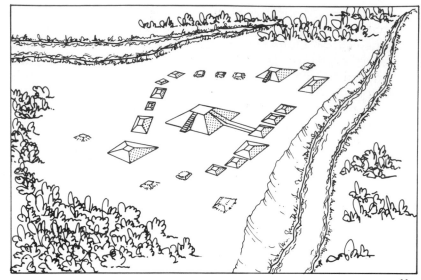

Winterville

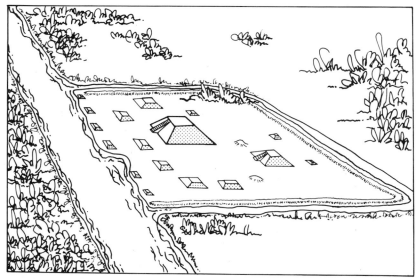

Lake George

FIGURE 12.3. *Primary mound centers of the Winterville phase in the Lower Yazoo Basin. Both sites have nearly identical site plans, except that Lake George was fortified with palisade and moat during the declining occupation of the Lake George phase.*

ples, the principal mounds at the Anna and Feltus sites were located at the bluff edge so that a single 61-m slope from mound summit to valley floor was formed. These sites were meant to be seen and to command. They faced the world (or what must have been the symbol of it—the Mississippi River) and were in close communication with each other.

The archeological evidence is convincing in detailing the fact that the series of mound sites illustrated in Figure 12.4 was the result of a massive public works campaign (Table 12.3). All the major construction seems to have occurred within a relatively brief period of 50–100 years. Such evident organization of the local societies is itself an important change from the comparatively modest level of organization to be inferred for the Coles Creek culture.

Since the mounds are assumed to have served a primarily socioreligious function, it is reasonable to suggest the introduction at this point in time of a strong religious belief system as the inspiration for these developments. Because of the dramatic evidence of mound-construction activities an hypothesis was formulated that the motivation for the Cahokia intrusion was some sort of fervid proselytism (Brain 1969). That this introduction of a religious belief system, regardless of its actual nature, was welcomed by the inhabitants of the Yazoo Basin is evident, although we cannot yet explain why. Whatever the reason, the hypothesis in question provides an explanation for the vast construction projects. The organization required for such projects, which was replicated over a wide area and in very different contexts, may have been derived from a central elite, perhaps symbolized by the great focal mounds at the primary sites. But the motivations of this elite may have been far more complex than is evident in the theocratic trappings. This suspicion takes on substance when specific geographic correlations are made.

Referring again to Figure 12.4, the site distributions of the Winterville phase in the Lower Yazoo region and the Anna phase in the Natchez Bluffs region provide some intriguing clues. These distributions must be considered on the local level, as well as in terms of the broader patterns of extraregional relationships. It will be noted that comparatively large population densities are manifest in the Yazoo Basin and Natchez Bluffs regions at this time. Also manifest (although perhaps not as clearly in Figure 12.4) is a change in demographic patterning as the settlement pattern appears to show a nucleation around the special centers under construction. These centers also increased somewhat in population, although they do not seem to have become true towns with large numbers of permanent residents. In this deviation from the usual Mississippian pattern, they are faithful to the Coles Creek precedent—another interesting example of the blend of traditions.

Beyond demography, these centers demonstrate a very special topographic relationship with the land. All of the major centers of these phases,

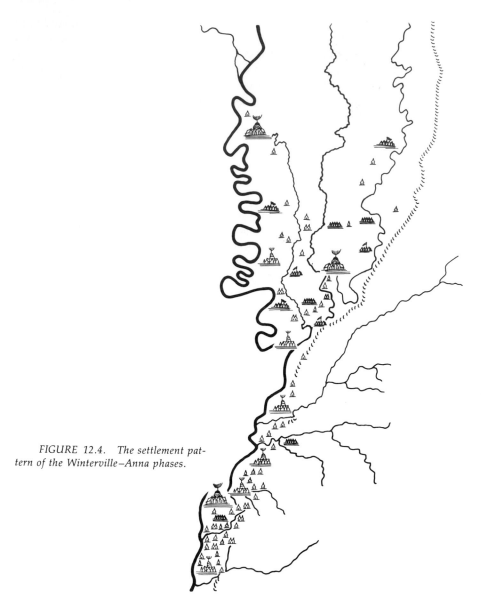

FIGURE 12.4. *The settlement pattern of the Winterville–Anna phases.*

with the single exception of the Lake George site, are located along the Mississippi River. Furthermore, they are strategically situated at what were then the major confluences or distributaries of the Mississippi River, the major points of control of the entire riverine system in these regions. Winterville was at the Arkansas confluence and Deer Creek distributary, Mayersville at the Bayou Macon and Steele Bayou distributaries, Duck

TABLE 12.3
Phases of Principal Mound Construction and Usage at Primary and Secondary Sites in the Lower Yazoo and Natchez Bluffs Regions

Site	Winterville	Lake George	Wasp Lake	Russell
Winterville	XXXXXXXXXXXxxxxxxxxxxxxxxxxxxxx			
Lake George	XXXXXXXXXXXxxxxxxxxxxxxxxxxxxxx			
Mayersville	xxxxxxxxxxxxxxx			
Duck Lake	xxxxxxxxxxxxxxx			
Lake Dawson		xxxxxxxxxxxxxxxxx		
Leland		xxxxxxxxxxxxxxxxxxxxxxxxxxxxxxxxxxxxx		
Arcola		xxxxxxxxxxxxxxxxxxxxxxxxxxxxxxxxxxxxx		
Magee		xxxxxxxxxxxxxxxxxxxxxxxxxxxxxxxxxxxxx		
Jaketown		xxxxxxxxxxxxxxxxxxxxxxxxxxxxxxxxxxxxx		
Rolling Fork		xxxxxxxxxxxxxxxxxxxxxxxxxxxxxxxxxxxxx		
Grace		xxxxxxxxxxxxxxxxxxxxxxxxxxxxxxxxxxxxx		
Haynes Bluff		xxxxxxxxxxxxxxxxxxxxxxxxxxxxxxxxxxxxxxxxxxxxxxxxxx		

Site	Anna	Foster	Emerald	Natchez
Anna	XXXXXXXXXXXxxxxxxxxxxxxxxxxxxxx			
Emerald		xxxxxxxxxxxxxxxxxxx	XXXXXXXXXX	
Yokena	xxxxxxxxxxxxxx			
Windsor	xxxxxxxxxxxxxx			
Feltus	xxxxxxxxxxxxxx			
Shieldsboro	xxxxxxxxxxxxxx			
Glass		xxxxxxxxxxxxxxxxxxxxxxxxxxxxxxxxxxxxx		
Foster			xxxxxxxxxxxxxxx	
Fatherland			xxxxxxxxxxxxxxxxxxxxxxxxxxxxxxxxxx	

Lake at the Yazoo confluence, Yokena at the Big Black confluence, Windsor at the Bayou Pierre confluence, Anna and Feltus at the Fairchild–Coles-Creek confluence and Tensas distributary (this location may have had a double significance in communication, for it was also on the principal east–west land route, which crossed the river at this point, known in historic times as the "Natchez Portage"), and Shieldsboro at the confluence of the Homochitto. Quite clearly, there was a strong orientation toward the Mississippi, and perhaps even a conscious attempt to control movement along it.

These centers may have been more than control points at critical junctures; following popular economic theories, they may also have functioned as regional "redistribution" centers that were part of, but not necessarily subject to, a larger interactive network. Such an interpretation is consistent with the evidence. It explains the location of secondary centers at intermediate points along the river, and it also explains the Lake George site as a primary center for a secondary river system, for the Yazoo is actually the most important river on the east bank of the Mississippi south of the Ohio. Furthermore, it suggests a local development, which is consistent with the concept of the Plaquemine culture that was so relatively homogeneous (like its Coles Creek parent) in its archeological manifestation in the regions involved. Regional interaction on a grander scale is testified to by the continuing introduction of new Mississippian traits, especially evident in ceramic and lithic types of northern origin. In the other direction, such distinctive Lower Valley artifacts as the Alba, Scallorn, and Bayogoula point types and L'Eau Noire pottery have been found at Cahokia and related sites in the north (O'Brien 1972). The relationship with Cahokia, however, fades during this phase. Whether this is to be interpreted as a weakening of Cahokia as a prime mover and direct influence or as an indication of a strengthening of a broader based interaction sphere requires more perspective than is available in this study. The question should be the object of wider inquiry and synthesis.

Eventually, in the broader perspective, a generalized Mississippian pattern was to become established as far south as the Yazoo River. The Plaquemine frontier fell back to the Natchez region. We cannot say by what processes of acculturation this was accomplished until the right questions are asked within the context of an appropriate research design. It is clear, however, that the severe demographic displacements that occurred in the concluding centuries of prehistory played a significant role in this process. These changes first become evident on the regional level during the Lake George and Foster phases.

LAKE GEORGE—FOSTER

During the later stages of the prehistoric record, some major changes occurred in the settlement patterns for the Yazoo Basin and Natchez Bluffs regions. First, there was a fragmentation of the homogeneous Plaquemine culture sphere. Although there was direct continuity of the Plaquemine in the Foster and Emerald phases of the Natchez region, the populations of the Yazoo Basin became increasingly "Mississippianized." The delicate balance of the Plaquemine culture was slowly overwhelmed as the Yazoo Basin was subjected to new influences in the Lake George and Wasp Lake phases (Brain 1969, Phillips 1970).

Although the populations in the Yazoo Basin and Natchez Bluffs regions seem to have remained relatively stable, a dramatic change in settlement pattern orientation began to evolve (Figure 12.5). Starting in the Lake George and Foster phases, and increasingly thereafter, a definite shift away from the Mississippi River and toward the interior is evident.

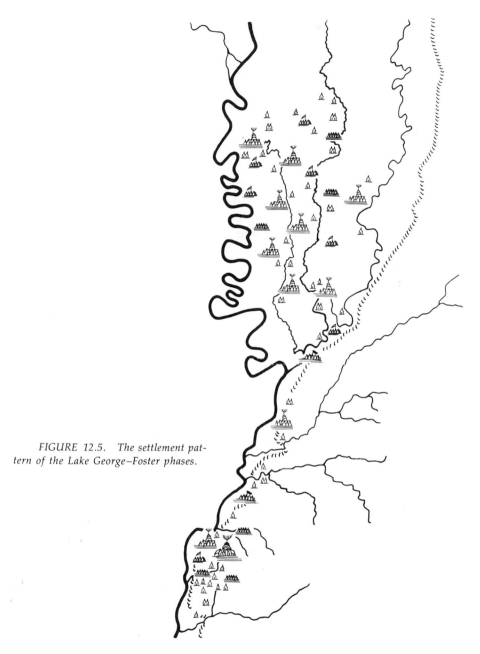

FIGURE 12.5. The settlement pattern of the Lake George–Foster phases.

Most of the great centers on the river were abandoned during these phases, being replaced by others located on interior drainages.

Thus, by the end of the fourteenth century, Mayersville, Duck Lake, Yokena, Feltus, and Shieldsboro were completely deserted, whereas

Windsor and Anna were in the process of being abandoned (Table 12.3). An apparent exception to the pattern is the intermediately placed Glass site, which gained prominence at this time. It alone seems to cling to the river, filling a role as yet unexplained. A tentative hypothesis is that the Glass site was more closely associated with the occupation on the west bank than any of the other Yazoo or Natchez sites, an hypotheses that derives some support from later associations to be described in what follows. But with this exception there is a notable rejection of the main channel of the Mississippi River.

In the Yazoo Basin this major change in the focus of the settlement patterning is especially marked. The basic pattern of the Winterville phase featured large, strategically placed centers which were inferred to have exercised strong, but as yet ill-defined, control over a widely dispersed population. During the Lake George phase, however, these large centers suffered a decline. At both Winterville and Lake George there was a manifest depopulation, with a concomitant reduction of emphasis on mound construction and a decrease in the extent of site utilization (Brain 1969, n.d., Williams and Brain in press). It is clear that although both of these sites may have retained some importance, the principal focus of mound construction (and presumably other activities) was shared by a number of secondary sites built at intervals along the Yazoo and other interior streams. For some reason, the population turned inward and concentrated in more numerous but smaller centers. What all this means in sociopolitical terms is moot, but a change in the cultural structure is evident. It would seem that the population was increasingly organized around smaller, competing local centers, rather than being dispersed and dominated by the large regional centers of the Winterville phase.

In the Natchez region, however, the preeminence of the primary center (and a centralized sociopolitical structure?) was dramatically reinforced. The Natchez populations did not focus their efforts on secondary centers. Rather, as the Anna site was being abandoned, construction was underway concurrently at the great Emerald Mound (Brain *et al.* n.d.). Second in magnitude only to Monks Mound at Cahokia as a single late prehistoric earthwork construction, Emerald not only replicates the site plan of Anna but in a remarkable physiographic recreation, is placed upon a man-made bluff top, the so-called "mound" (Figure 12.6). Clearly, the populations who built Emerald wanted a duplicate of Anna, but at a safe distance from the river.

The suggestion of "safety" probably provides only part of the explanation for the basic reorientation of settlement patterns that occurred during these phases. It may be that the primary reason for the shift lay in the fact that the river became less and less of an open, interregional avenue of

Anna

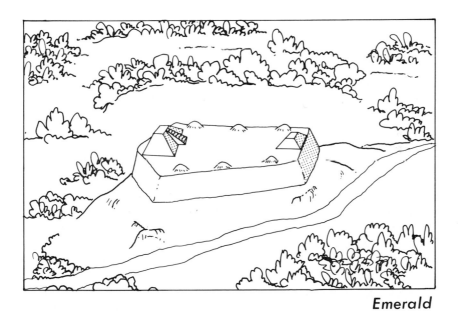

Emerald

FIGURE 12.6. *Primary mound centers of the Natchez Bluffs. Anna on its natural bluff dominated the Mississippi River during the Anna phase; Emerald on its artifical bluff along the Natchez Trace began to replace Anna during the Foster phase and achieved its final form during the Emerald phase.*

communication as interaction became increasingly localized. This certainly does not mean that extraregional interaction ceased, but that its scale and control was of a lower order and more contingent upon local instigation. A regionalization occurred.

But in the Lower Yazoo, at least, this regionalization was not purely local in inspiration. As noted, it was at this time that the basin became increasingly acculturated to the Mississippian pattern. The evidence is especially abundant in the artifactual inventories, which become almost entirely Mississippian in content. But there are also concurrent behavioral changes of distinctive character, such as a more nucleated settlement pattern and a subtle shift of the dominant mound adjacent to the northwest quadrant of the plaza (Williams and Brain in press). Although the prerequisite for this process may have been the breakdown of the earlier patterns, the explanation is probably to be found in various undirected small-scale interactions, apparently including small demographic movements at the regional level (Brain in press). The entire Yazoo Basin was slowly drawn into the Mississippian culture sphere. The Natchez region, on the other hand, continued to maintain the indigenous traditions.

WASP LAKE—EMERALD

The Wasp Lake and Emerald phases are the latest prehistoric phases in the respective regions. Actually, *protohistoric* is the better characterization, for this part of the Southeast experienced a "false dawn" of historic contact as the early sixteenth-century Spanish explorers made brief entradas into the unknown wilderness. These were not enduring affairs, and contact was soon broken, so that the area again receded into the realm of the unknown until European contact was reestablished and the historic period truly begun at the conclusion of the seventeenth century. But during that brief interval of Spanish exploration a glimpse of the native Indian cultures, many still at their zeniths, is recorded. The most ambitious of these expeditions, resulting in the most informative record, was that of De Soto. In the narratives of that entrada, great native chiefdoms are described which impressed even the usually arrogant conquistadores. The Lower Valley was found to be divided into populous, and often contentious, "provinces." Each of these was ruled by a chief who lived in the principal village, which was usually a fortified town with multiple mounds and plazas.

Archeologically, there is some confirmation of these reports, as well as the continuation of trends already observed in preceding phases. The sites plotted in Figure 12.7 reveal a very interesting distribution. There is a noticeable decline from the previous phases in the number of sites, and these are nearly all restricted to interior locales away from the Mississippi

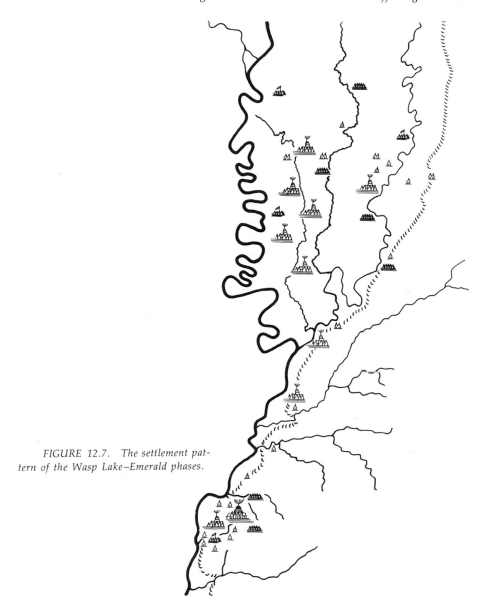

FIGURE 12.7. *The settlement pattern of the Wasp Lake–Emerald phases.*

River. This pattern holds especially to the major sites, with only the Glass site continuing as an exception. That the Glass site is an exception is probably due to the fact, already alluded to, that it was an important center of the proto-Taensa, who in historic times occupied the *west* bank of the river.

In the Yazoo Basin, the Winterville and Lake George locales had been completely deserted. Instead, the demographic focus appears to have shifted to the most interior water courses in the central part of the basin, especially the more newly settled parts (compare Figures 12.2, 12.4, 12.5, and 12.7). Perhaps these were not subject to the same cultural or ecological fatigue that partly explain the depopulation that seems to have been occurring in the rest of the region at that time. Whatever might have been the case, these locales formed a tightly circumscribed core around which the latest prehistoric–protohistoric events revolved.

That some mound construction was still being carried on even at this late date in the Yazoo Basin is apparent from the site plans of some of the important centers. The small, multimound site pattern continues, with the single dominant mound now shifted to the north side of the plaza. Examples of this basic site plan are found at the Law, Magee, Silver City, and Haynes Bluff sites. The Haynes Bluff site has the latest plan of all, with the dominant mound there located in the northeast quadrant. Excavation in 1974 determined that the mound was largely constructed during this phase (Brain 1975).

In the Natchez Bluffs, there is little evidence of occupation south of the Glass site until one reaches the concentration around the modern city of Natchez. There, too, the focus had definitely shifted away from the river. The Anna site had finally been completely abandoned, and the primary center in the region was now the Emerald site, located on that great interior land trail later known to history as the Natchez Trace (thus, Emerald displays a change in the form of external contact, not necessarily the lack thereof). Excavations by the Lower Mississippi Survey in 1972 revealed that the final great stages of Emerald were built during this phase—be it noted again, in grand imitation of Anna, probably accounting for its more traditional site plan. The Foster site as well as an undetermined portion of the Fatherland site were also constructed during this phase, and both exhibit the later plan with the principal mound on the north side of the plaza (Brain et al. n.d.).

The archeological picture of these phases and some of the events inferred are greatly enhanced by the tantalizing descriptions in the historical documentation of the De Soto entrada. In early May 1541, the weary Spanish army straggled into the Yazoo Basin and discovered the native "province" of Quizquiz, which was located some leagues inland from the Mississippi River near the Arkansas confluence (Brain et al. 1974). Taking the inhabitants by surprise, they quickly invested the principal town, which is clearly described as a major mound center (Garcilaso 1951):

> Off to one side of the town was the dwelling place of the Curaca. It was situated on a high mound which now served as a fortress. Only by means of two stairways could one ascend to this house. Here many Indians gathered while other sought refuge in a very wild forest lying between the town and the Great River [p. 423].

The Indians soon recovered and, astoundingly, "almost four thousand armed warriors had gathered around the Cacique within less than three hours after their arrival in this town; and they were afraid that since these men had assembled in such a brief time, many more would come later [*ibid*.:425]." Garcilaso's account was written long after the expedition and is considered untrustworthy in factual details, especially as difficulties encountered were exaggerated to the glory of the conquistadores. However, in this instance, the figures in the other extant narratives (Bourne 1922) tend to support Garcilaso's estimate, and the fact that the Spaniards uncharacteristically backed down, seeking peace rather than confrontation (their proven tactic to success), confirms the magnitude of the opposition. Quizquiz had a very large population, which, moreover, could be rallied quickly to the protection of central authority.

A fascinating glimpse of the power and confidence of such a central authority is provided by the Cacique of Quigualtam a year later. In response to De Soto's typically arrogant demand for subservience, this chief (referred to in the narrative as "the greatest of that country") sent a marvelous message, which with equal arrogance bade De Soto mind his manners (Bourne 1922, I:154–155):

> It is not my custom to visit anyone, but rather all, of whom I have ever heard, have come to visit me, to serve and obey me, and pay me tribute, either voluntarily or by force: if you desire to see me, come where I am; if for peace, I will receive you with special goodwill; if for war, I will await you in my town; but neither for you, nor for any man, will I set back one foot.

This was supreme power, and apparently intimidating enough that the Spaniards never pressed their demands nor actually visited Quigualtam. A most unfortunate turn of events for this study, because Quigualtam was the proto-Natchez "province" of the Emerald phase; and the Emerald site itself was probably the seat of that great chief (". . . I will await you in my town . . .").

Events were soon to affect all these discoveries profoundly. Clues to those events are also contained in the accounts of the Spanish witnesses. After crossing the Mississippi River opposite Quizquiz, De Soto encountered a clear case of sociocultural confrontation (Brain 1977). Very different peoples lived as hostile neighbors in the same region. The differences are most clearly described in the settlement patterns: One pattern was composed of a large number of small open villages, whereas the other was characterized by bigger towns that were fortified. The hostilities were apparently occasioned by the fact that the latter peoples were actively "pushing" into the region (Garcilaso 1951:435). It is unlikely that this was a unique event, but rather was one of a series of disruptions occurring in the Lower Valley as far south as the Arkansas River at that time. A direct consequence of these disruptions was demographic displacements, the most important of which was the forced migration of whole tribal groups. These mass migrations became the vanguard of yet a new Mississippian intrusion into the southern reaches of the Lower Mississippi Valley. It would seem that new developments were in the making before they were overwhelmed by the even greater events of European intervention.

RUSSELL—NATCHEZ

With the Russell and Natchez phases, we enter the historic period, which is defined as beginning with established and continuing European presence, and is confirmed archeologically by the appearance of European artifacts. For the Indians of the Yazoo and Natchez regions, this was a brief phase, lasting only from 1699 to 1730. By this point, the great aboriginal climax witnessed by De Soto had passed, and the cultural inventory of the indigenous tribes was a poor reflection of the developments of the Lake George, Wasp Lake, Foster, and Emerald phases. But the greatest change was demographic. The disruptions already described continued into this period.

For some as yet unknown reason, the Yazoo region experienced a dramatic depopulation in the late protohistoric period, whereas the Plaquemine-derived populations located in the Natchez Bluffs region immediately to the south managed to hold the line at a greatly reduced state. The causes of the depopulation have not been determined, but the introduction of European diseases and an increase in aboriginal warfare have been hypothesized as major contributing factors. Whatever the causes, and surely they were both multiple and cumulative, the effect was to encourage population displacement on a large scale, although the groups themselves may have decreased markedly in size. The valley was opened to long-distance migrations, and many can be cited in the protohistoric and early historic periods: the Michigamea, Quapaw, Kaskinampo, Koroa, Tioux, Ofo, Tunica, Grigra, Taensa, Houma, and Bayogoula can all be demonstrated to have made a major move at least once (Swanton 1946). Of the major tribes, only the Natchez remained in their ancestral home until forced out by the French.

The only occupation of the Yazoo region during the Russell phase seems to have consisted of a remnant population clinging to a short stretch of the bluff margin along the lower course of the Yazoo River (Figure 12.8). The tribal units encountered in this region by the French in 1699 included a number of different ethnic groups. In mixed villages lived the Tunica, Yazoo, and Ofo. The Tioux and Koroa were also present, although there is evidence that population segments had already started moving farther downriver by this time. The Ibitoupa and Chakchiuma were established farther upstream in the vicinity of what is now Greenwood, Mississippi.

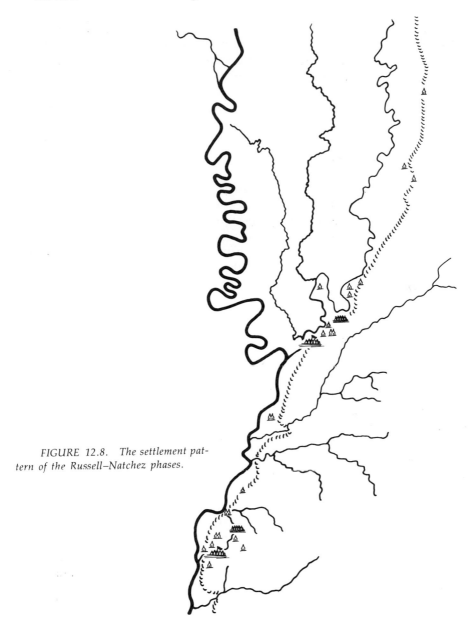

FIGURE 12.8.   The settlement pattern of the Russell–Natchez phases.

All of these were "Mississippian" groups, but there is indeed more to be told. Some, like the Yazoo and Chakchiuma, may have been remnants of the great prehistoric populations from the interior of the basin—mere vestiges of the Lake George and Wasp Lake occupations—whereas others, such as the Tunica and Ofo, were newly immigrant to the region. Thus, a demographic input is evident. The new peoples had a vague cultural affiliation with the indigenous natives, but they were distinct in actual artifactual inventories, and they were distinct as sociopolitical entities.

The tribes just enumerated were small and unimpressive as sociopolitical groups. According to eighteenth-century French accounts, each was independent politically and was organized at the tribal level; the great chiefdoms that must have been operative in the late prehistoric phases had disappeared, along with large population aggregates. The comparatively few souls clinging to the valley edge in small, widely scattered villages were almost a mockery of the great events that had been witnessed.

The geographic focus of the Russell phase was the Haynes Bluff site. Haynes Bluff appears to have been the only major Wasp Lake phase mound site that continued to be occupied into the historic period. Although the site plan at Haynes Bluff achieved its final form at a very late period, it is doubtful that any significant mound construction was carried out during the Russell phase. Nevertheless, the custom of mound usage was well preserved: No matter who had built the mounds, the peoples of the Russell phase, whatever their origins, were quite accustomed to using them. This custom, apparently not observed by other contemporary Indian groups, with the notable exception of the Natchez, is amply recorded in the early eighteenth-century French records: In 1702, Father Gravier noted that the Tunica had a "small temple raised on a mound of earth" and even later, in 1722, La Harpe observed that the houses of the Yazoo, Koroa and Ofo were mostly "situated on mounds of earth . . . made by hand."

The occupation of the Natchez region may have been somewhat more substantial than the Yazoo during this period, but it, too, showed a marked decline from earlier periods. Except for an ephemeral—historically undocumented, but archeologically confirmed (Ford 1936:71, Moore 1911:378–381)—continuity in the vicinity of the Glass site, itself now abandoned, all evidence of occupation is concentrated in the south around the historic home of the Natchez Indians (Figure 12.8). Even there, only a small number of villages are recorded by the French (5 to 12 depending upon the source; these figures, however, must be used with caution, since they seem to refer more to sociopolitical centers than population concentrations). At least two of these villages were composed of non-Natchezan (i.e., Mississippian) refugee groups, a clear indication of the disruption of the times (Brain 1971a). Proud Quigualtam had faded, and, although there is some historical evidence to the contrary, the Foster and Emerald sites appear to have been abandoned. Excavations at both sites in 1972 failed to produce a single historic artifact (Brain et al. n.d.).

According to the French, the focus of Natchez sociopolitical life was the Fatherland site (Neitzel 1965). This shift from Emerald, or even Foster, is significant, for Fatherland is a modest site with only a few small mounds. That these were of very late construction is confirmed by the site plan, which places the dominant mound in the northeast quadrant of the plaza, exactly parallel to the arrangement at Haynes Bluff. Fatherland was the seat of the "Great Sun," the paramount chief of the Natchez, but it apparently had a small resident population, most of the people being scattered over the countryside in small villages and hamlets. A reason for this kind of settlement patterning was offered by Father Charlevoix, re-nowned historian of New France, who visited Natchez in December 1721: "The savages, from whom the great chief has a right to take all they have, get as far from him as they can; and therefore many villages of this nation have been formed at some distance from this [French 1851:159]." If the accuracy of this observation may be trusted, it throws some shadows on theories of redistribution, for it would seem that the settlement pattern was determined primarily by distant removal from the tax collector. This may have been no small matter, especially when the not always willing sacrifices at the funeral of a Sun are contemplated, but cannot provide the sole explanation for a general pattern, which has great antiquity in the Natchez region.

In 1729, after an experiment of three decades, the Indians tired of French colonialism and grew restless. The Natchez were the first to rebel. After one injustice too many, they rose up in November of that year and massacred the French colony almost to a man. Emulating this successful venture, the Yazoo performed a nearly identical feat on the French outpost in their midst the following month. Their independence was short-lived, however, and within a year, while they themselves dealt with the Natchez, the French persuaded the Quapaw to attack and scatter all the Yazoo tribes, whether they had participated in the massacre or not. The Quapaw accomplished this, and the Yazoo tribes are generally lost from history thereafter; the French exacted their revenge from the Natchez by forcing them out of their ancient land, and ultimately out of Louisiana. Thus, effective Indian occupation of the Yazoo and Natchez regions came to a close on some unknown day in A.D. 1730. From that point on, parties of Choctaw and Chickasaw probably passed through, and some ghostly refugee groups may have held out for a while in some of the more inaccessible locations, but there was no more permanent settlement—that is, until Euro-American colonization gained momentum toward the end of the century.

Summary

There are no conclusions to be offered here, but a brief review and summary of thoughts is in order. As noted at the outset, the objective of this study has been to take one period of aboriginal occupation, usually analyzed as a single synchronous body of data, and to break it down into a series of component parts that truly approach relatively contemporary events. This is obviously only the first step. But it is a major one that should be continually refined if the sophisticated models of human development and interaction proposed elsewhere are to be applied with credibility.

The concluding half millennium of aboriginal occupation in the Lower Mississippi Valley was fraught with change. The impetus for many of the major observable changes appears to have been foreign in origin, specifically identified as "Mississippian" for purposes of this study. Thus, it was with a strong contact from the great Mississippian center of Cahokia that the period began, and it was with a major influx of new Mississippian peoples that the period ended. These events were but two of the more dramatic that give particular distinction to this climactic period in the Yazoo and Natchez regions.

The direct Cahokia contact occurred within the indigenous late Coles Creek context, and it was to affect that context profoundly. Whatever the reasons for the contact might have been, the distribution was distinctive: manifest only at widely separated sites, those sites were generally located at critical junctures of the riverine system. It would seem that small numbers of people were involved, but that they were in positions of great influence. The Cahokia diagnostics soon disappear from the archeological record in the area, and an intensely viable development ensued, which represented the reaction of the Coles Creek peoples and their culture to the strong, organized, external influence. Whatever the Cahokians had to offer was accepted, adapted, and transformed by indigenous groups into a new expression that became the late prehistoric climax.

The Winterville and Anna phases were hybrids of the Mississippian and Coles Creek cultural traditions, the result referred to as the Plaquemine culture. In the Natchez region, the Plaquemine culture remained dominant into the historic contact period. But the Yazoo Basin was subjected to continuing influence from the north, until the Mississippian pattern eventually came to dominance during the Lake George phase. Although some southern elements were retained, the overall settlement patterns, site plans, artifact inventories, inferred sociopolitical organizations, and economic activities, were more Mississippian, as defined in these pages, than indigenous in tradition.

During the final phases of aboriginal occupation, new Mississippian influences were literally brought in by new Mississippian peoples. The pattern observed was one of migrations of entire, but modestly sized, tribal groups. These seem to have overwhelmed the Yazoo, and broke upon and around the Natchez. The relative viability and stability of the Natchez sociopolitical structure is clearly indicated by their continued existence in the midst of such population movements (Brain 1971a). The nature and actions of this tail end of the Coles-Creek–Plaquemine tradition contrast sharply with the fragmented and confused picture presented by the contemporary Mississippian manifestations. Yet this may be an unfair assessment. There are indications of more order in the chaos, more purpose of mind, than had originally been perceived in these late migrations.

The Tunica, the vanguard of this terminal Mississippian "expansion," provide some fascinating clues. Of all the known groups, their migrations were the most extensive: Beginning during the Wasp Lake phase in or near the province of Quizquiz (Brain *et al.* 1974), they ultimately achieved the southernmost penetration by an organized Mississippian tribal group into the Lower Valley. According to their own legends (Haas 1950), these moves were occasioned in each case by exterior pressures rather than interior design. But once committed, there is the strong suggestion that the moves were directed by a very special ulterior consideration. There is repeated reference in the contemporary French accounts to the fact that the Tunica were entrepreneurs of the first order. They were excellent traders, who apparently held their own in matters of commerce with Indian and European alike. Perhaps they held an advantage, because they seem to have controlled the production and exchange of some vital resources, such as salt. Altogether, their success may be measured by their unusual accumulation of material goods (Brain 1970b, 1978). This entrepreneurial proficiency must have had some bearing on the movements of the Tunica, and indeed the choice of settlement in each case would seem to confirm expectations: The Tunica started out at the confluence of the Arkansas and the Mississippi; they moved first to the Yazoo confluence, and then to the vicinity of the mouth of the Red River. Their choice of settlement location may have been dictated by the procurement of such prime resources as salt. But for whatever reason, the fact remains that they sequentially chose to settle at the three most important river junctions within the area of their travels. It is remarkably reminiscent of earlier patterns. There was quite a difference in scope and execution, of course, but the replication of the basic theme is striking. And that is the point: It may not have been coincidence. Such adaptability and vision may have been a major component in the various successes of the Mississippian movement through time and space.

There are other thoughts in this category. It will be noted that ecological factors have not been emphasized in this review. Although ecologically oriented studies are certainly important, the focus here has been upon other nonenvironmental factors that seem to have been operative. Not only does this approach afford additional perspective, but, in some situations, these factors often seem to have been of overriding importance. In the rich natural environment of the Lower Mississippi Valley, subsistence would rarely have played an important role in the events described here.

These events were often motivated by other concerns, and the local subsistence potential of the land was more than adequate to support them. This is the crux of the point being made: The gross archeological patterns observed here are perhaps better interpreted in terms of the broader perspective of cultural geography, rather than the specific interaction between subsistence systems and the natural environment, per se (e.g., Mosenfelder 1975).

However, the perspective offered here is not to be understood as ignoring the importance of a highly efficient and productive subsistence base, which was integral to the patterns and supportive of the events discussed. Such a base must have been fully agricultural, as well as widely exploitive of the rich natural environment (cf. Price in press: his "smorgasbord" subsistence strategy). The surpluses of maize at Quizquiz reported by the De Soto army—in the spring, before the new crops could have matured—testify to the success of late prehistoric bottomland farming. A way of life so successful could be expected to change basic cultural priorities. Indeed, a fundamental change in lifestyle is indicated by the observation that the men of Quizquiz tended the fields. Thus, the notion that agriculture beyond the clearing of the land was exclusively women's work among the North American Indian seems to have been another mistaken stereotype. At least one society in the Lower Valley had reached the point where values had dictated that men must farm. Such a development is not to suggest that the results were necessarily any better or that this sparked an "agricultural revolution" and greater productivity. In fact, it may have weakened the dietary base, as there may have been an overall decrease in the amount of meat available per capita, leading to some deficiencies—especially salt, the manufacture and trade of which had become a necessary and important business by this period (and which contributed substantially to the success of those Quizquiz descendants, the Tunica). But the ever-increasing importance of intensive corn agriculture did affect priorities and roles. How far back into the prehistoric record this lifestyle can be projected must remain hypothetical at this point. But it may well have been the spark that contributed to the success of the whole Mississippian phenomenon, and which dramatically sets it apart from the superficial homology of the Coles Creek culture.

This is, perhaps, what Mississippian was all about: a basic change in production that may have supported greater populations, but, more importantly, increased the requirements of those populations qualitatively as well as quantitatively. Thus, intensified interactions and other activities were necessary to procure and exchange necessities. The success of each Mississippian venture, then, depended upon how adequately the cultural system in that particular context satisfied the requirements. In the rich alluvial valley of the Mississippi, success was apparently easy—even to allowing the existence of competing systems, such as Coles Creek—

although eventual population growth brought about demographic pressures, which caused other problems. Beyond the broad floodplains of the Mississippi and its major tributaries, it must have been more difficult to meet the requirements. In regions where, in fact, the needs could not be fulfilled, or the system eventually failed for whatever reason, changes would have been forced in the economic, sociopolitical, and/or religious[1] systems, depending upon the particular problem. Thus, we have a model for Mississippian interaction and expansion, and for its often different, heretofore unpredictable behavior in different regions. For all its apparent success, it was a closely balanced adaptation that required constant maintenance, or else it would wither, which it often did after being initially established. The late prehistoric occupation of the Lower Mississippi Valley is a special case of social and natural adaptation: another facet of native developments during the Mississippi period.

It must be clear in this volume that the total range of "Mississippian" developments comprise a very complex set, and that future archeological research must emphasize the interplay of all variables to be found in each late prehistoric context. Since settlement pattern studies are one of the more direct ways to assess such matters as subsistence strategies, social organizations, and political structures, it is necessary to detail the great variety in such patterning through time and space. Only then can the search for common denominators leading to explanatory mechanisms truly begin.

Acknowledgments

This chapter obviously owes a considerable debt to my predecessors and colleagues of the Lower Mississippi Survey. Especially to be mentioned are the contributions of Stephen Williams (1956), Philip Phillips (1970), Ian Brown (1973), and Vincas Steponaitis (1974). The detailed archeological data upon which this chapter is based will be presented in the following publications: Brown and Brain (1977), Williams and Brain (in press), Brain (n.d.). Illustrations were prepared by the talented hands of Barbara Westman, Nancy Fernald, and Hillel Burger.

References

Bourne, Edward G.
    1922   *Narratives of the career of Hernando de Soto.* Two volumes. New York: Allerton.

[1] There is an intuition that some part of the so-called Southern Cult reflects just such a reaction. Those elements which have pan-Southeastern expression are concentrated on the margins of Mississippian development in contexts which the author believes to be very late in the prehistoric period. That the Cult is not *the* Mississippian religion is clearly indicated by the rarity of diagnostic artifacts in the primary Mississippi River system, regardless of temporal placement.

Brain, Jeffrey P.
  1969   Winterville: A case study of prehistoric culture contact in the lower Mississippi
         Valley. Ph.D. dissertation, Department of Anthropology, Yale University, New
         Haven.
  1970a Early Archaic in the lower Mississippi alluvial valley. *American Antiquity* **35**:104–
         106.
  1970b The Tunica treasure. *Lower Mississippi Survey, Bulletin* **2**. Peabody Museum, Cam-
         bridge.
  1971a The Natchez "paradox." *Ethnology* **10**:215–222.
  1971b The lower Mississippi valley in North American prehistory. Manuscript on file at
         the Southeastern Archaeological Center, National Park Service, Tallahassee.
  1975   The archaeology of the Tunica: Trial on the Yazoo. *Lower Mississippi Survey,
         Preliminary Report.* Peabody Museum, Cambridge.
  1977   The archaeological phase: Ethnographic fact or fancy? In *Archaeological essays in
         honor of Irving Rouse,* edited by R.C. Dunnell and E.S. Hall. New York: Mouton.
  1978   *Tunica treasure.* Cambridge: Peabody Museum Press.
  in press Cultural dynamics in the lower Mississippi Valley, A.D. 1000–1700: A case study
         of Mississippian impact on the southern periphery. In *Reviewing Mississippian
         Development,* edited by S. Williams. Santa Fe: University of New Mexico Press.
  n.d.   *Winterville.* Cambridge: Peabody Museum Press.
Brain, Jeffrey P., Alan Toth, and Antonio Rodriguez-Buckingham
  1974   Ethnohistoric archaeology and the De Soto Entrada into the lower Mississippi
         Valley. *Conference on Historic Site Archaeology, Papers* **7**:232–280.
Brain, Jeffrey P., Ian W. Brown, and Vincas P. Steponaitis
  n.d.   *Archaeology of the Natchez Bluffs.* Cambridge: Peabody Museum Press.
Brown, Ian W.
  1973   Settlement patterns in the bluff areas of the lower Mississippi Valley. B.A. thesis,
         Department of Anthropology, Harvard University, Cambridge.
  1975   Archaeological investigations at the historic Portland and St. Pierre sites in the
         lower Yazoo basin, Mississippi. M.A. thesis, Department of Anthropology, Brown
         University, Providence.
  1978   Early 18th century French–Indian culture contact in the Yazoo Bluffs region of the
         lower Mississippi Valley. Ph.D. dissertation, Department of Anthropology, Brown
         University, Providence.
Brown, Ian W., and Jeffrey P. Brain
  1977   Archaeology of the Natchez Bluff Region, Mississippi: Hypothesized cultural and
         environmental factors influencing local population movements. *Southeastern Ar-
         chaeological Conference, Bulletin* **20**.
Brown, James A.
  1971   The dimensions of status in the burials at Spiro. *Society for American Archaeology,
         Memoir* **25**:92–112.
Christaller, W.
  1966   *Central places in southern Germany,* translated by C.W. Baskin. Englewood Cliffs,
         New Jersey: Prentice-Hall.
Cotter, John L.
  1951   Stratagraphic and area tests at the Emerald and Anna Mound sites. *American
         Antiquity* **17**:18–32.
Ford, James A.
  1936   Analysis of Indian village site collections from Louisiana and Mississippi. *Louisiana
         Geological Survey, Anthropological Study* **2**.
  1951   Greenhouse: A Troyville-Coles Creek Period site in Avoyelles Parish, Louisiana.
         American Museum of Natural History, Anthropological Papers **44**(1).

Ford, James A., Philip Phillips, and William G. Haag
  1955   The Jaketown site in West–Central Mississippi. *American Museum of Natural History, Anthropological Papers* **45**(1).
French, Benjamin F.
  1851   *Historical collections of Louisiana, Part III.* New York: D. Appleton and Co.
Garcilasco de la Vega, El Inca
  1951   *The Florida of the Inca*, translated and edited by J.G. Varner and J.J. Varner. Austin: University of Texas Press.
Greengo, Robert E.
  1964   Issaquena: An archaeological phase in the Yazoo Basin of the lower Mississippi valley. *Society for American Archaeology, Memoir* **18**.
Griffin, James B.
  1967   Eastern North American archaeology: A summary. *Science* **156**:175–191.
Haas, Mary R.
  1950   Tunica texts. *University of California Publications in Linguistics* **6**(1):1–174.
Holmes, William H.
  1885   *Ancient pottery of the Mississippi valley.* Washington: Judd and Detweiler.
  1886   Ancient pottery of the Mississippi valley. *Bureau of American Ethnology, Annual Report* **4**.
  1903   Aboriginal pottery of the eastern United States. *Bureau of American Ethnology, Annual Report* **20**.
Lewis, R. Barry
  1974   Mississippian exploitative strategies: A southeast Missouri example. *Missouri Archaeological Society, Research Series* **11**.
McKern, William C.
  1939   The midwest taxonomic method as an aid to archaeological culture study. *American Antiquity* **4**:301–313.
Moore, Clarence B.
  1911   Some aboriginal sites on the Mississippi River. *Academy of Natural Sciences of Philadelphia, Journal* **14**:367–478.
Mosenfelder, Clara M.
  1975   The Mississippian settlement system in the lower Yazoo Basin: An analysis of the impact on the natural and social environments on site location. Manuscript on file, Museum of Anthropology, University of Michigan, Ann Arbor.
Neitzel, Robert S.
  1965   Archaeology of the Fatherland site: The Grand Village of the Natchez. *American Museum of Natural History, Anthropological Papers* **51**(1).
O'Brien, Patricia J.
  1972   A formal analysis of Cahokia ceramics from the Powell Tract. *Illinois Archaeological Survey, Monograph* **3**.
Phillips, Philip
  1970   Archaeological survey in the lower Yazoo Basin, Mississippi, 1949–1955. *Peabody Museum of Archaeology and Ethnology, Papers* **60**.
Phillips, Philip, James A. Ford, and James B. Griffin
  1951   Archaeological survey in the lower Mississippi alluvial valley, 1940–1947. *Peabody Museum of Archaeology and Ethnology, Papers* **25**.
Price, James E.
  in press Mississippian settlement systems of the central Mississippi valley. In *Reviewing Mississippian Development*, edited by S. Williams. Santa Fe: University of New Mexico Press.
Quimby, George I.
  1942   The Natchezan culture type. *American Antiquity* **7**:255–275.

1951   The Medora site, west Baton Rouge Parish, Louisiana. *Field Museum of Natural History, Anthropoligical Series* **24**:81–135.

Reed, Nelson A.
1969   Monks and other Mississippian mounds. In Explorations into Cahokia archaeology, edited by M. Fowler. *Illinois Archaeological Survey, Bulletin* **7**:31–42.

Smith, Bruce D.
1975   Middle Mississippi exploitation of animal populations. *Anthropological Papers, Museum of Anthropology, University of Michigan* **57**. Ann Arbor.

Steponaitis, Vincas P.
1974   The late prehistory of the Natchez region: Excavations at the Emerald and Foster sites, Adams County, Mississippi. B.A. thesis, Harvard University, Cambridge.

Swanton, John R.
1946   The Indians of the southeastern United States. *Bureau of American Ethnology, Bulletin* **137**.

Willey, Gordon R., and Philip Phillips
1958   *Method and theory in American archaeology.* Chicago: University of Chicago Press.

Williams, Stephen
1956   Settlement patterns in the lower Mississippi valley. In *Prehistoric settlement patterns in the New World,* edited by G.R. Willey. New York: Viking Fund Publications in Anthropology. Pp. 52–62.
in press Some definitions and history of the concept of Mississippian. In *Reviewing Mississippian development*, edited by S. Williams. Santa Fe: University of New Mexico Press.

Williams, Stephen, and Jeffrey P. Brain
1970   *Philip Phillips, lower Mississippi Survey, 1940–1970.* Peabody Museum of Archaeology and Ethnology, Cambridge.
in press Excavations at the Lake George site, Yazoo County, Mississippi, 1958–1960. *Peabody Museum of Archaeology and Ethnology, Papers* **68**.

13

Determinants of Settlement Size and Location in the Moundville Phase

CHRISTOPHER S. PEEBLES

*The meanings—or as Weber calls them, the ideal types—
that the historian introduces into the facts must not be taken
as keys to history. They are only precise guideposts for
appreciating the divergence between what we think and
what has been, and for bringing into the open what has been
left out of our interpretation. Each perspective is there only
in order to prepare for others. It is well founded only if we
understand that it is partial and that the real is still beyond
it. Knowledge is never categorical; it is always conditional*
[Merleau-Ponty 1964:195].

This chapter analyzes the relationship between settlements of the
Moundville phase and the physiographic diversity, biotic productivity,
and agricultural potential of the landscape in which the inhabitants of
these settlements lived out their lives. The patterns extracted from the
covariation of settlement size and location with the natural and social
environment are both ideal and conditional in nature. They are ideal
because they represent the common and repetitive elements and measures
of the remains of a society that spanned some 300 years. They are conditional because they will be modified and refined by new discoveries, new
questions, and additional analysis. Nonetheless, these patterns, these

369

models of the Moundville settlement system have value as benchmarks against which new knowledge can be assayed and to which the settlement systems of other societies can be compared.

The Moundville phase, which was defined originally by DeJarnette (DeJarnette and Wimberly 1941) and later redefined by McKenzie (1966), is among the most extensive and complex of the Mississippian societies in the Southeast. The temporal span of this phase extends from approximately A.D. 1200 to 1500. Its areal extent encompasses a large group of settlements located in the Black Warrior River Valley south of Tuscaloosa in West–central Alabama and a smaller cluster of settlements situated in the Tennessee River Valley in Northwest Alabama. Between these two points to the north and west, that is, between the fall line at Tuscaloosa and the Tennessee River, there may be additional clusters of Moundville phase sites; however, in the absence of systematic site survey, this area is a blank on the map of Alabama's prehistory. To the north and east of Tuscaloosa no sites have been found that can be assigned to the Moundville phase, although the Cahaba River Valley should contain some sites of this phase. The distinctive Moundville-style ceramics occur in sites as far south as the Alabama Gulf Coast; however, on the basis of the total ceramic assemblage, these sites cannot be assigned to the Moundville phase proper (see Holmes 1963, Trickey and Holmes 1971, Trickey 1958). In addition, much of the pottery from the several unnamed Mississippian phases of southern Alabama and northwestern Florida have been characterized as "Moundville-derived" (Sears 1964).

Like most of the later archeological phases in eastern North America, the criteria used to define the Moundville phase consist mainly of pottery types. The standard utilitarian wares, which make up approximately 90% of the sherd scatter and midden contents at most Moundville phase sites, are designated *Warrior Plain* and *Moundville Incised.* The former are undecorated, shell-tempered elongated and hemispherical jars, which usually have strap handles attached to the vessel shoulder and lip. These vessels fall within the broad class which Phillips (1970:131) has designated Mississippi Plain. *Moundville Incised* differs from *Warrior Plain* only in the incised arched line on the shoulder of the vessel and the incised geometric motifs parallel to this line.

The decorated wares of the Moundville phase, apart from imported pottery, some effigy vessels, and some vessels with shapes that defy easy classification, fall into one or another of the black-filmed types: *Moundville Black Filmed, Moundville Filmed Engraved, Moundville Engraved-Indented,* and *Moundville Filmed Incised.* Shell-tempered bottles and bowls make up the majority of vessel forms in these categories. However, only the bottle is found in the *Moundville Engraved-Indented* type, and a few additional vessel forms make up a minority of the examples found in the other types. Vessels in these black-filmed categories were given a black organic wash after the initial firing. The vessels were then refired, and then the surfaces were polished to a high luster. No additional decoration was applied to *Moundville Black Filmed* vessels. Scrolls and parallel-line motifs were incised on *Moundville Filmed Incised* vessels before the first firing; various geometric designs and the iconographic motifs of the Southern Cult were engraved on the body of *Moundville Filmed Engraved* vessels after the second firing; thumb-sized indentations were impressed into the body of *Moundville Engraved Indented* vessels at the point at which they were leather-dry, and then, after the second firing, interlocked curvilinear motifs were engraved around the indentations. Whereas the greater percentage of vessels associated with the burials are the decorated variety, less than 15% of the sherd count from one of the largest excavations at Moundville is made up of these types, and even smaller percentages of decorated sherds are found in the village middens of sites near Moundville. (For a discussion of Moundville phase pottery see DeJarnette and Wimberly 1941, Heimlich 1952, McKenzie 1965, 1966, Wimberly 1956.)

In addition to the formal similarities in ceramics, a wide range of other artifacts serves to link together the several Moundville phase sites. The most distinctive group of items whose form and archeological context are generally similar from site to site are those artifacts included as definitive characteristics of the Southern Cult (see Williams 1968). Of these items, copper axes, oblong copper gorgets, stone palettes, and feline effigy pipes take on distinctive forms in the Moundville phase. In addition, these and other items, when taken in the context of mortuary ceremonialism, serve as a mirror of the social organization of the Moundville phase.

Analysis of 2053 burials from the Moundville site showed two distinctive dimensions of mortuary ritual. The numerically smaller, superordinate dimension, which can be associated with the chiefly lineage, is defined by burials interred with most of the Southern Cult artifacts. This dimension, with two exceptions noted on page 372, cannot be partitioned on the basis of age and sex: Infants and children have most of the items and symbols found with adults. This pattern suggests that in this dimension an individual's superordinate rank is dependent in the first instance on the situation into which he or she was born; that is, the superordinate dimension measures ascription. The second, subordinate dimension, which contains the majority of the burials, can be partitioned on the basis of age and sex. That is, in this dimension the mortuary ritual accorded individuals is associated with the age of the burial, and, to a lesser extent, with the sex of the burial. This pattern suggests that on this second dimension, rank is dependent on an individual's life history and achievement rather than ascription at birth (Peebles 1974, Peebles and Kus 1977).

Within the superordinate, ascriptive dimension, there are two clearly defined groups of adult male burials whose mortuary ritual point to their association with either political or ritual "offices." One group of burials ($N = 7$) clearly represents the highest statuses and the highest political offices in the society. These individuals are interred in the truncated mounds and are the products of an elaborate mortuary ritual that included the use of infants and skulls as part of the burial ceremony. Large copper axes were placed in the graves of these burials, and these artifacts are probably the material representations of the office held by these individuals. The second group of burials ($N = 17$) are interred in or near truncated mounds and have, among other items, paint palettes and red, white, green, and black mineral-based "paints" as part of their grave goods. The individuals in this group of burials probably held second-order ritual or political offices, the duties of which included the application of body paint or tatoos to individuals at appropriate seasonal or situational junctures.

It should be noted that individuals representing the highest offices (copper axes and infant ceremonialism) are found only at Moundville, although the infant ceremonialism does define lesser offices in central-mound burials at other Moundville phase sites (Peebles 1971). The offices mirrored by the paint palettes occur at Moundville and other Moundville phase sites. As such, these offices were probably a necessary adjunct to the ongoing life of most Moundville phase settlements. The spatial and ritual segregation of these offices is paralleled by the hierarchical arrangement of settlements discussed in the body of this chapter.

At present, more is known about the social and spatial organization of the Moundville phase than is known about its chronology, development, and decline. That is, the culture–history of this phase is known only in the broadest and most imperfect of outlines. Ultimately the roots of the Moundville phase probably can be traced to one or another Early Mississippian phase in Alabama. One such phase has been identified by Jenkins (1976, and references therein) and has been designated the West Jefferson phase. Settlements of this phase, which can be placed in the period from approximately A.D. 900–1050, are located in the Black Warrior River Valley from west of Birmingham to south of Tuscaloosa and in the upper reaches of the Cahaba River Valley south of Birmingham. The ceramics of the West Jefferson phase are typically Early Mississippian forms made from clay-grit tempered Late Woodland paste. These ceramics are probably linked to the earlier McKelvey phase, Late Woodland ceramic assemblage. Although predominantly hunter–gatherers, West Jefferson phase populations did grow a small amount of corn. Settlements ($N = 4$) in the northern part of the phase's range seemingly consisted of a single round dwelling that was surrounded by various types of pit features used for storage and food preparation. The surface scatters of artifacts from sites of this period in the lower part of the Black Warrior River Valley seem to indicate larger, multiple-dwelling settlements.

At some point after A.D. 1000 the small ceremonial center at Bessemer, Alabama, was constructed on the banks of a tributary of the Black Warrior River. This site, which has two truncated mounds and one small burial mound, was excavated in the late 1930s (DeJarnette and Wimberly 1941). The material recovered from this excavation suggests that, in terms of social complexity and ceramic typology, the site stands midway between the West Jefferson phase and the beginning of the Moundville phase. [The chronological position of Bessemer used to construct a small model in Peebles (1971) is, as is the model, incorrect.] The ceramics from the Bessemer site are made from both clay-grit and shell-tempered paste. The form and decoration of these vessels are prototypic of later Moundville phase types, especially *Warrior Plain, Moundville Incised, Moundville Black Filmed*, and *Moundville Filmed Incised.* The mortuary ceremonialism at the Bessemer site is more like that of the Early Mississippian site at Macon Plateau (Fairbanks 1956) than that of the later Moundville phase. At both Macon Plateau and Bessemer, interment in the burial mound was reserved for a small segment of the total population, and the complexity of the mortuary ritual suggests that only a very few discrete status positions— either achieved or ascribed—were mirrored by this mortuary ritual. It should be noted that there is a small burial mound similar to the one at Bessemer located on the southwest margin of the Moundville site (Peebles 1971). This mound may mark the beginning of Moundville as a Mississippian ceremonial center. These data suggest that in the broad scale it can be argued that between A.D. 900 and 1200, the basic technological, structural, and symbolic elements that were combined into the Moundville phase had begun their indigenous growth and evolution within the Black Warrior River Valley (see Jenkins 1976 for a contrasting point of view.)

The period from A.D. 1200 to 1500 brackets the life-history of the Moundville phase. The demise of this phase is marked by the 100-year span centered on A.D. 1500. In Sheldon's (1974) chronology, this period can be characterized as "Moundville Decline," and the subsequent period—from A.D. 1550 to 1700—is occupied by the "Burial Urn Cultures," of which the Alabama River phase (Cottier 1968, 1970) is the best-known representative. The areal extent of the Alabama River phase includes the Black Warrior River Valley south of Tuscaloosa, the Alabama River Valley west of Montgomery, and the Tombigbee River Valley from a point near its confluence with the Black Warrior River to a point below its confluence with the Alabama River.

Although there is a marked change in the ceramic assemblage between the Moundville and Alabama River phases, broad continuities can be traced in several of the ceramic categories. Sheldon (1974:45) has traced the development of *Moundville Filmed Incised* bowls into *Foster Filmed Incised* and *Alabama River Incised* carinated bowls and *Warrior Plain* into

Alabama River Plain and *Alabama River Applique*. Neither the remainder of the black-filmed types nor the Southern Cult iconographic motifs survive the transformations that led to Alabama River phase ceramic types.

There seems to be no major shift in crops grown or animals hunted between the Moundville and Alabama River phases. However, the complex social, political, and ritual organization that characterized the Moundville phase is not apparent in the remains of the Alabama River phase. The marked settlement hierarchy of the former gives way to smaller, undifferentiated settlements in the latter. The settlement system of the Alabama River phase seems to encompass more settlements that, in total, probably contained a population equal in size to that of the Moundville phase at any one point in time. In brief, it appears that there was a marked redistribution of people over the landscape at the end of the Moundville phase.

There is, as the name "Burial Urn Culture" suggests, a change in mortuary ceremonialism between the Moundville phase and the Alabama River phase. In the latter phase, a significant (but, because of a biased sample, unmeasurable) proportion of the burials was interred, either as primary (infants and children) or as secondary burials, in large carinated bowls. The remainder of the population was buried as either primary or secondary interments in pits. An analysis of the available cemetery data (Sheldon 1974) shows that there are few distinct statuses mirrored by these mortuary practices. Moreover, the patterned variability present is closely correlated with the age and sex of the burial. Such a pattern suggests that life history and achievement are the major determinants of status in the Alabama River phase.

As Sheldon (1974:115) argues, the changes that lie between the Moundville phase and the "Burial Urn Cultures" are primarily sociopolitical in nature. The complex mound–plaza, Southern Cult focus of political and ritual life is terminated. The hierarchical statuses and offices associated with ritual and social control are eliminated. The complex lineage-based pyramid of prestige and power is truncated. What remains are segmentary jural communities, loosely united by cross-cutting ties of consanguinity and common ritual (Peebles 1970). In essence, the foundations of the Creek Confederacy, which itself was composed of disparate independent villages, were laid during this period. If, in fact, the changes from the complex, hierarchical organization of the Moundville phase to the relatively egalitarian organization of the Alabama River phase began prior to European contact, then, among other constructs, the model developed by Friedman (1972, 1975) to understand the cyclical changes from ranked to egalitarian societies in highland Burma might be applied in this case.

In summary, the Moundville phase was a structural moment in the development of native American societies in the Southeast. The elements and transformations that led to this complex chiefdom began in the pro-toagricultural societies of the Early Mississippian period. From this be-ginning, the gradual development of agriculture and ritual–regulatory mechanisms (Peebles and Kus 1977) can be observed, if only in the broadest of outlines. At least the next 200 years encompass what seems to have been a period of organizational stability and cultural complexity. At approximately A.D. 1500, however, the social, political, and religious hierarchy—and the symbols associated with these offices and statuses—ceased to be an integrative force in the society. It is possible that the costs (surplus) used to support the hierarchically ordered regulatory mecha-nism had risen to the point at which the social reproduction of the society itself was at stake.

Moundville Phase Sites and Settlements

The majority of the sites that can be assigned to the Moundville phase are located in the Black Warrior River Valley of West Central Alabama. These sites extend from a point just south of the Fall Line, near Tuscaloosa, to a point where the river enters the Black Belt, some 75 river miles (120 km) downstream. The locations of these sites are shown in Figure 13.1.

The Moundville site is central to this group of settlements. It is situated on a bluff overlooking the Black Warrior River at 33°00′ north latitude, 87° 38′ west longitude. The areal extent of the site exceeds 300 acres (121.5 ha), and its 20 large platform mounds have survived the ravages of time and excavators. Approximately 5% of the surface area of Moundville has been excavated: B. Moore made two excursions to Mound-ville, and partially excavated many of the mounds (Moore 1905, 1907). The Alabama Museum of Natural History conducted excavations at Mound-ville almost continuously from 1929 to 1941. Their work, which was as innovative as it was extensive, has been reported by Peebles (1973).

Although a complete description and analysis of the settlement is reserved for a forthcoming paper, a sketch of the community organization can be presented here. The 20 platform mounds outline a plaza of approx-imately 100 acres (40.5 ha) in area, and these features dominate the site (Figure 13.2). The mounds on the margins of the plaza alternate between those with large platforms and no burials and those with relatively smaller platforms and richly accompanied burials. On all but the river side of the plaza, buildings of varying sizes and functions were erected. An interpo-lated map of structure floor area per unit of excavation, Figure 13.2, shows that the most densely built-upon areas of the site were at the east and west sides of the plaza, and along the southern margins of the site.

The types of structures erected varied with respect to their location in

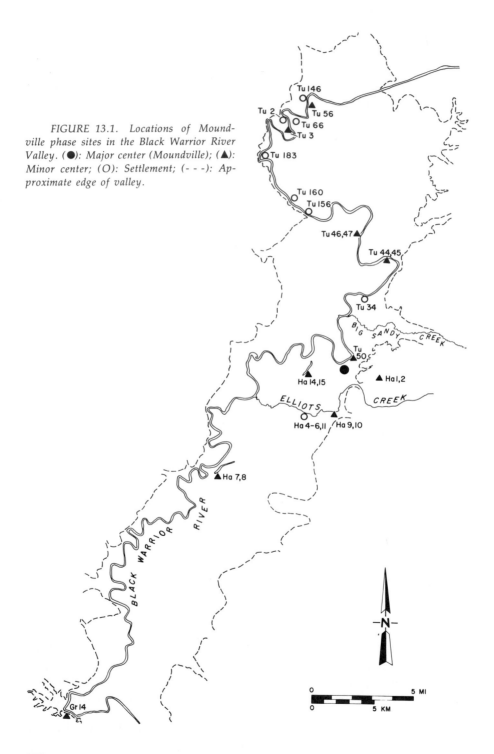

FIGURE 13.1. Locations of Moundville phase sites in the Black Warrior River Valley. (●): Major center (Moundville); (▲): Minor center; (O): Settlement; (- - -): Approximate edge of valley.

376

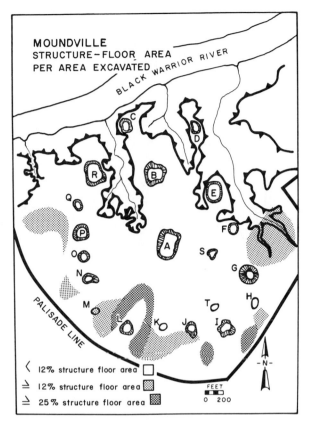

FIGURE 13.2. *Isopleth map of percentage of each excavation unit covered by a structure floor:* $\bar{x}$ = 13.53%; SD = 16.90%; N = 44 *points.*

the community. Large "public" buildings were placed near the northeast and northwest corners of the plaza. One of these structures, which was located just north of Mound Q, is shown in Figure 13.3. The caches of skulls buried near the north wall of this building were the usual correlates of ritual structures at Moundville. Other special-purpose structures, which included a charnal house and a "sweathouse," were situated just inside the southern boundary of the plaza. Common residential areas were located away from the plaza, but within the palisade wall, in the western and eastern sectors of the site. Portions of two of these village areas are illustrated in Figures 13.4 and 13.5. The Administration Building excavation (Figure 13.4) was located southeast of Mound T, the Museum Parking Lot excavation (Figure 13.5) was located northwest of Mound P. A large residential and mortuary area, which was an "elite" living space as defined by its burials, was located east of Mound E and F, on the east bank of the creek that runs by these mounds. This area was designated the Rhodes

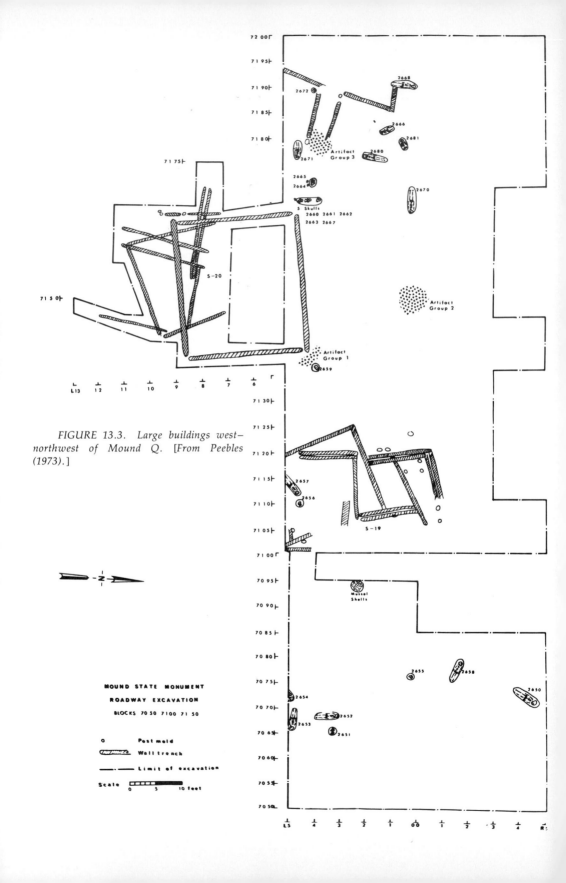

FIGURE 13.3. Large buildings west–northwest of Mound Q. [From Peebles (1973).]

MOUND STATE MONUMENT

ROADWAY EXCAVATION

BLOCKS 70 50 7100 71 50

○   Post mold

〰〰〰   Wall trench

———— Limit of excavation

Scale ▭▭▭▭▭▭
0   5   10 feet

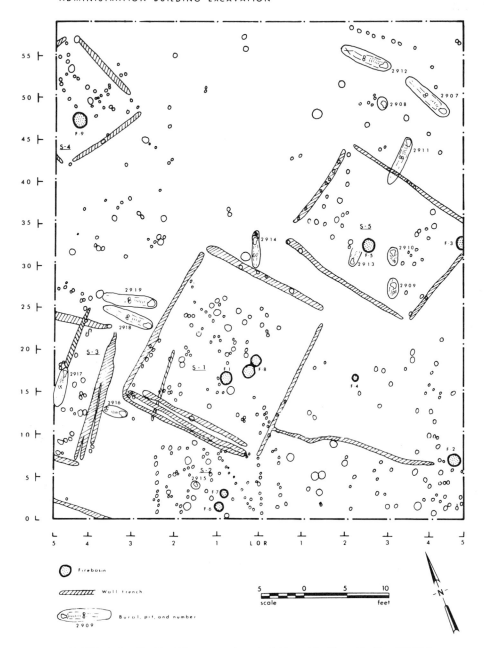

FIGURE 13.4. *Residential area southwest of Mound I.* [*From Peebles (1973).*]

MOUND STATE MONUMENT
MUSEUM PARKING LOT EXCAVATION

FIGURE 13.5. *Residential area West–Northwest of Mound P.* [*From Peebles (1973).*]

site, and Figures 13.6 and 13.7 show the seven-room building, burial area, and northeast extension of the palisade wall recorded in this area.

The density and distribution of artifacts recovered from the several excavation units at Moundville show that most of the day-to-day debris was discarded into the river and ravines, but that the residue of items that remained can be used to define activity areas. The density of artifacts (exclusive of sherds) per 100 ft^2 (9.3 m^2) of excavation was used to create an interpolated artifact density map for the site as a whole (Figure 13.8). In general, the densest concentrations of artifacts were along the slopes leading to the river at the northeast boundary of the site. When individual artifact types were plotted by site-area, several independent groupings were apparent. Debitage from shell-bead manufacture occurred north of Mound F and east of Mound E. Bone awls and grooved sharpening stones were found only in the northeast quadrant of the site. Ceremonial items such as paint pigments and copper fragments were found near the "public" buildings at the northeast corner of the plaza. Pottery-working materials, that is, caches of shell and clay, were located in an area of large open hearths (kilns) west of Mound P. Heavy processing tools, projectile points, and other household debris were found in the village areas of the site.

The burials excavated at Moundville comprise the major class of archeological features at that site. To date, 3051 burials have been excavated. Although interments were placed in most areas of the site except the plaza, the majority of the burials were located in the northeast and southern sectors of the settlement (Figure 13.9). These burials, as discussed earlier, have been analyzed—perhaps overanalyzed—(Peebles 1971, 1972, 1974, 1977; Peebles and Kus 1977), and the results will not be discussed further. At Moundville, the highest-status burials are found in the mounds, and, in general, as the distance from the northernmost mounds increases, the average status of the burials decreases. In brief, the *status-space*, defined by the burials, is paralleled by the distribution and variety of dwellings and artifacts.

Within 2 miles (3.2 km) of Moundville, four small, truncated mounds, three of which have associated village areas, and a cluster of four villages are found. The nearest of these sites to Moundville is Tu-50, a small, truncated pyramidal mound, .5 miles (.8 km) to the north of Moundville. Jones noted in his survey of 1933 that this mound measured 35 × 35 feet (10.7 × 10.7 m) at its base and 30 × 30 feet (9.1 m) at the platform. The height of this mound varied from 12 feet (3.65 m) at the north side to 10 feet (3 m) at the south side to 21 feet (6.4 m) at the east side. No village area has yet been found associated with this mound. However, a nearby historic site, Tu-52, has yielded burials with European grave goods.

A mound and village complex, Ha-1 and Ha-2 is located 1.6 miles southeast of Moundville. Both the mound and the village area are located on a flat ridge overlooking an unnamed tributary of Elliots Creek. W. B.

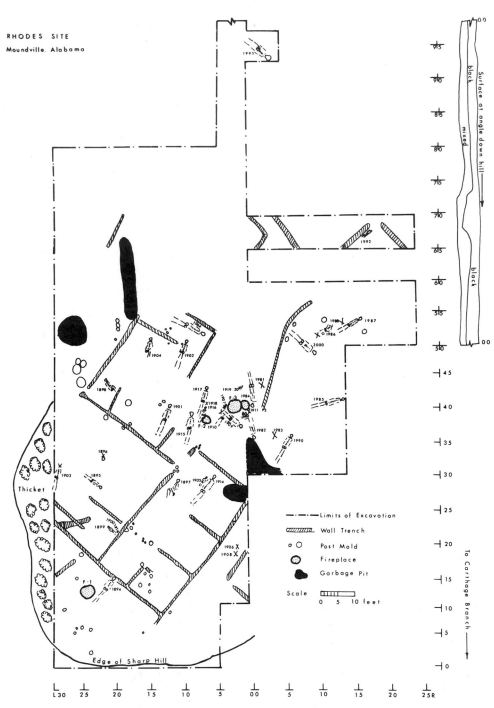

FIGURE 13.6. *Multi room structure on the east bank of Carthage Branch, East of Mound E.* [*From Peebles (1973).*]

382

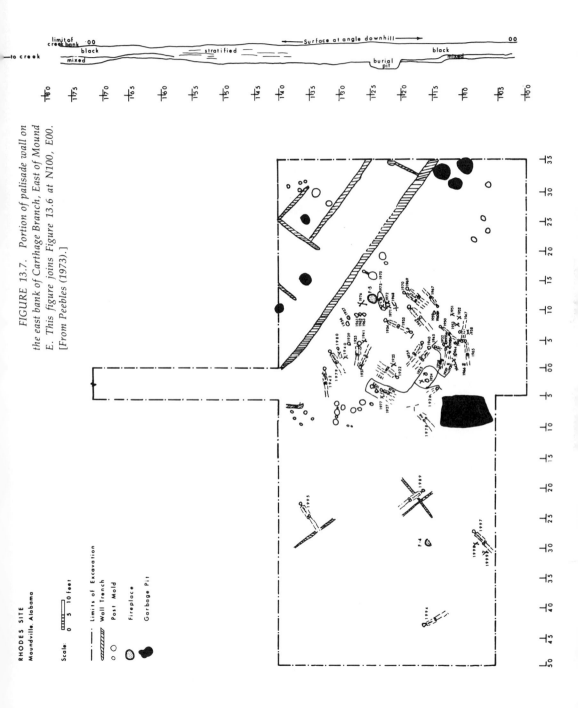

FIGURE 13.7. Portion of palisade wall on the east bank of Carthage Branch, East of Mound E. This figure joins Figure 13.6 at N100, E00. [From Peebles (1973).]

383

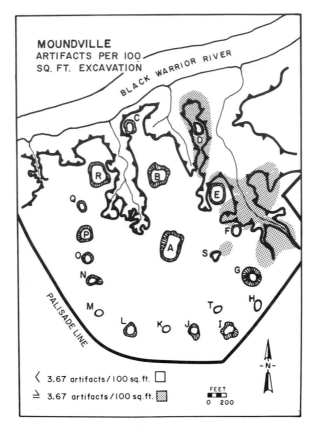

FIGURE 13.8. *Isopleth map of artifact density per 100 square feet of excavation:* $\bar{x} = 1.54$; SD = 2.51; N = 44 points.

Jones noted in his survey of 1933 that the mound was conical in shape, that its base measured 70 × 70 feet (21 × 21 m), and that it was 8 feet (2.4 m) high. Jones measured the extent of the surface scatter of artifacts and found that it covered an area of approximately 200 × 400 feet (ca. 1.8 acres or .73 ha). Nielsen (Nielsen *et al.* 1973:71–73) had assigned both these sites to the Moundville phase on the basis of Jones's collections.

Another mound and village pair, Ha-9 and Ha-10, is located on a terrace overlooking Elliots Creek, about 2.1 miles (3.4 km) south–southeast of Moundville. When Jones surveyed the mound in 1933, it measured 20 × 20 feet (6 × 6 m) at its base and was 6 feet (1.8 m) high. The surface scatter indicative of a village cover an area approximately 150 × 200 feet (ca. 1.0 acres or .4 ha). Nielsen (Nielsen *et al.* 1973:82–83) assigned these sites to the Moundville phase on the basis of Jones's collections.

A third mound and village pair, Ha-14 and Ha-15, is located on an oxbow lake, about 1.7 miles (2.7 km) east–southeast of Moundville. When

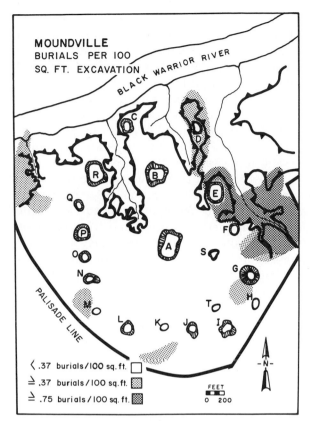

FIGURE 13.9.   Isopleth map of number of burials per 100 square feet of excavation: $\overline{X}$ = .34; SD = .55; N = 44 points.

Jones recorded these two sites, the mound had a barn on its summit, and no dimensions were recorded for it. During the spring of 1970, floodwaters from the Black Warrior River cut through the village area of the site and exposed several burials.. The staff of Mound State Monument, in the wake of local pothunters, managed to salvage some of the endangered material. Most of the sherds in the 1970 collection are *Warrior Plain*; minority types include *Moundville Incised* and *Black-Filmed* sherds. There is also a Late Woodland component as shown by a number of clay-tempered sherds on the village portion of the sites.

A cluster of four villages, Ha-4, Ha-5, Ha-6, and Ha-11, was recorded by W. B. Jones on the second terrace above Elliots Creek. This cluster of sites is located 2.8 miles (4.5 km) due south of Moundville. Jones's surface collection from Ja-4 contained numerous *Moundville Black Filmed* and clay-tempered sherds. The surface scatter at Ha-4 measured 165 × 220 feet (50 × 67 m). Site Ha-5, the surface scatter of which measured 280 × 225 feet (85 ×

69 m), yielded predominantly clay-tempered sherds and a minority of shell-tempered *Warrior Plain* sherds. Pitted stones and stone discoidals were also collected from Ha-5. Site Ha-6, by contrast, was strung out along the terrace for approximately 625 feet (190 m) and was 125 feet (38 m) wide. In addition to surface collecting this site, Jones put in a few small test-pits. The artifacts from both the surface collection and the test pits at Ha-6 are missing from the collections at Mound State Monument; therefore, the assignment of Ha-6 to the Moundville phase must be considered provisional. Site Ha-11 was also an elongated village that overlooked Elliots Creek from the same terrace as the other three sites. This site measured 820 × 130 feet (250 × 40 m). The surface collection from this site "consisted of almost equal amounts of shell tempered and clay tempered pottery sherds [Nielsen *et al.* 1973:84]. "In aggregate, the surface scatters from these four sites, covered more than 6 acres (2.4 ha). These four sites, considered for the moment as one site, are the largest village area associated with the Moundville phase. Through the ceramics in their surface collections, these sites provide an important link with the preceding Late Woodland period. Clay-tempered, *McKelvey* pottery cannot now be viewed as just an aberrant inclusion on these and several other Mississippi period sites in the Black Warrior River Valley.

The southernmost sites assigned to the Moundville phase are the White Mound and Village, Ha-7, Ha-8, and Gr-13. The White Mound, first visited by C. B. Moore in 1905, was described by him as follows:

> This mound, the sides of which almost correspond with the cardinal points of the compass, is 13.5 feet in height. Neighboring trees show a deposit of mud left by freshets almost 8 feet from the ground; hence this mound must have afforded a welcome refuge to the aborigines in flood time. The western end of the mound is raised about 2.5 feet higher than the rest of the mound. The maximum diameter of the mound, E. and W., is as follows: 25 feet under each slope; the lower part of the summit plateau, 34 feet; beneath the slope leading to the higher part of the summit plateau, 18 feet; higher part of the summit plateau, 27 feet; total 129 feet. The maximum diameter N. and S. is 115 feet, 65 feet of which belongs to the summit plateau. Considerable digging to a depth of from 4 to 5 feet yielded in one place fragments of a human skull [Moore 1905:127].

Jones tested this mound in 1933 and had little better luck than did Moore. Jones also excavated the village area that adjoins the White Mound, with better results. These excavations yielded 28 burials with which were associated a number of *Moundville Filmed Engraved* vessels, copper ornaments, and shell beads. An abundance of *Warrior Plain* sherds were also obtained in the general digging. Nielsen's survey crew collected at this site in 1972 and reported 43 *Warrior Plain* sherds, five *McKelvey* sherds, and two *Mulberry Creek Cordmarked* sherds (Nielsen *et al.* 1973:81).

The southernmost site clearly within the Moundville phase is Gr-14, a mound and village combination located 45 river miles south of Moundville. O'Hear (personal communication) has found both *Warrior Plain* and *Moundville Black Filmed* ceramics at that site.

Upstream from Moundville the first site encountered after the Tu-50 mound is a small village, Tu-34, which is 3.5 (5.6 km) miles to the north–northeast. Jones's field notes and collection from this site clearly place it in the Moundville phase. *Moundville Black Filmed* and *Warrior Plain* sherds are in the surface material. Jones says of this site, "Another unmistakable tie between Moundville and Snow's Bend [Field notes, M.S.M.]." Jones paced the surface scatter and recorded it as 70 × 120 feet (21.3 × 36.6 m). Later field notes (1968), however, show Tu-34 to be much larger; and aerial photographs of the field in which this site is located suggest that about 3 acres (1.2 ha) would be a reasonable estimate of site size.

A mound and village pair, Tu-44, Tu-45, are 6.0 miles (9.7 km) north–northeast of Moundville, and are located on the interior of an un-named bend in the river. Jones's 1933 survey notes that the mound was about 4 feet (1.2 m) high, that its base measured 59 × 98 feet (18 × 30 m), and its plateau measured 51 × 91 feet (15.5 × 27.7 m). The long side of this mound was oriented approximately 10° west of north. The village area, which is immediately adjacent to the mound, measured 200 × 200 feet (ca. .9 acres or .36 ha). The surface collection from this village area was composed of *Warrior Plain* sherds. Moore (1905:243) lists this site as the mound at Jones Ferry.

The next sites upriver from Moundville are another mound and village pair—Tu-46, Tu-47—located 7.0 miles (11 km) due north of Moundville. Moore (1905:243) tested this mound and found nothing. Jones surveyed the mound and gave its height as 7 feet (2.1 m), its base as approximately 100 × 133 feet (30.5 × 40.5 m), and its summit dimensions as 69 × 91 feet (21 × 28 m). The village area, which is on a low ridge near the mound, covered an area approximately 100 × 270 feet (ca. .6 acres or .24 ha).

At the Foster Ferry Bridge, which is 8.4 miles (13.5 km) north–northeast of Moundville, there is a large Moundville phase village—Tu-156. The surface scatter, which was on a ridge in the river bottoms and which Jones characterized as "Moundville culture," covered an area 270 × 555 feet (ca. 3.4 acres or 1.4 ha). Just to the north of Tu-156 is another village, Tu-160, which Jones also identified as belonging to the "Moundville culture." This village is on a low ridge in the river bottoms. The surface scatter of this site covered an area approximately 75 × 110 feet (ca. .2 acres or .08 ha).

A small village, Tu-183, was found by Jones on the interior of Robinson's Bend, about 11 miles (17.7 km) north–northeast of Moundville. Jones clearly identifies this site as part of the "Moundville culture." The surface scatter that defined this site extended along a low ridge and covered an area of about 150 × 280 feet (ca. 1.0 acres or .4 ha).

The Snow's Bend site, a mound and village pair numbered Tu-2 and Tu-3, is 12.3 miles (20 km) north–northeast of Moundville. The Alabama Museum of Natural History excavated a portion of the cemetery at Snow's Bend during 1929–1931; these excavations were reported by DeJarnette and Peebles (1970).

Another large Moundville phase village, Tu-66, is located 13.1 miles north–northeast of Moundville on the outside of Clement Bend. This site, which is on a horseshoe-shaped terrace that almost fills the open part of the bend, measured 250 × 800 feet (ca. 4.6 acres or 7.4 ha).

The northernmost mound upstream from Moundville is Tu-56. When Jones surveyed this mound in 1933, its base measured 190 × 45 feet (58 × 14 m) and its height varied from 18 feet (5.5 m) on the west to 12 feet (3.65 m) on the south to 9 feet (2.75 m) on the north to 7 feet (2.13 m) on the east. The area around Tu-56 is a well-filled oxbow lake which has silted up heavily since being shut off from the river channel. Jones noted several sites, including a 200- × 200-foot (61- × 61-m) surface scatter near this mound. However, there are presently no data available on the materials he collected from any of these sites.

Although there is some evidence for sites north of the fall line, the northernmost Moundville phase site yet found on the Black Warrior River is a large village, Tu-146. This site is located 14 miles (22.5 km) due north of Moundville. Jones characterized the location of Tu-146 as being on a terrace that placed it above all but the highest rivers. He also clearly assigned the material collected from this site to the Moundville phase. The surface scatter from Tu-146 covered an area approximately 330 × 830 feet (ca. 6.3 acres or 2.5 ha). Thus, this site is only slightly smaller than the Ha-4, Ha-5, Ha-6, and Ha-11 combination.

Physiography and Biogeography of Moundville Phase Sites

Lewis Larson (1971a,b) has noted that Mississippi period sites are associated with areas of marked physiographic and ecological complexity.

> If the major sites of the Mississippi period are plotted on maps whereon there are also plotted physiographic provinces, forest regions, climatic areas, or other environmental distribution data, the sites, almost without exception, are found only on the boundaries of natural areas. . . .

Thus they come to occupy positions that allowed access to two or more significantly contrasting ecological zones. Apparently, as a consequence of this patterned distribution of Mississippi Period sites a factor other than agriculture was considered in the selection of the locations of these sites. While all were located on rivers, they were located only at those points where rivers flow out of one ecological zone into another [Larson 1971b:21].

These generalizations fit perfectly the distribution of Moundville phase sites in the Black Warrior River Valley.

Figure 13.10 shows the locations of these sites. The northernmost sites are located near the point where the river leaves the Piedmont and flows across the fall line and into the fall line hills of the Coastal Plain province. All but one of the sites are located in this transitional region which Fenneman describes as follows:

> Altitudes in this belt reach more than 700 feet in northern Alabama, but the level declines toward the Black Belt on the south and west. This is sometimes called the central pine belt of Alabama, a dissected upland with a few broad or flat divides. Much of the area is carved to maturity by valleys 100 to 200 feet deep. An exceptional cuesta near the middle of the belt in Alabama contains some areas of rugged wilderness. Relief near the larger streams may reach 250 feet within a half mile. Such areas, while belonging properly in the Coastal Plain province, are not "coastal plain" as that term is commonly used by the residents. The underlying rock formations of this zone are the Tuscaloosa next to the fall line and Eutaw farther out. Both are sandy and poorly consolidated but support steep slopes. Except for some fair red soils on the Eutaw the district is unproductive. Two-thirds of it remained woodland in 1913 [Fenneman 1938:67].

The southernmost of the sites, Gr-14, is located on the edge of the Black Belt, an area of deep residual prairie soils overlying the Selma chalk. This physiographic complexity is mirrored by the biotic variety in the Moundville area.

The Moundville phase sites in the Black Warrior River Valley are located on the northernmost edge of the Ecotone Province of the Temperate Deciduous Forest Biome (Southern Region). "The ecotone area is the pinelands which under primeval conditions showed transitions to oak–hickory, maritime, and magnolia forsts [Shelford 1963:Fig. 201, fn]."

Immediately to the north of Moundville, the ecotone region grades into the oak–hickory forest, and this region runs from north and west of Moundville to the other side of the Mississippi River. Eastward from Moundville, the oak–hickory forest extends along the fall line to the Cahaba River, where it again grades into the ecotone. To the north, about half the distance from Moundville to the Tennessee River, the oak–hickory

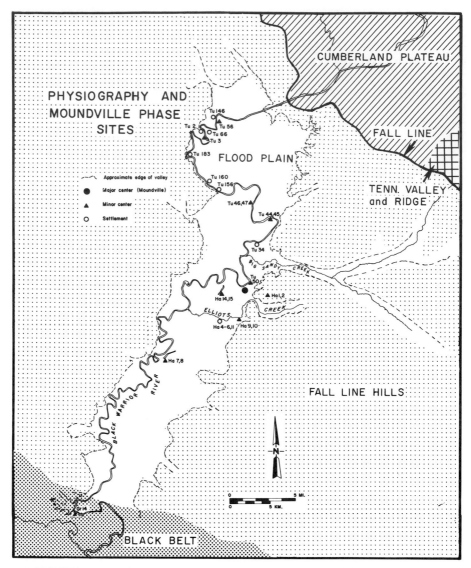

FIGURE 13.10. *Physiographic zones (after Fenneman 1938) and sites of the Moundville phase in the Black Warrior River Valley.*

forest turns into the mixed mesophytic forest of Tennessee and extreme northern Alabama.

An analysis of the dominant plant and animal species in the forest regions that surround Moundville phase sites shows that most species of flora and fauna exploited by the historic Indians and Euro-American settlers of the Upper Southeast were not only present, but also were, in some cases, abundant. In the northernmost forest region of interest here, the mixed mesophytic forest (tulip–oak–deer faciation of Shelford), dominant trees include the tulip tree, white oak, beech, basswood, yellow buckeye, sugar maple, American oak, and red oak. The dominant animal species was the faunal staple of the Southeastern Indians, the white-tail deer, *Odocoileus virginianus*. In fact, deer were most densely distributed in the mixed mesophytic forest during the early Euro-American period (Shelford 1963:36).

The oak–hickory forest (post-oak–turkey–hickory faciation of Shelford) is, with the exception of the ecotone, the closest forest region to Moundville. As its name suggests, the dominant trees are post, white, black, blackjack, and scarlet oaks. Also represented are shagbark, mockernut, and occasionally pignut hickory (Shelford 1963:57). The turkey, which along with the white-tail deer was one of the faunal mainstays of the native Americans, "may have had its largest population in the oak–hickory because of the edibility of the acorns of post oak and blackjack oak [Shelford 1963:59]." A small bear population, gray fox, raccoon, opossum, and striped skunk were also represented in the oak–hickory forest. However, "few mammals appear to have had large populations in oak–hickory forest or in pine land [Shelford 1963:59]."

The ecotone, which was the immediate setting for the Black Warrior River sites, would, under pristine conditions, have had the biotic forms from the oak–hickory, magnolia, and pine forests. Roland F. Harper (1913, 1928, 1943) has classified the ecotone forests of the Moundville region as part of the central pine belt region. He further divides this region into: (*a*) a short-leaf pine division, (*b*) the long-leaf pine hills, and (*c*) the Eutaw division. The stretch of the Black Warrior River from the fall line at Tuscaloosa to the area of the White Mound and Village, Ha-7, Ha-8, in Hale County lies within the short-leaf pine division; south of the White Mound and Village the forest grades into the Eutaw division. The long-leaf pine hills are shown by Harper (1943:Fig. 4) as forest islands within the short-leaf pine division.

In reconstructing the oak–hickory, magnolia, and maritime forests and the ecotone, Shelford and his students had only remnant forest areas with which to work. Nevertheless, the conclusions they reached about the dynamics of succession in this region are relevant not only to the Moundville phase but to any archeological study of this region.

> Succession in the ecotone area was probably making considerable progress in 1600 toward a broad-leafed forest climax. Magnolia forest and maritime forest were extending up the stream valleys to meet the oak–hickory forests in the upper portions of these valleys. Oak–hickory forest was also invading the broad-leaved bogs. In the upland between the streams, elements of the post oak faciation were probably present, with

blackjack oak important. Where fire occurred, there were, of course, fire climaxes, but had the pristine condition continued, climax forest would probably have been attained over a considerable part of the area of Magnolia faciation [Shelford 1963:88].

In effect, the location of the Moundville phase sites in the Black Warrior River Valley maximized the relationship of these sites to the number of nearby forest edges and proximity to a number of major forest areas. As a result, the major extra-agricultural foodstuffs exploited by the aboriginal inhabitants of these sites were not only available locally, but in the case of deer and turkey, the two most economically important animal species, they were especially abundant in nearby forest areas. Turkey abounded in the oak–hickory forest; deer reached their maximum density in the mixed mesophytic forest; bear, one of the major sources of edible oils, were present in the oak–pine facies; major species of nut trees (for flour and oil) grew in several nearby forest areas; finally, the Black Warrior, its tributaries, and local lakes were important sources of fish.

If, for the moment, we take the presence of an agricultural base as a given for the communities that make up the Moundville phase and view the location of these groups of sites in relation to the natural productivity of the landscape, then it is clear that the Moundville phase subsistence base had two strings to its bow—wild and agricultural resources. That is, Mississippian communities, contrary to some popular archeological thought, were not completely agricultural.

Examination of both the archeological and ethnohistoric materials from the Southeast support a conclusion that the time devoted to hunting and gathering, but especially to hunting, was almost equal to that devoted to agriculture. The Natchez, for example, made two crops of corn plus crops of beans and squash in a summer and also intensively exploited their natural surroundings. They systematically hunted deer and were one of the few tribes in the interior of the Southeast to do so in communal hunt. The Natchez also hunted bison and migratory waterfowl, gathered seeds, nuts, berries and fruits, and fished the rivers (Swanton 1946:290–291).

The Alabama, to give an example geographically closer to Moundville, engaged in widespread hunting in addition to their agricultural round.

> The savages usually set out on the hunt at the end of October. The Allibamons go to a distance of 60, 80, and even 100 leagues from their village and they carry along with them in their pirogues their entire family; they return only in March which is the season for sowing their fields. They bring back many skins and much smoked meat. When they have returned to their village, they feast their friends, and make presents to the old people who have been unable to follow them, and who have protected the cabins of the village during the hunting period [Bossou 1768 quoted in Swanton 1946:262].

Swanton notes that the above description "would undoubtedly hold good for all other tribes of the Creek Confederation [Swanton 1946:263]."

Although this and other eighteenth-century descriptions of native hunting practices probably reflect the effects of the deerskin trade on the Indians and a disengagement into settlements separated by "buffer zones" (Hickerson 1970), the observations of wide-ranging hunting limited to a few animal species in all probability holds for the late prehistoric period as well.

Larson (1971a:18) noted that 95% of the identifiable bone fragments from Etowah were deer and turkey. Smith's (1975) analysis of the faunal collections from several Mississippian sites in the central Mississippi Valley shows both selectivity and seasonality in hunting practices. He concludes:

> The Middle Mississippi groups being studied selectively exploited a restricted segment of the biotic community [Deer, Turkey, Raccoon, Fish, Migratory Waterfowl]. By concentrating on those species that occurred in high densities in small geographical areas (resulting in localized high biomass values), Middle Mississippi groups maximized their annual meat yield in relation to the energy necessary to exploit them (Smith 1975:139).

My own limited observation of the faunal collections from Moundville agrees with Smith and Larson's observations. Most of the readily identifiable bone fragments are deer and turkey. The locations of the Moundville phase sites, when viewed on the regional scale, maximizes access to habitat situations favored by these species.

Locational Analysis: The Black Warrior Sites

The Moundville phase sites in the Black Warrior River Valley can be visually grouped into three clusters plus two isolated sites. The northernmost, tightly clustered group contains two mounds, Tu-3 and Tu-56, a village, Tu-2, which is associated with Tu-3, and three additional villages, Tu-146, Tu-66, and Tu-183. The second, a widely dispersed group, is composed of three villages, Tu-160, Tu-156, and Tu-34, plus two mound-and-village pairs, Tu-46, Tu-47, and Tu-44, Tu-45. The third and largest group of sites is arranged in a semicircle around the Moundville site. In addition to Moundville, this group contains a mound, Tu-50, three mound-and-village pairs, Ha-1, Ha-2, Ha-9, Ha-10, and Ha-14, Ha-15, and a cluster of four sites, Ha-4, Ha-5, Ha-6, and Ha-11, which probably are one large village. South of the Moundville group are two isolated mound-and-village pairs, Ha-7, Ha-8, and Gr-14.

The straight-line and river distances between each of these sites and their first through third nearest-neighbors are given in Table 13.1. The spatial discontinuities between these three groups of sites are shown very clearly in this table. There are marked breaks between Gr-14 and Ha-7, between Ha-7 and the southernmost sites in the Moundville group, Ha-4, Ha-5, Ha-6, Ha-11, between the northernmost site in the Moundville group, Tu-50, and Tu-34, and between Tu-160 and Tu-183. The order–neighbor statistics for the sites in Table 13.1, excluding Gr-14, are given in Table 13.2. On the average, and via a straight-line route, each site is slightly more than 1 mile (.6 km) from its first nearest neighbor, about 2 miles (1.2 km) from its second nearest neighbor, and a little more than 2.5 miles (4.0 km) from its third nearest neighbor. The coefficients of variability [$CV = (S/\bar{x})(100)$] for these three nearest-neighbor measures are 82.01, 65.37, and 50.0%, respectively. The decreasing variability from first through third nearest neighbors suggests that these sites were not randomly placed on the landscape.

A number of methods, which are generally called nearest-neighbor analyses, have been developed by geographers and ecologists to test for randomness in point patterns distributed in one or more spatial dimensions. These methods have been summarized by King (1969), Haggett (1965), and Garner (1967) for geographical problems, and by Greig-Smith (1964) and Pielou (1969) for ecological analysis. Archeological applications include works by Clarke (1968), Hodder and Hassall (1971), Hodder (1972), Whallon (1973, 1974), and Hodder and Orton (1976). Two of the many variants of nearest-neighbor analysis will be used to analyze the distribution of Moundville phase sites in the Black Warrior River Valley.

The first method, developed by Clark and Evans (1954), compares the observed distance between first nearest-neighbor sites to the expected distance that is derived from a Poisson probability function. Clark and Evans define, although with a slightly different set of symbols, the following variables and equations to measure the distribution of nearest neighbors: Given N sites in an area of size A, then the density of sites, is defined as

$$\lambda = N/A. \tag{1}$$

The distance from site i to its first nearest-neighbor is symbolized as r_i, and the average nearest-neighbor distance, $\bar{r}_0$, becomes

$$\bar{r}_0 = \frac{\sum_{i=1}^{n} r_i}{N} \tag{2}$$

The expected average distance between sites can be shown to be

$$\bar{r}_E = 1/(2\lambda^{1/2}) \tag{3}$$

and the standard error of $\bar{r}_E$ is

$$\theta_{r_E} = .26136/(N\lambda)^{1/2} \tag{4}$$

The ratio

$$R = r_0/r_E \tag{5}$$

can then be used as a measure of the degree to which the observed distribution approaches or departs from random expectation. In a random distribution, $R = 1$. Under conditions of maximum aggregation, $R = 0$, since all of the individuals occupy the same locus and the distance to nearest neighbor is therefore 0. Under conditions of maximum spacing, individuals will be distributed in an even, hexagonal pattern, and every individual (except those at the periphery of the population) will be equidistant from six other individuals. In such a distribution, the mean distance to nearest neighbor will be maximized and will have the value

$$1.0746/\lambda; \tag{6}$$

when this is the case, $R = 2.1491$ [Clark and Evans 1954:447].

The measure R can be expressed as a standard variate of the normal curve by the equation

$$C = (\bar{r}_0 - \bar{r}_E)/\theta_{\bar{r}_E} \tag{7}$$

An additional stricture is that for the points under consideration, any point that is nearer the border of the area than it is to its nearest neighbor must be eliminated from the analysis.

For this and the subsequent nearest-neighbor analysis, 18 of the sites in the Black Warrior River Valley will be considered. GR-14 was eliminated because of its nearness to the boundary. In the absence of more information, sites Ha-4, Ha-5, and Ha-6 and Ha-11 will be treated as a single site. All contiguous mound-and-village pairs will be treated as single sites. The area to be used for density determinations will be the Black Warrior River Valley proper. That is, the eastern and western borders of the study area will be defined by the limits of alluvial and terrace deposits. The northern border will be set at the fall line; the southern border will be set at the Warrior Lock and Dam, the point where both banks become swampy. These borders yield a "natural" study area of approximately 246 mi^2 and a site density (λ) of .0771 sites per square mile.

By Clark and Evans's method, the expected distance value ($\bar{r}_E$) is 1.8007; the observed mean distance (r_0) is 1.389; $R = \bar{r}_0/\bar{r}_E = .7714$. The standard variate of the normal curve (c) is -1.8553; the probability (p) of a greater difference between $\bar{r}_0$ and $\bar{r}_E$, using the Pearson Type III distribution, because of the small sample size, is less than .1. The null hypothesis of a random distribution for these sites cannot be rejected, but the R value of

TABLE 13.1
Order-Neighbor Measures in Miles (Kilometers) for Moundville Phase Sites in the Black Warrior River Valley

Base site	First			Second			Third		
	Site	Land	River	Site	Land	River	Site	Land	River
Tu-146	Tu-56	.5(.8)	.3(.5)	Tu-66	1.2(2.0)	—	Tu-2	1.4(2.3)	2.7(4.3)
Tu-56	Tu-146	.5(.8)	.3(.5)	Tu-66	1.1(2.0)	—	Tu-2	1.5(2.4)	2.4(3.9)
Tu-66	Tu-3	.6(1.0)	—	Tu-2	.6(1.0)	—	Tu-56	1.1(1.8)	—
Tu-2	Tu-3	.6(1.0)	.7(1.1)	Tu-66	.6(1.0)	—	Tu-146	1.4(2.3)	2.7(4.3)
Tu-3	Tu-66	.6(1.0)	—	Tu-2	.6(1.0)	.7(1.1)	Tu-183	1.7(2.7)	4.1(6.6)
Tu-183	Tu-3	1.7(2.7)	4.4(7.1)	Tu-2	2.1(3.4)	5.1(8.2)	Tu-66	2.3(4.2)	—
Tu-160	Tu-156	1.0(.6)	1.0(.6)	Tu-183	2.5(4.0)	3.2(5.1)	Tu-3	3.3(5.3)	7.6(12.3)
Tu-156	Tu-160	1.0(.6)	1.0(.6)	Tu-46,47	2.7(4.3)	5.5(8.9)	Tu-183	3.5(5.6)	4.2(6.8)
Tu-46,47	Tu-44,45	1.9(3.1)	2.9(4.7)	Tu-156	2.7(4.3)	5.5(8.9)	Tu-34	3.1(5.0)	5.9(9.5)
Tu-44,45	Tu-46,47	1.9(3.1)	2.9(4.7)	Tu-34	2.1(3.4)	3.0(4.8)	Tu-156	4.5(7.2)	8.4(13.6)
Tu-34	Tu-44,45	2.1(3.4)	3.0(4.8)	Tu-50	3.1(5.0)	4.8(7.7)	Tu-46,47	3.1(5.0)	5.9(9.5)
Tu-50	Moundville	.5(.8)	.5(.8)	Ha-1,2	1.6(2.6)	—	Ha-14,15	2.4(3.9)	4.4(7.1)
Moundville	Tu-50	.5(.8)	.5(.8)	Ha-1,2	1.6(2.6)	—	Ha-14,15	1.7(2.7)	3.9(6.3)
Ha-1,2	Moundville	1.6(2.6)	—	Tu-50	1.6(2.6)	—	Ha-9,10	2.9(4.7)	—
Ha-9,10	Ha-4,5,6,11	1.5(2.4)	1.7(2.7)	Moundville	2.1(3.4)	15.4(24.8)	Ha-14,15	2.5(4.0)	11.5(18.5)
Ha-4,5,6,11	Ha-9,10	1.5(2.4)	1.7(2.7)	Ha-14,15	2.1(3.4)	9.8(15.8)	Moundville	2.8(4.5)	13.7(22.0)
Ha-14,15	Moundville	1.7(2.7)	3.9(6.3)	Ha-4,5,6,11	2.1(3.4)	9.8(15.8)	Tu-50	2.4(3.9)	4.4(7.1)
Ha-7,8	Ha-4,5,6,11	5.3(8.5)	12.3(19.8)	Ha-9,10	6.5(10.5)	14.0(22.6)	Ha-14,15	6.7(10.8)	14.8(23.8)
Gr-14[a]	Ha-7,8	13.9(22.4)	26.1(42.0)	Ha-4,5,6,11	18.9(30.4)	36.7(59.1)	Ha-9,10	19.8(31.9)	38.4(61.8)

[a]Excluded from all summary statistical calculations.

TABLE 13.2
Order-Neighbor Statistics in Miles for Sites in the Black Warrior River Valley

Order j	N		$\sum\limits_{i=1}^{N} r_{ij}$		$\sum\limits_{i=1}^{N} r_{ij}$		$\bar{r}_j$		s_j	
	Land	River	Land	River	Land	River	Land	River	Land	River
1	18	15	25.00	37.10	56.64	220.63	1.39	2.47	1.14	3.03
2	18	11	36.90	76.80	106.15	754.52	2.05	6.98	1.34	4.67
3	18	15	48.30	96.60	159.97	845.64	2.68	6.44	1.34	4.00

.7714 suggests that these sites are clustered, and that the average distance between them is about 25% less than would be expected if they were randomly located.

Clark and Evans's method, despite their statement (Clark and Evans 1954:446) that it would be generalized to K dimensions, is only applicable to first nearest-neighbors in two dimensions. Thompson (1956) and Dacey (1963, 1964) have generalized and refined this method for application to a point's jth nearest neighbors and have related the observed and expected distance values to the χ^2 distribution. Dacey has shown that for the jth nearest neighbor when there is a "random pattern with a theoretical density of λ points per unit area, . . . the quantity $2\pi\lambda r^2$ is a chi-square variable with $2j$ degrees of freedom [Dacey 1964:46]." This quantity, for a homogeneous random pattern obeying a Poisson probability function, measures the probability of a jth nearest neighbor being within a unit radius of a single point. Utilizing the additive nature of χ^2, for N points, the formula becomes

$$2\pi\lambda \sum_{i=1}^{N}/r_j^2 \tag{8}$$

This quantity is also distributed as chi-square with $2jn$ df. The resulting χ^2 value can be converted to a standardized normal variate by the formula

$$[(2\chi^2)^{1/2} - (2n - 1)^{1/2}]. \tag{9}$$

It should be noted that (8) is correct and that (23) of Dacey (1963:511); reprinted in King (1969) is incorrect (Dacey personal communication).

Table 13.3 gives the order-neighbor statistics for the first through third nearest neighbors for the 18 Moundville phase sites in the Black Warrior River Valley. For the second and third nearest neighbors, these sites show marked clustering; the observed distances are significantly less than the expected distances. The χ^2 value of 51.42 for $j = 2$ and 77.49 for $j = 3$ both have a probability $p > .995$. Thompson accepts a value of over .95 as an indicator of clustering, "the distance being smaller than expected [Thompson 1956:392]." The statistic for the first nearest-neighbor, which includes the outlier (Ha-7) shows that the distribution, although clustered, is tending to randomness.

TABLE 13.3
Nearest-Neighbor Statistics

Order j	N	$2\pi\lambda\sum_{i=1}^{N}r_{ij}^2$ (X^2)	$df = 2jn$	Standard deviation units	p
1	18	27.44	36	−1.02	$9 \geqslant p \geqslant 0.5$
2	18	51.42	72	−1.82	$p \approx .95$
3	18	77.49	108	−2.21	$p \geqslant .995$

The next step is to investigate what lies behind the clustering of these sites. Obviously there are correlations of site location with various habitat factors such as topography, water, and soils, and these correlations will be examined in the next section. For the moment the focus will remain on the sites, their typology, and the relationship between site types and their nearest neighbors.

There is a clear hierarchy among these 18 sites. The smallest site covers about .2 acres (.08 ha); the largest covers more than 300 acres (121 ha). One site has 20 ceremonial mounds; a number of sites have only one ceremonial mound; and several sites have no associated mounds. Based on previously established typologies of Mississippi period sites (Phillips, Ford, and Griffin 1951, Sears 1968), the Moundville phase sites in the Black Warrior River Valley can be placed into a descending hierarchy, based on site size, of a single major ceremonial center, several minor ceremonial centers, and a number of village–hamlet units.

Table 13.4 gives a cross-tabulation for first and second nearest-neighbors for each type of site. The result of the cross-tabulation shows that the major ceremonial center, Moundville, has minor ceremonial centers for its first and second nearest-neighbors; and, in fact, Moundville's first four nearest-neighbors are minor ceremonial centers. All but one of the village–hamlet units have minor ceremonial centers for either their first or second nearest-neighbors. The single village–hamlet without a minor ceremonial center for either its first or second nearest-neighbor, Tu-160, is the smallest site (.2 acres or .08 ha) in the sample. Minor ceremonial centers have the major ceremonial center, other minor ceremonial centers, and village–hamlet units as first and second nearest-

TABLE 13.4
Cross-Tabulation of First and Second Nearest–Neighbors by Site Type

	First nearest–neighbor			Second nearest–neighbor			
	Major ceremonial center	Minor ceremonial center	Village– hamlet	Major ceremonial center	Minor ceremonial center	Village– hamlet	Total
Major ceremonial center		1	0		1	0	2
Minor ceremonial center	3	2	4	1	3	5	18
Village– hamlet	0	5	3	0	4	4	16
Total	3	8	7	1	8	9	36

neighbors. These relationships among the types of sites strongly suggest that the village–hamlet units are related to the major ceremonial center only through the minor ceremonial centers, and that the minor ceremonial centers are related equally to each other, to the major ceremonial center, and to the village–hamlet units. The nature of this pattern is explored by Steponaitis (Chapter 14 of this volume) and his analysis details one aspect of these spatial relationships.

Soils and Site Locations in the Black Warrior River Valley

Ward (1965) examined the relationship between 24 Mississippi period sites in Tennessee, Georgia, and Mississippi and the soils on which these sites were located. He found that all the sites were situated on fertile and friable soils; that is, they were located on seasonally inundated silt loams and fine sandy loams. Larson (1972) has taken Ward's findings and suggested, in addition, that the percentage of such valuable soils was so low that Mississippian sites were fortified to assure a group's hold on this irreplaceable asset. The association of Moundville phase sites in the Black Warrior River Valley with the several soil types of Hale and Tuscaloosa counties confirms the expectations generated by Ward's analysis. All Moundville phase sites are located on silt loams, fine sandy loams, and clay loams. Moreover, there is a delicate balance between the height of the land and the average flood crest of the Black Warrior River. However, the relationships between the soils and the settlements are not exhausted by this single set of associations. The location, size, and variety of settlements in this valley are determined not only by soil type, but by the productivity of the soils that could be exploited easily by each settlement.

The soils of Hale and Tuscaloosa counties were mapped in the early twentieth century (U.S.D.A. 1912, 1914; Rowe *et al.* 1912; Winston *et al.* 1914). The major soil areas of Tuscaloosa County are shown in Figure 13.11. These major soil areas, which can be extended southward into Hale County, reflect soil derivation from three distinct geological formations. The soils in the southwestern portion of the county are derived predominantly from Upper Coastal Plain deposits; soils in the northeastern part of the county are derived from the sandstones and shales of the Appalachian spur, which extends into Tuscaloosa County; the soils in the extreme eastern portion of the county are derived from the limestones of the Limestone Valley area (C.E.S. 1967:29).

These major divisions are further broken down into soil areas. Soil Area 1 (Figure 13.11) is composed of materials derived from the extreme southwestern terminus of the Appalachian Mountain Chain. This area is

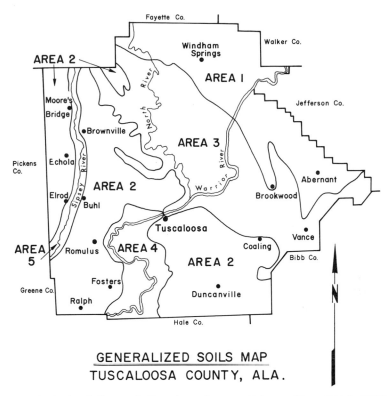

GENERALIZED SOILS MAP
TUSCALOOSA COUNTY, ALA.

FIGURE 13.11.   Soil areas in Tuscaloosa County, Alabama. [From C.E.S. (1967).]

characterized by narrow valleys and steep ridges; the soils are generally shallow and stony. Forest covers this area today. Soil Area 2 comprises the hilly, rolling topography of the northern Coastal Plain. These soil deposits, derived predominantly from Cretaceous ocean sediments, are deep and range from heavy clays to loamy sands. Forests also cover most of this area today. Soil Area 3 is composed of soils derived from the Tuscaloosa formation; soil deposits in this area are deep on ridge caps and shallow elsewhere. Soil composition ranges from red sandy clays to clay loams. The majority of this area is also presently forested. Soil Area 5 comprises the floodplain of the Sipsey River. Soils there are deep and poorly drained, and lands in this area have generally been left in an unimproved state. Soil Area 4 is of the greatest interest here:

> This soil area comprises the flood plain and river terraces of the Warrior River from the city of Tuscaloosa to and beyond the Green County line. About half of this area is so subject to flooding that it has been left in forest. The remaining half is excellent farm land and is the most productive and intensively farmed area of the county. Soils are deep and well-drained or moderately well-drained. Farms in this area are large, gener-

ally. Corn and cotton are the major crops, but large acreages are devoted to cattle and hog production [C.E.S. 1967:31].

Within Soil Area 4, the valley of the Black Warrior River, 8 soil groupings, 12 soil series, and 18 soil types have been identified and mapped (U.S.D.A. 1912, 1914; Rowe *et al.* 1912; Winston *et al.* 1914). The Huntington series is found on the first bottoms of the Black Warrior and its tributaries. The Kalmia and Bibb series are located in the bottoms in areas of poor drainage. The Cahaba series is found on the second bottoms of the principal streams. The Ochlockonee series is confined to stream banks with courses entirely within the Coastal Plain. The Greenville series is found on the oldest terraces and in the uplands. The principal upland soils include the Orangeburg group—Greenville, Orangeburg, Ruston, and Guin series—plus the Susquehanna and Norfolk series.

These soils vary in their mechanical properties, fertility, and productivity; as a result, their suitability for agriculture differs markedly. In the early twentieth century, *the baseline for all measures used herein*, the Huntington series of soils and the Waverly clay loams were among the most productive soils in the valley. Corn was the principal crop grown on these soils, and yields often reached 90 bushels per acre. The Kalmia and Bibb soils generally were not used for agriculture because they were poorly drained. The Ochlockonee series soils, when their natural drainage was sufficient, would produce up to 60 bushels of corn per acre. The Cahaba series soils were well suited to cultivation and yielded up to 40 bushels of corn per acre. The Greenville soils, which were probably the remains of an ancient river terrace, were highly productive, and yielded an average of 40 bushels of corn per acre; yields of 100 bushels per acre were reported. The upland soils on the margins of the valley, including the Orangeburg and Susquehanna soils, were not considered good corn soils: yields range from 10 to 25 bushels per acre. On the coastal plain the Ruston series soils produced up to 40 bushels of corn per acre in the early twentieth century.

From these soil summaries it is apparent that the Huntington, Cahaba, Greenville, Waverly, Ochlockonee, and perhaps Ruston series soils would have been the most attractive to prehistoric residents of the Black Warrior River Valley. The almost yearly redeposition and renewal of the Huntington series soils and the periodic flooding of the Cahaba series soils would have maintained their constant productivity and thus their attractiveness to agriculturalists. Within each of these types, the silt loams, loams, and fine sandy loams would have been the most easily worked and productive.

The yields in bushels per acre just given in the soil descriptions are probably within the range of yields obtained by aboriginal farmers. Although Winston *et al.* (1914) strongly argue for "modern" soil conservation practices such as terracing, green manuring, and the use of chemical fertilizers, it is clear that only the exceptional yields they report are the result of such practices. The reported average yields clearly result from plowing and planting alone. Furthermore, both average and exceptional yields were produced with nonhybrid corn. It was not until after World War II that Alabama farmers started planting hybrid corn (Andrews 1959:Table 3).

Table 13.5 scales the soils of the Black Warrior River Valley by scoring each soil with the midpoint of the average yield in bushels per acre for that soil as reported in Rowe *et al.* (1912), Winston *et al.* (1914), and Stroud *et al.* (1938). As an estimate of prehistoric yields this table is no doubt generous by some constant factor; however, as a scale of expected productivity for each soil type it is probably accurate (i.e., the interval ordering of the soil types is probably correct). It now remains to relate these soils and their productivity to site location and size.

C. Vita-Finzi, E. S. Higg, and M. R. Jarman have demonstrated the utility of systematic and comparable analyses of the relationship between a site and the kinds and productivity of the land that surrounds that site (Vita-Finzi and Higgs 1970, Jarman, Vita-Finzi and Higgs 1972, Jarman

TABLE 13.5
Midpoints of Average Yields of Corn per Acre by Soil Type

Soil type	Yield in bushels per acre		
	Tuscaloosa County 1911	Hale County 1909	Greene County 1923
Huntington fine sandy loam	30.0		
Huntington silt loam	45.0		
Waverly clay loam		35.0	
Greenville loam	40.0	17.5	
Greenville fine sandy loam	25.0		
Cahaba loam	32.5[a]	32.5	
Cahaba fine sandy loam	27.5	15.0	15.0
Cahaba sandy loam	20.0[a]		
Cahaba silt loam	30.0		
Cahaba clay loam			22.5
Ochlockonee fine sandy loam	17.5[a]	17.5	30.0
Ochlockonee clay loam			45.0
Ruston fine sandy loam	35.0		
Guin sandy loam	10.0[a]		
Orangeburg gravelly sandy loam	17.5[a]	10.0[a]	
Orangeburg fine sandy loam	17.5	12.0	
Susquehanna fine sandy loam	20.0[a]		
Oktibbeha fine sandy loam			11.5
Kalmia fine sandy loam	8.0[a]		8.0

[a]Estimated.

1972). They have proposed that the unit of analysis be the "site catchment" or "site exploitation territory."

> Studies of modern agricultural [Chisholm 1968] and hunting gathering [Lee 1969] economies have shown that the territory exploited from a site tends to lie within certain well defined limits. Other things being equal the farther the land is from the site the less likely it is to be exploited from it. In the former case the costs of exploitation rise to oppressive heights at a distance of 4–5 km from the settlement. Among the !Kung Bushmen the site exploitation territory lies within a radius of about 10 km; beyond this exploitation becomes uneconomic and the home base has to be moved. Clearly distance has to be qualified in terms of local topography; the operative factor is the time and effort involved in travelling rather than absolute distance. For the purposes of preliminary study we have adopted the distance covered in two hours' walking as the critical threshold for hunting and gathering economies, and in one hour's walking for agricultural exploitation. These figures approximate to the geographical limits proposed by Lee and Chisholm, and seem reasonable in that they would permit an effective working day after discounting walking time [Jarman, Vita-Finzi, and Higgs 1972:63].

Thus for analytical purposes, habitual subsistence activities are viewed as being carried on within a circumscribed area around an archeological site. Hunters and gatherers may shift through an "annual territory" (Jarman 1972:709) and within this annual territory the group may inhabit several sites, each with its own catchment.

Agricultural villages may also shift location through time as soil fertility declines or the supply of available firewood is exhausted. However, for a single site at a single point in time, the field around the site can be viewed as a series of concentric effort-lines across which, as one leaves the center, effort increases; and beyond some point, subsistence activities fall off to zero. The task, then, is to analyze the catchment in terms of the potential it held for the population occupying the site within it.

Jarman, Vita-Finzi, and Higgs (1972:63) have suggested that land within an hour's walk (4–5 km) should entail the majority of an agricultural village's exploitive domain. Chisholm has shown that the 4–5-km radius is an outside limit. "All studies agree to show that at a distance of 1 kilometre the decline in net return is large enough to be significant as a factor adversely affecting the prosperity of a farming population . . . [Chisholm 1968:66]." In their study of Middle Bronze Age through Saxon period agriculturalists in southern England, A. Ellison and J. Harris (1972) chose catchments of 2 km in radius for analysis, and catchments of varying size have been used with excellent results in the analysis of Mesoamerican agricultural systems (Flannery 1976, Brumfiel 1976). For the Moundville phase sites in the Black Warrior River Valley, catchments of both .6 and 1.2 miles radius were employed.

These figures approximate, to the nearest .1 mile, catchments of 1 and 2 km radius.

Circles of .6- and 1.2-mile radius were inscribed on sheets of drafting film and transferred by means of a thermofax machine to overhead transparency film. A transparency film was then centered on each site location on the soil maps and the soil boundaries were sketched on the film. (This process prevented any damage to three old and rare soil maps.) In defining the limits of each catchment, only land within walking distance of .6 and 1.2 miles were included. That is, catchments were carried neither across the river nor around oxbow lakes when the opposite shore was greater than a .6 or 1.2 mile walk. A polar planimeter was used to determine the extent of the soil types within each catchment and the total size of the catchment. These figures are given here as *total* measures. If a site's catchment overlapped with another site's catchment, then an *adjusted* figure was given in which the common part of the catchment was divided equally between the two sites.

The smallest catchment within a .6-mile walk of any site encompassed 184 acres; the adjusted catchment figure included only 84 acres. The largest catchment of .6-miles radius for both total and adjusted measures contained 723 acres. The average total size of catchments of .6-mile radius was 472.9 acres ($SD = 164.1$ acres); the average adjusted size of catchments of .6-mile radius was 447.9 acres ($SD = 169.3$ acres). The least extensive catchment of 1.2 miles radius contained 492 acres, and the adjusted figure fell to 184 acres. The largest catchment of 1.2 miles radius contained 3349 acres, and the adjusted measure was 2511 acres. The average total size of the 1.2-mile-radius catchments was 1741.1 acres ($SD = 816.83$ acres); the average adjusted average was 1442.3 acres ($SD = 676.52$ acres).

The soils in both the .6- and 1.2-mile-radius catchments around all but one site were predominantly Huntington, Waverly, and Cahaba soils. The exception, Ha-1, Ha-2, was surrounded by Greenville loam, itself an excellent corn soil. That is, not only are these sites located on the best, perpetually river-renewed, corn soils, but their catchments also are composed predominantly of such soils. To turn the site–soil association around, all but two significant parcels of Huntington silt loam in Tuscaloosa County were occupied by Moundville phase sites. The exceptions are an approximately 600-acre parcel of Huntington silt loam located on the interior of the river bend just to the north of Tu-46, Tu-47, and a large area of Huntington silt loam east of Tu-3.

Although the Hale County sites are located on Waverly clay loam, there are broad expanses of this soil along the river in Hale County on which no Moundville phase sites have been located. The only plausible explanation that can be offered for this absence of sites is the elevation of these soils above the river. North of Moundville in Tuscaloosa County, the Cahaba and Huntington soils that were occupied were sufficiently elevated to prevent complete and deep inundation of the village area by the spring floods. However, south of Moundville, which itself is elevated sufficiently to be above any flood recorded in modern history, the 100- through 150-foot contour lines are back so far from the river that the floodplain and Waverly clay loams are readily flooded. Only at the White mound and village, Ha-7, Ha-8, is the coincidence of soils and elevation seemingly compatible with permanent occupation. The elevation at which the perceived flood risk was acceptable to the inhabitants could probably be ascertained if measurements more accurate than those of the extant topographic maps (50- and 20-foot contours) were available.

Given that there are data on the average yield of corn in bushels per acre (Table 13.5) and that for each catchment the acreage extent of each soil type is known (Table 13.6), then a measure of productivity can be obtained for each catchment in each county. The gross median productivity of a catchment can be defined as the sum of the products of the midpoints of the range of the average yields of bushels of corn for each soil type in the catchment multiplied by the number of acres of that soil present in the catchment. The results of these calculations for *total* and *adjusted* catchments are presented in Table 13.6. These measures of catchment productivity are not meant to imply that they were the actual production figures for the catchments during the Mississippi period. They are calculated both so that the various catchments can be scaled and to facilitate comparison of catchments and sites within catchments.

The measures of catchment productivity range from a low value of 3535 bushels in an adjusted catchment of .6 mile radius, to a high of 84,553 in a catchment of 1.2 mile radius that had not been reduced to reflect areas shared with other catchments. The average productivity of unadjusted catchments of .6 mile radius is 14,780 bushels (SD = 4699.6 bushels), and the average for adjusted catchments of .6 mile radius is 13,892 bushels (SD = 4602.1 bushels). The average productivity of unadjusted catchments of 1.2 mile radius is 49,908 bushels (SD = 18,486 bushels), and the average for adjusted catchments of 1.2 mile radius is 40,743 bushels (SD = 17,217 bushels).

Among the most productive catchments are those occupied by Moundville and its nearest neighbors. Moreover, all of Moundville's nearest neighbors, except Ha-1, Ha-2, have adjusted productivity measures that are of the same order of magnitude as Moundville's. This implies that Moundville, the major ceremonial center, which is some 50 times larger than the largest of the other sites, had other villages and their catchments as part of its catchment. That is, Moundville's sustaining area included not only the products of its own catchment, but also the lands and products of its neighbors (see Chapter 14 of this volume).

If three assumptions can be made, then the data in Table 13.6 on site size and productivity can be turned to further use. The first assumption is

TABLE 13.6
Site Size, Catchment Size, and Catchment Productivity

Site	Site size in acres (hectares)	Acres (hectares) in catchment				Catchment productivity (bushels of corn)			
		.6 mile		1.2 mile		.6 mile		1.2 mile	
		Total	Adjusted	Total	Adjusted	Total	Adjusted	Total	Adjusted
Tu-146	6.3(2.55)	494(200)	494(200)	1877(760)	1749(708)	18,085	18,085	57,363	53,368
Tu-56	Mound	382(155)	380(154)	1236(500)	824(334)	15,210	15,120	43,665	29,120
Tu-66	4.6(1.86)	469(190)	467(189)	1241(502)	930(377)	17,820	17,730	45,538	34,550
Tu-2	No data	455(184)	371(150)	1477(598)	1227(497)	18,138	14,603	41,178	28,348
Tu-3	Mound	184(74)	84(34)	492(199)	184(74)	8,017	3,535	23,928	8,035
Tu-183	1.0(.40)	322(130)	322(130)	1041(421)	1041(421)	11,703	11,703	37,400	37,400
Tu-160	.2(.08)	312(126)	295(119)	1024(415)	799(323)	11,270	10,610	34,305	26,628
Tu-156	3.4(1.37)	290(117)	272(110)	924(374)	666(270)	10,860	10,170	32,518	23,368
Tu-46,47	.6(.24)	490(198)	490(198)	1801(729)	1801(729)	13,240	13,240	54,053	54,053
Tu-44,45	.9(.36)	303(123)	303(123)	694(281)	694(281)	10,950	10,950	23,340	23,340
Tu-34	3.0(1.21)ᵃ	438(177)	438(177)	1712(693)	1712(693)	13,258	13,258	55,398	55,398
Tu-50	Mound	543(220)	428(173)	2148(870)	1189(481)	18,740	15,640	61,393	40,830
Ha-1,2	1.8(.72)	723(293)	723(293)	2837(1149)	2511(1017)	10,708	10,708	45,491	38,426
Ha-4,5,6,11	6.5(2.63)	723(293)	723(293)	2837(1149)	2282(924)	21,143	21,143	77,953	65,975
Ha-7,8	5.0(2.02)ᵃ	559(226)	559(226)	2103(851)	2103(851)	19,458	19,458	72,613	72,613
Ha-14,15	.7(.28)	541(219)	541(219)	2368(959)	2059(834)	17,980	17,980	78,888	69,003
Ha-9,10	1.0(.40)	723(293)	723(293)	2837(1149)	2351(952)	11,913	11,913	46,895	36,717
Gr-14	No data	328(133)	328(133)	1255(508)	1255(508)	7,597	7,597	31,795	31,795
Moundville	300.0(121.45)ᵃ	706(286)	569(230)	3349(1356)	2027(821)	24,731	20,506	84,553	45,153

ᵃEstimated.

407

that there is a relationship between population size and subsistence base. There is sufficient confirmation for this proposition in the literature to accept it, at least in its most general form, as a viable assumption. The second assumption is that there is a systematic relationship between settlement size and the size of the population resident therein. In the absence of other data, population cannot be directly estimated from site size, nor can direct comparisons of settlement size be made cross culturally. However, within a single cultural system located in a relatively homogeneous habitat, sites on which similar sets of activities took place ought to vary in size in relation to the resident population (cf. Cook and Heizer 1968).

The third assumption is that the surface scatter reported for all the sites but Moundville is an accurate reflection of settlement size. Such an assumption relates the maximum extent of the surface scatter to the maximum extent of the settlement and its population. This assumption makes intuitive sense and it certainly follows much past archeological practice.

The estimation of Moundville's size poses special problems. As already noted, the area of Mound State Monument is a little over 300 acres. However, much of the park is occupied by the plaza and the mounds. Neither the Rhodes site, which is to the northeast of the park, nor the roughly 125 other acres outside the park boundaries which show surface material, have been included in estimates of the site's size. Therefore, until exact limits are established for the Moundville site, the 300-acre (121-ha) figure will be used. As an estimate of the site's total extent it is surely low; as an estimate of the residential area it is no doubt inflated.

Given these assumptions—the systematic relations between subsistence base and population, population and settlement size, settlement size and surface scatter—the following hypotheses can be put forward. First, if the primary criterion for individual site location is the presence of suitable soil for corn agriculture, then site size should vary systematically with the measure of productivity of the soil within a reasonable distance. That is, the population ought to be rationally distributed by the law of least effort with respect to areas of high productivity. Second, if Moundville served a number of settlements as a ceremonial center, then its size and location will not be a direct function of its catchment productivity, but instead will be related to the productivity and locations of the settlements which it served. Therefore any measure of correlation between site size and catchment productivity should be positive and significant for all sites, but the addition of Moundville to the site sample should lower the correlation between these variables.

Pearson product—moment correlation coefficients were calculated between the measure of site size and the several measures of catchment size and productivity. The results of this analysis are presented in Table 13.7.

TABLE 13.7
Correlation Coefficients Site Size by Catchment Measures

Site size	(1) All Sites (N=14)	(2) Minor ceremonial centers (N=6)	(3) Village–hamlets (N=7)	(4) Minor ceremonial centers and village–hamlets (N=13)
Total acres .6 mile	.3562	.1502	.8040*	.2811
Adjusted acres .6 mile	.1430	.1502	.8025*	.2807
Total acres 1.2 miles	.4953	.1114	.7488*	.2209
Adjusted acres 1.2 miles	.1811	.2437	.6752*	.1927
Total productivity .6 mile	.6159*	.5815	.8747**	.7342**
Adjusted productivity .6 mile	.4184	.5815	.8685*	.7243**
Total productivity 1.2 miles	.4819	.3828	.7713*	.4570
Adjusted productivity 1.2 miles	.0064	.4886	.6536	.4098

* $p \leq .05$.
** $p \leq .01$.

The first set of correlation coefficients, which includes Moundville (Column 1 of Table 13.7), shows a single significant correlation between site size and total productivity in the .6-mile radius catchment ($r = .6159, p < .05$). When, however, the productivity is adjusted to take into account overlapping catchments, the correlation coefficient falls markedly ($r = .4184$). The exlusion of Moundville from the sample results in significant correlations between site size and the total productivity of .6-mile radius catchments ($r = .7342, p < .001$) and the adjusted productivity of catchments of .6-mile radius ($r = .7243, p < .01$) (Figure 13.12). That is, excluding Moundville, approximately 52% of the variability in settlement size can be explained by the variability in the productivity of land within a .6-mile walk that does not cross into another catchment.

Further division of the sites into minor ceremonial centers and village–hamlet units yields additional patterned variability in these measures. Minor ceremonial centers (Column 2 of Table 13.7) show only a moderate correlation with productivity and no correlation with catchment size. Village–hamlet settlements (Column 3 of Table 13.7) are correlated with catchment size and highly correlated with catchment productivity. Approximately 75% of the size of these settlements can be explained by the variability in the adjusted productivity of the .6-mile radius catchments. The difference in the relationship of settlement size to catchment productivity probably can be understood by reference to the functions of the two types of settlements. The population size of the village–hamlet units probably was governed by productivity, the length of the walk to the fields, and an organization factor that set upper population limits for this type of settlement. Minor ceremonial centers, in contrast, seem to have

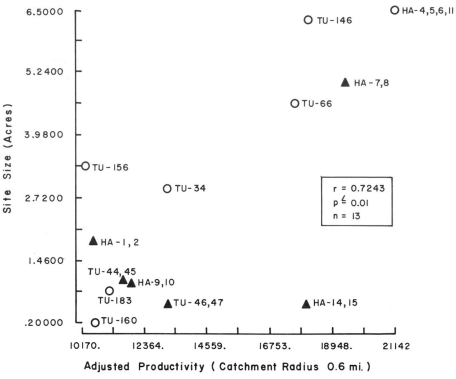

FIGURE 13.12.   *Scatter plot of site size versus the adjusted productivity in bushels of corn in the .6-mile radius catchments for (○) villages and (▲) village–mound pairs.*

been both administrative units and primary producers. As a result, population size in these settlements could have been set by administrative decisions rather than by the marginal yields of agriculture.

Moundville Phase Settlements: A Summary

Three categories of settlement are evident among the Moundville phase sites in the Black Warrior River Valley. Moundville, by measures of size, internal settlement complexity, variety of social statuses and political offices represented in the burials, and productive specialization, stands alone as the major ceremonial center. The second category, that of minor ceremonial center, is evidenced by 10 sites, each with a single platform mound, and all but one having an adjacent village area. The third category of site, villages and hamlets, seems to be the locus of primary agricultural production in the system; they show little evidence of internal status differentiation or variety in productive specialization.

Measures of the distribution of Moundville phase sites in the Black Warrior River Valley show that these sites were placed on the landscape in a nonrandom manner. For example, Moundville, the major settlement in the system, had only minor ceremonial centers for its first through fourth nearest neighbors, and all but one of the villages and hamlets had a minor ceremonial center for their first nearest neighbor. A statistical analysis of the distances between nearest neighbor sites shows that first nearest neighbors show moderate clustering, and second and third nearest neighbor sites are significantly and markedly clustered.

As Chisholm (1968:103) has noted, the location of an agricultural village is a compromise between (*a*) a set of resource factors, which are weighted on a cost of transport basis and (*b*) communication links with the wider community outside the village. Included in the first set of factors are proximity and access to arable land and water, which have the highest weights; access to various industrial raw materials, which have moderate weights; and access to fuel and building materials, which have the lowest weights. The locations of Moundville phase sites were chosen to minimize the "costs" of all these commodities.

All these sites were located on the most productive, easily tilled, self-renewing agricultural soils, and the size of the villages varied in relation to the productivity of the soils in their catchments. All sites had unrestricted access to water, and Moundville had, in addition to the river, four man-made lakes and several free-flowing artesian wells within its walls. All sites had access to the resources of the ecotone in which they were located, and all were proximate to the oak–hickory forest biome. The numerous "edges" of the ecotone and adjacent forests would have supported large populations of the animal species which Mississippian cultural systems seasonally harvested. All these sites were near sources of building materials, and the spring flood brought part of the year's firewood.

Communication links between these sites are accomplished easily either by land or by river. As Steponaitis shows (Chapter 14 of this volume) the pattern of site location minimizes the cost of transporation of material and information from the minor ceremonial centers to Moundville, and presumably, from Moundville back to these centers. There are, in addition, links from the group of sites on the Black Warrior River to the major east–west transcontinental trail system. The northernmost Moundville Phase sites in the valley of the Black Warrior River are situated near the Fall Line, and thereby near the Alabama–Chickasaw trail that ran from Montgomery to Memphis. The southernmost site lies on a branch of the

Alabama–Choctaw–Natchez trail which ran from Montgomery to Jackson (Myer 1928).

The locational analysis of these sites can best be concluded by drawing an analogy with a series of nested boxes, each box exponentially smaller than the preceding box. The initial box entails all the land in West-Central Alabama. Inside this first box is a second marked "only in river valleys." Inside the next box is one marked "only when the area is one of marked ecological and physiographic complexity." Next is a box labeled "politically optimal location" (see Chapter 14). Inside that box is yet another box marked "only where there are either Waverly clay loams, or Huntington, Cahaba, or Greenville loams, silt loams, or fine sandy loams." The final box is marked "only when these soils are sufficiently elevated to be immune from deep flooding and water logging at planting time." Each box has reduced the available land by at least a factor of 10; each has more narrowly circumscribed the area of potential settlement locations than the one before. These, then, are some of the factors which interacted with and shaped the form and substance of the Moundville phase's adaptation to the external world. The following chapter by V. Steponaitis deals with another aspect of the relations among these settlements, that of tribute flow.

Acknowledgments

The paper from which this chapter derives was written initially in 1970. A "ditto" version, *Moundville Paper No. 7*, was distributed in 1973. That version of the paper was cited kindly by David Clarke in his book *Spatial Archaeology* (Academic Press, 1977) and inadvertently was awarded the status of a published monograph by an anonymous editor who had the responsibility of checking the bibliography in Ian Hodder and Clive Orton's book *Spatial Analysis in Archaeology* (Cambridge 1977). For the present volume, the paper was reduced to about one-half its length and the catchment and distance measures were checked and recalculated. This quality-control task was taken on by Vincas Steponaitis, and he has my gratitude for cheerfully finding and correcting several errors.

At several points in its history, this paper has benefited from the constructive critiques of C. H. Fairbanks, L. Binford, A. C. Spaulding, C.-A. Moberg, J. A. Brown, S. Williams, J. Cottier, C. Sheldon, N. Jenkins, L. S. Alexander, H. T. Wright, III, J. B. Griffin, A. Rasoabemanana and S. M. Kus.

My work at Moundville was made possible only by the many kind acts of David L. DeJarnette to whom I will always owe a great debt. Partial funding for this work was provided by NSF Grant GS-2837.

References

Chisholm, M.
    1968   *Rural settlement and land use*. London: Hutchison.
Clark, P.J. and F.C. Evans
    1954   Distance to nearest neighbor as a measure of spatial relationships in populations. *Ecology* **35**(4):445–453.
Clarke, D.L.
    1968   *Models in archaeology*. London: Methuen.
Cook, S.F., and R.F. Heizer
    1968   Relationships among houses, settlement areas, and population in aboriginal California. In *Settlement archaeology*, edited by K.C. Chang. Palo Alto: National Press Books. Pp. 79–116.
C. E. S.
    1967   *Overall economic development program: Tuscaloosa County, Alabama*. Auburn: Cooperative Extension Service, Auburn University.
Cottier, J.W.
    1968   Archaeological salvage investigations in the Miller's Ferry lock and dam reservoir. Report on file, University Museums, University of Alabama. Tuscaloosa.
    1970   The Alabama River Phase: A brief description of a late phase in the prehistory of south central Alabama. Report on file, University Museums, University of Alabama. Tuscaloosa.
Dacey, M.F.
    1963   Order neighbor statistics for a class of random patterns in multidimensional space. *Annals of the Association of American Geographers* **53**:505–515.
    1964   Two-dimenstional random point patterns: A review and an interpretation. *Papers of the Regional Acience Association* **13**:41–55.
DeJarnette, D.L., and S.B. Wimberly
    1941   The Bessemer site. Museum Paper Number 17. Geological Survey of Alabama, University, Alabama.
DeJarnette, D.L., and C.S. Peebles
    1970   The development of Alabama archaeology—the Snow's Bend site. *Journal of Alabama Archaeology* **16**:77–119.
Fairbanks, C.H.
    1956   Archaeology of the funeral mound Ocmulgee National Monument, Georgia. *Archaeological Research Series* No. 3. Washington, D.C.: National Park Service.
Fenneman, N.E.
    1938   *Physiography of eastern United States*. New York: McGraw-Hill.
Friedman, J.A.
    1972   System, structure and contradiction in the evolution of "Asiatic" social formations. Doctoral dissertation, Department of Anthropology, Columbia University. New York.
    1975   Tribes, states, and transformations. In *Marxist analyses and Social Anthropology*, edited by M. Bloch. New York: John Wiley and Sons. Pp. 161–202.
Garner, B.J.
    1967   Models of urban geography and settlement location. In *Socioeconomic models in geography*, edited by R.J. Chorley and P. Haggett. London: Methuen. Pp. 303–360.
Grieg-Smith, P.
    1964   *Quantitative plant ecology*. London: Buterworth.
Haggett, P.
    1965   *Locational analysis in human geography*. London: Edward Arnold.

Harper, R.M.
   1913   Economic botany of Alabama, Part 1. Monograph No. 8. Geological Survey of
           Alabama, University, Alabama.
   1928   Economic botany of Alabama, Part 2. Monograph No. 9. Geological Survey of
           Alabama, University, Alabama.
   1943   Forests of Alabama. Monograph No. 10. Geological Survey of Alabama, University,
           Alabama.
Heimlich, M.D.
   1952   Guntersville basin pottery. Museum Paper No. 32. University, Alabama: Alabama
           Museum of Natural History.
Hodder, I.R.
   1972   Locational models and the study of Romano–British settlement. In *Models in ar-
           chaeology,* edited by D.L. Clarke. London: Methuen. Pp. 887–909.
Hodder, I.R., and M. Hassall
   1971   The nonrandom spacing of Romano–British walled towns. *Man* **6**(3):391–407.
Hodder, I.R., and C. Orton
   1976   *Spatial analysis in archaeology.* London: Cambridge University Press.
Holmes, N.H., Jr.
   1963   The site on Bottle Creek. *Journal of Alabama Archaeology* **9**:16–27.
Jarman, M.R.
   1972   A territorial model for archaeology: a behavioral and geographical approach. In
           Models in archaeology, edited by D. L. Clarke. London: Methuen.
Jarman, M.R., C. Vita-Finzi, and E.S. Higgs
   1972   Site catchment analysis in archaeology. In *Man, Settlement, and urbanism,* edited by
           P.J. Ucko, R. Tringham, and G.W. Dimbleby. London: Duckworth. Pp. 61–66.
Jenkins, N.J.
   1976   Terminal Woodland–Mississippian interaction in northern Alabama: the West
           Jefferson Phase. Paper presented at the annual meeting of the Southeastern Ar-
           chaeological Conference. Tuscaloosa, Alabama.
King, L.J.
   1969   *Statistical analysis in geography.* Englewood Cliffs, New Jersey: Prentice-Hall.
Larson, L.H., Jr.
   1971a   Transcribed discussion. *Newsletter of the Southeastern Archaeological Conference*
           10(2):28–34.
   1971b   Settlement distribution during the Mississippi period. *Southeastern Archaeological
           Conference Bulletin* **13**:19–25.
   1972   Functional considerations of warfare in the southeast during the Mississippi
           period. *American Antiquity* **37**(3):383–392.
Lee, R.B.
   1969   !Kung Bushmen subsistence: An input output analysis. In *Contributions to an-
           thropology: Ecological essays,* edited by D. Damas. National Museums of Canada,
           Bulletin No. 230. Ottawa. Pp. 73–94.
McKenzie, D.H.
   1965   Pottery types of the Moundville Phase. *Southeastern Archaeological Conference Bulle-
           tin* **2**:55–64.
   1966   A summary of the Moundville Phase. *Journal of Alabama Archaeology* **12**:1–58.
Merleau-Ponty, M.
   1964   *The Primacy of Perception.* Evanston, Illinois: Northwestern University Press.
Moore, C.B.
   1905   Certain aboriginal remains of the Black Warrior River. *Journal of the Academy of
           Natural Sciences* 2nd Series **13**(2):124–244.
   1907   Moundville revisited. *Journal of the Academy of Natural Sciences* 2nd Series
           13(3):334–405.

Myer, W.E.
1928   Indian trails of the southeast. *Forty-Second Annual Report of the Bureau of American Ethnology*. Washington, D.C.: Smithsonian Institution. Pp. 726–857.

Nielson, J.J., J.W. O'Hear, and C.W. Moorehead
1973   An archaeological survey of Hale and Green Counties, Alabama. Report on file, University Museums, University of Alabama. Tuscaloosa, Alabama.

Peebles, C.S.
1970   Moundville and beyond: Some observations on the changing social organization in the southeastern United States. Paper presented at the 69th annual meeting of the American Anthropological Association.
1971   Moundville and surrounding sites; some structural considerations of mortuary practices. In "Approaches to social dimensions of mortuary practices," edited by James A. Brown. *Society for American Archaeology Memoir* **25**:68–91.
1972   Monothetic-divisive analysis of the Moundville burials: An initial report. *Newsletter of Computer Archaeology* **8**(2):1–13.
1973   Excavations at Moundville: 1905–1951. Manuscript on file at the Museum of Anthropology, University of Michigan, and at Peabody Museum, Harvard University.
1974   Moundville: The organization of a prehistoric community and culture. Doctoral dissertation, Department of Anthropology, University of California, Santa Barbara.
1977   Biocultural adaptation in prehistoric America: An archaeologist's perspective. *Southern Anthropological Society Proceedings* **11**:115–130.

Peebles, C.S., and S.M. Kus
1977   Some archaeological correlates of ranked societies. *American Antiquity* **42**(3):421–448.

Phillips, P.
1970   Archaeological survey in the lower Yazoo basin, Mississippi, 1949–1955. *Papers of the Peabody Museum of Archaeology and Ethnology* **60**. Cambridge: Peabody Museum.

Phillips, P., J.A. Ford, and J.B. Griffin
1951   Archaeological survey in the lower Mississippi valley, 1940–1947. *Papers of the Peabody Museum of Archaeology and Ethnology* **25**. Cambridge: Peabody Museum.

Pielou, E.C.
1969   *An introduction to mathematical ecology*. New York: Wiley.

Rowe, R.W., W.G. Smith, and C.S. Waldrop
1912   Soil survey of Hale County, Alabama. *Field Operations of the Bureau of Soils, 1909*. United States Department of Agriculture, Eleventh Report. Pp. 677–703.

Sears, W.H.
1964   The southeastern United States. In *Prehistoric man in the new world*, edited by J. D. Jennings and E. Norbeck. Chicago: University of Chicago Press. Pp. 259–287.
1968   The state and settlement patterns in the new world. In *Settlement archaeology*, edited by K.C. Chang. Palo Alto: National Press Books. Pp. 134–153.

Sheldon, C.
1974   The Mississippian–Historic transition in central Alabama. Doctoral dissertation, Department of Anthropology, University of Oregon. Eugene.

Shelford, V.E.
1963   *The ecology of North America*. Urbana: University of Illinois Press.

Smith, B.D.
1975   Middle Mississippi exploitation of animal populations. *Anthropological Papers, Museum of Anthropology, University of Michigan* **57**. Ann Arbor.

Smith, C.A.
1976   *Regional Analysis*, 2 volumes. New York: Academic Press.

Swanton, J.R.
1946   The Indians of the southeastern United States. *Bureau of American Ethnology, Bulletin* **137**. Smithsonian Institution, Washington, D.C.

Thompson, H.R.
    1956   Distribution of distance to *N*th neighbor in a population of randomly distributed individuals. *Ecology* **37**(2):391–394.
Trickey, E.B.
    1958   A chronological framework for the Mobile Bay region. *American Antiquity* **23**(4):388–396.
Trickey, E.B., and N.H. Holmes, Jr.
    1971   A chronological framework for the Mobile Bay region, revised 1970. *Journal of Alabama Archaeology* **17**(2):115–128.
United States Department of Agriculture
    1912   Soil map, Hale county sheet, Alabama. Washington, D.C.: Bureau of Soils, United States Department of Agriculture.
    1914   Soil map, Tuscaloosa County sheet, Alabama. Washington, D.C.: Bureau of Soils, United States Department of Agriculture.
Vita-Finzi, C., and E.S. Higgs
    1970   Prehistoric economy in the Mount Carmel area of Palestine: Site catchment analysis. *Proceedings of the Prehistoric Society* **36**:1–37.
Ward, T.
    1965   Correlation of Mississippian sites and soil types. *Southeastern Archaeological Conference Bulletin* **3**:42–48.
Whallon, R., Jr.
    1973   Spatial analysis of occupation floors I: Application of dimensional analysis of variance. *American Antiquity* **38**:266–278.
    1974   Spatial analysis of occupation floors II: The application of nearest neighbor analysis. *American Antiquity* **39**:16–34.
Williams, S. (editor)
    1968   The Waring papers: The collected works of Antonio J. Waring, Jr. *Papers of the Peabody Museum of Archaeology and Ethnology* **57**. Cambridge: Peabody Museum.
Wimberly, S.B.
    1956   A review of Moundville pottery. *Newsletter of the Southeastern Archaeological Conference* **5**(1):17–20.
Winston, R.A., W.J. Latimer, L. Cantrell, W.E. Wilkinson, and A.C. McGehee
    1914   Soil survey of Tuscaloosa, Alabama. *Field Operations of the Bureau of Soils, 1911.* United States Department of Agriculture, Thirteenth Report. Pp. 5–74.

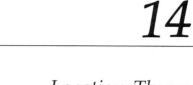

14

Location Theory and Complex Chiefdoms: A Mississippian Example

VINCAS P. STEPONAITIS

The man–land approach has been highly productive especially when dealing with cultural systems of relatively low complexity. I would suggest however that when dealing with systems of greater complexity, man-man relationships take on increasing importance in the determination of the spatial distribution of activity loci and thus of settlements. In emphasizing basically economic man-man relationships, Central Place Theory furnishes a potentially useful analytical model for dealing with these systems [Johnson 1972:769]

Central place principles provide a complete statement of urban location only when urban centers are supported exclusively as market centers by the retail and service functions they provide [Berry 1967:35].

In recent years, archeologists have devoted a great deal of attention to central place theory in the analysis of prehistoric settlement systems. Generally using the formulations of Christaller (1933, 1966), studies have examined the structure of central place hierarchies in the ancient Near East (Johnson 1972, 1975), Roman Britain (Hodder 1972), and prehispanic Mesoamerica (Flannery 1972, Hammond 1974, Marcus 1973, 1976). Such

417

applications have met with varying degrees of success, but overall have shown the utility of the approach, at least in certain situations.

Central place theory consists of a set of related models that were originally developed to explain certain regularities in the sizes and distribution of urban centers. Christaller defined a central place as a locus where centralized goods and services are available to a populace living in a surrounding hinterland, or "complementary region." Christaller's model assumes that central places form a hierarchy in which each lower-order center supplies only a certain subset of the services provided by each higher-order center. Higher-order centers not only supply a wider range of services than lower-order centers, but also have larger complementary regions, each of which encompasses a number of smaller, lower-order regions. It was predicted that under certain conditions, central places would form a regularly spaced, hierarchically nested lattice, with each place centrally located in a complementary region of hexagonal shape. (For a more complete summary, see Berry 1967, Berry and Pred 1961, or Haggett 1965).

It is not difficult to see why archeologists have found Christaller's formulation so attractive. His model is elegant, and it links certain aspects of economic behavior with a type of archeological data that is often easily recoverable—the distribution of sites over the landscape. Yet the model's many attractions should not be allowed to obscure its general limitations. As Berry's quote at the beginning of this chapter indicates, most workers have come to the conclusion that Christaller's model and its various derivative forms are relevant only to the analysis of *market* locations (see also Smith 1974:171).

The purpose of this chapter is to develop a locational model that is applicable to settlement hierarchies in complex prestate societies or complex chiefdoms. Although it has been suggested that Christaller's model, perhaps with minor modifications, can be used in the context of chiefly settlement systems (e.g., Lafferty 1976), I find this view to be questionable. Christaller's central place theory is based on a set of restrictive assumptions which do not hold true in premarket contexts. Since true market economies are absent in complex chiefdoms, these societies are clearly beyond the theory's reach. Thus, a different model is called for, one founded on premises more appropriate to the level of sociopolitical integration being considered.

I will begin by examining the organization of complex chiefdoms and the relations that structure settlement hierarchies within them. Next I will formulate a locational model for chiefly centers, at the same time showing in more detail why Christaller's central place theory is inappropriate. Finally, I will use the model to analyze the spatial distribution of centers in an archeologically known complex chiefdom—the Moundville phase of west-central Alabama.

Complex Chiefdoms: Organization, Tribute, Political Centers

The use of a typological approach in categorizing societies poses the problem of having to define discrete units in what is essentially an evolutionary continuum. The general evolutionary concept of chiefdom, as formulated by Service (1962) and Fried (1967), has been widely used and sometimes misunderstood. Thus, it is necessary to clarify the concept as it is used here. I focus particularly on complex chiefdoms, a category that includes only a subset of the societies traditionally classified under Service's rubric of *chiefdom*.

Chiefdoms are distinguished from politically less complex societies by the fact that they exhibit institutionalized and permanent offices of leadership. These offices are associated with well-defined jurisdictions, and exist independently of the individuals who occupy them at any given time. Each office is endowed with a relatively fixed set of duties and prerogatives, not entirely dependent on the incumbent's degree of competence (Service 1975:72). That is, a chief's mandate to lead derives primarily from the authority vested in the office he holds. This authority is maintained and sanctified by means of a pervasive religious ideology and by conspicuous sumptuary ritual. In politically more developed chiefdoms, sacred authority is supplemented by considerable power of sheer physical coercion, secular punishment, in order to ensure compliance (Sahlins 1958:11, *passim*). Chiefs do not, however, control the institutionalized monopoly of force which has been said to characterize the political apparatus of states. In a society where the ability to use force legitimately is held by various constituent subunits in severalty, the chief does not have exclusive access to force, only the most extensive access (Earle 1973:27).

Individuals who fill chiefly offices are most often recruited, at least in part, with reference to their position in a social hierarchy, wherein differential statuses are ascribed at birth. The ranking of individuals relative to one another is often cognized in terms of genealogical distance to a mythical common ancestor. The closest living descendent of that ancestor is assigned the highest rank, the ranks of other members of society being reckoned in proportion to the proximity of their relationship to this highest-ranking person. The resulting social form has been termed by Kirchhoff (1955) a *conical clan*, and by Firth (1936) a *ramage*.

Chiefdoms are further characterized by what has been termed *redistribution*. In essence, redistribution is based upon an institutionalized relationship of reciprocity between subject and chief (Sahlins 1972:188). The subjects place their surplus goods and labor at the disposal of the chief, and in return, the chief is expected to provide goods and services for the benefit of his subjects. Both Sahlins (1958) and Service (1962, 1975) have argued that redistribution in all chiefdoms exists primarily to coordinate specialized production within a diversified regional economy. More recent work, however, has shown this view to be questionable. Ethnographic evidence suggests that in many chiefdoms, local units of production were self-sufficient in most goods needed for subsistence (Earle 1973, 1977, Finney 1960). Whatever goods were not available locally could be obtained by means of small-scale exchanges organized on the household level (Peebles and Kus 1977). Indeed, it is not very useful to regard redistribution as a unitary phenomenon in all chiefdoms, because its function can vary greatly from one context to another (Earle 1977). Much of this variation is related to differences in the degree of political complexity and centralization in the societies where redistribution is found.

The simplest chiefdoms are characterized by only one level of superordinate political offices. Chiefs who fill these offices are only part-time administrators, and are not exempt from having to engage in the manual labor of subsistence production. Because the chief's household is expected to be self-sufficient, a chief does not live off the surplus food and gifts brought him by his subjects; most of the surplus collected thus gets distributed back to the populace. The flow of material goods between hierarchial levels is balanced, or sometimes even weighted in favor of the commoners. The chief, in living up to his role as a superiorly generous kinsman, is often forced to give away more than he takes in, the difference being made up by his household having to work harder at production.

Complex chiefdoms, on the other hand, have two- or three-tiered political hierarchies. Their social systems exhibit a well-developed class structure, in which nobles are clearly differentiated from commoners. Because most of the nobility are not required to engage in production, the burden of the latter pursuit falls entirely on the commoners. The nobility consume, for their own subsistence and political needs, most of the goods the commoners pass up the hierarchy. Relatively few goods remain available for redistribution to the commoners, so the reciprocal obligation is typically fulfilled in either of two ways: (*a*) by means of secular or religious services that only nobility can perform, or (*b*) by means of presentations that are more symbolic than substantial, such as token redistribution of insignificantly small amounts of food. A semblance of reciprocity between chiefs and commoners is thus maintained, but as Sahlins (1972:140) aptly points out "the cycle has all the reciprocity of the Christmas present the small child gives his father, bought with the money his father had given him." What formally appears to be redistribution in complex chiefdoms is functionally more akin to the collection of tribute than the insitutionalized sharing of surplus (Earle 1973:23, Oliver 1974:1008).

Complex chiefdoms are usually organized according to a principle wherein a higher-ranking chief has control over a number of lower-ranking chiefs, each of whom, in turn, directly controls a certain territorial district or social unit. In such a hierarchical system, political control implies the right to collect tribute, and vice versa. These two processes are inextricably linked, primarily because they are mutually reinforcing. A chief commands the payment of tribute by virtue of his political power. At the same time, however, a large part of the chief's power rests on his ability to maintain continued access to a sufficiently large pool of tribute (Sahlins 1963). A lower-ranking chief collects tribute from his underlings, but in turn he owes tribute to his political superior. The apex of a chiefly political hierarchy is effectively defined by the level at which all upward payments of tribute stop.

What is important for the purposes of this chapter is that different nodes in the political hierarchy are usually associated with spatially discrete (and archeologically recognizable) central settlements. Insofar as administrative control and collection of tribute are the major activities that structure the political hierarchy, these activities may also have some correlates in spatial terms, influencing the locations of central settlements relative to one another and to the populations they serve. Yet before we can build a model to describe these spatial correlates, we must examine how the network of administration and tribute flow is organized vis à vis the political centers in a chiefly system. This question will now be explored with reference to two ethnographically documented complex chiefdoms—the Natchez of the Lower Mississippi Valley, and the Society Islanders of Polynesia.

THE NATCHEZ

The Natchez political hierarchy was composed of two administrative levels. The nation as a whole was governed by a supreme chief called the Great Sun, and also had a supreme war chief called the Tattooed Serpent. Below this upper level, the chiefdom was subdivided into a number of smaller administrative districts, each placed under the immediate control of a lower-ranking chief, with the exception of the district in which the Great Sun and Tattooed Serpent resided, which they themselves administered directly (Swanton 1911, White *et al.* 1971:369, 382).

Some of the earlier accounts mention nine or more of these districts, but after 1716 there seem to have been only six (Swanton 1911:45–48). Information concerning their size is scanty, although one was described as having been more than a square league (9 mi^2) in extent (DuPratz 1774:73). Swanton (1911:43–44) estimates that in 1698 the nation as a whole comprised 3500 souls, but by 1730 had been reduced to some 2100.

Within each district was a single permanent center, referred to by the French somewhat misleadingly as a village. Such a center consisted of a temple and the dwellings of the chiefs and other important personages arranged around a plaza. It was marked by monumental architecture insofar as the temple and/or some of the important dwellings were placed upon pyramidal mounds artificially constructed of earth (Neitzel 1965; Swanton 1911:158, 190–191, 213–214; Thwaites 1900:135). Contrary to what the word "village" implies, these centers did not have nucleated populations. Only the high-ranking officials and perhaps a few others lived here. In 1700, for instance, the Grand Village, political capital of the Natchez, was described as having, in addition to the temple, only nine cabins by one count, and only four by another. Most of the population was widely dispersed over the countryside, living in isolated households or small hamlets situated in the midst of their own agricultural fields (Du-Pratz 1774:33; Swanton 1911:108).

The Natchez had a two-tiered hierarchy of centers, which directly reflected their political structure. At the apex of this hierarchy was the Grand Village, where the Great Sun and the Tattooed Serpent lived. This place served as the administrative and religious center not only of its own district, but also of the nation as a whole. Subordinate to the Grand Village were at least four lower-order centers, each of which directly administered the scattered population living within its district.

Collection of tribute within this system took a number of different forms. At one extreme was sporadic tribute, which stemmed from a chief's right to demand goods or labor from the people under his jurisdiction at any time. It is clear from the accounts that such sporadic demands were not uncommon (e.g., Swanton 1911:110, 135, 166, 221, 217). More regularly scheduled tribute collections also took place, however, the people usually bringing their goods to a place in or near the political center of the district in which they lived. The focus of many of these payments seems to have been the local temple:

> The fathers of families never fail to bring to the temple the first fruits of everything they gather; and they do the same by all the presents that are made to the nation. They expose them at the door of the temple, the keeper of which after having presented them to the spirits carries them to the great chief, who distributes them to whom he pleases [Charlevoix, quoted in Swanton 1911:166].

Most of the goods at the disposal of the chiefs were probably acquired through the agency of large-scale organized feasts (Swanton 1911:109ff). Such feasts were regularly celebrated at least once a month, which to the Natchez meant 13 times a year. Each district held its own feasts separately, although it seems that the harvest feast, which took place annually near the Grand Village, may have involved participation from all the other districts as well. Feasts embodied religious ritual (including some token distribution of food), games, and public dancing, yet their important political function was not overlooked by the early observers. DuPratz remarked:

The feasts are equally religious and political, religious in that they appear to be instituted to thank the Great Spirit for the benefits he has sent men, political in that the subjects then pay their sovereign the tribute which they owe. . . [quoted in Swanton 1911:110].

Similarly, Penicaut wrote:

It is ordinarily the great chief who orders the dance feasts . . . in all the villages of his dominion. These feasts are ordinarily undertaken when the great chief has need of some provisions such as flour, beans, and other such things, which they place at the door of his cabin in a heap the last day of the feast. . . . The chiefs of the other villages send him what has been obtained from the dances in their villages [quoted in Swanton 1911:121].

The last passage is of particular interest, for it tells us how the lower-order centers were linked to the capital in the overall flow of tribute. The dominant pattern was apparently this: Individual households would bring their goods to the central settlement of the district in which they resided. There, the goods would be bulked, and the local chief would send a certain fraction of the revenue to the Grand Village, keeping the rest for his own subsistence and political needs. In this way, the Grand Village would receive tribute directly from its own district, but indirectly from the households elsewhere, the goods first being channeled through the lower-order centers.

It is also interesting to note that the flow of administrative information often followed the same channels as the flow of goods, albeit in the opposite direction. Decisions made by the Great Sun were first transmitted to the lower-order centers, from where the local chiefs would be expected to enforce them on the people within their respective districts (McWilliams 1953:88–89, Swanton 1911:100).

THE SOCIETY ISLANDERS

The political structure of the Society Islands at the time of European contact was somewhat more complex than that of the Natchez. The basic political unit was the *fenua*, or "tribe." There were from 17 to 20 of these units on the island of Tahiti alone, a few more or less at any given time owing to the vicissitudes of political consolidation and fragmentation. *Fenua* were quite variable in size. According to Oliver's estimates, their populations on Tahiti ranged from 940 to over 4000 individuals, with a mean of approximately 2080 (Oliver 1974:Table 3).

Each *fenua* was internally composed of smaller administrative districts called *patu*, which were further subdivided into even smaller units called *rahui*. Corresponding to this territorial structure was a three-tiered hierarchy of political offices. The *fenua* as a whole was ruled by a chief. Directly below him were a number of subchiefs, each of whom had jurisdiction over a *patu*. Officials of lowest rank were stewards (*ra'atira*) who each had charge of a *rahui*. Although the larger *fenua* exhibited all three tiers of this hierarchy, the smaller *fenua* tended to have only two (Oliver 1974:969).

Several supratribal alliances existed on the island, each composed of a number of adjacent *fenua* united under the hegemony of a militarily superior chief. This paramount chief could collect some tribute from his weaker allies and expect their support in times of war. Yet to call all of these alliances "princedoms" as some European writers did would be misleading. Some, if not all, of these aggregates were relatively fragile entities in which the paramount chief's centralized political power was never very well consolidated. Moerenhout described these units as:

> invariably divided into [several] major districts each with its own chief, and only temporarily—and at that not absolutely—subordinated to the chief of one of them. Moreover, it appears that each district's own chief had more authority locally than did the chief whose overlordship had been established by conquest. The overall power of the latter was so limited by the jealousy and unity of the former that he was never able to annex their districts to his own domain . . . [quoted in Oliver 1974:991].[1]

Political centers associated with administrative districts at all levels were characterized by the presence of *marae*—structures used in religious ritual. These *marae* were rectangular courtyards, usually paved with stones, and sometimes surrounded by a masonry wall (Oliver 1974:177ff). Within the courtyard were a number of upright stones, and generally a stone platform at one end. *Marae* of many types were built (Emory 1933), but it is quite clear that their size and elaboration were directly tied to the status of the chiefs who used them. Thus, the "tribal" *marae* of a *fenua* chief would be a larger and more complex structure than that of a subchief, which in turn would be more elaborate than that of a steward (Oliver 1974:186, 1010, *passim*). Indeed, such a three-tiered hierarchy of *marae* has been identified archeologically on Mo'orea (Green *et al.* 1967:224–225). Other architecturally distinctive features associated with these centers were chiefly dwellings, assembly houses, and/or assembly platforms, all of which are recognizable archeologically (Green *et al.* 1967:Table 13, Oliver 1974:170ff).

Most of the population on the islands lived in scattered households within several kilometers of the coast. Each household would typically have several buildings constructed for different purposes, and would be set off from other households by a good distance, sometimes hundreds of meters. There was, however, a general tendency for households to form loose spatial clusters of 10 or so (Oliver 1974:44).

---

[1] Quoted material on this page and on pages 425, 426, and 429 is from Oliver, D. L., *Ancient Tahitian Society*. Honolulu: University Press of Hawaii.

Collections of chiefly tribute were occasioned by various circumstances. Chiefs could, of course, demand goods or labor from their subchiefs and commoners at any time. Large-scale levies would be imposed at the commencement of public works projects, at the arrival of visiting dignitaries, and for the equipping of war parties. More regular contributions from commoners were received as first fruits offerings and at various other ceremonial and ritual occasions (Oliver 1974:1001ff, *passim*).

The tribal (*fenua*) chief always seems to have received tribute from each subtribe (*patu*) as a unit. Sometimes, each subtribe would make separate presentations and on different occasions; other times, all the subtribes would be present and make their contributions jointly (Oliver 1974:1006). A chief could sometimes collect tribute away from his center while traveling, but most of these presentations apparently took place at or near the tribal *marae,* the highest-order chiefly center within the *fenua*.

Collection of tribute at the subtribal level is much more poorly documented, so that the channels through which it generally flowed are difficult to reconstruct with confidence. The only good clue comes from Morrison's description of an offering of first fruits:

> the fruits being ripe the Towha [subchief] . . . informs the Ratirra [steward] . . . that on such a day the offering is to be made and it is proclaimed through the district by a cryer to inform their respective tenants . . . who on the day appointed each gather some of every species and having put them in a basket [also taking a suckling pig, they] repair to the house of their respective Ratirra who then heads his own people and proceeds to the house of the Towha, who with his priest and orator heads the whole and the procession proceeds to the house of the Chief, sometimes four or five hundred in a body, where being arrived [some rituals are performed, after which] the fruits are deposited before the Chief and they retire and return home. When this ceremony is performed to the King [i.e., paramount chief], the Chiefs of the District always head the procession.
>
> This ceremony is then performed by the Ratirras to their respective Towha and afterwards by the Tenants to their Ratirras . . . [quoted in Oliver 1974:262–263].

This passage is noteworthy, because it suggests to us that goods generally moved along regular social channels: commoners to steward to subchief to chief. In spatial terms, this movement would translate as follows: from household to lower-order center to higher-order center, and so on up.

Corvee labor in some instances seems to have been mobilized along the same lines as the flow of goods. In executing corvee projects of a tribal scale, much of the initial work would be allocated and carried out at the subtribal level, the final work being completed at the tribal chiefly center. This process is illustrated in the following passage:

The *upea ava* or salmon net, is the longest and most important, and is seldom possessed by any but the principal chiefs; it is sometimes four fathoms long, and twelve or more feet deep. One of this kind was made by Hautea, the governor of Huahine, soon after our arrival. . . . As is customary on all occasions of public work, the proprietor of the net required other chiefs to assist in its preparation. Before he began, two large pigs were killed and baked. When taken from the oven, they were cut up, and the governor's messenger sent with a piece to every chief; on delivery the quantity was stated which each was desired to prepare towards the projected net . . . .

The servants of the chief furnished their quantity of netting . . . as other parties brought in their portions, the chief and his men joined them together . . . [Ellis, quoted in Oliver 1974:999–1000].

Similarly, thatch plates for a public building to be put up at the tribal capital were manufactured by each subtrial unit in advance, and pooled at the site of construction:

The people from different parts are assembling in our neighborhood in order to thatch the big house called Nanu which is built at the public expense. . . . The people of both Huahines are gathered together . . . [and] they have brought their several divisions of thatch . . . [Davis, quoted in Oliver 1974:997].

Whether the netting and the thatch plates that arrived at the tribal capital were sent from the chiefly centers of the subtribal districts is never explicitly stated, but it is extremely likely that they were. Thus, once again the same spatial channels would appear to have been used: Corvee labor destined for a higher-order center often had to be mobilized first at the lower-order centers.

And finally, as in the preceding passage, we find that administrative information was also passed along the same channels, the movement often being in a direction opposite to that of tribute:

Whenever a measure affecting the whole of the inhabitants was adopted, the king's *ve'a* or messenger was despatched with a bundle of *niaus* or leaflets. On entering a district, he repaired to the habitation of the principal chiefs, and, presenting a cocoanut leaf, delivered the orders of the king. . . . When the chiefs approved of the message, they sent their own messengers to their respective tenants and dependents with a cocoanut leaf for each, and the orders of the king [Ellis, quoted in Oliver 1974:1032].

A Locational Model for Chiefly Centers

Having examined the types of interaction that take place among centers in a chiefly hierarchy, we are now prepared to move to a more general level, and formulate a locational model. First, however, let us examine in more detail why a market-based model like Christaller's is inappropriate for the analysis of chiefly systems as those I have just described. When the characteristics of settlement hierarchies found in market as opposed to chiefly systems are compared, a number of fundamental differences become apparent. These differences do not merely have to do with the types of commodities or services being exchanged. Rather, they are primarily structural, involving the manner in which the centers are articulated with their hinterlands and with each other.

The first of these differences can be seen in how the hinterland served by each central settlement is formed. The hinterland or "complementary region" of a market center arises basically from the statistical outcome of numerous individual decisions. When choosing between market centers which offer equivalent goods, people generally go to the one that is nearest (see Berry 1967:10–23). Thus, the complementary region of a market center consists de facto of the area closer to it than to any other equivalent central place. If a market center were to change its location relative to other centers (all else remaining constant), the size and shape of its complementary region would shift accordingly.

The hinterlands of chiefly centers, on the other hand, are formed de jure as clearly delineated territories. In effect, they are administrative districts, defined in terms of established political boundaries, and often in terms of corporate land-use rights vested in a particular kin group. Such a district owes its existence to social and political factors that are independent of preferential decisions made by commoners. It is imposed from above, as it were, and retains its integrity no matter where within its boundaries the chiefly center is located.

The second difference between market and chiefly systems lies in the nature of the relations among centers of equivalent order. Market centers offering equivalent goods compete with one another for the traffic of the outlying populace. As a result, market centers tend to be evenly spaced over the landscape in a configuration which minimizes their direct competition and maximizes their profits (Berry 1967:86).

The relations among centers in a chiefly system can be quite different. While some degree of competition surely exists among chiefly centers that are independent of each other politically, the amount of competition among centers *within* a single, well-integrated political system should be considerably less pronounced. This lack of competition stems from the fact that the boundaries of internal administrative districts are fixed, de jure, by the social and political parameters of the system as a whole. The size and shape of a center's administrative district remains unaffected by that center's nearness to other politically affiliated centers of equivalent order. Thus, there appears to be no process operating that consistently favors spatial repulsion between such centers, and so it should not be surprising to find a great deal of variance in their relative spacing.

Finally, perhaps the most important difference between market and chiefly systems lies in the configuration of the spatial channels by which rural households are linked to higher-order centers. In a market system, movements between the household and all central places which service it are direct. A consumer travels to a nearby lower-order center for frequently needed goods, and to a higher-order center for less frequently needed goods. In each case, the consumer goes to and from the market directly, and generally by the shortest route (Figure 14.1A).

The links between households and higher-order centers in a chiefly system, on the other hand, are often *not* direct. A household brings its tribute in goods and labor to the lower-order center of the administrative district in which the household is established. From the lower-order centers, a part of this tribute then passes up to the higher-order center. Political messages and administrative information tend to follow the same spatial channels as tribute, but often travel in the opposite direction. In this way, movements between households and higher-order centers are mainly channeled through centers of lower order, intermediate in the political hierarchy. The highest-order center interacts with relatively few households directly: those in its immediate district (as H in Figure 14.1B).

SPATIAL EFFICIENCY IN COMPLEX CHIEFDOMS

Given that a market-based central place theory is inappropriate for analyzing the spatial relationships among centers in a chiefly system, an alternative model is called for. Let us therefore discuss some of the factors

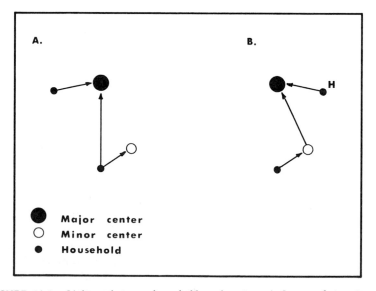

FIGURE 14.1. *Linkages between households and centers. A. In a market system. B. In a chiefly system. H Indicates a household in the immediate district of the major center.*

likely to serve as constraints on the location of chiefly centers. We can take as a point of departure a statement by Blanton:

> For our purposes here, the most salient characteristics of central institutions are that they require energy to function, and that the transactions take time. Energy is supplied by subsystems of producers, who must work more than would necessary in the absence of such institutions. The fact that there is a finite amount of energy in the environment of any society, and that producers can be pushed or otherwise encouraged to produce only so much surplus means that central institutions always have a maximum size and are always limited to a finite number of transactions per unit time. . . . We might expect, therefore, given time and energy constraints, that in all societies we will find the presence of strategies that minimize both the time and energy costs of central institutions. . . . Although there undoubtedly will be considerable cross-cultural variability in the form of these strategies and the extent to which minimization is actually achieved, there is probably no society in which there is complete disregard for the energy and time costs of these mediating central institutions [1976:251–252].[2]

The central institutions of complex chiefdoms, it will be remembered, were supported by the surplus production and corvee labor of the commoners. Yet Sahlins' (1963, 1972) work has convincingly shown that each producer was willing to expend only a limited amount of effort above the minimum required to fulfill his own and his household's needs.

> In other words, the chiefly toll on the household economy had a moral limit consistent with the kinship configuration of the society. Up to a point, it was a chief's due, but beyond that, highhandedness. The organization set an acceptable proportion between the allocation of labor to the chiefly and domestic sectors [Sahlins 1972:147].

The cost of maintaining the central institutions in complex chiefdoms was quite high. In addition to the nobility, whose numbers could be quite sizable, there were various other nonproducers who derived their support, directly or indirectly, from tribute brought in by the commoners. Among these nonproducers were various religious functionaries and craft specialists subsidized by the chiefs, in addition to a large number of servants, warriors, entertainers, and other "hangers-on," who would gather around the residences of important chiefs and live off their largesse. The entourage of a Tahitian chief, for example, consisted of "many of his friends and their families often amounting to near 100 principals besides their attendants [Banks, quoted in Oliver 1974:971]." Also contributing to the cost of these central institutions was their need to maintain an aura of awesomeness and sanctity, which served to validate the authority vested in them. Monumental architecture, costly sumptuary

[2] This is quoted from Blanton, R., Anthropological Studies of Cities. *Annual Review of Anthropology* 5.

goods, and elaborate religious ritual were all part and parcel of the chiefly apparatus, the brunt of whose maintainance fell on the commoners. The elaborateness of this sumptuary complex and the size of the chiefly administrativereligious superstructure were directly related to the level of political centralization and complexity within the system. As the centralization and complexity increased, so did the cost of maintaining its central institutions.

Returning to the energy constraints I spoke of earlier, it appears that the most complex chiefdoms attained a level of consumption that came quite close to the "moral limit" of household surplus production, and even tended to occasionally surpass it. "The major Polynesian paramounts seemed inclined to 'eat the power of the government too much', as the Tahitians put it, to divert an undue proportion of the general wealth towards the chiefly establishment [Sahlins 1963:297–298]." If a chief continued to make unacceptable demands on the goods and labor of his subjects for too long, the usual response was rebellion, the offending chief being deposed by another who was more moderate in his exactions (ibid.). The fact that such rebellions occurred (or at least were said to occur) means the chiefly apparatus was well aware that its access to tribute was limited, and that it had to be concerned with staying within certain bounds. Thus, as Sahlins (1968:93) notes, "The Hawaiian paramounts worried about [the people most subject to tribute] and devised all manner of means to relieve the pressure on them."

One way to relieve this pressure without curtailing the size of the chiefly establishment would be to make more efficient use of the effort which the people were legitimately willing to put to chiefly ends. Speaking in general terms, this "public" effort consisted of two major components: (a) effort invested in surplus production and corvee labor, and (b) effort invested in movement of people and goods (such as tribute) to and from the chiefly centers. The chiefs could maximize the former, without increasing the burden on the commoners, only by minimizing the latter. One of the most effective and obvious ways to minimize the latter might have been to locate chiefly centers efficiently over the landscape.

In order to see how such spatial efficiency is optimally achieved, we can construct an idealized model based on the parameters already discussed. Consider a chiefly system consisting of five administrative districts each of which has a political center (Figure 14.2). The administrative hierarchy is of two levels, with one major center, or capital, and four politically subordinate minor centers. Each center collects tribute from the settlements in its own district. In addition, the capital collects tribute from each of the minor centers.

Let us assume that the "cost" or effort involved in moving over a certain distance is proportional to the distance squared.[3] Let us also

---

[3] The "cost" we are concerned with here is not simply measurable in terms of energy

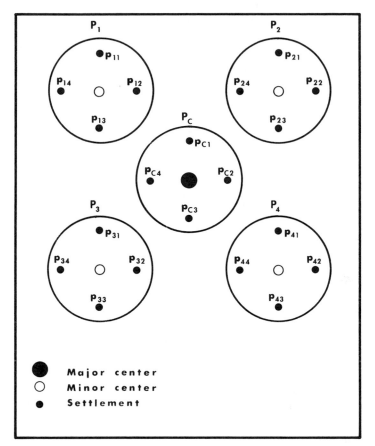

FIGURE 14.2. *An idealized chiefly system consisting of five administrative districts. The populations of individual settlements (p_{ij}) and of districts (p_i) are noted symbolically.*

assume that the demand for goods and services placed by a district center on a particular settlement is proportional to the settlement's population; similarly, that the demands the capital places on a minor center are proportional to the population of the district which the minor center controls. We can then express the aggregate yearly effort invested in movement between the settlements in a single district and their center as:

$$m_i = \sum_{j=1}^{J} tp_{ij}d_{ij}^2, \tag{1}$$

expenditure (which would be directly proportional to distance), but rather involves people's perception of how much effort and trouble a trip of given length involves. Empirical studies have shown that the frequency of travel (or other kinds of interaction) between two points often diminishes in proportion to a value very close to the distance squared (Haggett 1965:35–37), suggesting that the latter measure may well approximate the variable we are interested in. Using distance squared has the added advantage of having a mathematically simple solution for finding the point at which "cost" is minimized.

where m_i is proportional to the aggregate yearly effort expended in intradistrict movement, that is, in movement between the political center of the ith district and the settlements tributary to it, t is proportional to the average yearly amount of tribute, in goods and labor per capita, that is channeled into (or through) the minor centers, p_{ij} is the population of the jth settlement in the ith district, and d_{ij} is the distance from the jth settlement in the ith district to that district's political center.

Similarly, the yearly cost of movement between the minor center of the ith district and the capital is expressed as follows:

$$m_i' = T_i P_i D_i^2, \tag{2}$$

where m_i' is proportional to the aggregate yearly effort expended in interdistrict movement, that is, in movement between the minor center of the ith district and the capital, T_i is proportional to the average yearly amount of tribute, in goods and labor per capita, sent to the capital from the minor center of the ith district, P_i is the population of the ith district, and D_i is the distance between the minor center of the ith district and the capital.

The symbols t and T_i represent measures of how much tribute flow takes place at the intra- and interdistrict levels, respectively, and thus are related to the degree of political centralization at each level. Each value increases as the intensity of interaction at that level increases, that is, as there are more man-trips per person per year. In addition, these values are related to the amount of goods (tribute) flowing at each level, measured in terms of bulk. As the flow of goods increases, so do these values, because the more goods are being carried, the greater is the effort to move a certain distance. In most cases, t is greater than T_i, because all tribute destined for the capital must first pass through the minor center.

Movements to and from minor centers thus involve costs on two levels: (*a*) costs deriving from interaction with settlements within their districts (m_i), and (*b*) costs deriving from interaction with the capital (m_i'). A measure of the total costs of movement to and from the minor center of the ith district (M_i) can be expressed as follows:

$$M_i = m_i + m_i', \tag{3}$$

$$M_i = \sum_{j=1}^{J} t p_{ij} d_{ij}^2 + T_i P_i D_i^2. \tag{4}$$

The ideal location for a minor center is the place where M_i is minimized. If there were no interdistrict tribute flow ($T_i = 0$ and $m_i' = 0$, as is the case in simple chiefdoms), then M_i equals m_i. Under these conditions, M_i is minimized when the minor center is geographically centered with respect to the population in its own district (Figure 14.3). This ideal location is the district's *demographic center of gravity* (henceforth referred to as DCG; for a procedure to calculate the DCG see the Appendix).

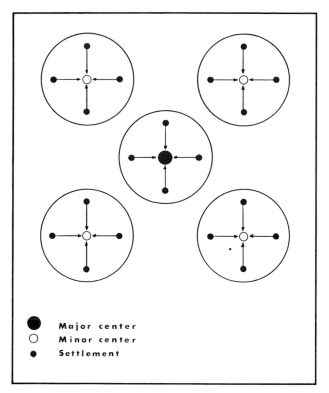

FIGURE 14.3. *The ideal locations of centers with no tribute flowing from minor centers to the capital (i.e., $T_i = 0$). Each center is located at the demographic center of gravity (DCG) of its administrative district. Arrows indicate the flow of tribute.*

If, however, the lower-order center pays tribute to the higher-order center ($T_i > 0$ and $m_i' > 0$, as in complex chiefdoms), then the ideal location of a minor center is no longer at the DCG, but is closer to the capital (Figure 14.4). The greater the degree of political centralization, the greater is the ratio of T_i to t, and the farther is the optimal location deflected away from the DCG and toward the capital. (A procedure to calculate this ideal location is given in the Appendix.)

The implications of the latter finding are quite interesting, because they are contrary to what one would expect in a market situation. As we have seen, the optimal location for a chiefly center is often *not* at the geographical center of the population within its district, whereas a market (if it is to minimize movement costs) is always ideally located at the geographical center of its complementary region. Moreover, our model predicts that lower-order chiefly centers would tend to cluster *toward* their capital. This is in opposition to the empirically observed tendency in market systems, where lower-order central places are prone to be dis-

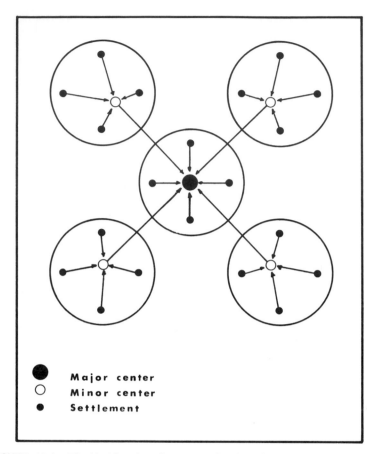

FIGURE 14.4.   *The ideal location of centers with tribute flowing from the minor centers to the capital (i.e., $T_i > 0$). Note that each minor center is not at the DCG of its district, but rather is closer to the capital. Arrows indicate the flow of tribute.*

persed *away* from higher-order central places because of the latter's competitive advantage in attracting customers (Hodder 1972:897–900; Brush 1953).

The next aspect of the model to be considered is the optimal location of the chiefly capital. As in Eq. (1), we can express the yearly cost of intradistrict movement to and from the capital (m_c) as:

$$m_c = \sum_{j=1}^{J} tp_{cj}\, d_{cj}^2, \tag{5}$$

where p_{cj} is the population of the jth settlement in the capital's immediate district, and d_{cj} is the distance between the capital and the jth settlement in the capital's immediate district. Since the capital collects tribute from all the minor centers as well, the interdistrict component of the movement costs can be written, following Eq. (2), as:

$$m_c' = \sum_{i=1}^{I} T_i P_i D_i^2. \tag{6}$$

Combining Eqs. (5) and (6), we get the expressions for the total yearly cost of movements to and from the capital (M_c), analogous to Eqs. (3) and (4):

$$M_c = m_c + m_c', \tag{7}$$

$$M_c = \sum_{j=1}^{J} tp_{cj} d_{cj}^2 + \sum_{i=1}^{I} T_i P_i D_i^2. \tag{8}$$

The capital is ideally located at the place where M_c is minimized. If it were to optimize with respect to the first term (m_c) only, the capital would locate at the DCG of its district. If, on the other hand, it were to optimize with respect to the second term (m_c') only, the capital would be situated at the *center of gravity of the minor centers* (CGMC), each being weighted according to $T_i P_i$. (A procedure to calculate CGMC is presented in the Appendix.) In fact, the capital would be expected to optimize with respect to both m_c and m_c' at the same time, its ideal location being somewhere between the DCG and CGMC, a spatial comprise between the two.

This is not to say, however, that the two terms are of equal importance. When a high degree of political centralization exists, the ideal location of the capital is primarily determined by the positions of the lower-order centers, rather than by the distribution of local settlements within its own district. If the value of T_i is not small relative to t, m_c' will generally be large in comparison with m_c. This is true because $\bar{D}_i$ is likely to be very much greater than $\bar{d}_{cj}$, and $\bar{P}_i$ very much greater than $\bar{p}_{cj}$ (D_i being the mean value of D_i, $\bar{d}_{cj}$ the mean value of d_{cj}, etc.). The resulting implication is that in order to keep movement costs from becoming excessive, the location of the capital must always be near the CGMC.

In an empirical situation, finding the optimal location for the capital requires, among other things, complete data on the distribution of population, and a knowledge of where the boundaries between the administrative districts lie. However, such complete data are almost never available to the archeologist. This problem can to some extent be circumvented by using the CGMC as an approximation of the ideal locus, for as we have just shown, in theory these two points should always be relatively close to each other. If we can assume that the tribute flow from each of the minor centers is the same (i.e., the value of $T_i P_i$ is the same for all i), then calculating the CGMC is a considerably more practical undertaking, especially in an archeological context, because it requires only that we know the spatial distribution of the minor centers (see Appendix). Since such centers tend to be archeologically conspicuous sites, complete recovery of their locations within a region is often not difficult to accomplish.

Using the CGMC as an approximation, we can empirically determine the degree to which a capital's observed location approaches its theoretical ideal. Assuming that the annual tribute flow from each of the minor centers is the same, we can use an index of spatial efficiency (E) expressed as follows:

$$E = \frac{\sum^{I}_{i=1} R_i^2}{\sum^{I}_{i=1} D_i^2} \tag{9}$$

where R_i is the distance from the CGMC to the minor center in the ith district, and D_i is the distance from the capital to the minor center in the ith district. Because by definition $\sum R_i^2$ is less than or equal to $\sum D_i^2$, this index equals 1.0 when the capital is ideally located, and becomes smaller as the distance between the observed and ideal location increases (see Massam 1972:6).

In constructing this model, we have dealt with finding the ideal location of a minor center and that of the capital as two separate problems. In fact, the two problems are closely related, because the optimal location of a minor center depends upon the location of the capital, and vice versa. Although it should be possible to build a model that takes both aspects into account simultaneously, I do not feel it would substantially change the nature of the predictions. The approach adopted here is heuristically sound, and has the advantage of being much less complicated mathematically.

Briefly summarizing this section, we have examined a number of factors which are likely to influence to location of political centers in a complex chiefly society. The following general conclusions have emerged, based on the model just developed:

1. Chiefly centers within a stable, politically unified system engage in little competition among themselves, and there is no direct process which consistently favors mutual repulsion between adjacent centers. Hence, we should not necessarily expect to find regular spacing among centers within such systems.
2. In order to minimize movement costs, lower-order centers would tend to cluster toward the higher-order center (or capital). The ideal location for a subordinate center is therefore not in the geographical center of the population within its own district, but rather is closer to the superordinate capital to which it pays tribute.
3. Where political centralization at the capital is strong and incoming tribute flows are high, the optimal location of the capital is principally determined with respect to the lower-order centers within its political control. The degree to which the actual location of the

capital approximates the ideal can be measured by means of an index of spatial efficiency (*E*).

The Model Applied: The Moundville Phase

Having derived a model for the location of chiefly centers, we can now apply it to a body of empirical data. Before we proceed, however, it is important to make clear what this application should accomplish. The model is based on a set of ideal assumptions which may not hold perfectly true in any real situation. An empirically observed pattern can be expected to be more or less like the one predicted by the model only to the extent that other factors, which the model does not take into account, do not intervene. The model is primarily useful in helping us ask meaningful questions of our data, and in allowing us to generate hypotheses which can be tested by other means (Hodder 1972, Johnson 1972:769, 1975:291).

It is in this light that we now examine the settlement data from the Moundville phase of west-central Alabama. This phase, thought to date approximately between A.D. 1200 and 1500, was a variant of the Mississippian culture found in many parts of the southeastern United States in late prehistoric times. On the basis of an extensive burial analysis and various other lines of evidence, Peebles (1971, 1974, Chapter 13 of this volume) has argued that the Moundville phase represents the archeological manifestation of what we have defined as a complex chiefdom.

The sites we are specifically concerned with are found along the Black Warrior River between the fall line at Tuscaloosa and the confluence with the Tombigbee River near Demopolis (see Figure 14.5; Peebles Chapter 13 of this volume, Nielsen *et al.* 1973). On formal grounds, these sites can be classified into three categories; major center, minor center, and residential site. The first category has only one example, the site of Moundville itself. This major center is by far the largest site in the valley, and is one of the largest in the southeast as a whole. It contains at least 20 mounds, and covers over 120 ha. Sites of the second category are considerably more modest in size, each exhibiting only a single mound, with or without evidence of an immediately adjoining village. There are ten such minor centers in the Black Warrior River Valley. The third category consist of all settlements which are not associated with mounds. The six largest of these residential sites range in size from .4 to 2.6 ha (Peebles, Chapter 13 of this volume). These larger settlements probably do not, however, represent the entire picture. There is evidence to indicate that some part of the population may have lived in dispersed farmsteads (cf. the sites referred to as "camps" in Nielsen *et al.* 1973). Exactly what proportion of the people may have lived in these small settlements is not known. Residential sites,

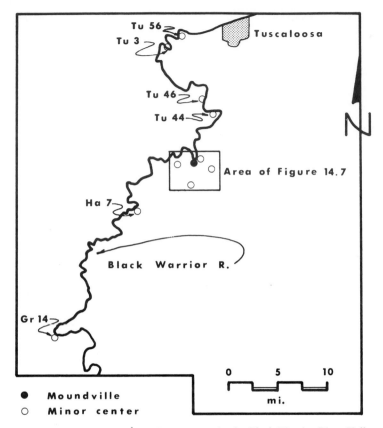

FIGURE 14.5. *Moundville phase centers in the Black Warrior River Valley.*

especially the smaller ones, are relatively inconspicuous and difficult to locate archeologically. Hence, it is probable that only a small fraction of those present in the valley have been recorded.

The Black Warrior settlement system was thus characterized by a clearly defined two-level hierarchy of centers. The fact that only one major center existed and that all the minor centers were of equivalent size (that is, they each had only one mound) strongly suggests that the valley was politically unified, with the administrative capital being Moundville. Indeed, Moundville's function as the highest-order center has been documented on grounds other than its relative size. Burial analyses have suggested that while persons of elite status were associated with both Moundville and the lower-order centers, individuals of the highest rank were interred only at Moundville (Peebles 1971).

Having established the background of the chiefly settlement system being considered, let us now examine the degree to which these data conform to the model's expectations.

LACK OF REGULAR SPACING

The straight line and river distances between adjacent Moundville phase centers are presented in Table 14.1. If spatial competition of the kind found in market systems were present, we would expect to find a high degree of regularity in the spacing of these centers relative to one another. Among the Moundville phase centers, such regularity is clearly not seen. Distances between centers along a straight line range from .8 to 22.3 km. While the mean distance is 6.3 km, the standard deviation of these measurements is 5.5 km, almost as large as the mean. Using river kilometers as a measure of distance produces similar results, with a mean spacing of 14.6 km and a standard deviation of 13 km. Although this irregularity in spacing could admittedly be caused by many different factors, it is quite consistent with the chiefly model, which postulates that

TABLE 14.1
Distances between Adjoining Centers

Adjoining centers	Straight-line distance in miles (km)	Distance along river in miles (km)[a]
Tu-56–Tu-3	1.7(2.7)	3.1(5.0)
Tu-3–Tu-46	6.2(9.8)	14.1(22.7)
Tu-46–Tu-44	1.9(3.1)	2.9(4.7)
Tu-44–Tu-50	5.2(8.4)	7.8(12.6)
Tu-50–Ha-1	1.6+(2.6)	—
Moundville–Tu-50	.5(.8)[b]	.5(.8)
Ha-1–Moundville	1.6(2.6)[b]	—
Ha-1–Ha-9	2.9(4.7)	—
Ha-9–Moundville	2.1(3.4)[b]	—
Moundville–Ha-14	1.7(2.7)[b]	3.9(6.3)[c]
Ha-14–Ha-9	2.5(4.0)	—
Ha-7–Ha-9	6.5(10.5)	—
Ha-14–Ha-7	6.7(10.8)	14.8(23.8)
Ha-7–Gr-14	13.9(22.4)	26.1(42.0)
	$\mu = 3.93(6.32)$	$\mu = 9.15(14.73)$
	$\sigma = 3.42(5.50)$	$\sigma = 8.09(13.02)$

[a] All river distances are measured along the present channel from the point where the river comes closest to the site.

[b] Distances to Moundville are measured with respect to the nearest of the mounds surrounding its plaza.

[c] Ha-14 is presently located on an oxbow lake which might possibly have been part of the active river channel when the site was occupied, although Nielsen *et al.* (1973:90) think this possibility is unlikely.

there is no direct process necessarily favoring mutual repulsion between centers.

SPATIAL EFFICIENCY: MOUNDVILLE

The degree of political centralization in the Black Warrior system appears to have been quite high. The capital, Moundville, was extremely large in comparison to each of the minor centers. Moundville had a total of 20 mounds, and each of the minor centers had only one. Indeed, the tribute in goods and labor needed to support a capital the size of Moundville must have been substantial. In addition, some of this tribute would have had to have been transported over long distances. The Black Warrior system was over 117 river kilometers (51.5 air kilometers) in extent, with the most distant minor center, Gr-14, being 72 river kilometers from Moundville. Such a system was extensive by prestate standards, approximating the size of some of the "supratribal" alliances on Tahiti (see Oliver 1974:Figure 23–1). Under such circumstances, the pressure to achieve an optimal state of spatial efficiency would probably have been great.

In order to measure the degree to which Moundville's location approximates the theoretical optimum, we can use the index of spatial efficiency (E) presented in Eq. (9). Measuring straight line distances, we find that Moundville's spatial efficiency with respect to the minor centers is very high, E taking a value of .94. The practical significance of this result can be highlighted by comparing it to values of E calculated for each of the other site locations (Figure 14.6). Nine of the 10 other centers have lower spatial efficiencies than Moundville; one site, Ha-14, does have a higher spatial efficiency (.98), but the increment by which it exceeds Moundville's value is rather small.

Straight line distances can in this case serve only as a first approximation, however. Given the heterogeneous, nonisotropic landscape in the area being dealt with, the effort expended in movement per unit distance cannot be expected to be the same between all pairs of sites. It seems reasonable to assume, for example, that for any given distance movement by river entails a different amount of effort than movement by land. Although there is no way of assessing the relative difference in precise quantitative terms, we can to some extent control for the difference by calculating our index of spatial efficiency with regard to the two modes of movement separately. To this end, the minor centers can be divided into two groups: those that were probably connected to Moundville mainly by river, and those that were probably linked with Moundville by land. The former group is composed of Gr-14, Ha-7, Tu-44, Tu-46, Tu-3, Tu-56; the latter group of Tu-50, Ha-1, Ha-9, and Ha-14. The distances between

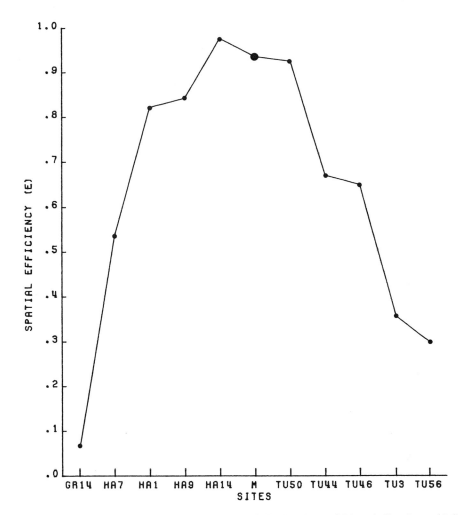

FIGURE 14.6. *The Spatial Efficiency (E) of the locations of Moundville phase chiefly centers, calculated using straight line distances. Note that the Moundville site has a very high spatial efficiency of .94, higher than that of all other sites except one (Ha-14).*

Moundville and sites in the former group are best expressed in river kilometers, whereas the distances between Moundville and sites in the latter group are best measured in land kilometers.

With respect to the river sites (Table 14.2), Moundville's location has an extremely high spatial efficiency of .996. In relation to the four land-connected centers (Figure 14.7), a similarly high value of .89 is obtained. As can be clearly seen in Figure 14.8, Moundville's location generates the highest value of E within each group. We thus find that Moundville's location closely approximates the ideal predicted by our model, suggest-

TABLE 14.2
River Distances from Moundville to Selected Minor Centers

Site	Direction from Moundville	Distance along river in miles (km)
Gr-14	South	44.8(72.1)
Ha-7	South	18.7(30.1)
Tu-3	North	25.3(40.7)
Tu-44	North	8.3(13.4)
Tu-46	North	11.2(18.0)
Tu-56	North	28.4(45.7)

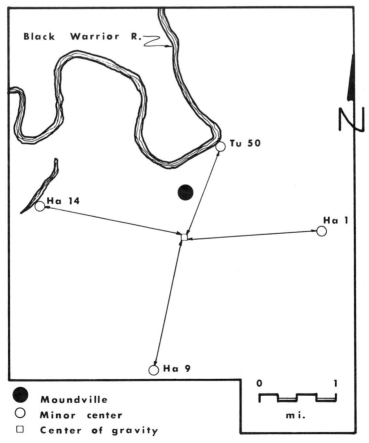

FIGURE 14.7. *Moundville and its four nearest neighbors. The square denotes the center of gravity of the four minor centers in this group.*

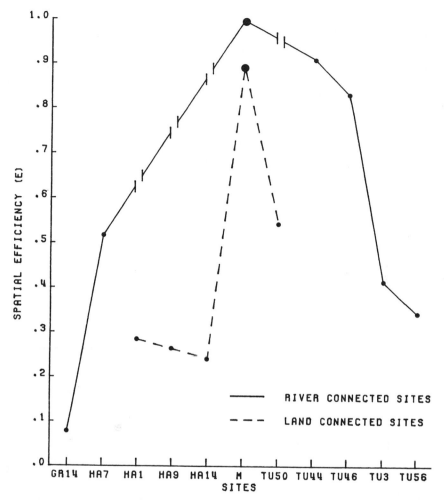

FIGURE 14.8. *The spatial efficiency (E) of the locations of Moundville phase chiefly centers, calculated separately for river and land connected sites. Note that Moundville has the highest spatial efficiency within each group.*

ing that minimization of movement costs between Moundville and the minor centers was an important factor influencing the spatial configuration of the Black Warrior system.

SPATIAL EFFICIENCY: THE MINOR CENTERS

In order to measure precisely the degree to which the locations of minor centers conform to the predicted ideal, we would require complete information on the boundaries of administrative districts, and on the distribution of population within them. Because data of this sort are not available in the case at hand, the model must be assessed with regard to its more general prediction that minor centers would have a tendency to cluster toward the capital. Such clustering does seem to have taken place in the Black Warrior system. Of the 10 minor centers, four have Moundville as a nearest neighbor (Table 14.3). This cluster, consisting of Ha 1, Ha 9, Ha 14, and Tu 50, can easily be seen in Figure 14.5. The mean distance between Moundville and each of the four surrounding centers is 2.4 km, whereas the mean nearest-neighbor distance for centers not in this cluster is 6.6 km.

It does not appear likely that the proximity of these four centers to Moundville can be explained with reference to the distribution of good agricultural soils within the valley. Based on data provided by Peebles (Table 13.6), an index of the mean agricultural productivity per acre was calculated for the lands within a 1-km (.6 mile) walk of each minor center (Table 14.4). The results are presented graphically in Figure 14.9. The average mean productivity per acre for sites within the cluster is 25.3 units, whereas that for the outlying sites is 33.8 units. The centers clustered around Moundville were generally located near poorer agricultural soils than the centers found elsewhere. Thus, our evidence is consistent with the notion that sociopolitical factors related to the minimization of movement were influencing the spatial distribution of the minor centers.

Departure from the Model: Flow of Tribute in Relation to Distance from Moundville

In initially formulating the model, it was assumed that the amount of tribute per capita being transported to the major center from each of the

TABLE 14.3
Nearest Neighbor Distance in Miles (Kilometers)

Site	Nearest neighbor	Straight-line distance in miles (km)
Gr-14	Ha-7	13.9(22.4)
Ha-1	Moundville	1.6(2.6)[a]
Ha-7	Ha-9	6.5(10.5)
Ha-9	Moundville	2.1(3.4)[a]
Ha-14	Moundville	1.7(2.7)[a]
Tu-3	Tu-56	1.7(2.7)[a]
Tu-44	Tu-46	1.9(3.1)
Tu-46	Tu-44	1.9(3.1)
Tu-50	Moundville	.5(.8)[a]
Tu-56	Tu-3	1.7(2.7)
Moundville	Tu-50	.5(.8)[a]

[a] Distances to Moundville are measured with respect to the nearest of the mounds surrounding its plaza.

TABLE 14.4
Catchment Productivity[a]

Site	Acres (ha) of arable land in Catchment (1 km walk)	Index of catchment productivity	Average productivity per acre
Tu-3	84(34)	3,535	42.1
Tu-44	303(123)	10,950	36.1
Tu-46	490(198)	13,240	27.0
Tu-56	380(154)	15,120	39.8
Ha-7	559(226)	19,458	34.8
Gr-14	328(133)	7,597.5	23.2
			$\mu = 33.8$
Ha-1	723(293)	10,708	14.8
Ha-9	723(293)	11,913	16.5
Ha-14	541(219)	17,980	33.2
Tu-50	428(173)	15,640	36.5
			$\mu = 25.3$

[a] Based on data presented by Peebles (Chapter 13).

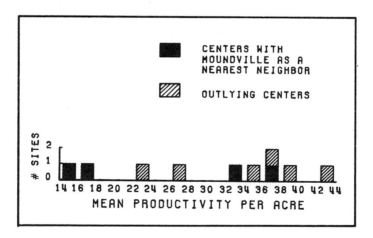

FIGURE 14.9. *Histograms of minor centers showing mean productivity per acre of arable land within a 1-km walk of each site (the catchments of adjacent sites do not overlap). The four centers with Moundville as a nearest neighbor (dark squares) average 25.3 units per acre, whereas the outlying centers (hatched squares) average 33.8 units per acre.* [Based on Table 14.4.].

minor centers was the same, in other words, that T_iP_i was constant for all i. There is reason to believe, however, that in some complex chiefdoms the per capita levy of tribute (T_i) might not be uniformly distributed among the various districts. For instance, Sahlins (1968:93) has pointed out that in Hawaii, "people near the paramount chief's court were most subject to its predation." Indeed, it would be logical to expect that in a large chiefdom, such would be the case. We have assumed that the cost of transport increases as do (a) the amount of goods being moved, and (b) the square of the distance. Remember also that the chiefs had to be concerned with staying within the "moral limit" of what effort the people were willing to expend on the nobility's behalf, otherwise being faced with the possibility of being deposed from office. Under such conditions, it is likely that the largest amounts of tribute would be demanded from the subordinate centers within a certain limited distance, beyond which transport costs (and the costs of enforcing compliance) would become too burdensome.

It is therefore possible that the minor centers closest to Moundville were supplying a greater amount of tribute per capita than those farther away. If we tentatively assume (for the sake of argument) that the population in each of the districts was approximately the same, this proposition can perhaps be tested archeologically in the following manner: The more surplus goods and corvee labor a minor center was forced to allocate to the purposes of the capital, the less would have been available for expenditure locally. Minor centers sending a disproportionately large share of tribute to Moundville would probably have had a severely curtailed ability to engage in mound construction. Thus, if the proposition were true, one would expect that the minor centers closest to Moundville would also have the smallest mounds.

Table 14.5 presents the available data on the sizes of the mounds at the minor centers. An index of the volume of earth used to build each mound

TABLE 14.5
Sizes of Mounds at Minor Centers[a]

Site	Date described	Basal length (L) in feet (m)	Basal width (W) in feet (m)	Height (H) in feet (m)	Index of size (L × W × H)
Gr-14	1905[b]	195(59.4)	150(45.7)	9.7(3.0)	283,725(8,144)
	1973[c]	159(48.5)	118(36.0)	9(2.7)	168,858(4,714)
Ha-1	1933[d]	70(21.3)	70(21.3)	8(2.4)	39,200(1,089)
Ha-7	1905[b]	129(39.3)	115(35.1)	13.5(4.1)	200,272(5,656)
Ha-9	1933[d]	20(6.1)	20(6.1)	6(1.8)	2,400(67)
Ha-14	1933[d]	78(23.8)	78(23.8)	5(1.5)	30,420(850)
Tu-44	1933[d]	98(29.9)	59(18.0)	4(1.2)	23,128(646)[f]
Tu-46	1933[d]	133(40.5)	100(30.5)	7(2.1)	93,100(2,594)
Tu-50	1933[d]	35(10.7)	35(10.7)	14.3(4.4)[e]	17,558(504)
Tu-56	1933[d]	190(58)	45(13.7)	11.5(3.5)[e]	98,325(2,781)

[a] Measurements are not available for the mound at Tu-3.
[b] Moore (1905:127).
[c] Nielsen et al. (1973:34).
[d] Site survey files, Mound State Monument, Moundville, Alabama.
[e] Where several different measurements of height were recorded, the mean is used.
[f] Field notes indicate this mound had probably been "flattened down for stock" in recent times.

is computed by multiplying its basal dimensions by its total height. Since these mounds were originally pyramidal rather than rectangular, and have undergone a considerable amount of erosion since the time they were being used, the index does not represent an exact measure of volume, but rather a figure that is proportional to the volume by some more or less constant factor. Thus, the index should accurately reflect the sizes of the mounds relative to one another.

Figure 14.10 shows the value of the index for each minor center arranged in order of increasing distance from Moundville. Clearly, the five

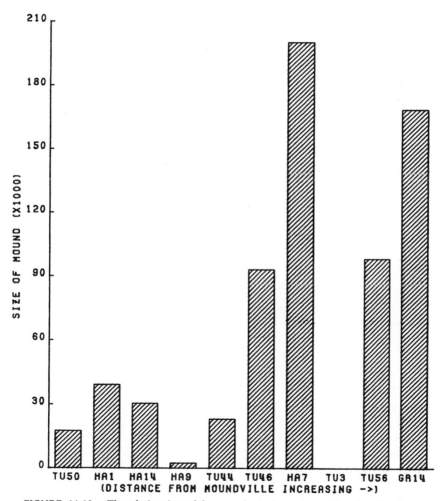

FIGURE 14.10.   *The relative sizes of the mounds at minor centers. Note that the sites nearest to Moundville (on the left side of the histogram) all have mounds that are comparatively small.* [Based on Table 14.5.]

sites closest to Moundville have mounds significantly smaller than the sites farther away. This difference in size does not appear to have been dictated by differences in the natural productivity of the soils on which these sites were located. Figure 14.11 clearly indicates that mound size is not correlated either with the total productivity or with the mean productivity per acre of the land within a 1-km walk of the site. It thus appears possible that a major variable dictating mound size is the site's distance from Moundville, a result consistent with our tentative hypothesis that Moundville exacted the largest tribute from the minor centers closest at hand. Based on the range within which the smaller mounds occur, it appears that 14.5 river kilometers may have been the approximate distance beyond which continual large-scale movement of tribute was made impractical by the high costs of transport and/or enforcement. The observed differences in mound size may, of course, have been due to other factors such as differences in the size of locally available labor pools and/or different temporal spans of occupation. These questions, however, will only be

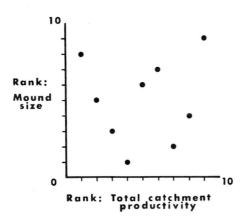

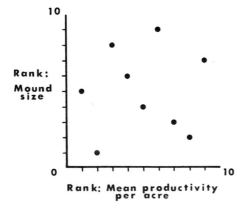

FIGURE 14.11. *Scatter plots showing no rank correlation between mound size and (top) total productivity of 1-km Catchment; (bottom) mean productivity per acre of arable land in a 1-km catchment. Only the nine minor centers for which mound size is known are included.* [Based on Table 14.5.]

resolved when further excavation at the minor centers and additional survey in the valley are undertaken.

Summary

In the preceding pages, I have discussed some of the sociopolitical relations in complex chiefdoms that link territorial units together, and the effects that these relations might have on the spacing and distribution of chiefly centers. A model expressing these relations was formalized, and was applied to settlement data from the Moundville phase of the Black Warrior River Valley. In a number of respects, the data were found to be consistent with the expectations generated by the model. It now remains for me to mention briefly some of the limitations of the model, probably already apparent to the reader, and certain possibilities it might present for future research.

Perhaps the greatest shortcoming of this model is that it does not take sufficiently many factors into account to be justifiably labeled "predictive." It considers the ideal location of centers only with regard to a fairly restricted set of sociopolitical variables, that is, the flow of tribute and administrative information. It takes no account of various other factors, which, in many cases, may also have a significant influence on the location of chiefly centers. For example, one such factor might be intensive warfare, which could cause the major center to be located as far as possible from the enemy frontier. Another might be interpolity alliance, which might influence the capital to be located where its direct access to major political centers elsewhere would be maximized. A third possibly relevant factor is "locational inertia," which refers to the fact that in some cases a political center, once firmly established, might tend to remain where it is even if changing circumstances render its location less than optimal.

Clearly, much more work needs to be done before the variables influencing chiefly settlement location are adequately understood. The utility of the model presented here lies in the fact that it provides us with a way to measure spatial efficiency objectively vis-à-vis a clearly defined and important set of internal political processes. To the extent that any empirical case deviates from this theoretical optimum, it is hoped that the investigator will be led to examine other variables and formulate better models which might help account for the observed divergence.

Appendix

To find the demographic center of gravity of the ith administrative district, begin by imposing a two dimensional grid over the distribution of sites. Any units of measurement can be used for this grid, even purely arbitrary ones. The coordinates of the DCG can then be calculated as follows:

$$x_i' = \frac{\sum_{j=1}^{J} x_{ij} p_{ij}}{\sum_{j=1}^{J} p_{ij}},$$ (10)

$$y_i' = \frac{\sum_{j=1}^{J} y_{ij} p_{ij}}{\sum_{j=1}^{J} p_{ij}},$$ (11)

where x_i', y_i' are the coordinates of the DCG in the ith district, x_{ij}, y_{ij} are the coordinates of the jth settlement in the ith district, and p_{ij} is the population of the jth settlement in the ith district.

In the preceding computations, the actual administrative center should not be counted as one of the J settlements. For a more extended discussion and a simple example of how these formulas are applied, see Massam (1972:5 or 1975:24ff).

Using the same two-dimensional grid, the coordinates of the ideal location for a minor center that pays tribute to a higher-order center can be calculated as follows:

$$x_i'' = \frac{t \sum_{j=1}^{J} x_{ij} p_{ij} + T_i X_c P_i}{t \sum_{j=1}^{J} p_{ij} + T_i P_i},$$ (12)

$$y_i'' = \frac{t \sum_{j=1}^{J} y_{ij} p_{ij} + T_i y_c P_i}{t \sum_{j=1}^{J} p_{ij} + T_i P_i},$$ (13)

where t is a constant proportional to the per capita rate of tribute flow from settlements to minor center (see page 432), T_i is proportional to the per capita rate of tribute flow from a minor center of the ith district to the capital (see page 432), x_i'', y_i'' are the coordinates of the ideal location for the minor center of the ith district, P_i is the total population of the ith district, and x_c, y_c are the coordinates of the capital or higher-order center. As in Eqs. (10) and (11), the actual minor center should not be included as one of the J settlements when computing x_i'' and y_i''.

To find the center of gravity of the minor centers (CGMC), a two-dimensional grid must once again be used (any units of measurement will suffice). The coordinates of the CGMC are computed as follows:

$$X' = \frac{\sum_{i=1}^{I} T_i \, x_i \, P_i}{\sum_{i=1}^{I} T_i T_i P_i},$$ (14)

$$Y' = \frac{\sum_{i=1}^{I} T_i \, y_i \, P_i}{\sum_{i=1}^{I} T_i T_i P_i},$$ (15)

where X', Y' are the coordinates of the CGMC, and x_i, y_i are the coordinates of the minor center in the ith district. Assuming, as we do in this chapter, that $T_i P_i$ is the same for all i, Eqs. (14) and (15) become equivalent to

$$X' = \frac{\Sigma^I_{i=1} x_i}{I}, \tag{16}$$

$$Y' = \frac{\Sigma^I_{i=1} y_i}{I}, \tag{17}$$

where I is the total number of subordinate minor centers. The coordinates of the capital and the population of its district should be excluded when calculating Eqs. (14)–(17).

Acknowledgments

I wish to thank the following individuals who critically read earlier drafts of this paper and provided many useful suggestions: John Alden, J.P. Brain, I.W. Brown, L. Cameron, W. Cowan, R.I. Ford, K.L. Hutterer, K.W. Kintigh, W. Macdonald, J. Marcus, D.F. Morse, J. Parsons, C.S. Peebles, B. Smith, W.R. Tobler, and H.T. Wright. Responsibility for the final product, or course, rests entirely with me. Thanks also go to W. Macdonald for preparing most of the illustrations, and to L. Cameron for typing the various drafts.

References

Berry, Brian J.L.
   1967   *Geography of market centers and retail distribution.* Englewood Cliffs, New Jersey: Prentice-Hall.
Berry, Brian J.L., and A. Pred
   1961   Central place studies: A bibliography of theory and applications. *Regional Science Research Institute, Bibliographic Series,* **I**.
Blanton, Richard
   1976   Anthropological Studies of Cities. *Annual Review of Anthropology* **5**.
Brush, John E.
   1953   The hierarchy of central places in southwestern Wisconsin. *Geographical Review* **43**:380–402.
Christaller, W.
   1933   *Die Zentralen Orte in Süddeutschland.* Jena.
   1966   *Central places in southern Germany.* C.W. Baskin, Translator. Englewood Cliffs, N.J.: Prentice-Hall.
DuPratz, M. LePage
   1774   *The history of Louisiana.* (Reprinted 1972, Claitor's Publishing Division, Baton Rouge, La.)
Earle, Timothy K.
   1973   Control hierarchies in the traditional irrigation economy of Halelea District of Kauai, Hawaii. Ph.D. dissertation, Department of Anthropology, University of Michigan, Ann Arbor.
   1977   A reappraisal of redistribution: Complex Hawaiian chiefdoms. In *Exchange Systems in Prehistory,* edited by T.K. Earle and J.E. Ericson. New York: Academic Press. Pp. 213–227.

Emory, K.
  1933   Stone remains in the Society Islands. *Bernice P. Bishop Museum Bulletin*, No. **116**. Honolulu.
Finney, B.
  1966   Resource distribution and social structure in Tahiti. *Ethnology* 5:80–86.
Firth, Raymond
  1936   *We, the Tikopia*. London: Allen and Unwin.
Flannery, Kent V.
  1972   The cultural evolution of civilizations. *Annual Review of Ecology and Systematics* 3:399–426.
Fried, Morton H.
  1967   *The evolution of political society*. New York: Random House.
Green, Roger C., Kaye Green, R.A. Rappaport, Ann Rappaport, and Janet M. Davidson
  1967   Archaeology on the Island of Mo'orea, French Polynesia. *Anthropological Papers of the American Museum of Natural History* **51**, Part 2.
Haggett, Peter
  1965   *Locational analysis in human geography*. London: Edward Arnold
Hammond, Norman
  1974   The distribution of Late Classic Maya major ceremonial centers in the central area. In *Mesoamerican archaeology: New approaches*, edited by N. Hammond. London: Duckworth.
Hodder, I.R.
  1972   Locational models and the study of Romano-British settlement. In *Models in archaeology*, edited by D. Clarke. London: Methuen. Pp. 887–910.
Johnson, Gregory
  1972   A test of the utility of central place theory in archaeology. In *Man, Settlement, and Urbanism*, edited by P. Ucko, R. Tringham, and G. Dimbley. London: Duckworth. Pp. 769–786.
  1975   Locational analysis and the investigation of Uruk local exchange systems. In *Ancient civilization and trade*, edited by J. Sabloff and C.C. Lamberg–Karlovsky. Albuquerque: University of New Mexico Press. Pp. 285–339.
Kirchhoff, Paul
  1955   The principles of clanship in human society. *Davidson Anthropological Journal* **1**:1–10.
Lafferty, Robert H.
  1976   Kincaid and other Mississippian sites: A central place perspective. Paper read at the 41st annual meeting of the Society of American Archaeology, St. Louis.
Marcus, Joyce
  1973   Territorial organization of the Lowland Classic Maya. *Science* **180**:911–916.
  1976   *Emblem and state in the Classic Maya Lowlands: An epigraphic approach to territorial organization*. Washington D.C.: Dumbarton Oaks.
Massam, Bryan H.
  1972   The spatial structure of administrative systems. *Commission on College Geography Resource Paper* No. 12.
  1975   *Location and space in social administration*. New York: Wiley.
McWilliams, Richard Gaillard
  1953   *Fleur de Lys and Calumet: Being the Penicaut narrative of French adventure in Louisiana*. Baton Rouge: Louisiana State University Press.
Moore, Clarence B.
  1905   Certain aboriginal remains of the Black Warrior River. *Journal of the Academy of Natural Sciences of Philadelphia*, **13**.

Neitzel, Robert S.
  1965   Archaeology of the Fatherland site: The Grand Village of the Natchez. *Anthropological Papers of the American Museum of Natural History* **51**, Part 1.
Nielsen, Jerry, John W. O'Hear, and Charles W. Moorehead
  1973   An archaeological survey of Hale and Greene Counties, Alabama. Final Report to the Alabama Historical Commission for Contract AHC 52472. University of Alabama: University Museums.
Oliver, Douglas L.
  1974   *Ancient Tahitian Society.* Honolulu: University Press of Hawaii.
Peebles, Christopher S.
  1971   Moundville and surrounding sites: Some structural considerations of mortuary practices II. *Memoirs of the Society for American Archaeology* **25**:68–91.
  1974   Moundville: The organization of a prehistoric community and culture. Ph.D. dissertation, Department of Anthropology, University of California, Santa Barbara.
Peebles, Christopher S., and Susan Kus
  1977   Some archaeological correlates of ranked societies. *American Antiquity* **42**:421–448.
Sahlins, Marshall D.
  1958   *Social Stratification in Polynesia.* Seattle: University of Washington Press.
  1963   Poor man, rich man, big man, chief: Political types in Melanesia and Polynesia. *Comparative Studies in Society and History* **5**:285–303.
  1968   *Tribesmen.* Englewood Cliffs, New Jersey: Prentice-Hall.
  1972   *Stone age economics.* Chicago: Aldine.
Service, Elman R.
  1962   *Primitive social organization.* New York: Random House.
  1975   *Origins of the State and civilization.* New York: W.W. Norton.
Smith, Carol A.
  1974   Economics of marketing systems: Models from economic geography. *Annual Review of Anthropology* **3**:167–202.
Swanton, John R.
  1911   Indian tribes of the lower Mississippi Valley and adjacent coast of the Gulf of Mexico. *Bureau of American Ethnology Bulletin* **43**.
Thwaites, Reuben Gold
  1900   *The Jesuit relations and allied documents,* Vol. 68.
White, Douglas, R., George P. Murdock, and Richard Scaglion
  1971   Natchez class and rank reconsidered. *Ethnology* **10**:369–388.

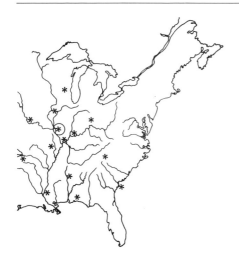

15

Cahokia and the American Bottom: Settlement Archeology

MELVIN L. FOWLER

Archeological surveys and discussion of settlement patterns have long been a part of Cahokia studies. These surveys, however, have been carried out at different levels of sophistication and for different goals. It is only in the past decade and a half that intensive controlled surveys have been made of the Cahokia region.

Although earlier investigators had noted sites other than Cahokia in the American Bottom region of the Mississippi River Valley (see McAdams 1881, 1882, 1883, 1887, 1895, Snyder 1894, 1895, 1909, 1913, 1914, 1917, Thomas 1894, 1907, and others), Bushnell (1904, 1917, 1922) was the first to put these discussions into specific terms in publishing a map of the American Bottom region with the major sites marked on it. Previously A.J.R. Patrick had made detailed maps of the major sites but these were never published and are stored in the Missouri Historical Society.

In the late 1950s the University of Michigan began a site survey of the region as part of their research sponsored by the Viking Fund. The results of this work and the Excavations at Cahokia and Pulcher have been published in preliminary form (Griffin and Spaulding 1951).

The first intensive survey of the Cahokia region was carried out by Alan Harn (1971) in 1961–1963, working under the auspices of a National Science Foundation grant to the Illinois Archaeological Survey and Southern Illinois University. In this survey, Harn attempted to walk all of the open land in the area and to map the location of sites, as well as delineat-

455

ing those areas where no evidence of sites was found. Harn's survey was complemented by a similar survey conducted by Patrick Munson (1971) on the Wood River Terrace and bluffs bordering the American Bottom.

Both of these surveys were enlarged upon by Keith Brandt (1972) working under my direction for the University of Wisconsin—Milwaukee Cahokia project. Whereas our goals under this NSF-sponsored program were to work primarily at Cahokia, we felt that data were needed on the supporting settlements. Analyzing the collections of Harn and Munson, and adding to them himself, Brandt was able to increase our insights into Cahokia settlements. Using much of the data already mentioned, and other site surveys Elizabeth Benchley (1976) prepared a summary of the cultural resources of the greater St. Louis area.

In all these surveys there were no definitions of sampling goals and strategy. In general, the emphasis was upon locating all the archeological sites present in the area. This was never accomplished and probably never could be. More recent surveys in the southern portion of the American Bottom by archeologists from Southern Illinois University-Edwardsville have greatly increased the total site inventory. Current work in the path of interstate highway construction is also adding to the data base. These last-mentioned surveys are being conducted on a much more systematic basis than any of the previous surveys, but are limited to proposed right-of-way areas.

There are some very definite limitations to the conclusions that can be reached on the basis of the surveys carried out to date. Since no attempt has been made in any of these surveys to assure representativeness of the materials sought or collected, there is no way that we can propose a settlement system for Cahokia and its surrounding communities in the American Bottom that represents much more than our idea of how things might have been. I do not mean to criticize the work of those investigators just mentioned, who were sometimes working in a manner that was, until recently, common in archeology. With the increasing understanding by archeologists of the nature of the data base they have to cope with, and the appropriate sampling methods for dealing with the data base, new and exciting approaches to the whole question of site surveys and settlement pattern studies are being developed.

Another limitation to the site survey data available for the American Bottom is that the collections from these sites were unsystematic. As was common, these collections fall largely into the "grab bag" category. That is, sherds and other artifacts were picked up more or less over the entire site area. If an attempt had been made to collect materials systematically, we might be able to make more confident statements concerning both the chronology and the function of sites. As it is, the materials we have provide us with, at best, only a crude measure of these factors.

There is, then, a real need in Cahokia studies for the design and implementation of a systematic site survey of the area, based upon sound sampling strategies. This could be a stratified sampling procedure, perhaps based upon the delineation of physiographic zones similar to that proposed by Gregg (1972). Careful formulation of the methodologies for selecting areas within these zones for intensive surveys should then be established, along with sampling strategies to be utilized for collecting materials within the sites that are located. When this is done, it will be possible to say something about the total settlement system of the Cahokia region with some degree of confidence.

Despite all these limitations, I will discuss in this chapter some aspects of a possible Cahokia settlement system in the American Bottom. The model is based upon research carried out prior to 1972. Site data recovered since 1972 may well necessitate some modification of the interpretations to be presented but it has not yet been analyzed sufficiently to warrant inclusion.

The American Bottom

The geographic region to be discussed here is an area of the Mississippi River Valley known as the American Bottom (sometimes referred to as the American Bottoms, but the older usage is the singular) (Figure 15.1). The area referred to when the term American Bottom was coined is to the northeast, east, and southeast of St. Louis, Missouri, and extends approximately from the mouth of the Illinois River near Alton, Illinois southward to the mouth of the Kaskaskia River. More recently we have tended to use the term to refer to a smaller area reaching only as far south as Dupo, Illinois, just north of the mouth of the Meramac River. This pocket of land is a portion of the river valley approximately 18 km (11 miles) at its widest point and extending from north to south a little over 40 km (25 miles). Both to the north and the south of the American Bottom, the river valley is relatively narrow, being on the order of 5 km (3 miles) in width.

The American Bottom region was probably formed by the channels of the Mississippi and Missouri Rivers fluctuating back and forth through time. Many oxbow lakes and other remnants of now extinct channels suggest this activity. Munson (1974) has analyzed the relationships of these extinct channels to each other and to archeological sites. Based upon his analysis and that of Bareis (1964), it seems probable that at the time of the Mississippian cultural utilization of the American Bottom the main channel of the Mississippi River was very close to its present course. Only minor channel changes are documented by Munson as occurring after Mississippian times. One major channel cut-off episode may have taken place during the development of Cahokian Mississippian, resulting in

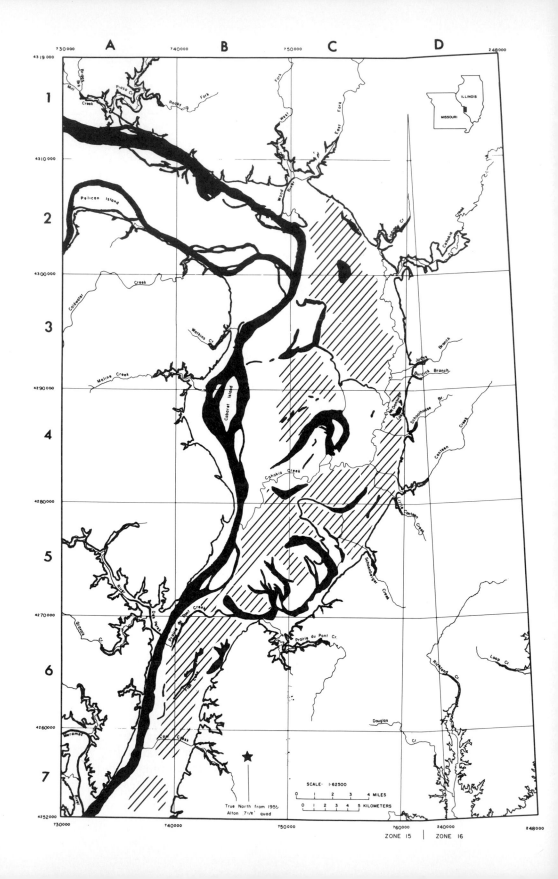

SCALE: 1:62500

0   1   2   3   4 MILES

0   1   2   3   4   5 KILOMETERS

True North from 1955
Alton 7½' quad

ZONE 15 | ZONE 16

Horseshoe Lake (Figure 15.1, C-4). Munson suggests that the formation of Horseshoe Lake occurred prior to 900 years ago, at approximately A.D. 1100.

Although the American Bottom is today covered largely by open farm land and areas of urban and industrial blight, it was, in the past, an area of diverse natural zones. These zones provided a variety of exploitive niches for Mississippian populations. Working with land survey witness tree records of the early nineteenth century, as well as with travelers' accounts and early topographic maps, Gregg (1972) has identified several biogeographic zones within the American Bottom. Basically the area can be initially subdivided into three broad regions: the bottomlands, the bluff banks, and the upland zones. Our primary concern is with the bluff banks and bottomland regions.

The bottomlands region contains the greatest environmental diversity. Approximately the eastern two-thirds of the bottomland region was covered by a lowland wet prairie habitat. This prairie area was nearly bisected by the Horseshoe Lake area. The evidence for this prairie comes from several sources. One of these is the Collot map of the region, which shows what appears to be a large nonforested area just east of St. Louis (Tucker 1942, Plate XXVIII). How far back in time this proposed prairie can be extended is not known. Other large habitat areas within the bottomlands region were the aquatic resource zones of the sloughs, oxbow lakes, and streams.

The bluff banks, along the eastern edge of the bottomlands region were covered largely by mixed hardwood forests. The bluff edges supported hill prairies and cedars. Back away from the bluff edges was the long-grass prairie upland.

A major feature of significance in the American Bottom was the numerous creeks that connected oxbow lakes and sloughs and the upland regions with the Mississippi River. One of the longest of these is Cahokia creek, which flows out of the uplands at the north end of the American Bottom (Figure 15.1, D-2) and then turns southward, paralleling the bluff until it reaches the central area of the region (Figure 15.1, C-4). At this point it turns westward, cutting across the bottom and flowing into the main channel of the Mississippi River at East St. Louis, Illinois (Figure 15.1, B-5). These creeks or small rivers must have represented important avenues of transportation during prehistoric times.

The American Bottom region is also located at the border of several broad physiographic zones, which were probably significant in the de-

FIGURE 15.1. *The American Bottom region of the Central Mississippi River Valley. The bluffs are delineated by the black line, representing the 450-foot elevation above sea level. The major river channels, oxbow lakes, and creeks are represented in solid black. The approximate extension of the lowland prairie is indicated by cross-hatching. The grid is in 10,000-m units of the UTM grid for zones 15 and 16.* [Sources: Gregg (1975b:Figures 2–14), Benchley (1976:Figure 2).]

velopment of the settlement systems (Figure 15.2). To the southeast is the large southern deciduous hardwoods forest zone; on the northeast is the prairie peninsula area; to the southwest are the Ozark mountain regions; and to the south is the lower Mississippi Valley region.

American Bottom Chronology

Chronological controls are a necessity in studying settlement pattern developments in a given region. Despite recent statements to the contrary, we have begun to make some progress toward understanding the chronological framework of the American Bottom region and the Cahokia site in particular. The first development of a concern with chronology occurred in the 1930s with the discovery by the late Gene Stirling of a

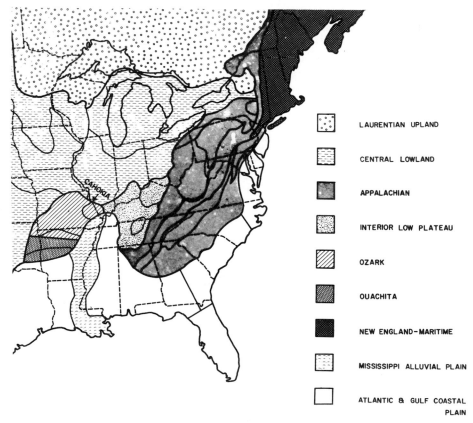

LAURENTIAN UPLAND

CENTRAL LOWLAND

APPALACHIAN

INTERIOR LOW PLATEAU

OZARK

OUACHITA

NEW ENGLAND-MARITIME

MISSISSIPPI ALLUVIAL PLAIN

ATLANTIC & GULF COASTAL
PLAIN

FIGURE 15.2. *The location of the Cahokia site and the American Bottom in relation to Major Physiographic provinces of eastern North America.* [Source: Lobeck (1950).]

premound midden area in the western portion of the Cahokia site proper. This early occupation was termed *Old Village,* and contrasted with the later material, which came to be called *Trappist.* Griffin subsequently elaborated on this simple temporal scheme, and specified some of the types belonging to these two "phases" in his now historic paper (Griffin 1949). During the 1950s and 1960s there was increased concern with this simplistic chronology and some efforts were made to improve upon it. There was talk of an Early Mississippian phase and increasing finds suggested a strong presence of Woodland ceramic types and Bluff Culture material (Hall 1966, 1967, O'Brien 1972, Vogel 1975). The 1971 and 1973 Cahokia Conferences were held to deal specifically with this problem of chronology (Fowler and Hall 1975). Based upon their presentations and discussions of then-recently excavated materials, the conferees agreed upon and defined a sequence of eight phases for the Cahokia site, dating from before A.D. 800 through to the Historic or contact period. These phases are

Patrick phase before A.D. 800
Unnamed phase I (Jarrot Phase, Gregg 1975a) A.D. 800–900
Fairmount phase A.D. 900–1050
Stirling phase A.D. 1050–1150
Moorehead phase A.D. 1150–1250
Sand Prairie phase A.D. 1250–1500
Unnamed phase II A.D. 1500 1700
Historic phase A.D. 1700—

Robert Hall (1975) has correctly pointed out that these phases are only current approximations, and will undoubtedly be modified and refined in the future. He also raises valid questions concerning the danger of attempting to apply these phases too rigidly outside the Cahokia area proper in the American Bottom, let alone to the whole Midwest, as some individuals would like to do. In this chapter, the chronology suggested by the Cahokia Ceramic Conference of 1971 will be used in discussions of the Cahokia site itself, and with proper caution, it will also be used in the discussion of settlement patterns throughout the American Bottom.

The Cahokia Site: Settlement Organization

The dominating prehistoric community in the American Bottom was Cahokia. It is not only the location of the largest earthen structure in North America, but was probably the largest population concentration and most complex community north of the Rio Bravo. To understand or even talk about the American Bottom settlement system it is necessary first to look at Cahokia.

The Cahokia site has been examined by numerous persons for the past

170 years, and descriptions of its size and complexity abound in the extant literature (see Fowler 1969). In 1966 we began a long-range project centering on the Cahokia site. As part of this research program we examined all the published literature and maps pertaining to the Cahokia site. New and old aerial photographs of the site area were also collected. A 1-m contour-interval map of the site was prepared. Examination of these data led us to identify certain research problems in terms of mound form and locations, which we tried to resolve in the field. This was not always satisfactory, as many landowners were reluctant to have us walk their property and, of course, many of the mounds have been destroyed since they were first described in the nineteenth century.

Two very valuable sources were available. The first of these was the unpublished map of Cahokia commissioned by A.J.R. Patrick around 1880. On this map, 71 mounds of the Cahokia site were very carefully described as to location and shape. The Patrick map is now in the Missouri Historical Society archives in St. Louis. The second valuable resource was the collection of oblique aerial photographs of the Cahokia site made in 1922 by then Lt. George Goddard (Goddard 1969:93, Hall 1968). Both the Patrick map and the Goddard photographs presented details of the site as it was before major agricultural and urban development destroyed large portions of Cahokia.

Based on all these data, mounds have been classified as to shape. Utilizing Patrick's and Goddard's data, along with that of more recent investigators (for example Moorehead 1922, 1923, 1929) and our own fieldwork, the number of identifiable locatable mounds has been currently fixed at over 100 (Figure 15.3). Based this information, the following interpretive comments can be offered concerning the nature of the Cahokia community.

At its peak of development, the Cahokia site extended over an area of more than 5 square miles. Over 100 earthen mounds of various sizes, shapes, and functions were scattered throughout this area. These mounds were not randomly scattered, but were constructed in a patterned distribution that signifies to us the organization of the community (Figure 15.4). The majority of these mounds cluster along a natural ridge that is the major east–west axis of the site and the highest, driest land in the area. These mounds are arranged in groups around what may have been plazas (Figure 15.5). The largest of these groupings centers around Monks Mound which, with its height (more than twice that of the next tallest mound), its four terraces, and the large building on its summit, must have been the dominating center of the community both in its physical and functional aspects. The grouping around Monks Mound was made up of some of the largest mounds in the site, which were laid out in two rows on either side of Monks Mound. To the south of Monks Mound was what appears to have been a plaza area (Figure 15.5A). About 750 m south of Monks

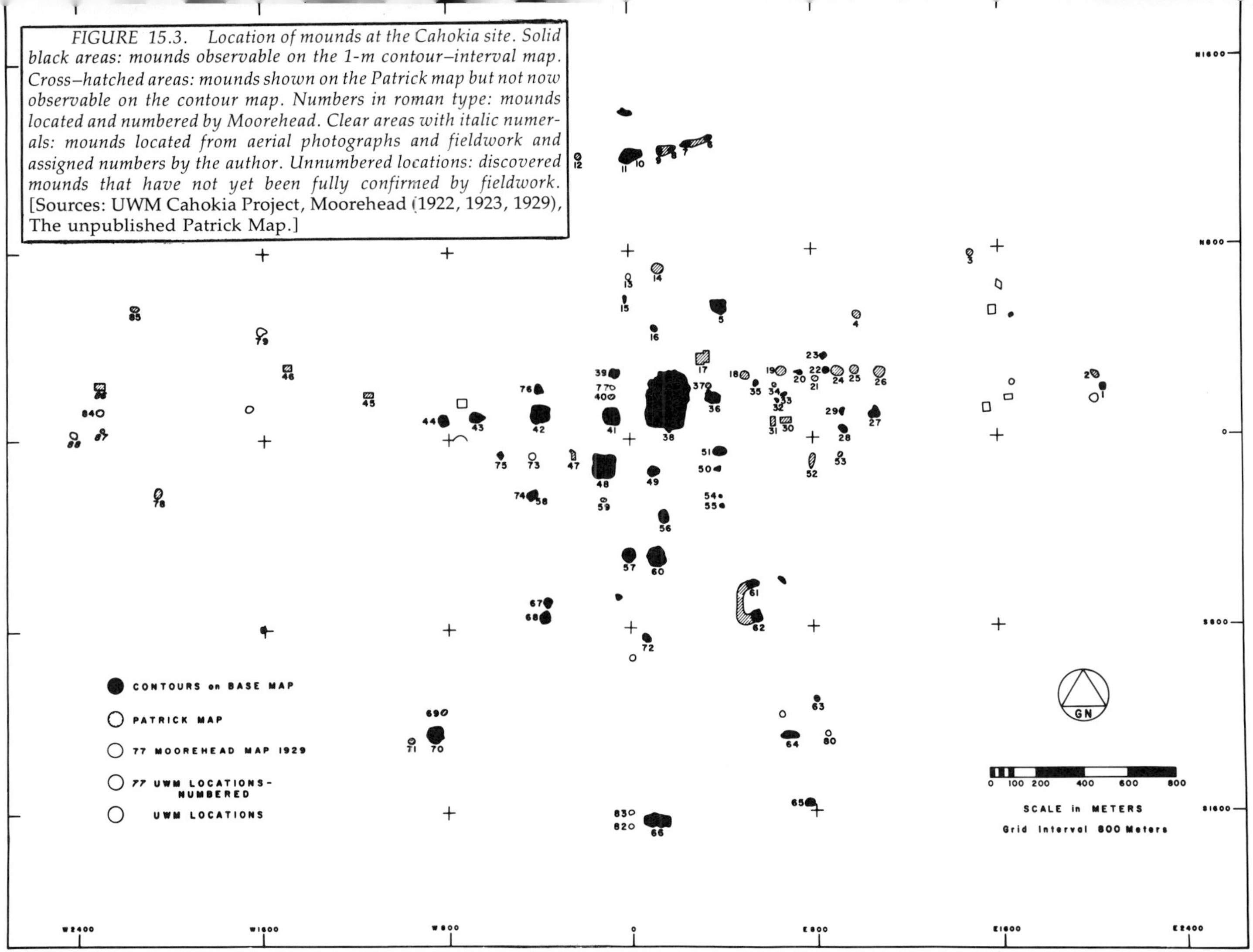

FIGURE 15.3. Location of mounds at the Cahokia site. Solid black areas: mounds observable on the 1-m contour–interval map. Cross-hatched areas: mounds shown on the Patrick map but not now observable on the contour map. Numbers in roman type: mounds located and numbered by Moorehead. Clear areas with italic numerals: mounds located from aerial photographs and fieldwork and assigned numbers by the author. Unnumbered locations: discovered mounds that have not yet been fully confirmed by fieldwork. [Sources: UWM Cahokia Project, Moorehead (1922, 1923, 1929), The unpublished Patrick Map.]

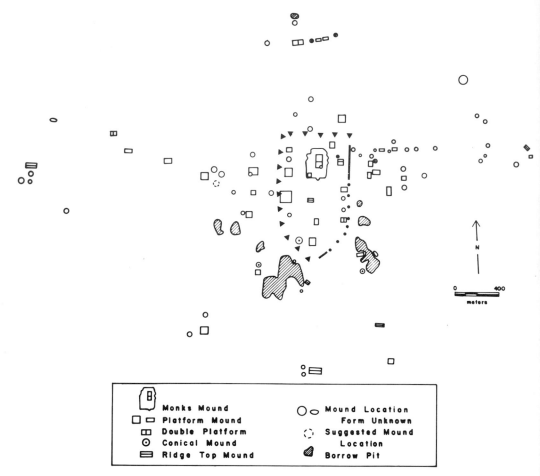

FIGURE 15.4. A schematic map of the Cahokia site indicating mound distribution and the author's interpretation of mound form. The approximate location of the palisade is indicated as follows: solid lines indicate the areas where the palisade has been confirmed by excavation. Dotted line indicates the palisade location that shows clearly on aerial photographs. The line of triangles is my suggestion of the location of the remaining portions of the palisade as suggested by aerial photo interpretation.

Mound were two mounds, one a square platform or truncated pyramid and the other having a conical shape. Most of the mounds associated with Monks Mound were platform mounds, and may have been the location of important public buildings or possibly the residences of high-status persons. The major exception to this pattern is the associated conical mound type, which may have been the charnal house and burial mound where the remains of high-status persons were kept and buried at ceremonially determined intervals.

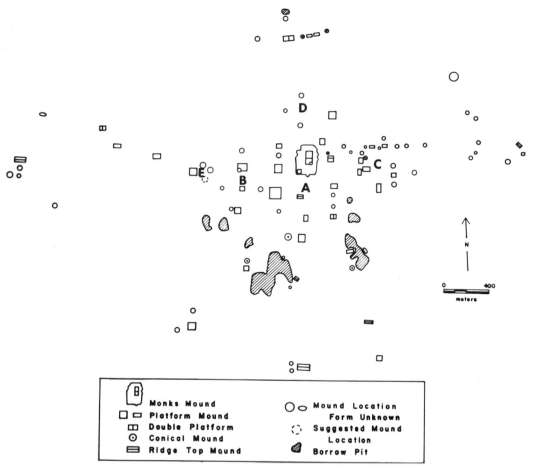

FIGURE 15.5. *Possible plaza locations at the Cahokia site: A. Central plaza; B. Merrell plaza; C. Ramey plaza; D. North plaza; E. West plaza.*

This entire central area appears to have been enclosed by a large wall (Anderson 1969) (Figure 15.4). Indications of this wall were first noted on aerial photographs, some taken in 1922. Lines on the aerial photos indicated where prehistoric disturbance of the subsoil had taken place. By excavating these linear features indicated on aerial photos, the University of Wisconsin—Milwaukee's research team exposed the trenches in which this great wall was built. Only small portions of the total wall have been excavated, but the indications on the various aerial photos suggest its total length. It appears to have enclosed the central 80 ha (200 acres) of the Cahokia community, and was constructed of large logs placed upright in a deep foundation trench. Watchtowers and gates were spaced at regular intervals along the wall. The wall was apparently rebuilt at least four different times during the twelfth century.

The presence of watchtowers or bastions strongly suggests that the wall was built for defensive purposes. Perhaps the central portions of the community could have served as a walled retreat to which the residents of the community could flee in times of danger. However, the wall may well have served another function: to screen off and isolate the high-status central core of the community.

Outside the walled inner core of Cahokia were many mounds and residences. These appear to have been organized in clusters, each with its own platform mounds, burial mounds, and plazas (Figure 15.6). These clusters may represent subcommunities within the large metropolis.

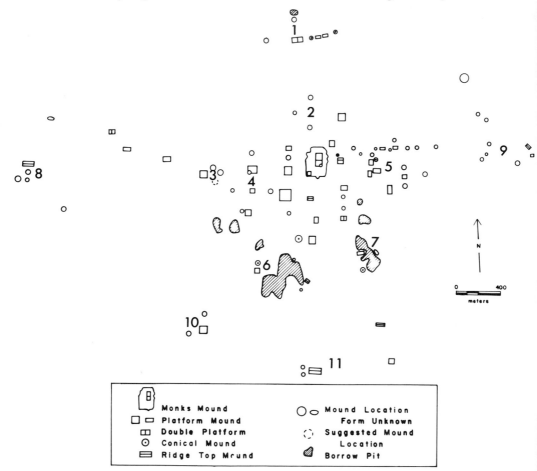

FIGURE 15.6.   Possible mound groupings at the Cahokia site: 1. Kunneman group; 2. North group; 3. West group; 4. Merrell group; 5. Ramey group; 6. Borrow Pit group; 7. Listerman group; 8. Powell group; 9. East group; 10. Rouch group; 11. Rattlesnake group.

Various areas within the Cahokia site have been excavated, revealing the nature of residential areas. Such residential utilization of the site area seems to have been concentrated in the central east–west axis ridge over an area of about 800 ha (2000 acres). The houses were of pole and thatch construction, usually having a rectangular floor plan. These houses were constructed at regular intervals, several to an acre. Once a building spot was chosen, a series of such structures were built in the same locality, indicating that one building site was used for several generations. There was a wide range of variation among these houses, however. Some may have been the residences of relatively high status persons and others of craftsmen and farmers. One house excavated about 400 m east of Monks Mound contained over 20 pottery vessels of various sizes.

Based on the known density of houses in excavated areas, and the amount of land useful for housing, it has been estimated that nearly 30,000 persons inhabited Cahokia at its peak of occupation (Gregg 1975a).

Further evidence of the complexity of the Cahokia site comes from various excavations that show the changing use of land, particularly in areas close to the central core area. In some cases, land that was residential became the location of large public buildings and compounds. The palisade surrounding the central core area appears to have been built right through an active and dense residential area—a form of urban renewal. These facts all suggest the power of a coercive central authority directing the destiny of the Cahokia community.

Although many archeological excavations have been carried out within the Cahokia site, we do not have sufficient control of the data base to state conclusively how much of the site was occupied at any one time, and which mounds were used contemporaneously. In almost all areas where excavations have been made, there is evidence to suggest that these areas were first occupied during the Fairmount phase, and continued through the history of the site. For example, the early stages of Monks Mound were built in the Fairmount phase (Reed, Bennett, and Porter 1968) and the final reworkings occurred during the Sand Prairie phase. Earlier Patrick phase occupation of the area has been found in the western portions of the Cahokia site (O'Brien 1969) and in deep stratigraphic deposits near the eastern edge of Monks Mound (Williams 1975). Most investigators agree that although Cahokia was a large complex site during the Fairmount phase, it probably reached its maximum level of complexity during the Stirling–Moorehead occupations. Cahokia was still utilized during the Sand Prairie phase, but this use was probably less intensive than earlier occupation.

The site appears to have been essentially abandoned by Historic times, although historic Indian burials have been found, among other places, on the first terrace of Monks Mound (Benchley 1975) and in the Rattlesnake Mound (Moorehead 1929).

Only a carefully planned sampling program will allow us to be more specific about the sequence of site utilization, population growth, and mound construction at Cahokia. It is hoped that such a testing program can be carried out in the next few years.

American Bottom Settlements

The Mississippian occupation of the American Bottom area is represented by cultural materials similar to those defined for the Fairmount, Stirling, Moorehead and Sand Prairie phases at the Cahokia site, representing a time period of roughly A.D. 900 to 1500.

The sites shown in Figure 15.7 represent the distribution of all of the Mississippian sites located in the American Bottom area. Physically, these sites vary in size and internal characteristics. I have divided the sites into four categories, based upon their size and relative complexity.

FIRST-LINE COMMUNITY

There is only one first-line community—the Cahokia Site itself. It was obviously the dominant community during the Mississippian utilization of the American Bottom.

SECOND-LINE COMMUNITIES

These are relatively large sites covering more than 50 ha (124 acres) and having several mounds. The sites known of this line are the Mitchell site, about 11 km north of Cahokia, the Pulcher site, near the southern end of the American Bottom, the East St. Louis site, and the St. Louis site. Of these, only the Mitchell site has been studied archeologically in any detail (Porter 1969, 1974).

The Mitchell site was probably more than 50 ha in size, with several mounds surrounding a plaza. Because of railroad construction in the late 1800s and interstate highway construction in the 1960s only one mound and a small portion of the original site exists. Rather extensive house or

---

FIGURE 15.7.   *The Location of Mississippi period sites in the American Bottom. Cahokia, the first-line community, is indicated by the large solid circle. The four second-line communities are represented by stars. The single—mound third-line communities are indicated by triangles. The small villages, hamlets, and farmsteads, or fourth-line communities, are represented by small solid circles.* [Sources: Harn (1971), Munson (1971), Brandt (1972), Benchley (1976).]

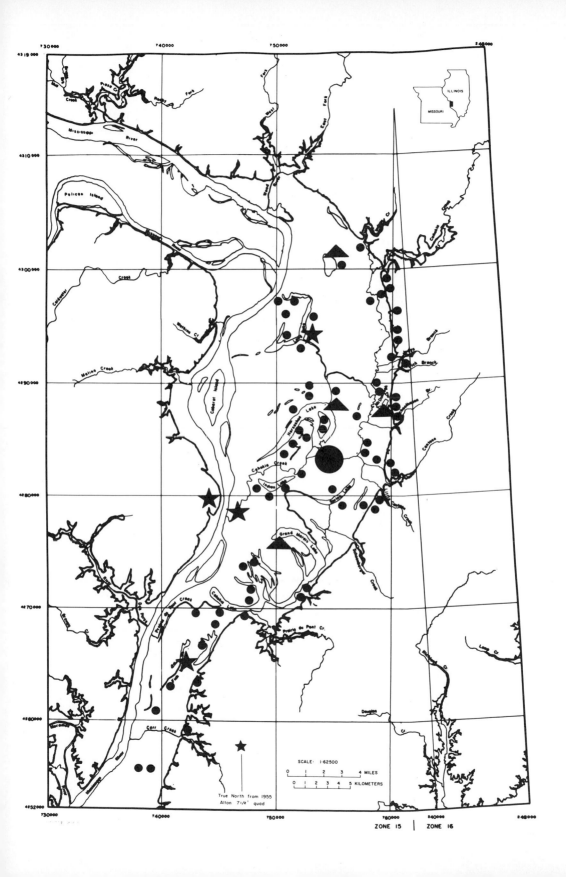

SCALE: 1·62500

0   1   2   3   4 MILES

0 1 2 3 4 5 KILOMETERS

True North from 1955
Alton 7½' quad

ZONE 15 | ZONE 16

residential construction was uncovered during excavation in the area surrounding the plaza and mounds. Porter feels that the site was occupied for only a short period of time, perhaps 100 years, during the twelfth century A.D.

The East St. Louis, or Metro site, was a large group of mounds. In the early 1800s one observer (Brackenridge 1814) reported 45 mounds, but when they were mapped by Patrick in the latter part of that century, only 15 mounds were recorded. Most of the mounds were destroyed during construction of the city of East St. Louis. Others may have been buried when the grade of the city in that area was raised to place it above flooding. It is possible, however, that some of the Metro site was preserved as the area of East St. Louis was filled in to raise it above the flood level. Brandt (1972:67–78) suggests that in some places this fill may be as deep as 3 m. Moorehead (1929:26) says that habitation debris where he tested was from "20 inches to 3 feet" below the surface. Some observations were made when the mounds were razed. In one of these mounds Dr. John Francis Snyder (1909:249–250) reported what he called a charnal house with upright cedar posts still preserved.

Prior to the large-scale modification of the American Bottom, mounds existed along the banks of Cahokia Creek extending from the East St. Louis group right up to the westernmost section of the Cahokia site. In some ways, one might suggest that the natural ridge on the south margin of Cahokia Creek extending from near its mouth to beyond the Cahokia Site was, in fact, a single continuous site. Some of the earlier investigators described a continuous high density of cultural debris along the ridge.

The St. Louis group was on the west bank of the Mississippi River channel in the heart of what is now downtown St. Louis (Long 1823). The mounds were largely destroyed during the middle of the nineteenth century, although records of the mounds and finds within them exist (Williams and Goggin 1956). The site was composed of several mounds in what is now the heart of downtown St. Louis. The Long Nose God masks found at this site suggest that it may have been occupied at least during the later portion of the Mississippian occupation of the area. No firm data exist that might allow us to say anything more specific about these two sites on either side of the main channel of the Mississippian occupation.

The fourth second line community in our classification is the Pulcher site (Flagg 1838:225, Fowler 1969:317, Griffin and Spaulding 1951:80 and Snyder 1909). Some excavations have been carried out at the Pulcher site by the University of Michigan in 1951, and by the Southern Illinois University Museum in the 1960s. The site covers approximately 120 ha (300 acres), and contains several mounds. The bulk of archeological material from the site seems to pertain to the earlier portions of the Mississippian settlement, but later materials are also known.

THIRD-LINE COMMUNITIES

Third-line communities are indicated by those sites having only one mound surrounded by habitation debris. Five third-line communities have been identified, scattered through the Bottom, usually associated with lake-edge environments. The Horseshoe Lake site (Gregg 1975b) is the only one to have been tested by limited archeological excavation. It was Gregg's conclusion that the site was a farming community with a platform-mound public center. His interpretation was that the site was largely developed during the earlier part of the sequence at Cahokia, that is, the Fairmount phase.

FOURTH-LINE COMMUNITIES

Fourth-line communities are those localities, without mounds, which could be considered hamlets or farmsteads. They are only a few hectares in extent. Some of the small dots shown in Figure 15.7 are mounds along the bluff edge, burial mounds (Melbye 1963) with apparent relationships to the large sites in the Bottom. Other mounds are conical in shape and Snyder (1909:74) and other early investigators referred to them as *signal mounds*. It is possible that they were located along the bluff edge, which would have been the effective horizon, as markers for calendrical observations. Some previous investigators have already looked into this possibility (Wittry 1969), and it is currently being investigated further. The mound site locations should be removed from our consideration as we are presently more interested in the habitation sites.

SITE LOCATIONS

The settlement map (Figure 15.7) shows the generalized locations of these different types of communities in the American Bottom. It treats them as if they were all occupied at the same time. For the present, we shall make this assumption and look at the distribution of sites accordingly.

Almost all the sites are located within the bottomland wet prairie zone. The major exceptions to this pattern are the sites situated around Horseshoe Lake, which at the time of the first land surveys of the area was what Gregg (1972:Fig. 3, p. 42) called the sugarberry–elm–sweetgum–wapiti zone. According to Munson (1974) this may also have been a zone that was associated with one of the more recent channel changes of the Mississippi River.

Within the prairie zone, all types of sites were located near aquatic resources. These were either lakes, creek channels, or sloughs. Fourth-line communities were located near all these different types of aquatic resource zones. The other types of communities, however, show more limited distribution. Third-line communities all seem to be located at the edge of major lakes. Thus, they appear as specialized exploitive communities, perhaps for food production for the greater population at Cahokia and other communities in the Bottom.

Second-line communities were even more specially located. They appear to be in localities of direct communication with the Mississippi River. The Mitchell site on the north is located on Long Lake, which probably gave transportation access to the Mississippi River. The Mitchell site is also located just a few miles to the south and east of the mouth of the Missouri River. It therefore was situated in a very significant control location for any communication, trade, etc. moving up the River. It perhaps stood as guardian of the northern frontier of the greater Cahokia settlement system. The two very large sites on each side of the main channel of the Mississippi, the Metro and St. Louis Sites, are unique in location. No other sites are known so close to the main channel. These two sites appear to have been possible control communities on the main channel of the river, perhaps monitoring the movement of goods and people. The East St. Louis or Metro site is also located at the mouth of Cahokia Creek, the longest-flowing water course in the American Bottom.

The fourth of the second-line communities is Pulcher, which is located in the south end of the Bottom on the banks of Fish Lake. This lake is part of an extensive slough and channel system, which Munson suggests was cut off some time prior to 2000 years ago, and which provides direct water access to the main channel of the Mississippi.

Thus the distribution of these different types of sites in the American Bottom suggests a hierarchical relationship of the communities involved in the settlement system. Cahokia was the major and dominating community. It was centrally located in the American Bottom both geographically and in terms of transportation routes. Thus, it probably served both as the major population center and as the center of distribution and control.

Second to Cahokia were four large sites whose location within the American Bottom suggests that they may have been communities in control of major access routes to the region. The Mitchell site is on the north near the mouth of the Missouri River, the Pulcher site is situated to the south near the mouth of the Meramac and at the point where the American Bottom narrowed. The St. Louis and Metro Sites are located on either bank of the Mississippi channel and at the mouth of Cahokia Creek. Perhaps they served the same function as St. Louis and what is now East St. Louis did in the nineteenth century, that is, as major transshipment communities for goods coming from the west to the east and vice versa.

Smaller, single-mound sites were located in situations suggesting that they might have been specialized food-producing and procuring communities. This type of location was the edge of large oxbow lakes in the wetland prairie zone.

The largest number of sites were the small village, hamlet, and farmstead sites without mounds. These were located on the edges of creeks and small lakes, and more or less evenly scattered throughout the Prairie area of the American Bottom. All the locations of sites of this size and proposed function are obviously not known, but those sites illustrated in Figure 15.7 may well be a representative sample. It can be stated with a fair degree of confidence that most of the second- and third-line communities have been located.

SUMMARY

This hierarchical model for an American Bottom settlement system is based on the assumption that all these sites were occupied more or less contemporaneously. The available data are not sufficiently detailed and controlled either to support or to reject this assertion. This model is implied by Porter's (1974) suggestion that differences in ceramics may suggest different contemporary areas of production. Some of the data, however, suggest that not all of these sites are contemporaneous.

Harn found evidence to suggest that most of the sites he examined were not occupied after what we now call the Fairmount phase. He did point out the problems of preservation of shell-tempered pottery in heavily plowed agricultural fields. The destruction of this pottery would skew the data in the direction of the earlier phases. This caused Harn to propose the urbanization or nucleation of the American Bottom populations into Cahokia. Some confirmation of this hypothesis seems to come from Gregg's (1975b) research at the Horseshoe Lake site suggesting that the mound at that site may have been built during the Fairmount phase. Griffin (personal communication) has suggested for years that Pulcher was early and he probably would agree that it lasted only into the Fairmount phase at Cahokia. Thus, two of the major communities in our hierarchical model, and many if not most of the fourth-line communities, were abandoned by the end of the Fairmount phase.

The data from the Mitchell site as presented by Porter (1969, 1974) suggest that this site was largely occupied in the later period of Cahokia's development. The radiocarbon dates and other information place Mitchell during the Stirling and Moorehead phases. We feel that the St. Louis and Metro sites also belong to the later part of the Cahokia development; but of course, this cannot yet be adequately demonstrated.

Alternative Models

We can propose another settlement system model for the later part of Cahokia, which is that which Harn proposed, that is, a nucleation model. In this system, there were perhaps ony two types of communities. The first line community was Cahokia. Only the second-line communities were present to support Cahokia and to control the distribution of resources. It may be that the Cahokia, St. Louis, and Metro sites could be considered as one large community extending from central Cahokia Creek along the ridge to the Mississippi River and to the bluffs on the west shore.

A third possibility is that both models are correct and represent a developmental sequence in the growth of the Mississippian utilization of the American Bottom area. This model incorporates the development of Mississippian in the region out of local farming communities of the Patrick phase. The Patrick phase appears to represent the first intensive agricultural utilization of the region. With population growth, the number of such communities increased in the American Bottom. To control the distribution of goods and resources, both within the American Bottom and to and from the outside, a central first-line community, with growing dominance over the others, evolved. To produce special goods and to serve as regional control centers, second-line specialized communities developed. At this point, probably during the Fairmount phase, the hierarchical settlement system had evolved.

With further population growth and the need for full exploitation of the immediate hinterland, a process of population nucleation began, reaching a climax in the Stirling and Moorehead phases. Contemporary with this may have been the specialized development of the Mitchell site. It may be that trade with the upper Missouri area had grown to the point where this became a significant location.

This is suggested by the data that Porter has from the Mitchell site indicating central plains relationships (Porter 1974:647–648). O'Brien (1969) has reported on other central plains like materials from the Cahokia area. Harn and others have also pointed out the plains relationships of the Spoon River and central Illinois River Valley areas during this time period.

This is to be contrasted with data from the Fairmount phase, where materials are found that seem to suggest connections with the Caddo area. For example, Caddoan projectile points and pottery have been found in Mound 72. We can hypothesize then that in the earlier periods of Cahokia's development its relationships were to the south. This may explain the location of the Pulcher site as the important second–line community. Later, the emphasis shifts and Mitchell becomes the more significant second-line community.

The ultimate climax of the nucleation model may be in the shift of emphasis in later times away from Cahokia itself to a prehistoric St. Louis, that is, the concentration of population in the East St. Louis–St. Louis areas on both banks of the Mississippi River. Since there is little possibility of testing this idea, it must remain as conjecture. There is no doubt though, that by historic times the Cahokia area was insignificant and unknown to the French as a location of Indian populations.

Future Research

Despite the different surveys that have been done in the American Bottom we do not yet have sufficient understanding to assess the relative strength of these three models, that is, the hierarchical, the nucleation and the developmental. On the basis of these ideas, however, hypotheses can be developed and their test implications outlined. Then a probablistic sampling survey of the American Bottom could be conducted. Data from this type of controlled survey would allow us to accept or reject these hypotheses. This is the status and current need of settlement pattern studies in the Cahokia region.

References

Anderson, James
   1969   A Cahokia palisade sequence. In *Investigations in Cahokia archeology*, edited by M.
           Fowler *Illinois Archaeological Survey Bulletin* 7:89–99. Urbana.
Bareis, Charles J.
   1964   Meander loops and the Cahokia site. *American Antiquity* **30**:89–91.
Benchley, Elizabeth D.
   1975   The first terrace of Monks Mound. In *Cahokia archaeology: Field reports*, edited by
           M. Fowler. *Illinois State Museum Research Series*, No. **3.** Springfield
   1976   An overview of the prehistoric resources of the metropolitan St. Louis area. Cul-
           tural Resource Management Studies, National Park Service, United States Depart-
           ment of the Interior. Washington, D.C.
Brackenridge, Henry Marie
   1814   *Views of Louisiana together with a journal of a voyage up the Missouri river, 1811.*
           Pittsburg. (Modern edition published 1962, by Quadrangle Books, Inc., Chicago.)
Brandt, Keith
   1972   American Bottom settlements. Paper presented at the 37th annual meeting of the
           Society for American Archaeology May 4–6, 1972 Bal Harbor, Florida.
Bushnell, David I. Jr.
   1904   The Cahokia and surrounding mound groups. *Papers of the Peabody Museum of
           American Archaeology and Ethnology (1904–1913)*, Vol. III, No. 1.

1917　The origin and various types of mounds in eastern United States. *Proceedings of the Nineteenth International Congress of Americanists.* Washington, 1915. Pp. 43–47.

1922　Archaeological reconnaissance of the Cahokia and related mound groups. Explorations and Fieldwork of the Smithsonian Institution in 1921. *Smithsonian Miscellaneous Collections* **72**(15):92–105.

Flagg, Edmund
1838　*The far west: Or, a tour beyond the mountains,* Vol. 1. New York: Harper and Brothers.

Fowler, Melvin L.
1969　The Cahokia site. In *Investigations in Cahokia archaeology,* edited by M. Fowler. *Illinois Archaeological Survey Bulletin 7.* Urbana.

1975　(editor) *Cahokia archaeology: Field reports. Illinois State Museum Research Series,* No. 3. Springfield.

Fowler, Melvin L., and Robert L. Hall
1975　Archaeological phases at Cahokia. In Perspectives in Cahokia Archaeology. *Illinois Archaeological Survey Bulletin* **10**:1–14. Urbana.

Goddard, George
1969　*Overview.* New York: Doubleday and Company.

Gregg, Michael
1972　Biological resource base and area ecology. In The University of Wisconsin—Milwaukee Cahokia archaeology project, edited by Melvin Fowler. Department of Anthropology, University of Wisconsin–Milwaukee. Mimeo.

1975a　A population estimate for Cahokia. In *Perspectives in Cahokia archaeology, Illinois Archaeological Survey Bulletin* **10**:126–136. Urbana.

1975b　Settlement morphology and production specialization: The Horseshoe Lake site, a case study. Ph.D. dissertation, Department of Anthropology, University of Wisconsin—Milwaukee.

Griffin, James B.
1949　The Cahokia ceramic complexes. *Proceedings of the 5th Plains Conference for Archaeology.* Notebook No. 1. of the Laboratory of Anthropology, The University of Nebraska, Lincoln.

Griffin, James B., and Albert C. Spaulding
1951　The central Mississippi valley archaeological survey, season 1950—a preliminary report. *Journal of the Illinois State Archaeological Society* 1(3):74–81.

Hall, Robert L.
1966　Cahokia chronology. Paper prepared for distribution at the annual meeting of the Central States Anthropological Society. St. Louis, Missouri. On file at the Illinois State Museum. Mimeo.

1967　The Mississippian heartland and its Plains relationships. *Plains Anthropologist* **12**(36):175–183.

1968　The Goddard–Ramey Cahokia flight: A pioneering aerial photographic survey. *The Wisconsin Archaeologist* **49**(2):75–79.

1975　Chronology and phases at Cahokia. In *Perspectives in Cahokia archaeology, Illinois Archaeological Survey Bulletin* **10**:15–31. Urbana.

Harn, Alan D.
1971　An archaeological survey of the American Bottoms in Madison and St. Clair Counties, Illinois. In An archaeological survey of the American Bottoms and Wood River terrace. *Illinois State Museum Reports of Investigations* No. **21**:19–39. Springfield.

Lobeck, A.K.
1950　*Physiographic diagram of North American. New Jersey: The Geographical Press.*

Long, Stephen H.
 1823   *Account of an expedition from Pittsburg to the Rock Mountains performed in the years 1819, 1820. Complied from the notes of Major Long, Mr. T. Say, and other gentlemen of the party by Edwin James in early western travels 1748–1846*, Vol. XIV, edited by Reuben Gold Twaites. Clevland: Arthur H. Clark.

McAdams, William
 1881   Ancient mounds of Illinois. *Proceedings of the American Association for the Advancement of Science. 29th meeting held at Boston, Massachusetts, August, 1880.* Salem.
 1882   Antiquities. In *History of Madison County, Illinois* Edwardsville, Illinois: Brink and Company. Pp. 58–64.
 1883   *Antiquities of Cahokia or Monks' Mound in Madison County, Illinois.* Edwardsville, Illinois: Brink and Company.
 1887   *Records of ancient races in the Mississippi valley.* St. Louis: C.R. Barns Company.
 1895   Archaeology. *Report of the Illinois Board of World's Fair Commissioners at the World's Columbian Exposition.* Springfield: H.W. Rokker, Printer and Binder. Pp. 227–304.

Melbye, F. Jerome
 1963   The Kane Burial Mounds. *Archaeological Salvage Report,* **15.** Carbondale: Southern Illinois Museum.

Moorehead, Warren K.
 1922   The Cahokia Mounds: A preliminary report. *University of Illinois Bulletin* **19**(35). April 24, 1922. Urbana.
 1923   The Cahokia Mounds: Part I A report of progress by Warren K. Moorehead and Part II some geological aspects by Morris M. Leighton. *University of Illinois Bulletin* **21**(6). Urbana.
 1929   The Cahokia Mounds. *University of Illinois Bulletin* **26**(4). Urbana.

Munson, Patrick J.
 1971   An archaeological survey of the Wood river terrace and adjacent bottoms and bluffs in Madison county, Illinois. In Archaeological surveys of the American Bottoms and adjacent bluffs, Illinois. *Illinois State Museum Reports of Investigations* No. **21**(1):100–120.
 1974   Terraces, meander loops, and archaeology in the American Bottoms, Illinois. *Transactions of the Illinois State Academy of Science* **67**(4):384–392. Springfield.

O'Brien, Patricia J.
 1969   Some ceramic periods and their implications at Cahokia. In *Explorations into Cahokia archaeology*, edited by M. Fowler. *Illinois Archaeological Survey, Bulletin* 7:100–120. Urbana.
 1972   A formal analysis of Cahokia ceramics from the Powell Tract. *Illinois Archaeological Survey Monograph*, No. 3. Urbana.

Porter, James W.
 1969   The Mitchell site and prehistoric exchange systems at Cahokia. In *Explorations into Cahokia archaeology*, edited by M. Fowler. *Illinois Archaeological Survey Bulletin* 7. Urbana.
 1974   Cahokia archaeology as viewed from the Mitchell site: A satellite community at A.D. 1150–1200. Ph.D. dissertation. Department of Anthropology, University of Wisconsin—Madison.

Reed, Nelson A., John W. Bennett, and James W. Porter.
 1968   Solid core drilling of Monks Mound: Technique and findings. *American Antiquity* **33**(2):137–148.

Snyder, John Francis
 1894   An Illinois "Teocalli." *The Archaeologist* **2**(9):259–264. Waterloo, Indiana.
 1895   A group of Illinois mounds. *The Archaeologist* **3**(3):77–81. Waterloo, Indiana.

1909   Prehistoric Illinois. Certain Indian mounds technically considered. *Journal of the Illinois State Historical Society,* Vols. 1 and 2, pp. 31–40, 47–65, 71–92. Springfield.

1913   *The prehistoric mounds of Illinois.* Published by the "Monks of Cahokia."

1914   Prehistoric Illinois—The great Cahokia mound. *Illinois State Historical Society Journal* **6**:506–508. Springfield.

1917   The great Cahokia mound. *Illinois State Historical Society Journal* **10**:256–259. Springfield.

Thomas, Cyrus

1894   Report on the mound explorations of the Bureau of Ethnology. *Twelfth Annual Report of the Bureau of Ethnology, 1890–1891.* Washington, D.C.

1907   Cahokia or Monks Mound. *American Anthropologist* **9**:362–365.

Tucker, Sara Jones (compiler)

1942   *Indian villages of the Illinois country, Vol. II, Scientific Paper, Illinois State Museum. Part I, Atlas.* Springfield, Illinois: State of Illinois.

Vogel, Joseph R.

1975   Trends in Cahokia ceramics. In *Perspectives in Cahokia archaeology,* edited by M. Fowler. *Illinois Archaeological Survey Bulletin* **10**:32–125. Urbana.

Williams, Kenneth

1975   Preliminary summation of excavations at the East Lobes of Monks Mound. In *Cahokia archaeology: Field reports,* edited by M. Fowler. *Illinois State Museum Research Series* **3**:21–24.

Williams, Stephen, and John Goggin

1956   The Long-Nosed God Mask in eastern United States. *The Missouri Archaeologist* **18**(3):1–72.

Wittry, Warren L.

1969   The American woodhenge. In *Explorations into Cahokia archaeology,* edited by M. Fowler. *Illinois Archaeological Survey Bulletin* **7**:43–48. Urbana.

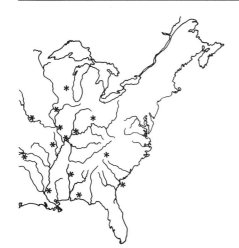

16

Variation in Mississippian Settlement Patterns

BRUCE D. SMITH

Taken together, the preceding chapters of this volume serve to illustrate a number of important points concerning Mississippian settlement patterns.

First, there is, in some ways, an apparent wide range of diversity of settlement patterning during the Mississippi period. Although this may seem like a rather obvious statement to make, there has been a tendency over the last 10 years to think of a single static model of Mississippian settlement patterning that could be successfully applied over a wide geographical area. Although this interpretive focus upon the overall uniformity of Mississippian settlement patterns has certainly been justified to some extent in terms of the similarities that have been found to exist, it has at the same time diverted attention from the related research question of variation in Mississippian settlement patterning.

Second, although the preceding chapters certainly demonstrate variation in the spatial patterning of human populations in the Eastern Woodlands during the Mississippi period, they also indicate the amount of further research that will have to be carried out before any adequate level of understanding can be reached concerning both the basic similarities between Mississippian settlement patterns and the existent dimensions of variation. Each of the settlement-pattern–settlement-system models presented in this volume is based largely upon site data obtained through

479

surface survey. The degree to which these models reflect reality can only be assessed through long-range excavation programs.

Finally, a number of the chapters contain interesting attempts to identify and determine the relative importance of those environmental and cultural variables that influenced the size and spatial distribution of the Mississippian sites comprising a specific settlement system. The fact that these attempts produced very promising results suggests that it would also be worthwhile to discuss environmental and cultural variables that might be expected to account for temporal and geographical similarities and differences between all Mississippian settlement systems.

The objective of this final chapter is to consider the complex question of variation in Mississippian settlement patterning, and to propose a tentative model that serves to explain, at least to some extent, why such similarities and differences exist in the spatial distribution of Mississippian populations. It should perhaps be made clear that the model to be presented here is not meant to be a final, complete, and definitive solution to this complex research problem. It is quite possible that such a definitive, detailed explanation of the variation in Mississippian settlement patterning may never, in fact, be achieved. It is hoped, however, that the model to be presented will not only provide a partial explanation of the problem, but will also serve to focus attention upon those aspects of the problem that seem to represent potentially promising avenues for future research.

The Adaptive Niche of Mississippian Populations

In attempting to identify aspects of underlying uniformity in Mississippian cultural systems, one is, in fact, establishing boundary conditions or criteria for a definition of "Mississippian." Prehistoric human populations in the Eastern Woodlands have, in the past, usually been categorized as being "Mississippian" on the presence or absence of a number of material culture characteristics such as rectangular, truncated, substructural pyrimidal mounds and shell-tempered pottery. I would like to propose a different set of boundary conditions that will serve to define "Mississippian" as a cultural adaptation to a specific habitat situation, and as a particular level of sociocultural integration. I am sure that this proposed new definition of "Mississippian" will not meet with unanimous approval, and that it will also involve declassifying some groups previously identified as being Mississippian. These negative consequences will be outweighed, it is hoped, by the degree to which this new definition will provide insight into geographical variations in Mississippian subsistence–settlement systems.

It was within the meander-belt zone of the lower alluvial valley of the Mississippi River that the Mississippian cultural adaptation first appeared, and where the major development of Mississippian communities took place. Subsequent expansion of the Mississippian cultural adaptation was primarily along the major floodplain valley corridors formed by the tributaries of the Mississippi River. Even those Mississippian settlements established outside of the drainage of the Mississippi River were situated, with few exceptions, within the valley of a major river. It has been recognized for a number of years that the Mississippian cultural adaptation was largely restricted to the meander-belt zones of the river valleys of the Eastern United States. What has not generally been recognized is that this restriction of Mississippian populations to floodplain situations was not simply because of the availability of easily tilled alluvial soils. Rather this restriction was a function of the specific, complex adaptation by Mississippian populations to this habitat zone composed of linear bands of circumscribed agricultural land and concentrated biotic resources. Before describing the niche that Mississippian populations occupied, a number of significant characteristics of such meander-belt habitat zones should be discussed.

The first point I would like to emphasize concerning this meander-belt habitat zone is that it can be classified as a "naturally subsidized solar-powered ecosystem [Odum 1975:18]." The term "naturally subsidized" refers to the fact that, in addition to being powered by solar energy, this meander-belt habitat zone receives a power subsidy in the form of a constant waterborne flow of nutrients through the zone. This energy subsidy "reduces the unit cost of self-maintenance of the ecosystem, and thereby increases the amount of solar energy that can be converted to organic production [Odum 1975:18]." This increased productivity index translates into unusually high sustained biomass values for species of plants and animals within meander-belt habitat zones and a higher carrying capacity for predator populations (including humans) that occupy the higher trophic levels within the ecosystem. The significant extent to which Mississippian populations depended upon this energy subsidy will be elaborated upon later in this chapter. The rivers that carry this energy, in the form of suspended nutrients, into and through meander-belt habitat zones are also largely responsible for the confusing and complex topography characteristic of such areas.

Most of the major rivers in the Eastern United States can be described as aggrading streams, because the floodplain slopes away from the river rather than toward it. This is due to differential deposition of soil during flood stages. As floodwaters leave the river bed, large amounts of silt, sand, and nutrients are deposited as the velocity of the floodwater drops. The lighter sediments such as clay are carried greater distances from the river. This rapid deposition of large amounts of soil along the edges of the river bed forms asymmetrical natural levees that slope back gradually into the level floodplain. Rivers do not stay within the confines of these naturally formed sand and silt levees, but periodically break through, forming new channels. This constant lateral shifting occurs within a zone of predictable width, which is called a "meander belt." The constant formation of new meanders and associated natural levees eventually forms an almost continuous ridge of superimposed and coalesced former levees. These linear meander-belt zones are paralleled on both sides by back swamp areas that contain poor clay soils and which are inundated by floodwaters during much of the year.

Meander shifting often creates isolated channel remnants that are called cutoff or oxbow lakes. Most of these cutoff channels will eventually be filled in, but the depositional process and associated vegetational succession is relatively slow.

The resultant topography of the meander-belt habitat zone is a complex undulating pattern of superimposed former natural levees interspersed with channel remnant–oxbow-lake–swamps in various stages of being filled in. Although there may be relatively little variation in elevation within such meander-belt zones, slight variations in elevation are associated with significant differences in soil type, drainage, and vegetation associations. These differences in relief are especially significant in terms of the occurrence of distinctive vegetation types. A wide variety of plant communities can be found in close association to each other, with areas that differ in elevation by only a few feet supporting quite different species of plants. Not only do these meander-belt habitat zones contain a variety of distinct biotic communities stacked in close vertical juxtaposition, but the complex curvilinear nature of the topography results in long, linear interface or edge areas between adjacent biotic communities. These two factors of variety of biotic communities within a small, circumscribed area, and maximum linear interface between communities combine to produce a habitat zone that will support a variety of species of animals at relatively high population densities.

A final point that should be made in reference to these meander-belt habitat zones is that they are environmentally circumscribed (Carneiro 1970, Hall 1973:15–16). These energy-subsidized linear bands of high quality, easily tilled soils that support high biomass levels of plants and animals are partially isolated from upland areas by parallel tracts of low backswamp areas. Beyond these backswamp areas, unsubsidized upland regions often contain less fertile soils that would be more difficult to clear and farm and would not be renewed by flood waters. An important exception to this general occurrence of lower quality soils in upland areas should be noted. The relatively narrow linear bands of wind deposited (Loess) soils, which are present along the bluff edges of a number of river valleys in the Eastern Woodlands, often have all of the advantages of levee ridge soils, and were invariably utilized by Mississippian populations when available (see Chapters 9 and 12). The biomass values of plant and animal populations would also be lower in upland areas.

Although Carneiro (1970:735) states that the Eastern Woodlands of North America provided extensive tracts of uncircumscribed agricultural land, his subsequent description of the "circumscribed" meander-belt zone of the Amazon River (Caneiro 1970:736–737) closely parallels the description provided here of the meander-belt habitat zone of the major rivers of the Eastern United States. In both situations, what Carneiro terms a "steep ecological gradient [1970:736]" separates linear bands of highly prized agricultural land containing high biotic resource concentrations from surrounding less productive and less promising habitat zones.

In summary, the habitat situation to which Mississippian populations developed a complex, yet very flexible cultural adaptation can be generally characterized as environmentally circumscribed linear bands. These river floodplain zones contained a confusing patchwork of oxbow lakes, seasonally flooded low areas, and coalesced natural levee ridges composed of a wide range of different soil types, and supporting a wide variety of species of plants and animals at high biomass levels.

The niche filled by Mississippian populations within this specific habitat situation involved selective utilization of a limited number of species groups of wild plants and animals that represented dependable, seasonally abundant energy sources that could be exploited at a relatively low level of energy expenditure. The five wild species groups that were of primary importance to Mississippian populations as energy sources are the following:

1. Backwater species of fish.
2. Migratory waterfowl.
3. The terrestrial trinity (white-tail deer, raccoon, and turkey).
4. Nuts, fruits, and berries (primarily hickory nuts, walnuts, acorns, persimmons, cherries, plums and hackberries).
5. Seed-bearing pioneer plant species (primarily *Polygonum*, and *Chenopodium*).

In addition to selectively exploiting these optimum energy sources existing within the floodplain ecosystem, Mississippian populations also selectively destroyed the natural vegetation growing on certain preferred soil types, replacing this vegetation with a number of domestic cultigens that also represented dependable, seasonally abundant energy sources. Maize (*Zea mays*), beans (*Phaseolus* sp.), and squash (*Cucurbita pepo*) were the most important crops grown. In addition to this "horticultural trinity," three crops of secondary importance were grown—sunflower (*Helianthus annuus*), marsh elder (*Iva* sp.), and gourd (*Largenaria siceraria*).

Although all Mississippian populations occupied the same general niche within floodplain habitat zones, any specific Mississippian population would have had to adjust this basic adaptive strategy to conditions existing in the specific segment of the linear habitat zone that they occupied. The floodplain habitat zones of different river valleys, and even different segments along the same river floodplain, would obviously not have been equally attractive to Mississippian populations in terms of providing optimum occurrence of, and access to, potential energy sources.

The relative degree to which any segment of a river floodplain approached the optimum habitat situation for the adaptive niche of a Mississippian population can be measured in terms of a single variable: the size of the net energy subsidy that it received. The adaptive niche of Mississippian populations therefore not only involved selective utilization of a limited number of dependable, seasonally abundant energy sources within a naturally subsidized floodplain ecosystem, it also involved orientation toward a certain habitat configuration that enabled the successful capture of the power subsidy that literally flowed through the floodplain. One of the most interesting aspects, then, of the Mississippian adaptive niche is that it was to a great extent both focused upon and dependent upon energy sources that were "externally powered." This variable of net external energy subsidy would, of course, be related to the total energy subsidy entering any floodplain segment, which in turn could be roughly quantified in terms of streamflow volume. This relationship between the total energy subsidy entering a floodplain segment and the net external energy subsidy available for Mississippian populations was not, however, a constant. Two floodplain segments having comparable streamflow volumes could differ significantly in terms of the net energy subsidy available for Mississippian populations. Topographic configuration, along with spring flooding and subsequent summer drain off characteristics, were just as important as total energy subsidy values in determining the net external energy subsidy level of any floodplain segment.

Spring flooding would have been of obvious importance in that it was the primary way in which external energy was seasonally diverted from the main channel of the river and distributed over the floodplain. The degree to which nutrient rich floodwaters would have provided an external energy subsidy would not have been uniform along all segments of a floodplain corridor. Summer drain-off characteristics and topographic considerations would, in turn, have determined the extent to which this seasonally distributed energy subsidy was captured within a specific segment of the floodplain, and made available for utilization by Mississippian populations. The degree to which any floodplain segment was able to capture this seasonal energy subsidy in a form that could be successfully utilized by a Mississippian population can be quantified in terms of two variables:

1. The total area of well drained, easily tilled land within the flood-plain segment-support area of a Mississippian population that received an energy subsidy in the form of nutrient rich flood waters on a dependable, but not necessarily a yearly, basis, and which was also free of floodwaters in time for the spring planting of cultigens. The maximum energy yield from harvested domestic crops that a Mississippian population could obtain from any floodplain segment on a continual basis would have depended to a significant extent upon the degree to which the external energy subsidy was captured in the form of nutrient rich soil, which in turn could be transformed into an energy form (cultigens) that could be directly consumed by the human population. Thus one way of viewing Mississippian horticulture is in terms of a deliberate modification and simplification of the ecosystem in order to capture more effectively the external energy subsidy that was seasonally distributed across the flood-plain. Although it is difficult to determine accurately the extent to which domestic cultigens contributed to the diet of Mississippian populations, most Eastern North American archeologists would agree that these exter-nally subsidized energy sources comprised a significant portion of the total Mississippian caloric intake.

2. The total area of permanent lakes and seasonally flooded low areas occurring within the floodplain-segment support area of a Mississippian population. In addition to nutrients, spring flood waters also carried a wide variety of different species of fish out of the main channel into shallow water areas to spawn. A large percentage of these fish would have subsequently been stranded in oxbow lakes and shallow water areas as floodwaters retreated back within the natural levees of the main channel. These stranded fish would have represented an externally subsidized energy source in that much of their lives would have been spent within the main channel of the river, where nutrients carried by the current would have powered their food base. This significant seasonal (spring–early summer) increase in the fish biomass levels of oxbow lakes, com-bined with the large number of fish trapped and easily captured in shallow-water areas, combined to produce a dependable, easily exploited, externally powered energy–protein source for Mississippian populations. Migratory waterfowl, moving through the Mississippi flyway in the spring and fall of the year, stopping at oxbow lakes to rest and feed, would have represented another such seasonally abundant energy–protein source for Mississippian populations.

Although fish and waterfowl have previously not been recognized as being a very important component in the subsistence base of Mississip-pian populations, recent research has indicated that taken together, these two species groups may well have contributed *at least* 50% of the total protein intake of Mississippian populations living within the meander-belt habitat zone of the Mississippi River. The maximum energy yield that a Mississippian population could have obtained from these two externally powered species groups within any floodplain segment would have been determined largely by the total area of permanent oxbow lakes and seasonally flooded areas occurring within that floodplain segment. The relative potential of migratory waterfowl as an energy source would not, of course, have been purely a function of the occurrence of oxbow lakes, but would have also been influenced by the proximity of any floodplain segment to the Mississippi flyway corridor.

Although the preceding description of the niche of Mississippian populations is not as detailed as it could be (see Smith 1974, 1975 for a more complete consideration of this topic), it does serve to emphasize a limited number of boundary conditions that can be employed to define "Mississippian," partially, and will, it is hoped, go a long way toward explaining some aspects of the regional variation in Mississippian settlement patterning.

I would like to propose that the term "Mississippian" be used to refer to those prehistoric human populations existing in the eastern deciduous woodlands during the time period A.D. 800–1500 that had a ranked form of social organization, and had developed a specific complex adaptation to linear, environmentally circumscribed floodplain habitat zones. This adaptation involved maize horticulture and selective utilization of a limited number of species groups of wild plants and animals that represented dependable, seasonally abundant energy sources that could be exploited at a relatively low level of energy expenditure. In addition, these populations depended significantly upon an even more limited number of externally powered energy sources. Defining "Mississippian," in part, in terms of an adaptive niche is useful, I think, for a number of reasons.

First, although it clearly indicates that the general term "Mississippian" encompasses all those populations having a similar subsistence subsystem (populations that adapted to a similar habitat zone in a similar manner), it does not at the same time imply the degree to which "Mississippian" populations may have had similarities in other aspects of their overall cultural systems. Therefore, it not only allows for cultural systems that may be very different in terms of social and ideological subsystems to be subsumed under the general heading "Mississippian," it also recognizes that this may well be the case.

Second, this definition serves to raise a number of potentially interesting research questions concerning the range of subsistence–settlement-pattern variation existing between different Mississippian populations. These interrelated research questions would involve comparison of Mississippian populations in terms of the degree of concomitant variation in three variables:

1. The total net external energy subsidy that any floodplain-segment support area was able to capture in a form that could be successfully

utilized by Mississippian populations. This variable could be quantified in terms of (a) the total energy subsidy flowing through any floodplain segment (streamflow volume); (b) the total area of well-drained, easily tilled land within the floodplain segment; and (c) the total area of permanent lakes and seasonally flooded low areas occurring within the floodplain segment.

2. The subsistence pattern of the Mississippian population. This variable could be quantified in terms of (a) the relative importance of different species of plants and animals as energy sources; (b) the degree to which these energy sources were selectively utilized; and (c) the seasonality of exploitation of these energy sources.

3. The settlement pattern of the Mississippian population. This variable could be quantified in terms of (a) the number of different categories of Mississippian settlements in terms of size (rank–size hierarchy) and the relative size of settlements in each of these categories; (b) the number of settlements within each size category (rank–size ratio); and (c) the spatial distribution of settlements within the floodplain segment support area.

The reader will, I am sure, recognize that these three variables of total-net-external-energy-subsidy–topographic-configuration, subsistence patterning, and settlement patterning have been demonstrated to be clearly related in a number of the preceding studies of specific local Mississippian populations and their floodplain-segment support areas.

There is no reason why these same three variables should not be expected to covary along predictable dimensions as Mississippian populations occupying different floodplain-segment support areas are compared. According to the model being presented, floodplain segments that are similar in terms of Variable 1 (total-net-external-energy-subsidy–topographic-configuration) might be expected to have supported Mississippian populations with similar subsistence patterns. Such similar subsistence patterns reflect parallel adjustment of the basic adaptive strategy already outlined to conditions existing in the specific floodplain segment being occupied. Similarly, Mississippian populations occupying floodplain segments that are comparable in terms of Variable 1 would be expected to share similar settlement patterns, reflecting their parallel adjustment to similar patterning in the spatial distribution of important energy sources, especially those externally powered energy sources already discussed.

It should perhaps be pointed out that whereas the model being proposed could qualify as environmental possibilism, it is not meant to be an environmental deterministic statement. In comparing Mississippian populations located in different floodplain-segment support areas in terms of these three variables, I am not suggesting that similar environments produce or cause similar cultural systems. Rather, I am suggesting that it would be worthwhile to consider the extent to which variation in Mississippian subsistence–settlement patterns can be predicted in terms of variation in certain habitat characteristics. One of the most interesting aspects of attempting to determine accurately the strength of this relationship between habitat characteristics and Mississippian subsistence–settlement patterns is that it will, it is hoped, serve to not only focus attention upon those aspects of subsistence–settlement patterns that cannot be explained in terms of habitat characteristics, but will also to identify those Mississippian populations that appear to deviate strongly from the predictions of the model. Thus, the model is designed only not to analyze the degree to which environmental variables can be used to explain Mississippian subsistence–settlement pattern variation, but also to identify those aspects of subsistence–settlement patterning that can only be explained in terms of variables within the social and ideological subsystems of Mississippian populations.

Having described both the habitat zone occupied by Mississippian populations and the general adaptive niche they filled within that habitat zone, and having proposed a partial new definition of "Mississippian," which serves to focus attention upon the interrelationships between habitat, adaptive niche, and settlement patterning, a more specific consideration of variation in the spatial distribution of Mississippian populations can now be presented.

Mississippian Settlement Patterning

BALANCING ENERGY EFFICIENCY AND BOUNDARY MAINTAINANCE: A BASIC MODEL

The location of almost any Mississippian settlement within a floodplain habitat zone can, to a great extent, be generally explained as a result of two energy-capture factors:

1. The availability of well-drained, easily tilled, energy-subsidized natural levee soils suitable for horticultural garden plots.
2. Easy access to the rich protein resources of fish and waterfowl in channel-remnant oxbow lakes.

The natural levees adjacent to active main channels appear to have been avoided by Mississippian populations, most likely because of the severity of spring flooding. Mississippian populations preferred, instead, the natural levees that paralleled former-channel oxbow lakes. Although proximity to optimum soil types and oxbow lakes appear to be important variables in explaining the location of Mississippian settlements within the floodplain habitat zone, these two energy-capture factors do not serve to explain completely the range of variation in the size of Mississippian settlements, nor do they explain the internal complexity of Mississippian settlement systems.

The optimum spatial distribution of Mississippian populations in terms of efficient energy-source utilization would involve a dispersed pattern of small settlements situated on preferred soil types, adjacent to channel-remnant oxbow lakes. In a typical floodplain situation like the Black Bottom (Chapter 10), one would expect a linear patterning of small settlements along the natural levees adjacent to oxbow lakes (Figure 10.1, p. 277). In more patchy environmental situations such as the Powers phase area (Chapter 8), one would expect such small settlements to be located on small isolated pockets of preferred soils, adjacent to low-lying oxbow lakes, swamps, or seasonally flooded areas (Figure 8.9, p. 220).

These small homestead settlements, representing the minimum economic unit, would be occupied by a single to several nuclear–extended-family groups on a year-round basis. The number of individuals occupying these small settlements would, at least in some instances (e.g., the Black Bottom—Chapter 10) be largely a function of the number of hectares of high-quality soil available within close proximity. The garden plots of each household would be located adjacent to settlements, minimizing energy expenditure in terms of horticultural activities and facilitating protection of the fields from animal pests. Each small settlement would also have had easy access to the rich protein resources of oxbow lakes.

Early historic descriptions of such dispersed settlement patterns are common for Indian groups in the Eastern Deciduous Woodlands (see the discussion by Green and Munson, Chapter 11, p. 320–322). If the existence of the Kincaid site is ignored for the moment, the Mississippian settlement pattern of the Black Bottom (Figure 10.1) is a good archeological example of a dispersed pattern of small settlements, representing an optimum solution to problems of efficient energy-resource utilization. The Steed–Kisker settlement pattern in the Brush Creek Valley (Figure 1.4, p. 12) is another well-documented archeological example of such an energy-efficient dispersed pattern of settlement. If the pressure for efficient utilization of energy sources was the single causative factor in determining the spatial distribution of Mississippian populations, such a settlement pattern as already described would be expected to have been fairly prevalent. Since such a dispersed pattern of small settlements has rarely been observed in pure form in a Mississippian context, it is obvious that factors additional to energy efficiency influenced the distribution of Mississippian populations.

These factors, which acted counter to the pressure for population dispersal, involved the need for Mississippian populations to be organized as competitive cultural entities, with the ability to maintain and defend the boundaries of their support areas. The structural organization of Mississippian populations into such competitive cultural entities involved mechanisms to deal both with the internal problem of social cohesion and cooperation and the external problem of defense of land and people. One of the most obvious and effective mechanisms for dealing with these twin problems is nucleation of a population into fortified villages. Although such a nucleated settlement pattern would represent the optimum solution to the problem of defense, it would be an inefficient pattern in terms of energy capture. Similarly, although a dispersed pattern of small settlements would represent an optimum solution to the problem of energy capture, it would be a very poor solution to the problem of group defense and boundary maintainance, and would not encourage internal cultural cohesiveness.

Many Mississippian populations appear to have developed a compromise settlement system that not only balanced these two opposing pressures, but was also flexible in terms of dynamic adjustment to the shifting pressure for boundary-maintainance capabilities. This compromise settlement system involved relatively large, often fortified settlements, located centrally to a dispersed settlement pattern of small homesteads. These centrally located settlements, which will be referred to as "local centers," would also be expected to be located adjacent to sufficient high-quality soil to support the horticultural gardens of the inhabitants, as well as having easy access to the protein resources of channel-remnant oxbow lakes. Local centers would serve as the foci for the local populations, living in homesteads distributed within a reasonable walking distance (movement between homesteads and local centers in many situations may have actually been by watercraft, along oxbow lakes), and would function to maintain internal social cohesiveness. The local center would have been the location of public ceremonial areas (e.g., plazas, public structures, mounds), and would also have been the residence of individuals occupying important ceremonial–political positions. The local center would have had a relatively small segment of the local population living within its walls on a permanent basis, but also would have had the capability of containing the total local population within its fortifications during periods of hostility with neighboring populations.

If the hypothetical settlement system model being presented is, to any degree, an accurate reflection of reality, then the large, impressive Mississippian village sites that have been the focus of archeological research over the last half century represent relatively small components in the overall settlement systems that existed, with a significant percentage of any local population living in small, dispersed homesteads on a permanent basis (for a detailed analysis of such a homestead, see Smith 1978).

Individual family units living in dispersed homesteads would have visited the local center, where they may well have maintained a second, temporary, habitation structure, only in certain situations:

1. For scheduled seasonal ceremonies of renewal and cultural integration.
2. For burial, or other rites of passage ceremonies of kinsmen or high-status individuals.
3. For payment of labor–energy demands (corporate labor construction projects, primarily fortification construction and maintenance, and mound construction).
4. For mutual defense, during periods of short- or long-term hostility with neighboring populations.

When combined with the Mississippian subsistence strategy model described earlier in this chapter, I think the settlement system model outlined here could perhaps be employed to define further the boundary conditions of "Mississippian." Many, if not all, Mississippian populations could be generally characterized as having a settlement system consisting of dispersed farmsteads surrounding a local center, with this system representing a flexible compromise solution to the opposing pressures of optimum energy utilization and optimum social-cohesion–boundary-maintenance-abilities.

Although local-center Mississippian subsistence–settlement systems were undoubtedly very numerous during the Mississippi period, the Kincaid system of the Black Bottom (Chapter 10) is one of the few such systems that has been carefully documented and analyzed within the framework of a long term regional research project. Such a settlement system also suggests a ranked or chiefdom level of cultural complexity, with the existence of ceremonial–political power positions at local centers. This is not to say, however, that such local center systems (what Steponaitis, Chapter 14, would refer to as simple, one-level chiefdoms), represent the highest level of cultural complexity achieved by Mississippian populations. That such is not the case is clearly demonstrated by a number of the preceding chapters in this volume.

Before turning to a consideration of the settlement patterning of Mississippian populations organized at higher levels of cultural complexity, it is first worthwhile to point out some of the difficulties that await archeologists interested in describing and analyzing the structure of Mississippian settlement systems organized at the local center level of complexity. The difficulties in question involve the kinds of variation from the basic model just presented that might be expected to occur in reality.

Let us first consider the kinds of change in the settlement patterning of a Mississippian local population that might be expected to occur through time.

TEMPORAL VARIATION

Short-Term Seasonal Variation

If the seasonal pattern of warfare described ethnohistorically for areas of the Eastern Woodlands was prevalent during the Mississippi period, there might well have been a resultant seasonal change in the spatial distribution of local populations. During the summer warfare season, homesteads would often be abandoned for short periods as family groups took up temporary defensive occupation of fortified local centers. This seasonal nucleation of local populations would be followed in the late-summer–early-fall by a reoccupation of outlying homesteads.

Longer-Term Variation in the Basic Pattern

A similar cyclical oscillation (although not of predictable or uniform length) of nucleation and dispersal might be expected to occur over longer periods of time as local populations adjusted to changing levels of hostility with neighboring populations. During periods of relative peace, the defensive function of a fortified local center would cease to be an important aspect of its role in the settlement system. It would, however, continue to be the focus of ceremonial and political activities of the local population, with a small resident population. In such period of minimal hostility, maintenance of local center fortifications might be neglected, necessitating rebuilding if and when hostilities subsequently ensued. Similarly, local centers established during long periods of chronic peace, or in newly colonized areas lacking formidable potential competition, may well have had minimal or no fortification walls. With most of the family units distributed in small scattered homesteads, and only occasionally visiting the local center, Mississippian populations during peaceful times could be best characterized as having a partially occupied ceremonial-center–dispersed-homestead settlement pattern.

During periods of prolonged hostilies, on the other hand, homesteads would be all but abandoned as the entire local population took up residence either in close proximity to, or actually within the fortification walls of, the local center.

Temporary shelters, in addition to abandoned homesteads, would be scattered among outlying garden plots, providing short-term shelter for families tending crops. With most of the family units residing within, or in close proximity to, the local center, and only occasionally visiting outlying garden plots, Mississippian populations during times of hostility could be best characterized as having a nucleated-village–field-house settlement pattern.

The settlement pattern of Mississippian populations in some floodplain situations might also change through time if soil depletion necessitated shifting the location of homesteads, and perhaps even local centers.

Finally, the settlement pattern of a Mississippian population at a local center level of complexity would change through time if and when it was drawn into short-term political alliances with neighboring populations. The kinds of settlement pattern changes that might be expected to occur as supra-local political systems emerged and subsequently fragmented again into autonomous local-center systems will be considered later in this chapter.

First, however, it is necessary to consider the implications of such temporal change in the analysis of the settlement patterning of Mississippian populations. If the Mississippian settlement pattern model being described comes at all close to reality, there exists the distinct possibility of Mississippian populations modifying their settlement systems in response to cultural pressures over very short periods of time. This in turn means that a very fine grain chronology is necessary before the basic problem of contemporaneity of occupation of settlements can be dealt with. Even within as short a period of time as 200 years, a Mississippian settlement system may change a number of times in response to environmental and cultural pressures. Unless the archeologist has reasonable control of the chronology within that 200-year span, it would be very easy, if not unavoidable, to assume that the evidence for a number of different system states or structural poses in fact reflected a single contemporaneous system (see the discussions of this problem by Harn, Chapter 9; Muller, Chapter 10; Green and Munson, Chapter 11; Brain, Chapter 12; and Fowler, Chapter 15).

GEOGRAPHICAL VARIATION

In addition to the dimension of temporal variation, one could also expect geographical variation to exist in the settlement patterning of Mississippian populations at the local center level of complexity.

Variation in Energy Resource Distribution

A certain degree of the variation in the spatial distribution of different local Mississippian populations can be expected, and explained, in terms of environmental variation. If a Mississippian population at a local center level of organization sequentially occupied two different floodplain segments, their settlement patterning would change as a result of their adjustment of a basic adaptive settlement–subsistence strategy to the specific topographic–resource distribution characteristics of their support areas.

2. Variation in the Level of Hostility

Geographical variation in settlement patterning can also be expected to occur, reflecting different levels of hostility in different areas. Two local Mississippian populations that were very similar in all other respects could exhibit quite distinct variations of the dynamic, flexible settlement system just outlined if one was located in an area of chronic hostility, and the other in an area of relative peace.

It would be possible, then, for local Mississippian populations with very similar cultural systems and the same basic subsistence–settlement strategy to have distinctly different settlement patterns due to differences in hostility levels and the distribution of energy resources in their respective support areas. It is therefore of obvious importance that archeologists be able to discriminate between those differences in Mississippian settlement patterns that reflect significant differences in the structure of the cultural systems being compared, and those that can be explained in terms of variation in hostility levels and energy resource distribution.

The third and final dimension of variation in the settlement patterning of Mississippian populations is the dimension of sociopolitical complexity.

VARIATION DUE TO SOCIOPOLITICAL COMPLEXITY

Although there is obviously a wide range of variation in the degree of complexity of Mississippian socio-political systems, I would agree with Peebles and Kus (1977) that Mississippian populations were organized at a chiefdom or ranked level of complexity. I also agree with Peebles and Kus that a ranked form of organization can be employed as a boundary condition in defining "Mississippian": "In summary it is both a mode of adaptation—maize agriculture—plus a ranked form of organization that are the defining characteristics of Mississippian cultural systems. [Peebles and Kus 1977: 435]." Although Peebles and Kus are primarily concerned with proposing archeological correlates of ranked societies, this chapter focuses on the subsistence–settlement systems of Mississippian populations. Taken together, these three factors: (*a*) adaptive niche; (*b*) settlement system; (*c*) structure and level of complexity of the sociopolitical organization) can be used to define the boundary conditions of "Mississippian."

Even though all Mississippian populations, by definition, had a ranked form or organization, this still leaves a lot of room for variation in the structure of Mississippian sociopolitical systems: "It should be understood that not all of these chiefdoms comprised comparable numbers of people, nor were they equally centralized. Chiefdoms may have small populations or large, and their chiefs may be relatively weak or strong.

[Hudson 1976:203]." The local center level of organization (what Steponaitis, Chapter 14, terms a simple chiefdom), described earlier in terms of settlement patterning, probably represents the lower end of the range of variation in complexity of Mississippian societies, in that it has a single level of administration or control (the local center).

More complex ranked societies (what Steponaitis, Chapter 14, terms complex chiefdoms) are defined in terms of having two or more levels of administration or control. Such complex chiefdoms can be characterized as consisting of a number of local populations, one of which has managed to bring the others under political hegemony. The ceremonial center of the dominant local population represents a second level of administration or control (a regional center) within the chiefdom. Decision making would, to a great degree, be centralized at the regional center, with information and energy flowing to such regional centers through the lower-level local centers. Such regional centers, when compared with local centers, could be distinguished on the basis of larger overall size, larger and more numerous mounds, larger plazas, and higher-status occupants. Regional centers, like local centers, were probably occupied on a permanent basis by only a segment of the total local population, with the majority of family units distributed in small homesteads within the support area of the regional center.

Judging both from ethnographic and archeological examples, complex chiefdoms with a two-level hierarchy of administrative control are rarely composed of more than six or seven local populations brought under the control of an emergent regional center. The prehistoric and historic two-level chiefdoms of the Eastern Woodlands do not appear to have been very stable political entities, with breakdown or fragmentation being a constant possibility. This constant possibility of fragmentation was to a great extent a result of the relative autonomy of local populations comprising such chiefdoms. Each maintained its own support area, and was economically self sufficient. Each maintained its own local center, with its resident administrative-control hierarchy at the local level.

> If powerful chiefdoms or small primitive states did exist in the Southeast in Mississippian times, they were probably not very stable, as is the case in such societies elsewhere in the world, the reason being that their local communities remained almost completely self sufficient [Hudson 1976:205].

See Peebles and Kus (1977) and Steponaitis (Chapter 14) for more detailed descriptions of the organization of complex chiefdoms.

Analysis of the settlement patterning of the complex chiefdoms that occupied floodplain habitat situations during the Mississippi period often involves dealing with a relatively large geographical area, since a number of interrelated local populations, rather than a single local population, comprise the unit of study (see Chapter 13). This is not always the case, however. In optimum floodplain habitat situations with high carrying capacity, complex chiefdoms may cover relatively small geographical areas (see Cottier 1974:85–88; Morse 1973:72–76).

With a limited number of important exceptions, the settlement patterning of such two-level Mississippian chiefdoms would be very similar to what one would expect for a number of spatially contiguous local center or single-level simple chiefdoms. Based on the model proposed by Steponaitis (Chapter 14), the following differences in the settlement pattern might be expected to exist.

1. The emergence of a regional center, distinct from local centers in terms of:
   (a) larger overall size,
   (b) evidence of greater corporate labor expenditure in the form of mounds, plazas, public structures, and fortifications,
   (c) the presence of high status burials and goods not occurring at local centers,
   (d) a reasonable high spatial efficiency with respect to local centers [see Eq. 14.9].
2. A tendency for local centers to cluster toward the regional center.
3. A tendency for local centers closest to the regional center to have less evidence of corporate labor investment than local centers located further away (see Chapter 14).

With the possible exception of the American Bottom (Chapter 15) Mississippian complex chiefdoms do not appear to have developed a hierarchical structure that involved more than two levels of administration. Although there are certainly a number of other contributing factors to the uniqueness of Cahokia and the American Bottom, it is interesting to note that nowhere else in the Eastern Woodlands is there a more optimum setting for Mississippian occupation in terms of net energy subsidy. The American Bottom, an environmentally circumscribed, unusually wide floodplain segment of the Mississippi River, contains large areas of suitable horticultural land, is covered with a series of large and small oxbow lakes, ponds, and seasonally inundated areas, and is located directly on the Mississippi flyway corridor. Although it certainly cannot be stated that these optimum conditions in terms of available energy "caused" the development of a unique Mississippian cultural system in the American Bottom, I think most archeologists would agree that such an optimum situation in terms of energy resources was a necessary prerequisite to such development. The range of variation in the complexity of Mississippian sociopolitical systems in terms of hierarchical structure, then, is limited, with perhaps a single exception, to from one to two levels of administrative control.

Mississippian cultural systems at both the local center and regional center level of complexity can be further characterized and compared along two additional dimensions of complexity: (a) the overall size of the cultural entity, and (b) the degree of centralization of the sociopolitical system. The overall size of a Mississippian sociopolitical entity could be quantified either in terms of the geographical space incorporated in its support area, or in terms of the number of individuals comprising its population. While neither of these measures of the overall size of a Mississippian sociopolitical entity can be observed directly, both can be approximated archeologically. The total horticultural support area of either a local or a regional Mississippian population could be approximated by determining the number of hectares of suitable horticultural land within the catchment area of the settlements of the chiefdom (see Chapter 13), assuming that the contemporaneity of occupation of homesteads and local and regional centers could be established. The number of people comprising a Mississippian chiefdom could be approximated through analysis of the number and size of domestic living structures present at settlements (see Chapters 8, 10, 11), as well as by analysis of burial populations (Black 1973).

The degree of centralization of decision making in Mississippian chiefdoms could be approximated in a number of ways. At the local-center level of organization, the amount of corporate labor expenditure contributed to the local center, expecially labor contributed to nondefensive projects, could perhaps be used as a measure of the control maintained over the local population. Similarly, the degree to which any large-scale construction projects appear to have been organized and carried out under centralized control could also be employed to measure centralization of decision making. Analysis of the number of, and variation in, status positions represented in burial populations, of course, continues to be the most commonly used method of assessing centralization of decision making at both the local-center and regional-center levels of organization. Finally, for Mississippian chiefdoms having a two-level administrative structure, Steponaitis (page 440) has suggested that comparison of a regional center and associated local centers in terms of their relative size and the evidence for corporate labor expenditure could be employed as a measure of centralization of decision making at the regional center.

By using a number of measures of cultural complexity, including those described briefly in the preceding paragraphs, it should be possible at some point in the future to place different Mississippian sociopolitical systems on a scale of complexity and centralization ranging from the most simple single-level chiefdom to the most complex two-level chiefdom.

Once this has been accomplished, we will be in a much better position to assess the relative importance of both environmental variables (e.g., net energy subsidy levels and spatial distribution of energy resources) and cultural variables (e.g., boundary maintenance and the size, level of complexity, and degree of centralization of sociopolitical systems) in determining the settlement patterning of Mississippian populations.

This level of analysis of Mississippian settlement patterning is theoretically possible, but it can only be accomplished if future Mississippian research is directed toward a number of important and as yet poorly understood research problems.

Suggestions for Future Research

It is undoubtedly apparent to the reader by this point that Mississippian cultural systems can be characterized as being dynamic, flexible systems, allowing Mississippian populations not only to adapt successfully to different floodplain habitat situations, but also to make necessary adjustments to sometimes abrupt shifts in local political situations. Many of these adjustments of the cultural system to variations in the surrounding natural and cultural environment, are, as described earlier, reflected in changes in the spatial distribution of populations, changes in the patterning of settlements.

If early descriptive accounts of Indian populations in the Eastern Woodlands hold any validity for the late prehistoric period, one might expect fluid and unstable political situations to have been fairly common during the Mississippi period, with local populations making frequent necessary adjustments as short-term alliances were established and broken, as complex chiefdoms emerged and subsequently fragmented. If this was in fact the case, frequent shifts in the settlement patterning of Mississippian populations should also be expected to have occurred. Mississippian settlement patterns therefore represent a potential research avenue for documenting and analyzing regional shifts in sociopolitical organization during the late prehistoric period.

This obvious research potential of Mississippian settlement pattern analysis is balanced by the fact that such settlement systems also represent very subtle, very complex archeological puzzles that are difficult to analyze and interpret accurately. Because settlement system analysis of Mississippian populations represents such a complex research puzzle, it necessitates a long-term commitment of time and energy by any archeologist who hopes to gain a reasonably accurate and detailed understanding of a settlement system. The necessity of approaching Mississippian settlement system analysis within the framework of a long-term regional research design is clearly demonstrated by the preceding chapters of this volume. There is no fast and simple way to unravel and understand such complex and dynamic settlement systems. They cannot be understood by limited observation of single sites, floating free of any systemic or chronological context.

The most obvious and most difficult problem involved in Mississippian settlement system analysis, even within a regional research design framework, involves establishing the contemporaneity of occupation of settlements. This issue of contemporaneity has been raised by almost all of the contributors to this volume, yet there does not at the present time appear to be a dependable and widely applicable method to deal with the problem.

Archeomagnetism has, for the last decade, been held up as the ultimate solution to the problem, in that it theoretically allows for the dating of individual hearths and other baked clay features within a very narrow range of accuracy. Eastern North American archeologists are still waiting, however, for the obvious potential of the method to be transformed into usable dates.

There has also been some discussion concerning the possibility of developing "floating" dendrochronological sequences that would allow for accurate relative dating of settlements belonging to the same settlement system. This method too, while certainly having clear potential, has yet to be successfully applied in the Eastern Woodlands.

Finally, there exists the possibility that short term changes in ceramic design elements and temper characteristics might be successfully employed to establish a relative chronology of settlements within a research universe. This potential application of microseriation techniques appears currently to be the most promising avenue for dealing with the research problem of establishing the contemporaneity of occupation of Mississippian settlements.

A second obvious problem area in the analysis of Mississippian settlement systems exists in our almost total lack of knowledge of the "lower end" of such systems. With a few notable exceptions, most research efforts have tended to focus on village-sized Mississippian sites, with smaller than village sized sites being known only through surface survey. These numerous, but poorly known, small sites that comprise the lower end of Mississippian settlement systems represent, I think, one of the most promising avenues of research in terms of learning more concerning such systems. Expanded research on the lower end of Mississippian settlement systems should be focused initially on the interrelated problems of identifying the variety of functionally different site types that exist within different systems, and establishing the range of variation that is to be expected within each site category.

The homestead settlement type, characterized earlier in this chapter as being the permanent year-round settlement of one to several nuclear–extended families, for example, is represented by less than a dozen excavated sites. It is, as a result, difficult to determine the expected range of variation for Mississippian homesteads in terms of duration of occupation, spatial patterning of features, the variety and kind of activities carried out, and the size and composition of the occupying group.

There is, at the same time, no clear set of boundary conditions for distinguishing between homesteads and similar but functionally distinct settlement types. What criteria, for example, can and should be used to distinguish among homesteads and archeologically similar "field houses," which would have been occupied only seasonally for short periods of time? Similarly, what is the upper limit in terms of spatial area and population size that is to be expected for Mississsippian homesteads? It may well be, as Muller (Chapter 10) has suggested, that the number of family groups occupying a homestead settlement is a function, at least in some situations, of the amount of horticultural land available immediately adjacent to the settlement location. Settlements occupied by as many as 8 to 10 family groups might well exist that would be the functional equivalent of single-family homesteads. The homesteads within any settlement system could well exhibit a fairly wide range of variation in terms of size, and the composition of the occupying groups could quite likely change through time. The criteria for determining whether a settlement fits within the homestead settlement category should therefore not necessarily be based on site size along, but rather on the variety and/or the kinds of activities that were carried out at the site.

The homestead settlement category is not, however, the only lower-end Mississippian settlement type that is inadequately understood. Although short-term-occupation–limited-activity sites such as hunting and butchering camps, plant collection and processing camps, and raw material procurement sites have been both proposed as possible functional site categories and tentatively identified on the basis of surface collections, very few have actually been excavated.

A third problem area in the analysis of Mississippian settlement systems involves establishing whether or not functionally distinct site categories exist that are intermediate in size and complexity between local centers and homesteads. Although the existence of such settlement types would be a significant departure from the basic settlement system model just presented, there is a limited amount of archeological evidence that suggests that they may be present in some situations.

The hamlet settlement type is usually characterized as consisting of from 10 to 20 domestic structures, and has usually been identified on the basis of area of surface scatter of artifactual materials. There are, however, several excavated Mississippian sites that appear to fall within this general size range (Morse 1968, Rolingson and Schwartz 1966). Because of the limited amount of excavation that has been carried out at sites believed to be in this size range, it is not presently possible either to determine how common such sites are in Mississippian settlement systems, or to establish their functional role. Do they represent the upper end of the homestead settlement category, or a functionally distinct type of settlement with a wider range of activities being carried out? This question, like the others raised in the concluding section of this chapter, will be answered only after much more excavation of lower end Mississippian settlements has been carried out.

A second settlement type that may exist below the local-center level in some Mississippian settlement systems is the village. The village designation is usually applied to sites that cover from .25 to 2 ha in size, and that do not have any mounds present. Mississippian sites that fall into this size category may well have filled a number of different functional roles within the context of different settlement systems. It is quite possible, for example, that many such village sites represent local centers in settlement systems, even though they do not contain substructural pyramidal mounds. Such mounds are certainly not a universal prerequisite for local-center status. Many of the described village sites appear to be very similar to local centers in terms of internal settlement patterning, in that they have centrally located plaza areas bounded by one or more large ceremonial structures and high-status domestic structures. It is certainly a reasonable possibility that for some Mississippian settlement systems, mound construction was not present at local centers. Similarly, within Mississippian settlement systems organized at the regional-center level of complexity, it is possible that some local centers would have mound construction present, whereas others would not.

It is also possible that in some situations, such village settlements filled some of the defensive functions of local centers without having any of the corresponding administrative functions. Village settlements filling this limited defensive function might be expected to occur when a local population is distributed over a fairly wide geographical area, making rapid access to the local center difficult for outlying homesteads, or in situations where natural obstacles such as swamps would cut off some homesteads from the local center. The sand ridges of the Power phase area (Chapter 8), for example, would have been partially isolated through the spring and summer by intervening low swampy areas, making movement from ridge to ridge rather difficult. Is Powers Fort, then, the local center of the Powers phase, with fortified villages such as the Snodgrass site serving a limited defensive role for homesteads situated on ridges to the east of Powers Fort? Or are these fortified villages, with central plazas and adjacent public structures, more accurately characterized as being the local centers of a two-level complex chiefdom, with Powers Fort being a regional rather than a local center? The answers to these kinds of questions, as well as the other questions raised concerning the existence and functional roles of village settlements can be answered only by further excavation of such sites within the framework of a long-term regional research project.

A fourth and final problem area that should be addressed in future research into the nature of Mississippian settlement patterns involves obtaining a much better understanding of the internal structure and developmental history of local and regional centers. How many individuals occupied such settlements on a permanent basis, and what were their relative status positions? What areas inside fortification walls were occupied on a temporary basis, and what was the frequency, duration, and seasonal scheduling of such temporary occupation episodes? What was the magnitude and the timing of corporate labor projects? How frequently were fortification walls rebuilt or expanded? Did such rebuilding efforts take place during temporary occupation episodes? How many sequential additions to mounds were made, and when in the occupational sequence did these additions occur?

These problem areas represent, of course, only some of the avenues of future research that should be considered. I am sure that the other contributors to this volume, as well as the reader, can add to this short list. Hopefully this volume demonstrates that although we are certainly a long way from gaining an understanding of the complexity and range of variation of Mississippian settlement systems, we have at least reached the point where we can seek answers to some of the right questions.

References

Black, Thomas
    1973   Population estimation from burial data of a Middle Mississippian society. Paper on file at the Museum of Anthropology, University of Michigan. Xerox.
Carneiro, Robert L.
    1970   A theory of the origin of the state. *Science* **169**:733–738.
Cottier, John W.
    1974   The area archaeological reconstruction. In Investigation and comparison of two nationally registered Mississippian archaeological sites in southeast Missouri. Final report submitted to the National Endowment for the Humanities. Carl Chapman, principal investigator, Columbia, Missouri.
Hall, Robert L.
    1973   An interpretation of the two-climax model of Illinois prehistory. Paper prepared for the IXth International Congress of Anthropological and Ethnological Sciences. Chicago.
Hudson, Charles
    1976   *The Southeastern Indians.* Knoxville, Tennessee: University of Tennessee Press.

Morse, Dan F.
  1968   Mapping a Mississippian community near Marked Tree. *The Arkansas Archaeologist* **9**:37–39.
  1973   The Nodena Phase. In Nodena: An account of 75 years of archaeological investigations in southeast Mississippi County, Arkansas, edited by Dan F. Morse. *Arkansas Archaeological Survey Research Series* **4.** Fayetteville, Arkansas: Arkansas Archaeological Survey.
Odum, Eugene P.
  1975   *Ecology.* Second edition. New York: Holt.
Peebles, Christopher S., and Susan M. Kus
  1977   Some archaeological correlates of ranked societies. *American Antiquity* **42**:421–448.
Rolingson, Martha A., and Douglas Schwartz
  1966   Late Paleo-Indian and Early Archaic manifestations in western Kentucky. *The University of Kentucky Studies in Anthropology,* **3.**
Smith, Bruce D.
  1974   The emergence and expansion of the Mississippian cultural adaptation: A subsistence strategy viewpoint. Paper presented at an advanced seminar on Mississippian development. Santa Fe: School of American Research.
  1975   Middle Mississippi exploitation of animal populations. *Anthropological Papers, Museum of Anthropology, University of Michigan,* **57.** Ann Arbor, Michigan.
  1978   *Prehistoric patterns of human behavior: A case study in the Mississippi valley.* New York: Academic Press.

Subject Index

STUDIES IN ARCHEOLOGY

Consulting Editor: Stuart Struever

Department of Anthropology
Northwestern University
Evanston, Illinois

Charles R. McGimsey III. **Public Archeology**

Lewis R. Binford. **An Archaeological Perspective**

Muriel Porter Weaver. **The Aztecs, Maya, and Their Predecessors: Archaeology of Mesoamerica**

Joseph W. Michels. **Dating Methods in Archaeology**

C. Garth Sampson. **The Stone Age Archaeology of Southern Africa**

Fred T. Plog. **The Study of Prehistoric Change**

Patty Jo Watson (Ed.). **Archeology of the Mammoth Cave Area**

George C. Frison (Ed.). **The Casper Site: A Hell Gap Bison Kill on the High Plains**

W. Raymond Wood and R. Bruce McMillan (Eds.). **Prehistoric Man and His Environments: A Case Study in the Ozark Highland**

Kent V. Flannery (Ed.). **The Early Mesoamerican Village**

Charles E. Cleland (Ed.). **Cultural Change and Continuity: Essays in Honor of James Bennett Griffin**

Michael B. Schiffer. **Behavioral Archeology**

Fred Wendorf and Romuald Schild. **Prehistory of the Nile Valley**

Michael A. Jochim. **Hunter-Gatherer Subsistence and Settlement: A Predictive Model**

Stanley South. **Method and Theory in Historical Archeology**

Timothy K. Earle and Jonathon E. Ericson (Eds.). **Exchange Systems in Prehistory**

Stanley South (Ed.). **Research Strategies in Historical Archeology**

John E. Yellen. **Archaeological Approaches to the Present: Models for Reconstructing the Past**

Lewis R. Binford (Ed.). **For Theory Building in Archaeology: Essays on Faunal Remains, Aquatic Resources, Spatial Analysis, and Systemic Modeling**